CULTURE, POWER AND PERSONALITY
IN MEDIEVAL FRANCE

CULTURE, POWER AND PERSONALITY IN MEDIEVAL FRANCE

JOHN F. BENTON

EDITED BY
THOMAS N. BISSON

THE HAMBLEDON PRESS
LONDON AND RIO GRANDE

Published by The Hambledon Press, 1991

102 Gloucester Avenue, London NW1 8HX (U.K.)

P.O. Box 162, Rio Grande, Ohio 45672 (U.S.A.)

ISBN 1 85285 030 2

© The estate of John F. Benton 1991

Introduction: Thomas N. Bisson 1991

British Library Cataloguing in Publication Data

Benton, John F.
  Culture, power and personality in medieval France
  1. French civilisation, 987-1589
  I. Title   II. Bisson, T.N. (Thomas Noel)
  944'.02

Library of Congress Cataloging-in-Publication Data

Benton, John F.
  Culture, power and personality in medieval France:
  John F. Benton: edited by Thomas N. Bisson.
  Includes bibliographical references and index
  1. France – Civilization – 1000-1328
  2. Latin literature – to 1500 – France –
  2 History and criticism
  3. French literature – to 1500 – History and
    criticism
  I. Bisson, Thomas N.   II. Title.
  DC33.2.B44   1991
  944'.021 – dc20   91-6576 CIP

Printed on acid-free paper and bound in Great
Britain by Bookcraft Ltd., Midsomer Norton, Somerset

Preface

The present volume contains most of John Benton's substantial articles, perhaps all he would have chosen to republish himself. Of full-length studies, only those applying electronic technology to problems of textual analysis, decipherment, and image-enhancement have been omitted, as being provisional inquiries in a fast developing field of applied methodology. There had been talk of such a collection for more than a decade. Benton knew how much he had invested in these articles and surely knew even better than his readers what coherence they had. But he would have wished to make revisions – adjustments of allusive words in conference papers, cross-references, and, above all, the up-dating of arguments and documentation in studies extending back more than twenty-five years – that are now impossible. Minor corrections have been made even in photographically reprinted pieces, some stylistic adjustments have seemed warranted in Chapter 14, here printed for the first time. The publisher's willingness to set or re-set five of the articles is a valuable contribution to this work that is warmly appreciated. The author's acknowledgements are reproduced as he first wrote them.

Some words of characterization and personal reminiscence are attempted in the Introduction. Here it remains for me to thank Elspeth Benton for her help and encouragement in this project; the California Institute of Technology for providing a subsidy in aid of publication; Rosy Meiron for her expert and devoted administrative assistance; Martin Sheppard for his capable editorial collaboration; as well as friends of John Benton who have shared with me their knowledge of his ways and works: Robert L. Benson, Elizabeth A.R. Brown, Michel Bur, Giles Constable, Berthe Marti, Eleanor Searle, and Norman Zacour. If something of our lamented friend tugs at us again in these pages, enlivens our remembrance, it is owing to their fidelity, aid, and good counsel.

T.N.B.
South China, Maine
August 1990

Contents

Preface	v
Acknowledgements	ix
Bibliography of John F. Benton	x
John F. Benton	xii
Introduction	xiii
Abbreviations	xix

PART I: LETTERS AND LOVE

1	The Court of Champagne as a Literary Center	3
2	Nicolas of Clairvaux and the Twelfth-Century Sequence, with Special Reference to Adam of St. Victor	45
3	Nicolas de Clairvaux à la recherche du vin d'Auxerre, d'après une lettre inédite du XIIe siècle	77
4	The Evidence of Andreas Capellanus Re-examined Again	81
5	Qui étaient les parents de Jacques de Vitry?	89
6	Clio and Venus: a Historical View of Medieval Love	99
7	An Abusive Letter of Nicolas de Clairvaux for a Bishop of Auxerre, Possibly Blessed Hugh of Mâcon	123
8	Theocratic History in Fourteenth-century France: the *Liber bellorum domini* by Pierre de la Palu	129
9	'Nostre Franceis n'unt talent de fuïr': the *Song of Roland* and the Enculturation of a Warrior Class	147
10	Collaborative Approaches to Fantasy and Reality in the Literature of Champagne	167

PART II: MONEY AND POWER IN FRANCE AND CHAMPAGNE

11	The Revenue of Louis VII	183
12	Philip the Fair and the *Jours de Troyes*	191
13	The accounts of Cepperello da Prato for the Tax on *nouveaux acquêts* in the Bailliage of Troyes	255
14	Written Records and the Development of Systematic Feudal Relations	275

PART III: SELF AND INDIVIDUALITY

15	The Personality of Guibert de Nogent	293
16	Individualism and Conformity in Medieval Western Europe	313
17	Consciousness of Self and Perceptions of Individuality	327
18	Les entrées dans la vie: étapes d'une croissance ou rites d'initiation	357
19	Trotula, Women's Problems, and the Professionalization of Medicine in the Middle Ages	363
20	Suger's Life and Personality	387

PART IV: ABAELARDIANA

21	The Paraclete and the Council of Rouen of 1231	411
22	Fraud, Fiction and Borrowing in the Correspondence of Abelard and Heloise	417
23	Philology's Search for Abelard in the *Metamorphosis Goliae*	455
24	A Reconsideration of the Authenticity of the Correspondence of Abelard and Heloise	475
25	The Correspondence of Abelard and Heloise	487

Index	513

Acknowledgements

The articles reprinted here first appeared in the following places and are reprinted by kind permission of the original publishers.

1. *Speculum*, 36 (1961), 551-91.
2. *Traditio*, 18 (1962), 149-79.
3. *Annales de Bourgogne*, 34 (1962), 252-55.
4. *Studies in Philology*, 59 (1962), 471-78.
5. *Le Moyen Age*, 70 (1964), 39-47.
6. *The Meaning of Courtly Love*, ed. Francis X. Newman (Albany: State University of New York Press, 1968), pp. 19-42.
7. *Mediaeval Studies*, 33 (1971), 365-70.
8. *Bibliographical Studies in Honor of Rudolph Hirsch*, ed. William E. Miller and Thomas G. Waldman (Philadelphia, 1975); The Library Chronicle, 40 (Winter, 1974), 38-54.
9. *Olifant*, 6 (1979), 237-58.
10. *Selected Proceedings of the Third Congress of the International Courtly Literature Society (Liverpool, 1980)*, ed. Glyn Burgess (Liverpool, 1981), pp. 43-57.
11. *Speculum*, 42 (1967), 84-91.
12. *Studies in Medieval and Renaissance History*, 6 (1969), 281-344.
13. *Order and Innovation in the Middle Ages: Essays in Honor of Joseph R. Strayer*, ed. William C. Jordan, Bruce McNab and Teofilo F. Ruiz (Princeton, 1978) pp. 111-35, 435-57.
14. This is published here for the first time. Lecture delivered at conference on 'Language and History in the Middle Ages' at Centre for Medieval Studies, University of Toronto, November 7 1981.
15. *Psychoanalytical Review*, 57 (1971), 563-86.
16. *Individualism and Conformity in Classical Islam*, ed. Amin Banani and Speros Vryonis, Jr. (Wiesbaden, 1977), pp. 145-58.
17. *Renaissance and Renewal in the Twelfth Century*, ed. Robert L. Benson and Giles Constable (Cambridge, MA., 1982), pp. 263-95.
18. *Annales de l'Est*, 34 (1982), 9-14.

19. *Bulletin of the History of Medicine*, 59 (1985), 30-53.

20. *Abbot Suger and Saint-Denis: A Symposium*, ed. Paula Gerson (New York: Metropolitan Museum of Art, 1986), pp. 3-15.

21. *Bulletin of Medieval Canon Law*, n.s. 4 (1974), 33-38.

22. *Pierre Abélard – Pierre le Vénérable*, Colloques internationaux du Centre de la Recherche Scientifique, 546 (Paris, 1975), pp. 471-506.

23. *Speculum*, 50 (1975), 199-217.

24. *Petrus Abaelardus: Person, Werk und Wirkung*, ed. Rudolf Thomas (*Trierer Theologischen Studien*, xxxviii, 1980), pp. 41-52.

25. *Falschüngen im Mittelalter*, Monumenta Germaniae Historica, Schriften, 33: V (Hanover, 1988), 95-120.

Articles and Books by John F. Benton not Included in the Present Collectioin

'Two Twelfth-Century Charters from Rural Catalonia in the Lea Library', *The Library Chronicle*, 28 (1962), 14-25; 'Cartularies and the Study of French Medieval History', *ibid.* 30 (1964), 1-6; 'The University of Pennsylvania Manuscript Catalogue: Notes for a New Edition', *ibid.* 23-35.

[Assistant editor] *Catalogue of Manuscripts in the Libraries of the University of Pennsylvania to 1800*, compiled by Norman P. Zacour and Rudolf Hirsch (Philadelphia: University of Pennsylvania Press, 1965), viii + 279 pp.

[Co-author with Jeannine Fohlen] 'A.-A. Monteil et les comptes de Franche-Comté', *Le Moyen Âge*, 74 (1968), 495-506.

'A Bernardine Manuscript in Claremont, California', *Analecta Cisterciensia*, 24 (1968), 39-46.

[Editor] *Self and Society in Medieval France: The Memoirs of Abbot Guibert of Nogent* (New York and Evanston: Harper & Row, 1970), rpt. Medieval Academy Reprints for Teaching, 15 (University of Toronto Press, 1984. Partially translated into Japanese by Norio Moriyama in *Nara Shigaku*, no. 3 (1985), 78-95, and no. 4 (1986), 38-55.

[Co-author, with James Greenlee] 'Montaigne and the 110 Guillaumes: A Note on the Sources', *Romance Notes*, 12 (1970), 1-3.

[Co-editor, with Thomas N. Bisson] *Medieval Statecraft and the Perspectives of History: Essays by Joseph R. Strayer* (Princeton: Princeton University Press, 1971).

'Comment' on Lloyd de Mause, 'The Evolution of Childhood' in *History of Childhood Quarterly*, 1 (1974), 585-589.

[Co-author, with Fiorella Prosperetti Ercoli] 'The Style of the *Historia Calamitatum*: A Preliminary Test of the Authenticity of the Correspondence Attributed to Abelard and Heloise', *Viator*, 6 (1975), 59-86.

Historical preface to *Charters of St. Fursy of Peronne*, ed. William M. Newman (Cambridge, MA, 1977), pp. vii-xxiv.

'Nouvelles recherches sur le déchiffrement des textes effacés, grattés ou lavés' in *Comptes rendus des séances de l'Académie des Inscriptions et Belles-Lettres*, année 1978, 580-594.

[Co-author, with Alan R. Gillespie and James M. Soha] 'Digital Image-Processing Applied to the Photography of Manuscripts', *Scriptorium: International Review of Manuscript Studies*, 33 (1979), 40-55.

Translation: 'Descartes's *Olympica*', *Philosophy and Literature*, 4 (1980), 162-166.

'Nicolas de Clairvaux', *Dictionnaire de Spiritualité*, 11 (1981), 255-259.

'The Birthplace of Arnau de Vilanova: A Case for Villaneuva de Jiloca near Daroca', *Viator*, 13 (1982), 245-257.

'Abelard, Peter' and 'Arnald of Villanova', *Dictionary of the Middle Ages*, 1 (1982), 16-20 and 537-538; 'Trota and Trotula' (in press).

[With Peter Dronke and Elisabeth Pellegrin] 'Abaelardiana: Poems from Orléans, Bibl. mun. MS 284, 183-184', *Archives d'histoire doctrinale et littéraire du Moyen Age*, 49 (1982), 273-295.

[With Brian Patrick McGuire] Edition of letter of Guibert of Gembloux in McGuire, 'A Letter of Passionate Friendship by Guibert of Gembloux', *Cahiers de l'Institut du moyen-âge grec et latin [de l'Université de Copenhague]*, 53 (1986), 11-14.

'Independence, Money, and the Walls of Academe', *The Independent Scholar: A Newsletter for Independent Scholars and their Organizations*, I, no. 1 (Winter 1987), 1-5.

'Electronic Subtraction of the Superior Writing of a Palimpsest', to appear in *Techniques de déchiffrement des écritures effacées*, ed. Jean Irigoin (Paris: C.N.R.S., in press).

John F. Benton. (*Photo: Richard Kee*)

Introduction

T.N. Bisson

The voice burst in – it would have been in 1978 – with that note of boisterous cheer to which one learned to accord a wary welcome: 'Tom, I've recanted!' It was a disarming *captatio*, and a becoming one, even if it left one (or me) groping for the right orthodoxy to congratulate: not courtly love, not the revenues of Capetian kings, but (this time) the authenticity of the *Historia calamitatum*. John F. Benton was an *engaged* scholar as some of the learned seekers and heretics of the Middle Ages had been. He throve on debate because he believed passionately in historical truth, in documented persuasion – and because he devoted himself instinctively to big questions. He was at his best in conferences, stalking colleagues with well sharpened questions, listening with mingled skepticism and sympathy, probing good humouredly for weak points, and contributing himself with challenging erudition and irresistible charm. He was forever making friends (and not only scholarly ones); he remembered people and their queries and replied to them; and he sought written answers to his questions from students, colleagues, archivists, and librarians in a worldwide network of *amicitia docta*. But he was no mere controversialist, still less a dogmatist; he won assent to his findings or, as in the case of Abelard and Heloise, rethought his questions in the light of worthy criticisms. Where conviction eluded him, he did not shrink from saying so, setting forth the possibilities. He spoke and wrote from a cultivated familiarity with medieval history and a searching knowledge of the culture and institutions of northern France in its grandly creative twelfth century. His death on 25 February 1988 deprived his family, friends, students, and colleagues of a singularly cherished and talented individual.

John Frederick Benton was born on 15 July 1931, the only son of Quaker parents devoted to the intellectual life. Educated at the Westtown School and Haverford College (A.B. 1953), he received his Ph.D. from Princeton University in 1959. He taught first at Reed College (1957-9), then at the University of Pennsylvania (1959-65), before moving to the California Institute of Technology in 1965. There he rose through the professorial ranks, becoming Doris and Henry Dreyfuss Professor of History in 1987.

He was a Fulbright Scholar (1955-6), a John Simon Guggenheim Memorial Fellow (1963-4), and a John D. and Catherine T. MacArthur Prize Fellow (from 1985). He was elected Fellow of the Medieval Academy of America in 1978.

Although long handicapped by ill health, he was riding a tide of creative success at the time of his death. His life-long project to edit the charters of Count Henry the Liberal (and his successors) of Champagne (1152-97) was advancing toward completion, his new work on the physician Trotula was bearing first fruits, and his latest study of the correspondence of Abelard and Heloise was in press. These subjects are well represented in the present volume, for almost all of John Benton's published research took the form of articles. He was none the less the editor of two books highly valued by teachers: *Town origins: the evidence from medieval England* (Boston: Heath, 1968), a well conceived anthology of secondary studies and documents; and *Self and society in medieval France: the Memoirs of Abbot Guibert of Nogent* (New York: Harper & Row, 1970), a thorough rewriting of the Swinton Bland translation preceded by a highly original introduction of which the gist was also published as an article, reprinted in the present volume (chapter 15). He coedited a collected of Joseph R. Strayer's articles (Princeton University Press, 1971). Benton's major book will be his edition of the charters of Champagne, which is being completed for publication in France.

The main directions of John Benton's research and teaching were determined by his interest in literature. Trained in classical and medieval Latin by Berthe Marti, then at Bryn Mawr College, and drawn thence to the study of medieval vernacular verse with D.W. Robertson Jr., he found a congenial research subject in the court of Champagne under Henry the Liberal and the Countess Marie. Congenial not simply because learned and creative clerks were known to have enjoyed the patronage of these princely lords, but also because the extent and nature of their engagement in this courtly culture proved far less clear than historians had assumed. 'The court of Champagne as a literary center' (*Speculum*, 1961; reprinted here, chapter 1), based on this research, was a characteristically searching and critical study that set the courtly prosopography of medieval France on a newly secure foundation. It opened the prospect of an historical approach to medieval literature. Benton explored this domain in critical studies of courtly love as well as of monastic culture, Latin poetry, and the Old French epic and romance (chapters 2, 6, 9, 10). If his radical critique of 'courtly love' has not won universal acceptance among literary specialists, it has compelled a more cautious recognition of the historical problems entailed by overly literal readings of Chrétien's romances or of Andreas Capellanus. Another characteristic habit of his method was revealed by this work. By using diplomatic evidence to establish personal associations, Benton was led not only to seek out the originals of printed charters but especially the originals and early copies that had eluded

Henri d'Arbois de Jubainville. Chapters 3, 5 and 7 convey useful gleanings of this approach, while the textual discovery that underlies 'The revenues of Louis VII' (chapter 11) may be regarded the work of an inspired sleuth. In this case a simple misreading by a modern editor had led to useless speculation on the amount of the king's income in 1180, speculation which Benton disposed of at a stroke.

In his interest in finance as well as his ability with charters, John Benton was virtually a *chartiste*. His long study of 'Philip the Fair and the *Jours de Troyes*' (chapter 12) is a masterly reconstruction of lost registers known from scattered and incomplete copies. 'The accounts of Cepperello da Prato for the tax on *nouveaux acquêts* in the bailliage of Troyes' (chapter 13) provided the first careful edition of a record of an Italian agent in the service of Philip the Fair; of an agent who, as it happens, was the subject of a misleading tale in Boccaccio's *Decameron*. Both these studies were dedicated to Joseph R. Strayer, whose work on Philip the Fair and whose insistence on sound method and clarity of exposition Benton carried on. 'Written records and the development of systematic feudal relations' (chapter 14), a paper hitherto unpublished, belongs in this same class of studies even as it points to a new strain of interest in technology.

In the 1970s Benton turned increasingly to the investigation of persons and personality while adopting electronic techniques to the solution of historical problems. His work with computers and digital image-processing was that of a pioneer; experimental, engaged, and widely stimulating. It began with a co-authored preliminary paper on 'The style of the *Historia calamitatum* . . .' (*Viator* 1975), then shifted to an applied study in manuscript decipherment, 'The birthplace of Arnau de Vilanova: a case for Villanueva de Jilóca near Daroca' (*Viator* 1982), in which an electronically enhanced reading of a fourteenth-century palimpsest preserved in southern California led to a novel and plausible historical revision. Benton drew resourcefully on the scientific expertise of his colleagues at CIT and he explored the methodological implications of image enhancement technology in other studies (Bibliography, nos. 24, 29, 36, 45) 'Written records . . .' (chapter 14) is, in its way, a theoretical reflexion on the historical background of computer literacy. Several of these studies together with 'Theocratic history in fourteenth-century France: the *Liber bellorum Domini* by Pierre de la Palu' (chapter 8) illustrates Benton's creative curiosity with manuscripts in collections accessible to him.

Later work on personality and individualism owed something to theoretical interests. Benton was drawn experimentally to 'psychohistory' when he examined the self revelations of Guibert of Nogent; the result was a powerfully suggestive reading of Guibert's emotional dependence on his mother (chapter 15). Erik Erikson was invoked in a brief study of stages of life (chapter 18), while quite diverse social scientific and medical findings figure in major studies of individuality (chapters 16, 17) and women's medicine (chapter 19). The two former papers constitute admirably erudite and judicious surveys of their large and timely theme. But great individuals interested Benton as much in their personal character as in their cultural attributes. After Guibert he turned to Abelard and Heloise, then to the enigmatic figure of the physician Trotula, finally to the Abbot Suger. Manuscript discoveries were central to this research on all three. Benton's identification of the source for two canons relating to nuns in MS Troyes 802 in a council of 1231 supported his argument that the compiler of the earliest source of the Abelardian letters was no friend of the Paraclete (chapter 21). His discovery of Madrid Complutense 119, a French or English manuscript of about 1200, enabled him to prove the existence of a woman physician named Trota (or Trotula) who wrote a treatise *De practica* (chapter 19). And his research in the archives and cartulary of Chaalis resulted in a firm identification of Suger's pettyknightly origins for the first time (chapter 20).

In these works Benton's critical faculties are placed in the service of larger problems. The study of Suger, without quite superseding Panofsky's famous introduction, moves beyond it in almost every way. The pioneering article on Trotula will surely be the *fons et origo* of future work on this intriguing figure in the history of medicine. As for Abelard and Heloise, it can only be said that they were the challenge of John Benton's life. He wrote five articles on or about them (Part IV, chapters 21-5), three of which (22, 24, 25) were devoted to the baffling question whether they were – or in what sense, one or both could have been – the authors of the famous letters preserved in MS Troyes 802. Here above all one recognizes Benton's insistence on setting truth above emotion. Second to none in his admiration of Heloise, fascinated by the medieval women – Hildegarde of Bingen, Eleanor of Aquitaine, Marie of Champagne, the shadowy Trotula – he encountered, he was a sympathetic expositor of women's experience. But the romantic veil falls. Guibert's mother is exposed as well as heard; Marie and her mother are demythologized. As for Heloise, her testimony is accepted strictly in the context of the institutional life through which we know her.

The three essays on the correspondence well disclose the tendency of Benton's thought. Led in 1972 to resurrect the radical scepticism of Bernhard Schmeidler, he argued that the whole correspondence was a thirteenth-century forgery by 'a falsifying anti-feminist at the Paraclete [working] from both authentic and inauthentic materials in an attempt to change the traditional administrative structure of the abbey' (p. 475; chapter 22). By 1979 he had all but abandoned this argument – this was his 'recantation' (more exactly, a retractation) – and it is worth noticing why. It was partly because he had failed to persuade most other scholars; and partly because, upon reconsideration, he found the discrepancies to which he had at first drawn attention either too circumstantial or too slight to bear much weight. Yet one senses that a deeper implicit cause of doubt was Benton's powerfully historical sense of the letters' nature; of the inherent probability of their twelfth-century authorship. In the paper of 1979 (chapter 24) he returned to a theory of Abelardian authorship for the letters, presenting newly supportive evidence from Fr. Chrysogonus Waddell's research on the liturgy of the Paraclete, while admitting to lingering 'doubts and problems' (p. 486). By 1986 he was ready to argue strongly for Abelard's authorship of all the letters, drawing on computer-assisted studies of style that went beyond his own first efforts (chapter 25).

There John Benton left the question, ever open to debate, but far better examined and posed than he found it. His late work, like his first, sought to explain how people did things as well as how they thought. The two at once, that is; inseparable parts of a richly conceived history. Few American scholars since Charles Homer Haskins have so well explored the culture *and* institutions of twelfth-century France. Benton addressed large problems while shunning large solutions. Magnanimous, learned, persuasive, he wrote as he spoke: clearly, modestly, and with humane doses of spice and wit. He brought common sense to all he touched. His articles wear well. They form a major contribution to the study of medieval history.

John Benton was my earliest academic friend. He and I set out together on what Rufus M. Jones called 'the trail of life in college', for we were placed firmly in adjoining seats by William E. Lunt in his alphabetically dominated course in English history on our first day at Haverford College. From there we were drawn alike to work under Theodor E. Mommsen and Joseph R. Strayer at Princeton (1956-7). Elspeth Hughes, whom John had married in 1953, easily took her place in this association. How well I remember post-seminar meals in their rooms in Blawenberg, N.J., where we shared a genial discourse of the oppressed! In later years we were often in each others' homes. For by the time our professional ways parted, our aims and styles – and jokes – had long since assumed the vulgate forms of lasting friendship.

Yet in this respect I was but one of many. It bears repeating that John's gift for friendship was at the heart of his experience. I have mentioned some special friends in the Preface, but they know as well as I how many others there were! No one of us who knew him can pretend fully to evoke this man who gave himself to us all and to others we academics never met. Born into Quakerism, he never lost the outgoing sympathies, the outrage at oppression, in which he had been educated. Nor did he lose his sense of humour or his caustic, often self-deprecating, wit in which we delighted. He enjoyed telling on himself of encounters with his seniors in which John typically unhorsed his adversary with a witty thrust, only to absorb a healthy cuff or two in return. His way of speaking through laughter was memorable. He seldom mentioned the physical pain that was his other life-long companion. To be sure, he was not mute about his afflictions. He would talk of them clinically, taking keen interest in the remedies, yet without self pity. Elspeth knew better than we others what a toll they took.

In what he could not have known were his last hours, John Benton composed an inspirational letter to his oldest daughter. He concluded by saying 'I feel at peace with myself', then wondered in his typically sensitive way whether he was not sounding 'complacent'. It was so like him. *Requiescat in pace*. We remember him as a friend and scholar of rare quality.

Abbreviations

AA.SS.	*Acta sanctorum*, ed. J. Bollandus et al. (Antwerp, etc., 1643-)
A.D.	Archives départementales
AH	*Analecta hymnica medii aevi*
AHR	*American Historical Review*
AN	Archives nationales
AS	AA.SS.
Aube (Marne, Seine-et-Marne, etc.)	A(archives départementales de l') Aube
BN	Bibliothèque nationale
CC(L, Cont. Med.)	Corpus Christianorum (latinorum, Continuatio Mediaevalis)
CCMe	*Cahiers de Civilisation médiévale*
CFMA	Les Classiques français du Moyen Age
C.N.R.S.	Centre national de la Recherche scientifique
CSEL	Corpus Scriptorum ecclesiasticorum latinorum
CTSEEH	Collection de Textes pour Servir à l'Etude et à l'Enseignement de l'Histoire
DHGE	*Dictionnaire d'histoire et de géographie ecclésiastiques*
EETS	Early English Text Society
EHR	*English Historical Review*
EPM	Etudes de Philosophie médiévale
GF	Otto of Freising and Rahewin, *Gesta Friderici I imperatoris*, ed. G. Waitz, B. von Simson, MGH, SS rerum Germanicorum (Hanover, 1912)
JWCI	Journal of the Warburg and Courtauld Institute
MGH, SS (*Capit., Const., Epist.*)	*Monumenta Germaniae Historica, Scriptores* (*Capitularia, Constitutiones, Epistolae*). See also SS
MP	*Modern Philology*
MPL	See P.L.
P.-C.	Alfred Pillet, Henry Carstens, *Bibliographie der Troubadours* (Halle, 1933)
P.L.	*Patrologiae cursus completus . . . Series latina*, ed. J.-P. Migne, 221 vols. (Paris, 1844-64)

SB	Sitzungsberichte
RS	Rolls Series
SATF	Société des Anciens Textes Français
SS	*Scriptores rer(um) germ(anicarum), in us(um) schol(arum)*

I

LETTERS AND LOVE

1

The Court of Champagne as a Literary Center

THE remarkable literary flowering of twelfth-century France grew from the fruitful meeting of representatives of different intellectual traditions, the collaboration of the laymen of the feudal courts and of those trained in monastic and cathedral schools.[1] This mixing occurred most often at the courts of great lords, either because authors met personally in that varied and changing society or because they wrote for an audience which they knew had sophisticated and eclectic tastes. Among these centers the court of Henry the Liberal and Marie of Champagne was one of the most important, notable for the education and patronage of its count and countess, for the prominence of the many scholars and authors associated with it in one way or another, and for the quality of its literary remains.

Ever since 1883, when Gaston Paris declared that it was a northern center for the dissemination of the doctrines of *l'amour courtois*,[2] the court of Champagne has interested literary and social historians alike. It is therefore surprising that there is no historical study of the court of Champagne more recent or more concerned with literary matters than that which Henri d'Arbois de Jubainville in-

---

* This article was originally prepared as part of my doctoral dissertation, "The Court of Champagne under Henry the Liberal and Countess Marie," submitted to the Department of History at Princeton University in May 1959 and reproduced photographically by University Microfilms, Ann Arbor, Michigan. My gratitude to Professor Joseph R. Strayer for his supervision, to the Fulbright Exchange Program for making possible a year's work in France, and to many others is acknowledged in the dissertation itself. For this reworking I gratefully acknowledge the kind assistance of Mlle Jeanne Vielliard and the staff of the Institut de Recherche et d'Histoire des Textes for continuing to send me microfilms, transcriptions, and points of information, and of Professors Berthe M. Marti and William J. Roach, who read my article in manuscript and improved it greatly, without having any responsibility for its contents. The financial aid of a Special Faculty Research Grant from the University of Pennsylvania was most welcome.

[1] See the summary statement of Reto R. Bezzola, *Les Origines et la Formation de la littérature courtoise en occident*, 2: *La Société féodale et la transformation de la littérature de cour* (Paris, 1960), p. 129. The third part of this great work will cover the courts of the later twelfth century. Cf. the opinion summarized by Urban T. Holmes, Jr, "The Idea of a Twelfth-Century Renaissance," SPECULUM, XXVI (1951), 644.

[2] "Etudes sur les romans de la table ronde. Lancelot du Lac: II. Le Conte de la Charrette," *Romania* XII, 523.

cluded in his *Histoire des ducs et des comtes de Champagne* a century ago.[3] Literary historians have had to work with an insufficient knowledge of the court personnel, its administrative practice, and even of basic chronological data. The greater attractions of French studies over Latin and of romances over pious tracts and commentaries have led modern scholars to concentrate on special interests, leaving us without a survey of the literature of the court of Champagne as a whole.[4] Historians of mediaeval society have meanwhile often accepted without critical review the conclusions of their colleagues in literature about the relationship between life and imaginative writing at this particular court. In the absence of a historical treatment of questions of literary importance, a number of unfounded assumptions and loose generalizations have become a part of modern discussions of the court of Champagne.[5] A study which stays close to the available evidence may help to establish more firmly our knowledge about courtly literature and the society for which it was written.

The ways in which a court influenced literary activity can not always be easily established, but close attention to the authors themselves provides some useful clues. The major portion of this paper will be devoted to individual authors, classified in four groups according to their relationship to the court. Some few authors and scholars can be found among those who were in regular attendance at the court; a much larger number dedicated their works to the count or countess, wrote letters to the count, or mentioned the court and its rulers in their writing. A fifth section is reserved for those whose connection with the court is doubtful or mistaken. Such a classification is useful in showing that all the authors associated with the court were not uniformly intimate with its rulers. Dr Johnson's experience with Lord Chesterfield and his definition of a patron as "commonly a wretch who supports with insolence and is paid with flattery" are reminders that a dedication may be direct evidence only of the hopes of the author and not of the inclinations of the dedicatee; more evidence than a simple dedication is needed to prove a close relationship between a patron and an author. Probably an author who dedicated a work to the count or countess appeared at court to present his composition and to receive whatever reward was offered, but this does not mean that he was regularly a member of the court. The author of a letter, of course, may never have met the person to whom he wrote. Finally, it should be remembered that an author might mention the rulers of Champagne without being in any way connected with them.

The question of whether or not an author regularly attended the court is of

[3] 6 vols. in 7 (Paris, 1859–67). This was a pioneering work by a distinguished archivist at Troyes, but much more archival material has since become systematically available. I have been able to add over 150 charters to his catalogue for the period 1152–98.

[4] Recent studies concentrating on Marie are provided by Rita Lejeune, "Rôle littéraire de la famille d'Aliénor d'Aquitaine," *Cahiers de Civilisation Médiévale*, I (1958), 324–328, and Françoise Bibolet, "Marie, comtesse de Champagne," in *Almanach 1957 de l'Indépendant de l'Aube* (Troyes, 1957), pp. 64–73. I owe my thanks to both these scholars for their personal assistance.

[5] A representative though not exhaustive number of the opinions here challenged are cited in the footnotes in order to show the reason for considering some of these matters so fully.

great importance for this study, and only a fortunate combination of circumstances provides satisfactory evidence for an answer. Throughout most of the twelfth century the clerks of the court of Champagne concluded their charters with a list of the witnesses to the legal act described. Over four hundred such witness lists from this court in the second half of the twelfth century have survived in its well-preserved records. At places with different notarial practices, such as the royal court, witnesses were not commonly named, and as the evidential value of sealed documents became more generally accepted, even chanceries which had listed witnesses abandoned the practice. In Champagne, at the count's court, witness lists were usually omitted after 1187, so that, in spite of richer documentation, we know less of the administrative personnel of the court in the thirteenth century than in the twelfth.

The witness lists permit a thorough study of the nature of the court of Henry and Marie and of the persons who composed their entourage. Over six hundred people witnessed at least one court charter which did not apparently pertain to them personally, and some names recur over one hundred times. The frequency and circumstances of these listings allow us to know the names of a relatively small group of men who were often at court, and to differentiate those who traveled with the itinerant ruler, those who attended the court when it was resident near their homes, and those who traveled from a distance to attend its sessions. While men of importance and high social standing were those most likely to be named as witnesses, simply knights and clerics appear frequently, and even serfs, court menials, and burghers are listed occasionally. If, during the time in which witness lists are abundant, the name of a man of any importance is never recorded, we cannot conclude that he never visited the court, but we may be reasonably sure he was not a regular member of the court circle. It should be noted that the documentation of court personnel is rich for the period before 1181, fair from 1181 to 1187, and poor after 1187.[6]

A chronological outline introduced at this point will provide some biographical data about the rulers and clarify the following discussion of the court authors. Henry the Liberal, eldest son of Thibaut the Great of Blois, was born in 1127 and became count of Champagne at his father's death in 1152. Marie, eldest daughter of Louis VII and Eleanor of Aquitaine, was born in 1145.[7] Newly recovered evidence shows that their engagement was contracted in 1153 and not before, so that

---

[6] The validity of witness lists as evidence, chancery practice at the court of Champagne, and the locations and editions of the court charters are discussed in appendices of my dissertation. The number of charters with witness lists analyzed there is as follows: from Henry I (1152–81), about 370; from Countess Marie in the same period, 7; from Marie's first regency (1181–87), 32; from Henry II while in Champagne, 5; from Marie after the accession of her son (1187–98), 13. The figures are affected by the regrettable tendency of mediaeval and early modern copyists to omit witness lists, and by their apparent preference for recording the acts of men rather than women.

[7] Edmond-René Labande, "Pour une image véridique d'Aliénor d'Aquitaine," *Bulletin de la Société des Antiquaires de l'Ouest*, 4th ser., II (1952), 180. This thoughtful summary is the best available presentation of the personality and career of Marie's mother. Unannotated material in this paragraph may be found in H. d'Arbois de Jubainville's *Histoire*.

one of Henry's first independent acts as count was to form an alliance with the Capetian monarchy which his father had generally opposed.[8] That the marriage had taken place by 1159 seems to me established by a charter of that year in which Henry referred to Marie as "comitissa sponsa mea" and "Trecensis comitissa." "Sponsa" could mean either bride or fiancée, but the title of countess indicates that the marriage had been solemnized. Marie's youth and the use of "sponsa" rather than "uxor" suggest that the marriage was celebrated not long before the charter was issued.[9] The later date, 1164, commonly cited for this marriage was proposed by Henri d' Arbois de Jubainville on the basis of the chronicle of Robert de Torigny, who said under 1164 that Count Henry "iterum assumpsit filiam Ludovici regis, quam prius dimiserat."[10] Since we know now that this passage is not a garbled account of the marriage, it may be evidence of an actual separation of the spouses, perhaps brought about by the count's temporary estrangement from Louis VII after the failure of the meeting between the king and Frederick Barbarossa at Saint-Jean-de-Losne in 1162.

After returning from a pilgrimage to Jerusalem, Henry died on 16 March 1181, leaving Marie a thirty-six-year-old widow with four children: Henry (born 29 July 1166), Thibaut (born in the spring of 1179), and Marie and Scholastique, whose birth dates are uncertain. From 1181 until Henry II's majority in 1187 Marie had direct control of the affairs of the county; for some years she sided with her relatives in opposition to young Philip-Augustus, and at one point Count Philip of Flanders, another rebel, negotiated with the pope for a dispensation to marry her.[11] Marie acted again as regent after Henry II departed for the Third Crusade in 1190. When her elder son died at Acre in September 1197, his brother Thibaut had not yet reached his majority and Marie continued to govern the county until her death early in March 1198.

---

[8] H. d'Arbois de Jubainville, *Histoire*, III, 12–13, places the engagement at the time of the Second Crusade and discounts the statement of the learned editors of the *Art de vérifier les dates* (4th ed., in 18 vols. [Paris, 1818–19], XI, 370) giving the date as 1153. The Benedictine scholars used charters which Arbois de Jubainville did not consult, so that he based his statement on a grammatical technicality in a late and unreliable chronicle. The two elusive charters of Count Henry, in which he notes that 1153 was "anno illo quo filiam ipsius regis affiduciavi," appear in B. N. ms. fr. 12021, fol. 13 r° and 15 r°.

[9] Professor Urban T. Holmes accepted the analysis of the implications of the charter of 1159 which I sent him personally, and conveniently reprinted the document in his *Chrétien, Troyes, and the Grail* (Chapel Hill, 1959), p. 18. Although the charter is known only in a late copy, the date is supported by a reference to Archbishop Samson of Reims, who died in 1161. It is gratifying to see how quickly and thoroughly Jean Misrahi developed the implications of the revised dating for Arthurian scholarship in "More Light on the Chronology of Chrétien de Troyes?," *Bull. bibl. de la Soc. Int. Arthurienne*, XI (1959), 109–113. Working independently, Professor Misrahi reached the same conclusions about Arbois de Jubainville's date of 1164 as I did in my dissertation, pp. 30–31.

[10] Arbois de Jubainville, *Histoire*, III, 96.

[11] Both the negotiation of the marriage and its termination were surely politically determined. A contemporary explanation of the change of plans, that Marie granted her favors to the count too soon and had nothing left to tempt him into marriage, sounds like idle gossip and did not convince the chronicler who reported it. See William of Ardres in *MGH SS*, XXIV, 715.

I. AUTHORS WHO APPEARED OFTEN AT COURT

Although many authors may have attended the court occasionally,[12] the witness lists show that only a few were regularly in the entourage of the count or countess. We know for certain of only two authors who were often in the company of Count Henry, and both of these men were more closely attached to their ecclesiastical posts than they were to the court. Andreas Capellanus, who is discussed in the fifth section, may have been Countess Marie's chaplain, and Henry's chancellor may have been a literary man. An author might, of course, have talents which would recommend him as a court official; we need not conclude from these less certain cases that an author was given a court position because he was an author. The conclusion that authors were seldom regular attendants at the court of Champagne is not surprising; this was the normal situation at mediaeval courts.[13] If Henry or Marie wanted to reward an author with a living, the grant of a quiet prebend as a canon would encourage more future writing than a post at the busy court.

Maître Nicolas de Clairvaux (also known as Nicolas de Montiéramey) received his early education at the Benedictine monastery of Montiéramey ten miles from Troyes.[14] His subsequent career reveals an ambitious man with a talent for ingratiating himself with influential patrons. In his youth he was chaplain to Bishop Hatto of Troyes and conducted business at Rome for both Peter the Venerable of Cluny and Bernard of Clairvaux. In 1145 he abandoned his black robe and entered Clairvaux, where he became Saint Bernard's secretary. There he dealt with part of the monastery's voluminous correspondence, became adept at writing in the style of his master, and probably also composed many of his extant sermons and liturgical pieces. This productive period at Clairvaux ended in 1151, when Nicolas was expelled from the monastery for theft and the improper possession and use of the seals of Bernard and the prior. Bernard wrote to Pope Eugene III about Nicolas, denouncing him in the strongest terms.[15] With this letter a matter of public knowledge, it would seem that only unusual personal charm could have allowed Nicolas to advance his career.

After Bernard's death Nicolas received the favor of Adrian IV at Rome, by 1158 he was back at his old monastery of Montiéramey, and by 1160 he had become the prior of Saint-Jean-en-Châtel, a dependency of Montiéramey at Troyes. From then until his death some time between 1175 and 1178 he lived at Troyes,

---

[12] Walter Map, for instance, stopped at the court in 1179, without ever leaving any record of his visit in the local documents. See below, p. 28.

[13] See Samuel Moore, "General Aspects of Literary Patronage in the Middle Ages," *The Library*, 3rd ser., IV (1913), 369–392.

[14] On Nicolas see the summary of Augustin Steiger, "Nikolaus, Mönch in Clairvaux, Sekretär des hl. Bernhard," *Studien und Mitteilungen zur Geschichte des Benediktiner-ordens*, XXXVIII (1917), 41–50 and the contributions of Jean Leclercq, "Etudes sur Saint Bernard," *Analecta Sacri Ordinis Cisterciensis*, IX (1953), 62–67 and "Les collections de sermons de Nicolas de Clairvaux," *Revue Bénédictine*, LXVI (1956), 269–302. Dom Leclercq very kindly sent me the proofs of this latter article before it was published.

[15] The letter is in Migne, *P.L.*, CLXXXII, 500–501.

where he appeared on occasion at the court of the count. As prior of Saint-Jean, Nicolas witnessed six charters of the count, all apparently enacted at Troyes. Count Henry made several substantial donations to Nicolas directly or to Montiéramey "pro amore carissimi mei magistri Nicolai." In 1160 Henry gave Nicolas the income from a house in the market place at Troyes, and in the next year he granted an income to Montiéramey from two houses at Bar-sur-Aube on condition that during his life Nicolas should have the income "ad facienda negocia sua." In 1170 the count recorded a grant to Nicolas of an annual income of one hundred sous at Saint-Etienne-de-Troyes; this probably had some connection with Nicolas' position as canon of that church. Henry made other grants to Saint-Jean-en-Châtel, which the prior naturally received, but the presents mentioned here stand out because they were of personal benefit to Nicolas.[16]

Nicolas dedicated two collections of his literary endeavors to Henry, each prefaced by a letter of eulogy. One, of which only the introductory letter is known, was a collection of letters which Nicolas probably presented to the count about 1161 and which he had recently written to the pope and other great people.[17] The other work dedicated to Henry was a manuscript which contained a group of nineteen sermons, some other sermons, a collection of commentaries on verses of the Psalms, and some liturgical pieces, including ten sequences. Nicolas' works show an author well read in the Bible and the classics, not an original thinker but a man abreast of the thought of his time, whose passion for style and rhetorical devices led to the repetition of clichés and commonplace quotation. They also show a man whose pretentious labors were not impeded by intellectual integrity. Nicolas mentioned casually in the letter introducing this second collection to Count Henry that it was his own work except for the contribution of others "paucis in locis." In fact, a number of the sermons were written by Saint Bernard and the commentaries on the Psalter were the work of Hugh of Saint-Victor, in which Nicolas changed only the words "frater carissime" to "comes dulcissime."[18]

In this instance we can see quite clearly the relationship between author and

---

[16] Arbois de Jubainville, *Histoire*, III, 146–147, 457–458; his "Recueil des chartes d'Henri le Libéral," in *Trésor des pièces rares et curieuses de la Champagne et de la Brie*, ed. J. Carnandet (Chaumont, 1863), I, 282–283; and Charles Lalore, *Collection des principaux cartulaires du diocèse de Troyes*, 7 vols. (Paris, 1875–90), VII, 73–76. Maître Nicolas witnessed a charter of 1158 involving the abbot of Montiéramey, Aube 6 H 705. As canon, Nicolas established masses for himself at St-Etienne with an endowment of sixty livres. See *Recueil des historiens de la France: Obituaires*, ed. Auguste Molinier, *Obituaires de la province de Sens*, IV: *Diocèses de Meaux et de Troyes* (Paris, 1923), p. 529 B.

[17] Migne, *P.L.*, CXCVI, 1651–52. For the dating of the letter see Arbois de Jubainville, *Histoire*, III, 199, n. 3. Nicolas' own estimation of his career is summed up in this letter by the statement, "ab ineunte aetate mea placui magnis et summis principibus hujus mundi." Nicolas compared Henry to Plato's philosopher-king, beginning his letter with this rephrasing, "Philosophus dicit: 'Ego tunc humanarum rerum statum arbitror esse felicem cum aut philosophus principari aut principes philosophari contigerit.' " William of Malmesbury also quoted Plato (*Republic*, v, 473), in a form closer to the original, when he praised the learning of King Henry I in *De Gestis Regum*, ed. William Stubbs, (London, 1887–89), II, 467. Nicolas' alteration of kings to princes was presumably intentional.

[18] An analysis of this second manuscript with identification of the borrowing is provided by Dom Leclercq, *Rev. Bén.*, LXVI (1956), 270–279, 300–302. I have prepared an edition of the sequences in this manuscript; see below, ch. 2, p. 45-75.

patron. Nicolas dedicated some of his works to the count and praised him fulsomely; Henry rewarded Nicolas liberally and addressed him as "dearest." Since Nicolas lived in Troyes he could attend the court easily when it was in town, and the two men may have conversed frequently and at length. But Nicolas did not travel with the court or take any significant part in its administration. One curious reference shows that at least once Nicolas acted as private secretary to the count. We have the reply to a letter which Nicolas wrote to Bishop Arnulf of Lisieux complaining about a young canon of Saint-Etienne-de-Troyes whom he charged with forging the seal of the count of Champagne to obtain a loan. In his reply Arnulf referred to a letter which he had received from Count Henry and thought Nicolas had written. In Arnulf's identification of the style and handwriting of the letter we may suspect a touch of sarcasm: "Porro littere ille stilum vestre peritie redolebant, apicesque his, quos noviter a vestra sanctitate recepi, identitatem manus michi certis indiciis penitus expresserunt."[19]

Pierre de Celle, one of the finest spiritual writers of the twelfth century, was another literary churchman who might sometimes be found at Henry's court. Pierre's life was one of contemplation, writing, and ecclesiastical administration. He was born into a noble family of Champagne about 1118, and in his youth entered the Cluniac priory of Saint-Martin-des-Champs near Paris. By 1145 he had been chosen abbot of the Benedictine monaster of Celle on the outskirts of Troyes, and in 1162 he became abbot of the important church of Saint-Rémi-de-Reims. In 1181 he was named bishop of Chartres, succeeding his friend John of Salisbury; he died soon after 1183. He has gained the attention of posterity, not for his administrative activities, but because of his spiritual writings. His education was similar to that of Nicolas de Clairvaux, and he knew the classics, the Fathers, and (first and always foremost) Scripture. Both Pierre and Nicolas wrote monastic sermons and spiritual letters, and in fact the two men had an extensive and friendly correspondence over doctrinal and exegetical matters. Their writings, however, are in striking contrast. Pierre had little concern for rhetoric, and though he could achieve the heights of poetry, it is not likely that he took much care to polish his writing. His letters are direct and forceful, with no trace of hypocrisy. Pierre does not parade his knowledge of the classics. His self-effacing stylistic goal was to write like the Bible, and his text is often a cento of scriptural words and phrases. Above all, he was a symbolist in the monastic tradition; Dom Leclercq has called him the Claudel of his time.[20]

Pierre dedicated a treatise on monastic discipline to Count Henry. The praise usual in dedications is of course present, but it is not effusive, and restraint lends it dignity. The subject of the treatise was of no particular concern to Henry, and it was actually written for a canon regular who had requested it from the author. Pierre made no claim that this work was written for Henry, and said that he

---

[19] *The Letters of Arnulf of Lisieux*, ed. Frank Barlow, Camden Society, 3rd series, LXI (London, 1939), Letter 66, p. 117.

[20] On Pierre see Jean Leclercq, *La Spiritualité de Pierre de Celle* (Paris, 1946). For his style see in particular pp. 17, 53, 93, and 101. The correspondence with Nicolas is discussed by M. D. Chenu, "Platon à Cîteaux," *Archives d'hist. doctr. et litt. du moyen âge,*" XXI (1954), 99–106.

dedicated it to the count in order to add luster and make it publicly acceptable. He did not even say that he expected the book to interest Henry, but advised him to put it down as soon as it began to drag.[21]

Pierre's name as witness to six of Henry's charters between 1152 and 1178 is evidence of continuing contact between the two men.[22] Since ecclesiastical affairs could easily bring the abbot of Celle or of Saint-Rémi into the count's presence, these charters are not in themselves indicative of personal friendship. Dom Leclercq, who does not consider Pierre's restrained dedication an evidence of intimacy, says that his words "semblent ici empreints de déférence plutôt que de véritable affection."[23] Henry made a few grants which favored Pierre as abbot of Celle, but they did not have the personal character of his donations to Nicolas. The one surviving letter from Pierre to Henry is a rather curt note dealing with finances, but in Pierre's correspondence with others the two men appear on good terms. Soon after Henry became count, Pierre wrote to the pope to support William of Champagne's candidature to the office of provost of Soissons, emphasizing how well he would be protected and supported by his brothers Henry and Thibaut. The abbot also acted as Henry's agent in writing to the Carthusians to support the count's attempt to get an outpost of that order to settle in his estates. In one of these letters Pierre stated that he was writing for Henry because the count was at the time too much occupied with his own and the king's business.[24]

The count of Champagne and the abbot of Celle were naturally brought together by their affairs, but we cannot see that the personal or literary relationships between Henry and Pierre were particularly close. It is noteworthy that Henry was the only layman to whom Pierre addressed a dedication, and probably Henry's education and interests were to some degree responsible for this. Henry may well have rewarded Pierre for the dedication, but literary patronage is not as clearly established here as it was in the case of Nicolas de Clairvaux.

Maître Etienne "de Alinerra." When writing about the controversy St Bernard had with Gilbert de la Porrée in 1148, the Cistercian monk Helinand de Froidmont reported that certain overzealous disciples of Gilbert and Peter Abelard later began to denigrate Bernard and the whole Cistercian order.

Quorum unus magister Stephanus, cognomento de Alinerra, dixit mihi, seipsum interfuisse illi Remensi concilio, et Bernardum nostrum nihil adversus Gislebertum suum praevaluisse; sed econtrario ipsum Gislebertum opinionem suam rationibus et auctoritatibus per omnia confirmasse: quosdam vero episcopos et abbates Galliae privata gratia Bernardi nostri somnium illius sententiae praetulisse, et papam Eugenium ad ejus damnationem induxisse. Adjiciebat etiam Bernardum nostrum eo tempore magnam confusionem passum fuisse apud Antissiodorum: ubi quemdam mortuum, quem coram omni populo suscitandum praedixerat, post multas orationes incassum fusas suscitare non praevaluit. Erat autem iste Stephanus de clericis Henrici comitis Campaniae, canonicus Bel-

---

[21] The dedication is in *P.L.*, ccii, 1097–1100.

[22] To the four acts cited in Arbois de Jubainville, *Histoire*, iii, 147 (in which, for no. 6 read no. 2) add Lalore, *Cartulaires*, vi, 40–41 and Cart. de St. Thierry, Reims Bibl. mun. ms. 1602, fol. 71 v°-72 r° (1162 at *Minziacum*).

[23] Leclercq, *Spiritualité*, p. 42.

[24] These letters are in *P.L.*, ccii, 438–439, 408, 472–473.

vacensis, et Sancti Quiriaci apud Prevignum, et exercitatissimus in omni genere facetiarum utriusque linguae, Latinae et Gallicae; avarissimus tamen; velut qui semper secutus fuerat otium, et cibum alienum: qui eodem anno quo mihi haec narravit, mortuus est, credo in ultionem sancti Bernardi, cui detraxerat.[25]

The search for Maître Etienne "de Alinerra," clerk of Count Henry and canon of Beauvais and of Saint-Quiriace-de-Provins, is inconclusive. The only Maître Etienne known to have been closely associated with Count Henry is a man usually identified in our charters as Maître Etienne de Provins, who was elected provost of Saint-Quiriace in 1169, replacing the count's brother William.[26] This Etienne was named as a witness in nine of Count Henry's charters between 1164 and 1174, almost all enacted at Provins.[27] He was also a canon of Saint-Etienne-de-Troyes, and it is possible that such a collector of prebends may also have been a canon of Beauvais. Maître Etienne became Count Henry's regular chancellor in 1176, and as chancellor he travelled about Champagne with the count, in contrast to his earlier stationary witnessing at Provins and Troyes. He accompanied Henry on his pilgrimage in 1179 and reached the Holy Land, but he is not known to have returned.[28]

Since a man might easily be known by more than one cognomen, a name associating the chancellor with Provins is no bar to his identification as the subject of Helinand's account. The name of "Magister Stephanus de Aliorra" appears in one of Henry's charters of 1161 as a canon of Saint-Etienne, and since Chancellor Etienne was also a canon of that church, a variant spelling of the cognomen given by Helinand would seem to have been found. In a charter of 1186, however, "Stephanus de Aliotra" is listed as a priest and canon of Saint-Etienne.[29] Possibly the variation of one letter here distinguishes two men; perhaps we have to do with a coincidence or a pair of relatives with the same name. But if Etienne "de Aliotra," alive in 1186, was the man named by Helinand, then that man was presum-

---

[25] *P.L.*, ccxii, 1038. Helinand's allusion to the story of Bernard's embarrassment at Auxerre suggests a much more scurrilous version of what is apparently the same anecdote, reported by Walter Map, *De Nugis Curialium*, ed. M. R. James (Oxford, 1914), p. 39. Walter visited the court of Champagne in 1179, the same year in which Maître Etienne de Provins presumably died and therefore the year in which he told his story to Helinand, if he was the one who did so. See below, p. 576.

[26] John R. Williams, "William of the White Hands and Men of Letters," in *Haskins Anniversary Essays*, ed. Charles H. Taylor and John L. La Monte (Boston, 1929), pp. 380–381. I see no reason why this Etienne de Provins should not have been a witness to the charter Williams cites in n. 104.

[27] Add to the references noted in Arbois, *Histoire*, iii, 131: Elizabeth Chapin, *Les Villes de foires de Champagne* (Paris, 1937), pp. 282–284; Lalore, *Cartulaires*, v, 35; original charter of 1174 in Yonne H 198 (liasse); Marne G 1308 (orig.); and AN K 192 #212 (copy).

[28] Arbois de Jubainville, *Histoire*, iii, 133. Doubts that Maître Etienne the Chancellor might not have been the provost of St-Quiriace are allayed by references in the charters in Félix Bourquelot, *Histoire de Provins* (Provins, 1839–40), ii, 400, and AN K 192 #71.

[29] Both of the original charters exist today. That of 1161 is in Aube 6 H 286 (liasse), and is printed in Lalore, *Cartulaires*, vii, 73–74; that of 1186 is in Aube 6 G 7 (carton 2). In Helinand's *Chronicle* the spelling "Alinerra" is that given by Migne and his printed source. The autograph manuscript of the *Chronicle*, once kept at the seminary of Beauvais, can no longer be located, in spite of a diligent search by the Institut de Recherche et d'Histoire des Textes. Cf. *Comptes-rendus des séances de la Société académique de l'Oise*, April 1920.

ably not the chancellor, who appears not to have come back from the crusade in 1179. One solid link of identification could resolve these doubts, but at present our knowledge is unsatisfactory.

In the chance that the chancellor was the learned clerk of Helinand's story, some other information about him may be useful. Before he became chancellor Etienne de Provins appeared as often at court as other important churchmen who were not court officers but who were frequent attenders. He acted occasionally as chancellor before he took regular office, and since the count controlled appointments to prebends at Saint-Etienne and Saint-Quiriace, his positions there are signs that he enjoyed Henry's favor. During his life he amassed a certain amount of property including an oven, a mill and a field which he owned outright, a house at Provins, and a stone house near the count's palace at Troyes; this may support Helinand's charge of avarice.[30]

Whatever "clerk" Helinand had in mind, this student of Abelard and Gilbert de la Porrée, skilled in both Latin and French, is the most scholarly individual identified as a member of the court. J. R. Williams has suggested that he was the Master Stephen of Reims, canon of Beauvais, under whom the poet Gautier de Châtillon studied, and thinks it probable that he was a grammarian cited as Stephen of Beauvais and Stephen of Reims in the notes of a twelfth-century student of Priscian.[31] Unfortunately he was a scholar whose works, if there were any, have not survived, and all that we can say is that Count Henry had as a clerk a man with a reputation for learning.

Geoffroi de Villehardouin took the office of marshal at the court of Countess Marie in 1185. In the succeeding years his official duties must have brought him often to the court of Champagne, but he can in no way be considered a court author, for Villehardouin dictated his celebrated history of the Fourth Crusade long after he had left Champagne. It would be pleasant to think that the influence of a cultured court affected his later work, but there is no way to demonstrate this thesis.[32]

II. AUTHORS WHO WROTE FOR THE COURT

A sure indication of the importance of a court as a literary center is the list of authors who wrote for its patronage. Besides Nicolas de Clairvaux and Pierre de Celle, we know of a number of authors who addressed works (other than letters) to the count or countess, or who wrote at their command. Three of the pieces discussed in this section, the *Eructavit*, the *Venjance Alixandre*, and the song of Richard the Lion-Hearted, have dedications which do not claim that the person addressed encouraged their composition. The most effective demonstration of the literary influence of Henry and Marie is that Chrétien de Troyes, Evrat, Gace Brulé, Gautier d'Arras, and Simon Chèvre d'Or all acknowledged their personal

---

[30] For Etienne's property see Arbois de Jubainville, *Histoire*, III, 134; Victor Carrière, *Histoire et cartulaire des Templiers de Provins* (Paris, 1919), pp. 46–47; *Obituaires de Sens*, IV, 477 C; and an undated act of William, archbishop of Sens, Yonne H 935.

[31] "The Quest for the Author of the *Moralium Dogma Philosophorum*," SPECULUM, XXXII (1957), 740–741.

[32] For details on the marshal and author see Jean Longnon, *Recherches sur la vie de Geoffroy de Villehardouin* (Paris, 1939).

intervention. This influence should not be exaggerated, however, since Gace Brulé wrote only one of his many songs specifically for Marie, and she was not the principal patron of Gautier d'Arras.

Chrétien de Troyes. After years of investigation all attempts to identify the author Chrétien with Chrétiens named in contemporary documents have failed to provide more than interesting speculation. A man named Chrétien appeared as a canon of Saint-Loup-de-Troyes in 1173 and another (or possibly the same man) was a canon of Count Henry's church of Saint-Maclou at Bar-sur-Aube. If it could be shown that either of these men was an author, or even that he was connected in some special way with the court of Champagne, some support would exist for an identification. Professor Holmes has constructed an ingenious argument based on handwriting to show that the canon of Saint-Maclou was the father of Countess Marie's chancellor Gautier.[33] Unfortunately this link of identification is not possible, for clear evidence establishes that the chancellor Gautier was a younger son of Clarembaud III de Chappes, viscount of Troyes.[34] We are left with no secure knowledge of the author Chrétien outside of that provided by his writing.

Two passages in his own works connect the author Chrétien with Champagne. The first is his use of the cognomen "de Troies" in *Erec* (l. 9); the second is the introduction to *Lancelot* in which he states:

> Puis que ma dame de Chanpaigne
> vialt que romans a feire anpraigne,
> je l'anprendrai molt volentiers
> come cil qui est suens antiers
> * * * *
> Mes tant dirai ge que mialz oevre
> ses comandemanz an ceste oevre
> que sans ne painne que g'i mete.
> Del CHEVALIER DE LA CHARRETE
> comance Crestïens son livre;
> matiere et san li done et livre
> la contesse, et il s'antremet
> de panser, que gueres n'i met
> fors sa painne et s'antancïon.[35]

---

[33] Professor Holmes discusses previous suggestions (including that of L. A. Vigneras) and his own research in *Chrétien, Troyes, and the Grail*, pp. 52-61. While I agree with him that Chrétien was a rare name (no witness of that name appears in the court charters of Champagne), I do not share all his conclusions about the identification of the author. When I wrote to him about the Chrétien, canon of St-Maclou, whose name I found in two charters (not from the court), I suggested that the problem of identity must remain uncertain until further evidence is found. Such evidence has not yet been produced. I can see no justification for Philipp A. Becker's assumption that a knight named Chrétien mentioned in the *Feoda Campanie* was the author. See his "Neues über Chrestien de Troyes," *Romanische Forschungen*, LX, (1947), 536-545.

[34] On Gautier de Chappes see Lalore, *Cartulaires*, I, 117-118; V, 57-58, 117-118; and *Obituaires de Sens*, IV, 238 F and 453 A.

[35] *Le Chevalier de la charrete*, ed. Mario Roques, (Paris, 1958), ll. 1-29. On the literary significance of this passage see D. W. Robertson, Jr, "Some Medieval Literary Terminology, with Special Reference to Chrétien de Troyes," *Studies in Philology*, XLVIII (1951), 669-692. On the interpretation of Lancelot note p. 691. But see also Faith Lyons, "'Entencion in Chrétien's *Lancelot*," *Studies in Philology*, LI (1954), 425-430.

This introduction alone establishes Marie's importance as a literary patron; it clearly informs us that Chrétien was in personal communication with the countess, that she encouraged him to write, and that she suggested the story which Chrétien developed. He therefore can be called a court author, that is, someone who wrote for the court. But we are not justified in calling Chrétien a member of the court. A thorough search of the charters of Henry and Marie has failed to turn up any mention of any person named Chrétien. This absence should not surprise us, since, as has been said, few other authors appeared often at the court, and then not simply because they were authors. In view of Chrétien's dedication of his *Perceval* to Count Philip of Flanders it may also be noted that no one has found any trace of the author's name in the numerous documents of the court of Flanders.

Since Marie was involved in the composition of *Lancelot*, one might expect the poem to be of great value as an indication of her literary and social ideas. Because the hero of the romance has an illicit affair with the wife of his lord and sovereign, it has often been assumed that the countess of Champagne advocated a new concept of love and commissioned Chrétien to disseminate a revolutionary doctrine.[36] It is not possible, however, to move directly from the existence of a romance about adultery to the conclusion that it expressed Marie's views. We are dealing with a literary work of subtle construction; modern critics have suggested that Chrétien's romances are as full of symbolism as mediaeval sculpture and that we must beware of a strong strain of irony.[37] It is not surprising that current interpretations of *Lancelot* are not in agreement,[38] since irony, symbolism, allegory, or other literary devices can be demonstrated convincingly only by reference to conventions independent of the story itself. I have suggested elsewhere that *Lancelot* is a humorous satire in which the hero reveals how an improper love turns him away from the ideals of Christian and feudal society.[39] This is not the place to develop such a thesis, and I mention it only as one possible alternative to the view

---

[36] This is one of the major theses of the article by Gaston Paris in *Romania*, XII (1883) cited above, n. 2. Its influence can be seen in a statement from the introduction to John J. Parry's translation of *The Art of Courtly Love by Andreas Capellanus*, (New York, 1941), p. 14: "The poem [*Lancelot*] is an elaborate illustration of the doctrine of courtly love as it was introduced into northern France by Eleanor and Marie. Here for the first time in Chrétien's extant works we find the glorification of the love of one man for another man's wife. . . . Chrétien clearly found the theme distasteful and left the poem unfinished."

[37] Reto R. Bezzola cites Louis Bréhier's conclusions about religious art and applies them to Chrétien in *Le Sens de l'aventure et de l'amour* (Paris, 1947), p. 6; D. W. Robertson, Jr, raises some most challenging questions about Chrétien's use of ironic humor in "Chrétien's *Cligès* and the Ovidian Spirit," *Comparative Literature*, VII (1955), 32–42.

[38] Mario Roques cites some of the views with which he disagrees in "Pour l'interpretation du *Chevalier de la Charrete* de Chrétien de Troyes," *Cahiers de Civilisation Médiévale*, I (1958), 148.

[39] In my dissertation, "The Court of Champagne," pp. 236–245. Part of that argument was based upon an attempt to show that the proper names would have had meaning to an audience listening to Old French. Professor Roach has pointed out to me that *gorre* as a common noun is not attested before the fourteenth century and that *bade* occurs at this time only in the phrase *en bades*; I therefore withdraw my entire etymological adventure, while still feeling that ample evidence of humorous irony remains. Cf. Holmes, *Chrétien, Troyes, and the Grail.* p. 45–46.

that Chrétien's romance shows that the author or Marie idealized adultery. Rather than use a work of imaginative literature as a key to the social standards of a court, the more secure procedure is to investigate the historical evidence to see what light it sheds on literature. In any case, we should avoid hypotheses based on assumptions about the personal life of an author unknown to us. Jean Frappier has appropriately warned us against imagining that Chrétien left *Lancelot* unfinished because he was ordered to write a work unsuited to his tastes.[40]

Evrat. In 1192 a man named Evrat began to write a verse translation of Genesis at Marie's request.[41] The poem, which contains much commentary and incidental material, runs to over 20,000 lines and was not completed until after Marie's death in 1198. Of its author, active in a time when witness lists were no longer common, we know nothing except his name and the little which can be drawn from the poem itself. The learning displayed proves him a well-read cleric, and his fulsome praise of Henry the Liberal, Marie, and young Henry shows that he aspired to favor from the court. Evrat refers to himself often in the poem, but he gives almost no personal information in the process.[42]

Jean Bonnard, the only scholar to publish an analysis and criticism of this unedited work, concluded that it was not poetry but versification and dismissed Evrat with the judgment that Marie was not fortunate in her choice of an author.[43] Bonnard's evaluation of the literary quality of the work was accurate, for Evrat's style is banal and monotonous and he seldom achieves the rhetorical effects for which he strives. But, as Bonnard recognized, symbolic exegesis and moral applications were of greater interest to the author than the surface qualities of his presentation; it is therefore only fair to judge Evrat and, by extension, the taste of his patroness, principally in terms of his own intention. His announced goal is to lead his audience, both clergy and laity, to understand the significance of his Biblical material. Following the usual mediaeval practice, the text is presented with a gloss which explains the difficult words and concepts, explicates the symbolic levels of the text, and points out both hidden and obvious morals. In so doing, Evrat draws on previous commentators, and frequently cites by name Eusebius, Josephus, Bede, Augustine, and above all, Jerome. Other authorities

---

[40] *Chrétien de Troyes* (Paris, 1957), p. 124–125.

[41] "De la gentis contesse encor / Ki l'estoire en romans fist faire. . . . " There is an analysis of this unpublished poem in Jean Bonnard, *Les Traductions de la Bible en vers français au moyen âge* (Paris, 1884), pp. 105–119; the lines quoted here are on p. 107.

[42] There is some reason to connect Evrat with Le Mans, and possibly with the cathedral church there. The only personal reference I have found beyond the name is: "Se cil le peut metre en romanz / Ja par Saint Julien del Mans / S'anrme ne sera mais perdue / n'espoentee, n'esperdue." Paris, B. N. ms. fran. 12456, fol. 2 v°. Saint Julien was the patron saint of the cathedral of Le Mans.

[43] Bonnard, *Traductions*, pp. 118–119. The reader can judge the style from these opening lines:

> Cil ki toz biens fait commancier
> Soit a cest livre enromancier.
> Le prologes ici commance
> Del romanz q'Evraz enromance.
> Comment donc senz enromancier
> Ne peut romanz encommancier? (fol. 2 r°)

and traditions appear in his work, and much of Evrat's labor of over six years must have gone into weighing the different glosses available to him.[44]

For what audience did Evrat intend his translation? His references to clergy and laity and to his auditors suggest that he expected the poem would be read aloud to a group. But besides stating that Marie requested the translation, Evrat says that the countess, who would know how to understand and read his work, could read it in her library.[45] Presumably the author wrote with both the countess and her court in mind.

Evrat's commentary provides a slight but illuminating clue to the views about women which might be found at Marie's court. Not surprisingly, Evrat gives no approval to anything like "courtly love." God ordained marriage and created love between man and woman so that they might keep faith with one another, Evrat states, and no one, not even a monk or a hermit, should separate what God has joined together.[46] When telling the story of the Fall, Evrat compares the guilt of Adam and Eve. In a couplet he sums up his sense of a man's responsibility for the direction of family affairs:

> Hom doit avoir et sens et force;
> N'est pas hom cant femme l'esforce. (9 v°)

But though Adam foolishly allowed himself to be deceived, Eve's guilt was greater, for she had suggested the sin to which Adam assented. The author accepts Adam's excuse and reveals something of the influence expected from a wife by saying that Adam acted reasonably in believing Eve. Evrat's condemnation of Eve led him to make a few unchivalrous remarks about women in general. They are unable to hold back from doing something a man has forbidden; they extract secrets from a man and then quickly pass them on; if a man says anything which displeases a woman, never will he have any peace. It is true that Evrat may well have found these criticisms in whatever source he was using, that his comments are less bitter than much mediaeval anti-feminism, and that he hails the role of the Virgin in bringing into the world the remedy for Eve's sin. Nevertheless, that a flattering poet included any critical remarks in a composition intended for a powerful woman suggests that such comments were commonplace and could be made without exciting any particular attention, even at the court of the countess of Champagne.[47]

---

[44] *Ibid.*, pp. 105, 110–113. On Biblical exegesis see Beryl Smalley, *The Study of the Bible in the Middle Ages*, 2nd ed. (New York, 1952), and Henri de Lubac, *Exégèse médiévale*, 2 vols. (Paris, 1959).

[45] "Quant la contesse de Champaigne / Ki bien lo sout entendre et lire / Lo peut en son armaire eslire . . . " (fol. 2 r°). Bonnard quotes a passage referring to an audience of clergy and laity on p. 110. Before citing a passage directed to auditors, Bonnard (p. 117) denied its significance by saying, "Une assemblée de barons n'aurait pris que fort peu de goût aux gloses interminables qui retardent la marche de son récit." One suspects that Bonnard has extended to the mediaeval audience his own dislike of allegorical explication. He does not take account of the tastes either of a learned layman like Count Henry or of his contemporary, the illiterate count of Guines, who listened to Scripture and understood both literal and mystical meanings. See the *Chronicle* of Lambert of Ardres in *MGH SS*, xxiv, 598.

[46] The passage is quoted by Bonnard, *Traductions*, p. 114.

Evrat's future editor will need to be widely read in Biblical exegesis, since the poem includes glosses, apocryphal material, and variations from the text of the Vulgate whose sources cannot be easily identified. Moses Gaster attempted to explain these puzzles by arguing that Evrat was a heretic and that his *Genesis* was derived from the mediaeval Slavonic *Palaea*, in which the Old Testament story was embellished with many legends and apocrypha which are part of the literature of Bogomilism.[48] If this hypothesis could be proved it would be of great importance, since it would point to a literary and scholarly link between northern France and the Eastern heretics and would call into question the orthodoxy of Countess Marie and the court of Champagne. But Gaster worked only from Bonnard's scanty analysis, and if he had read the text itself he presumably would not have made his suggestion. In addition, he was not sufficiently familiar with the Biblical commentaries of Western Christendom. He considered it a sign of the influence of the *Palaea* that Evrat includes Cain's murder by Lamech, the legend of Antichrist, the denunciation of arrogant clergy, the change of Joseph's sale price from twenty pieces of silver to thirty, and other explanations of Old Testament passages by reference to the New Testament. All of these matters are commonly found in western literature of undoubted orthodoxy, however, and we do not need the *Palaea* to explain their appearance. In one significant detail Evrat departs from the orthodox tradition: he places the creation of the beasts on the fifth day, so that Man does not share his day of creation with any other animal. Although this variant also occurs in the *Palaea*, the rest of Evrat's text shows that he was not following that version of Creation, since the *Palaea* differs widely from Genesis, and in all other respects Evrat follows the Vulgate faithfully and almost literally.[49] A fuller reading of Evrat's texts, moreover, demonstrates the author's orthodoxy. His continual references to Holy Church, his belief that confession in the Church wards off the Devil, and his views on marriage are enough to show that Evrat was not a Bogomil or even a Waldensian. The translation of the Bible into the vernacular was condemned by the hierarchy at this time because un-

---

[47] The commentary on the fall is on fols. 9 v°-10 r°. Evrat bases his greater condemnation of Eve on a hairsplitting distinction which is only made clear by the context of the comparison. The woman, he says, "consenti / lo mal ou li hom s'asenti" (9 v°). Mr Richard O'Gorman kindly aided me with a transcription of this passage.

[48] *Ilchester Lectures on Greeko-Slavonic Literature* (London, 1887), pp. 164–171.

[49] Evrat's decision to place the creation of the beasts of the field on the fifth day was deliberate and not a matter of confusion: "Tot ce fist Deus sens devinailhe / al quint joor, ce sachies sens failhe" (fol. 5 v°). In this point Evrat differs from the text of Genesis and from all the Western Christian commentaries I have read. But no other aspect of the cosmogony of the *Palaea* as analyzed by Gaster (pp. 28 and 154), including the creation of Satanael and the other angels on the first day and of paradise on the third, appears in Evrat. Gaster never published his planned English translation of the *Palaea*. Father Francis Dvornik of Dumbarton Oaks and Mr Ivan Korowytsky of Temple University kindly introduced me to the literature on the *Palaea*. Possibly the creation of the beasts on the fifth day came to Evrat through Jewish Biblical studies going back to the Hebrew sources of the *Palaea*. Cf. "The Book of the Secrets of Enoch," xxx, 7–8, in R. H. Charles, *Apocrypha and Pseudoepigrapha*, II (Oxford, 1913). There are suggestions in the *Zohar* that the beasts of the field were created at the same time as the flying and creeping animals. See *Zohar*, 34 and 47a, trans. by Harry Sperling and Maurice Simon, 5 vols. (London, 1931–1934), I, 129–130, 147.

instructed people might be led into error. Evrat's translation, on the other hand, presented a full commentary to insure that Genesis would be read with the help of the traditional and orthodox glosses.[50]

Eructavit. A third literary work written for Marie is a poetical paraphrase of the psalm *Eructavit cor meum*, number forty-four of the Vulgate text. *Eructavit*, as the poem is known, was written after Philip Augustus became king, and since the author makes no mention of the fall of Jerusalem when speaking of the Turks, it was probably concluded before the catastrophe of 1187. This would place the probable time of its composition in the years of Marie's early widowhood and regency. There is no claim that Marie requested the poem, but in the dedication and conclusion the poet addresses the countess directly and presents the work to her. He presumed to give the countess personal and spiritual advice, including the comment, rare in mediaeval works addressed to wealthy patrons, that she should avoid excessive generosity. This suggests that the author was familiar with the countess and was in a position of some religious responsibility, but there is nothing in the poem to indicate a positive identification of this spiritual adviser, who certainly need not have been a regular member of the court.[51]

Eructavit is artistically superior to Evrat's *Genesis*. The verse is clear and flows smoothly, and the metaphors, often extended, are picturesque and sharply drawn. In approach, however, the two poems are similar. Like Evrat, the anonymous author of *Eructavit* presented a Biblical text with an extended allegorical and moral gloss. His method was that of an exegete, quoting a Latin verse and then adding a paraphrase and commentary in French. Like Evrat, he took his material from a number of different commentators, and his most impressive talent lay in the skill with which he combined what might have been random comments into a unified presentation.[52]

The Forty-fourth psalm was held to symbolize the marriage of Christ and the Church. Saint Jerome used it as a text for a letter to the noble lady Principia, and the French poem with its comments on earthly marriage was probably considered especially suitable for a woman. It is a joyful psalm, part of the liturgy of Christmas morning, and the French paraphrase was built on a theme of divine love and joy. This emphasis on love and joy brings the vocabulary and phrasing of the poem close to that of secular love literature, reminding us of the interplay to be found between secular and religious material.[53]

Gace Brulé. One lyric poet belongs on the list of those who wrote something at Marie's command. The knight Gace Brulé began one of his poems with the statement that the countess of Brie had commanded him to sing.

---

[50] Evrat's presentation of the story of Tamar (fols. 118 v°-129 r°) illustrates these points about his outlook and his use of allegory to explain the text of Scripture.

[51] *Eructavit*, ed. T. Atkinson Jenkins, Gesellschaft für romanische Literatur, 20 (Dresden, 1909). On *largesse* see ll. 7-14. For dating and discussion of the poem, see Jenkins' introduction. His attribution of the poem to Adam de Perseigne is discussed below, pp. 582-584.

[52] The sources have been studied by George F. McKibben, *The Eructavit; The Author's Environment, his Argument and Materials* (Baltimore, 1907).

[53] Particularly joyful is the commentary on "Afferentur in laetitia et exultatione" in ll. 1753 ff. The phrase "joie de la cort," so important in Chrétien's *Eric et Enide*, occurs in l. 34.

> Bien cuidai toute ma vie
> Joie et chançons obli̇er,
> Mais la contesse de Brie,
> Cui comant je n'os veer,
> M'a commandé a chanter,
> Si est bien drois que je die,
> Cant li plaist a conmander.[54]

In official documents Marie was always called countess of Troyes, but since she held part of Brie as her dower, the title countess of Brie could be used in a poem (when it helped the rhyme and meter) as properly as countess of Champagne. The argument which dates the poem and identifies the countess as Marie and not Blanche of Navarre seems to me reasonable but not entirely conclusive.[55]

Gace Brulé was one of the most prolific poets active at the end of the twelfth and beginning of the thirteenth century in northern France. His poems, almost all about love, are usually addressed to a male audience of "companions" or "lords" or dedicated to a circle of noble men. They do not convey a feeling of personal passion, and, in endlessly celebrating the love of his lady, Gace gives the impression of writing to please his courtly audience. His great popularity in his own day is hard to understand critically when one reads through a book of his lyrics, but the same could be said for most modern song writers. His commonplace thought and expression are not so obvious, of course, when the lyrics are sung.

The fact that he wrote one song at the command of the countess of Brie does not make Gace Brulé Marie's court poet, or even indicate that he ever visited her court. The poem itself is a piece of polite and conventional flattery; its complaint that the countess did not return or even recognize his love was the sort of praise which a writer could tactfully offer to any lady. Gace's poems were usually not very witty, but the one line attributed to the countess turns the song into a piece supporting the crusading movement, in which Marie's son became one of the leaders. Part of the author's complaint is that when he wishes to plead his case with his lady, she stops him by asking when he is going overseas, "Cant ireis vos outre mer?"

This song is attributed to Gace by the manuscript usually known as *C* and by the author of the *Roman de la Rose ou de Guillaume de Dole*. In opposition to this strong claim, manuscript *T* attributes it to the poet Aubouin de Sézanne, who is considered in a later section.

Richard the Lion-Hearted, when he was held in captivity by Henry VI in 1193, wrote a song in which he complained of the slowness with which his ransom was being collected. The song, which up to that point had concerned his vassals

---

[54] Holgar Peterson Dyggve, *Gace Brulé*, Mémoires de la Société Néophilologique de Helsinki, XVI (Helsinki, 1951), Song LXV, ll. 1–7, p. 396.

[55] *Ibid.*, pp. 18–23. Except for the matter of Marie's dower, noted by Mme Lejeune (*Cahiers de Civilisation Médiévale*, I, [1958], 325, n. 51), this model edition provides all the factual information given here on Gace Brulé. It is only fair, however, to warn the reader that Peterson Dyggve's statements about dating and identifications are sometimes surmises placed on top of probabilities. Robert Fawtier's opposing argument that Gace and Thibaut IV of Champagne were contemporaries has not yet been effectively refuted. See his "Thibaut de Champagne et Gace Brulé," *Romania*, LIX (1933), 83–92.

and subjects, closes with an address which modern editors give as follows:

> Contesse suer, vostre pris souverain
> vos saut et gart cil a cui je me clain
> et par cui je sui pris.
> Je ne di pas de celi de Chartain,
> La mere Looys.[56]

This may be translated as "Sister countess, may he to whom I appeal, and through whom I am made prisoner, save and guard for you your sovereign worth. I do not speak of her of Chartres, the mother of Louis." Marie of Champagne and Alix of Blois and Chartres were Richard's half-sisters, and were at that time the only sisters who were countesses. The final two lines are clear enough in denying any concern for Alix, who was the mother of Louis of Blois, but the address to Marie is less easily understood. As it stands the text asks that someone to whom Richard appealed and through whose actions he had been captured might protect Marie. The poem as a whole is addressed to Richard's barons, and it is hard to see how these lines could apply to them or to such men as Henry VI or Philip Augustus. The editors might, however, have adopted another version of the text in which the third line is given as "por ce que je sui pris."[57] This change permits one to translate the passage as, "May he to whom I appeal because I am captive save and guard for you your sovereign worth," suggesting that the appeal is addressed not to any earthly potentate, but to God. In either case, we do not know why Richard should favor Marie over Alix, but the implications of the poem seem to be political rather than literary.

Gautier d'Arras was the author of two romances, *Eracle* and *Ille et Galeron*. *Eracle*, which concerns us here, is the entertaining and edifying story of a young man divinely endowed with a talent for judging the value of stones, women, and horses, who eventually became emperor and recovered the Cross from pagan hands. A sub-plot is devoted to the amorous adventures of an empress who, against the advice of Eracle, was too closely guarded by her jealous husband. The clear moral of this episode is that jealous confinement will drive even the virtuous wife astray. Gautier began his romance with praise of Count Henry's brother, Thibaut of Blois. He acknowledged broader patronage before he reached the end, where he stated that he had put his work into rhyme for Thibaut and also for Countess Marie and then praised Baudouin of Hainaut, who had led him to complete the work.[58] The composition is often dated about 1165, but there is not enough evidence to justify such precision.

Frederick Cowper has devoted much of his scholarly life to the study of Gautier d'Arras and his works, and has pointed out the likelihood that the poet was a well-known officer of the same name at the court of Flanders. This Gautier d'Arras,

---

[56] Karl Bartsch, *Chrestomathie de l'ancien français*, 12th ed. by Leo Wiese (reprinted New York, 1951), song 43, ll. 37–41. More variant readings are given in Hans Spanke, *Eine altfranzösische Liedersammlung*, Romanische Bibliothek, 22 (Halle, 1925), #cix, pp. 201–203.

[57] Spanke, *op. cit.*, p. 203.

[58] *Oeuvres de Gautier d'Arras*, i: *Eracle*, ed. E. Löseth, Bibliothèque française du moyen âge, vi (Paris, 1890), ll. 1–94 and 6548–93.

a member of the family of the castellans of Arras, appeared in over one hundred documents beginning in 1160; he probably died or retired after 1184. His fiefs, his wife and children, and his court offices are known and show that he was an important and trusted member of the higher nobility of Flanders. This identification seems to me solidly based and entirely convincing.[59]

Professor Cowper's attempt to date the composition and associate it with Provins is neither so judicious nor so convincing as his identification of the author.[60] It is his thesis that Gautier's description of Rome as the setting of the story is really a lightly veiled picture of Provins and its May Fair. It is quite possible, of course, that Gautier's description of Rome was based on the urban life of his homeland, but the particular links which Dr Cowper cites with respect to Provins are not sound. His argument begins with Félix Bourquelot's description of the way the dome of Saint-Quiriace dominates Provins and reminds travellers of Rome, but he passes over the information that the present monstrous dome was built to replace the original tower which burned in 1662.[61] It is difficult to understand what connection Dr Cowper sees between Gautier's twelfth-century poem and the piece of the Cross and the Rose of Sharon which Thibaut IV brought back from Jerusalem in 1240. A round tower is prominent in *Eracle* and Dr Cowper says that the great square and octagonal fortified tower at Provins "presents substantially the appearance of being round." It is easy to disagree with this judgment. Dr Cowper's suggestion that the two feast days of the poem were Pentecost and Trinity Sunday is reasonable, but he is not justified in saying that they occurred "*just* before Saint John's Day" (italics mine). This statement is derived from the lines:

> Un cerisier ot fait planter,
> Dont ele souloit presenter
> Le dame un present chascun an,
> Devant le feste saint Jehan. (ll. 4236-42)

Such a general comment, which applies to every year as well as to the one in question and which does not say how close to the feast the present was made, provides no reason for searching for years in which Trinity Sunday fell on the Sunday before Saint John's Day, and the suggestion of 1166 or 1177 as likely dates of composition therefore has no basis.

Moreover, Dr Cowper's most important source of information about Provins, Bourquelot's *Histoire de Provins* (1839), is imprecise in its dating, and it is unlikely that many of the practices identified by local historians as mediaeval occurred in the twelfth century. And if Gautier was really "a good publicity man," as Dr Cowper suggests, would he have failed to make specific reference to the church of Saint-Quiriace-de-Provins when he referred to its patron saint?

---

[59] There are recent summaries of information about Gautier in the introduction to Cowper's edition of *Ille et Galeron* (Paris, 1956), and William C. Calin, "On the Chronology of Gautier d'Arras," *Modern Language Quarterly*, xx (1959), 181-196.

[60] "Gautier d'Arras and Provins," *Romanic Review*, XXII (1931), 291-300.

[61] Lucien Morel-Payen, *Troyes et Provins* (Paris, 1910), p. 132. There is a picture of the great tower at Provins on p. 125.

Neither the witness lists of charters nor Gautier's poem provide any evidence for associating the author with Provins. The date of the poem has not yet been precisely established. Countess Marie was only mentioned in passing, while Gautier praised his two other patrons extensively. The significance of the two lines relating to the countess should not be exaggerated.

Maître Simon Chèvre d'Or. The only author known to have written at Count Henry's request is Simon Chèvre d'Or (Capra Aurea), a canon of Saint-Victor of Paris. Simon composed a series of short poetic epitaphs for St Bernard (d. 1153), Hugues de Mâcon, bishop of Auxerre and formerly abbot of Pontigny (d. 1151), Suger of Saint-Denis (d. 1152), Count Thibaut of Blois (d. 1152), and Pope Eugene III (d. 1153). According to the heading given in the manuscript, these poems were written at the command or request of a certain Count Henry.[62] The Count Henry who would commission epitaphs for Thibaut the Great and the friends of his family was obviously Henry the Liberal. Presumably the poems were written shortly after the deaths they commemorate and in the early years of Henry's rule. The establishment of the identity of Simon's patron also allows us to conclude that the count of Champagne was the Count Henry who commissioned one of Simon's longer and more significant works.

Simon wrote three Latin poems treating the Trojan War. The shortest was probably the first and related only the adventures of Paris and the siege of Troy. The second was a more extended work of 430 lines which amplified the first and added a summary of the *Aeneid*. It was this second poem which Count Henry commissioned. It is probable that Simon wrote this poem for Count Henry before 1163, that is, within a decade of the composition of the epitaphs.[63] The third poem doubled the length of the second by adding a few episodes and some rhetorical embellishments. A note at the end of this manuscript states that Simon wrote an *Iliad* when he was not yet a canon, and that after he became a canon he wonderfully corrected and amplified it.[64] The manuscripts identify Maître Simon only as a canon of Saint-Victor, and no trace of him has been found in the records of that distinguished congregation.[65] Possibly at one time Count Henry appointed Simon to one of the prebends at his disposal, but there is no evidence of it.

Jehan le Nevelon or Jehan le Venelais. Among the most popular of the classical adventures was the story of Alexander, told in various versions in Latin and the

---

[62] The epitaphs are printed in Migne, *P.L.*, CLXXXV, 1251-1254, from a manuscript from the abbey of La Charité (Hte-Saône). The heading there reads: "Versus magistri Symonis, cognomento Capra aurea, canonici Sancti Victoris Parisiensis summi et celerrimi versificatoris, quos composuit precibus comitis Henrici." An eighteenth-century antiquary saw another manuscript which gave the same information in its similar heading, but which stated that the epitaph for Hugues de Mâcon was written at the request of the monks of Pontigny. See Abbé Jean Lebeuf, *Dissertations sur l'histoire ecclésiastique et civile de Paris*, II, (Paris, 1761), 262-263. Neither of these manuscripts has been identified.

[63] "Explicit Aurea Capra super Yliade rogatu comitis Henr[ici]." The date is established from external evidence. See André Boutemy, "La Geste d'Enée par Simon Chèvre d'Or," *Moyen Age*, LII (1946), 254.

[64] Boutemy, "La version parisienne du poème de Simon Chèvre d'Or sur la Guerre de Troie," *Scriptorium*, I (1946-47), 286.

[65] Fourier Bonnard, *Histoire de l'abbaye royale de . . . St. Victor de Paris*, I (Paris, 1904), 139, n. 1.

vernacular. A cycle of adventures was created, including two tales about the vengeance taken on Alexander's murderers. One of these, the *Venjance Alixandre*, was introduced with this praise of a certain Count Henry:

> Encor sera il bien du conte Henri loiez.
> Cil est sus tot le mont de doner enforciez,
> Sages est et cortois, preus et bien afetiez,
> Et aime les eglises et honore clergiez.
> Les povres gentils homes n'a il pas abessiez,
> Ançois les a trestouz et levez et hauciez,
> Et donnees les rentes, les terres et les fiez;
> En cuer de si haut home n'ot ains si grant pitiez,
> Ja ses pers de doner n'ert mes apareilliez,
> Des le temps Alixandre ne fu tel, ce sachiez;
> Quanque Diex a el monde li fust bien emploiez.[66]

This praise is very similar to a number of eulogies of Henry the Liberal, leading various editors and commentators to conclude that the poem was presented to the count of Champagne.[67] The problem of attribution and dating is complicated by a double reading of the name of the author, editors having the choice of Jehan le Nevelon or Jehan le Venelais. A number of men with the former name have been recorded, including the archdeacon of the cathedral chapter of Arras between 1181 and 1193. The name of Jehan le Venelais is unknown.[68] Neither name appears in the witness lists of the court of Champagne. Count Henry's interest in Simon Chèvre d'Or's *Iliad* supports the suggestion that the *Venjance*, an adventure story of antiquity, was also presented to him. It is likely that the author was not a familiar of the court of Champagne, and he may never have had any personal contact with Henry, if indeed the poem was written for him and not for some other count.

Count Henry of Champagne was the most renowned count of that name in his generation, but care must be exercised to avoid attributing to him more than his due. Among his contemporaries and neighbors were Count Henry of Bar, Count Henry of Grandpré, and Count Henry of Namur and Luxemburg. The recipient of the praise of the *Venjance Alixandre* was identified at one time as that Count Henry of Luxemburg who became Emperor Henry VII.[69] The *Venjance* was probably written toward the end of the twelfth century, and if this is correct Henry of Champagne is the most likely candidate. Proper caution must always be observed in making attributions, as J. R. Williams did when he noted that "ad comitem

---

[66] Jehan le Nevelon, *La Venjance Alixandre*, ed. Edward B. Ham (Princeton and Paris, 1931), ll. 46-55.

[67] Edward C. Armstrong, *The Authorship of the Vengement Alixandre and of the Venjance Alixandre* (Princeton and Paris, 1926), pp. 43-45.

[68] On the disputed reading, see Ham, *Textual Criticism and Jehan le Venelais* (Ann Arbor, 1946). He discusses the case for Jehan le Nevelon in the introduction to the edition cited above in n. 66. George Cary, *The Medieval Alexander*, ed. D. J. A. Ross (Cambridge, England, 1956), p. 31, shows the relationship of the *Venjance* to the other Alexander material of the period.

[69] For criticism of this view see Bateman Edwards, *A Classification of the Manuscripts of Gui de Cambrai's Vengement Alixandre* (Princeton and Paris, 1926), pp. 2-3.

Henricum" is found in the margin of one of the poems of Gautier de Châtillon, who dedicated his Latin *Alexandreis* to Archbishop William of Reims.[70]

III. AUTHORS OF LETTERS ADDRESSED TO COUNT HENRY

Most mediaeval letters have survived in collections made for later reference, instruction, or edification and enjoyment. The selectivity of time has been most harsh to that highly personal or ephemeral correspondence which was never recopied. The letters we have today show us that their writers looked upon their compositions as destined to have a large audience: the authors, who often kept drafts for future publication, probably expected letters sent to a court or religious congregation to be read aloud and perhaps preserved. This expectation of a large audience may explain why those letters discussed in this section often sound like contributions to the editorial pages of a newspaper. Simple business letters written without literary pretentions are not considered here; the dedicatory letters of Nicolas de Clairvaux and Pierre de Celle have already been considered.

Guido de Bazoches, one of the foremost Latin authors of Champagne, produced a collection of verse, a collection of letters, a personal apology or defense against his detractors, a tract on geography, and a world history which included his own experiences on the Third Crusade and was used by the later historian of Champagne, Albéric de Trois Fontaines. Most of the poetry and extracts of other works have been published, but Guido still awaits the full-scale treatment which will establish him as he deserves in the history of mediaeval Latin literature.[71] He came from the noble family of Bazoches, who were major vassals of the counts of Champagne and held the office of *vidame* of Châlons-sur-Marne. Guido was one of the canons prominent in the administration of the church of Châlons. He accompanied the expedition of Henry II of Champagne in 1190 and gave a place of honor to Henry I in his world history.[72] The fullest statement of his respect and admiration for Henry the Liberal, however, is to be found in his letters.

From the state of the unique manuscript it is difficult to determine whether portions of more than two letters to Henry have survived.[73] Letter XV of Guido's collection is a eulogy which compares Henry to the sun in an extended and involved metaphor. The burden of the letter is to thank Henry for some unspecified but important favor which the count had publicly given to the author. Guido concludes most of his letters with a poem for his correspondent, and this letter ends with a gracious little poem of gratitude.[74]

---

[70] See his article cited above (n. 31), SPECULUM, XXXII (1957), 741 and n. 50.

[71] Carter G. Jefferis, in his "Guido de Bazoches," University of California (Berkeley) doctoral dissertation deposited February 1943, was unfortunately unable to make use of unpublished materials. For a convenient summary on Guido see Max Manitius, *Geschichte der lateinischen Literatur des Mittelalters*, 3 vols. (Munich, 1911–31), III, 914–920.

[72] "Palatinus Campanie comes Henricus florebat in Francia, quin potius illa per illum . . . " Paris, B. N. ms. lat. 4998, fol. 63 v°. This passage was quoted almost exactly by Albéric de Troisfontaines, *MGH SS*, XXIII, 847.

[73] The manuscript of these letters, possibly corrected by the author himself, is in the National Library of Luxemburg. The two letters to Count Henry are on the folios now numbered 45–49. Portions of the second letter are printed by W. Wattenbach, "Aus den Briefen des Guido von Bazoches," *Neues Archiv*, XVI (1891), 79–81.

The next entry, labeled number XVI, is also addressed to Count Henry. It is interrupted at the end of the first folio, leaving a break where at least one leaf is missing. The continuation has been copied in a different hand and also breaks off at the end of a leaf. The content shows that the continuation is addressed to Henry the Liberal, but there is no way to determine if it truly continues the first part or is a section of another letter. The first part is largely occupied with a denunciation of one of Count Henry's knights who had attacked and devastated a religious house of the Parisian monastery of Saint-Martin-des-Champs whose care had been committed to Guido. If a letter of Alexander III refers to the same event, this passage shows that the letter was composed about 1171.[75] The second section is devoted to genealogy. With a great show of learning, Guido traced Henry's ancestry along different lines to Clovis, Charlemagne, Henry I of Germany, Robert of France, and William the Conqueror. One wonders if Guido had been commissioned to produce this genealogy or if the idea was his own. The genealogy of the house of Champagne had its political importance, for by the marriage of Henry's sister Adèle to Louis VII the blood line of the Carolingians was united with that of Hugh Capet. Most of the genealogy stands the test of modern criticism and demonstrates considerable historical knowledge, though the relationship with Henry of Germany was based on an erroneous identification.[76]

John of Salisbury's letter to Henry provides our surest evidence of the count's own theological and literary interests. Fortunately, John's lengthy epistle contains a review of the circumstances which led to his writing. In 1165–66 the noted English scholar and supporter of Thomas Becket was exiled from England and was staying at Reims with his old friend Pierre de Celle. He was there sought out by a certain Albéric de Reims, also called Albéric de la Porte de Venus, who came accompanied by several learned men to pose some questions on divine letters and

---

[74]
    Quo candore nivem, quo munere floris aprilem,
        Qua potero tamen luce iuvare diem?
    Set iuvat ora tuis michi laudibus esse minora,
        Nilque tuis laudes addere posse meas.
    Hoc tamen, hoc unum, si quid valet amplius addi,
        Addi posse nichil laudibus adde tuis.
    Te tua poscenti semper manus obvia talem
        Esse vel a tali reddit abesse parum.
    Talem te probitas morum probat esse tuorum
        Et genus et genere mens generosa magis.
    Talis es et talis dici credique mereris.
    Talem te vatum multa talia canit.   (fol. 47a)

[75] In a letter of 11 July 1171 or 1172 the pope wrote to Archbishop Henry of Reims: "Conquerente nobis G. Catalaunensi canonico accepimus quod Wermundus miles, nepos archidiaconi, ipsum et homines villae de Alneto, irrationabiliter depraedatus, eis damna gravia irrogavit." See Migne, *P.L.*, cc, 838–839). One place which bore the name *Alnetum* is Annet-sur-Marne, near Meaux, which was a priory of St-Martin-des-Champs. See L. H. Cottineau, *Répertoire topo-bibliographique des abbayes et prieurés*, 2 vols. (Mâcon, 1939), *s.v.*

[76] The genealogy is printed with notes by Wattenbach, *loc. cit.*, pp. 79–81. It is an open question whether Guillaume le Breton had the lineage of Adèle de Champagne in mind when he called her son "Karolide" in his *Philippide*, ed. H. François Delaborde (Paris, 1885), prologue, l. 28.

philosophical matters on Henry's behalf. John stated that he was astounded and had refused to believe in the sincerity of the mission until Pierre de Celle, then abbot of Saint-Rémi-de-Reims, had told him that Henry was not given to joking in these matters and had testified to the great pleasure which the count took in discussing literary subjects with learned men. John added that Pierre, whom he called Henry's most faithful and devoted friend, had whispered in his ear that Henry took such pleasure in his studies that he often displeased those whom affairs had brought to his court, "vos inde saepissime imperitae multitudinis offensam contrahere, quia vos a studendi exercitio nequeunt revocare, et pro arbitrio suo negotiorum et tumultuum procellis immergere."[77]

The queries which Henry directed to this learned visitor show something of the intellectual and literary matters which interested the count. These are his questions, of which John answered only the first three:

1. What do you believe to be the number of books in the Old and New Testaments?

2. Who were their authors?

3. What is the Table of the Sun seen in the sand by the philosopher Apollonius, mentioned by Jerome in his letter on Holy Scripture to the priest Paulinus?

4. What are the centos of Vergil and Homer mentioned in the same letter?

5. What is the source and meaning of the oft-quoted statement, "Those things which do not exist are more God-like than those things which do exist" (*Deiformiora sunt ea quae non sunt, quam ea quae sunt*)?

The third and fourth questions arose from a well-known letter on Scripture by Saint Jerome, and the first two may also have been suggested by this letter, which comments on each of the books of the Bible and their authors.[78] As far as he went John answered clearly and simply, treating the questions as those of a novice and not of an intellectual equal. The third and fourth questions do indeed show that Henry's knowledge of classical literature was not deep. The first two questions may also have been a request for simple information which should have been easily available to Henry, but on the other hand they may have been asking for John's personal opinion about a matter on which patristic authors did not agree. The fifth question, however, shows that Henry's queries were not all superficial. The statement about which the count wanted more information is philosophically sophisticated and may have been derived from the writing of John the Scot (Eriugena).[79] That such a doctrine was a subject of discussion at the court of

---

[77] *P.L.*, CIC, 124. The full letter is on cols. 123–31.

[78] Saint Jérôme, *Lettres*, ed. Jérôme Labourt, 6 vols. (Paris, 1949–1958), III, letter LIII, pp. 8–25, esp. 9 and 16.

[79] The word *deiformis* and its derivatives are rare. John the Scot used it to translate θεοειδής and ἀγαθοειδής in *De caelesti hierarcha* of Denis the pseudo-Areopagite; see P. G. Théry, "Scot Érigène traducteur de Denys," *Bulletin du Cange*, VI (1931), 246. Although I have not found the phrase quoted by Count Henry in John the Scot's work, it may well have been derived from his theology. *De caelesti hierarcha*, which greatly influenced John, is ordered by the degree to which its subjects are "deiformis" or "in Dei similitudinem;" in his own *De divisione naturae* John distinguishes between the classes of "ea quae sunt et quae non sunt" and says that insofar as inferior beings are unable to know them, God and the celestial orders are in the class of non-being. See Migne, *P.L.*, CXXII, 1049–50 and 413–414. I am indebted for the suggestion that the quotation in question might be in the work of John the Scot to Prof. P. O. Kristeller.

Champagne indicates that Henry was a serious student of affairs not usually cultivated by laymen. The letter gives no sign of personal or literary familiarity between the two men. John did not know Henry's interests from personal experience and controlled his amazement only after Pierre de Celle's explanation.

Herbert of Boscham. Further evidence of Count Henry's interest in Biblical and doctrinal matters is provided by a letter from another English scholar, Herbert of Boscham, who served for a time as personal secretary to Archbishop Thomas of Canterbury. The text of Herbert's letter has been preserved in a late copy which omits any address or explanation of the circumstances of its composition.[80] The letter discusses a complicated question of Biblical criticism which arises from different lists of the women who were present at the Crucifixion, since the Gospel of John names three Marys and that of Mark has the name of Salome in place of one of the Marys. These texts have been the subject of heated discussion since they were used in the fourth century by Helvidius to question the virginity of the mother of the Lord. Saint Jerome replied to Helvidius in an extended tract which dealt with these passages, and they have naturally received many other commentaries.[81] Herbert's own discussion of the identity of Salome and the three Marys begins with Jerome, cites among others Bede, Origen, and John Chrysostom, and concludes with the tradition related by a certain brother named Master William who knew a church dedicated to the Three Marys.

Although we do not know why Herbert of Boscham wrote this letter to Count Henry, it is reasonable to assume that he, like John of Salisbury, was answering a question posed by the count. Herbert was an able Biblical commentator who had a command of Hebrew.[82] His service to the exiled archbishop of Canterbury brought him to the neighborhood of Henry's domains and to the count's attention. In 1166-67 Herbert wrote a number of letters pleading Becket's case which were to be sent in the name of various French dignitaries. This activity explains why a letter supporting Archbishop Thomas, written in the name of Count Henry of Troyes to Pope Alexander, was included in a collection of Herbert's correspondence.[83] Perhaps the little Biblical commentary was a gracious return by Herbert for the help which the count had rendered his patron.

Philippe de Harveng, first prior and then abbot of the Premonstratensian monastery of Bonne-Espérance near Cambrai, was the author of a handbook on the training of the clergy, a commentary on the Song of Songs, some verse, saints' lives, and other pieces. One letter in his collected correspondence is directed to a

---

[80] British Museum, Royal MS. 6 E III, fols. 250ᵇ-251. Gerald I. Bonner, Assistant Keeper of Manuscripts at the British Museum, kindly sent me photostats and a description of the manuscript. The letter does not appear in Herbert's *Opera Omnia*, ed. J. A. Giles, 2 vols. (Oxford, 1845-46).

[81] Jerome, *De Perpetua Virginitate B. Marie adversus Helvidium*, *P.L.*, XXIII, 193-216. Helvidius was also challenged by Augustine and Isidore.

[82] Smalley, *Study of the Bible*, pp. 186-195.

[83] Herbert also wrote letters in the name of Bishop Etienne of Meaux and of Mathieu, precentor of Sens, who appeared often at Henry's court. See J. C. Robertson, ed., *Materials for the History of Thomas Becket*, (London, 1875-85), VI, 38-44, 140-143. About this time Pope Alexander III recommended Herbert to the bishop of Troyes to fill the office of provost left open by the resignation of William of Champagne. See Jules Mathorez, "Guillaume aux Blanches-Mains," *Revue des Archives Historiques du Diocèse de Chartres*, 1912, p. 197.

layman named Henry. The existing text has no more informative address, but all commentators agree that it was written to Count Henry of Champagne.[84] The father of the person addressed is praised for his liberality, which would apply to Thibaut the Great, who supported both Saint Bernard and the founder of the Premonstratensian order, Saint Norbert. The letter lauds its subject for his learning, which surpasses that of other counts, for his support of the clerical order, and for his foundation of collegiate churches. Everything in the letter accords perfectly with what we know of Count Henry the Liberal and is similar to other eulogies which he received. But we are not justified in going beyond the letter to say that Philippe de Harveng was one of Henry's counselors.[85] Nothing in the letter suggests a personal relationship or that the author had even seen the count. Perhaps Philippe wrote in recognition or in hope of some particular liberality, or perhaps his letter shows only that he felt it beneficial to praise the uncommon learning and clerical orientation of a layman.

IV. AUTHORS WHO WROTE ABOUT THE COURT

The historian's search for references to Henry and Marie in contemporary writing produces a harvest rich in number though limited in what it reveals of their character and daily life. The rulers of Champagne were important and powerful people, and the authors of their day wrote about them either from hope of favor or simply because the subject was naturally interesting. Collectors of *exempla* related anecdotes about them, chroniclers recorded their deeds, and poets mourned their deaths or heralded their names. This section is not a catalogue of mediaeval references to the count and countess; it records those contemporary authors, not discussed elsewhere, whose comments on Henry and Marie are of greatest literary interest. It should be noted, however, that any princely family might have been the subject of similar references, and that these accounts and allusions were not the product of the literary interests or patronage of the count and countess.

Walter Map, the English courtier and author, attended the Third Lateran Council in 1179. On his way to Italy from England, Walter enjoyed the hospitality of Count Henry and conversed with him, as he reported later, about the proper limits of generosity. In this instance, since we know the reason for the journey, we can see that literary concerns were not responsible for bringing a famous author to Henry's court. This visit may have been the occasion for an exchange of anecdotes with a local raconteur, since both Walter and Henry's clerk, Maître Etienne, related scurrilous stories about Saint Bernard which seem to be versions of the same tale.[86]

Pierre Riga, who later wrote a versified and moralized version of the Bible in Latin, came from the region of Reims. In 1165, when Pierre was a student in

---

[84] Philippe's works are collected in *P.L.*, CCIII; the letter to Henry is in cols. 151-156. For a discussion of the abbot's life and works see G. P. Sijen, "Philippe de Harveng," *Analecta Praemonstratensia*, XIV (1938), 37-52, 189-208.

[85] As John Mahoney does in *Analecta Praemonstratensia*, XXXI (1955), 167.

[86] Walter Map, *De Nugis Curialium*, ed. M. R. James, pp. 225-226. See above, n. 25.

Paris, Adèle of Champagne, Count Henry's sister, bore a son to Louis VII and thereby assured succession to the throne. A poem on the birth of this child has been attributed to Pierre Riga, who had previously written a collection of verse for the archbishop of Reims. This poem concludes with an account of the way in which gifts were presented when the joyful news was announced, and pays special attention to the pre-eminent generosity of a Count Henry. Everything accords with the reputation and position of Henry the Liberal, and the assumption that the audience would understand this as a reference to the count of Champagne is safe.[87]

Guiot de Provins. Both Henry the Liberal and his eldest son are mentioned in passing in an extended poem by Guiot de Provins. Guiot was a successful poet who traveled widely in courtly circles. He eventually left the world and entered monastic life, first at Clairvaux and then at Cluny. Around 1206 he wrote a long composition, known as his *Bible*, which contains a list of great lords whom he had known and who were then dead. Over eighty lords are mentioned, including Count Henry of Champagne, "li plus larges hom dou mont," and young Count Henry, who went overseas.[88] It should be noted again in passing that these references do not show that the counts of Champagne were particular patrons of the poet.

Huon III d'Oisy, castellan of Cambrai and viscount of Meaux, was one of the great vassals of the county of Champagne. Around 1189 Huon wrote two poetic compositions, one clearly a crusading song and the other a strange piece called the *Tournoiement des dames*. This poem recounts the events of an imagined tournament held near Lagny in western Champagne at which all the contestants were noble ladies of the north of France. The theme of the poem is apparently political satire on behalf of the crusade. The countess of Champagne, identified by the date of composition as Marie, appears briefly in the tournament and performs in an honorable fashion.[89] Huon's two major offices show the close feudal ties between Champagne and Flanders and his poetry illustrates some of the literary talents and interests to be found among highly placed laymen.

Conon de Béthune, a pupil in song-writing of Huon d'Oisy, wrote vernacular verse for courtly audiences. In one well-known song Conon wrote of the criticism he had received from Queen Adèle and her son King Philip because his language was that of Artois. The poet was particularly sensitive to this reproach, he said, because people from Champagne, including the countess, were present. At one time or another Conon could be found at a number of northern courts and he is listed as a vassal of Champagne in one of the registers of the fiefs of the county. The poem cited here does not show that Marie was a patroness of the author; her

---

[87] H. François Delaborde, "Un poème de Pierre Riga sur la naissance de Philippe-Auguste," in *Notices et Documents publiés pour la Société de l'Histoire de France* (Paris, 1884), pp. 121-127. On Pierre see Manitius, *Geschichte*, III, 820-831.

[88] *Bible*, ll. 324-325 and 349-350 in *Les Oeuvres de Guiot de Provins*, ed. John Orr (Manchester, 1915).

[89] Alfred Jeanroy, "Notes sur le *Tournoiement des dames*," *Romania*, XXVIII (1899), ll. 82-89, p. 242. On the identification of Marie see H. Petersen Dyggve, "Les dames du 'Tournoiement' de Huon d'Oisi," *Neuphilologische Mitteilungen*, XXXV (1935), 72.

role in the poem is simply that of an important visitor to the royal court, which Conon was also attending.[90]

Verse by anonymous authors. Three poems or songs honoring the house of Champagne in this period have been preserved in collections which do not identify their authors. Two of these are funeral elegies, one for Marie and Henry II, who died within months of each other, and the other for Henry the Liberal. The third calls for support for the crusading movement, laments the fall of Jerusalem, and hails Henry II of Champagne for alone sustaining hope in the Holy Land. All three of these poems are of mediocre quality and conventional in their praise. Marie is called a model widow and Henry the Liberal is lauded, as usual, as an exemplar of generosity. The author of the elegy for Henry I regrets that Philip Augustus was not goverened by his uncle, to which cause he attributes the troubles of the kingdom.[91]

V. AUTHORS WHOSE ASSOCIATION WITH THE COURT IS DOUBTFUL OR ERRONEOUS

Andreas Capellanus. The identification of Andreas Capellanus, author of the celebrated treatise *De Amore*, as the chaplain of Countess Marie is so commonly repeated that it is easy to forget the uncertain nature of the evidence and the doubts of a number of critics. The present discussion is not intended to assert that the author Andreas was not or could not have been Marie's chaplain, but simply to show that the question is still open.

Within the text of *De Amore* Andreas refers indirectly to himself as chaplain of the royal court. The incipit of MS. C (thirteenth century?) calls the author "Andreas capelanus [sic] regis francie" and the explicit of F (fifteenth century) repeats this statement. The incipit of D (fourteenth century) identifies him as "magister Andreas francorum aulae regie capellanus;" it concludes with the statement: "editum a magistro Andrea regine capellano." Another mediaeval tradition, demonstrably unreliable, identifies Andreas as the chaplain of Innocent IV. The weightiest evidence, therefore, places the author at the royal court of France.[92] If we could find a chaplain named Andreas attending the king or queen about the time *De Amore* was composed, we could reasonably think the author had been discovered.

Since *De Amore* contains a letter dated 1174, this year is the *terminus a quo*.

---

[90] *Les Chansons de Conon de Béthune*, ed. Axel Wallensköld (Paris, 1921), song III, p. 5. For Conon's vassalage see Auguste Longnon, *Documents relatifs au comté de Champagne et de Brie, 1172–1362*, 3 vols. (Paris, 1901–14), I, #2594. On the strength of this song Gaston Paris (*Romania*, XII [1883], 523) wrote of Marie, "C'était pour lui que Conon de Béthune, entre 1186 et 1190, composait ses premières chansons."

[91] These three poems are printed by C. L. Kingsford, "Some Political Poems of the Twelfth Century," *English Historical Review*, v (1890), 319–320, and 324–325.

[92] In one of the dialogues a lover supports his proposition by saying that "amatoris Andreae, aulae regiae capellani, evidenter nobis doctrina demonstrat." *Andreae Capellani De Amore*, ed. E. Trojel (Hanover, 1892), p. 148. This is the only edition with a full critical apparatus. The information given by the manuscripts is reviewed in this edition, pp. xxi–xxxi. Trojel's conclusion about the author is on p. xli.

The *terminus ad quem* may be surely placed at 1238, since in that year Albertano da Brescia made use of Andreas' work. Evidence for making these limits more precise is not entirely conclusive, but the most comprehensive dating of *De Amore* by its references to Hungarian affairs places its composition between 1186 and 1196.[93] At no time in the period between 1150 and 1250, however, has a chaplain named Andreas been identified at the royal court. There is nothing surprising about this absence of information, since the royal notaries did not ordinarily list witnesses in their charters, and we have less data about the minor personnel of the royal court at this time than we do for courts, like that of Champagne, where witnesses were recorded.

Seventy years ago Pio Rajna pointed out that Countess Marie of Champagne, who plays a prominent part in *De Amore* and about whose judgments the author claims personal knowledge, had a chaplain named Andreas.[94] He suggested tentatively that Marie's chaplain may at some time have served at the royal court, where he composed his book. A number of scholars have taken the correlation of name and date and the apparent appropriateness of the employment as sufficient proof that the elusive author has been identified. This line of argument is quite possible, but it is by no means conclusive, and some scholars have not accepted it.[95]

The name of the "Andreas Capellanus" cited by Rajna appears in nine of Countess Marie's charters between 1182 and 1186. In these years of relatively scanty charter evidence nine appearances are enough to establish that this André was a regular and probably important member of the court. Since his name does not appear after 1186, while those of other chaplains do, it is reasonable to suppose that he died or left Marie's service about that time. The title "dominus" which he was given a few times and his consistently high ranking among the witnesses show that he was a priest, but we know nothing else of his life or background. The other court chaplains about whom we have any information held modest or humble positions in the social order (one was the son of a serf) and advanced in ecclesiastical preferment through the influence of the court. There is no way to determine whether André and his colleagues had similar careers.[96]

---

[93] Andreas referred (p. 62) to a Hungarian king who had long, round thighs and broad, flat feet. Alexandre Eckhardt shows convincingly that this was Bela III (whose skeleton measures almost 6′ 3″) in *De Sicambria à Sans-Souci* (Paris, 1943), pp. 113–124. Arpad Steiner in SPECULUM, IV (1929), 92–95, placed the composition before 1186 on the grounds that a prudent author would not comment unfavorably on the looks of a patron's relative by marriage. But why believe that brothers-in-law were protected from humorous sallies at either the royal court or that of Champagne? Andreas praised the Hungarian king's virtue if not his beauty. The more general limits of time are discussed in Trojel's introduction, pp. v–ix.

[94] "Tre studi per la storia del libro di Andrea Capellano," *Studj di filologia romanza*, v (1891), 258.

[95] In the introduction (p. 17) to his influential translation, *The Art of Courtly Love*, Parry accepted the view that the author was Marie's chaplain and questioned the claim that he was a royal chaplain. Manitius, *Geschichte*, III, 282, identifies the author only as chaplain of the French king.

[96] Five of the charters are printed: Lalore, *Cartulaires*, I, pp. 101–103; *ibid.*, v, p. 58; and A. Harmand, "Notice historique sur la léproserie de la ville de Troyes," *Mémoires de la Société . . . de l'Aube*,

Since we know so little of Marie's chaplain, his possible identification as the author of *De Amore* would not materially advance our understanding of the book. If correct, it would show that he was a priest without telling us anything of his personal standards. It would support the author's claim of personal knowledge about Marie. But since the book was probably written about 1186 when the chaplain André no longer appears in court records, we could not assume that the author wrote for Marie. Such an opinion as "it is clear that Andreas, like Chrétien, wrote his book by direction of the countess," goes beyond what is justified by our evidence.[97]

Because Andreas referred to certain noble ladies by name, *De Amore* has been used as historical evidence, particularly to show that Eleanor of Aquitaine assembled a court of noble ladies at Poitiers and that Marie visited her there.[98] This conclusion is based on a series of judgments about amatory affairs which Andreas records under the names of such ladies as Marie, Eleanor, the countess of Flanders, and Ermengarde of Narbonne. But the form of presentation is that of a legal case book, which may include decisions made at various times and places. Nothing in the text indicates that Marie and the other ladies visited Eleanor in Poitiers or came together anywhere else. Even if these "judgments" were actually delivered, they are not evidence of continuing contact between Eleanor and Marie.[99] In addition, there is the distinct possibility that Andreas was not recording anything which actually happened.

Literary historians have not been able to agree about the meaning of *De Amore*. One school of thought accepts it as a serious book, an "exposition of courtly love;" another considers that Andreas wrote "tongue-in-cheek" descriptions of actual courtly practices without any intention of condemning them; a third school sees *De Amore* as a humorous and ironic condemnation of concupiscence not concerned with "courtly love" at all.[100] As long as this disagreement is unresolved,

---

XIV (1847–48), 531, 532, and 535. The other charters are all originals: Marne H 98 (1183); Aube 6 G 7, carton 2 (1185); Aube 9 H 21 (1186); and Marne G 1308 (1186). The charter of 1185 shows Andreas in the presence of Marie's half-sister, Marguerite, who married Bela III of Hungary in the next year. This material is discussed more fully in an article to appear in *Studies in Philology*, "The Evidence for Andreas Capellanus Re-examined Again." The suggestion that the author was a certain André de Luyères (made by John F. Mahoney in the same journal, LX [1958], 1–6) is there considered critically.

[97] Parry, *Art of Courtly Love*, p. 17.

[98] Amy Kelly, *Eleanor of Aquitaine and the Four Kings* (Cambridge, Massachusetts, 1950), pp. 160 and ch. 15, n. 5: "The clue to the presence of Marie in the court of Poitiers is the fact that André the Chaplain mentions her specifically as taking part with Eleanor in 1174 in judgments under the rules of the *Tractatus*." This is simply not so; the letter of 1174 (ed. Trojel, pp. 152–155) gives no indication of place or that Marie and Eleanor were there together. Charters of 1173, 1174, and 1175 show Marie in Champagne with her husband. Cf. her "Eleanor of Aquitaine and Her Courts of Love," SPECULUM, XII (1937), 5: "Nothing that we know of Marie's life precludes the assumption that she was in Poitiers in the period of question." Miss Kelly made very little use of charter evidence.

[99] I know of no other evidence for the statement of Gaston Paris, *Romania*, XII (1883), 523: "[Marie] était fille d'Alienor de Poitiers, et resta toujours en commerce avec elle."

[100] The three approaches in this order are expressed by Parry, *Art of Courtly Love*, esp. p. 19; W. T. H. Jackson, "The *De Amore* of Andreas Capellanus and the Practice of Love at Court," *Romanic Review*, XLIX (1958), 243–251; and D. W. Robertson, Jr, "The Subject of the *De Amore* of Andreas Capellanus," *Modern Philology*, L (1953), 145–161, and "The Doctrine of Charity in Mediaeval

De Amore, like Chrétien's *Lancelot*, will be an unsure guide to the literary attitudes or practices of feudal courts. Andreas' book is not a source of unambiguous historical evidence, but is itself to be interpreted in the light of what we know about mediaeval society and literature.

With good reason a number of modern historians have been unwilling to believe in the existence of actual "courts of love" as described by Andreas.[101] If Andreas' account contains imaginative elements, it is possible that he did not intend to give a serious presentation of the views of the women in question. Mediaeval chroniclers and collectors of gossip provide little evidence with which to test this hypothesis, but in the case of Eleanor of Aquitaine we are well enough informed to see that some of the decisions attributed to her may be ironic comments upon her own behavior. When Eleanor judged the problem of the woman who has to choose between a young man devoid of worth and an adult knight of complete probity, she decided, according to Andreas, that a woman would act less wisely (*minus provide*) if she chose the less worthy one.[102] The mediaeval audience would have been perfectly aware that Eleanor had actually rejected the love of her husband Louis VII, whom she compared to a monk, and had quickly married Henry Plantagenet when he was just nineteen and she was near thirty. In *De Amore* Eleanor also gives a judicial decision which condemns consanguineous marriage.[103] Again, it was well known that Eleanor's separation from Louis was pronounced for consanguinity after the marriage had been blessed by the pope, and that Henry was almost as closely related to Eleanor as Louis. These two cases may lead us to suspect that there is more humor or satire than faithful quotation in the decisions of women about whom we are less well informed.

It is very difficult to know what effect Andreas expected to create through the quotations he attributes to Countess Marie. Taken out of their strange context, some of the statements he puts in her mouth make good sense in terms of conventional morality, such as the judgment that it is improper for a woman to seek to be loved and yet to refuse to love.[104] Most crucial to an understanding of Andreas' treatment of the woman who may possibly have been his employer is the letter he attributes to her on the subject of love and marriage. This letter, supposedly written in 1174, says in part that love can have no potency between two spouses: "Dicimus enim et stabilito tenore firmamus, amorem non posse suas inter duos iugales extendere vires. Nam amantes sibi invicem gratis omnia largiuntur nullius necessitatis ratione cogente. Iugales vero mutuis tenentur ex

---

Literary Gardens," SPECULUM, XXVI (1951), 36–39. A book which surveys these contradictory opinions and suggests that "courtly love" "co-existed" with mediaeval Christianity is Felix Schlösser, *Andreas Capellanus* (Bonn, 1960).

[101] Cf. Paul Remy, "Les 'cours d'amour': légende et réalité," *Revue de l'Université de Bruxelles*, VII (1955), 179–197.

[102] *De Amore*, ed. Trojel, pp. 278–279.

[103] *Ibid.*, p. 279: "Satis illa mulier contra fas et licitum certare videtur, quae sub errois cuiuscunque velamine incestuosum studet tueri amorem. Omni enim tempore incestuosis et damnabilibus tenemur actibus invidere, quibus etiam ipsa humana poenis novimus gravissimis obviare."

[104] *Ibid.*, p. 277.

debito voluntatibus obedire et in nullo se ipsos sibi invicem denegare."[105] Was Andreas reporting what he thought Marie would actually have said or did say on this question? Was the letter intended to tell us anything of the state of Marie's marriage in 1174? By making the quotation did the author imply criticism or approval of the countess? The answers to these questions are presumably connected with the author's opinion of love, which he defines at the beginning of his book as passion or suffering, "passio quaedam innata procedens ex visione et immoderata cogitatione formae alterius sexus. . . . "[106] If Andreas considered love as here defined desirable, then he probably was presenting Marie as an open advocate of adultery, but if he considered such love as something to be avoided, he may have intended the quotation attributed to Marie as a veiled praise of marriage, which provides a remedy for love. It is worth noting that this letter echoes the Pauline doctrine of marriage, where marriage is permitted as a defense against fornication, and the point at issue is whether the quotation was intended to subvert or support that doctrine. Some help in treating these literary questions may be provided by other evidence about Marie and the court of Champagne.

Adam de Perseigne. In his edition of *Eructavit*, published in 1919, T. Atkinson Jenkins argued that the poem was written by the Cistercian abbot and author Adam de Perseigne, who preached a sermon at Countess Marie's deathbed. Jenkins thought the poet showed unusual familiarity with Marie and that in its theology, exposition, and attitude toward the Virgin Mary *Eructavit* is similar to known writings of Adam de Perseigne.[107] This attribution has no substance. The anonymous poem does not in fact suggest a particularly close relationship between its author and the countess, and even if it did, Marie's deathbed summons to Adam and his subsequent sermon do not demonstrate such closeness.[108] Jenkins freely admitted that there was nothing personal about the theology, exposition, and concern for the Virgin which he found in Adam's work and in *Eructavit*, since he called them characteristically Cistercian. He even noted that Adam gave a different application to the phrase "Eructavit cor meum" in prose works than the verse has in the poetical translation.[109] The similarities of ideas and texts which he cited are commonplaces, and he was not specific about details of expression.[110] While it is difficult to prove that Adam, of whom we know little, was not the author of *Eructavit*, it can be said that such a claim is unlikely.

---

[105] *Ibid.*, p. 153.

[106] *Ibid.*, p. 3.

[107] *Eructavit* (cited above, n. 51), pp. xiii-xviii.

[108] The account of Marie's summons and Adam's sermon is given by Thomas de Cantimpré, *Bonum Universale de Apibus*, ed. Georgius Colivernerius, 2nd ed. (Douai, 1627), I, vii, 7, pp. 31-32. Adam's sermon as quoted is thoroughly conventional and does not suggest a life-long connection. Marie could have known of Adam de Perseigne's reputation as a spiritual counsellor for women from her sister Alix.

[109] *Eructavit*, p. xvii and n. 3.

[110] The reader may study these citations in the introduction, p. xvii, nn. 2 and 3. Many phrases, ideas, and favorite verses were common to monastic authors, many of whom owed their style to St Bernard. I see nothing striking, for instance, in such matters as the statement that the Virgin conceived at the words *Dominus tecum* or in "a certain indelicacy" of expression.

The author of *Eructavit* set out to write a work of spiritual edification for a noble lady which she could understand in the vernacular. But when Countess Blanche of Champagne, Marie's successor, wrote to Adam de Perseigne to ask him for a copy of his sermons, he replied that the request would be praiseworthy if Blanche could understand Latin or if the sermons could be interpreted for her, but he warned her against translations by asserting that any expression of thought may lose its savor or structure in passing from one language to another.[111] In another letter Adam expressed his pleasure to Marie's sister, Alix of Chartres, at being able to write to her in Latin.[112] There is a large corpus of edifying works surely attributed to Adam and all of it is in Latin prose. It would be strange if an author with such an opinion of translation wrote one of the first French translations of a part of Scripture, and one which was particularly graceful and well-composed.

Jenkins noted that Marie had a chaplain named Adam, but avoided asserting that this man was Adam de Perseigne. Canon Jean Bouvet has been less hesitant and has based his recent biographical sketch of Adam de Perseigne on the assumptions that he was both the author of *Eructavit* and the chaplain of the countess.[113] For this reason we may consider what can be known of the life of Marie's chaplain. He was the son of a serf, Aceline, whom Henry II of Champagne gave to the lepers' colony of Deux-eaux near Troyes in 1188. He witnessed charters for Marie in 1188, 1189, and 1191;[114] since after 1187 witness lists were rarely noted, there is no significance to the small number of references. He became a canon of Saint-Etienne-de-Troyes and retained that position after Marie's death. A charter of 24 February 1201 (N.S.) recorded that one of the canons of Saint-Etienne who arbitrated a dispute was "dominus Adam Capellanus quondam Comitisse Trecensis."[115] The title "dominus" shows that he was a priest, and it is therefore likely that he was the priest and canon of Saint-Etienne named Adam who issued a charter in 1220.[116] Canon Bouvet feels that the word *rusticus* which Adam de Perseigne applied to himself is more than simple self-deprecation and is evidence that the abbot was born a serf. Other elements of biography are more surely contradictory. Adam de Perseigne became abbot of the important Cistercian abbey in 1188 at the latest, and in one of his letters he says that before he became a Cistercian he had been a canon regular and then a Benedictine monk. On the other hand, Marie's chaplain was presumably a member of the secular clergy

---

[111] *P.L.*, CCXI, 691-692.

[112] *Ibid.*, col. 686.

[113] The biography introduces his edition and translation of Adam de Perseigne, *Lettres*, Sources Chrétiennes, 66, to be published in three vols., I (Paris, 1960), 7-29. This sketch contains the information on the abbot given here.

[114] To the charters cited in Arbois de Jubainville, *Histoire*, IV, 544, add one of 1191 printed by Charles Lalore, *Documents sur l'abbaye de Notre-Dame-aux-Nonnains de Troyes* (Troyes, 1874), #9, p. 13, and a charter of the bishop of Meaux of 1189 which refers to an action of Countess Marie, Seine-et-Marne H 492 (Cart. de Fontaines), fol. 4.

[115] Paris, B.N. ms. lat. 17098 (Cart. de St-Etienne), fol. 116 r°-v°. When Canon Bouvet wrote to me in 1957 for information about the chaplain, this was not among references I was able to send him. Cf. his introduction, p. 7, n. 1.

[116] Cart. de St-Etienne, fol. 150 v°.

and was a canon as late as 1201. At that time Adam de Perseigne was one of the most influential churchmen in Western Christendom. Though an abbot could also be a canon of Saint-Etienne, it is inconceivable that a scribe would not have identified the abbot of Perseigne by his well-known title if he had occasion to name him in a charter.

The identification of Adam de Perseigne as the author of *Eructavit* and as Marie's chaplain is unconvincing. The former is based on a few similarities commonly found among clerical authors of the day, and the latter is in turn based on the first and supported by a common first name. Neither argument seems likely when all the available evidence is weighed in the balance.

Rigaut de Barbezieux. Because they have been more widespread and authoritative, the scholarly pronouncements on the troubador Rigaut de Barbezieux have had more serious effects than those on Adam de Perseigne. Rigaut's poems provide almost no biographical information and the mediaeval biographies and commentaries are vague in their chronology. Modern scholars therefore have had little material for dating or describing the poet's life, but their consensus has been to place his activity between 1175 and 1215.[117] In large part these dates were influenced by the *tornade* of one song whose text was established by Anglade as:

> Pros comtessa e gaia, ab pretz valen
> Que tot avetz Campanh' enluminat,
> Volgra saupsetz l'amor e l'amistat
> Que us port car lais m'arm'e mon cors dolen.[118]

The countess who illumined Champagne and was honored by Rigaut could only be Marie, it was thought, and Gaston Paris even stretched the meaning of this passage to the point of asserting that Rigaut actually attended Marie's court, which was thus a link between the poetry of the north and south.[119]

We are fortunate that at last a meticulous article by Mme Rita Lejeune has placed the study of Rigaut de Barbezieux on a sound footing.[120] Working on the basis of all available information, Mme Lejeune has identified the poet as a knight of that name who was *viguiers* (*vicarius*) of the stronghold of Barbezieux in Charente, who appeared in charters between 1140 and 1157, and who had apparently died or retired from the world by 1163. Such a biography does not accord with a poem addressed to Countess Marie, and Mme Lejeune meets the problem head-on with the following argument. The *tornade* in question is found only in a few late manuscripts and is therefore of doubtful authorship; the reading *Campanh'* is itself suspect, being only one of a number of variants; and even if Champagne is the proper reading, it is more likely that the poet was referring to the Champagne de Cognac, which is next door to Barbezieux, rather than to the northern county.

---

[117] J. Anglade and C. Chabaneau, "Les chansons du troubadour Rigaut de Barbezieux," *Revue des langues romanes*, LX (1920), 227-228.

[118] *Ibid.*, Song X, ll. 41-44, p. 284. I have not yet seen Rigaut de Berbezilh, *Liriche*, ed. Alberto Varvaro (Bari, 1960).

[119] In his introduction to *Le Roman de la Rose, ou de Guillaume de Dole*, ed. Gustave Servois (Paris, 1893), p. cxx.

[120] "Le Troubadour Rigaut de Barbezieux," *Mélanges István Frank*, published as *Annales Universitatis Saraviensis*, VI (1957), 269-295.

Rigaut de Barbezieux must therefore be dropped from the list of the court authors of Champagne, and with him disappears the only personal contact between Marie and the poets of the south.

Aubouin de Sézanne. Although the song "Bien cuidai toute ma vie" is attributed to Gace Brulé in two usually reliable collections, it is ascribed to Aubouin de Sézanne in another manuscript. Almost nothing is known of the life of this poet, but two charters of Thibaut IV of Champagne show that Aubouin died between 1221 and 1229. If he wrote the poem, which is unlikely, the countess of Brie addressed in it was more probably Blanche of Champagne than Marie. In any case we are left with one song and two attributions, so that if Aubouin de Sézanne should be added to a list of court authors then Gace Brulé should be removed.[121]

VI. CONCLUSIONS: THE LITERARY ROLES OF HENRY, MARIE, AND THEIR COURT

By the middle of the twelfth century many rulers read and understood Latin, or at least saw to it that their sons did. The contemporary monarchs Louis VII, Frederick I, Henry II, and William II of Sicily were all educated men who could make use of Latin. In France some of the families which ruled the great principalities had a tradition of learning. The dukes of Aquitaine and the counts of Anjou valued education; Philip of Alsace, count of Flanders, was praised for his literacy. Education was therefore part of the equipment of a man who took a position of great power seriously, and it is in this context that we are to understand the references to the learning of Count Henry of Champagne.[122]

Count Thibaut the Great provided his son with a tutor in his boyhood, and Henry showed himself to be an apt pupil. When Philippe de Harveng wrote to him as an adult, he congratulated the count on the solicitude of his father and on his own diligence as a student, which had been combined to produce his remarkable education: "Horum concursu scholarum disciplinam per annos aliquot prosecutus sub magistrali ferula, liberalem es scientiam assecutus, et juxta modum temporis et personae, tantis, ut aiunt, literis es imbutus, ut quamplures clericos transcendas in eorum nequaquam numero constitutus."[123] Both Philippe and John of Salisbury pictured Henry turning from the cares of administration to the solaces of serious literature, and there is much evidence of his reading in the classics and religious writing. A codex of Valerius Maximus copied at Count Henry's order is still in existence, and the literary correspondence which he received shows his interest in religious literature.[124] The count also commissioned

---

[121] The song is cited above, n. 54. For the few established facts about Aubouin see Auguste Longnon, "Chartes relatives aux trouvères Aubouin de Sézanne, Gilles de Vieux-Maisons, et Thibaut de Blaison," *Ann.-Bull. de la Société de l'Histoire de France*, 1870–71, pp. 85–90.

[122] On this subject see James Westfall Thompson, *The Literacy of the Laity in the Middle Ages* (Berkeley, 1939), V. H. Galbraith, "The Literacy of the Medieval English Kings," in *Proceedings of the British Academy*, XXI (1936), and a recent highly valuable article which cites Henry of Champagne specifically, Herbert Grundmann, "Litteratus-illitteratus," *Archiv für Kulturgeschichte*, XL (1958), 52.

[123] *P.L.*, CCIII, 152. On Henry's tutor see Arbois de Jubainville, *Histoire*, III, 10.

[124] BN ms. lat. 9688: "Descriptum Pruvini, jussu illustris comitis Henrici. Willelmus Anglicus. Anno incarnati Verbi MCLXVII, indictione XV." See Léopold Delisle, *Cabinet des manuscrits de la*

Simon Chèvre d'Or to write a classical adaptation, and he may have enjoyed the *Venjance Alixandre*. As far as we know, Henry's literary tastes were conservative, and we have no evidence that he enjoyed current history, legal studies, romances, or French lyric verse.

Count Henry sought the conversation of men of letters, but he did not therefore give them positions in his court. He was on good terms with Pierre de Celle and a patron of Nicolas of Clairvaux, both of whom held ecclesiastical posts in the neighborhood of Troyes. He may have appointed a man with a reputation for learning as his chancellor, thereby strengthening his administrative staff. We have no proof that Maître Etienne was actually an author, and before his appointment the chancellor was apparently no closer to the count than other well-educated churchmen of the region. Henry commissioned Simon Chèvre d'Or to write epitaphs and a version of the fall of Troy for him in Latin, but preferment at the count's court or even in his domains does not appear to have been among Simon's rewards. Guido de Bazoches, a canon of Châlons-sur-Marne, wrote letters and a poem for the count and received some unspecified gift from Henry. The *Venjance Alixandre* was probably written for Henry of Champagne, but we are uncertain of the identity of its author and know nothing of the circumstances of its composition. In short, Count Henry's education was solid, his literary interests were serious, and he encouraged a few authors in their endeavors. As a literary patron he outshone many of his contemporaries, including the king of France, but his court did not come up to the example of either Henry Plantagenet or of his own brother, Archbishop William of Reims.[125]

We have less information about the education of Countess Marie than of her husband. The name of her teacher, Alix de Mareuil, who was at one time connected with the convent of Saint-Pierre d'Avenay near Epernay, is recorded.[126] A line in the poem of Evrat implies that Marie could read French.[127] There is no direct evidence that she could read Latin, though some well-educated women could. Adam de Perseigne felt free to write to Marie's sister, Alix, in Latin because he knew that she had some knowledge of the language.[128] So far as we know, however, no author who addressed Marie in his work wrote for her in Latin, and the translations into French of Biblical texts and commentaries for her benefit suggest that her knowledge of Latin, if existent, was weak. The question of Marie's

---

Bibliothèque Impériale, 3 vols. and atlas (Paris, 1868–81), II, 352, and Arbois de Jubainville, *Histoire*, III, 190 n. 3. In his letter to the count discussed above, John of Salisbury referred to "vester Vegetius" (col. 131). Since John was not familiar with Henry's intellectual pursuits, this may simply mean that he associated a military writer with the interests of a count.

[125] Cf. Charles H. Haskins, "Henry II as a Patron of Literature," *Essays in Medieval History Presented to Thomas Frederick Tout* (Manchester, 1925), pp. 71–77, and the article on William of Champagne by John R. Williams cited above, n. 26.

[126] It appears in the charter cited above, n. 9. See Louis Paris, *Histoire de l'abbaye d'Avenay*, I (Paris, 1879), 59 and 68–69. Alphonse Roserot suggested that Alix de Mareuil came from the house of Châtillon-sur-Marne in *Dictionnaire historique de la Champagne méridionale (Aube)*, 3 vols. (Langres, 1942–48), p. 45.

[127] See above, n. 45.

[128] See above, n. 112.

Latinity bears on the intended audience of Andreas' *De Amore,* for if Marie could not understand *De Amore* without the help of translation, there is little reason to think that it was written for her delectation. The obvious audience for a Latin treatise would be clerics and a few well-educated laymen, who might have found the first two books of *De Amore* amusing rather than instructive.

The statements of various authors show that Marie was one of the outstanding literary patrons of her day. Chrétien's *Lancelot,* Evrat's *Genesis,* and one song by Gace Brulé were written at her direct request; Gautier d'Arras was encouraged in writing his *Eracle* by the countess; and *Eructavit* was written specifically for her. Presumably these authors received suitable rewards for their labors, though there is nothing to show that any of them regularly attended Marie's court, and for the period before 1187 when witness lists are abundant negative evidence has some value. Andreas Capellanus may have been Marie's chaplain at one time, though the identification is far from sure. Unlike her husband's, Marie's known literary tastes were *avant-garde.* Gace Brulé was one of the first lyric poets writing in the vernacular in the north of France; Chrétien de Troyes was one of the great innovators in the creation of Arthurian romance; Gautier d'Arras, though a lesser light, was also a pioneer; and even the idea of translating Scriptural material into French was new and exciting in the twelfth century.

Can we move from the conclusion that Marie encouraged authors of the new genres in both secular and religious literature to the assertion that she was the propagator of doctrines which, to use the words of Amy Kelly, "undermine all the primary sanctions and are subversive of the social order"?[129] Gaston Paris thought so, and credited Marie with introducing into northern France the ideals of *l'amour courtois,* to which he called attention.[130] Such an assertion has a double basis: that Marie encouraged Chrétien to write a work which seemingly praised Lancelot, a knight who committed adultery with his sovereign's wife, and that Andreas Capellanus, whether or not he wrote in Marie's service, quoted her as making pronouncements on love which seemed to advocate adultery and to elevate women to the rank of high priestesses of a cult of love. The reader who takes Chrétien and Andreas seriously and sees no irony or satire in their work may reasonably conclude that Marie was a great social innovator. Enough serious questions have been raised about the nature of the work of these two authors, however, that it is important to know if Marie's contemporaries came to the same conclusions about her social role as do some modern literary specialists.

If Marie's views on love were complacent about man's part in adultery, she would have been accepting the double standard of her society and would have attracted no particular attention. A man's fidelity was a matter to note, not his lapses, and the chronicler Gislebert de Mons reported with surprise that Marie's son-in-law, Baldwin of Hainaut, disdaining all other women, loved his wife alone, "although it is rarely found in any man that he should cleave so much to one woman and be content with her alone."[131] But if Marie actually favored and

---

[129] *Eleanor of Aquitaine,* p. 166.
[130] See above, n. 2.
[131] *La Chronique de Gislebert de Mons,* ed. Léon Vanderkindere (Brussels, 1904), pp. 191–192.

defended the adultery of women of respectable station, she was affronting the lords and churchmen with whom she was in daily contact. The known or suspected infidelity of a noblewoman called forth the strongest reactions. Count Thibaut the Great was able to join the county of Troyes to his other domains because his uncle Hugues suspected his wife of adultery, repudiated her, and disinherited the son whom she bore.[132] When Count Philip of Flanders, who at one time negotiated for Marie's hand, suspected that his wife had committed adultery with Gautier de Fontaines, he put the young nobleman to death in a most unpleasant fashion.[133] In *Eructavit* a bride, after being advised to rise when her husband approaches, to forget her father and mother, and above all to love her husband with a pure love (*fin amors*), is reminded of the custom of the world about infidelity. When a woman deserts the love of her husband for another, the poet states, either through sin or through a mistake, even though she repents fully, her husband has no obligation to take her back, and in fact, she would be better off in the grave.[134] The very charge of immorality against a married woman was considered a serious affront to her husband's honor. The custumal of Champagne provided that if anyone made the baseless charge that an unmarried woman was a whore, he should pay the moderate fine of five sous, but if the same charge was made about a married woman in her husband's presence, the fine might be as high as sixty sous.[135]

If the doctrines implied by the "courtly love" interpretation of Chrétien and Andreas were openly proclaimed at the court of Champagne and disseminated in its literature, writers who did not accept them would not have passed them over in silence. It is therefore of considerable interest that Marie received no comment or criticism on this matter from any of her contemporaries. Pierre de Celle knew her personally, but all we learn from him about the countess is that she once so shrewdly flattered a visiting abbot at her dinner table that he forgot the business which brought him to court.[136] The Cistercian abbot Adam de Perseigne held clearly stated views on a married woman's proper subservience, but when he preached a sermon at Marie's deathbed, he spoke in conventional terms of human vanity and of the worldly pride of the great lady who found no pomp or honor in death.[137] The pious author of *Eructavit* himself praised Marie's piety and reproached her only for excessive generosity.[138] The list of orthodox authors who praised Marie could be extended, and the number of those who failed to comment upon her alleged scandalous theories is even greater. What impressed contempo-

---

[132] Arbois de Jubainville, *Histoire*, II, 135–136.

[133] J. Johnen, "Philipp von Elsass, Graf von Flandern," *Bull. de la Commission royale d'histoire [de Belgique]*, LXXIX (1910), 418–420. This article answers the problems raised in *Revue des Langues Romanes*, XXXII (1888), 286–288, and *Romania*, XVII (1888), 591–595.

[134] *Eructavit*, ll. 1428–50, 1577–94.

[135] Paulette Portejoie, ed., *L'ancien coutumier de Champagne* (Poitiers, 1956), section XLII, pp. 198–199.

[136] *P.L.*, CCII, 552.

[137] Cited above, n. 108.

[138] *Eructavit*, ll. 1–14.

raries about Marie was the vigor and ability with which she exercised the power of her feudal position; chroniclers reported admiringly that she ruled Champagne *viriliter*.[139] Here we have her true inheritance from Eleanor of Aquitaine.

During Henry's life Countess Marie regularly traveled about the county with her husband, moving from one administrative center to another. Since only women of high rank were named as witnesses, we know almost nothing of her female retainers. Three men were attached to her personal service; a chaplain Dreux, a clerk Laurent, and a certain Nevelon, *miles comitisse*. Other men who witnessed her charters usually appeared also in those of her husband. All available information indicates that Marie played no important independent role in court life while Henry was alive. Many regular members of the court failed to return with Henry from his final expedition in the Levant, where he was defeated in battle, captured by the Turks, and ransomed by the Emperor Manuel. It is therefore not surprising that many new names appear in the witness lists of his widow's acts. The names showing continuity of court personnel are also frequent, and there is no evidence to show that Marie changed the nature of the court significantly while she was in charge of its administration.[140]

Besides revising and classifying the list of known court authors, this study of the available evidence from the court of Champagne suggests a reconsideration of two currently accepted views about the literary significance of the court. First of all, it questions the belief that the court of Champagne in particular served as a point of literary interchange between north and south.[141] The troubadour Rigaut de Barbezieux, we now know, had nothing to do with the court of Champagne or Countess Marie. There is no evidence to show that Marie ever saw her mother or communicated with her after Eleanor left the court of France when Marie was seven, and it is quite possible that at the royal court Marie was brought up to despise her mother. I have found no indication that there were southerners among the court personnel of Champagne. It is true that ideas and literary styles which have been labelled "southern" are found in Champagne, but they are also found in other northern courts, like those of the king or the count of Flanders. The travels of thousands of pilgrims, merchants, and knights were surely more effective than any activities of the countess of Champagne in bringing knowledge of the culture of southern France to the north. The literary connections of the court of Champagne were not with the south but with northern France and Flanders.[142]

Secondly, the evidence assembled in this paper does not support the opinion

[139] Chronicle of Tours, *Recueil des historiens des Gaules et de la France*, ed. Dom Bouquet, XVIII, 293, and Annales de Rouen, *MGH SS*, XXVI, 500.

[140] See my dissertation, "The Court of Champagne," pp. 172–175 and 259–260.

[141] Cf. Alfred Jeanroy, *La Poésie lyrique des troubadours*, 2 vols. (Toulouse and Paris, 1934), I, 273–274.

[142] Chrétien de Troyes wrote for both Marie and Philip of Flanders. Huon d'Oisy was a vassal of both Flanders and Champagne. Gautier d'Arras was also a vassal of Flanders. The abbot of Bonne-Espérance near Cambrai wrote to Count Henry. The author of the *Venjance Alixandre* may have been an archdeacon of Arras. These instances show that the literary intercourse, like the political and the economic, was largely to the north.

that Marie's court was a center for "courtly love" as either a social or a literary phenomenon. "Courtly love" was sufficiently revolutionary to attract attention if it were advocated in any serious fashion. If Chrétien de Troyes and Andreas Capellanus truly and seriously reflect Marie's beliefs, then it must have been common knowledge that she was openly subversive of the position upheld by the men of her day. Yet none of the abundant letters, chronicles, laudatory songs, and pious dedications suggests that Marie or her court was in any way unusual or unorthodox. Modern theorists of "courtly love" owe us an explanation of these contradictions. My own inclination is to accept the suggestion of a few critics that the intentions of Andreas and Chrétien when they wrote about worldly love were conventionally moral and humorous or ironic.[143] Problems of sex and love were clearly common topics at a court such as that of Champagne, interesting both the worldly-wise and the morally sensitive. If Chrétien and Andreas were indeed ironic moralists, they used this interest to hold the attention of their audience. A sophisticated audience may well have enjoyed and understood such an apporach. This is not the place to raise all the questions connected with "courtly love," but the questions which are considered do have broader implications, for if "courtly love" is not to be found at the court of Champagne, where then did it exist?

It is important to know if a courtly audience was able to understand a sophisticated literary approach. At the court of Champagne about a third of the witnesses to court charters were clerics, and there was a small nucleus of churchmen, mainly canons, who traveled with the count and countess and attended them regularly. A somewhat larger body of laymen was regularly at the court and in the company of these churchmen. A courtly audience was therefore partly composed of clerics, who may to some degree have shared the literary interests and attitudes which they had learned in monastic and cathedral schools. The learning of the count and countess was probably even more important. We know that Count Henry read extensively in religious and classical literature. Marie's training was presumably not as deep, but her commissioning of Evrat's *Genesis* shows that she found allegorical exposition congenial. Obviously, few laymen had the educational advantages of the count and countess, but there is no reason to think that all courtly literature was written for an unlettered and unsophisticated audience.

Our evidence provides some slight indication of the ways in which one author who wrote for the court influenced another. Since a great court was a center where people came together, it would have been quite possible for authors to meet there to exchange stories and to discuss literary techniques. But if, as this study suggests, most authors spent comparatively little time at court, then the importance of direct personal contact was probably slight. An author who attended the court of Champagne and others like it would have had an opportunity to hear the recitation of works written by his contemporaries. In this way, for instance, Chrétien de Troyes may have heard the *Eracle* without necessarily meeting

[143] Cf. the articles of D. W. Robertson, Jr, cited above in notes 37 and 100.

Gautier d'Arras himself.[144] Less direct as an influence and yet still of importance was the knowledge which one author writing for the court would have of other courtly literature. When an author thinks of his audience, he thinks of the literary background and understanding which will be brought to his own work. The variety and complexity of the literature written for a court gave the mediaeval author, as it gives us, an indication of the literary sophistication of the audience. In this respect the court of Champagne was indeed outstanding. There one could find the classical reconstruction of Simon Chèvre-d'Or and the scriptural allegory of Evrat, the *fin amors* of *Eructavit* and (perhaps) the *amor mixtus* of Andreas Capellanus, the letters of Hebraic scholar Herbert of Boscham and of rhetorician Nicolas de Clairvaux, the fanciful adventures of Lancelot and of Eracle, the French lyrics of Gace Brulé and the Latin verse of Guido de Bazoches. By considering this courtly literature as a whole we may be better prepared to understand its individual parts.

---

[144] Cf. Th. Heinermann, "Zur Zeitbestimmung der Werke Gautiers von Arras und zu seiner Stellung zu Chrétien von Troyes," *Zeitschrift für französische Sprache und Literatur*, LIX (1935), 242. The relationship of common elements in the work of Chrétien and Andreas is not clear. See K. G. T. Webster, "The Water-Bridge in Chrétien's 'Charrette'," *Modern Language Review*, XXVI (1931), 73, n. 1.

Fig. 1. Countess Marie of Champagene represented in an initial to Chretien de Troyes' *Lancelot*, dedicated to her, as preserved in Guiot's manuscript of Chretien's works (early thirteenth century). See above pp. 13-15.

2

Nicolas of Clairvaux and the Twelfth-Century Sequence, with Special Reference to Adam of St. Victor

The vast number and variety of sequences, those liturgical interpolations which in the middle ages commonly followed the repetition of the Alleluia in the Mass, and the freedom of their development, show that they were an outlet for the creative talents of musicians and poets. A sample of sequences from successive periods allows the literary historian to trace the development of rhyme and accentual meter, and a musicologist has described the sequence 'as the parent of oratorio and the grandparent of modern drama.'[1] But while a view which encompasses centuries reveals to us variety and change, the compositions of any given time were largely shaped by inherited traditions. Not the least value of studies on the early history of the sequence is their demonstration of the close connection between various Alleluia melodies and their sequences and the way in which appropriate texts were fitted to melodies for specific feasts.[2]

A distinction between the technical terms 'sequence' and 'prose' is necessary for a clear discussion of their interrelated development. The chants which follow the Alleluia are called sequences, whether the melody is sung as a wordless extension of the final -*a*, or is accompanied by a text, full or partial, fitted syllable by syllable to the notes of the music. The text alone is called a prose, and once the melody of a sequence was established, many different proses might be written to fit it. By the twelfth century, different styles of proses had been developed. The proses of the first period, written by such ninth-century authors as Notker Balbulus of St. Gall, are simple lines of text, determined in their form by the music; the only usual formal characteristic is a repetition of the musical line and a consequent parallelism of the text. Accentual meter, assonance, and rudimentary rhyme were next developed by authors of what is now called the Transitional Style, and many proses of this style were written in the eleventh century. The final stylistic stage, which appeared in the late eleventh or early twelfth century, is that of the 'regular' sequence, marked by regular accentual meter and two-syllabled rhyme. The acknowledged master of the regular sequence was Adam of St. Victor at Paris in the middle of the twelfth century. Although these

---

[1] Anselm Hughes, *Anglo-French Sequelae edited from the papers of the late Dr. Henry Marriott Bannister* (Nashdom Abbey 1934) 1.

[2] For current accounts see Bruno Stäblein, 'Zur Frühgeschichte der Sequenz,' *Archiv für Musikwissenschaft* 18 (1961) 1-33 and Paul Evans, 'Some Reflections on the Origins of the Trope,' *Journal of the American Musicological Society* 14 (1961) 119-130.

three styles represent changes of poetic taste, sequences in the earlier styles continued to be enjoyed in the later middle ages, and early melodies were often used as a vehicle for new proses. Often the composition of a sequence can be dated approximately by its appearance in an early manuscript, but neither the melody nor the style of the prose can be a sure guide to the time of the composition.[3]

The early history of the sequence reveals some of the traditions and possible choices of melodies and styles which would govern the composition of a twelfth-century author. But unfortunately our knowledge of the work of individual authors, and consequently our understanding of individual musical and poetic creativity, suffer from one severe limitation: almost all medieval sequences have survived in chant books in which they are anonymous and undated. As will be seen, we are not even sure of the compositions of such an author as Adam of St. Victor, and scholars have been reduced to using stylistic criteria to determine the canon of his work. But without an understanding of the way individual authors worked, stylistic criteria may be seriously misleading. It is therefore important to examine carefully those few collections of sequences which can be with certainty attributed to an individual author, such as the recently discovered sequences of Nicolas of Clairvaux.

The author of this collection has already been studied on the basis of his published letters and sermons.[4] Nicolas, monk of Clairvaux and Montiéramey, has received a certain notoriety as the unfaithful secretary of St. Bernard, the literary companion of Count Henry I ('the Liberal') of Champagne, and an author whose works exhibit a taste for classical learning and plagiarism. Nicolas spent his early years at the Benedictine monastery of Montiéramey in the diocese of Troyes and was active at the episcopal court as chaplain to Bishop Hatto of Troyes about 1144. Between 1145 and 1151 he was a

---

[3] For survey accounts which will direct the reader to more specialized literature see, in addition to the works cited above in notes 1 and 2, F. J. E. Raby, *A History of Christian-Latin Poetry* (2nd ed. Oxford 1953) 210-219, 223-229, 345-375; Jacques Handschin, 'Trope, Sequence, and Conductus' in *Early Medieval Music up to 1300*, ed. A. Hughes (New Oxford History of Music 2; Oxford 1954) 128-174; Willi Apel, *Gregorian Chant* (Bloomington, Ind. 1958) 442-464.

[4] There is no up-to-date summary on Nicolas. Much has come to light since Augustin Steiner wrote 'Nicolaus, Mönch in Clairvaux,' in *Studien und Mitteilungen zur Geschichte des Benediktiner-Ordens* 38 (1917) 41-50. The two most important additions are by Dom Jean Leclercq, 'Études sur S. Bernard et le texte de ses écrits,' *Analecta S. Ordinis Cisterciensis* 9 (1953) 62-67, and 'Les collections de sermons de Nicolas de Clairvaux,' *Revue bénédictine* 66 (1956) 269-302. For Nicolas' relationship with the count of Champagne see the section on him in Benton, 'The Court of Champagne as a Literary Center,' *Speculum* 36 ; above, pp. 7-9. Nicolas' return to Montiéramey by 1158 is established by MS Aube 6 H 705.

monk at Clairvaux, where he served as St. Bernard's personal secretary, ending his career there when he was expelled for theft and the misuse of his master's seal. He may have returned to Montiéramey directly after this reversal, and he is known to have appeared at the papal court in the good favor of Adrian IV. By 1158 he was back at Montiéramey; soon after he became prior of one of the abbey's dependencies, St. Jean-en-Châtel in Troyes. At Troyes he often appeared in Count Henry's entourage. Both as prior and on his own behalf, Nicolas received a succession of grants which indicates that until his death in 1178 (or shortly before) he remained one of Count Henry's favorites. He dedicated two manuscripts of his works to the count: one a letter-book from which only a few letters have survived,[5] and the other a collection which has been recently identified.

Dom Jean Leclercq's fruitful research on the writings of St. Bernard has brought to light a manuscript of this second collection. This manuscript, British Museum Harley MS 3073, is of medium size (250 by 160 mm.) and on paleographical grounds can be dated to the twelfth century. It contains a letter of dedication to Count Henry, a collection of nineteen sermons (the work of Nicolas himself), some other sermons (actually the work of St. Bernard), a collection of commentaries on verses of the Psalms (plagiarized from Hugh of St. Victor), and, as announced in the introductory letter, 'responsoria et lectiones de Cruce, responsoria et lectiones de Virgine, et decem sequentias de Christi festivitatibus et sanctorum suorum.'[6] All of the liturgical material has remained unpublished; the text of the sequences, which occupy fols. 129v-140v, is edited for the first time at the end of this article.[7]

The Virgin Mary occupies the place of honor in the collection. Nicolas addresses the first prose to her directly without reference to any particular feast day. The honoring of Mary continues in the third prose (for the Nativity) and in the fourth (for the Assumption of the Virgin), in both of which

---

[5] The introductory letter to Count Henry is in Migne, PL 196.1651-52; it announces, among others, a letter to Chancellor Roland before he became Alexander III. This unedited letter is in Berlin MS Phillipps 1719, fols. 117v-118r, along with a collection of letters which for the most part are in the letter-book made while Nicolas was at Clairvaux (printed in PL 196).

[6] Dom Bertrand Tissier edited Nicolas' sermons and his introductory letter in *Bibliotheca patrum Cisterciensium* (Bonnefont 1660) III 193-236. Dom Leclercq has described and analyzed this manuscript, re-edited the introductory letter to Count Henry, and provided a note on the unedited offices in *Rev. bén.* 66.270-279, 300-302. Throughout this article Dom Leclercq shows how frequently Nicolas plagiarized the work of others. He points out (p. 279) that in presenting Hugh of St. Victor's commentaries as his own, Nicolas was content to change the address from *frater carissime* to *comes dulcissime*.

[7] I have worked from a microfilm provided by the courtesy of the British Museum and wish to thank the Trustees for their permission to publish the text.

the author addresses Mary directly as intercessor with her Son. In the second prose (for the Resurrection) Mary plays little part, however, and the emphasis is on the contrast of the two natures of Christ. The following proses are for the feast days of specific saints. The fifth lauds Sts. Peter and Paul (June 29), who made Rome greater than it had been under the Caesars; formerly the city subjugated lands, the poet says, but now it occupies heaven itself. The sixth prose honors St. John the Evangelist (Dec. 27), the seventh St. Stephen (Dec. 26), and the eighth St. Sebastian (Jan. 20). The final two proses detail the miracles of St. Victor (Feb. 26), a Merovingian confessor from Champagne, whose relics were transferred to Montiéramey in 837.

Topical references to specific congregations in four of the proses are explained by Nicolas' career and help to prove that he was actually the author. One of the proses to St. Victor addresses the saint as 'Victor noster' (9.5.3) and both contain the phrase 'tua familia' (9.11.4, 10.11.2). Another prose refers to Sts. Peter and Paul, 'quorum in memoria fulget hec ecclesia' (5. 19.3-4), and the one which honors St. Stephen states: 'nos tui famuli tua familia sumus et erimus in hac ecclesia tibi data' (7.13.2-4). It was natural that a monk of Montiéramey should write in honor of St. Victor of Champagne. At the request of the abbot of Montiéramey, St. Bernard composed an office for St. Victor, and one of Nicolas' sermons is for the feast of the local saint.[8] The phrase 'tua familia' in the final proses therefore refers to the monks of Montiéramey. The reference to a particular church of Sts. Peter and Paul is explained by the fact that the cathedral church of Troyes was dedicated to them.[9] The designation of a church 'given' to St. Stephen suggests the collegiate church of St. Étienne de Troyes which Count Henry endowed as a private chapel in 1157. Nicolas was a canon of this church at the time of his death, as a listing in its obituary roll shows.[10] These references to churches closely connected with Nicolas' life and with the diocese of Troyes should confirm his authorship of the proses, for if Nicolas had appropriated works written by someone else for use in these churches, a manuscript dedicated to Count Henry and presented at his court could easily reveal the plagiarism.

---

[8] On St. Victor see AS 6.670-672. St. Bernard's office is printed there (673-674) and in PL 182.609-612. Nicolas' sermon is in PL 144.732-736. It may be noted that the abbey of St. Victor in Paris was dedicated, not to this saint, but to St. Victor of Marseilles.

[9] Alphonse Roserot, *Dictionnaire historique de la Champagne méridionale* (*Aube*) *des origines à 1790* (Langres 1942-48) I 59. This list shows the number of other churches in the department of Aube dedicated to Sts. Peter and Paul and St. Stephen for which Nicolas *might* have written these proses. The probability that he wrote for churches of the city in which he and the count lived is, of course, great.

[10] Auguste Molinier (ed.) *Obituaires de la province de Sens* 4 (Paris 1923) 529 B. For the charter of foundation in 1157 see Elizabeth Chapin, *Les villes de foire de Champagne* (Paris 1937) 279-282.

Additional confirmation of Nicolas' authorship is that seven of the proses are written for saints or festivals honored by Nicolas in sermons which appear in the same manuscript, and that, as will appear in the notes to the proses, they share phrases and ideas with the sermons.[11]

The important question of the date of composition of the proses cannot be determined precisely. In his letter of introduction, which may have been written any time from his return to Troyes about 1160 until his death, Nicolas says he composed the works collected in the manuscript 'in viridiori aetate.' The sermons show strongly the influence of the style of St. Bernard, and were probably written after Nicolas became the abbot's secretary. It is clear, however, that at least some were composed for use at Montiéramey and not Clairvaux, and so they were probably written after Nicolas left Clairvaux in 1151.[12] The offices were also apparently composed after 1151.[13] We cannot be sure that the proses were written at the same time as the other works. Bishop Hatto of Troyes, who died in 1145 and whom Nicolas served as chaplain about 1144, wrote a regular sequence or hymn of high technical quality preserved in a collection for St. James of Compostella,[14] and Nicolas may have begun to write proses under his influence. If Nicolas intended his prose for St. Stephen to be sung in Count Henry's church, then he must have written it after the foundation of that church in 1157. Since he may have written his introductory letter as late as the 1170's, we cannot know what period of time seemed like a *viridior aetas*. The proses may well have been written at different times, perhaps as early as the 1140's, probably in the 1150's or 1160's.

The author's literary equipment as revealed by his letters and sermons also appears in his proses. Nicolas wrote often of his early reading of classical

---

[11] The nineteen sermons of the Harley MS were printed among the sermons of St. Peter Damiani in PL 144. For a careful discussion of this confusing situation and a table showing the various places where these sermons have been printed see J. J. Ryan, 'Saint Peter Damiani and the Sermons of Nicholas of Clairvaux: a Clarification,' *Mediaeval Studies* 9 (1947) 151-161. Leclercq also gives a table of references to PL in *Rev. bén.* 66.273-276. Nicolas worked a bit of verse into his sermon for St. Stephen, PL 144.853: 'Scintillat sidus, magus adorat, exsultat polus, tellus resultat.'

[12] The sermon on St. Victor was composed for delivery at Montiéramey, and another one applies more to Benedictines than to Cistercians (see Leclercq, *Rev. bén.* 66.276 n. 1). On dating the sermons after Nicolas' expulsion from Clairvaux, see *ibid.* 291-292.

[13] So I am informed by Fr. M. Chrysogonus Waddell, O.C.S.O., Master of Chant at the Abbey of Our Lady of Gethsemani, Trappist, Ky., who is preparing a study of Nicolas' offices. Fr. Chrysogonus has aided me greatly in the preparation of this article, particularly in the notes to the proses.

[14] Peter Wagner, *Die Gesänge der Jakobus-Liturgie zu Santiago de Compostela* (Fribourg en Suisse 1931) 48 and 112; *Liber Sancti Jacobi, Codex Calixtinus*, II: *Musica*, ed. G. Prado (Santiago de Compostela 1944) plate 29 and pp. 68-69.

authors, but the way in which he quotes classical phrases suggests that much of his familiarity was superficial and gathered at second hand.[15] This same suspicion is not justified for his Biblical allusions. In this respect Nicolas was a true disciple of St. Bernard, and the influence of Scripture permeates his work. The same orientation is found in his proses. The greatest source of allusions, as one would expect, is Scripture, and classical overtones are minimal. I note as an exceptional case the Ovidian phrase *fons illimis* (*Metam.* 3.407) in reference to the Virgin; even this may have been a common epithet, since it was used in the same way by Adam of St. Victor.[16] The influence of the liturgy as a source of Biblical quotations is strong, and the echoes of Patristic sources which appear in the proses were probably derived from monastic lectionaries.

The proses for the different saints obviously derive, either directly or indirectly, from saints' lives.[17] All the miracles of St. Victor related in the proses are contained in a life of the saint preserved at Montiéramey. It is highly likely that Nicolas had read the *Acta Sancti Sebastiani* by Pseudo-Ambrose, since it contains all the details related in the prose and Nicolas echoes a number of phrases and uses the rare word *holovitrea* which occurs therein. Nicolas obviously relied on the New Testament for his story of St. Stephen, but the sources for the other saints are less certain. The apocryphal details about St. John are all in the work of Pseudo-Abdias, but they also occur in other common accounts about the saint. The specific events which Nicolas relates about Sts. Peter and Paul are so few that it is impossible to trace them to a single source, and with such widely diffused legendary material there is little point in looking for particular sources.[18]

The evidence to show that Nicolas used the sequences of others as models will be discussed in detail later. Even a superficial reading shows that his proses sound very much like others written in the same style. Since Nicolas is known for his plagiarism and incorporated the work of Hugh of St. Victor in the collection of his own *opera* dedicated to Count Henry, the suspicion arises that Nicolas modeled his work directly on that of Hugh's colleague, Adam of St. Victor. The discussion of this question may help to illuminate

---

[15] For a reference in a sermon to an early love of classics (presumably applying to study at Montiéramey) see PL 144.852. Many of Nicolas' classical quotations are mere tags which he could easily cull from *florilegia*. For instance, when he quotes Plato on philosopher-kings in order to praise Count Henry (PL 196.1651), this quotation can not be based on any direct knowledge of the *Republic*.

[16] See 3.7.1 and note.

[17] These sources are discussed in the notes to the proses.

[18] The intricate passage of themes from one prose in honor of St. Peter to another is discussed by J. Szövérffy, 'Gaude Roma... (Marginal notes on some St. Peter sequences attributed to Adam of St. Victor),' *Proc. Royal Irish Acad.* 57 C (1955) 1-27.

the work of both Nicolas and Adam. To begin with, we must review what little is known of Adam's career.[19]

There is no sure record of when Adam entered the house of St. Victor, though a Victorine chronicler writing at the end of the twelfth century says that he was a pupil of Gilduin, who became abbot in 1113 and died in 1155. One late tradition states that Adam became a Victorine about 1130, and a charter of 1139 records that a man named Adam was currently choirmaster. In one of his sermons Hugh of St. Victor (d. 1141) quotes as the work of an *egregius versificator* a regular sequence, *Ave virgo singularis*, which some editors have attributed to Adam.[20] If this sequence is truly one of Adam's, then his reputation was established in Hugh's lifetime. An epitaph for Bernard of Clairvaux (d. 1153) is ascribed to Adam, and his editors credit him with a sequence honoring St. Thomas of Canterbury, who was canonized in 1173.[21] Tradition relates that Adam died during the prelacy of Guérin, who was abbot from 1173 to 1193. From this outline it can be seen that there is no way to tell if Adam wrote the bulk of his compositions as early as the 1130's or as late as the 1170's; he and Nicolas were contemporaries, and their uncertain biographies do not settle the question of priority and influence.

One reason why so many of Nicolas' proses sound like those of his contemporaries, including Adam, is that with the exception of two compositions in the transitional style they follow the 'rules' we associate with the regular sequence. This form of sequence, which appeared about the end of the eleventh century, most commonly has strophes composed of two or three eight-syllable trochaic lines, followed by a seven-syllable line which is usually trochaic. The eight-syllable lines are consistently linked by double rhyme, and they are broken after the fourth syllable by a pause falling at the end of a word.[22]

---

[19] For the evidence on Adam's career which can be gleaned from the records of St. Victor's, see Fourier Bonnard, *Histoire de l'abbaye royale et de l'ordre des chanoines reguliers de St. Victor* (Paris 1904-08) I 128-132. The earliest printed edition of Adam's sequences by Clichtoveus, *Elucidarium ecclesiasticum* (Basel 1517), is reprinted in PL 196.1423-1534. Léon Gautier included many spurious proses in his two-volume edition, *Œuvres poétiques d'Adam de Saint-Victor* (Paris 1858-59); following the criticism of Misset he eliminated many of these from his 3rd ed. (1 vol. Paris 1894). Eugène Misset and Pierre Aubry, *Les proses d'Adam de Saint-Victor: texte et musique* (Paris 1900) contains the critical essay by Misset first published in 1881. Clemens Blume and H. M. Bannister re-edited Adam's proses along with many others in AH 54 and 55 (1915-22). Franz Wellner (ed. and trans.), *Adam von Sankt Viktor, Sämtliche Sequenzen* (2nd ed. Munich 1955) is the most recent edition, but the best critical edition is still that in the *Analecta hymnica*, which will be cited throughout this article.

[20] AH 54 No. 204. On the attribution of this prose, see below, n. 36.

[21] PL 196.1534-35 and AH 55 No. 328.

[22] These principles of composition are discussed in AH 54.vi-vii, and Raby, *Christian-Latin Poetry* 347-348.

Nicolas clearly wrote with these principles of composition in mind, though his meter is occasionally awkward and he does not always break the line regularly.[23] The compressed form of the prose lends itself to a certain lapidary expression, like this verse by Nicolas:

> Sic est Christo Petrus mixtus,
> ut quod ligat, liget Christus —
> audi mirabilia. (5.11)

This verse form, like that of the vernacular romances, permits the author to stress his word play through rhyme:

> Verbum Dei carnem sumit,
> nec in carne se consumit,
> sed consummat quod assumit
> in mundi presentia. (3.2)

When two authors express the same idea in this tight form, the results may seem remarkably similar.

Nicolas (5.15)	*Adam* (AH 55 No. 289.14)
Petrus princeps in honore,	Petrus praeit principatu
Paulus primus in labore,	Paulus pollet magistratu
duo luminaria.	Totius ecclesiae.

This similarity may indeed be the result of copying, or it may be the result of coincidence compounded by verse form and alliteration. Besides resemblances of this sort, there are a number of single lines cited in the notes to the proses which are actually common to Adam and Nicolas. These common phrases suggest that one author was familiar with the work of the other, and since Adam's proses received much wider circulation than Nicolas',[24] it is likely that Nicolas had some familiarity with the work of the Victorine. But these points of similarity are not sufficient to show that Nicolas modeled his work directly on that of Adam.

Another area in which Nicolas' compositions are very similar to those of Adam is that of allegorical symbolism, particularly in reference to the Virgin. In the following strophe, for instance, Nicolas compares Mary to the burning bush, Gideon's fleece, and the flowering rod of Aaron or Jesse:

---

[23] There are over twenty lines in which the end of a word does not coincide with the end of the second trochee. Prose 9 contains six of these 'faults,' but 2 is perfect in this respect. Metrical 'faults,' some of them intentional, are discussed in n. 32.

[24] Adam's proses are widely diffused in existing manuscripts, while Nicolas' are unknown except for the Harley manuscript. They are not indexed in the massive catalogues of Ulysse Chevalier, *Repertorium hymnologicum* (Louvain 1892-1912), and Hans Walther, *Initia Carminum* (Göttingen 1959). Perhaps they were not even sung regularly in the churches for which they were written; Mlle F. Bibolet, librarian of the municipal library of Troyes, has examined a number of the graduals from Montiéramey and Troyes in her care without finding any of Nicolas' proses.

> Rubus ardet novo more,
> vellus madet novo rore,
> virga gaudet nova flore,
>   renovantur omnia. (3.4)

Adam's commentators have shown how such a use of symbolism, especially Old Testament typology, is one of the striking characteristics of his poetic art.[25] But they also show that this style was commonly used by many contemporary authors; St. Bernard, who had such a strong influence on Nicolas, is one of many writers who continuously develop this sort of symbolic allusion.[26] Similar references can also be found throughout the anonymous proses of the period. Nicolas' symbolism is worthy of attention, but symbolism is in no way peculiar to any one author of the twelfth century.

The form of the sequences themselves provides our surest guide to Nicolas' relationship to other authors. The music supplies the most revealing information, and this point takes us back to the Harley manuscript. The proses are all written under a four-line staff, and seven of the ten are supplied with music in notation apparently contemporary with the rest of the manuscript. The music, where it is present, shows the duplicating antiphonal pattern characteristic of sequences. The duplication is nearly exact, and a misplacement of the movable C-line accounts for almost all of the variants. The music is sometimes the only clue to the form of the sequence, showing that in one instance (6) Nicolas followed the old practice of beginning with an unmatched verse and that in three cases (2, 4, 5) he ended in that fashion. Sequence 6 is particularly complex, ending with a matched pair which follows a single verse. Stanzas 11 and 12 of sequence 2 and Stanzas 4 and 5 of sequence 6 are composed of six lines instead of three because that is the form imposed by the music.

Nicolas did not claim that he composed the music of the sequences, and in four cases there is direct evidence that he did not. The final prose for St. Victor (10) uses the melody of an eleventh-century sequence of the transitional style, *Laetabundus exsultet*.[27] The melody of the prose for St. Sebastian (8) is that of another transitional sequence, *Congaudentes exsultemus*, which honors St. Nicolas of Myra.[28] The prose for St. John the Evangelist (6) uses the

---

[25] Misset and Aubry, *Proses* 56-110; Raby, *Christian-Latin Poetry* 363-375.

[26] For examples of St. Bernard's use of the same images see PL 183.432-433.

[27] For the music see C. A. Moberg, *Über die schwedischen Sequenzen* (Uppsala 1927) II No. 4. The text is in AH 54 No. 2. Since other derivatives of this famous sequence used this melody and the same opening words, Nicolas may have used another version as a model.

[28] The music is in Moberg, *op. cit.*, II No. 22, the text in AH 54 No. 63. Blume attributes to Adam of St. Victor a prose which follows the strophic scheme of *Congaudentes*, AH 55 Nc. 178. Nicolas' model was probably neither of these but *Clara chorus dulce panget*,

melody of a regular sequence, *Laudes crucis attollamus*, which was once attributed to Adam of St. Victor, but which specialists now place before his time in the early twelfth or late eleventh century.[29] And Nicolas follows the melody of a widely circulated regular sequence, *Potestate non natura*, for the first five musical lines of his prose for the Nativity (3); his own contribution to the form and music of this sequence is apparently in the last four stanzas, where he wrote twelve-syllable lines which do not match any of the verses of his model.[29a] As has been said before, it was a common practice to use traditional melodies, and we know that Adam of St. Victor used earlier melodies for at least eight of his sequences.[30] For most sequences the melodies preceded the text, and there were hundreds of texts written to the melody of *Laetabundus* alone.[31] In his *Laetabundus* sequence Nicolas advertised

---

(AH 54 Nc. 94), which omits the concluding strophes found in the other two sequences. In addition, a few words and constructions of *Clara chorus* appear in Nicolas' text. The prose attributed to Adam is by far the most developed and 'regular' of the group.

[29] The music is in Moberg, *op. cit.* II No. 1, the text in AH 54 No. 120. For details of correspondence see below, n. 32. Note that Nicolas has one more pair of three-line strophes than the printed text, but has an unpaired four-line strophe where the original has a pair. The three-line strophes suggest that a pair of verses printed in AH 54.191 as variants were part of the sequence known to Nicolas in the mid-twelfth century. The note on p. 192 discusses the early date of *Laudes crucis* as established by an early and wide diffusion of its manuscripts, and rules against Adam's authorship. This opinion is accepted by Raby, *Christian-Latin Poetry* 347. Nicolas Weisbein re-edits the prose and attributes it to Hugh Primas of Orléans in *Revue du moyen-âge latin* 3 (1947) 5-26. Franz Wellner includes *Laudes crucis* in *Sämtliche Sequenzen* 357 and 376, basing his argument largely on the music, but on this see Hans Spanke, 'Die Kompositionskunst der Sequenzen Adams von St. Victor,' *Studi medievali* n.s. 14 (1941) 26.

[29a] *Potestate non natura* (AH 54 No. 96), which appears in twelfth-century manuscripts from many countries, was sung to more than one melody. Prof. Bruno Stäblein has very kindly identified and transcribed for me the melody which Nicolas followed from Assisi Com. MS 695, fols. 170ᵛ-171ᵛ. As Fr. Rembert Weakland informed me, variations of this melody were used for the proses *Ave virgo singularis* and *Virgo mater salvatoris* in *Le Prosaire de la Sainte-Chapelle*, ed. R. J. Hesbert (Monumenta Musicae Sacrae 1; Mâcon 1952), plates 187-190 and 19-23. None of these proses contains twelve-syllable lines, and Nicolas' melody differs from all of them for the final two pairs. The melody of Nicolas' sequence is transcribed at the end of this article in order to make clear the extent of his musical contribution. It should be noted that the melodies of *Ave virgo singularis* and *Virgo mater salvatoris* recorded in the graduals of St. Victor's were variations of another sequence, *Verbum bonum et suave*, and they are therefore not an indication of a link between Nicolas and Adam. On this see Misset and Aubry, *Proses* 243-246, 294-297 and Spanke, *Studi med.* n.s. 14.11.

[30] Spanke, *Studi med.* n.s. 14.26.

[31] Dreves and Blume, *Ein Jahrtausend lateinischer Hymnendichtung* (Leipzig 1909) II 17-18. For the spread of the melody beyond the limits of liturgy and into vernacular tongues see Friedrich Gennrich, 'Internationale mittelalterliche Melodien,' *Zeitschrift für Musikwissenschaft* 11 (1929) 274-278.

the relationship with the earlier composition by beginning with its opening words. Such use of a model was not 'plagiarism' but was intended to honor the saint by adapting a beloved sequence to his service. I have not been able to identify the other three melodies and cannot tell whether Nicolas composed them himself or borrowed them from other sequences. These melodies are published at the end of this article in the hope that someone may be able to establish either Nicolas' originality or his further indebtedness.

The use of a previous melody created the form for the words of a new prose. The phrasing of 10 is choppy, for instance, because the musical lines of *Laetabundus* are short and require phrases of this sort. The music fully explains why Nicolas, writing after the regular sequence had been developed, composed two proses in the traditional style. The form of 8 and 10 is transitional because that was the form of their melodies, though where the music allowed him the option, Nicolas sometimes wrote with rhyme not found in his models. When Nicolas wrote in a developed, regular form, as he did in the prose for St. John, this form was also determined by his melody. Nicolas followed his models so closely that in a few places he departed from the regularity of meter which the musical pairing of verses would otherwise require.[32] These deviations from regular meter and the verbal echoes from the texts of *Laetabundus* and *Clara chorus* cited above in notes 27 and 28 suggest that Nicolas composed his proses by using other proses as models, and not by working directly with the melody of an earlier sequence. Such a method of composition would explain why three of his proses are not accompanied by music, for if Nicolas used a prose alone as a model, he may not have had the music available to add to the manuscript. Since musicologists often stress the congruence of music and prose in medieval sequences, it is important to see that Nicolas may have written with his eyes on the text and not on the music of his model.

An analysis of form will explain why some of his proses have the same structure as some proses written by Adam of St. Victor, and at the same time will show that Nicolas' work was largely independent of that of Adam. As Hans Spanke has shown, Adam used the melody of *Laudes crucis* in a number of his sequences,[33] and since Nicolas used the same melody, both authors

---

[32] In 6.4.4-5 Nicolas matches two ten-syllable lines against a pair of seven-syllable lines; this is exactly the form of the corresponding verses of *Laudes crucis*. In verse 13 Nicolas follows the model with a pair of seven-syllable lines and even rhymes with the same words. The musical model does not justify a six-syllable line paired with one of five syllables in 8.11.2 and 8.12.2. Probably the missing syllable in 7.14.3 (for which there is no music) is the result of an author's slip, though possibly the scribe omitted a 'hac' before 'presentia.'

[33] Spanke, *Studi med.* n.s. 14.22-23. For Blume's suggestion that Adam, too, modeled a sequence on *Congaudentes* see above, n. 28.

naturally wrote some proses with the same form. There are sufficient differences of form in other proses, however, to establish that Nicolas did not copy Adam's style of composition.

(1) Adam's strophes and his meters are much more varied in form than those used by Nicolas. Much of Adam's poetic power comes from the variety he introduces into his 'regular' sequences. Nicolas' poetry, on the other hand, is highly predictable. Outside of his 'transitional' sequences, Nicolas varies his verses composed of eight- and seven-syllable trochaic lines in only one way. The exceptional verses are in 1, 3, and 7, where Nicolas closes with strophes composed of three lines which approximate dactylic tetrameter, with a fourth line of four syllables.[34]

(2) These twelve-syllabe lines are indeed unusual. They may be Nicolas' single claim to originality, for we know that he departed from the melody of his model in order to write twelve-syllable lines in prose 3. Lines of twelve syllables are rare in sequences, and they are particularly rare in the work of Adam of St. Victor. Although Adam often uses a long line, his few twelve-syllable lines are usually broken into halves by an inner rhyme. One instance in which he uses dactylic tetrameters stands out as an extreme rarity.[35]

(3) With the exception of only one pair of strophes (5.13-14), every one of Nicolas' verses ends with an *a*. This was the usual practice in early Gallic proses; *Congaudentes exsultemus*, *Laetabundus*, and *Clara chorus*, for instance, follow this rule without exception, and there are only a few deviations in *Laudes crucis*. Adam, on the other hand, held to no such practice as a regular principle of composition. Terminal *a*'s predominate in the *Ave, virgo singularis* cited by Hugh of St. Victor, however, so that if Adam was the author of that prose, it can be said that he once observed the convention but abandoned it later in his career.[36]

His other works show that Nicolas was a highly imitative writer, incorporating the felicitous phrases of others into his own work and even repeating himself upon occasion.[37] This study shows that he used at least four sequences very carefully as models, and doubtless he studied other proses as

---

[34] The form of all his regular sequences is very similar. Over four-fifths of the verses are composed of two, three, or four eight-syllable lines followed by one of seven syllables. Prose 9 has no variation of strophes; 2 and 4 close with two strophes of seven-syllable lines, followed by one of alternating eight and seven-syllable lines; and 5 has almost the same form. As stated in the text, 1, 3, and 7 close with twelve-syllable lines.

[35] AH 55 No. 337.7 and 8. Cf. Misset and Aubry, *Proses* 34.

[36] Two other factors which show either that Adam did not write the prose or that he changed his style as he matured are that there is no variety in the form of the strophes and that, as the editors point out (AH 54.324), the meter is awkward in 13.3 and 17.3.

[37] For examples of Nicolas' use of sources and repetition, see Leclercq's notes in *Rev. bén.* 66.271-273. Nicolas repeats the essence of one of his own verses in 5.1 and 6.3.

well. Other points of his style are also imitative: the allegorical images and the word plays which enliven his work are commonly found in authors of his day. But although Nicolas was an imitator, it cannot be shown that Adam of St. Victor had a major influence on his work. The chronology of both authors is uncertain, but it is possible that Nicolas wrote the bulk of his proses before Adam composed the majority of his. While points of similarity are evidence that Nicolas may have known some of Adam's proses, the points of formal difference, on the other hand, are striking. Nicolas was much more conservative than Adam and he did not follow Adam's attractive metrical schemes, his freedom from the restriction of the terminal *a*, or his music.

The proses of Nicolas of Clairvaux provide us with a new point of comparison from which to view Adam of St. Victor. Other studies have already discredited the idea that Adam led the way in the creation of regular sequences, by showing that regular sequences were written toward the end of the eleventh century and that Adam, like Nicolas, had his models.[38] The existence of Nicolas' collection is one more proof that by the middle of the twelfth century the regular sequence was established as a conventional form. But while Adam did not invent the form, the comparison with Nicolas emphasizes how much he was a master of it. Nicolas slavishly followed his models, and his greatest weakness is the sameness and jingling predictability of his poetry. Adam, on the other hand, composed strophes of much greater variety, showed the master's touch in his deviations from rigid meter, and apparently adapted the music of earlier melodies to suit his own constructions.[39]

The greatest problem in any study of Adam's work is to establish which proses came from his pen. Three different methods of determining authenticity have been used by modern editors.[40] When Léon Gautier published his first edition of Adam's proses in the middle of the nineteenth century, he relied heavily on the lists of Adam's proses preserved at St. Victor's. But these lists were compiled centuries after Adam's death, and in many instances they are demonstrably unreliable. This criticism was presented by Eugène Misset, who instead turned to the earliest chant-books of St. Victor's and picked out the proses which fitted the stylistic criteria which he believed governed the work of Adam. In his third edition Gautier accepted most of Misset's arguments, and based his attributions on the Victorine graduals,

---

[38] Gautier (in his 1st ed.) and Misset attributed to Adam such sequences as *Laudes crucis* and *Hodiernae lux diei* (AH 54 No. 219). The early manuscripts noted in AH for these and other regular sequences show that the form was established before Adam's time.

[39] The variations with which Adam adapted earlier melodies are shown by Spanke, *Studi med.* n.s. 14.

[40] These editions are listed above, n. 19. Each edition contains a criticism of the previous attributions.

the lists of proses, and conformity to certain stylistic criteria. But 'rules' of style are uncertain as evidence of authorship, for other poets may have written in Adam's style, or he may have written in a variety of styles. These difficulties seemed so great to Blume and Bannister that they attempted no fixed list of Adam's compositions for the final volumes of the *Analecta Hymnica*. Stylistic grounds were used in part for such judgments as 'würdig Adams' or 'ascribenda videtur Adamo de S. Victore'; but these editors made their greatest contribution rather through analyzing the date and origin of an overwhelmingly large number of manuscripts. Thereby they could show that a given prose had been written earlier than Adam's period, or that certain proses apparently had their origin at St. Victor's. When all methods of determination are combined, a relatively small number of proses remains which may confidently be attributed to Adam. Franz Wellner has not, however, been so highly restrictive in compiling the latest edition of Adam's proses, but has used Misset's collection as a core and added a few more sequences which accord with his stylistic criteria.

The information provided by Nicolas' collection supports the hesitations of Blume and Bannister, for Nicolas' proses show that a contemporary could on occasion write verses which on stylistic grounds cannot be differentiated from those of Adam.[41] More significantly, the collection shows us a twelfth-century author writing proses in the transitional style in order to fit an earlier melody. If Nicolas could write two of his ten proses in the transitional manner, why not expect the same variety of composition from Adam?[42] These considerations suggest that as yet no sure means of determining the composition of Adam's *corpus* has been found.[43] This *caveat* does not, of course, affect the fact of Adam's reputation in his own day and in the traditions of St. Victor's, and if we continue to be unsure of the authorship of the 'Victorine' proses, the proses themselves remain available for investigation and appreciation.

The preceding analysis of the relationship of text and music shows something of the method of composition which one twelfth-century author followed. He began by choosing an established melody, either in the transitional or the regular style. Then he composed a prose to fit the form which the melody required. As far as we can tell, Nicolas did not compose to fit

---

[41] See the statements in AH 54.viii-xvi and 55.vii-ix. These views are supported by Raby, *Christian-Latin Poetry* 351. While in general Nicolas is not the equal of Adam, prose 2 fits all the stylistic criteria used to determine Adam's work.

[42] This point supports Blume's arguments for the attribution to Adam of AH 55 No. 178. The attribution was accepted by Wellner, *Sämtliche Sequenzen* 357 and 360-361.

[43] Any uncertainty about whether Adam wrote some of the proses attributed to him should not weaken the central arguments of this article, since the generalizations about style are based on a large number of proses.

the music directly, but used the text of an earlier prose as a model of the poetic form to follow. Thus it was possible for the music and the scheme of both meter and rhyme to be completely derivative. An author like Nicolas could choose one of a number of forms, but once the choice was made, he wrote within its limitations and, by following its conventions, continued a conservative and traditional style. Only in the introduction of twelve-syllable lines did Nicolas depart from the form of his models.

The proses of Nicolas of Clairvaux are here edited so that the reader may judge them for himself. The deficiencies of Nicolas' style, when compared with the very best work of the twelfth century, have already been noted. But when his work is compared with the average prose written in his day, his achievement stands out in his careful general construction, the purity of his rhyme, his appropriate allusions, and the forcefulness of his expression.

The Harley manuscript was written with great care and provides a text requiring very few corrections.[44] As an indication of scribal procedure it is worth noting that the rubricator was not given a written indication of the initials he was to add, but was left to determine them from the context.[45] In editing I have expanded the few simple abbreviations and supplied modern punctuation and capitalization. Though I have differentiated *u* and *v*, vagaries of orthography have been maintained, even when the same word is spelled differently in succeeding lines (4.6, 5.18). The repetition of a musical line is here indicated by printing paired verses opposite each other; when a verse stands alone it is because it does not have a musical pair. The annotation of sources and comparisons is not exhaustive, but is intended to illustrate Nicolas' methods of composition.[46]

---

[44] The correctness of the text, the attractiveness of the manuscript, and the exact correspondence of its contents to that announced in the introductory letter suggest that the Harley MS may be the actual presentation copy. The introductory letter as edited by Leclercq (*Rev. bén.* 66.271-272) raises some questions which cannot at present be answered. The manuscript omits the author's name from this letter, while the seventeenth-century editor Tissier (n. 6 *supra*) includes it. Was this because the name was not needed in a personal presentation copy? Did Tissier have a better copy in front of him? Or did Tissier add the name as an unannounced emendation? The answers to these questions might tell us if the Harley MS was the one presented to Count Henry.

[45] In one instance an initial *O* was corrected by inscribing an *S* (8.6.1), another initial was erased and left blank (3.11.1), and a third was never entered, presumably because the rubricator could not decide whether to make the word *Iam* or *Nam* (4.2.1).

[46] So many specialists in medieval literature or music have aided me with this article that I cannot thank them all here, but I must give special recognition to Prof. Berthe Marti, who aided me with her criticism and started me on this project by telling me that every young medievalist should edit a text as a lesson in humility. I am grateful for the financial aid of the University of Pennsylvania Commitee on the Advancement of Research.

[1] Sequentia de Sancta Maria

fol. 129ᵛ [1] Salve, virgo, salus rerum,
salve, dies, lux dierum,
in qua parit lumen verum
genitrix et filia,

[2] Dies, renovatrix mundi,
terre, maris et profundi,
dies, scala redeundi
ad celi palatia.

[3] Verbi virtus incarnati
regnum mortis et peccati,
mortis legem, cogit pati
celeri victoria.

[4] Commutatur nox in lucem;
virga floret et fert nucem,
quia virgo parit ducem,
virgo viri nescia.

[5] Puer iste nobis natus,
nobis ad salvandum datus,
quando fodit eius latus
militaris lancea;

[6] Hinc fons vite cursum cepit,
lumen cecus hinc recepit,
hic deceptus qui decepit,
hic est fracta rumphea.

130ʳ [7] Hoc foramen, hec / caverna
nos reduxit ad eterna,
terram iunxit et superna
sociali gratia;

[8] Hic columba ponit sedem,
hic secura figit pedem,
hinc ad celi volat edem
cum pennarum gloria.

[9] Counitur Deo limus,
unum fiunt summus, imus,
ut nos per hoc unum simus
in Christi milicia.

[10] Venter ille, fons bonorum,
quo mixtura fit istorum,
in quo fecit sibi thorum
Dei sapientia.

[11] Hic novem mensium quiescit
[spacio,
hic agit nuptias rex pater filio,
hic carnis, anime, verbi fit unio
in Maria.

[12] Hic sumit angelus honoris
[gloriam,
hic iustus accipit virtutis gratiam,
peccator impetrat peccati veniam
in Maria.

130ᵛ [13] Stupent archangeli, mirantur
[sydera,
tremit humanitas hec videns
[opera,
quod Deum virginis includunt
in Maria. [viscera

[14] O fili virginis, qui salvas omnia

trahe nos miseros ad illa gaudia

quibus aspergitur celestis curia
cum Maria.
Amen.

---

1 1.4 Cf. Nicolas, PL 144.721: 'illa mater et filia Creatoris.' On this topos see A. L. Mayer, 'Mater et filia,' *Jahrbuch für Liturgiewissenschaft* 7 (1927) 60-82.   3.2-3 Cf. Rom. 8.2.   4.2 Num. 17.8.   4.4 Cf. Adam, AH 55 No. 191.4.3: 'virgo viri nesciam.'   5.1 Isai. 9.6. Cf. Bernard, PL 183.78.   5.3-4 Joan. 9.34.   6.1 Ps. 35.10. Cf. Bernard, PL 183.439.   6.2 Joan. 9.1-35.   6.3 Cf. Leo the Great, PL 54.201.   6.4 Cf. Adam, AH 54 No. 149.6.4.   7-8 Cf. Cant. 2.13-14 and Gen. 7.8-12.   9.1 Cf. Bernard, PL 183.98 and Adam, AH 54 No. 99.3.1: 'Verbum carni counitum.'   10 Cf. Nicolas, PL 144.558: 'O venter ... in quo Deus gloriae reclinatur.'   11.3 Cf. Bernard, PL 183.98-99: 'Verbum enim, et anima, et caro in unam convenere personam...'

[2] De Resurrectione

[1] Hec est dies expectata,
dies felix et beata
et dierum gloria,

[2] Dies plena gaudiorum,
in qua Christus rex celorum
fecit mirabilia.

[3] Mortem morte superavit
et infernum spoliavit
nobili victoria.

[4] Corpus suum suscitavit
et latronem coronavit
singulari gratia.

[5] Vir dolorum, vir leprosus,
vir percussus, vir perosus
Iudee malicia.

[6] Vide quantum gloriosus,
quantum surgat et formosus
de / mortis angustia.

[7] O Maria, noli flere,
resurrexit Christus vere,
surrexerunt omnia.

[8] Iam fit iudex iudicatus,
reos solvit condempnatus
sublimi potentia.

[9] Sol resurgit orto sole.
Synagoga, semper dole,
solis huius nescia.

[10] Et tu, gaude, sponsa Christi,
que de sponso credidisti
quicquid negat impia.

[11] Puer, iussus immolari,
prohibetur vulnerari,
dum mutatur hostia.
Caro Christi sensit dura;
splendor patris et figura
non senserunt talia.

[12] Dum Egyptum Ioseph servat
et frumentum coacervat,
aperit cellaria.
In hoc loco granum sevit
alter Ioseph de quo crevit
frumentorum copia.

[13] O sepulcrum gloriosum,
celis ipsis / preciosum,
domus Dei propria,

[14] Ex te surgit soporatus
Christus tanquam crapulatus
de cella vinaria.

[15] Flos Marie Christus natus,
flos sepulcri suscitatus,
sed est differentia:

[16] Illa dedit moriturum;
istud reddit regnaturum
regna super omnia.

[17] Locus ammirabilis,
sanctus et terribilis,
iustorum victoria,
peccatorum venia.

[18] Laudes redde debitas,
regis magni civitas,
ad te currunt secula
tanta per pericula.

[19] Tu qui mortem superasti
tua morte propria,
fac ut tecum resurgamus
ad beata gaudia,
ubi puri puro purum
cantemus alleluia.

---

2 1.1 Ps. 117.24 Cf. Adam, AH 54 No. 149.2.1.   4.2 Cf. Leo the Great, PL 54.324.
5.1-2 Isai. 53.3-4.   6.2 Cf. Isai. 63.1.   7.1-2 Cf. AH 54.366.13: 'O Maria, noli flere; Iam surrexit Christus vere' (with variant: Resurrexit). Cf. Adam, AH 54 No. 149.17.2.   11.5 Adam, AH 54 No. 100.1.1; cf. Heb. 1.3.   12 On Joseph as a type of Christ see Bernard, PL 185.141. Cf. Adam, AH 54 No. 149.8.1-2: 'Ioseph exit de cisterna, Christus redit ad superna.'   13.1 Isai. 11.10.   14.1 Ps. 3.6.   15.1 Cf. Bernard, PL 183.42.   16 Cf. Nicolas, PL 144.563: 'Illic vivens terram irrigat viventium, hic moriens terram morientum.'   18.1 Cf. Adam, AH 54 No. 155.26.3: 'Laudes reddit debitas.'

132r

[3] DE NATIVITATE DOMINI
[melody: Potestate non natura]

[1] Ad archanum huius rei
convocentur omnes rei,
pleni fide, pleni spei,
summa cum fiducia.

[2] Verbum Dei carnem sumit,
nec in carne se consumit,
sed consummat quod assumit
in mundi presentia.

[3] Nemo terram operatur
in qua Deus generatur;
de supernis fecundatur
speciali gratia.

[4] Rubus ardet novo more,
vellus madet novo rore,
virga gaudet novo flore,
renovantur omnia.

[5] Flos suavis, flos iocundus,
cuius fructu vivit mundus,
candidus et rubicundus,
solus inter milia,

[6] Flos de campo non arato,
flos de loco consecrato,
flos ex orto consignato,
flos illustrans omnia,

[7] Virgo, virga recta nimis,
porta clausa, fons illimis—

132v
tu superna iungis imis
caritate media.

[8] Per te celum restauratur,
per te tellus reparatur,
per te fortis exarmatur,
sua perdens spolia.

[9] Virgo sancta, mater sancti,
virgo, sponsa regis tanti,
miserere supplicanti
populo, dulcissima,

[10] Lux et splendor angelorum,
consolatio iustorum,
una sola spes lapsorum
misericordissima.

[11] Exora filium, precipe filio,
nam utrumque potes respectu
[proprio,
ne nos inveniat torpentes ocio
dies illa,

[12] Dies miserie, dies plorantium,
dies angustie, dies clamantium,

qua separabitur turba letantium
a dampnata.

[13] O virgo virginum et mundi
[gloria,
tunc assit miseris tua presentia,

133r
que nos eripiat ab hac / miseria

tam timenda,

[14] Nec hoc sufficiat tutum refugium,

sed omnes pertrahat ad tuum
[filium,
ubi cum ipso sit commune gau-
[dium
in secula.
Amen.

---

3   4.3 *ms* virgo   5.2 *ms* vivit vivit   11.1 *ms* xora, E *in rasura*

---

3 On the melody see above, note 29a.   2.1 Joan. 1.14.   4 Cf. Bernard, PL 183.42
and 432-433.   4.1 Exod. 3.2.   4.2 Iud. 6.36-38; Ps. 71.6.   4.3 Isai. 11.1
or Num. 17.8. Cf. Nicolas, PL 144.720-721.   5.3 Cant. 5.10.   7.1 Porta clausa:
Ezech. 44.2. Fons illimis: Ovid, *Metam.* 3.407; the phrase appears in Adam, AH 54
No. 197.20.3.

[4] De Assumptione Beate Marie

[1] Voce dulci, mente pura,
plaudat omnis creatura
communi leticia.

[2] Nam communis amor rerum
ducitur ad lumen verum,
ad superna gaudia.

[3] Virga Iesse, mater Dei,
porta vite, portus spei,
transit ad celestia.

[4] Currit in occursum matris
leto vulto verbum patris
cum celesti curia.

[5] Stupet chorus angelorum
ad presentiam amborum
pro sublimi gloria;

[6] Admiratur descendentem,
ammiratur ascendentem
ad celi palatia.

[7] Fulget celum novo / sole,
nova matre, nova prole;
renovantur omnia.

[8] Spargitur imber rosarum,
liliorum, violarum,
per celorum atria.

[9] Intra sedem maiestatis
et abyssum claritatis
illa virgo regia

[10] In vestitu deaurato,
quem colore variato
cingit auri fimbria.

[11] Ibi natus hanc honorat,
ibi natum mater orat
pro nostra miseria.

[12] Nichil potest hic negare,
cum hec possit imperare
matris reverentia.

[13] Urbs beata, nunc bearis,
cum Mariam contemplaris
singulari gracia.

[14] Fontem tibi gaudiorum
fundit terra miserorum
affluenti copia.

[15] Ergo celum servi terre
debes vicem iam referre
pro tua potentia.

[16] Et cum nobis multa dabis,is
nunquam ta/men compensab
virginis magnalia.

[17] Quicquid enim Deus fecit,
in hac et per hanc refecit
mira providentia,

[18] Ut sit polus decor soli,
fit et solum honor poli,
mediante Maria.

[19] Virgo, mundi domina,
dele nostra crimina,
pande celi limina
post carnis certamina.

[20] Audi nostra cantica,
post Ihesum spes unica,
angelorum gloria,
peccatorum venia.

[21] Tibi virgo supplicamus
cordium instantia;
tibi laudes cumulamus
vocum elegantia,
ut nos tibi congregatos
congreges in gloria.
Amen.

---

4   2.1 Nam: *ms* am, *spatio relicto*

---

4   3.1 Isai. 11.1; cf. Nicolas, PL 144.558.   6.1-2 Gen. 28.12.   10.1 Ps. 44.10.
Nicolas uses the phrase in PL 144.717, Adam in AH 54 No. 105.15.3.

[5] De Apostolis Petro et Paulo
[without music]

134ᵛ [1] Psallat chorus et exultet,
 celum plaudat et resultet
 ad tanta sollempnia.

[2] Summi regis / senatores,
 orbis terre defensores,
 transeunt ad gaudia.

[3] Morte quidem triumphali
 sed uterque speciali
 coronatur laurea.

[4] Petrus cruce consummatur,
 Paulus vero decollatur,
 ambo morte rosea.

[5] Roma, custos tante rei,
 que partiris sanctos Dei
 cum celesti curia,

[6] Tibi datur corporalis,
 illi vero spiritalis
 et viva substantia.

[7] Plus hii tibi contulerunt
 quam Augusti reliquerunt
 armis et potentia.

[8] Sanguis horum subiugavit
 que Romanus ignoravit
 insularum spacia.

[9] Nunc es vere caput rerum,
 nunc es mundi lumen verum
 Christi providentia.

[10] Olim terras subiugasti,
 sed nunc celos occupasti
 dulci violentia.

[11] Sic est Christo Petrus mixtus,
135ʳ ut quod ligat, liget Christus —
 audi mirabilia.

[12] Nec precedat sed sequatur,
 sicut ipse protestatur
 sua voce propria.

[13] Ad archanum trinitatis,
 predicator veritatis
 et magister gentium,

[14] Modo quodam singulari
 meruisti presentari,
 celum intrans tercium.

[15] Petrus princeps in honore,
 Paulus primus in labore,
 duo luminaria,

[16] Duo filii splendoris
 et corone dignioris
 in superna patria,

[17] Per hos mundus informatur,
 per hos Christus conformatur
 in misericordia.

[18] Hiis patronis iustus gaudet;
 his patronis reus audet
 sperare de venia.

[19] Vobis ergo cantica
 sonet vox organica,
 quorum in memoria
 fulget hec ecclesia.

[20] Vobis, principes celorum
 et terrarum gloria,
135ᵛ sup/plicamus ut hunc chorum
 ducatis ad atria,
 ubi quies, ubi dies,
 una super milia.
 Amen.

---

5 4.1-2 Cf. Nicolas, PL 144.636. 11.2 Matth. 16.19. 13.2-3 2 Tim. 1.11.
 14.3 2 Cor. 12.2; cf. Nicolas, PL 144.649. 15.3 Nicolas, PL 144.636: 'duo coeli luminaria'; *ibid*. 649: 'Ecclesiae luminaria.'

[6] De Sancto Iohanne Euvangelista
[*melody*: Laudes crucis]

[1] Dulci laudis melodia
replicemus alleluia
vocis elegantia.

[2] Dies instat hodierna
quam Iohannes sempiterna
cumulavit gratia.

[3] Gaudet tellus et exultat,
celum plaudit et resultat
ad tanta sollempnia.

[4] Unicus euvangelista
mortem vincit die ista
nobili victoria.
Nam amoris hic privilegio
dilectus est a Dei filio
speciali gratia.

[5] Virgo carne, mente purus,
virgo Virgini futurus,
fidelis custodia,
Vocatus a nupciis
dulcibus indiciis,
dulci spreta copula.

[6] Princeps factus secretorum,
filius tonitruorum,
tonans super secula,

[7] Eructavit verbum / bonum,
verbum dulce, dulcem sonum
per quod fiunt omnia.

[8] Supra pectus salvatoris
magni signum in amoris
inter eius brachia,

[9] Declinatus obdormivit,
et ab ipso requisivit
tradentis indicia.

[10] Clavis fixus rex celorum
inter menbra peccatorum
Iudee nequicia,

[11] Huic matrem credidit
et servandam tradidit
de crucis angustia.

[12] Exultavit in tormentis
et tyranni sevientis
contempsit imperia,

[13] Dum ferventis olei
pro fervore fidei
pertulit incendia.

[14] Hic defunctum a defunctis
relevavit coram cunctis
cruce potentissima.

[15] Hunc venena non leserunt,
que bibentes occiderunt
morte velocissima.

[16] Virgas aurum esse iussit,
quod in virgas mox reduxit
fidei potentia.

[17] Lapides in gemmas vertit,
sed et rursus hoc convertit
simili fiducia.

[18] Sacram vidit visionem
in longinquam regionem,
longum perferens agonem
pro verbi constantia,

[19] In qua celum reseratur,
agnus Dei demonstratur,
annis mille religatur
serpentis astucia.

[20] Vivus intrat sepulturam
et sic carnem valde puram
reddit terre possessuram
infinita premia.

[21] O dilecte Iesu Christi,
qui iam celos ascendisti,

[22] Ora patrem pietatis,
ut nos salvet a peccatis

---

6 On the melody see above, n. 29.   4.4-5 Cf. AH 10 No. 276. 3b.1-2.   6.2 Marc. 3.17.   7.1 Ps. 44.2.   8-9 Joan. 13.25.   11.1 Joan. 19.26.
12-20 All this apocryphal material is in *Vita auctore pseudo-Abdia*, printed among other places in J. A. Giles, *Codex apocryphus novi testamenti* (London 1852) I 336-369.

voces audi nostre gentis
tuas laudes concinentis
communi leticia.

et adiungat nostrum chorum
summis choris angelorum
in eterna patria.
Amen.

137ʳ [7] DE SANCTO STEPHANO
[without music]

[1] Salvatorem heri natum
adoremus nobis datum
pietate nimia.

[2] Nunc levitam lapidatum
tanquam primum purpuratum
recolat ecclesia.

[3] Homo sanctus, homo tutus,
custodire constitutus
viduarum corpora,

[4] Signa magna faciebat
et Iudeos convincebat
per scripture tempora.

[5] Statim fremunt ad tumultum
nec adtendunt sancti vultum
plenum lucis gratia.

[6] Ardent, strident, dissecantur,
et currentes conglobantur
eius ad supplicia.

[7] Volant saxa quasi grando
nec lascescunt lapidando
Iudeorum brachia.

[8] Prothomartyr stat invictus
et frendentes suffert ictus
summa paciencia.

137ᵛ [9] Videt Ihesum sursum stantem,
celos sibi reserantem
in paterna gloria.

[10] /Et adsurgit primo testi
Christus, laudans manifesti
militis exordia.

[11] Flectit genu pro Iudeis,
orans ut ignoscat eis
in hac ignorantia.

[12] Et sic tandem consummatus,
celos intrat celo natus
celesti victoria.

[13] O gemma martyrum, lucens et
[previa,
nos tui famuli tua familia

sumus et erimus in hac ecclesia
tibi data.

[14] Nunquam nos deseret tua me-
[moria,
donec nos pertrahas ad illa
[gaudia,
que semper cumulat de presentia
tam beata.

[15] Ibi videbimus, ibi laudabimus,
ibi letabimur et exultabimus,
in domum Domini letantes ibi-
[mus
via recta.

[16] Nil ibi deerit — cessit cupiditas;
nil latebit — eat iam curiositas;
nil terrebit ibi — cedat infir-
[mitas
interfecta.

138ʳ [17] Tu, /qui tam dulciter et flexis
[genibus
rogasti Dominum pro tuis hos-
[tibus,

[18] Ut, cum deposita mundi super-
[bia,
mundum mundaverit maiestas
[regia,

---

7 1.1 Since the feast of St. Stephen is on Dec. 26, 'heri' refers to the Nativity; the idea is fully expressed by Fulgentius, PL 65.729. Cf. Adam, AH 55 No. 310.1.1: 'Heri mundus exsultavit.'   3.2-3 Act. 6.1-5.   4.1 Act. 6.8.   9.1 Act. 7.55-56. 11.1-3 Act. 7.60.   15.2 Ps. 65.6; Nicolas quotes this verse in PL 144.841. 15.3 Ps. 121.1.

adesto, quesumus te, collaudan-
[tibus
mente tota,

nobis subveniant tua suffragia
mundo nota.
Amen.

[8] De Sancto Sebastiano
[*melody*: Congaudentes exsultemus]

[1] Resonemus alleluia
concordi leticia
[3] *Cui* martir Sebastianus
sacra plenus gratia
[5] Confortando studiose
beatorum agmina,
[7] *O felix* martyr,
Marcus et Marcellianus
cuius eloquentia
[9] Super ipsum lux immensa
micuit et splendida,
iuxta stetit adolescens
palla tectus candida.
11] Nicostratus fundit vota
sanctumque martirem
tenens mente devota
querit baptismi merita.
13] Tranquillinus ut sanatur
cum uxore baptizatur
omnique familia.
15] Hic stellarum disciplinam
dissipavit in ruinam,
frangens olovitrea.
17] Tandem captus sagittatur
sagittarum copia,
19] Furit Diocletianus
et sentit Sebastianus
fustigantum brachia.
[21] Ergo martir preciose
qui tua sollempnia
voce pia

[2] *Ad* honorem summi patris,
quem collaudant *omnia*,
[4] Exhibebat sub absconso
clamidis obsequia,
[6] Spem promittens et honoris
infiniti culmina.
[8] Non timuerunt
momentanea tormenta,
spreta mundi gloria.
[10] Uxor Nicostrati muta
per annorum spacia
ad ipsius vocem lingue
recepit officia.
[12] Curat sacra medicina;
regenerantur
credentium agmina
Christi virtute munita.
[14] Et prefectum baptizatum
vidit Roma liberatum
podagre sevicia.
[16] Turba multa Romanorum
per hunc venit ad celorum
agmina purpurea.
[18] Sed illesus remonstratur
regis in presentia.
[20] Et sic carne liberatus,
celos intrat laureatus
cum summa victoria.
[22] Celebramus, posce nobis
sempiterna gaudia.
Alleluia.

---

8 6.1. *ms* Opem *corr. in* Spem   12.1 *ms* Currit

---

8 For the music and textual model see above, n. 28. The words here in italics are in the apparent model, *Clara chorus dulce pangat*, AH 54 No. 94. All the miracles related in the present prose are detailed in *Acta auctore S. Ambrosii*, AS 2.629-642. Some verbal similarities are cited in the following notes.   4 *Ibid*. 629b: '...sub chlamyde terreni imperii Christi militem agebat absconditum.'   8 *Ibid*.: '...momentanea tormentorum genera non timerent.'   15 *Ibid*. 638b: 'Tunc accesserunt ... holovitrea ... dum sanctorum manibus frangeretur.'

[9] DE SANCTO VICTORE
[without music]

[1] Gaude, Syon, et exulta
Dei tui laude fulta;
te natorum turba multa
circundat in gloria.

[2] Uni dies hodierna
servit lege sempiterna,
quem collaudat in superna
rex tuus milicia.

[3] Et tu, gaude, plebs honesta
tanti patris tanta festa,
voce sonans manifesta,
predi/cans alleluia.

[4] Dies redit letabunda,
dies felix et iocunda,
dies pura, dies munda,
mundans a nequicia.

[5] Mens peccati mole clausa
respirare iam sit ausa;
Victor noster est in causa
securus de venia.

[6] Intra ventrem matris signa
fecit mira laude digna,
vincens fortiter maligna
demonum collegia.

[7] O res mira sed divina!
Hic ex aqua fecit vina,
replens in virtute trina
vascula regalia.

[8] Huic gemmis adornata
crux in celis est monstrata,
voxque statim assignata,
pandens hec misteria.

[9] Angelorum in hac vita
sensit cantica mellita
pater noster inaudita
voce iubilantia.

[10] Carcerali fractum pena
furem deserit cathena,
/data libertate plena
eius in memoria.

[11] O lux orbis infinita,
Victor, vivens Christi vita,
voce poscimus unita
nos tua familia,

[12] Ut ad summi regis thronum,
ubi vivit omne bonum,
capiamus vite donum
per tua suffragia.
Amen.

[10] ITEM DE SANCTO VICTORE
[melody: Laetabundus exsultet*]*

[1] *Letabundus*
exultet fidelis cetus,
alleluia;

[2] De Victoris
festivo splendore letus,
res miranda.

---

9 6.1 *ms* infra

9-10 The details on St. Victor appear in an anonymous life printed in AS 6.671-672. There must have been a copy of this life (or a remarkably similar one) at Montiéramey. In a sermon for the feast of this saint, Nicolas wrote: 'Ad manum est patris nostri Victoris solemnitas, ad cujus sacratissimum corpus, si vera est antiquitatis fides, quotidie residemus. ... Quae et quanta sint [signa et mirabilia ejus], et quanta sublimitate fulgentia, libellus de vita et orta ejus latius exaratus sufficit indicare.' PL 144.732-733.
10 On the melody and textual model see above, n. 27. The words in italics are in the text of *Laetabundus*, AH 54 No. 2.

[3] Intra matris viscera
    terruit demonia
    tremefacta.
[5] Servo sensum reddidit,
    quem pro causa perdidit
    morte digna.
[7] Lapi/des sunt anime
    cruci Christi proxime
    super astra.
[9] Eius ad memoriam
    sensit latro gratiam;
    ferrum dat licentiam
    absque pena.
[11] O mundi gloria,
    tua familia
    tua celebrat
    sollempnia.

[4] Regi potum obtulit,
    quem ex aqua protulit
    vinum facta.
[6] Vidit in celestibus
    crucem cum lapidibus
    in hec signa.
[8] Angelorum cantico
    delectatus unico
    vidit castra.
[10] Fecit hec et alia
    Victor mirabilia,
    raptus ad palatia
    laude plena.
[12] Duc nos ad gaudia,
    que sunt in patria
    ubi redundat.
    leticia.
    Amen.

Four Melodies (Sequences 1-4)

For the transcription of these melodies I am indebted to Father Rembert Weakland, O.S.B., and his confrères at St. Vincent Archabbey, Latrobe, Pennsylvania. On the principles of his transcription, Father Weakland writes as follows:

> The music of the verses here coupled is written in full in the original manuscript. In the few cases where the same distinction between *punctum* and *virga* is not maintained by the scribe in both verses the transcription follows the first version. If one of the verses has a liquescent syllable, the transcription indicates the non-liquescent version, whether it be a *punctum* or a *clivis*; if both verses have liquescent syllables, the transcription uses the liquescent *clivis* (the *cephalicus*).

1. SEQUENTIA DE SANCTA MARIA

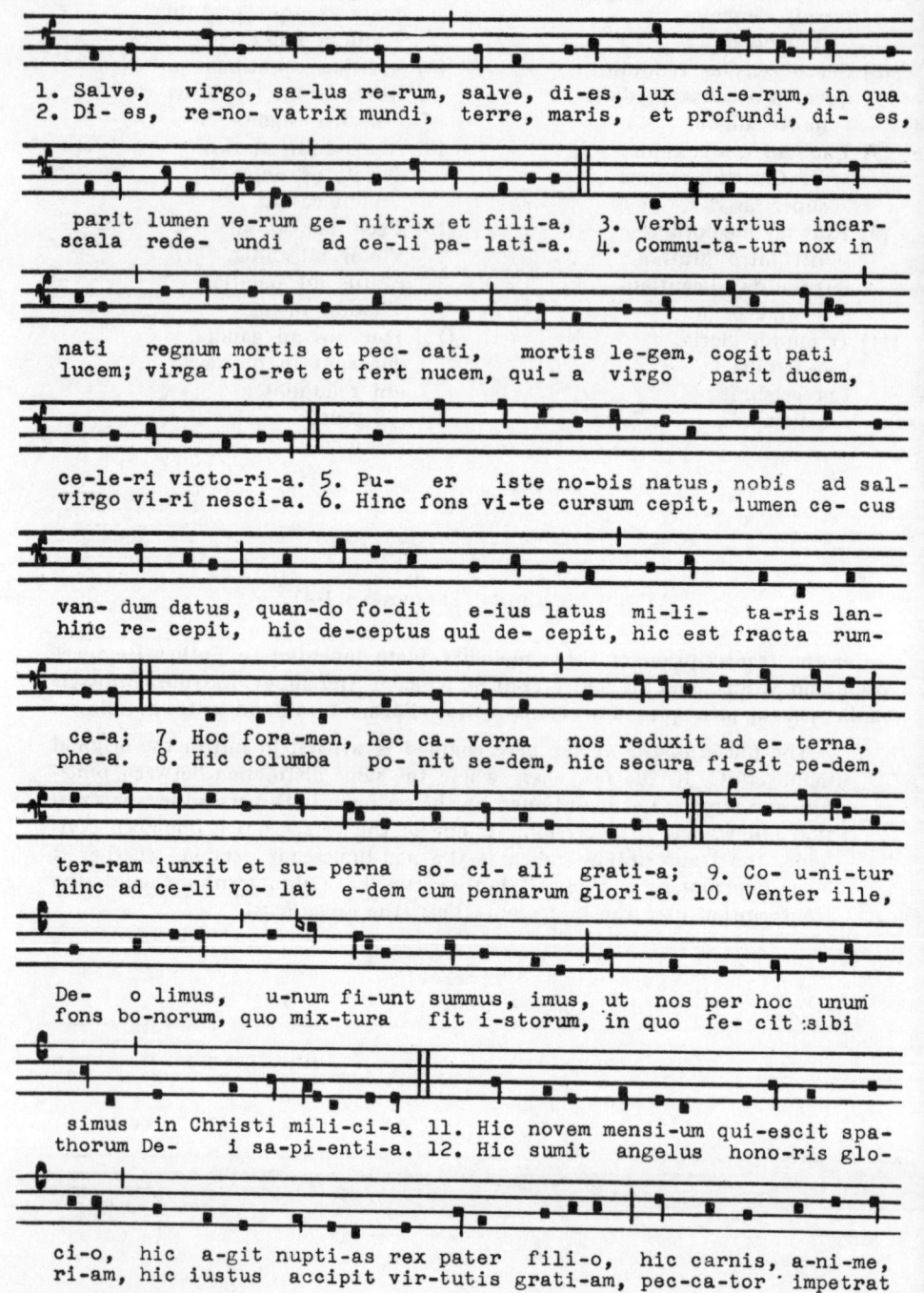

1. Salve, virgo, salus rerum, salve, dies, lux dierum, in qua parit lumen verum genitrix et filia,
2. Dies, renovatrix mundi, terre, maris, et profundi, dies, scala redeundi ad celi palatia.
3. Verbi virtus incarnati regnum mortis et peccati, mortis legem, cogit pati celeri victoria.
4. Commutatur nox in lucem; virga floret et fert nucem, quia virgo parit ducem, virgo viri nescia.
5. Puer iste nobis natus, nobis ad salvandum datus, quando fodit eius latus militaris lancea;
6. Hinc fons vite cursum cepit, lumen cecus hinc recepit, hic deceptus qui decepit, hic est fracta rumphea.
7. Hoc foramen, hec caverna nos reduxit ad eterna, terram iunxit et superna sociali gratia;
8. Hic columba ponit sedem, hic secura figit pedem, hinc ad celi volat edem cum pennarum gloria.
9. Counitur Deo limus, unum fiunt summus, imus, ut nos per hoc unum simus in Christi milicia.
10. Venter ille, fons bonorum, quo mixtura fit istorum, in quo fecit sibi thorum Dei sapientia.
11. Hic novem mensium quiescit spacio, hic agit nuptias rex pater filio, hic carnis, anime,
12. Hic sumit angelus honoris gloriam, hic iustus accipit virtutis gratiam, peccator impetrat

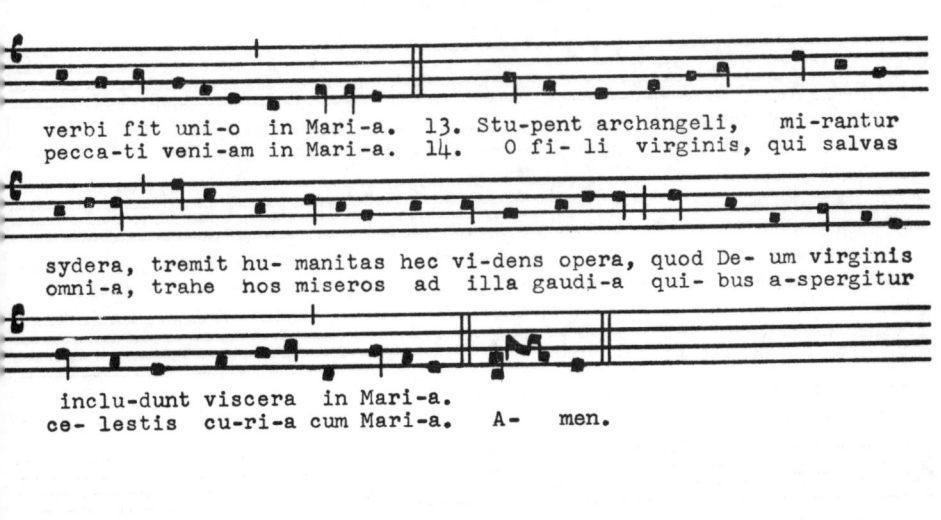

verbi fit uni-o in Mari-a. 13. Stu-pent archangeli, mi-rantur
pecca-ti veni-am in Mari-a. 14. O fi-li virginis, qui salvas

sydera, tremit hu- manitas hec vi-dens opera, quod De- um virginis
omni-a, trahe nos miseros ad illa gaudi-a qui- bus a-spergitur

inclu-dunt viscera in Mari-a.
ce- lestis cu-ri-a cum Mari-a. A- men.

2. DE RESURRECTIONE

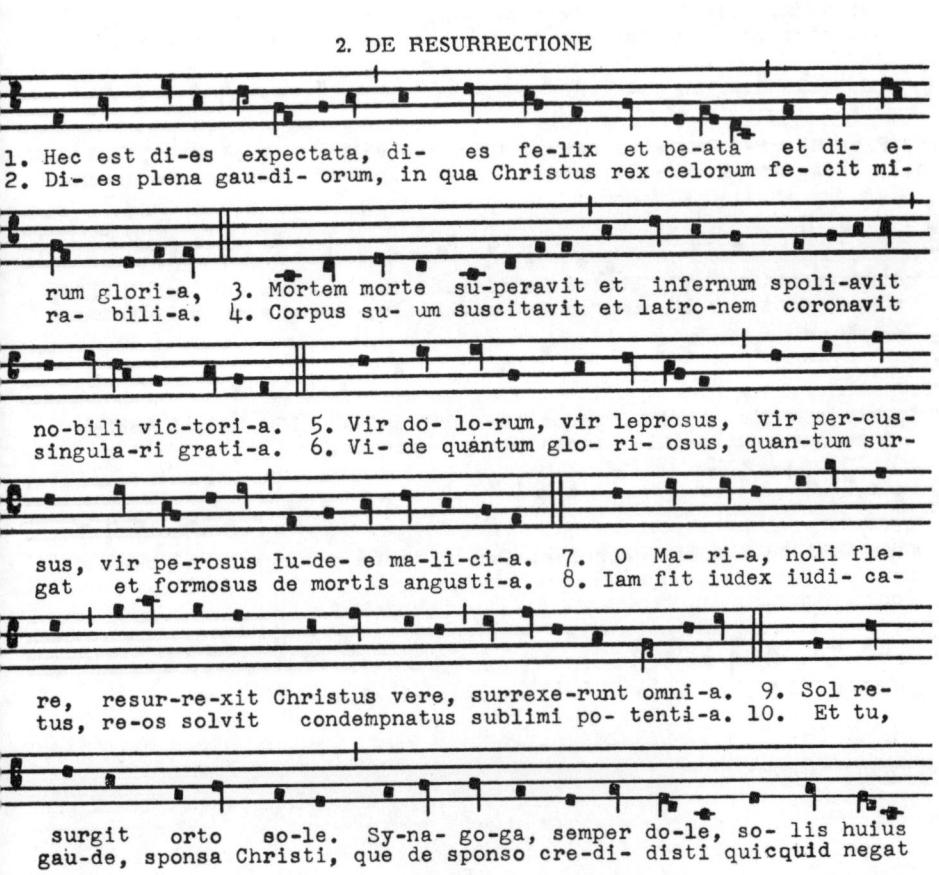

1. Hec est di-es expectata, di- es fe-lix et be-ata et di- e-
2. Di- es plena gau-di- orum, in qua Christus rex celorum fe- cit mi-

rum glori-a, 3. Mortem morte su-peravit et infernum spoli-avit
ra- bili-a. 4. Corpus su- um suscitavit et latro-nem coronavit

no-bili vic-tori-a. 5. Vir do- lo-rum, vir leprosus, vir per-cus-
singula-ri grati-a. 6. Vi- de quantum glo- ri- osus, quan-tum sur-

sus, vir pe-rosus Iu-de- e ma-li-ci-a. 7. O Ma- ri-a, noli fle-
gat et formosus de mortis angusti-a. 8. Iam fit iudex iudi- ca-

re, resur-re-xit Christus vere, surrexe-runt omni-a. 9. Sol re-
tus, re-os solvit condempnatus sublimi po- tenti-a. 10. Et tu,

surgit orto so-le. Sy-na- go-ga, semper do-le, so- lis huius
gau-de, sponsa Christi, que de sponso cre-di- disti quicquid negat

nesci-a. 11. Pu- er, iussus immo- la-ri, pro- hibe-tur vulnera-
impi-a. 12. Dum E- gyptum Io-seph servat et frumentum co- acer-

ri, dum muta- tur hosti-a. Ca- ro Christi sensit dura; splendor pa-
vat, a- perit cel-la-ri-a. In hoc loco gra-nam sevit alter Io-

tris et fi- gura non senserunt tali-a. 13. O se-pulcrum glo-
seph de quo crevit fru- mentorum copi-a. 14. Ex te· sur-git so-

ri-osum, ce-lis ip-sis preci-osum, do-mus De- i propri-a,
poratus Christus tanquam crapulatus de cel-la vi- na-ri-a.

15. Flos Ma-ri-e Christus natus, flos se- pulcri suscitatus, sed est
16. Il-la dedit mo-ri- turum; i-stud red-dit regnaturum regna

diffe-renti-a: 17. Locus ammi-rabilis, sanctus et terribilis,
su-per omni-a. 18. Laudes redde debitas, re- gis ma-gni civitas,

iu-sto-rum vic- tori-a, pecca-to- rum veni-a. 19. Tu qui mortem
ad te cur-runt secula tanta per pe- ricula.

superasti tu-a morte propri-a, fac ut tecum resurgamus ad be-ata

gaudi-a, ubi puri puro purum cantemus allelu-ia.

3. DE NATIVITATE DOMINI

1. Ad archanum huius rei convocentur omnes rei, pleni fidei, pleni spei, summa cum fiducia. 3. Nemo terram operatur in qua Deus generatur; de supernis fecundatur speciali gratia. 5. Flos suavis, flos iocundus, cuius fructu vivit mundus, candidus et rubicundus, solus inter milia, 7. Virgo, virga recta nimis, porta clausa, fons illimis tu superna iungis imis caritate media. 9. Virgo sancta, mater sancti, virgo, sponsa regis tanti, miserere supplicanti populo dulcissima, 11. Exora filium, precipe filio, nam utrumque potes respectu proprio, ne nos inveniat torpentes es angustie, dies clamantium, qua separabitur turba le-

2. Verbum Dei carnem sumit, nec in carne se consumit, sed consummat quod assumit in mundi presentia. 4. Rubus ardet novo more, vellus madet novo rore, virga gaudet novo flore, renovantur omnia. 6. Flos de campo non arato, flos de loco consecrato, flos ex orto consignato, flos illustrans omnia, 8. Per te celum restauratur, per te tellus reparatur, per te fortis exarmatur, sua perdens spolia. 10. Lux et splendor angelorum, consolatio iustorum, una sola spes lapsorum misericordissima. 12. Dies miserie, dies plorantium, dies angustie, dies clamantium,

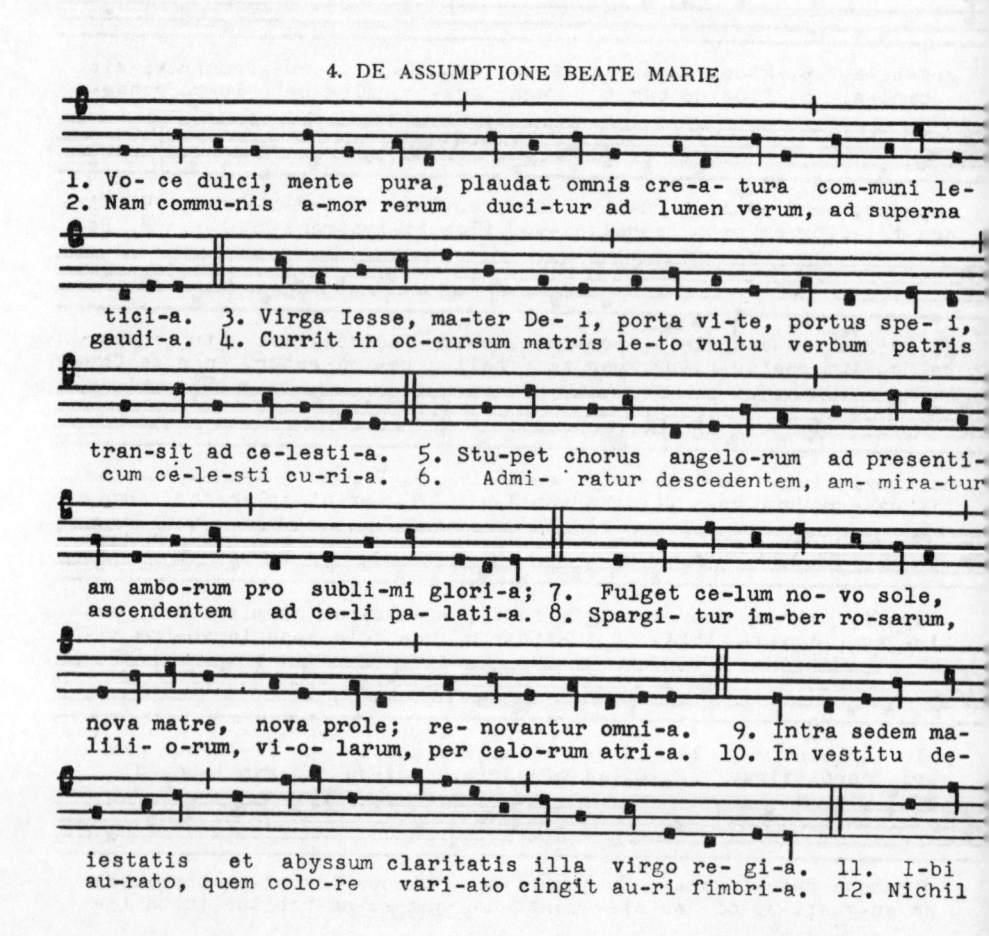

o-ci-o di- es il-la, 13. O vir-go virginum et mun-di glori-a,
tanti-um a dampna- ta. 14. Nec hoc suffi-ci-at tu- tum re- fugi-um,

tunc assit mi- seris tu- a pre-senti-a, que nos e-ri-pi-at ab
sed omnes pertrahat ad tu- um fi-li-um, u-bi cum ipso sit com

hao mi- seri-a tam timen- da,
mu- ne gaudi-um in secu- la. A- men.

4. DE ASSUMPTIONE BEATE MARIE

1. Vo- ce dulci, mente pura, plaudat omnis cre-a- tura com-muni le-
2. Nam commu-nis a-mor rerum duci-tur ad lumen verum, ad superna

tici-a. 3. Virga Iesse, ma-ter De- i, porta vi-te, portus spe- i,
gaudi-a. 4. Currit in oc-cursum matris le-to vultu verbum patris

tran-sit ad ce-lesti-a. 5. Stu-pet chorus angelo-rum ad presenti-
cum ce-le-sti cu-ri-a. 6. Admi- ratur descedentem, am- mira-tur

am ambo-rum pro subli-mi glori-a; 7. Fulget ce-lum no- vo sole,
ascendentem ad ce-li pa- lati-a. 8. Spargi- tur im-ber ro-sarum,

nova matre, nova prole; re- novantur omni-a. 9. Intra sedem ma-
lili- o-rum, vi-o- larum, per celo-rum atri-a. 10. In vestitu de-

iestatis et abyssum claritatis illa virgo re- gi-a. 11. I-bi
au-rato, quem colo-re vari-ato cingit au-ri fimbri-a. 12. Nichil

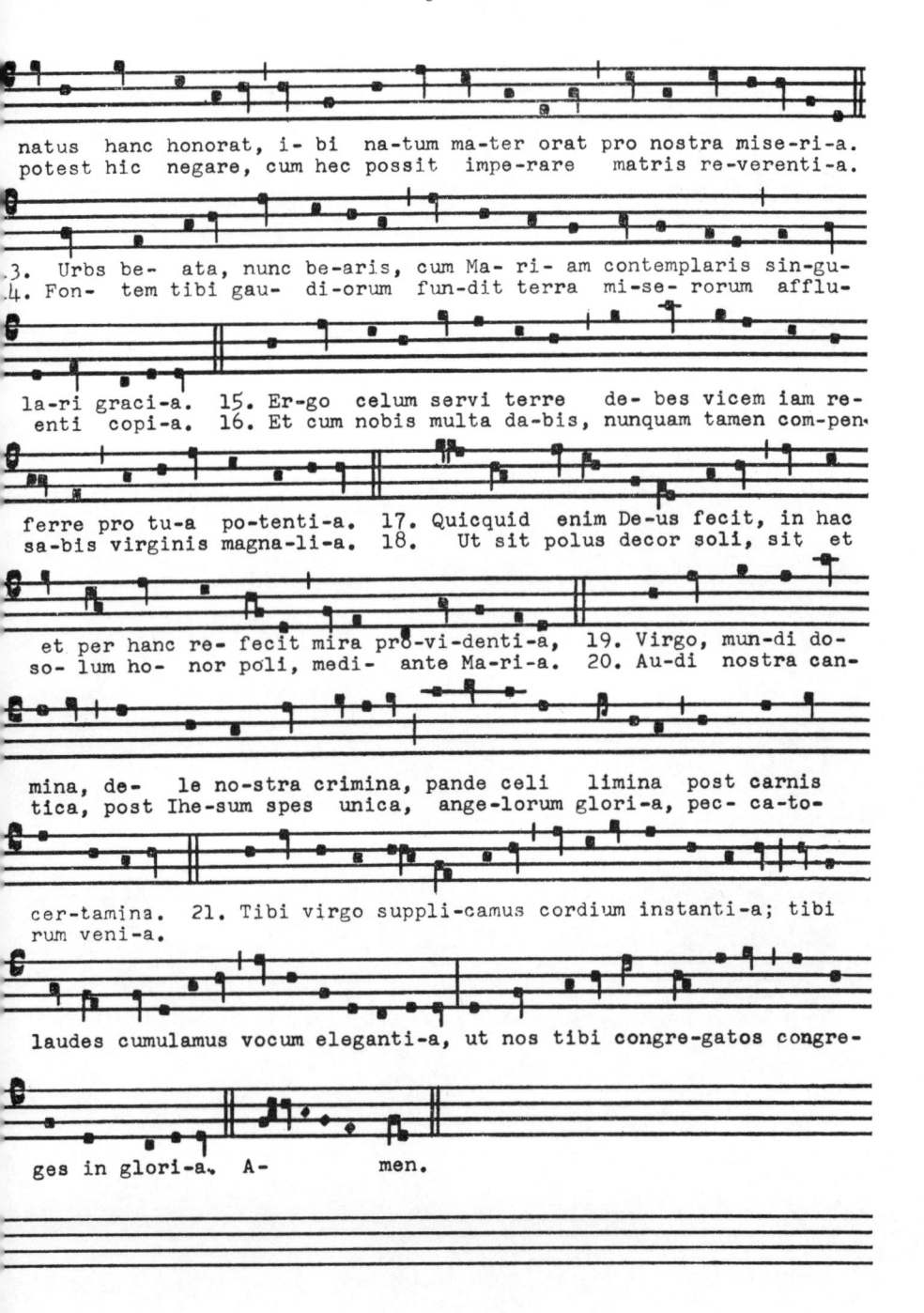

natus hanc honorat, i- bi na-tum ma-ter orat pro nostra mise-ri-a.
potest hic negare, cum hec possit impe-rare matris re-verenti-a.

3. Urbs be- ata, nunc be-aris, cum Ma- ri- am contemplaris sin-gu-
4. Fon- tem tibi gau- di-orum fun-dit terra mi-se- rorum afflu-

la-ri graci-a. 15. Er-go celum servi terre de- bes vicem iam re-
enti copi-a. 16. Et cum nobis multa da-bis, nunquam tamen com-pen-

ferre pro tu-a po-tenti-a. 17. Quicquid enim De-us fecit, in hac
sa-bis virginis magna-li-a. 18. Ut sit polus decor soli, sit et

et per hanc re- fecit mira pro-vi-denti-a, 19. Virgo, mun-di do-
so- lum ho- nor poli, medi- ante Ma-ri-a. 20. Au-di nostra can-

mina, de- le no-stra crimina, pande celi limina post carnis
tica, post Ihe-sum spes unica, ange-lorum glori-a, pec- ca-to-

cer-tamina. 21. Tibi virgo suppli-camus cordium instanti-a; tibi
rum veni-a.

laudes cumulamus vocum eleganti-a, ut nos tibi congre-gatos congre-

ges in glori-a. A- men.

3

Nicolas de Clairvaux à la recherche du vin d'Auxerre, d'après une lettre inédite du XIIe siècle

Nicolas de Clairvaux, qui fut un temps secrétaire de saint Bernard, fit carrière en écrivant pour d'autres que pour lui. Non seulement il composa pour l'abbé de Clairvaux des lettres et des sermons, mais il fréquenta par la suite la cour du comte de Champagne, Henri le Libéral, qui recourut à lui pour sa correspondance. Et, tandis qu'il était à Clairvaux, Nicolas composa nombre de lettres pour les moines ses compagnons, écrivant comme s'il avait adopté le nom et la personnalité d'un autre : la collection de sa correspondance écrite durant cette période comprend des lettres rédigées par lui pour l'abbé Bernard, le prieur Rualène, Henri de France (frère de Louis VII), Gérard de Péronne et bien d'autres moines. Cette activité littéraire prit fin lorsque Nicolas fut accusé d'avoir poussé trop loin son rôle d'écrivain pour le compte des autres, en écrivant des lettres sans en avoir reçu mission et en se servant abusivement du sceau de Bernard. En 1151, l'abbé l'expulsa de manière humiliante [1].

Cet échec ne mit cependant pas fin à la carrière de Nicolas ou à la collaboration, dont il se flattait, avec les grands de ce monde [2]. Quittant la France pour Rome, il entra au service du cardinal Roland Bandinelli — le futur pape Alexandre III — et du pape d'alors, Adrien IV. Vers 1158, il revint en Champagne et obtint la faveur du comte Henri, grâce auquel il devint prieur de Saint-Jean-en-Châtel, à Troyes (une dépendance de l'abbaye de Montiéramey dont il avait été moine avant son entrée à Clairvaux). Il resta à Troyes,

---

[1]. Pour compléter l'article d'Augustin STEINER, *Nicolaus, Mönch in Clairvaux*, dans *Studien und Mitteilungen zur Geschichte des Benediktiner-Ordens*, t. XXXVIII, 1917, p. 41-50, cf. Dom Jean LECLERCQ, *Les collections de sermons de Nicolas de Clairvaux*, dans *Revue bénédictine*, t. LXVI, 1956, p. 269-302, et J. BENTON, *The Court of Champagne as a Literary Center*, dans *Speculum*, t. XXXVI, ci-dessus, pp. 7-9. La plupart des lettres de Nicolas ont été publiées dans MIGNE, *P.L.*, t. 196, c. 1589-1654.

[2]. Nicolas écrivait au comte Henri, vers 1161 : *Ab ineunte aetate mea placui magnis et summis principibus hujus mundi* (*P.L.*, t. 196, c. 1652).

familier du comte Henri auquel il servait en quelque sorte de secrétaire, jusqu'à sa mort, survenue vers 1176.

On peut se demander quelles qualités d'esprit et de charme permirent à Nicolas de jouir de l'estime de tant de personnages, en dépit d'un caractère qui ne brille pas à nos yeux par l'honnêteté [1]. On peut aussi se demander en quoi son style faisait de lui un écrivain recherché par ses collègues qui étaient eux-mêmes parfaitement capables d'écrire leurs propres lettres. A la lecture de celles de Nicolas, nous les trouvons pour la plupart enflées, maniérées, surchargées de rhétorique et de mots rares. Jusqu'à un certain point, force nous est d'admettre que ses contemporains appréciaient ce style-là, et que la carrière littéraire de Nicolas s'est édifiée sur un style pompeux et une réelle habileté à emprunter des phrases et des idées à d'autres auteurs. Mais, dans son œuvre, certains morceaux révèlent un aspect plus attrayant de l'auteur et de l'homme : ainsi y a-t-il une beauté lyrique dans certaines des proses écrites par Nicolas, notamment dans celles qui honorent la Vierge [2]. Et, parmi les quelques lettres de lui qui demeurent encore inédites, il en est une qui retient l'attention par son style et par son humour.

A la différence de beaucoup des lettres de Nicolas, en effet, celle-ci le montre capable de s'exprimer sans trop s'étendre en longueur. Loin de pécher par un excès de sérieux, elle présente une requête avec une allure souriante, qui paraît avoir transformé l'auteur lui-même. Ce qui frappe le plus le lecteur, c'est la façon dont Nicolas se fait un jeu d'user de citations bibliques détournées de leur sens premier. L'usage inattendu du langage de l'Écriture était assez commun au XIIe s., mais ici, au lieu d'élever ses images au plan de l'allégorie, Nicolas les rabaisse jusqu'aux préoccupations très mondaines du ravitaillement en vin. Le lecteur est d'ailleurs très avancé dans sa lecture quand il s'aperçoit que Nicolas écrit dans un but très pratique, et non sur un sujet mystique. Qu'on en juge par ce texte :

A l'évêque d'Auxerre, son Nicolas [assure] qu'il est sien. Pour employer les mots de l'Évangile, ils n'ont plus de vin [3]. *Envoyez-moi non point* le vin de l'égarement [4], *mais le vin qui réjouit le cœur de l'homme* [5], *dont la couleur excellente, la saveur très douce et l'*agréable

---

1. LECLERCQ, *op. cit.*, p. 278.

2. Textes publiés dans *Nicolas of Clairvaux and the Twelfth-Century Sequence, with special reference to Adam of Saint-Victor* (*Traditio*, t. XVIII, 1962, p. 151-179).

3. Jean, II, 3. — Nous adoptons ici les traductions de *La Sainte Bible*, par Louis Segond.

4. Psaumes, LIX, 5.

5. Psaumes, CIII, 15.

odeur [1] *témoignent de la qualité. C'est en ces trois éléments que se manifeste sa perfection, et la corde à trois fils ne se rompt pas facilement* [2].

Envoyez-moi le vin, le tonneau et le chariot, puisque vous m'avez laissé sur cet espoir, comme vous me l'avez promis. Mais, si le chariot pose un problème (et j'ai peur qu'il en pose un), je préfère l'envoyer plutôt que de perdre [le vin]. Je crois ce que vous croyez. Différer serait me l'ôter.

Car les vins qui sont dans notre région sont troubles, et ne viennent pas de ces plants qui croissent chez vous dans la bénédiction ; leur jus n'est pas passé d'une nation à l'autre, et d'un royaume vers un autre peuple [3]. *Ordonnez que le tonneau soit net et propre, pour qu'une si noble boisson ne soit pas avilie par la rusticité du bois. Envoyez en séparément pour l'abbé et pour moi* ; les Juifs, en effet, n'ont pas de relation avec les Samaritains [4].

Cette lettre fait partie d'une collection de lettres de Nicolas incluse dans le manuscrit Phillipps 1719 de Berlin, manuscrit du XIIIe s. où figurent également des lettres d'Hildebert de Lavardin, et de Symmaque. On y trouve trente-sept lettres écrites par Nicolas à Clairvaux, et quatre plus tardives ont été transcrites à la fin de la collection. La lettre citée ici a été ajoutée pour remplir un vide, au f⁰ 96 v⁰, à la fin d'un groupe de lettres variées qui précèdent celles de Nicolas [5]. Cet emplacement suggère l'idée que cette épître est venue aux mains du copiste indépendamment du reste de la collection, qu'elle ne faisait pas partie du groupe bien connu des lettres écrites à Clairvaux, et qu'elle avait sans doute été rédigée après que Nicolas eut été chassé de ce monastère, et après son retour en Champagne vers 1158. Mais ni la date de la lettre, ni l'identification de l'évêque d'Auxerre ne sont assurées. Il semble cependant probable que la lettre a été écrite à Alain, évêque d'Auxerre entre 1152 et 1167, que Nicolas avait bien connu au temps où tous deux étaient moines à Clairvaux [6]. Si elle date du temps où Nicolas était prieur

---

1. Exode, XXIX, 18.
2. Ecclesiaste, IV, 12.
3. Psaumes, CIV, 13.
4. Jean, IV, 9.
5. Le manuscrit a été décrit par Valentin ROSE, *Verzeichnis der lateinischen Handschriften der kgl. Bibliothek zu Berlin*, I, *Die Meerman-Handschriften des Sir Thomas Phillipps*, Berlin, 1893, p. 418-422. Nous avons l'intention de publier les autres lettres inédites de Nicolas qui y figurent ; celle-ci a été éditée avec l'autorisation de la Deutsche Staatsbibliothek in Berlin et grâce à l'amabilité du Dr Helmut Boese et du Dr Hans Lülfing. Nous avons bénéficié de l'aide financière du Committee for the Advancement of Research de l'Université de Pennsylvanie et le professeur Lloyd Daly nous a aimablement apporté ses conseils sur un certain nombre de points.
6. *Gallia Christ.*, t. XII, c. 293-295. Nicolas, Alain d'Auxerre et Pierre de Celle figurent tous comme témoins d'une charte du comte Henri pour Larrivour, en 1161 (Arch. Aube, 4 H 29, éd. d'ARBOIS DE JUBAINVILLE, *Hist. des ducs et des comtes de Champagne*, t. III, 1861, p. 453).

de Saint-Jean-en-Châtel, l'abbé mentionné à la fin du texte serait celui de Montiéramey (à dix-huit km. de Troyes) dont dépendait ce prieuré. Cela semble plus vraisemblable que de supposer que Nicolas, secrétaire de l'abbé de Clairvaux, aurait demandé un tonneau pour saint Bernard et un autre pour lui personnellement.

Cette lettre apporte un témoignage de plus en faveur de la réputation du vin d'Auxerre, dont Roger Dion a noté le renom acquis dès le XIIe siècle [1]. Le transport par chariot depuis Auxerre jusqu'en Champagne méridionale n'aurait pas offert de difficulté, quand on songe qu'en 1178 le comte de Guines faisait servir du vin d'Auxerre au cours d'un repas offert à l'archevêque de Reims à Ardres, bien au nord de la Champagne [2]. Troyes, Montiéramey et même Clairvaux sont dans la même région géographique, la vallée de l'Aube. D'où que Nicolas ait écrit sa lettre, il faudrait conclure sur son témoignage que les vins des importants vignobles de la Champagne méridionale étaient de qualité médiocre au goût des connaisseurs du XIIe siècle [3].

APPENDICE

[Berlin, ms. Phillipps, 1719, f° 96 v°]

Domino Autusiodorensi suus N. quod suus. Ut verbis ewangelicis vos alloquar, *vinum non habent* [4]. Mittite mihi non *vinum compunctionis* [5], sed *vinum quod letificet cor hominis* [6], cui color optimus, sapor dulcissimus, *odor suavissimus* [7] testimonium reddant. In his enim tribus perfectio eius attenditur, et *triplex funiculus difficile rumpitur* [8]. Mittite vinum, dolium, et vehiculum, quia in hac spe dimisisti me, sic mihi promisisti. Quodsi de veiculo questio est (nam et ego hanc timeo questionem), antemittam quam amittam. Credo quod vos creditis. Differre auferre erit. Nam turbata sunt vina que in circuitu nostro sunt, nec sunt de radicibus illis que vivunt apud vos in benedictione, quarum succi non *transierunt de gente in gentem et de regno ad populum alterum* [9]. Precipite ut dolium liquidum sit et mundum, ne tante nobilitatis liquor ligni rusticitate degeneret. Seorsum abbati, seorsum mittetis et michi. *Non enim coutuntur Iudei Samaritanis* [10].

---

1. Roger DION, *Histoire de la vigne et du vin de France des origines au* XIXe s., Paris, 1959, p. 245.
2. Lambert d'Ardres, in *M G H*, *S S*, t. XXIV, p. 601.
3. Cf. DION, *op. cit.*, p. 185 et 234. — Nous remercions M. Sallé, assistant à la Faculté des Lettres de Dijon, et M. J. Richard de l'aide qu'ils ont bien voulu apporter à la traduction de notre article.
4. Joan., 2, 3.
5. Ps., 59, 5.
6. Ps., 103, 15.
7. Exod. 29, 18.
8. Eccle., 4, 12.
9. Ps., 104, 13.
10. Joan., 4, 9.

4

The Evidence of Andreas Capellanus Re-examined Again

In a recent article published in this journal[*] John F. Mahoney draws attention to eight charters enacted between 1158 and 1199 in the diocese of Troyes which refer to one or more clerics named Andreas.[1] Without asserting the identification categorically, Professor Mahoney suggests that André, the chaplain of Countess Marie of Champagne, may have been a local priest and canon named André de Luyères. At the same time he raises a question about the number of references to this André recorded by previous scholars. Since the establishment of any information about the Andreas Capellanus who wrote the celebrated treatise *De Amore* would be significant, a critical review of Professor Mahoney's tentative conclusions may not be amiss.[2]

Although the assumption is often presented as a fact, the identification of the author Andreas with the chaplain of Countess Marie has never been established from documentary evidence. The text

---

[1] "The Evidence for Andreas Capellanus in Re-Examination," LV (1958), 1-6. A recent monograph which reviews the extensive literature on the *De Amore* is Felix Schlösser, *Andreas Capellanus*, Abhandlungen zur Kunst-, Musik- und Literaturwissenschaft, 15 (Bonn, 1960).

[2] My conclusions about the witnesses to the charters of Count Henry the Liberal and Countess Marie are based on a study of over 600 of those charters available in print or in the archives of Champagne and Paris. The more general results of this study relating to literary history are presented in an article on "The Court of Champagne as a Literary Center," *Speculum*, XXXVI (1961), 551-591; see above, pp. 3-43.

[*]*Studies in Philiology*.

of the *De Amore* and the most reliable rubrics of its manuscripts tell us that the author was chaplain, not of the court of Champagne, but of the royal court of France.[3] Because Andreas gives a prominent place in his collection of amatory case histories to the "judgments" of Countess Marie, many scholars have felt that there was a close relationship between the author and the countess. When Pio Rajna suggested in 1891 that the author of the *De Amore* might early in his career have been the chaplain named Andreas who appeared in Marie's charters in the 1180's, the only serious opposition was raised over the question of the date of his writing.[4] The author of a recent survey of the evidence for dating the *De Amore* by its references to Hungarian affairs places its composition in the years from 1186 to 1196, thereby eliminating that particular objection.[5] But if there is no contradictory evidence to show that Marie's chaplain did not write the *De Amore,* the grounds for saying that he did are still slight. Many modern critics are suspicious of the existence of "courts of love"; if Andreas' account is fictional, then his familiarity with Marie's court may have been more imagined than real.[6] Andreas does not claim that he knew Marie personally, but only that he was familiar with her *dicta*.[7] There is no reason to think that the author *must* have been Marie's

[3] E. Trojel surveys the evidence of the manuscripts in the introduction to his edition, *Andreae Capellani regii Francorum De Amore libri tres* (Hanover, 1892), pp. ix-xii, xxi-xxxi. Although his text has since been republished, Trojel's edition remains the only one with full critical apparatus.

[4] Pio Rajna, "Tre studi per la storia del libro di Andrea Capellano," *Studj di filogia romanza*, V, 258-259. *Cf.* Trojel, *op. cit.,* p. xi.

[5] Alexandre Eckhardt, *De Sicambria à Sans-Souci* (Paris, 1943), pp. 113-124. Eckhardt here counters the argument of Arpad Steiner, "The Date of the Composition of Andreas Capellanus' De Amore," *Speculum*, IV (1929), 92-95.

[6] Paul Remy, "Les 'cours d'amour': légende et réalité," *Revue de l'Université de Bruxelles*, VII (1955), 179-197, is a useful survey of a subject on which too much loose writing has been produced.

[7] *De Amore,* ed. Trojel, p. 269: "Et hoc quidem Campaniae comitissam ex quibusdam suis dictis sensisse cognovimus." This is translated as "We know from some of her remarks that the Countess of Champagne knew this" by John J. Parry in *The Art of Courtly Love by Andreas Capellanus*, Records of Civilization, 33 (New York, 1941), p. 166. "Remarks" suggests intimate conversation, but the word *dictum* has the meaning of a formal judicial decision such as Andreas reports elsewhere in his book. See J. F. Niermeyer, *Mediae latinitatis lexicon minus* (Leiden, 1954-), *s. v.* dictum.

chaplain; a royal chaplain could just as well have written about Marie and the other great ladies. Rajna himself did not assert that Andreas was Marie's chaplain at the time he wrote the book. Unless evidence is discovered which more closely links the chaplain of Marie's court to the *De Amore*, we cannot be sure that Rajna and his successors have not been the victims of the coincidental appearance of a relatively common name. The author of the *De Amore* may well still be unidentified.

There has been some confusion about the minor matter of the number of charters from the court of Champagne witnessed by an Andreas Capellanus. That Marie was served by a chaplain named André was originally established by Henri d'Arbois de Jubainville from the evidence of four charters, three of which were then in print.[8] When Louis-André Vigneras wished to document his assertion that the author of *De Amore* was Marie's chaplain, he cited these earlier references and two more printed charters, but thought that he had referred to seven charters.[9] Professor Mahoney began his investigation with Vigneras' list, and he does not, in spite of his claim to the contrary, add to the number of known charters witnessed by Andreas Capellanus.[10]

The printed records of Champagne have probably now been fully exploited, but there is more work to be done in the archives. My own investigations have turned up three more charters of Countess Marie witnessed by her chaplain André, bringing the total to nine.[11] One of these, enacted at Provins in 1185, was witnessed by another chaplain named Pierre, showing that André shared his

[8] *Histoire des ducs et des comtes de Champagne*, 6 vols. in 7 (Paris, 1859-67), IV, 544. The reference numbers noted there are to the catalogue of acts at the end of volume III.

[9] "Chrétien de Troyes Rediscovered," *MP*, XXXII (1935), 342. The confusion over the number of charters may have arisen from the duplication of references to manuscripts which were later printed.

[10] I do not understand why Professor Mahoney says in his text that the document he prints as #7 has been overlooked and was not mentioned by Vigneras, when in note 6 he states, correctly, that Vigneras lists it in his note. All the charters in Vigneras' list contain specific reference to Andreas Capellanus.

[11] Marne H 98 (orig. charter of 1183); Aube 6 G 7, carton 2 (orig. charter of 1185); and Aube 9 H 21 (orig. charter of 1186). The unprinted charter of 1186 which Arbois de Jubainville catalogued as #348 has the modern archival number of Marne G 1308. Chaplain Pierre was also a witness to this latter charter.

office with a colleague. The charter was also witnessed by Marie's half-sister Marguerite, who married King Bela III of Hungary in the next year. This is the marriage which figures prominently in modern attempts to date the *De Amore*. Marguerite and her mother, Queen Adèle, were also present at Marie's court on December 21, 1184.[12] If it could be demonstrated that Marie's chaplain wrote the *De Amore*, his personal acquaintance with these ladies would be highly significant. But unfortunately the charters neither prove nor disprove the hypothesis of his authorship. From the witness lists we learn only that André was a priest and an important member of the court in the years from 1182 to 1186.[13]

Professor Mahoney bases his suggestion that the names *Andreas Capellanus* and *Andreas de Lueriis* refer to the same man on the assumptions that "Andreas was associated with the court of Champagne for some time before he became, or was appointed, chaplain to Marie" and "any Andreas explicitly connected with Marie or her husband, Henri le Liberal, in these documents may be references to him who became *capellanus* later."[14] Marie may well have chosen a chaplain from any of the hundreds of churches of her domains which she visited during the journeys of her peripatetic court, and she may have picked a young man rather than an older man who had been known to the court for years without receiving court appointment. In the present state of our knowledge too many imponderables prevent us from making easy assumptions about court appointment practices. The establishment of more points of identity than a common baptismal name and residence in the same town is needed for a possible identification to be anything more than speculation.[15] With these considerations in mind we can turn to what is known of the life of André de Luyères.

[12] Aube 27 H 3 (carton), an original charter enacted at the convent of Notre-Dame de Foicy outside Troyes.

[13] The customary order of witnesses in these lists places the clergy before the laity and ordained clergy before those in minor orders. This explains why the chaplain André appears first in seven of nine lists. In two instances he was given the title "Dominus," which when applied to a cleric indicates that the man in question was a priest. The establishment of this fact is important, since the ordination of a *capellanus* is not always certain. Cf. Schlösser, *Andreas Capellanus*, p. 29.

[14] *Op. cit.*, p. 2.

[15] The name André appears commonly in the records of Champagne; it is by no means as rare as the elusive name Chrétien.

Identified by his full name or as André, priest of St Etienne, André de Luyères was listed among the witnesses to nine charters of Count Henry of Champagne between 1159 and 1176.[16] Almost all of these acts were concerned with the affairs of the churches of Troyes, particularly St Etienne, where André's nephew Bonel was one of the two guardians of the treasure.[17] Count Henry had founded St Etienne and appointed many of its canons, but these references do not demonstrate any close personal relationship between the count and André; they are a product of the count's usual practice of including clerics, particularly canons of a favored church like St Etienne, among the members of his court when ecclesiastical matters were being treated. Although André de Luyères was not named in any extant court witness list after 1176, two charters of 1186 show that he was active in the affairs of St Etienne in that year.[18] In 1199, still named as a canon of St Etienne, he received as his share in the settlement of a claim made by a local convent against his father an annual income for as long as he should remain a secular clergyman.[19] When he died he left St Etienne a stone house in the church cloister.[20]

---

[16] Three of these are cited by Professor Mahoney as documents #1-3. The first of these was dated Feb. 1, 1158 (O. S.), and should be dated 1159 (N. S.). He omits a final phrase which shows that André and the other priests in the witness lists were canons of St Etienne. In the heading of his document #2 read 1161 for 1162. In answer to the question which Professor Mahoney raises in note 18 as to why André was called *clericus*: *clerici* are here constrasted with *milites*, meaning clergy as opposed to laity. For the other six charters see Charles Lalore, *Collection des principaux cartulaires du diocèse de Troyes*, 7 vols. (Paris and Troyes, 1875-90), I, #39, pp. 68-69; A. Harmand, "Notice historique sur la léproserie de la ville de Troyes," *Mem. de la Société . . . de l'Aube*, XIV (1847-48), 525-526 (1171 and 1175); E. Pérard, *Recueil de plusieurs pièces curieuses servant à l'histoire de Bourgogne* (Paris, 1664), p. 248; and Cart. de St Etienne (Paris BN ms, lat. 17098), fols. 35v⁰ and 337r⁰.

[17] Cart. de St Etienne, fol. 35v⁰.

[18] André and his nephew Bonel were among the witnesses to a transaction involving St Etienne; this charter is cited by Professor Mahoney as document #6. André and Bonel were also included in a list of priests who were canons of St Etienne in the body of a charter issued by Marie and her son Henry; see Aube 6 G 7, carton 2 (orig.) or Cart. de St Etienne, fols. 56v⁰-57r⁰ (copy).

[19] This charter is reprinted by Professor Mahoney as document #8.

[20] *Recueil des historiens de la France: Obituaires*, ed. Auguste Molinier, *Obituaires de la province de Sens*, IV (Paris, 1923), 451F. A charter of

The most interesting information we have about this man who achieved local distinction as a priest and canon is that he came from a family which was bound by the limitations of serfdom. The document of 1199 does not make the family's position clear, but it gives the impression that they were property holders.[21] A charter of 1191 shows, however, that Humbert de Luyères was the father of a serf involved in a marriage exchange and was therefore a serf himself, since the bond was hereditary.[22] This conclusion is reinforced by a charter of 1173 which records that one of the serfs given in a marriage exchange was the daughter of Jean, nephew of the canon André de Luyères.[23] André, undoubtedly freed from serfdom in order to become a priest, was a member of a family which perhaps was attempting to live like the lower nobility but which had to acknowledge its servile station.

It is unlikely that André de Luyères was Marie's chaplain. His servile origin is not a bar to the identification; Marie's chaplain Adam (who appeared in her charters in 1188 and 1191) is known to have been the son of a serf.[24] But the dates of André de Luyères' long career as a canon of St Etienne from 1159 through 1199 do raise serious questions. The chaplain André witnessed extant court charters only in the years from 1182 to 1186, and since we know of other chaplains who served at court before and after this period, it is probable that these dates come close to marking the limits of his court service. The evidence of the witness lists is most easily explained by the supposition that at about 1186 André lost

1218 refers to this house "que fuit defuncti Andree de Lueriis in qua mansit defunctus Andreas quondan canonicus ecclesie ipsius," Cart. de St Etienne, fol. 210r⁰-v⁰.

[21] On the basis of this document Alphonse Roserot, whose knowledge of Champagne was encyclopedic, concluded about Humbert de Luyères: " Ce n'était certainement pas un roturier." But he had not taken into account the other documents referring to Humbert. See his *Dictionnaire historique de la Champagne méridionale (Aube)*, 3 vols. (Langres, 1942-48), p. 824.

[22] Lalore, *Cartulaires*, I, #106, p. 148.

[23] *Ibid.*, #47, p. 76. This charter is cited as document #4 by Professor Mahoney.

[24] On Adam see the references in Arbois de Jubainville, *Histoire*, IV, 544 and a charter printed by Charles Lalore, *Documents sur l'abbaye de Notre-Dame-aux-Nonnains de Troyes* (Troyes, 1874), #9, p. 13. On the court chaplains in general see my dissertation, *The Court of Champagne under Henry the Liberal and Countess Marie*, deposited at Princeton in May 1959 and published photographically by University Microfilms, Ann Arbor, Mich.

Marie's favor, died, or was otherwise incapacitated. But, when supposing these events, we must wonder why an ex-chaplain should remain for at least thirteen years as a canon of a church at which Marie was the influential lay patron. It should also be remembered that witness lists were written so that the witnesses could be identified in later years. If a well-known local canon became the court chaplain, he probably would have been identified by his familiar and established name in at least one of nine court witness lists. And in 1186 when André de Luyères was listed among the canons of St Etienne in the body of a court charter, his court office would probably have been mentioned if he had held one.

If one accepts the suggestion that André de Luyères became Marie's chaplain, it is still more difficult to believe that he wrote the *De Amore*. As the son of a serf from rural Champagne, André de Luyères probably had no more education than that provided in the grammar school of Troyes. The ecclesiastical records of Troyes are quite full in this period, and there is no evidence to show that André de Luyères held any position in the administration of the diocese, in the cathedral school, or in the cathedral chapter. The *De Amore*, on the other hand, is written in fluent if not flawless Latin and shows the author's familiarity with an impressive amount of classical, patristic, and contemporary literature. One must have a high opinion of the Latinity and education of the average secular canon to believe that André de Luyères had the ability and the training to write the *De Amore*. In addition, the subject and tone of parts of the *De Amore* do not accord with what we know of André de Luyères. The author of the *De Amore* compared the love of peasants to that of animals and emphasized class differences in his dialogues in a way which, it seems to me, makes social climbers look ridiculous.[25] Such remarks would seem out of place from the pen of a man who was the son of a serf and was himself making his way up the social scale.

The present survey of the evidence concerning Andreas Capellanus to be found elsewhere than in the *De Amore* has added little to our knowledge. The citation of a few more witness lists containing the name of Marie's chaplain André brings their total to

---

[25] Under the heading *De amore rusticorum* Andreas says, "naturaliter sicut equus et mulus ad Veneris opera promoventur." See *De Amore*, ed. Trojel, p. 235. Much of the debate in the dialogues is developed from class differences.

nine. The appearance of these references only in the years from 1182 to 1186 supports the belief that the chaplain's service did not extend far beyond those limits. It has also been established that the chaplain André was a priest. But nothing in the documents of Champagne shows that Marie's chaplain wrote the *De Amore*. The results of this survey do not support Professor Mahoney's suggested identification and leave the state of our knowledge largely where it was before he wrote his article. But the danger of tentative conclusions growing with repetition into positive assertions is so great [26] that there may be value in reminding the reader of what we do not know.

[26] *Cf.* Urban T. Holmes, *Chrétien, Troyes, and the Grail* (Chapel Hill, 1959), p. 16, n. 29 and p. 17.

5

Qui étaient les parents de Jacques de Vitry?

L'étude de la biographie médiévale, toujours à court d'éléments, souffre surtout au départ. Les grands hommes du Moyen Age ont laissé davantage de traces de leur départ de ce monde que de leur arrivée, et nous en savons beaucoup plus sur les œuvres de leur maturité que sur les influences qui se sont exercées sur eux au début de leur vie. Au titre de prédicateur réputé, d'évêque d'Acre et de cardinal de Tusculum, Jacques de Vitry apparaît souvent dans les documents de son époque. Il nous a légué une œuvre composée de deux histoires de croisade, d'un recueil de lettres qui se rapportent à la cinquième croisade, d'une vie de sa patronne spirituelle Sainte Marie d'Oignies, et des sermons qui contiennent des *exempla* et fables anecdotiques. Mais cette profusion de matériaux nous laisse ignorants ou incertains sur sa région natale, le nom et la position de sa famille, sa classe sociale et la chronologie du début de sa carrière. Si nous connaissons la date de son décès d'après une chronique, le 1er mai 1240, les historiens ne peuvent que supposer qu'il naquit entre 1160 et 1170 (1).

En 1912, dom Ursmer Berlière écrivait, « L'obscurité règne toujours sur les origines de Jacques de Vitry » (2), et aucune

---

(1) La seule monographie sur Jacques de Vitry est celle de Philipp Funk, *Jakob von Vitry, Leben und Werke*, Leipzig et Berlin, 1909. La brève étude d'Ursmer Berlière, Les évêques auxiliaires de Liège, *Revue bénédictine*, XXIX, 1912, pp. 69-73, est aussi utile. Ernest W. McDonnell, qui traite de Jacques de Vitry dans son livre *Beguines and Beghards in Medieval Culture*, New Brunswick, 1954, a annoncé son intention d'écrire une biographie complète. R. B. C. Huygens a récemment publié une édition critique des *Lettres de Jacques de Vitry*, Leiden, 1960.

(2) Berlière, ouvrage cité, p. 69.

autre recherche plus récente n'a sensiblement amélioré nos connaissances. On peut cependant distinguer deux étapes dans le début de sa carrière, l'une à Paris et l'autre à Oignies. Dans ses *exempla,* Jacques parle souvent de ses études à Paris, et son titre de *magister* montre qu'il reçut la *licentia docendi.* Il se peut que le récit de l'*Historia Fundationis Ecclesiae Beati Nicolai Oigniacensis,* qui indique qu'il était étudiant à Paris à l'époque de la prise de Jerusalem en 1187, soit fondé sur une tradition authentique (3). On ne peut savoir de façon certaine quand et dans quelles circonstances Jacques devint prêtre et chanoine régulier de l'église Saint Nicolas d'Oignies près de Cambrai. Vincent de Beauvais affirme qu'avant d'aller à Oignies, Jacques fut curé de la paroisse d'Argenteuil près de Paris (4). Cependant, d'après le récit écrit du vivant de Jacques et attribué à Thomas de Cantimpré, Jacques fut attiré à Oignies par la réputation de Marie d'Oignies, devint chanoine régulier à sa demande, et fut ordonné à Paris sur son insistance (5). En tout cas, il est certain qu'il était établi à Oignies en 1211, année où, prêtre et maître, il souscrivit pour l'abbaye voisine d'Aywières une charte du duc de Brabant (6).

L'obscurité de la vie de Jacques avant son arrivée à Oignies est vexante. La contradiction qui sépare Vincent de Beauvais de Thomas de Cantimpré sur la question de savoir si Jacques était prêtre avant 1210 ou non, met en question le reste du récit de Thomas. Or, c'est là la source

---

(3) Martène et Durand, *Amplissima collectio,* VI, Paris, 1729, col. 327. Funk, p. 9 conclut que cela est en général « eine wenig wertvolle Quelle ».

(4) *Spec. hist., Liber* XXX, c. 10. *MGH SS,* XXIV, p. 165.

(5) *Vita Mariae Oigniacensis, Supplementum,* éd. D. Papebroek, *AA. SS.,* XXV (23 juin, V), 573 E. Sur l'identification de l'auteur de cette œuvre que les *AA. SS.* attribuent à *Frater N. Canonicus Cantipratensis,* voir Funk, *Jakob von Vitry,* pp. 16-17. Funk, pp. 18-19, critique durement la valeur de cette chronique, mais McDonnell, *Beguines and Beghards,* p. 22, la croit « plausible » et s'appuie beaucoup sur elle.

(6) Berlière, Jacques de Vitry. Ses relations avec les abbayes d'Aywières et de Doorzeele, *Revue bénédictine,* XXV, 1908, p. 185.

principale de notre connaissance du développement spirituel de Jacques. Le manque de précision dans la chronologie nous empêche de savoir s'il était encore jeune homme ou un érudit déjà mûr quand il tomba sous l'influence de Marie d'Oignies.

D'autre part, le problème de l'origine sociale est important pour comprendre l'œuvre d'un homme qui fit tant pour soutenir les premières béguines. Etait-ce un noble fortuné, comme l'affirment certains historiens, ou sortait-il d'une famille pauvre, comme d'autres le prétendent (7)? De plus, l'incertitude où l'on est de savoir si Vitry est le nom de sa famille ou celui de sa ville natale, et même de quel Vitry il s'agit, accroit la difficulté de se renseigner de façon précise sur ces questions énigmatiques.

Les premiers biographes de Jacques ne pouvaient que deviner quelle était, parmi tant d'autres, la ville nommée Vitry, qui lui avait donné son nom. L'affirmation de Vincent de Beauvais selon laquelle Jacques était curé d'Argenteuil (Seine et Oise) suggère qu'il venait de Vitry-sur-Seine (Seine). Les rapports que Jacques eut plus tard avec la Belgique amenèrent Philippe Funk à suggérer qu'il pouvait être originaire de Vitry-en-Artois. D'autres événements de sa vie et certains éléments de ses écrits relient Jacques à la région de Reims et à la Champagne, de sorte que Vitry-en-Perthois (appelée aussi Vitry-le-Brulé) doit aussi être pris en considération (8).

---

(7) François Duchesne, *Histoire de tous les cardinaux français de naissance*, Paris, 1660, I, p. 203, affirme que le père de Jacques était un pauvre paysan, mais il ne cite que Vincent de Beauvais. Funk, *Jakob von Vitry*, p. 8, croit que le fait qu'il ait pu payer ses frais en tant qu'évêque-élu d'Acre montre que Jacques était issu d'une famille aisée. McDonnell, *Beguines and Beghards*, p. 21, dit qu'il était de famille noble.

(8) Il y a dans Funk, pp. 4-7, une discussion critique ; cf. Berlière, *Rev. bén.*, XXIX, 1912, p. 69. Aucun des deux ne comprend le rapport entre Vitry-en-Perthois et Vitry-le-François. Au Moyen Age, Vitry-en-Perthois était une ville importante et le centre d'une châtellenie du comté de Champagne. Quand elle fut brûlée par les troupes Impériales en 1544, François Ier ordonna de refonder

Cette troisième possibilité est renforcée par un passage des *Sermones feriales et communes*. Jacques y relate l'histoire d'un certain Jean de Wambaix (à l'ouest de Cambrai), homme qu'il connaissait personnellement, qui fut reçu toute une nuit par Jésus et la Vierge. Le matin suivant, au moment de partir, Jean reçut de Saint Pierre l'ordre d'aller « ad magistrum Jacobum, Remensem nacione, canonicum Cameracensem » pour se confesser et raconter ce qui lui était arrivé. L'auteur, qui essaie souvent d'authentiquer ses histoires d'une touche personnelle, fait ici apparemment référence à lui-même. S'il en est ainsi, il est établi que le lieu de naissance de Jacques était dans la région de Reims. Si Jacques venait de Vitry-en-Perthois, qui est à plus de 45 km de Reims, de l'autre côté de Châlons-sur-Marne, pourquoi dirait-il qu'il est *Remensis natione* ? On peut répondre raisonnablement qu'il ne fournit pas une affirmation précise, mais seulement une approximation. Cette supposition se fonde sur le fait que si nous n'avons aucune preuve que Jacques de Vitry fût chanoine *de* Cambrai, comme l'affirme la citation, nous savons qu'il était chanoine *près* de Cambrai (9).

Le peu que nous savons avec certitude au sujet de Jacques de Vitry indique que toute référence de date convenable à un homme de ce nom, portant le titre de *magister*, et ayant quelque rapport avec Vitry-en-Perthois, peut avoir trait à notre auteur et est susceptible d'ajouter à nos connaissances

---

la ville à côté. Cette fondation, Vitry-le-François, est à présent une ville importante, tandis que Vitry-en-Perthois n'est plus qu'un village. Voir Auguste LONGNON, *Dictionnaire topographique du département de la Marne,* Paris, 1891, pp. 300-301. Joseph GREVEN, *Die Exempla des Jakob von Vitry,* Heidelberg, 1914, p. 7, n. 2, fournit une liste de sept *exempla* qui ont trait à Reims et à la Champagne.

(9) Ce passage et ses implications furent notés indépendamment l'un de l'autre par GREVEN, *loc. cit.*, et Goswin FRENKEN, *Die Exempla des Jakob von Vitry,* Munich, 1914, pp. 99 et 20-22. Mon argument qu'il s'agit d'une approximation élimine la question soulevée par Greven, à savoir comment Jacques pouvait être chanoine de Cambrai après être devenu chanoine régulier d'Oignies.

biographiques. Ces conditions sont remplies par une charte octroyée par la Comtesse Marie de Champagne en 1193, charte conservée aux Archives de la Marne et imprimée ici pour la première fois, en appendice. Cette charte rapporte que Maître Jacques, fils de Hamon de Vitry, donna sa maison et les terrains entourant l'hospice de Vitry à l'abbaye de Trois Fontaines, et reçut en retour une rente annuelle de 100 sous de Provins perçue sur l'usufruit pour le restant de ses jours. Si Jacques mourait ou abandonnait le clergé séculier, ou s'il acquérait un bénéfice de 20 livres par an, la propriété resterait à l'abbaye libérée alors du paiement de cette rente. Cet acte fut approuvé par Oda, mère de Jacques, et par ses frères, Henri, moine à l'abbaye de Huiron, et Pierre, laïque. L'abbé de Trois-Fontaines ajouta que Jacques, son père, sa mère et ses frères recevraient à perpétuité les bénéfices spirituels de l'abbaye. Il fut noté que Jacques avait auparavant tenu ce domaine du prieuré de Sainte Geneviève-de-Vitry pour un cens annuel. Cet acte fut enregistré dans l'inventaire du cartulaire de Trois-Fontaines, qui affirme que la donation fut faite en présence de Milon, doyen de Vitry, par « un nommé Jacques, clerc, fils de Haymon Latoye dudit lieu » et fut confirmée par des chartes octroyées par la Comtesse Marie et l'Abbé Guillaume de Saint-Pierre-du-Mont à Châlons-sur-Marne. Cependant, seule la charte de Marie a été conservée dans les archives du monastère de Trois-Fontaines (10).

S'il pouvait être démontré que cette charte a trait au futur cardinal de Tusculum, elle serait de la plus grande utilité pour la biographie de Jacques. Nous saurions alors sans aucun doute que son lieu d'origine était Vitry-en-Perthois, dans la région de Reims. Ce renseignement, à son tour, expliquerait pourquoi le chroniqueur Aubri de Trois-Fontaines a donné tant de renseignements sur Jacques de Vitry, et prouverait que lorsque l'évêque Hugues de Liège envoya Jacques à Reims pour annoncer qu'il refusait

---

(10) *Cart. de Trois Fontaines,* Paris, BN. Coll. Champ., vol. XLV, f. 223, n° 447.

l'archevêché, il envoyait son évêque auxiliaire dans sa région natale (11). La charte nous informerait également sur la classe sociale de Jacques. Au XIIe siècle, il n'y avait pas de ligne bien nette entre la noblesse et les familles commerciales des villes, mais le fait que Jacques payait un cens pour une propriété urbaine de valeur suggère qu'il venait de la bourgeoisie aisée. Le nom de son père n'apparaît pas dans les registres des vassaux de Champagne et n'est pas connu par ailleurs. La charte et l'inventaire montrent tous les deux que Vitry était un nom de famille désignant l'endroit d'origine, mais que le père de Jacques avait aussi un autre patronyme. La charte fournirait également des renseignements d'ordre chronologique qui confirment les dires de Thomas de Cantimpré, puisqu'elle montre qu'en 1193 Jacques avait reçu le titre de *magister,* mais qu'il n'était pas encore prêtre (autrement l'inventaire l'aurait appelé prêtre et non clerc). La charte nous donnerait aussi les noms d'autres membres de sa famille et nous permettrait de chercher des renseignements complémentaires sur sa jeunesse et son milieu.

La certitude que Jacques de Vitry grandit en Champagne durant la vie de la Comtesse Marie et de son époux Henri le Libéral éclaircirait un point d'histoire institutionnelle. On a remarqué que nombre des *exempla* de Jacques se situent dans la région de la Champagne et de Reims, et que deux d'entre eux font allusion à la générosité légendaire du Comte Henri. L'une de ces histoires est la plus ancienne version d'un conte qui fut reproduit indépendamment plus tard par l'historien Joinville, arrière-petit-fils du sénéchal du Comte Henri. La célèbre histoire de Joinville nous dit comment Artaud de Nogent, chambellan du comte, intervint lorsqu'un chevalier pauvre demanda de l'argent au comte. Artaud lui répondit que le comte avait déjà donné tout ce qu'il possédait. Vexé par cette réponse, Henri donna

---

(11) Aubri est la source de beaucoup de renseignements au sujet de Jacques de Vitry, en particulier la mission à Reims et la date de sa mort. Voir *MGH SS,* XXIII, pp. 919 et 948.

Artaud lui-même au chevalier. Cette histoire qui fourmille de détails a un accent de vérité, mais elle n'explique pas quel droit Henri avait de donner Artaud. Ce détail nous est fourni par la version de Jacques de Vitry qui ne nomme pas l'homme en question, mais le qualifie de « servus ». Jacques savait-il personnellement qu'Artaud de Nogent, qui était riche et qui vivait comme un noble, était serf du comte, ou se basait-il sur des renseignements de seconde main ? Si nous pouvions être certains du lieu de naissance de Jacques et de sa familiarité avec la cour du comte, nous saurions mieux comment évaluer son témoignage (12).

Malheureusement on ne peut pas établir que la charte de 1193 se réfère à la personne de Jacques de Vitry. Aucun des renseignements spécifiques de la charte ne coïncide avec les données certaines en notre possession, mais en même temps aucune information de la charte ne les contredit non plus. Les doutes mêmes qui entourent son origine, le silence qui enveloppe sa famille et qui donne à cette charte toute sa valeur, nous empêchent de savoir si l'intérêt que présente cette charte n'est pas le résultat d'une pure coïncidence. La meilleure façon de confirmer (ou d'infirmer) les informations de cette charte serait de connaître les noms du père et de la mère de Jacques, mais je n'ai trouvé aucun élément biographique qui mentionne l'un ou l'autre. Le cartulaire de Huiron (Marne H 1381), monastère situé près de Vitry, ne contient point de mention du frère Henri, et le nom de Pierre de Vitry a pu être si fréquent qu'on ne peut guère accorder d'importance à son apparition occasionnelle dans les documents champenois (13). L'obituaire de Trois-Fontaines,

---

(12) Le conte de Jacques est imprimé par GREVEN, *Exempla*, p. 17, et FRENKEN, *Exempla*, pp. 106-107. Les versions d'Etienne de Bourbon, de la collection anonyme de Tours, et de Joinville sont commodément rassemblées par A. LECOY DE LA MARCHE, *Anecdotes historiques d'Etienne de Bourbon*, Paris, 1877, pp. 124-125. L'histoire de Jacques est exempte des déformations et malentendus évidents qui gâchent les versions d'Etienne de Bourbon et de la collection de Tours.

(13) Un certain Pierre fut bailli de Vitry en 1228 et 1229 ;

qui devrait contenir les noms du donateur et de sa famille, n'existe plus.

La valeur de la charte imprimée ci-dessous reste à déterminer à l'aide de renseignements supplémentaires qui montreront si elle s'applique ou non au futur cardinal. Quelqu'un saurait-il qui sont les parents de Jacques de Vitry? (14).

1193

Marie de Champagne fait savoir que Maître Jacques, fils de Hamon de Vitry, a donné sa maison avec le fond sise à Vitry à l'abbaye de Trois-Fontaines.

A. Original, Archives de la Marne, 22 H 116, pièce 1, 24×21 mm, avec double queue de soie verte, sceau disparu.

Ind. Cart. de Trois-Fontaines, BN. Coll. Champ., vol. XLV, fol. 223 r°, n° 447; Inventaire des chartes et titres de l'abbaye de Trois-Fontaines (1787), Marne 22 H 1, fol. 265 r°, n° 1. D'ARBOIS DE JUBAINVILLE, *Histoire,* III, n° 423.

Ego Maria Trecensis comitissa notum facio universis presentibus et posteris quod magister Jacobus, filius Haymonis de Vitriaco, dedit ecclesie beate Marie Trium Fontium in perpetuam elemosinam domum suam cum fundo domui pauperum de Vitriaco contiguam, quam quietam et ab omni calumpnia liberam possidebat, sicut ab anteriori vico usque

---

c'était peut être le même personnage que Pierre de Vitry, chambrier de Thibaut IV de Champagne en 1235. Voir Henri d'ARBOIS DE JUBAINVILLE, *Histoire des ducs et des comtes de Champagne,* Paris, 1865, IV, pp. 484 et 504. Mais une charte de 1224, Archives de la Marne G 1611 (liasse), montre que Pierre de Vitry, sergent du comte de Champagne, était fils de Nicolas le Changeur. Son nom apparaît aussi comme garant dans le registre des fiefs de Champagne pour les années 1222 à 1243. Voir *Feoda Campanie,* n° 3730, dans Auguste LONGNON, *Documents relatifs au comté de Champagne et Brie,* Paris, 1901, I.

(14) Je suis reconnaissant de l'aide que m'ont apportée Mme Jacqueline LE BRAZ, de l'Institut de Recherche et d'Histoire des Textes et M. René GANDILHON, archiviste de la Marne.

in aquam porrigitur, et sicut inter dictam domum pauperum et domum que fuit Marie de Besa dilatatur, concedentibus matre sua Oda et fratribus Henrico monacho de Oyron et Petro laico, ita que idem Jacobus perfectam garantiam adversus omnes qui iuri stare voluerint portabit. Concessit autem predicte ecclesie abbas assensu capituli sui predicto clerico usumfructum domus quotannis dum seculo vixerit centum solidos pruvinensis monete sancti Johannis baptiste festo persolvendos. Hac tamen pactione que si idem clericus obierit aut seculo renuntiaverit vel Deo annuente beneficium xx^{ti} libras per annum valens adeptus fuerit, ecclesia Trium Fontium a predicta pensione omnino remanebit absoluta. Concessit etiam predictus abbas eidem clerico, patri, matri, fratribusque eius ecclesie sue Trium Fontium spirituale beneficium imperpetuum. Sciendum autem quod idem clericus predictam domum ab ecclesia sancte Genovephe sub annuo censu tenebat. Ut autem hec rata perpetuo permaneant, sygilli mei impressione munire curavi. Actum anno Incarnati verbi M° C° XC° III°.

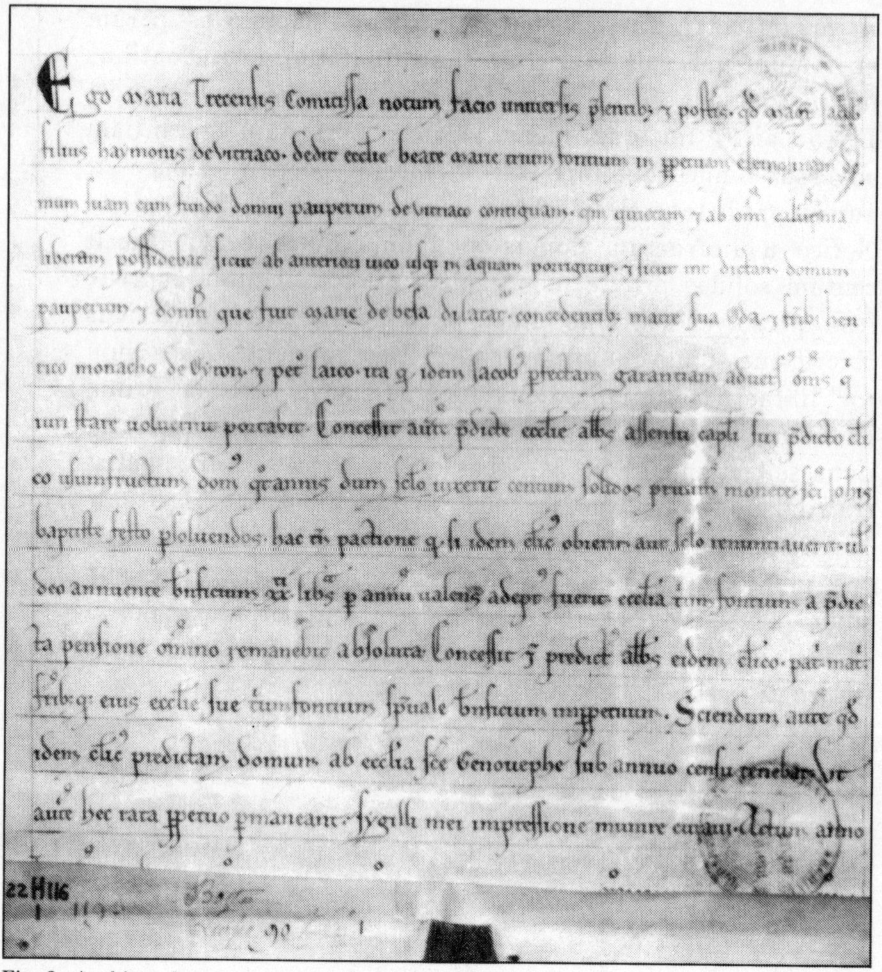

Fig. 2. Archives departmentales de la Marne, 22 H 116, no. 1

6

Clio and Venus: a Historical View of Medieval Love

To make a fresh start in the study of an established subject usually requires a difficult act of renunciation, to put aside, at least temporarily, the interpretations, assumptions, concepts, and sometimes even the vocabulary which have become accepted. The subject of love in the Middle Ages has long been treated by sensitive and influential authors. If we are now to avoid some of the difficulties they have left us, I must initially ask my audience to acquiesce in a willing suspension of preconceptions and to imagine for a time that Stendahl had not in 1822 presented his reading of Provençal literature in his *Essai sur l'amour*, that Gaston Paris had not introduced the term and concept of "courtly love," *amour courtois*, in his study of Lancelot in *Romania* in 1883, and that C. S. Lewis had never written *The Allegory of Love*. If you are willing to go along with me in this renunciation, perhaps you will also put aside for a bit a few other works, including the chapter on "Courtly Love" in Sidney Painter's *French Chivalry* and Denis de Rougemont's *L'amour et l'occident*, published in the United States as *Love in the Western World* and in Great Britain as *Passion and Society*.[1]

---

1. To cite authors with whom I have occasion to disagree throughout the footnotes of this paper would be both invidious and unnecessary. The informed reader will have no difficulty in recognizing opposing views, and the beginner will find his way more directly to the sources. To make those sources as accessible as possible I have noted translations wherever I could. For several helpful suggestions I owe thanks to Professors Elizabeth A. R. Brown, John W. Baldwin, and Thomas N. Bisson.

Most work on love in the Middle Ages has been based on literature, particularly lyric poetry and romances, works which may often be difficult to understand, or at least are subject to controversial interpretations. Fortunately, there is ample material for an elementary knowledge of medieval love, marriage, and sexual mores in more secure historical sources. Spiritual and canonistic writing, medical treatises, penitentials, letters, chronicles, law codes, court cases and much more provide a solid basis for understanding literary works. So let us begin with what Clio can tell us of Venus in her medieval garb.

In the first feudal age, when the authority of both church and secular government was very weak, marriage could be seen simply as a personal contract, enforced by the families of the people involved.[2] Financial considerations were always of prime importance. The Germanic tradition of marriage by capture *(raptus)* appears in the penalty to be paid to the father or other guardian who had lost his property, and ordinarily a legal marriage began with a financial contract between the two families. If there was a reason for separation and acceptable financial arrangements could be made, the marriage might end with a divorce by mutual consent.[3] Although in practice many marriages may have been based on the free choice of both parties, there was almost no legal authority to enforce the Romano-canonical principle that consent makes a marriage *(consensus facit nuptias)*. We may be sure that the weak commonly experienced abduction, repudiation, and uncontrolled brutality.

In contrast, the second feudal age delineated by Marc Bloch was a time of institutionalization. The same social and intellectual movements which brought increasing order to the ties of government, or which led to the numbering, clarification, and explanation of the sacraments, also brought greater order, principle, and control into marriage. Without idealizing the next stage of medieval marriage or ignoring the personal hardships which followed from laws based on an unstable mixture of scriptural injunctions, established customs, equity, and concern for human needs, it is

---

2. For quite different summary statements on medieval marriage see Gabriel Le Bras, s.v. "Mariage," *Dictionnaire de théologie catholique*, and Frederick Pollock and Frederic William Maitland, *History of English Law* (2nd ed.; Cambridge, Eng.: University Press, 1898), II, 364–99.

3. There are texts illustrating marriage contracts, divorce by mutual consent and a charter of composition for rape serving as a transfer of dowry in M. Thévenin, *Textes relatifs aux institutions privées et publiques aux époques mérovingienne et carolingienne* (Paris: A. Picard, 1887), #8, 17, 23, 41, 42, 48.

still clear that the institution of marriage was greatly strengthened, if not truly recreated, by the legal and social revival of the late eleventh and twelfth centuries. The consent of both parties, clearly expressed, was considered essential; marriage could follow rape only if the woman desired;[4] and there were courts to protect the rights of the weak and to limit the excesses of the brutal. Although the ecclesiastical prohibition of divorce made the termination of an unfortunate marriage difficult, the problem of unilateral repudiation was greatly reduced. In short, for the average bride the institution of marriage improved markedly in the twelfth and thirteenth centuries.

The preference for celibacy over marriage is so prominent in medieval religious writing that it is easy to overlook the underlying assumption that marriage was both normal and desirable for most people. Of course, St. Paul's teaching that marriage provides a remedy for a common weakness of the flesh appears regularly in dispensations to marry lest worse things ensue. But in addition to this apostolic concession, the influence of family alliances, property rights, desire for legitimate offspring, social status, and the prospect of companionship all worked to make marriage attractive to the participants. We cannot know how much our medieval ancestors looked forward to what we would call a satisfying personal relationship—surely much less than do modern Americans. But the ideal of marriage, if not always the reality, was that there should be love between the spouses.

The Epistle to the Ephesians, attributed to St. Paul throughout the Middle Ages, contains the exhortation (5:25), "Husbands, love your wives," and the prayer that the bride "be as loveable as Rachel to her husband" was included in the early medieval wedding service. In the twelfth century Hugh of St. Victor, one of the most sympathetic commentators on marriage, stressed that the sacrament of marriage was instituted before the Fall and from the beginning was based on mutual love. St. Thomas Aquinas called the affection between husband and wife "the greatest friendship" (*maxima amicitia*), and following Aristotle said it was based on delight in the act of generation, utility in domestic life, and, in

---

4. In the late twelfth century "Glanvill" maintained that men of good birth could not be forced into marriage by women of low estate, but Bracton in the next century permits this disparagement if the woman chooses it. See *The Treatise on the Laws and Customs of the Realm of England Commonly Called Glanvill*, ed. G. D. G. Hall (London: Nelson, 1965), Bk. XIV, 6, p. 176, and Henricus de Bracton, *De Legibus Angliae*, Rolls series, 70 (London: Longman, Trubner, 1878-1883), II, 491-93 (fol. 148).

some cases, the virtue of the husband and wife.[5]

But if it was expected that marriage should produce love, what of love before marriage? To raise the question in this way shows how the word love stretches to cover many different situations, including the settled affection of a married couple established in their intimacy, what Aquinas calls friendship, and the passionate desire for union of a couple whose physical relations are unconsummated or unsanctioned. What we are asking here is if it was common for a couple to marry after being attracted to each other by passion. A frequent answer is that there was no place in medieval society for premarital familiarity, or for passion to lead to marriage. No doubt in many cases this generalization is true. Although by law no marriage was valid until the partners were old enough to consent and had done so, and a considerate or prudent parent would not choose a spouse repugnant to his child, marriages were commonly arranged, often when the partners were mere infants, and the marital confrontation of frightened children must have been all too common. We are given a glimpse of such unhappiness in a decretal of Clement III which tells of a girl who was given in marriage by her step-father at the age of eleven, although she was "unwilling and objecting," and who ran away to another man after a year and a half. The pope ruled that the girl should be returned to her husband, since by living with him for so long "she seems to have consented" to the marriage.[6]

But the picture of marriage as loveless initially and perhaps forever is not completely representative, and is distorted in part because our records are almost entirely of marriages which came into court. Still for the later middle ages ecclesiastical registers reveal much premarital passion in a wealth of "breach of promise"

---

5. *Liber Sacramentorum Romanae Aeclesiae*, ed. Leo C. Mohlberg, Rerum ecclesiasticarum documenta, Fontes, IV (Rome: Herder, 1960), Bk. III, 52, p. 210; Hugh of Saint Victor in Migne, *Patrologia latina*, CLXXVI, 314-15, trans. Roy J. Defarrari, *On the Sacraments of the Christian Faith* (Cambridge, Mass.: Mediaeval Academy of America, 1951), pp. 324-25; Aquinas, *In X libros ethicorum Aristotelis ad Nicomachum expositio*, Bk. VIII, 12, ed. Raimondo M. Spiazzi (3rd ed.; Turin: Marietti, 1964), p. 452, and *Summa Contra Gentiles*, Bk. III, 123-24, trans. by Vernon J. Bourke as *On the Truth of the Catholic Faith* (Garden City, N.Y.: Image Books, 1956), III, pt. 2, 147-52. Aquinas uses the term *amicitia* along with *amor* to avoid any possible confusion with the "love of concupiscence." Cf. F. J. E. Raby, "Amor and Amicitia," *Speculum*, XL (1965), 599-610.

6. *Decretales Gregorii IX*, IV, 1, 21, ed. E. Friedberg, II, 668-69. See also Jean Dauvillier, "Pierre le Chantre et la dispense de mariage non consommé," *Études d'histoire du droit privé offertes à Pierre Petot* (Paris: Librairie générale de droit et de jurisprudence, 1959), pp. 99-100.

and clandestine marriage suits.[7] And if we look, we can find some evidence of marriages following the attraction of carnal passion in the twelfth and thirteenth centuries. As a witness let us call Philip the Fair's *bailli* from Beauvaisis, Philippe de Beaumanoir, who reports: "When a man has congress with a woman outside the bond of marriage and so has a child, and he marries her after the children are born or when she is pregnant, if the children are placed beneath the sheet which is customarily put over those who are ceremonially married in Holy Church, the legitimacy of the children should not be questioned, since they were placed there with the father and mother celebrating the marriage. . . . And through the grace which Holy Church and custom concede to such children, it happens often that their fathers marry their mothers out of pity for the children, so that less harm comes of it."[8]

As Professor Jackson points out in his paper, this explanation applies very well to the story of Rivalen and Tristan. And in real life, these so-called "mantle-children," heirs who were legitimated "*sub pallio*," appear as a common problem in the laws and court cases of Germany, France, and England, and are proof enough of the existence of carnal love before marriage. The public attitude of the English nobility toward these fruits of careless love is shown by the action of the English baronage assembled at the Council of Merton in 1236, who resoundingly denied Bishop Grosseteste's proposal that common law should treat "mantle-children" as legitimate heirs. Love before marriage was familiar, and the barons did not approve of it.[9]

---

7. Surprisingly little social history has been based on the voluminous records of ecclesiastical courts. The registers of the archdeacon's courts in England remain virtually untouched. For published French registers and a fruitful example of what can be done with them, see Jean-Philippe Lévy, "L'officialité de Paris et les questions familiales à la fin du XIVe siècle," *Études d'histoire du droit canonique dédiées à Gabriel Le Bras* (Paris: Sirey, 1965), II, 1265–94. A second great body of material even more surprisingly neglected by those concerned with the society of Chaucer are the Year Books, of which Maitland wrote, "It will some day seem a wonderful thing that men once thought they could write the history of mediaeval England without using the Year Books." The quotation is cited by William C. Bolland, *A Manual of Year Book Studies* (Cambridge, Eng.: University Press, 1925), p. 84.

8. *Coutumes de Beauvaisis*, Bk. XVIII, 23, ed. Amédée Salmon (Paris: Picard, 1899), I, 295–96.

9. R. Génestal, *Histoire de la légitimation des enfants naturels en droit canonique* (Paris: École Pratique des Hautes Études, 1905), and Albert Weitnauer, *Die Legitimation des ausserehelichen Kindes im römischen Recht und in den Germanenrechten des Mittelalters*, Basler Studien zur Rechtswissenschaft, 14 (Basel: Helbing und Lichtenhahn, 1940).

There should be no doubt that throughout the period we are considering some men chose wives they found physically and personally desirable, and women could presumably exercise some choice in how and to whom they seemed attractive. Among the causes of marriage Peter Lombard includes beauty, "which often inflames the soul with love."[10] At the same time that he advises against choosing a bride who can read, the author of *Urbain le Courtois* tells men not to marry for beauty.[11] The theme of the eventual marriage of lovers is common in medieval literature, more so, it seems to me, than that of adultery. Marrying for love was a good way to end a romance. Perhaps I may add, however, that even in literature love based on desire was not always assumed to be the ideal beginning to marriage and could be a source of trouble, as in the tale told by Chaucer's Franklin.[12]

Theoretical statements, literary examples, or exceptional cases did not overcome the social and economic pressure in the upper-classes to use marriage to join house to house and lay field to field. For the highly placed, the noble and the wealthy, arranged marriages remained the common pattern.[13] But for poorer people, often held back from early marriage by economic limitations, the personal choice of a partner based on familiarity and love could become increasingly routine. In 1484 Bernarde, daughter of a bourgeois of Troyes, told a neighbor that she was in love and had become engaged. The neighbor asked if she had the consent of her father. Bernarde replied that she didn't care about her father, that if he was upset by it he would calm down, and that several girls of better families than hers had married without parental consent and were very well off with their husbands.[14] Simple Bernarde! Her

---

10. *Sentences*, Bk. IV, 30, 3, in *Libri IV sententiarum* (2nd ed.; Quaracchi, 1916), II, 934. Peter considered beauty a less proper cause for marriage than making peace or reconciling enemies.

11. Ed. Paul Meyer, *Romania*, XXXII (1903), 72.

12. For anyone who took canon law seriously, the Franklin's Tale provided no model for a happy marriage. The condition to which Arveragus swore, which gave his wife license for adultery, came dangerously close to violating the canon *Si conditiones* in *Decr.*, IV, 5, 7, ed. Friedberg, II, 634. That one should not keep an illicit oath is set forth in II, 24, 18 (*ibid.*, p. 365).

13. On arranged marriages in the English upper classes in the sixteenth and seventeenth centuries see Lawrence Stone, *The Crisis of the Aristocracy, 1558-1641* (Oxford: Clarendon, 1965), pp. 594-612.

14. Aube, arch. dép., G 4184, fol. 306ᵛ, analyzed in the *Inventaire sommaire, série G* (Troyes-Paris, 1896), II, 293. This testimony is an example of the material for social history in these registers. The irony of this case is that it came into court when Bernarde later denied that she was engaged and her fiancé requested that she be adjudged to him.

appeal to the precedent of families higher in the social scale was misplaced. She should have claimed she was setting the style of the future.

After discussing love in marriage and love before marriage, let us turn now to extra-marital love. This subject bulks so large in current literary history that it is desirable to take a close look at how adultery was actually treated in the Middle Ages. To begin with, both Roman law and the Germanic codes punished adulterers very severely. The penalty provided in the Theodosian Code (XI, 36, 4) was that the violators of marriage should be sewed in a leather sack and burned alive, but Justinian tempered this to give the woman a scourging and send her to a nunnery, from which her husband might release her if he chose (Nov. 134, c. 10).[15] The barbarian codes often provide the penalty of death, or permit a father or husband to kill an erring daughter or wife, and a husband could kill his wife's seducer without incurring vendetta. Writing to King Aethelbald of Mercia in the mid-eighth century, St. Boniface reported: "In Old Saxony, if a virgin defiles her father's house by adultery or if a married woman breaks the marriage tie and commits adultery, they sometimes compel her to hang herself, and then over the pyre on which she has been burned and cremated they hang the seducer." Such extreme penalties were, of course, not always invoked or even sought. The law code of King Aethelbert of Kent, written around 600, provides for a reasonable, if expensive, composition: "If a free man lies with the wife of a free man, he shall pay [the husband] his wergild and buy a second wife with his own money, and bring her to the other man's home."[16]

While these references show that adultery could have serious consequences, two considerations must be kept in mind. In both

---

15. Percy E. Corbett, *The Roman Law of Marriage* (Oxford: Clarendon, 1930), pp. 145-46. There is an excellent translation of *The Theodosian Code* by Clyde Pharr (Princeton: Princeton University Press, 1952).

16. References to adultery in the Germanic laws are collected by Hermann Conrad, *Deutsche Rechtsgeschichte* (2nd ed.; Karlsruhe: C. F. Müller, 1962), I, 156; a good example is *The Burgundian Code*, trans. Katherine Fischer (Philadelphia: University of Pennsylvania Press, 1949), p. 68, § 68 and p. 45, § 34, 1. For the quotations see *Die Briefe des heiligen Bonifatius und Lullus*, ed. Michael Tangl, MGH, Epist. sel., I (Berlin, 1916), #73, p. 150, trans. by C. H. Talbot in *The Anglo-Saxon Missionaries in Germany* (New York: Sheed and Ward, 1954), p. 123; and F. L. Attenborough, *The Laws of the Earliest English Kings* (Cambridge, Eng.: University Press, 1922), p. 9, § 31. On penalties throughout medieval Europe see J. R. Reinhard, "Burning at the Stake in Mediaeval Law and Literature," *Speculum*, XVI (1941), 186-209.

primitive Roman and early Germanic law, only women were bound by the chain of marriage, and a man was considered an adulterer only if he seduced a married woman. Although Christian law denounced this double standard and treated both partners to a marriage as equally responsible, in this area the church had little effect on the secular law of medieval Europe and even less on behavior. Even in the second feudal age it was considered altogether unusual for a husband to remain faithful to his wife. A chronicler remarked with surprise that Baldwin of Hainaut, who married the daughter of Henry and Marie of Champagne, loved his wife exclusively, "although it is rarely found in any man that he should cleave so much to one woman and be content with her alone."[17] The second consideration is that if a man were sufficiently powerful he could easily put himself above both law and private vengeance and seduce the wives of his neighbors or subjects with impunity. St. Boniface was, after all, writing the letter just quoted to reprove King Aethelbald for his adulteries, and William IX of Aquitaine felt free to boast humorously about his conquests.[18]

The differences which developed during the post-Carolingian period between northern and southern Europe in the judicial treatment of adultery are striking. In the southern lands of written law adultery continued to be treated as a capital crime, along with such offenses as homicide, bloodshed, theft, and rape. In some charters of franchise the lord had the right to confiscate all the adulterer's goods and the offender's body was at the lord's mercy. The more common penalty in southern France was that the offending couple should run or be paraded naked through the town or village, sometimes tied together shamefully; in some places this punishment could be avoided by paying a heavy fine. Unfortunately, very little material exists to show how strictly these penalties were enforced.[19] In the north the legal situation was

---

17. *La Chronique de Gislebert de Mons*, ed. Léon Vanderkindere (Brussels: Kiessling, 1904), pp. 191–92.

18. The song in which William tells of tupping the wives of Lords Guarin and Bernart 188 times is edited by Alfred Jeanroy, *Les Chansons de Guillaume IX*, Classiques français du moyen âge, 9 (2nd ed.; Paris: Champion, 1927), pp. 8–13 (P.-C., 183, 12). There is a lively translation by Hubert Creekmore, *Lyrics of the Middle Ages* (New York: Grove, 1959), pp. 41–43. Whether the people in the song were recognizable individuals cannot now be known. On William's "courtly" songs see Peter Dronke, "Guillaume IX and courtoisie," *Romanische Forschungen*, LXXIII (1961), 327–338.

19. Auguste Molinier in *Histoire générale de Languedoc* (new ed.; Toulouse, 1872–1905), VII, 211; Jean Ramière de Fortanier, *Chartes de franchises du*

much less rigorous, for adultery was ordinarily not tried in secular courts, but was an ecclesiastical offense.[20] Church courts rarely imposed heavy fines, the most severe penalty was usually scourging, and it seems to have been quite simple to avoid censure for a long time if not altogether. In the late twelfth century one English couple, living adulterously in the eyes of the church, had ten sons before Pope Celestine III imposed perpetual continence on them, a penalty he thought appropriate "as they are both advanced in years and by knowingly continuing so long in public adultery and perjury have disturbed the church by grave scandal."[21] In 1302 the court of Edward I, brought into the matter by a suit for dower, found that a couple had notoriously lived together in adultery, although they had certificates from the archbishop of Canterbury and the bishop of Chichester that they had cleared themselves of the charge of adultery by compurgation in court Christian. All that the secular court could do was to enforce the provision of the Second Statute of Westminister (1285) that a woman who deserted her husband to stay with a paramour should have no dower unless reconciled with her husband.[22]

Although adulterers might easily avoid serious punishment from a court, the tradition of private vengeance was so strong that violators of marriage still ran grave risks. In a letter of 857 which became part of Gratian's *Decretum*, Pope Nicolas I referred to a husband's right "according to secular law" to kill his adulterous wife. No doubt such extreme revenge was accepted in the first feudal age; chroniclers report that in about 1000 Count Fulk Nerra of Anjou burned his adulterous wife Elizabeth. Even in the late thirteenth century Beaumanoir notes that if a husband has publicly warned a man to stay away from his home and then finds him lying with his wife, he can with impunity kill both of them or the man alone, so long as he does it immediately in hot blood.[23]

Lauragais (Paris: Sirey, 1939), p. 535, § 5. A thirteenth-century illustration in the custumal of Toulouse, Paris, Bibl. nat., ms. lat. 9187, fol. 30ᵛ, shows a tied couple preceded by a man with a trumpet.

20. In the late twelfth century Peter the Chanter noted that an injured husband who did not choose to kill an adulterer might bring him before a secular judge, but added that he had never seen such a case tried in a secular court. See Pierre le Chantre, *Summa de sacramentis et animae consiliis*, ed. Jean-Albert Dugauquier (Louvain-Lille: Éditions Nauwelaerts, 1954–), pt. III, 2, a, p. 351.

21. *Decr.* IV, 7, 5, newly edited by Walther Holtzmann and Eric W. Kemp, *Papal Decretals Relating to the Diocese of Lincoln in the Twelfth Century*, Lincoln Record Soc., 47 (Hereford: Hereford Times, 1954), pp. 60–61.

22. Pollock and Maitland, *History of English Law*, II, 395–96.

23. Gratian, C. XXXIII, qu. II, c. 6, ed. Friedberg, I, 1152; on Fulk see Pierre Daudet, *L'établissement de la compétence de l'Église en matière de divorce et de*

108 Culture, Power and Personality in Medieval France

In the second feudal age, however, the most extreme action taken against a wife was usually repudiation, as when Count William VIII of Montpellier put aside his wife Eudoxia, daughter of Emperor Manuel Comnenus. Churchmen viewed even this penalty as too severe. With respect to the case of William of Montpellier, Innocent III wrote in 1202, "although faithfulness to the marriage bed is one of the three goods of marriage, nevertheless its violation would not break the marital bond." Common custom was harsher. *Eructavit*, the translation and commentary on the 44th psalm dedicated to Countess Marie of Champagne, states as the custom of the world that when a woman deserts the love of her husband for another, either through sin or through a mistake, even though she fully repents her husband has no obligation to take her back and she would in fact be better off in the grave.[24]

Wives were usually treated more gently than their seducers. When Count Philip of Flanders suspected a young noble of adultery with the countess, he executed him by hanging him upside down in a latrine, while his wife, heiress of Vermandois, was simply disgraced. Besides the possibility of death, a man who came between a husband and wife also ran the risk of mutilation, for the brutal vengeance suffered by Abelard was a common form of private revenge for attacks on the sanctity of the home.[25]

One form of adultery was considered iniquitous beyond all the rest, and that was the crime of a vassal who betrayed his lord. Adultery with the lord's wife was a form of treason. The twelfth-century customs of Barcelona call it "the greatest felony," along with compassing the death of the lord or his legitimate son or taking a castle and refusing to return it. Death remained the accepted punishment for such treason; Ramon Vidal, a Catalan poet of the early thirteenth century, vividly describes a lord's retainers setting out to kill as a traitor a vassal believed guilty of adultery with the lord's wife. In the greatest scandal of the reign of Philip the Fair, when two nobles were accused of adultery with the wives of Prince Louis and Prince Charles, the king had the young

---

consanguinité (Paris: Sirey, 1941), pp. 23-24; Beaumanoir, *Coutumes*, XXX, 102, ed. Salmon, I, 472-73.

24. Innocent's "Per venerabilem," *Decr.* IV, 17, 13, trans. by Brian Pullan, *Sources for the History of Medieval Europe* (Oxford: Blackwell, 1966), pp. 68-72; cf. *Decr.* III, 32, 15. *Eructavit*, ed. T. Atkinson Jenkins, Gesellschaft für romanische Literatur 20 (Dresden: Niemeyer, 1909), ll. 1577-94.

25. J. Johnen, "Philipp von Elsass, graf von Flandern," *Bulletin de la commission royale d'histoire [de Belgique]*, LXXIX (1910), 418-20; Pollock and Maitland, *History of English Law*, II, 485.

men castrated, dragged behind horses to the gallows and hanged, since they were (as one chronicler put it) "not only adulterers, but the vilest traitors to their lords."[26]

Instances like these should have been enough to destroy the idea that medieval troubadours roamed about the countryside advocating adultery and addressing suggestive songs, more or less thinly disguised, to the wives of the local lords, for a poor troubadour was certainly a vulnerable rival. The best proof that the lords of medieval Europe saw no threat in love songs, even when addressed to their wives, is that troubadours, trouvères, and minnesingers not only survived but made a living.[27] If Bernart de Ventadorn had really been intimate with Eleanor of Aquitaine and had left court because of Henry's jealousy, is it conceivable that he would have made public a song about it?[28]

Having reiterated how serious the consequences of adultery could be, I should also stress the toleration of it which was so commonly found in some circles of medieval society. As we have seen, if a husband did not take action himself, adultery often went unpunished and perhaps even uncensured. Medieval literature can be quite complacent about adultery, as in the *fabliaux* stressing the foolishness of the cuckold or in the song attributed to the Countess of Die, in which a lady sings to her knight that she has "a strong desire to hold you in place of my husband, as long as I have your promise to do all that I would like."[29] Of course adultery was

---

26. *Usatges de Barcelona*, ed. Ramon d'Abadal I Vinyals and F. Valls Taberner, Textes de dret català, I (Barcelona, 1913), pp. 17-18, art. 40. Ramon Vidal's *Castía Gilos* is most recently printed in *Les Troubadours*, eds. René Nelli and René Lavaud (Paris: Desclée, De Brouwer, 1960-1966), II, 186-211; the lord had given the vassal in question a private residence, which is the meaning in l. 52 of *cassatz* < L. *casatus*. For the scandal of 1314 see Martin Bouquet, *Recueil des historiens des Gaules et de la France* (Paris, 1738-1904), XX, 609; XXI, 40; and XXI, 657.

27. This point was made over half a century ago, with all too little effect, by Stanislaw Stronski, *Le troubadour Folquet de Marseille* (Cracow: Académie des Sciences, 1910), pp. 61*-68*.

28. The song (P.-C., 70, 33) which Bernart addressed to Eleanor contains only conventional praise and no suggestion of improper conduct. "Per vos me sui del rei partitz" means simply that Bernart left the king because of her, and not specifically for her sake. If Bernart had fallen from the queen's favor and wished to return to court, what better song could he have written? See *The Songs of Bernart de Ventadorn*, ed. Stephen G. Nichols (Chapel Hill: University of North Carolina Press, 1965), pp. 138-40.

29. Gabrielle Kussler-Ratyé, "Les chansons de la comtesse Béatrix de Dia," *Archivum Romanicum*, I (1917), 173-74 (P.-C. 46, 4). Without some evidence of a particularly complacent Count of Die, the attribution of this song to any Countess of Die seems to me questionable.

offensive to anyone who valued the purity of noble bloodlines or took his (or her) religion seriously. But there were also nobles who shared Aucassin's preference to go to hell with the knights who die in tourneys and fine wars and with the beautiful, courteous ladies who have two or three lovers along with their lords. For such people the issue of adultery was not morality but honor, and their major concern was who wore the horns. For every woman who betrayed her husband there was a man who had made a conquest; the interest of the seducer was, of course, not in preventing adultery but in protecting his own honor through the virtue of his wife. In short, to make light of sexual adventures and adultery was more acceptable in the camp of William IX than in the sewing circle of his wife. We should not assume that a literature of loose morals was something which medieval women imposed on their men.

The great difficulties for modern understanding of medieval society have not been raised, however, by writings which express a light attitude toward adultery, but by those great works of literature like *Tristan* and *Lancelot* which treat it as a very serious subject indeed. An example of casual looseness is Ulrich von Zatzikhoven's *Lanzelet*, derived from an Anglo-Norman story of the twelfth century. In this version the hero, able both on the battlefield and in bed, has affairs with four women, ending with marriage to one, but he carefully stays away from King Arthur's wife. According to the mores of the time, this hero lived up to knightly expectations. The romance told by Chrétien de Troyes is in direct, and I think deliberate, contrast to this loose tale; Chrétien has gone out of his way to describe behavior he could be sure the courtly audience would condemn. In Chrétien's story the knight who rides in a shameful cart is no casual lover, but one who betrays his lord. In terms of the conventional standards of the court of Champagne, Chrétien's Lancelot was not more of a hero for loving Guinivere, but a felon. If we find Lancelot a sympathetic figure because he was guided by love rather than reason, it is because modern attitudes differ from medieval ones in ways Chrétien could not foresee.[30]

I am therefore in agreement with Professor Robertson that

---

30. *Lanzelet*, ed. K. A. Hahn (Frankfurt: Brönner, 1845), trans. and ed. by Kenneth G. T. Webster and Roger S. Loomis (New York: Columbia University Press, 1951); *Le chevalier de la charrette*, ed. Mario Roques (Paris: Champion, 1958), trans. by William Wistar Comfort in Chrétien de Troyes, *Arthurian Romances* (London: J. M. Dent, 1914).

Chrétien wrote courteously of Lancelot and left him locked in a tower, rather than condemning him explicitly, not because he found his behavior admirable but because he was writing in the medieval tradition of irony. This literary device was summed up simply by an early thirteenth-century teacher of grammar and rhetoric at Bologna, Boncompagno of Signa, in a definition which deserves a place at the beginning of every edition of *Lancelot*.[31]

"Irony is the unadorned and gentle use of words to convey disdain and ridicule. If he who expresses irony may be seen, the intention of the speaker may be understood through his gestures. In the absence of the speaker, manifest evil and impure belief indict the subject. . . . Hardly anyone can be found who is so foolish that he does not understand if he is praised for what he is not. For if you should praise the Ethiopian for his whiteness, the thief for his guardianship, the lecher for his chastity, the lame for his agility, the blind for his sight, the pauper for his riches, and the slave for his liberty, they would be struck dumb with inexpressible grief to have been praised, but really vituperated, for it is nothing but vituperation to commend the evil deeds of someone through their opposite, or to relate them wittily."

Up to this point I have been discussing love that has an obvious connection with sexuality, and this was hardly the only aspect of love which was important in the Middle Ages. Augustine, who thought there was something inherently evil about all carnal desire, explained carefully that in Scripture the word *amor* is used both of a good affection and of an evil love. As he put it in his influential *City of God*, "The right will is, therefore, good love, and the wrong will is evil love." This idea of a division of love was commonplace in the twelfth century; as Hugh of St. Victor put it succinctly: "two streams flow from the single fount of love, cupidity and charity." In the next century Thomas Aquinas ponderously demonstrated that it was proper to distinguish between the love of friendship and the love of concupiscence.[32] Note that for St. Thomas, as we have already seen, delight in the act of generation could increase friendship in marriage. Sexual pleasure

---

31. Paris, Bibl. nat., ms. lat. 8654, fol. 6ʳ. The Latin text follows as an appendix. Cf. D. W. Robertson, Jr., *A Preface to Chaucer* (Princeton: Princeton University Press, 1962), pp. 448–52.

32. *City of God*, Bk. XIV, ch. 7; Hugh of St. Victor, Migne, *PL*, CLXXVI, 15, trans. as "The Nature of Love" in his *Selected Spiritual Writings* (London: Faber and Faber, 1962), p. 187; *Summa theologica*, First Part of the Second Part, qu. 26, art. 4. Cf. Ovid, *Fasti*, IV, 1.

in marriage, fully consonant with reason, was a good thing. In short, Aquinas followed Aristotle in arguing that taking pleasure from any reasonable and appropriate behavior was natural and desirable.[33]

The idea that "love," expressed reasonably and appropriately, is a good thing can be found throughout medieval society. In religious terms, every Christian should love his neighbor, and in feudal terms, vassal and lord and their families should be bound by love. According to a ninth-century manual, a vassal should "fear, love, worship, and cherish" the relatives of his lord. Neither Christian charity nor feudal love necessarily involved an emotional or passionate personal attachment. Roland says that Charlemagne loved his vassals for the blows they struck. Love could express a purely formal relationship, a political alliance, the deference of a vassal before his lord, the bond of all the monks in a monastery, including those who disliked each other. In these terms, which have nothing to do with sexual desire, it increased one's worth to "love" another worthy person, as it increased one's honor to "love" a person of higher status.[34]

These theoretical statements provide a background for understanding medieval poetry in which a courtly writer says that he loves his lady. For a troubadour, traveling from court to court and singing to many ladies, these songs probably did not imply an emotional commitment, even when expressed in terms which sound quite passionate to us. Contemporaries could assume that the singer of love songs was not necessarily courting a woman, but only being courteous. The troubadour Elias Cairels defended himself against a forward lady, who was perhaps the creature of his imagination, by saying, "If I have sung your praise, it was not for dalliance *(drudaria)*, but for the honor and profit which I expected from it, as a jongleur does with a lady of worth."[35]

The love of friendship could also include those kisses and embraces which were often a part of medieval greetings, for in courtly circles it could be accepted as reasonable and appropriate to kiss a lady, to give her presents, to declare that one had become

---

33. For a full discussion see Josef Fuchs, *Die Sexualethik des heiligen Thomas von Aquin* (Köln: J. P. Bachem, 1949), pp. 21–30.

34. Edouard Bondurand, *L'Éducation carolingienne: le manuel de Dhuoda* (Paris: Picard, 1887), p. 103. See also the valuable semantic analysis of George F. Jones, *The Ethos of the Song of Roland* (Baltimore: Johns Hopkins Press, 1963), pp. 36–45.

35. P.-C. 133, 7, in Jules Véran, *Les Poétesses provençales* (Paris: A. Quillet, 1946), 152–57.

a better man through her friendship.[36] Such behavior should not be hard for us to understand, nor should we assume that it was concupiscent. If today a professor kisses his chairman's wife, or better yet the wife of a dean, gives her a present on her birthday, and treats her in a courteous fashion, no one need assume that he is not practicing "friendly love." If we today can distinguish between friendship and carnality, we should assume that medieval people could too. Of course, it is quite possible for a person to use the language of friendship with cupidinous desires in his heart. The danger of cupidity masquerading as proper love was the subject of a long discussion between the knight of La Tour Landry and his wife as to whether their daughters should court and kiss, and the hypocrisy of seduction provides much of the humor of the treatise on love by Andreas Capellanus.[37]

May I add in passing that since the lovers in Andreas' book were consistently unsuccessful, he can hardly have intended his work as a manual of seduction. What then was the purpose of his work? Perhaps we can judge from the view of Peter the Chanter, head of the school of moral philosophy at Paris at the end of the twelfth century. Peter was asked about the art of love, whether about Ovid's work in particular or the genre is not clear. He replied that "the art itself is good but its use is evil." The next question was then "does not he who teaches the amatory art use it and sin mortally?" To which it was replied that the teacher "does not use it but transmits it. He who corrupts women by its means uses it. Nevertheless, the teacher transmits it, not for use but as a warning."[38]

This part of the discussion may be summarized by attempting to be precise about terms. According to one group of medieval theorists there were two forms of love, one of which was reasonable and appropriate to the persons involved, could be practiced

---

36. For a straightforward statement approving this form of love see *Le Breviari d'Amor de Matfre Ermengau*, ed. Gabriel Azaïs (Béziers-Paris: Delpech, 1862), II, 413–16, ll. 27291 ff., trans. into modern French by Nelli and Lavaud, *Troubadours*, II, 664–71.

37. *Le Livre du Chevalier de La Tour Landry*, ed. Anatole de Montaiglon (Paris: Jannet, 1854), pp. 246–65, trans. from a medieval English version by G. S. Taylor, *The Book of the Knight of La Tour Landry* (London: Verona Society, 1930), pp. 248–70; and Andreas Capellanus *De Amore*, ed. E. Trojel (Havniae: Libraria Gadiana, 1892), trans. John J. Parry, *The Art of Courtly Love* (New York: Columbia University Press, 1941).

38. Munich, Staatsbibliothek, Clm. 5426, fol. 163ʳ, to be published by Jean Albert Dugauquier as ch. 332 in the fourth volume of his edition of Pierre le Chantre, *Summa de Sacramentis*. Cf. Andreas, *De Amore*, p. 313 (Parry, p. 187).

without sin or social affront, and was in fact good in itself; Aquinas called this the "love of friendship" and the troubadour Guillem Montanhagol said that chastity proceeds from it (*d'amor mòu castitatz*). There was a second form of loving directed toward the satisfaction of carnal desire, which Aquinas called the love of concupiscence and the troubadour Marcabru termed false friendship (*fals' amistat*). In theory love was the source of both branches, but they were very different in their ends and in their expression. We therefore create nothing but confusion for ourselves if we apply one technical term, other than the ambiguous word "love," to both forms of loving.[39] In particular I see no justification for combining aspects of one form of loving with aspects of the other and calling our creation "courtly love." While some authors wrote ambiguously about love, the literature I have read does not convince me that medieval people themselves inadvertently confused the categories and could not tell the difference between love which was concupiscent and that which was not. It seems to me that medieval authors and audiences enjoyed ambiguity in literature, not because they felt it reflected a basic ambiguity in the universe or the heart of man, but because their natural tendency was to think in very rigid categories. As the *Chanson de Roland* puts it (l. 1015), "Pagans are wrong and Christians are right."

An example of a passage in which some modern critics believe there is a combination of the two forms of love is that humorous dialogue by Andreas Capellanus in which a lover explains to a virgin that "pure love" proceeds "as far as kissing on the mouth and embracing and bashful contact with the nude lover, omitting the final solace."[40] The omission of the final act of Venus, which Andreas assumes may easily be reached later, preserves virginity, but it does not make the love chaste. How could anyone think it would? To do so requires the expectation that it is easy and in fact common for two naked lovers embracing together to avoid intercourse if one of them, presumably the woman, will only call a halt, thereby sublimating sexual desire into a spiritual relationship. This idea could be held in the Victorian period, when it was

---

39. *Les poésies de Guilhem de Montanhagol*, ed. Peter T. Ricketts (Toronto: Pontifical Institute of Mediaeval Studies, 1964), pp. 121–23 (P.-C. 225, 2); *Poésies complètes du troubadour Marcabru*, ed. J. M. L. Dejeanne, Bibl. mérid., 1st ser., 12 (Toulouse: E. Privat, 1909), Songs V and VI (P.-C. 293, 5 and 6). *Fin' amors*, meaning simply "true love," was not a technical term and was applied in various ways to both branches of love.

40. *De Amore*, p. 182 (Parry, p. 122). Cf. *De Amore*, pp. 264–65 (Parry, p. 164).

widely assumed that decent women did not enjoy sexual relations, and it still seems to linger on today. But it is a view which clashes with medieval views on physiology and the sexuality of women.

The medical theory inherited from antiquity was that both men and women are driven toward intercourse by their physiology. Women were thought to produce a seed (or *menstruum*) which collects in the womb and which gives rise to increasing sexual desire as it accumulates. Menstruation was considered the equivalent of a man's *pollutio* and to provide periodic relief; during pregnancy, when the *menstruum* was retained to nourish the fetus, a woman was at the peak of her sexual desire. Although medical treatises are imprecise in their terminology, orgasm seems to have been the indication of the emission of the female seed in intercourse. In any case, a woman's emission of seed, necessary for conception, was thought to be as pleasurable as that of a man; in fact, women were said to have twice the pleasure in intercourse as men, for they not only expelled seed but received it.[41] The natural consequence of this belief was the conclusion that a woman who conceived had taken pleasure in intercourse. Complacently, male judges denied any suit for rape brought by a woman who had become pregnant from the assault.[42] This theory of physiology explains the one strong area of medieval sexual egalitarianism. Since the sexual needs of women were thought to be as compelling as those of men, if not more so, a husband had as much responsibility to pay the marriage debt to his wife as she to him. The only woman who was not thought eager for sexual relations with someone was the unawakened woman. A woman would consequently choose a poor lover rather than have no man at all; as William IX put it, if denied wine anyone "would drink water rather than die of thirst." When contemplating other men's wives, as Duke William did, a man could take pleasure in this thought. But a man who brought back to his home the views of that bitter treatise, the *Quinze Joyes de Mariage*, must have viewed with horror the unquenchable sexuality of his wife.[43]

Since the force of sexuality was so compelling for both man and woman, it would be hard for chaste love to be just a little bit

---

41. The epitome of thirteenth-century female sexology is *De secretis mulierum*, which exists in many early printed editions. For references see Lynn Thorndyke in *Speculum*, XXX (1955), 427–43. See also Trotula of Salerno, *The Diseases of Women*, trans. Elizabeth Mason-Hohl (Los Angeles: Ward Ritchie, 1940).

42. *Year Books of Edward II*, vol. V, Selden Soc., 24 (London, 1910), p. 111.

43. P.-C. 183, 4, ed. Jeanroy, p. 4; *Les Quinze joyes de mariage*, ed. Fernand Fleuret (Paris: Garnier, 1936), trans. Elisabeth Abbott, *The Fifteen Joys of Marriage* (New York: Orion, 1959).

carnal. Frustrated desire was not thought preferable to satisfaction, for the natural end of desire was intercourse.[44] If carnal lovemaking stopped short of that goal, it was probably because the woman was a virgin, a state not likely to remain permanent if she found caressing pleasant enough. What preserved friendly love was virtue, aided by God's grace, or at least a sense of proper behavior. In a humorous song Daude de Pradas tells us that he divides his love in three. He has a lady from whom he receives small gifts and an occasional kiss; he loves her in order to increase his worth. He also likes to visit an honest virgin *(francha piucella)* who lets him kiss her cheek and doesn't jump up when he squeezes her breast. And finally, once or twice a month he beds down with a girl who works for wages, in order to learn what she knows of the game of love.[45] Daude could tell what was appropriate with each woman, and we should be careful to maintain his distinctions in our literary criticism.

Neither chaste nor cupidinous love has any direct or necessary connection with Catharism or other medieval heresies. The love of friendship was an expression of feudal or Christian values. The Cathars condemned Christian sexual morality and advocated a sexual purity far more rigorous than that actually found in Christian society; as a thirteenth-century Cathar ritual puts it, "Chastity places a man next to God."[46] There is, of course, no theoretical bar to thinking that some troubadours who celebrated chaste love were Cathars. Some southern French nobles were Cathars and many were sympathetic to at least some aspects of the religion. But admiring sexual purity was not peculiar to Cathars, and to assume that a poet advocating chastity was a heretic would be equivalent today to assuming that anyone advocating racial justice is a Communist.

The other side of the coin is that Cathars, opposed on religious

44. The twelfth-century Bolognese canonist Huguccio does mention the practice of *amplexus reservatus* in his *Summa*, Bk. II, 13 as a way for a married man to avoid the venial sin of pleasure in ejaculation. Comparison of his text with the *De Amore* shows that Andreas was not writing of the same thing when he discussed *amor purus*, for this form of intercourse could not be called "vererecundus contactus" for a woman. Other twelfth and thirteenth-century canonists ignore this passage in Huguccio, quite probably not understanding what he means. See John T. Noonan, Jr., *Contraception: A History of Its Treatment by the Catholic Theologians and Canonists* (Cambridge, Mass.: Harvard University Press, 1965), pp. 296-99.

45. *Poésies de Daude de Pradas*, ed. A. H. Schutz, Bibl. mérid, 1st ser., 22 (Toulouse: Privat, 1933), pp. 69-74 (P.-C. 124, 2).

46. Antoine Dondaine, *Un Traité néo-manichéen du XIIIe siècle* (Rome: Institutum Historicum FF. Praedicatorum Romae, 1939), p. 162; cf. *ibid.*, pp. 125-27.

grounds to procreation, were thought by their adversaries to have a stronger bar against generation than sexual activity itself. It may well be that some Cathars practiced sodomy and other non-generative sexual acts, but if they did, they kept it to themselves as best they could and did not write songs about it.[47] And a person did not have to be a Cathar to wish to avoid conception; various contraceptive devices, potions and practices were known and used throughout medieval Europe. All the same, contraception was not, as far as I can tell, the subject of any courtly literature.[48]

Catharism has been overrated as an influence on the sexual mores of medieval Europe. Publicly the Cathars preached sexual purity, but they were of course not alone in this. If they had an effect on most European Christians, it was probably to make it more difficult to be an advocate of chastity. Sometime in the 1180's the canon Gervase of Tilbury, then in the service of the archbishop of Reims, came upon a girl in a vineyard and, in the words of the man to whom he told the story, "courteously spoke to her at length of lascivious love." To these blandishments the girl replied, "Good young man, God doesn't wish me to be your lover or that of any man, since if I should lose my virginity and my flesh should once be corrupted, without doubt I should fall irredeemably into eternal damnation." Gervase immediately realized that she was a Cathar and began to reason with her. When the archbishop rode up he had the girl arrested and taken to Reims, where she was tried for heresy. When she refused to recant, she was burned at the stake, and died a martyr's death.[49]

This example of the treatment of a virtuous young woman raises the question of what effect the canons of courtesy had on the status of women. It is widely assumed that the twelfth century marks the beginning of a new period in the improvement of the social status of women. Of course, for the average person, man or woman, life in 1300 was more prosperous and more secure than it had been in 1000, and for the upper classes it was vastly improved.

---

47. St. Bernard thought that the public profession of chastity and continence made by the dualist heretics was hypocritical, and considered that for a man to remain continually with a woman and not know her carnally would be miraculous. See *Sermones super Cantica*, LXV and LXVI in *S. Bernardi Opera*, ed. Jean Leclercq et al. (Rome: Editiones Cistercienses, 1957-), II, 172-88, esp. pp. 175-76 and 179-81. These sermons and the letter of Eberwin of Steinfeld (*P.L.*, 182, 676-80) which solicited them show that the heretics preached chastity, whether or not they practiced it.

48. On Catharism and contraception see Noonan, *Contraception*, esp. pp. 179-93.

49. Ralf of Coggeshall, *Chronicon Anglicanum*, Rolls series, 66 (London, 1875), pp. 121-24.

And, as we have seen, the institution of marriage itself was strengthened. But these changes do not mean that the position of women had improved relative to that of men. If one judges by juridical status, the legal ability to inherit and administer property and bequeath it by will, to bring a suit in a court of law, to avoid remarriage if widowed, it is hard to see that the position of noble women improved between the first feudal age and the second, and Lady Stenton can even argue that for English women it went down after 1066.[50]

Why should one expect an improvement in status for women from a social code in which a man increased his honor by being polite? According to one French *lai* the ladies of a court in Brittany raised the question of why men liked to attend tourneys, why they adorned themselves and dressed in new clothes, why they sent presents of jewels and rings and other treasures, why they were honest and debonair, why they refrained from doing evil, why they liked gallantry and hugging and kissing. The answer, the ladies concluded in French, was a three-letter word.[51] Courtesy was created by men for their own satisfaction, and it emphasized a woman's role as an object, sexual or otherwise. Since they did not encourage a genuine respect for women as individuals, the conventions of medieval chivalry, like the conventions of chivalry in the southern United States, did not advance women toward legal or social emancipation. When men ignored chivalry, women were better off. Who would trade the position of Njal's wife for that of Isolt?

In this long but still abbreviated study I have attempted an introductory historical treatment of medieval love based largely on sources other than poetry and romances. In it I have not attributed any significant influence to the Cathars, and have not found it necessary to mention the Arabs, who may have contributed to the forms of Provençal songs but are not needed to understand the sexual mores or ideals of Christian Europe.[52] In addition, I have found no evidence of a dramatic change in social or sexual behavior or outlook spreading through southern France like a

---

50. It is instructive to compare the later medieval chapters in *La Femme*, Recueils de la Société Jean Bodin, XII, pt. 2 (Brussels: Editions de la Librairie encyclopédique, 1962), with F. L. Ganshof's introductory essay on Frankish women. See also Doris M. Stenton, *The English Woman in History* (London: Allen and Unwin, 1957), p. 28.

51. "Lai du Lecheor," ed. Gaston Paris, *Romania*, VIII (1879), 65-66, ll. 71-92.

52. The contrast between the position of women in Moslem and Western European society is well illustrated by Jean Richard in *La Femme*, pt. 2, p. 387.

plague, later to infect the north from a few centers like the court of Champagne or that of Eleanor of Aquitaine. Those changes in behavior I have noted occurred gradually, were moderate in their effect and can be understood as part of a general movement toward a more peaceful and better ordered society in the second feudal age. This paper attempts no systematic explanation of all medieval love literature, but the works I have mentioned seem to me consistent with Christian or feudal ideals, or with a society in which many people were not easily shocked by adultery but saw no reason to advocate it as a way of life for others. There was much discussion of love in various forms, and women were frequently honored by poets. Such poetry, we are told, increased the honor and profit of the singer, and in fact the service of ladies (which is hardly the same thing as the worship of women) does not seem to have significantly advanced their legal or social position. The second feudal age, like the first, remained a man's world.

Of course there were changes, and to see how literature and behavior acted on each other between 1100 and 1400 is a fascinating subject not attempted here. In treating it the greatest danger to avoid is that of working backward. There is, for instance, no doubt that in 1400 Charles VI founded a court of love, a serious literary and courtly assembly, but the existence of such a court should not lead us to think that the courts of love described by Andreas Capellanus were anything but humorous figments of his imagination.[53] As an example of the problem of historical perspective, let us take up a specific question. At the end of the Middle Ages a noble could depict himself on a tournament shield on his knees before a lady. What then is the earliest point where we can find evidence, outside of poetry, that a noble felt that it added to his honor to present himself as kneeling before a lady? Marc Bloch includes in his *Feudal Society* a picture entitled "The Lover's Homage" of the seal of Raymond de Montdragon, which shows a knight kneeling before a lithe figure in long robes. Is this early thirteenth-century seal our earliest evidence? No, for the figure in the long robes is actually not a woman but a man in civilian dress.[54] I mention this picture, not to point out a minor

---

53. Theodor Straub, "Die Gründung des Pariser Minnehofs von 1400," *Zeitschrift für romanische Philologie*, LXXVII (1961), 1-14; on the courts mentioned by Andreas see my "Court of Champagne as a Literary Center," *Speculum*, XXXVI (1961), 580-82.

54. *La société féodale, la formation des liens de dépendance* (Paris: A. Michel, 1939), trans. L. A. Manyon (London: Routledge, 1961), plate IV; cf. Germain Demay, *Le Costume au moyen âge, d'après les sceaux* (Paris: D. Dumoulin,

error in the work of a historian I greatly admire, but because it illustrates so well a familiar process. We see so often what we want to see, or expect to see, not what is there. Working backwards within the limits of a poorly defined concept could lead any historian to see a woman instead of a man.

Henry Osborne Taylor prided himself on writing two volumes on the sixteenth century without using the word "Renaissance," leading Charles Haskins to say of the forbidden term that "if it had not existed we should have to invent it." I have found the term "courtly love" no advantage in trying to understand the theory and practice of love in medieval Europe. It is not a medieval technical term. It has no specific content. A reference to "the rules of courtly love" is almost invariably a citation of Andreas' *De Amore*, a work which I think is intentionally and humorously ambiguous about love. The study of love in the middle ages would be far easier if we were not impeded by a term which now inevitably confuses the issue. As currently employed, "courtly love" has no useful meaning, and it is not worth saving by redefinition. I would therefore like to propose that "courtly love" be banned from all future conferences.

Appendix

Definition of irony by Boncompagnus de Signa from his *Rhetorica antiqua* (c. 1215)[55]

P = Paris, Bibl. nat., ms. lat. 8654, fol. 6ʳ
M = Munich, Staatsbibliothek, Clm 23499, fol. 4ʳ
V = Vatican City, Archivio della Basilica di San Pietro, H. 13, fol. 9ᵛ-10ʳ

Notula qua doctrina datur quid sit yronia et eius effectus.

Nota quod premissa narratio destinari potest etiam illi qui huc et illuc vagatur et studere contempnit, et dicitur hec species yronie in qua delinquens afficitur maiori pudore. Yronia enim est plana et demulcens verborum
5 positio cum indignatione animi et subsannatione. Verumtamen si videretur ille qui proponit yroniam, per gestus comprehendi posset voluntas loquentis. In absentia nempe manifestum delictum et immunda conscientia recipientem accusant. Gestus autem illorum qui subsannant et yronias proponunt subtiliter et utiliter in libro quem feci de gestibus et motibus corporum huma-
10 norum notavi. Ceterum vix aliquis adeo fatuus reperitur qui non intelligat si de eo quod non est conlaudetur. Nam si commendares Ethyopem de albe-

---

1880). There is a picture of a fifteenth-century tournament shield in Joan Evans, *The Flowering of the Middle Ages* (London: Thames and Hudson, 1966), p. 142.

55. I am grateful to Professor Robert L. Benson for collating the Munich and Vatican manuscripts.

dine, latronem de custodia, luxuriosum de castitate, de facili gressu claudum, cecum de visu, pauperem de divitiis, et servum de libertate, stuperent inenarrabili dolore laudati, immo vituperati, quia nil aliud est vituperium quam
15 alicuius malefacta per contrarium commendare vel iocose narrare. . . .

---

2   huc *om*. M   3   dicitur] quod *add*. V
4   efficitur M   9   quem] inquid V
11 si de—est] si non est de eo quod V
11 conlaudetur] laudetur M, laudatur V

7

An Abusive Letter of Nicolas de Clairvaux for a Bishop of Auxerre, Possibly Blessed Hugh of Mâcon

The next to the last piece in the collected letters of Nicolas of Clairvaux in Berlin Ms. Phillipps 1719 is a vigorous and scurrilous epistle which bears no rubric, heading or identification of sender or recipient. The references in the letter rule out the possibility that Nicolas wrote it in his own name, but since the collection contains many other letters which St. Bernard's well-known secretary wrote for other people, its presence here between two letters which are surely by Nicolas suggests that he wrote it *in persona* of someone else. Who this person might have been must be inferred from the text itself.[1]

(A)ngelus tenebrarum nunquam cessat a fidelibus impugnandis, qui principem illorum persecutus est ad mortem crucis.[2] Struit insidias de die in diem, et tali modo deponere membra nititur ne capiti suo per caritatis glutinum uniantur. Elegit iste antiquissimus serpens quosdam de capitulo Autusiodorensi et pessimos reddidit quos malignos invenit. Ad accusandam innocentiam meam nocentibus indigebat. Vidit lupos qui mentiebantur oves in domo Dei. Introivit in eos Satanas.[3] Insurrexerunt adversum me viri mendaces, qui gloriantur in malicia et potentes sunt in iniquitate.[4] Agerem in eos de eorum enormitate, nisi puderet me dicere, vos audire. Quantis redundat illorum vita flagitiis, quam turpiter utrumque[5] sexum libidinis imbre complueriunt, transeo, pater, quoniam vobis notum est et totius populi aures...[6]

Creavi eos in canonicos et filios Autusiodorensis ecclesie; ipsi autem spreverunt me.[7] Eram dominus illorum, sed ecce dicunt: Labia nostra a nobis sunt, quis noster dominus est?[8] Insurgunt filii contra patrem, oves impetum faciunt in pastorem, accusant vasa figulum.[9] Comminiscuntur mendacia, fabricant dolos. Meam nituntur deponere personam. Ne ergo credas eis, sanctissime pater, ne accommodes aurem pietatis

---

[1] The 13th-century manuscript is described by Valentin Rose, *Verzeichnis der lateinischen Handschriften der kgl. Bibliothek zu Berlin, I, Die Meerman-Handschriften des Sir Thomas Phillipps* (Berlin, 1893), 418-422. This letter, which is on fols. 117-117v, is published with the authorization of the Deutsche Staatsbibliothek in Berlin. I am grateful to Dr. Helmut Boese and Dr. Hans Lülfing for their assistance. For another letter in this collection see "Nicolas de Clairvaux à la recherche du vin d'Auxerre," *Annales de Bourgogne*, 24 ; above, 123-128. Giles Constable has made a fine study of Nicolas' early career in *The Letters of Peter the Venerable* (Cambridge, Mass., 1967), 2, 316-330.

[2] Philippians 2: 8.
[3] John 13: 27.
[4] Psalms 51: 3.
[5] Ms. is corrupt; it appears to read either utrimque or utriusque.
[6] Lacuna in Ms. (offenduntur ?)
[7] Isaiah 1: 2.
[8] Psalms 11: 5.
[9] Cf. Isaiah 29: 16.

sermonibus toxicatis. Filii Sathane sunt, vasa et instrumenta diaboli. Et tu, pater, bene legisti et intelligis, quia diabolus mendax est, et pater eius.[10]

Verbum est impositum a quorumdam detractorum malicia vestris auribus quod sorores mee castitatem Deo promissam fregerunt ad amplexus illicitos accendentes. Non debetis accedere sermoni talium, pater et domine, quorum lingua venenum evomit, et in suis excessibus est felicia perturbare.

Iure consilium ab illo queritur a quo solet consilium in rebus arduis emanare. Quod pie postulatur, iuste debet effectui mancipari.

Apud regem nostrum tantum evaluit quorumdam suggestio toxicata quod G., quem amore complectimur diligenti, horribili fecit in carcere[11] detineri. Eapropter actentius vos rogamus quatinus causa nostri vestra sedulitas sic laboret quod vestris precibus amicus noster a carcere liberetur.

Tradidistis nobis priorem inutilem et nimis inhonestum qui, relicta cura celle sibi commisse, bona nostra deportat ad tribades. Et polluta frequens est incola lupanaris. Revocate pollutum hominem si vobis est placitum, ne per eum nostra religio diffametur.

This letter clearly raises more questions than it answers. We learn that its sender was the *dominus* of some canons of Auxerre and that he had in fact made (*creavi*) them canons. Since the bishop of Auxerre held the right of appointment to canonries in the cathedral, we may conclude that the sender was bishop of that city. At the time of writing he was in conflict with these canons, who had, he said, accused him falsely and told lies about him. We also learn that he was responsible for some nuns who were accused of sexual laxity. He in turn denounced but could not replace a prior whose appointment was in the hands of the recipient of the letter, and for some reason he referred to the property of the cell or priory as "our" goods. The letter was written at a time when the king had just imprisoned someone named "G.", and the sender believed that the recipient could influence the king to have "G." released.

It is obvious that without external evidence, such as a letter which replies to this one, we cannot establish the sender, date or circumstances of this letter with certainty. There is, however, an historical setting into which the letter can be fitted neatly. Whether or not the situation about to be described is the actual setting of the letter, it seems at least to be a possible one.

Blessed Hugh of Mâcon had a long and distinguished ecclesiastical career. He was one of the original 30 Burgundian nobles who entered Cîteaux with St. Bernard in 1113, became the first abbot of Pontigny (1114-1136), and then served as bishop of Auxerre (1137-1151).[12] At the end of his life he provided both for the church of Auxerre and for his nephew, a canon of the cathedral, named Stephen. For Stephen he reinstituted the office of provost of the cathedral chapter, a grant which was confirmed by the pope.[13] To the cathedral chapter he left rights of usage in a wood which the canons had long been trying to acquire, some very rich sacerdotal vestments, a gilded chalice, an annual income of 30 *sous* from the village of Lindry, and the church of

---

[10] John 8: 44.

[11] Ms. carcarem.

[12] On Hugh's life and writing, see Abbé Barthélemy Rameau, "Hugues de Mâcon," *Revue de la Société littéraire, historique et archéologique du département de l'Ain*, 10 (1881), 60-70, and C. H. Talbot, "The Sermons of Hugh of Pontigny," *Cîteaux in de Nederlanden*, 7 (1956), 1-33; Gaetano Raciti, "Hugues de Mâcon," Dictionnaire de spiritualité (Paris, 1937 sq.), 7, 886-889.

[13] *Gesta pontificum Austissiodorensium*, ch. 55, in Migne, PL, 138, 299-300.

Lindry after the death or resignation of the incumbent. He also left an additional income of 10 *sous* for the use of the canons under the control of provost Stephen.[14]

The office of provost was the source of considerable trouble at Auxerre. Provost Ulgerius had opposed the election of Hugh of Montaigu, Hugh of Mâcon's predecessor, and when Hugh of Montaigu later had a chance to do so, he abolished the office and added its revenues to the income of the canons. When Hugh of Mâcon reestablished the office, he, had to endow it with episcopal revenues which he could otherwise have left to the chapter. From the canons' point of view, Hugh's appointment of his nephew was not only an act of nepotism but a novelty paid for out of their revenues. Even after Stephen had passed from the scene they continued to oppose the office, and the provostship was finally abolished by Hugh's successor, Alan, who again added its revenues to the collective income of the canons.[15] The appointment of Stephen split the chapter. According to a letter St. Bernard wrote not long after the bishop's death, Stephen's party consisted only of the cantor, the archdeacon, and the treasurer (whose incomes were probably separately funded), and one other canon, while 20 deacons and priests of the chapter were on the other side.[16]

Hugh of Mâcon died at Pontigny on 10 October 1151. St. Bernard wrote the pope that in the previous year when he had seemed to be on the point of death Hugh had granted the revenues of a church to his nephew. Bernard added that he had been informed on the best of authority that after Hugh recovered, he did not recognize what he had done. Whatever the truth of the charge that the bishop was out of his senses when he favored his nephew, we may conclude from this statement that sometime in the year before his death Hugh had begun to take steps to favor his nephew. Meeting resistance, he retired to friendly surroundings at Pontigny, taking his supporters with him. These circumstances would explain a mysterious note which Abbot Guichard of Pontigny wrote to Suger of St. Denis, recommending to him the treasurer of Auxerre, who was seeking Suger's support. Guichard ended by saying that since his own seal was not at hand, he would use that of the bishop of Auxerre.[17]

This story of Hugh and his nephew has been told in detail because it is usually recounted only on the basis of the letters of St. Bernard. Bernard found it hard to believe that such a saintly man as his old comrade could consciously commit nepotism, and he therefore explained to the pope that Hugh did not know what he was doing (*cum in morte aliquantum stupidus esset et turbatus*). Bernard declared that Stephen had made the bishop die practically intestate, leaving nothing or next to nothing to the poor and the churches. He specified that Stephen received the golden things in the bishop's

---

[14] Auguste Longnon, ed., *Obituaires de la province de Sens*. T. III. *Diocèses d'Orléans, d'Auxerre et de Nevers* (Paris, 1909), 242.

[15] *Gesta pontificum Autissiodorensium*, ch. 54, *loc. cit.*, 292, 297. For Alan's grant in 1166 see Yonne, arch. dép. G 1820, printed in Maximilien Quantin, *Cartulaire général de l'Yonne* (Auxerre, 1854-60), 2, 183-184.

[16] Bernard wrote a series of letters to Pope Eugene and Cardinal Hugh of Ostia, first supporting the nephew of his departed friend and then, after hearing more of the story of the dissident canons, denouncing Stephen and withdrawing his approval. The three surviving letters, nos. 274-276 in Mabillon's edition (PL, 182, 480-482), are the basis of the statements credited to St. Bernard here and in the next three paragraphs.

[17] *Recueil des historiens des Gaules et de la France*, 15 (2nd ed., Paris, 1878), 522-523. Suger died 13 January 1151; his death provides a terminal date for the letter.

personal property, his mounts, and seven churches and the tithes and fields in the bishop's woods. Of the legacy which Hugh actually left to the chapter Bernard said nothing, nor did he explain (what we must infer) that the income from the seven churches went to reestablish the provostship. While there is some exaggeration in Bernard's statement that Hugh had left next to nothing to the church, 30 or 40 *sous* and the expectation of one church must have seemed very little to the canons in comparison to what it took to endow Stephen's provostship.

Bernard placed all the blame for this unbalanced legacy on Stephen, saying that the bishop had been made to sin, and adding that "some people think" that Stephen had drawn up the will and sealed it. Perhaps the nephew did exercise improper influence on the old man, but the weight of the evidence does show that the bishop consciously favored his nephew. The author of the *Gesta Pontificum Autissiodorensium*, who disapproved of the re-creation of the provostship, states clearly that Hugh was responsible and that the pope confirmed the appointment. Abbot Guichard's letter to Suger also indicates that Hugh and the treasurer were seeking support before January 1151. The story that his favoring of his nephew was the act of an unsound or senile mind probably originated with the aggrieved canons, rather than with Bernard himself. It shows how bitter the division in the chapter of Auxerre had become, and provides a motive for the bishop to write with outrage that his sons had risen up against him and were trying to tear apart his person.

If Hugh did conclude in the year before his death that some of his canons were insubordinate and malicious, he had the opportunity to ask an established stylist like Nicolas of Clairvaux to compose a letter which would express these feelings. In the winter of 1150-51 Nicolas was sent by St. Bernard to attend the bishop of Auxerre, and since Nicolas fell ill, he was away from Clairvaux longer than anticipated.[18] This long visit with Hugh of Mâcon would have given Nicolas the occasion to be his temporary secretary.

The rest of the letter accords with what we know of Hugh of Mâcon's situation at the end of his life, though the references are so vague that no case can be built upon them. As bishop of Auxerre, Hugh held a position of oversight and authority over the nuns of Crisenon, who had been freed from the control of the monastery of Molesmes in 1140.[19] This relationship would explain why the bishop could feel called upon to defend his "sisters" from criticism, particularly if he was addressing a monastic correspondent. In the year or two before his death Hugh was also in conflict with the prior of La Charité-sur-Loire. The foundation grant to La Charité was made in 1059 by the bishop of Auxerre, and the bishops continued to take a close interest in the priory, but the prior was named by the abbot of Cluny and was responsible to him.[20] It is easy to understand how Hugh could become involved in the affairs of this eldest daughter of Cluny, both as bishop and because of his own experience as head of a monastery. In 1149 or 1150 the prior of La Charité wrote to Suger about the mistreatment he had received from Hugh, who had appropriated his tithes and churches, had seized and sold some of his cattle, and had incited the count of Nevers and Geoffroi of Donzy to attack him.[21] This letter shows how Hugh could have considered that the

---

[18] Ep. 265 (PL 182, 470). On the date see *Letters of Peter the Venerable*, ed. Constable, 2, 324.
[19] *Gallia christiana*, 12 (Paris, 1770), 425 and instr., col. 112 (Jaffé-Loewenfeld, no. 8104).
[20] René de Lespinasse, *Cartulaire du prieuré de la Charité-sur-Loire* (Nevers and Paris, 1887), 1-3, 76-82.
[21] *Recueil des historiens*, 15, 510. The letter is here dated 1149.

prior was wasting *bona nostra* and provides a motive for asking for his removal. If the author of the letter under consideration was not asking for the removal of the prior of La Charité-sur-Loire, he could have been.

The tissue of circumstantial evidence being wound around this letter would be greatly strengthened if it could be shown that in 1151 King Louis imprisoned a friend of Bishop Hugh's named "G." Unfortunately, the uncertainty of an initial can only be matched with other uncertain information. The most that can be said is that the mysterious reference may be related to the crisis at Saint-Denis after the death of Suger. This crisis brought the new abbot, Eudes of Deuil, into conflict with Suger's nephew Simon and a number of the former abbot's relatives and followers. The king became involved as an active supporter of Abbot Eudes, Suger's biographer Guillaume of Saint-Denis was temporarily exiled to Aquitaine, and someone known only as "G." met his death. St. Bernard wrote to the pope and Cardinal Hugh of Ostia on Eudes' behalf and declared that he was not responsible for the death of "G." Little can be built on such information, but it indicates a crisis which could have interested Hugh of Mâcon in 1151.[22]

If this letter was written for Hugh of Mâcon, to whom was it addressed? All we know is that the recipient was a leading ecclesiastic, addressed as *pater et dominus* and *sanctissimus pater*, that he was responsible for the appointment of the prior in question, that he was thought to have influence with the king, and that the sender felt that the recipient should listen to his side of the story rather than the canons. The reference to the prior suggests a monastic correspondent, and the names of three great abbots, all of whom could influence the king, come to mind: Peter of Cluny, Bernard of Clairvaux, and Suger of St. Denis. Peter's authority over the prior of La Charité makes him the most likely candidate, and Suger's death in early 1151 limits the likelihood that it was addressed to him.[23] We may well never know.

Although this letter is so unspecific that it cannot tell us anything about affairs in the diocese of Auxerre which we did not already know, its text is evidence of what its author, almost certainly Nicolas of Clairvaux, thought was appropriate for a great churchman to send. When writing for himself, Nicolas made a practice of urbanity, gracefulness and elaborate flattery. This letter is unusual in expressing outrage and distress, its message is brutal and even offensive, and its tone is not one of supplication but indignation. For vigor of denunciation it matches or surpasses the most outspoken letters of its time, including the letter St. Bernard wrote to Pope Eugene denouncing Nicolas himself.[24]

The letter deals with three ecclesiastical matters, the conflict between the canons and their lord, the conflict with a prior, and the defense against the charge of faulty supervision of a nunnery. Strikingly, all three of these affairs are expressed through allegations of sexual misconduct. The insubordinant canons are not only treacherous, but they are engaged in a torrent of lechery, including homosexuality. The prior

---

[22] On this crisis see Hubert Glaser, "Wilhelm von Saint-Denis: Ein Humanist aus der Umgebung des Abtes Suger und die Krise seiner Abtei von 1151 bis 1153," *Historisches Jahrbuch*, 85 (1965), 300-321, esp. 316.

[23] If Peter the Venerable was the recipient, the relatively unfriendly tone of the letter may have been in part the result of a conflict which Hugh and Peter had in 1148 over the church of Saint-Germain of Auxerre; see *Gall. christ.*, 12, instr., cols. 122-123 (Jaffé-Loewenfeld, no. 9259).

[24] Ep. 298 (PL 182, 500-501).

is not only wasting the goods of his church, but he is spending them on *tribades*, a word here oddly dredged out of the vocabulary of erotic insult, probably from Martial. And conversely, the charge of mismanagement which the sender has to face is that his sisters have broken their vows of chastity. Rather than deal directly with personal and ecclesiastical conflict, both the sender and his critics found it easier to circulate charges of sexual impurity and unnatural practice.

The letter may have been written to suit a sick and disturbed old man, but it had its interest for a wider audience in the twelfth century. If it was written by Nicolas of Clairvaux, it was probably he who kept a copy for the collection of letters made late in his lifetime. At some point in its transmission to us the author, collector or copyist discreetly removed all information which would allow us to be sure of the sender. The letter has come down to us in the form in which its copyist thought of it, not as the record of a particular historical circumstance but as a model of epistolary outrage and invective.

8

Theocratic History in Fourteenth-century France: the Liber bellorum domini *by Pierre de la Palu*

TO the degree that he is known at all today, Pierre de la Palu (ca. 1275–1342) is thought of as a Dominican controversialist who wrote extensively on theological issues, taught for his order at the Parisian convent on the rue Saint-Jacques, played some part in the political and ecclesiastical affairs of his time, was sent on a mission to Cyprus by John XXII and Philip VI, and was rewarded with the honorific office of Patriarch of Jerusalem.[1] His major published work is a commentary on the *Sentences* which contains a detailed refutation of Durand de Saint-Pourçain's criticism of Thomistic theses.[2] In the two centuries after his death, Pierre de la Palu was also remembered as something of an historian. In 1413 when the Dominican bibliographer Louis of Valladolid drew up a list of the authors of his order and their writings, he ranked La Palu ninth and noted the existence of a work which he had probably seen at Saint-Jacques: "Item librum historiarum, et intitulatur Liber bellorum domini."[3] Another Do-

---

1. The only detailed study of this politically active author is Paul Fournier, "Pierre de la Palu, théologien et canoniste," in *Histoire littéraire de la France*, XXXVII (Paris, 1938), 39–84.
2. *In quartum Sententiarum*, Venice, 1493 (Hain, 12286); to the manuscripts cited by Fournier, op. cit., pp. 53–54, n. 5, a reference should be added to an excellent fifteenth-century manuscript of Book IV alone in the Hoose Library of the University of Southern California. For a brief description and citation of sale catalogues see Seymour De Ricci and W. J. Wilson, *Census of Medieval and Renaissance Manuscripts in the United States and Canada* (New York, 1935–40), I, 1, p. 17, no. 3.
3. H. C. Scheeben, "Die Tabulae Ludwigs von Valladolid im Chor der Predigerbrüder von St. Jakob in Paris," *Archivum fratrum Praedicatorum*, I (1932), 254.

minican, Estevão de Sampayo, in his study of the life of Bl. Lawrence Menendez used this history to find the correct date of the sack of Antioch (1268), which had been garbled by other authorities, and Etienne de Lusignan cited the book frequently in *Les Droicts, auctoritez et prerogatives que pretendent au royaume de Hierusalem*, published at Paris in 1586–87. But the copy of La Palu's history which had long been preserved at Saint-Jacques was lost by the early eighteenth century when Fr. Jacques Echard was completing his work on the *Scriptores ordinis Praedicatorum*.[4]

Although no complete copy of the text has yet been found, copied extracts do exist. The longest is a manuscript which once belonged to the bibliophile Paul Pétau and is now preserved as Vatican, Reg. lat. 547. Ignazio Giorgi and Paul Riant published a long description of this manuscript in 1881, but unaware of the author's name, they were able to give only the title, which appears in this manuscript as *Liber bellorum Domini pro tempore Nove Legis*.[5] The Vatican manuscript is acephalous, containing only the *secunda pars principalis* in 107 chapters, followed by an appendix or *secunda particula* of 169 chapters. This long "second principal part" of the *Liber bellorum Domini*, devoted entirely to the history of the crusades in the Near East, reveals the author's limitations and intention. Regrettably, although La Palu had visited Cyprus and had both a deep interest in the crusading movement and unusual opportunities to make first-hand observations, Giorgi and Riant found that his history was simply an anthology of extracts from earlier authors such as Fulcher of Chartres and Baudry of Dol, as well as later authors of his own order such as Vincent of Beauvais and Bernard Gui. Except for a few introductory passages and the division of his sources into *articuli* and *conclusiones*, there does not appear to be an original word in the whole manuscript. Why should there be, when the author's goal was not historical but hortatory? Riant has aptly summed up the compiler's intention: "le but immédiat était d'amener—en excitant le zèle des fidèles par le récit des exploits des croisés,—le triomphe de l'Église

---

4. Jacques Quétif and Jacques Echard, *Scriptores ordinis Praedicatorum* (Paris, 1719–21), I, 608, a passage which cites the references of earlier authors.
5. "Description du *Liber bellorum Domini*," *Archives de l'orient latin*, I (1881), 289–322. Count Riant drew further information from this manuscript in "Déposition de Charles d'Anjou pour la canonisation de Saint Louis," in *Notices et documents publiés pour la Société de l'histoire de France* (Paris, 1884), I, 155–176.

sur les Musulmans infidèles, par le recouvrement des Lieux Saints."[6]

The work of Riant and Giorgi left open both the authorship of the text they described and the question of the contents of the first part of the book. The correct identification of the authorship of the *Liber bellorum Domini* was made by Paul Fournier in a magisterial study published in 1938, a study which also drew attention to MS. 865 of the Bibliothèque Sainte-Geneviève, a manuscript from the convent of the Capucins of Albi made in 1560, which according to the printed description gives a "résumé, accompagné de citations, des art. 105 à 115 de cette Ire partie dudit livre."[7] The extract in this manuscript deals with the Albigensian Crusade, and so shows that the distinction between the two parts of the *Liber bellorum Domini* is geographical rather than chronological, for the Vatican manuscript is devoted to crusades in the Near East, while all that exists of the first part is concerned with religious wars (or wars which might be so considered) on the mainland of Europe.

The published description of the manuscript in the Bibliothèque Sainte-Geneviève, which I have unfortunately not seen, gives the misleading impression that this sixteenth-century copy contains only a "résumé" of eleven chapters, though it actually contains the full text of a much larger number of chapters.[8] Study of this Parisian manuscript should add something to our knowledge of La Palu's

---

6. "Description du *Liber bellorum Domini*," p. 292.
7. Fournier, op. cit., pp. 80–82. The quoted description of MS. 865 is taken from Charles Kohler, *Catalogue des manuscrits de la Bibliothèque Sainte-Geneviève*, I (Paris, 1893), 420. According to this description the manuscript is paper, 72 pages, 278×200 mm.
8. *Petri Vallium Sarnaii monachi Hystoria Albigensis*, ed. Pascal Guébin and Ernest Lyon, Société de l'histoire de France (Paris, 1926–39), III, li–lii, describes this manuscript (here classified as *J*); pp. 48–72 give the full text of the *Historia* as printed in II, 252–323. The Bibliothèque Sainte-Geneviève manuscript therefore contains exactly the same portions of the *Historia Albigensis* as Lea MS. 45, and the variant readings given by Guébin and Lyon show that the two texts are closely related. It must be remembered, however, that according to Kohler's description (see above, n. 7), the Parisian manuscript contains *articuli* 105–115, while the Lea manuscript begins with *articuli* 105–112 and then skips to the *Historia Albigensis* (as the Sainte-Geneviève manuscript also does on p. 48). Unless Kohler's description is in error, the Sainte-Geneviève manuscript cannot have been copied from the Lea manuscript (since the earlier manuscript lacks *articuli* 113–115), but it seems obvious that the two manuscripts are most likely closely related. The Lea manuscript may therefore be of some use in tracing the evolution of the text of the *Historia Albigensis*.

history. Nevertheless, the manuscript on which the present article is based provides considerable material for an evaluation of the first part of the *Liber bellorum Domini*; publication of a summary of its contents may help in the identification of other manuscripts of the text and will make possible a comparison of a manuscript now in the New World with the one preserved in the Bibliothèque Saint-Geneviève.

The manuscript which is now shelved as number 45 of the Lea collection in the University of Pennsylvania libraries was purchased in April 1958, when Kenneth Setton was director of libraries and Rudolf Hirsch was associate director with particular responsibility for manuscript holdings. The University was then actively engaged in that remarkable wave of astute manuscript purchasing which finds its record in the *Catalogue of Manuscripts in the Libraries of the University of Pennsylvania to 1800*, compiled by Norman Zacour and Rudolf Hirsch. Of all the manuscript collectors and purchasers I have known, Mr. Hirsch has shown the greatest talent for finding at bargain prices manuscripts which had potential for contributing to scholarship and teaching. Lea MS. 45 was offered for sale by H. P. Kraus in list 189, *Text Manuscripts from the Middle Ages to the XVIII Century, for the Most Part from the Giuseppe Martini Collection*, item 183, for $285. That price, which must raise a feeling of nostalgia in collectors today, was doubtless a result of the fact that neither the previous owner (whether Giuseppe Martini or not, I do not know) nor the seller had identified the author or the title of the work. The catalogue description therefore called attention in its heading to the scribe (Rolandus de Monte, otherwise unknown) and called the text "commentaries on chapters 105–112, 192–195, and 142–148 of an unnamed historical work, perhaps a general history of France and the Crusades."

Physically the manuscript is not distinguished. It consists of 32 folios of paper, 29.5 × 21.5 cm., written in a Gothic cursive book hand of the early fifteenth century, 36–38 lines to a page. The writing gives some indication that the copy was made in southern France, and the manuscript may share a common ancestor with the one from Albi which is now in the Bibliothèque Sainte-Geneviève. Since Lea MS. 45 has been annotated by a later Spanish hand and is bound in a seventeenth-century vellum Spanish legal document, it appears that for some time it found a home in Spain before making the long trip which eventually brought it to Philadelphia.

The copyist, "Rolandus de Monte," ended his work with a complicated signature which suggests a notary's mark and a cheerful if unoriginal verse:[9]

> Explicit hic liber; de pena sum modo liber.
> Explicit hoc totum; pro pena da michi potum.
> Explicit expliceat; ludere scriptor eat.
> Finito libro sit laus et gloria Christo.

Fortunately, at the bottom of the last page a later cursive hand has added "Ita D. Petrus de Palude scripsit librum bellorum Domini, qui asservatur in bibliotheca nostra Parisiensi." The author's name was not easy to decipher, and I can still remember the day in 1966 when Rudolf Hirsch, Norman Zacour, and I, working in the old Lea Library overlooking 34th Street, puzzled out the information in that final sentence, turned to Quétif and Echard to learn more about Pierre de la Palu, and realized that we had in our hands a text of the history the Dominican bibliographers had been unable to find in Paris. Such moments are among the joys of a scholar's life. Usually they are filtered out of academic writing and go unrecorded, but in a volume dedicated to Rudolf Hirsch it seems appropriate to note my gratitude for one of many experiences of shared discovery.

What does Lea MS. 45 tell us about Pierre de la Palu and his history? A detailed knowledge of La Palu's use of his sources will have to take account of all available manuscripts of his work, but without such an investigation a simple comparison of the contents of Lea MS. 45 with the published description of the Vatican text of the *secunda pars* allows one to see that in both parts of his book La Palu was no more than a compiler, and a somewhat disorganized one at that. In the *secunda pars* he proceeds chronologically through 107 *articuli* and then, having at hand the text of Fulcher of Chartres for the first crusade, adds this new material in an appendix. Similar disorganization appears in the *prima pars principalis*, for *articuli* 105–112 contain a disjointed account of fighting from the beginning of the Albigensian crusade up to the beginning of the reign of Louis IX, taken entirely from the writing of Vincent of Beauvais and Bernard Gui, 142–148 are composed of the full text of the *Vita sancti Amici et Amelii*, with the action supposedly set in the time of Charlemagne, and 192–195 give the conclusion of the *Historia Albigensis* of Pierre

---

9. Cf. Lynn Thorndike, "Copyists' Final Jingles in Mediaeval Manuscripts," *Speculum*, XII (1937), 268, and "More Copyists' Final Jingles," ibid., XXXI, 324, 325.

des Vaux-de-Cernay. Chapter 195 is the end of the *prima pars principalis*, so we can see that in the opening part of his book La Palu worked through the Albigensian crusade on the basis of inferior sources (Vincent of Beauvais and Bernard Gui—both of whom were themselves compilers of earlier materials) and then completed his account with the continuous text of a far better history.[10]

The accidents of survival have given us only fragments of the first part of the *Liber bellorum Domini* and they are insufficient for us to see the structure of the composition. Why an account of a battle supposedly fought in the time of Charlemagne should fall between two descriptions of the Albigensian crusade is unclear, as is the nature of the material which made up the first 104 *articuli*. Both the Lea MS. and the one in the Bibliothèque Sainte-Geneviève were copied by or for people particularly interested in the Albigensian crusade, and as yet we have no evidence of the point at which La Palu began his work on the wars of the Lord. We cannot tell whether his compilation began with Jewish history, early Christian persecutions, or later history, perhaps taken from Eusebius or Gregory of Tours. But we do know from the material available that La Palu was simply a compiler of the scissors-and-paste school, so that the loss of parts of his work is scarcely an historical tragedy.

Although the existing fragments of his book have no more value as historical evidence than that of additional copies of the earlier works from which they were taken, the *Liber bellorum Domini* in itself is a curious witness to the mentality of the author. A mind which applied scholastic precision to splitting its sources into carefully labeled *articuli* and *conclusiones* brought together a disordered collection of odd fragments of history, made no apparent critical evaluation of his materials, and left a work which by modern standards has no value as history. La Palu's contemporary, Bernard Gui, was also a compiler, but he applied some critical standards, made comparisons between sources, and up-dated his text as new information became available.[11] La Palu liked a good story, as his inclusion

---

10. The specific sources from which La Palu took his material are indicated in the notes to the appendix.
11. Léopold Delisle, "Notice sur les manuscrits de Bernard Gui," *Notices et extraits des manuscrits de la Bibliothèque nationale*, XXVII, pt. 2, 165–455, is a remarkable monograph which makes clear the revisions Bernard Gui made in his work through a detailed study of his manuscripts. Though we now have critical editions of two of Bernard Gui's Dominican histories, edited by Thomas

of a version of the tale of Amis and Amiloun shows, for this account of friendship carried to the point where a father cuts off the heads of his sons to cure a friend of leprosy can find a place in a history of religious wars only by virtue of a dubious reference to a battle between Charlemagne and the king of the Lombards. The *Vita sanctorum Amici et Amelii* displays several instances of divine intervention, for Amiloun kills his children as a consequence of angelic instruction, and angels were also responsible for placing the tombs of the two heroes side by side, a miracle comparable to the column of fire which supposedly guided Simon de Montfort to the bodies of his dead comrades in the account which La Palu borrowed from Bernard Gui.[12]

From Herodotus on, the curiosity and critical judgment of historians have enriched the tradition of Western historiography. La Palu's *Liber bellorum Domini*, however, comes strikingly close to fitting the definition which R. G. Collingwood applied to the theocratic history of the ancient Near East, writing marked by an absence of scientific inquiry, "a statement of known facts for the information of persons to whom they are not known, but who, as worshippers of the god in question, ought to know the deeds whereby he has made himself manifest."[13] In the Western historiographic tradition distinguished by some of the writers he quotes verbatim, Pierre de la Palu himself stands out only as a noteworthy exception.[14]

Kaeppeli and P. A. Amargier, in Monumenta ordinis fratrum praedicatorum historica, 22 and 24 (Rome, 1949 and 1961), unfortunately the only printed text of the latter part of the *Flores chronicorum* is that published by L. A. Muratori, *Rerum italicarum scriptores*, III, pt. 1 (Milan, 1723), 351–684.

12. An informed discussion of the various medieval stories of the two friends is MacEdward Leach's introduction to *Amis and Amiloun*, E.E.T.S. 203 (London, 1937). The Latin version of the *Vita* given by La Palu is very close to the text of a thirteenth-century manuscript from St. Bertin published by F. J. Mone, in *Anzeiger für Kunde der teutschen Vorzeit*, v (1836), cols. 146–160. The story of the column of fire appears in *articulus* 107, 2 of the *Liber*. But why both La Palu and the scribe of the Lea MS. were so fascinated by the bloody story of Amis and Amiloun that they included it in a work in which its presence is most strange remains a mystery.

13. *The Idea of History* (Oxford, 1946), pp. 14–15.

14. Since this article went to press, I have received from Mlle. Elizabeth Dunan, to whom I am again happy to express my thanks for checking material in Parisian manuscripts, some notes comparing Bibliothèque Sainte-Geneviève MS. 865 with Lea MS. 45. Her work shows that Kohler's description (see above, note 8) is in error, that the later manuscript in the Bibliothèque Sainte-

Geneviève contains no material which does not also appear in the Lea MS., and that the two manuscripts "semblent avoir une source commune." More particularly, it should be recorded that MS. 865 contains *articuli* 105–112 (pp. 1–47), then an article numbered "Centesimus vigesimus secundus" (pp. 47–55), which is article 192 of the Lea MS., and then *articuli* 113–115 (pp. 56–72), which are the same as articles 193–195 of the Lea MS. Numerous differences between the two manuscripts make clear that any future editor should take account of both texts.

APPENDIX

Text of the headings of *articuli* and *conclusiones* in the
Liber bellorum Domini by Pierre de La Palu

The text which follows is given as it appears in University of Pennsylvania MS. Lea 45. In this transcription a differentiation has been made between *u* and *v*, and in some places *t* has been used in place of *c*, since the scribe has often been inconsistent and ambiguous in the form used for writing *t* (or *c*). Capitalization has been regularized, and abbreviations have been silently expanded. The scribe has been inconsistent in the use of a period and a virgule where we would use a comma, and I have regularized such instances by the use of commas. In a few places where the scribe has written *j* where a vowel is needed, a change to *i* has been made.

[105] Centesimus quintus articulus prime partis de bello Domini contra quosdam Sarracenos et contra Albigenses hereticos tam gladio spirituali quam materiali habet tres conclusiones: [fol. 1–2]

[1] Prima de legatione duodecim abbatum et Guallonis diaconis cardinalis contra Albigenses.[1]

[2] Secunda de peregrinatione nostrorum contra terram Albigensium.[2]

[3] Tertia de Memilini regis et Albigensium destructione.[3]

[106] Centesimus sextus articulus prime partis iterum de bello Domini contra Albigenses et Mediolanenses tunc scismathico hereticis et scismaticis faventes habet tres conclusiones: [fol. 2–3]

[1] Prima de bello Papiensium contra Mediolanenses tunc hereticos et scismathicos eximentes.[4]

[2] Secunda de bello nostrorum contra Albigenses et nece regis Arragonum.[5]

[3] Tertia de captione civitatis Avinionensis per regem Ludovicum.[6]

[107] Centesimus septimus articulus prime partis de bellis Simonis comitis Montis Fortis contra hereticos Albigenses habet tres conclusiones: [fol. 3–4ᵛ]

[1] Prima conclusio, quomodo captis civitatibus Biterris et Carcassone ab exercitu cruce signatorum, dux belli contra infideles Symon comes

---

1. Vincent of Beauvais, *Speculum historiale* (Strassburg, ca. 1473), bk. 30, ch. 93. I have used the former Phillipps copy in the Huntington Library (Copinger 6245).
2. Ibid., bk. 30, ch. 103.
3. Ibid., bk. 31, ch. 2.
4. Ibid., bk. 31, ch. 7.
5. Ibid., bk. 31, ch. 9.
6. Ibid., bk. 31, ch. 128.

Montis Fortis est ab omnibus constitutus.[7]

[2] Secunda conclusio de multis hereticis et castris que cepit idem comes in diocesibus Albigensi, Carcassonensi, Tholosana, et de columpna ignis apparente super corporibus aliquorum ab hereticalibus occisorum.[8]

[3] Tertia de aliis castris ab eodem comite captis, et Tholosa obcessa sed non capta.[9]

[108] Centesimus octavus articulus adhuc de bellis Symonis comitis Montis Fortis habet tres conclusiones: [fol. 4^v–7]

[1] Prima de victoria eius mirabili apud castrum Maurelli.[10]

[2] Secunda de castris aliis ab eo captis et quomodo in consilio celebrato in Montepessulano est in principem et dominum Tholose totiusque terre acquisite electus comes Symon Montis Fortis et per papam confirmatus.[11]

[3] Tertia de regis Francie Ludovici adiutorio.[12]

[109] Centesimus nonus articulus adhuc de bellis predicti comitis et fratris sui habet tres conclusiones: [fol. 7–9]

[1] Prima quomodo eidem comiti fuit adiudicatus per consilium generale et regem Francie comitatus Tholosanus, et quidquid acquisierat in illis partibus contra hereticos dimicando.[13]

[2] Secunda quomodo pro hiis opportuit fratrem eius et filium pugnare, et pacta quidem inire cum adversariis minus bona.[14]

[3] Tertia de iterata pugna comitis et morte eiusdem, et vana obsidione filii in qua fuit occisus alter filius comitis Montis Fortis.[15]

[110] Centesimus decimus articulus prime partis de bellis Ludovici regis contra eosdem Albigenses habet tres conclusiones: [fol. 9–10^v]

[1] Prima quomodo Ludovicus cepit Marmandam, et obsedit sed non cepit Tholosam, et de aggravatione guerre a rege.[16]

[2] Secunda de captione Avinionis plenius descripta quam superius.[17]

---

7. Bernard Gui, *Flores chronicorum*, anno 1209, in L. A. Muratori, *Rerum italicarum scriptores*, III, pt. 1 (Milan, 1723), 481.

8. Ibid., annis 1210–1211, ed. Muratori, pp. 481–482.

9. Ibid., annis 1211–1212, ed. Muratori, p. 482 (omitting paragraph concerning Miramolinus).

10. Ibid., anno 1213, ed. Muratori, pp. 482–483.

11. Ibid., anno 1214, ed. Muratori, p. 484; the blank in the second column should be *quindena*.

12. Ibid., anno 1215, ed. Muratori, pp. 484–485.

13. Ibid., anno 1215, ed. Muratori, p. 485.

14. Ibid., anno 1216, ed. Muratori, pp. 485–486.

15. Ibid., anno 1217, ed. Muratori, p. 568, followed by Vincent of Beauvais, *Spec. hist.*, bk. 31, ch. 85.

16. Bernard Gui, annis 1219–1224, with numerous omissions, ed. Muratori, pp. 568–569.

17. Ibid., anno 1226, ed. Muratori, pp. 569–570.

[3] Tertia de ordinationibus regis et legati pro fide et libertatibus ecclesie, et de regis morte.[18]

[111] Centesimus undecimus articulus prime partis de bellis et pace Albigensium Dei potentia domitorum habet quatuor conclusiones: [fol. 10^v–12^v]

[1] Prima de captione castri quod Beteca dicitur et castri Sarasseni et Montogio.[19]

[2] Secunda de obsidione Tholose et talatione [sic] et destructione omnium extra muros.[20]

[3] Tertia de pace et reconsiliatione comitis Tholosani.[21]

[4] Quarta de pace et captione Montis Securi, quod erat refugium hereticorum et omnium malorum.[22]

[112] Centesimus duodecimus articulus de bellis sancti Ludovici citra mare in quibus adiutus est pro quo pugnaturus erat ultra mare habet tres conclusiones: [fol. 12^v–15]

[1] Prima de discentione baronum Francie a rege Ludovico juniore.[23]

[2] Secunda de rebellione contra eundem regem in diocesibus Narbonensi et Carcass[onensi].[24]

[3] Tertia de itinere Ludovici regis in Pictaviam.[25]

[192] Centesimus nonagesimus secundus de destructione murorum Narbone et Tholose et comitatu Tholosano per papam et regem dato comiti Montis Fortis et rebellione comitis filii comitis Tholosani habet quinque conclusiones: [fol. 15–18]

[1] Prima quod muri Narbonenses ceperunt dirui de mandato legati et Ludovici primogeniti regis contra voluntatem archiepiscopi et civium.[26]

[2] Secunda de dirutione murorum Tholose et redditu Ludovici in

---

18. Ibid., anno 1226, extract, ed. Muratori, p. 570, followed by Vincent of Beauvais, *Spec. hist.*, bk. 31, ch. 129. This reference to the *Speculum historiale* is to the printed edition I have used. La Palu's text reads "libro xxxi°, capitulo c," indicating either an error on his part or another version of Vincent's *Speculum*.
19. Bernard Gui, annis 1226–1227, ed. Muratori, p. 571.
20. This and the following *conclusio* are taken from Bernard Gui, anno 1228, ed. Muratori, pp. 571–572, a text which contains long passages from Guillaume de Puylaurens, ed. Bouquet, *Recueil des historiens*, XIX, 219 and 223.
21. The break between *conclusiones* 2 and 3 is not marked in the text, but a marginal annotation suggests that it should fall on fol. 11^v in the quotation from Guillaume de Puylaurens, beginning "Interea venerabilis abbas Grandis Silve...."
22. Bernard Gui, anno 1244, ed. Muratori, p. 590, containing a passage from Guillaume de Puylaurens, ch. 46, ed. Bouquet, *Recueil*, XX, 770.
23. Vincent of Beauvais, *Spec. hist.*, bk. 31, ch. 130.
24. Bernard Gui, annis 1240 and 1242, ed. Muratori, pp. 574 and 589.
25. Vincent of Beauvais, *Spec. hist.*, bk. 31, ch. 148.
26. Pierre des Vaux-de-Cernay, *Historia Albigensis* (see article above, n. 8), par. 560–563, first sentence.

Franciam et legati in Romam, et terra commissa comiti Montis Fortis et captione Castrinovi.[27]

[3] Tertia quomodo Innocentius papa comitatum Tholosanum in consilio generali dedit comiti Montisfortis, et quomodo idem comes tamquam fidei deffensor a clero et populo ubique est honorifice susceptus, et a rege Francie in ducem Narbonensem et totius alterius terre per crucesignatos acquisite in dominium confirmatus est.[28]

[4] Quarta de occupatione provincie per Raymundum filium comitis condam Tholosani, que terra erat per consilium generale commendata comiti Montis Fortis, et de obsidione Bellicadri.[29]

[5] Quinta de captione Belle Gardie, et obsidione burgi Bellicadri contra hostes de burgo castrum obsidentes, de crudelitate hostium, quomodo captos clericos morte turpissima occidebant, suspendebant, mutilabant, cum machinis proiciebant.[30]

[193] Centesimus nonagesimus tertius de perditione Bellicadri et captione Castri Granarii et quibusdam aliis habet quinque conclusiones: [fol. 18–21]

[1] Prima de captione Bellicadri ab hostibus nostris obcessis inde exeuntibus, et cum superlectili sua tota, et quod comes noster diruit muros et turres Tholose, et quod cives Sancti Egidii apostate receperunt filium comitis condampnati. Propter quod abbas et conventus Corpus Christi de cathedra extrahentes nudis pedibus de villa processionaliter exierunt, villa suposita ecclesiastico interdicto.[31]

[2] Secunda de gravi obsidione Montis Granerii, quod castrum nostris dampna plurima inferebat, et non solum inexpugnabile, sed etiam inaccessibile videbatur, et maxime tunc temporis non tam penam quam martirum obsidentibus imminebat.[32]

[3] Tertia de captione et munitione Castri Granerii obcessis exeuntibus cum armis suis, et de appelatione ville Sancti Egidii ad legatum contra comitem nobilem Montis Fortis, qui appelationem detulit et ab illorum inpugnatione destitit, sed postquam legatus illos et alios rebelles et blasphemos excommunicavit, comes circum circa fere omnia castra cepit.[33]

[4] Quarta de iniuria ab hostibus fidei facta legato sedis apostolice contra quem septem vel octo quarellos proiecerunt, unum de sua familia vulneraverunt, et de turre Draconenti spelunca latronum super Rodanum quam comes cepit et diruit.[34]

---

27. Ibid., par. 563, second sentence, to 569.
28. Ibid., par. 570–573.
29. Ibid., par. 574–576 (p. 270, line 7).
30. Ibid., par. 576 (p. 270, line 7) to 582.
31. Ibid., par. 583–587.
32. Ibid., par. 588–589.
33. Ibid., par. 590–594.
34. Ibid., par. 595.

[5] Quinta de transitu Rodani mirabili, per quem territi sunt hostes fidei, et de compositione pacis inter comitem nostrum et Ademarum de Pictavia.[35]

[194] Centesimus nonagesimus quartus de proditione Tholose et Montis Albani et secunda obsidione Tholose et quibusdam miraculis que in ibi [sic] contigerunt habet quatuor conclusiones: [fol. 20ᵛ–22ᵛ]

[1] Prima de proditione Tholosanorum qui comitem deponitum receperunt, contra quos venerunt frater et filius comitis ad deffendendum munitiones que castrum Narbone a civibus appellatur.[36]

[2] Secunda de alia obsidione Tholose, quam comes ipse fecit, dum enim armatus sedensque super equo suo falerato navem intrare vellet ad fluvium Garone transeundum, eques cum equo cecidit in profundum aque, et eum ut mortuus plangeretur, subito ad celum manibus iunctis et erectis apparuit super aquam, qui tamen a suis in navem cum gaudio est susceptus.[37]

[3] Tertia de proditione frustratoria hominum Montis Albani, quia cum ipsi cum Tholosanis nocte senescallum comitis cum suis in lectis capere decrevissent illi tumultu invadentium excitati, se armantes, et in hostes irruentes omnes fugarunt, et quidam de muris precipitaverunt se ipsos. Cum autem Tholosani exeuntes unum militem cum uno socio obviante inclusissent et comes cum uno socio ad liberandum millitem occurisset, ab eis hinc inde aggressus se deffendit, quousque sui de exercitu venerunt, et hostes ad urbem retrocedere compulerunt.[38]

[4] Quarta de captione miraculosa burgi cum enim nostri fuissent a burgo depulsi, subito tanta pluvia inundavit, quod pontes sunt rupti, muri dissipati, et nostri burgum libere sunt ingressi.[39]

[195] Centesimus nonagesimus quintus articulus et ultimus de crudelitate Tholosanorum et morte preciosa comitis nobilis Montis Fortis et successorum eius primogenito suo et quibusdam aliis habet quatuor conclusiones: [fol. 22ᵛ–24]

[1] Prima de crudelitate Tholosanorum alias inaudita, quia nostros captos etiam clericos et sacerdotes diversis suppliciis perimebant mutilantes, vivos sepelientes, concremantes, sagittantes, cum machinis ad nostros proicientes, et lapiddes contra cardinalem ad castrum Narbonensem, quando sciebant missarum solempnia celebrari.[40]

[2] Secunda de ultimo bello comitis Montis Fortis in quo apparuit eius strenuitas unde missam audiens, suumque Redemptorem sacramentaliter

---

35. Ibid., par. 596–599.
36. Ibid., par. 600.
37. Ibid., par. 601–605.
38. Ibid., par. 606–606A.
39. Ibid., par. 606B.
40. Ibid., par. 606C–606D.

aspiciens flexis genibus et manibus elevatis in celum, eoque viso, dixit, "Nunc dimittis servum tuum, Domine, in pace etc." Interim autem exercitus noster pugnabat contra Tholosanos, et missa finita comes nobilis iterum subiungit, "Libera me, Domine, a tribulationibus et angustiis huius mundi, et me servum tuum fac ad evangelicam vitam pervenire," et tunc ait astantibus, "Eamus et pro Christo martirium subeamus, qui pro nobis mortem suscipere non expavit."[41]

[3] Tertia de comitis morte gloriosa, vel magis de victoria martiris preciosa, qui singulis diebus confitens, et ab obcessis ex quinque sagittis primo confixus, ad instar quinque plagarum Christi, ac ad instar prothomartiris Stephani lapidatus petra machine, super galeam in capite letaliter percussus, bis suum pectus percutiens, Deoque et beate Marie virgini se commendans, in Domino feliciter obdormivit.[42]

[4] Quarta de successore eius primogenito Amalrico, qui paterne probitatis per omnia imitator, licet obsidionem Tholosanam neccesse habuerit dimittere, tamen in omnibus aliis strenue se habuit suos potenter deffendens hostes suadens, destruens et prosternens. Ludovicus autem primogenitus regis Francie cum multis nobilibus veniens in auxilium comitis assumpsit signum crucis in pectore contra hereticos Albigenses, et in hoc terminatur totus liber.[43]

[142] Centesimus quadragesimus secundus articulus de bellis Domini per Amelium et Amicum Christi milites et martires gloriosos, et primo quo ad historie fundamentum habet tres conclusiones: [fol. 24^v-25]

[1] Prima quomodo parentes Amelii et Amici cum parvulis baptizandis in via Dei providentia ad[i]uvati Romam, simul corpore et animo pervenerunt.[44]

[2] Secunda quomodo pueris a summo pontifice honorifice baptizatis, datis eis ciphis paribus ligneis auro et gemmis ornatis ad propria sunt reversi.

[3] Tertia de documentis Bericani militis que moriens dedit Amico filio suo, a quo mortuus honorifice est sepultus.

[143] Centesimus quadragesimus tertius articulus de eodem, quomodo Amelius et Amicus se querentes et invenientes in curia regis Francorum sunt promoti, habet tres conclusiones: [fol. 25-26^v]

[1] Prima quomodo Amicus ab hereditate paterna et patria expulsus querens Amelium comitem, et ab eo quesitus, tandem cum hospitis sui filia nuptias celebravit.

41. Ibid., par. 607–609.
42. Ibid., par. 610–612.
43. Ibid., par. 613–620.
44. From here to the end of the manuscript, La Palu gives the text of the *Vita sanctorum Amici et Amelii* in a form very close to that published by F. J. Mone (see article above, n. 12), though with different paragraph divisions. La Palu's contribution is the detailed summary which appears in his headings.

[2] Secunda quomodo Amelius et Amicus mutuo se querentes peregrinum medium habuerunt, qui Amelium computans propter formam corporis indissimilem utriusque, Amicum misit Parisius ut ibi Amelium inveniret.

[3] Tertia quomodo sibi Parisius occurrentes, seque minime agnoscentes, qui se invicem agnoscentes fedus amicitie renovantes, et confirmantes juramento corporaliter prestito super sanctorum reliquias, quas in ense suo Amelius deferebat, simul curiam regis adierunt, a quo honorifice recepti, probitate morum suorum omnium gratiam obtinentes Amicus regis chamerarius et Amelius eiusdem dapifer sunt effecti.

[144] Centesimus quadragesimus quartus articulus de eodem, quomodo Amicus pugnans pro Amelio contra Aldericum illum vicit, adiutus amicitia caritatis, habet tres conclusiones: [fol. 26^v-28]

[1] Prima quomodo Amelius in curia regis remanens contra consilium Amici ad uxorem redentis, filiam regis oppressit, et cum Alderico proditore fedus iniens ab eo super hoc acturus duellum offerens, nullum adiutorem nisi piam reginam Hildegaldem potuit invenire, et tali pacto quod nisi Amelius ad diem assignatam rediret, regina regis thoro totaliter privaretur.

[2] Secunda quomodo invento Amico infortunium suum exponens, eius consilio, mutato habitu, ad domum eius ivit, uxoris osculum respuit, in lecto inter se et uxorem ipsam ensem nudum semper tenuit, donec Amicus qui loco eius duellum facturus erat in curia regis ad probandum veniens, fidem eum tenuisse cognovit.

[3] Tertia quomodo adveniente statuto die duelli Aldericus reginam quasi consciam stupri a thoro regis separare modis omnibus satagebat, que superveniente Amico loco Amelii cum viduis et virginibus Deo causam suam et filie cum precibus et lacrimis et elemosinis commendabat. Aldericus vero persuasus ab Amico quem Amelium credebat, ab incepta criminatione desistere, noluit acquiescere, jurans illum regis filiam violasse, Amico jurante illum mentitum. Tunc in campo devictus est capite amputato ab Amico, quem omnes astantes Amelium comitem extimabant.

[145] Centesimus quadragesimus quintus articulus de consequentibus ad victoriam Amici, et primo de prosperitate Amelii et adversitate Amici, habet quinque conclusiones: [fol. 28-29]

[1] Prima quomodo rex dedit in uxorem cum magna dote filiam suam Amelio comiti.

[2] Secunda quomodo Amicus lepra percussus, uxorique exosus, que machinata est plurimum in mortem Amici mariti eius, qualiter cum cipho Romano delatus est in castrum suum Bericanum.

[3] Tertia quomodo a familia patris servis suis verberatis non est admissus sed repulsus, sicut Job dicens, etc.

[4] Quarta quomodo a paterinis suis Rome et a summo pontifice

benigne susceptus est.

[5] Quinta quomodo fame orta Rome portatus a servis ad Amelium cum cipho, per consimilem siphum agnitus, quia species vultus eius propter morbum perierat, receptus est ab Amelio et regis filia agnoscentibus eius beneficia, et ab eis humanissime tractatus.

[146] Centesimus quadragesimus sextus articulus, quomodo pro salute Amici ad mandatum angeli Amelius duos filios suos infantes propriis manibus decollavit, habet tres conclusiones: [fol. 29-29^v]

[1] Prima quomodo angelus precepit Amico vix credenti quod peteret ab Amelio ut filios suos interficeret, quorum sanguine ipsum aspergeret et sanaretur, sicut Deus propter eum mori voluit, ut eius sanguine nos mundaret.

[2] Secunda quomodo Amicus invitus visionem Amelio retulit et ille affectu naturali egre tulit.

[3] Tertia quomodo Amelius non solum occidere voluit ut Abraham filium suum unum ad mandatum Domini sed duos filios licet cum dolore nimio interfecit, sine hoc quod ut haberet ut Habraham spem resurrexionis.

[147] Centesimus quadragesimus septimus articulus prime partis de mirabili effectu mortis puerorum pro custodienda fidelitate et ad mandatum Domini occisorum ut patuit per effectum, habet tres conclusiones: [fol. 30-31^v]

[1] Prima quomodo Amicus aspersus ab Amelio sanguine filiorum mundatus est non naturaliter sed miraculose a lepra.

[2] Secunda quomodo Deus miraculose illos pueros suscitavit cicatricibus in collo eorum remanentibus in testimonium miraculi perpetrati, quo facto parentes castitatem usque ad obitum servaverunt.

[3] Tertia quomodo uxor nequam Amici a diabolo vexata et precipitata expiravit, ut Amicus exercitum movens Bericanos obsedit, et deinceps in bello subegit, primogenitum Amelii secum tenens et in paterna domo restitutus. Et ecce quomodo Deus vult inviolabiter fidem amicitie observari, et observatam quomodo remunerat etiam in hac vita. Deus enim Amicum in bello servans, a lepra sanavit postmodum virtuose; Amelium a culpa et infamia liberans, filiamque regis sibi desponsans filios pro amicitia mortuos suscitavit. Et econtra quomodo ipse odit fidem violantes, Aldericus infideliter secreta revelans in duello ab Amico occiditur; uxor Amico viro suo fidem abnegans diaboli potestati subicitur.

[148] Centesimus quadragesimus octavus articulus de bello Domini per Karolum regem Francorum contra Desiderium regem Longobardorum oppressorem Romanorum in quo occisi sunt inter ceteros Amelius et Amicus, habet sex conclusiones: [fol. 30^v-32^v]

[1] Prima quo Karolus rex Francorum ab Adriano papa invitatus, Desiderium regem amicabiliter monuit, promittens etiam aurum et

argentum, ut ablata ab ecclesia Romana beatorum Petri et Pauli apostolorum restitueret pacemque daret, quod ille facere recusavit, occurrens cum excercitu ad montes, per quos Karolus transiturus erat.

[2] Secunda quomodo Karolo secundo et tertio rogante que ad pacem sunt, per nuntios missos regi Desiderio, ipse omnia contempnens Karolum audacter ad prelium expectabat, sed divina immi[n]ente gratia, ipse cum suo excercitu territus fugam adiit.

[3] Tertia quomodo Karolus cum multo maiore exercitu insequens Desiderium cum ipso tribus diebus pugnavit, nec vincere potuit paucis Longobardis, tot et tantis Francis et Theutonicis viriliter resistentibus, et adhuc ad prelium animatis.

[4] Quarta quomodo Franci a Karolo animati fortius pugnaverunt, et multis hinc inde occisis, Amicus et Amelius Deo digni milites obierunt, fugatumque Desiderium cum reliquo excercitu Karolus Papie obsedit.

[5] Quinta de sepultura interfectorum in ecclesiis a rege et regina fabricatis, et quomodo Amico et Amelio seorsum sepultis, sarcofagum unius ad sarcofagum alterius angelicis manibus est delatum, et quomodo in vita dilexerunt se, ita et in morte non sunt separati.

[6] Sexta quomodo Deus pestem in civitate obcessa misit, propter quam Karolus eam cepit, Desideriumque regem captum cum uxore in Franciam secum duxit, et sic Romanam ecclesiam ab illius tirannide liberavit.

9

'Nostre Franceis n'unt talent de fuïr': the Song of Roland and the Enculturation of a Warrior Class

During the German siege of Paris in December 1870, a learned and patriotic medievalist, Gaston Paris, delivered a set of lectures at the Collège de France on *La Chanson de Roland et la nationalité française*.[1] It would now be timely for a specialist in contemporary history and literature to prepare another study on the *Song of Roland* and modern nationalism, particularly in the period of World War I. Influential historians have blamed the newspapers and the popular press for inflaming public opinion on the eve of the Great War.[2] That 'yellow journalism' helped to indoctrinate the masses who marched enthusiastically to war cannot be doubted, but scholars and professors also played their part in the movement, and while the press harangued the future foot soldiers, the academic elite was addressing the officer class. Every *poilu* knew about Joan of Arc, but the officers had also learned in their *lycées* of the valor of the heroes of Roncevaux. While the greater part of this paper is devoted to the social and political values conveyed by the *Chanson* in the Middle Ages, the use of literature to buttress values can conveniently be illustrated by

---

* This is a revised version of a paper presented on October 6, 1978 at the conference *Roncevaux 778-1978* held at the Pennsylvania State University. The author wishes to express his gratitude to the organizers and the participants at that fruitful gathering. In addition, he owes special thanks to Professor Joseph J. Duggan of the University of California at Berkeley for generous bibliographic and critical assistance, and to Professor James W. Greenlee of Northern Illinois University for primary research on modern aspects of the topic. Besides the older, standard tools of *Roland* scholarship, I have made extensive and generally unacknowledged use of Duggan's *A Guide to Studies on the 'Chanson de Roland'*, Research Bibliographies and Checklists, 15 (London, 1976) with mimeographed supplements supplied by the compiler, and Gerard J. Brault, *The Song of Roland: An Analytical Edition*. 2 vols. (University Park, Pa., and London, 1978).

[1] Printed in his *La Poésie du moyen âge: leçons et lectures*. 2 vols. (I cite the 7th ed. of 1913), I, 87-118; *cf.* the partial English trans., *Patriotism vs Science* (New York, 1935).

[2] Sidney B. Fay, *The Origins of the World War*, 2 vols. (New York, 1928), I, 47-49: G. Lowes Dickinson *The International Anarchy, 1904-1914* (New York and London, 1926), pp. 40-47.

some reference to the *Song* in more modern times.

A dozen French translations of the *Roland* appeared between 1870 and 1914 and in 1880 it was assigned officially as a 'texte classique à l'usage des élèves de seconde.'[3] In 1900 a professor at the Lycée Henri IV told his audience at the École Spéciale Militaire at Saint-Cyr, 'La *Chanson de Roland* est notre *Iliade*' and concluded, 'Elle n'est pas seulement un sujet d'etude pour nos esprits: c'est une des sources vives où nous devons retremper nos âmes.'[4] During the summer of 1918 a professor at the École Normale of Fontenay-aux-Roses urged future teachers, when reading to future Rolands and Olivers from the *Chanson*, to show 'le lien toujours vivace qui joint au passé le présent' and the ideals inherited from 'nos aïeux du Moyen Age,' including 'ardent amour de la patrie,' 'culte souverain de l'honneur', and 'crainte de forfaire et d'être honni.'[5]

Joseph Bédier's love of medieval France and contempt for German culture, expressed in the great *Légendes épiques* he first published between 1908 and 1913, was shared widely by and with his countrymen.[6] Five days after Germany declared war on France, a friend of Charles Péguy, editorializing in a Parisian Catholic daily, offered his readers two inspirational (if technically incongruous) quotations, '*Finis Germaniae*' and the invocation of the Carolingian Salic (and therefore, Germanic) Law, 'Vive le Christ qui aime les Francs.'[7] Battle strategies for the war were created by military theorists like Ardent du Picq and the enthusiastic Colonel Grandmaison, rather than medievalists and their sympathizers,

---

[3] On Léon Gautier's classroom text and translation see Stephen G. Nichols, Jr., 'Poetic Reality and Historical Illusion in the Old French Epic,' *French Review*, 43 (1969), 23. In Rennes in 1889 students were asked to respond to the question, 'En quel sens la *Chanson de Roland* a-t-elle pu être appelée nationale?': see Abbé Blanoeil, *Baccalauréat: Histoire de la littérature française*, 31st ed. (Nantes, 1897), p. 515 for the 'Sujets de devoirs français donnés dans différentes facultés,' with 6 of 12 questions on the chansons de geste devoted specifically to the *Roland*.

[4] *L'Armée à travers les âges: Conférences faites en 1900* (Paris, 1902), lecture on '*La Chanson de Roland* by Paul Lehugeur, pp. 65 and 102.

[5] Henri Chamard, trans., *La Chanson de Roland* (Paris, 1919), pp. iii-iv, introductory letter to his students at Fontenay-aux-Roses dated 21 August 1918.

[6] On Bédiers 'fobia antitedesca' see Luigi Foscolo Benedetto, *L'epopea di Roncisvalle* (Florence, 1941), pp. 65-66: 'La teoria del Bédier non è in fondo che un episodio della campagna germanofoba condotta dagli intellettuali di destra negli anni che precedettero la guerra mondiale, campagna de cui la guerra mondiale venne come a legittimare la violenza e la passione.'

[7] *La Croix*, August 8, 1914 (n⁰ 9633), p. 1. The editorialist, who also cited Péguy's trust in 'saint Michel, sainte Geneviève et Jeanne d'Arc', was identified only by the initials R.T. The first 'quotation' is a reformulation of the late-eighteenth-century 'Finis Poloniae.' On the second quotation, which comes from the second and longer prologue to the Lex Salica written under Pepin, see Ernst H. Kantorowicz, *Laudes Regiae* (Berkeley and Los Angeles, 1946), p. 59, who punctuates as 'vivat qui Francos diligit Christus . . .' In the *Pactus Legis Salicae*, 12, Systematischer Text (Göttingen, 1957), p. 315, Karl August Eckhardt curiously punctuates as 'vivat qui Francos diligit, Christus eorum regnum custodiat, rectores eorum det . . .'

but all shared a common sense of national heritage and spirit. The Field Regulations of November 1913 declared: 'L'armée française, revenue à ses traditions, n'admet plus, dans la conduite des opérations, d'autre loi que l'offensive,' and stated formally, 'Les batailles sont surtout des luttes morales.'[8] On the battle-ground of morale, the *Chanson de Roland* could serve as a weapon.

As preparations for war against Germany developed, the *Song* leaped the Channel and two translations appeared in England in 1907, just three years after the Anglo-French Entente. Scott Moncrieff began his own translation as a 'solace' in the summer of 1918, and John Masefield in 1918 introduced each chapter of his apologetic *Gallipoli* with a hortatory passage from the *Song of Roland*.[9] The precise links connecting literature, ideals and actions are most uncertain, for it is so difficult to distinguish the determinants of behavior from their after-the-fact justification. Nevertheless, it seems clear to me that the *Chanson* played a part in the mentality of the Great War. The use of the *Roland* in modern times, either for inspiration or for solace, may be considered a part of the process of enculturation, a process which is probably harder to understand but easier to recognize in earlier or non-Western cultures than in our own.

'*Enculturation*' is a term recently created by anthropologists as an alternative to 'socialization' to distinguish different aspects of the educational process and its relationship to cultural change. Specialists differ over the distinctions between these terms and their specific meaning, and I will not insist on a matter of definition here. But since 'socialization' may lead one to think of children learning (however well) to listen respectfully to their elders or of a page being taught not to pick his teeth in public, I have preferred to use 'enculturation' here, defined as 'the process of acquiring a world view.'[10]

Great poetry both gives pleasure and teaches. The epic transmits information about the heroic past, and in either its oral form or in

---

[8] *Decret du 28 novembre 1913 portant règlement sur la conduite des grandes unites (service des armées en campagne)* (Paris: Librairie Militaire Berger-Levrault, 1914), p. 7 and Fernand Engerand, *Le Secret de la frontière, 1815-1871-1914: Charleroi* (Paris, 1918), p. 228; Engerand appears to have cited a fuller text of the decree than that published in 1914. On Col. Grandmaison see Barbara Tuchman, *The Guns of August* (New York, 1962), pp. 33-34, and on Ardent du Picq see John Keegan, *The Face of Battle* (New York, 1976), pp. 70-71.

[9] *La Chanson de Roland adapted into English Prose*, by Henry Rieu (London, 1907), and *The Song of Roland Newly Translated into English* by Jessie Crosland (London, 1907); C. J. Scott Moncrieff, trans., *The Song of Roland* (London, 1919), often reprinted. On Masefield see Paul Fussell, *The Great War and Modern Memory* (New York and London, 1975), pp. 87 and 147.

[10] See Margaret Mead 'Socialization and Enculturation,' *Current Anthropology*, 4 (1963). 184-188, and Nobuo Shimakara, 'Enculturation – A Reconsideration,' *ibid.*, 11 (1970), 143-154. The definition given here is that of Philip E. Leis, *Enculturation and Socialization in an Ijaw Village* (New York, 1972), p.5.

successive reworked texts, this information can change with circumstances. In non-literate societies, we are told by two field anthropologists, 'what continues to be social relevance is stored in the memory while the rest is usually forgotten', and in proof of this point they note how the Tiv people of Nigeria changed their 'traditional' genealogies over forty years. As a second example they cite the case of the state of Gonja in northern Ghana, which was divided into seven divisional chiefdoms in the early part of this century, at which time the local myths indicated that the founder of the state, Jakpa, had seven sons; sixty years later two of the divisional chiefdoms had disappeared and in the collective memory of the people Jakpa was said to have had only five sons.[11] We should expect analogous changes in an evolving story like that of Roland.

Information such as that just mentioned about genealogy and lineage is useful to a society in understanding its past or present political organization, but the transmission of techniques seems to play a very minor part in epic poetry. A young warrior would never learn how to fight in battle formation from hearing the *Song of Roland*.[12] He would not even learn how to use his sword. The 'fragment' from The Hague, dated about the year 1000, describes an 'epic stroke' which splits the middle of the opponent's head and body and even cleaves the spine of his horse.[13] This overhand stroke is used repeatedly in the *Chanson de Roland* (except that in the Baligant episode Charlemagne splits only the emir's head), the Bayeux tapestry depicts the beginning swing of such a stroke, and its consequences can be seen in numerous medieval illustrations.[14] Now if one reflects on this stroke, it is better suited to legendary heroes than to real-life survivors. If a warrior raises his arm like a tennis player about to serve, he exposes the vulnerable area of the armpit, loses the ability to

---

[11] Jack (John R.) Goody and Ian Watt, 'The Consequences of Literacy,' *Comparative Studies in Society and History*, 5 (1963), 307-310.

[12] On the need to fight in battle formation see R. C. Smail, *Crusading Warfare (1097-1193)* (Cambridge, Eng., 1956), pp. 126-130. Once the shock of a cavalry attack had occurred, however, combat between mounted warriors was necessarily individual or fought by small groups of men: see Brault, *Song of Roland*, I, 417, nn., 76, 80. The poem presents the 'new' method of using a lance without showing how to do it; see D. J. A. Ross, 'L'originalité de "Turoldus"': le maniement de la lance,' *Cahiers de Civilisation Médivale*, 6 (1963), 127-138.

[13] On the Fragment see Paul Aebischer, 'Le Fragment de La Haye, les problèmes, qu'il pose et les enseignements qu'il donne', *Zeitschrift für romanische Philologie*, 72 (1957), 20-37, and on the stroke itself, Menéndez Pidal, *Chanson*, pp. 376-378. According to the Pseudo-Turpin, Charlemagne characteristically used the full stroke; see *Historia Karoli Magni et Rotholandi*, chi. 20, ed. C. Meredith-Jones (Paris, 1936), p. 177.

[14] Many illustrations of split heads and even bodies are reproduced in Rita Lejeune and Jacques Stiennon, *La Légende de Roland dans l'art du moyen âge*, 2 vols. (Paris and Brussels, 1966), as well as D. D. R. Owen, *The Legend of Roland: A Pageant of the Middle Ages* (London, 1973). In the Bayeux tapestry the beginning of the stroke appears in the scene labeled 'Hic ceciderunt simul,' reproduced in Brault. *Song of Roland* 1, plate 49, *Cf.* the sword realistically raised for a cavalry thrust in the late twelfth-century *Rolandslied*, Heidelberg University, Pal. germ. 112, fol. 74. reproduced by Brault, *Song of Roland*, 1, plate 51.

parry all but a similar stroke, and gains nothing from the forward movement of the horse. According to those of my students who have fought with heavy swords on foot (I have not), a sweeping side-stroke is more powerful than an overhead smash, because it can be delivered with the torque of the whole body. And for a mounted warrior, a thrust is preferable to a cut, and the 'epic stroke' is particularly dangerous, because if the opponent veers, the stroke would then descend on the head of the rider's own horse. In short, the *Chanson de Roland* is not a manual of practical use for either a medieval warrior or a modern historian. It teaches not skills but values or morale. This is surely what the author of a thirteenth-century sermon had in mind when he wrote of the use of the deeds of Charles, Roland, and Oliver 'to give spirit to the audience.'[15]

The complex problems of dating, of different chronological 'layers' in the Oxford text, and of different versions of the *Chanson* which were produced and written after 'Turoldus' and completed his epic, are troublesome issues for any commentator. At this point I should say that I find compelling the major arguments of 'traditionalism' that the Oxford text does contain much material which entered the collective or poetic memory in earlier centuries, such as the 'epic stroke' or the episode of Charlemagne, like Joshua, making the sun stand still outside Zaragoza as reported in the *Annales Anianenses*.[16] Because it deals with traditional material, the poem of 'Turoldus' is notoriously hard to date precisely. The reference to Saracen battle drums in the poem helps to place its composition after 1086,[17] but beyond that point controversy rages. Some paleographers have dated the Oxford manuscript as late as ca. 1170, allowing other critics to place its composition in the 1150s. Others consider that the manuscript could have been written as early as 1125 and not later than 1150, thus ruling out a mid-twelfth-century composition and placing the text either shortly before the First Crusade or within a generation or so after.[18] For the purposes of this paper, dealing as it does

---

[15] 'Solent gesta Caroli, Rolandi et Oliveri referri ad animandum audientes' in a sermon attributed to Nicholas de Biard, cited by Edmond Faral in 'A propos de la *Chanson de Roland*', in *La Technique littéraire des chansons de geste* (Paris, 1959), pp. 277-278.

[16] The 'traditionalist' position is, of course, forcefully stated by Menéndez Pidal, *Chanson*, who discusses the Annals of Aniane on pp. 305-311. For those who respond to this particular point that the manuscript of this text was written in the early twelfth century and *could* have been 'contaminated' by the *Roland* itself, Menéndez Pidal provides an answer in his reference (p. 308, note 2) to the appearance of the same phrases in a continuation of the *Chronicon Isidorianum* from the year 1017 (*MGH SS*, 13, 262).

[17] The frightening and novel use of battle drums by the Almoravids at the battle of Zalaca in 1086, (*cf.* v. 3137) is noted by Martín de Riquer, *Los Cantares de gesta franceses* (Madrid, 1952), p. 81; French trans. by I.-M. Cluzel, *Les Chansons de geste françaises* (2nd ed., Paris, 1957), pp. 75-76.

[18] As stated above (n. 17), the reference to battle drums places the text after 1086. The paleographic arguments, still unresolved, about the Oxford manuscript are whether it was

with enculturative values, the precision of dating is not of great importance, so long as one accepts the principle that some portions of the epic entered the *Chanson*, in either oral or written form, well before the twelfth century, but that in a fluid tradition early material which does not have 'social relevance,' which goes against the cultural values of a later time, will tend to drop from sight. What is certain is that even if it were first written in the late eleventh century, the *Chanson de Roland* as we have it is culturally a twelfth-century poem, copied in the twelfth century, cited by twelfth-century authors, and popular enough to give birth to translations and other versions in the twelfth and thirteenth centuries. Moreover, a host of critical studies shows that the poem of 'Turoldus' is no mere pastiche of fragments from different epochs, but was intended by its author to have a unified form and meaning.[19]

The remainder of this paper is concerned with some of the ways in which the *Chanson* might have inspired or justified the behavior of its twelfth-century audience. Among the enculturative values which the *Song of Roland* displays, the most prominent is the glorification of warfare, a 'just war,' a 'Holy War,' to be sure, but warfare all the same. I doubt if many, if indeed any *bellatores* of the period when the *Chanson* was still a living epic needed to be reassured that warfare was a proper and honorable occupation. But when one looks outside the *Chanson* and the values of the warrior class, one can see that they are in contradiction to the lingering remnants of traditional Christian pacificism, a theme of great importance in many of the Fathers and clearly expressed by the quotation in Sulpicius Severus's popular *vita* of Saint Martin of Tours, 'I am a knight

copied in the period 1125-50 (Samaran, Marichal) or whether it could have been produced as late as 1170 (Bédier, Short); see Ian Short, 'The Oxford Manuscript of the *Chanson de Roland*: A Paleographic Note, '*Romania*, 94 (1973), 221-231, and Charles Samaran. 'Sur la date approximative du *Roland* d'Oxford,' *ibid.*, pp. 523-527. The Oxford text is clearly a copy, and in his edition of *La Chanson de Roland* (Milan-Naples, 1970), p. xiii, Cesare Segre has argued that at least one copy lies between 0 and the archetype. On this point André Burger, 'Leçons fautives dans l'archétype de la *Chanson de la Roland*,' '*Mélanges E.-R. Labande* (Poitiers, 1974), pp. 77-82 has raised doubts, suggesting that 0 could have been copied directly from the text of 'Turoldus'. On the basis of the evidence currently available it appears that the Oxford text could have been composed as well as copied in the early years of the reign of Henry II, but if this is the case, the author consciously maintained an archaic style and avoided obvious contemporary allusions. For arguments for a mid-twelfth-century dating of the *Chanson* see the unscholarly but suggestive work of Émile Mireaux, *La Chanson de Roland et l'histoire de France* (Paris, 1943), pp. 79-105, who places its composition c. 1158 in the circle of Henry II Plantagenet, and the articles of Hans-Erich Keller (some of which are cited below, n. 34), who considers it was written at Saint-Denis in the circle of Suger.

[19] On the unity of the poem of Turoldus see Bédier, *Légendes épiques*, 3rd ed., III, 410-453 or more recently, Brault, *Song of Roland*, I, 47-71. A 'remanieur' could of course be an excellent, indeed inspired, author.

(*miles*) of Christ, I am not permitted to fight.'[20] Whether or not a *Song of Roland* was chanted by a Taillefer to inspire the Norman army before the battle of Hastings, the twelfth-century authors William of Malmesbury and Wace considered the *Chanson* appropriate for such an occasion.[21] While the warrior of William the Conquerer or of the succeeding period can scarcely have been expected to have puzzled over Tertullian and Basil, and presumably gave no thought to the fact that Saint Martin deserted from the Roman army, not all bishops were warriors like the poetic Turpin or the historical Odo of Bayeux, who as members of the clergy were forbidden by canon law to bear arms.[22]

Attitudes toward warfare varied, of course, and I am not sure that the Gregorian Reform itself marks a great turning point on the issue of Christian pacifism. In the early eleventh century, Bishop Hubert of Angers was excommunicated for fighting at his king's command, while Bishop Wazo of Liège did lead troops in battle, but conscientiously did so unarmed.[23] When critics, with their own ideas about the nature of Christianity (medieval or modern), call the *Chanson* a devoutly Christian epic, a *Vita* or *Passio sancti Rolandi*, we need to remember that Archbishop Turpin provided an uncanonical model for any clergy who heard the poem.

---

[20] *Vita s. Martini* c. 4, ed. Jacques Fontaine, Sources chrétiennes, 133-135 (Paris, 1967-69), I, 260: see the editor's commentary on the *militia Martini*, II, 428-538. On Martin's changing rôle as a model see Barbara H. Rosenwein, 'St. Odo's St. Martin: the uses of a model,' *Journal of Medieval History*, 4 (1978), 317-331. On Christian pacifism in general see Roland H. Bainton, 'The Early Church and War', *Harvard Theological Review*, 39 (1946), 189-212, and his *Christian Attitudes toward War and Peace* (New York, 1960).

[21] On the testimony about the song chanted before the battle see David Douglas '*The Song of Roland* and the Norman Conquest of England,' *French Studies*, 14 (1960), 99-100. How we evaluate the story of Taillefer depends in large part on whether we conclude that the so-called *Carmen de Hastingae Proelio* was written shortly after 1066 or well into the twelfth century. The latest editors of the *Carmen*, Catherine Morton and Hope Munz, have argued that the work is both early and accurate: see their *The Carmen de Hastingae Proelio of Guy, Bishop of Amiens*, Oxford Medieval Texts (Oxford, 1972), pp. xv-xxx R. H. C. Davis contends that it is neither in '*The Carmen de Hastingae Proelio,' English Historical Review* 93 (1978), 242-261. The issue appears still to be *sub judice*.

[22] The often quoted admonition of St. Ambrose against the use of weapons by the clergy (Ep. 20, *MPL* 16, 1050) appears, among many other places, in the *Decretum* of Gratian (C 23 q. 8 c. 3, ed. Friedberg, 1, 954). It should be noted that the traditional prohibition against fighting by the clergy, which the Frankish kings included in their capitularies, specifically mentioned war against the infidels.

[23] For Hubert see *The Letters and Poems of Fulbert of Chartres*, ed. Frederick Behrends, Oxford Medieval Texts (Oxford, 1976), ep. 71, pp. 118-129. The letter or tract against any fighting by the clergy usually attributed to Fulbert (*MPL* 141, ep. 112) has been shown to be a twelfth-century forgery. See Behrends, 'Two Spurious Letters in the Fulbert Collection,' *Revue bénédictine* 80 (1970), 253-275; chronologically shifted by a century, the tract's contents remain significant. On Wazo see Anselm of Liege. *Gesta episcoporum Leodiensium* c. 54-56 (*MGH SS*, 7 [1846], 221-223).

154   *Culture, Power and Personality in Medieval France*

In what I have just said about the positive value placed on warfare I noted that the war commemorated in *Roland*, unlike those in the more common epics of revolt such as *Raoul de Cambrai*, was a 'Holy War' against the infidel. Practically all medievalists agree that there is a relationship between the *Chanson* and the development of the idea of crusade, the *Entstehung des Kreuzzugsgedankens*, though the chronology of that relationship has been hotly disputed. As Carl Erdmann has put it, 'Some say that "the *Chanson de Roland* would be impossible without the First Crusade," while others maintain that "the crusade would be incomprehensible without the *Chanson de Roland*".'[25] Erdmann did not attempt to date the poem, except to state that 'the *Chanson* cannot antedate the time of Alexander II.'[26] The theme of a *bellum domini* fits both the actual historical circumstances of the invasion of Spain and the period after the renewed religious expansionism of Christian Europe in the 1060s, that is, about the time of the writing of the *Nota Emilianense*, and so is of little help in dating either the Oxford *Roland* or its predecessors. While I feel that the *Chanson* accords well with a military-religious ethos common in the late eleventh and early twelfth centuries, what strikes me most is how difficult it is to find clearly demonstratable echoes of the crusade to recover Jerusalem in a text which took its present written form well after the First Crusade.[27] Equally, it is surprising how seldom the name of *Roland* or reference to the *Chanson* appears in the extensive literature

---

[24] See Edmond Faral, 'A propos de la *Chanson de Roland*: genése et signification du personnage de Turpin,' in *La Technique littéraire des chansons de geste*, pp. 271-280. The idea that there could be a sharp distinction between secular and religious culture in the crusading period seems to me a false dichotomy, but on this topic, see Julian White, 'La *Chanson de Roland*: Secular or Religious Inspiration?' *Romania*, 84 (1963), 398-408, and Gerald Herman. 'Why Does Oliver Die before the Archbishop Turpin?' *Romance Notes*, 14 (1972-73), 376-82. Mireaux, *Chanson de Roland*, pp. 59-63, argues that the Oxford *Roland* is an anti-pseudo-Turpin in emphasizing that Turpin was a warrior rather than a simple singer of masses. Whatever the chronology, the differing rôles of Turpin suggest some sort of dialectical relationship.

[25] Erdmann, *Die Entstehung des Kreuzzugsgedankens* (Stuttgart, 1935), p. 264: I have quoted the excellent new translation with additional notes and bibliography by Marshall W. Baldwin and Walter Goffart. *The Origin of the Idea of Crusade* (Princeton, 1977), pp. 284-285. See also Hans-Wilhelm Klein, 'Der Kreuzzugsgedanke im *Rolandslied* und die neuere Rolandforschung,' *Die neueren Sprachen* 6 (1956), 265-285.

[26] *Ibid.*, p. 265; English trans. p. 285. Menéndez Pidal, *Chanson*, pp. 244-248 stresses the counterargument of Charlemagne's actual 'Holy War' mission. The reservation that not *all* medievalists are agreed on a relationship between the ideas of the *Chanson* and those of the crusading period is necessary because of the same author's emphatic statement (p. 243): 'Toutes ces idées n'appartiennent pas au temps des croisades.'

[27] Clearly there are some echoes of military experience in the eastern Mediterranean theater of operations, notably the proper names in the Baligant episode, though the critical response received by Henri Grégoire makes the precise number uncertain: see on this point Joseph J. Duggan, 'The Generation of the Episode of Baligant,' *Romance Philology*, 30 (1976), 73. The argument of Rachel P. Rindone, 'An Observation on the Dating of the Baligant Episode,' *Romance Notes*, 11 (1967-70), 181-185, seems relatively weak to me.

written in support of the crusading movement.[28] Even in the early fourteenth century, when Pierre de la Palu turned to a literary source for his treatment of Charlemagne in his *Liber Bellorum Domini*, he used the story of Amis and Amiloun.[29] The *Chanson de Roland* must have been immensely popular in the twelfth and later centuries (as manuscripts, translations, and onomastics all attest), its ethos does support the militant expansion of Christianity, but the vigor of scholarly debate over precise dating suggests that it *could* have been composed before 1095, and the relative silence of crusading sources and propaganda with respect to Roland or the epic Charlemagne indicates that contemporaries could have understood, described, and advocated crusades quite well if the *Chanson de Roland* had never existed.

Besides the positive value placed on fighting itself and on militant Christianity, a third obvious but easily misunderstood cultural value transmitted by the *Chanson* is loyalty to king and country.[30] This point too has been amply treated in our literature on the *Chanson*, and in this brief discussion I wish particularly to express a caveat about an apparent 'French' or 'Capetian' nationalism. The 'patriotic' loyalties which I think the Oxford *Roland* exemplified for its listeners were loyalty to the warrior's highest recognized ruler, the ruler who led one's army into battle, a loyalty which we may call 'feudal' whether its object was an emperor, king, duke, or count, and willingness to fight and die for one's homeland, for *Tere Majur*, the familiar theme of *pro patria mori*, whatever that homeland or *pays* actually was. In addition, the *Chanson* also stresses *imperial* authority in terms which seem particularly appropriate to the Anglo-Norman 'empire', in part because William the Conqueror ruled to some degree in a Carolingian mode.[31] It may at first seem perverse not to emphasize the

---

[28] Raoul of Caen uses the names of Roland and Oliver to praise two heroes of the First Crusade, and Ordericus Vitalis compares Guiscard to Roland: Raoul of Caen, *Gesta Tancredi*, in *Historiens des croisades. Occidentaux* (Paris, 1866), 3, 627 and Ordericus, *Historia ecclesiastica*, Bk. 7, ed. Marjorie Chibnall. Oxford Medieval Tests (Oxford, 1969), IV, 36 (ed. Le Prevost, III, 186). As Menéndez Pidal has noted (*Chanson*, pp. 234-235), references to the story of Roland are strangely lacking in vernacular poetry intended to excite crusading zeal. I am unconvinced that the speech of Urban II as reported by Robert of Reims necessarily referred to the epic rather than the historical Charlemagne and his son (as suggested by Duggan. 'Generation', p. 70), since Charles and Louis did actually 'destroy pagan kingdoms and expanded in them the boundaries of the holy Church' in campaigns againsts the Saxons and the Avars.

[29] J. F. Benton, 'Theocratic History in Fourteenth-Century France: The Liber Bellorum Domini by Pierre de la Palu,' *The [University of Pennsylvania] Library Chronicle* 40 (1974) = *Bibliographical Studies in Honor of Rudolf Hirsch* (Philadelphia, 1974), pp. 38-54.

[30] *Cf.* D. D. R. Owen, 'The Secular Inspiration of the *Chanson de Roland*,' *Speculum*, 37 (1962), 390-400.

[31] Jacques Boussard, 'La Notion de royauté sous Guillaume le Conquérant, '*Annali della Fondazione italiana per la storia amministrativa*, 4 (1967), 47-77, compares the Salisbury oath to the oaths exacted by Charlemagne (pp. 68-69) and states (p. 64) that the concept of royalty in England in 1066 was 'beaucoup plus proche de l'idéal défini par Hincmar au

importance of *dulce France* and not to argue that the author of the Oxford *Roland* was trying to inculcate loyalty to the king of France (any king, from Henry I to Louis VII, depending upon the date assigned to the text). But let us consider the historical origins and context of the poem a bit more fully.

Whatever the means of transmission, the *Song of Roland* had to have its origin in the battle, the twelve-hundredth anniversary of which was commemorated in 1978. And when that event was celebrated in song, the ruler to whom highest honor was given had to be Charlemagne, and his warriors necessarily Franks. Charlemagne, the unifier of Christian Europe, became in legend and belief a universal hero, a Christian Alexander, but once the Capetians had overthrown the Carolingians, it took a long time for the Capetian monarchy to develop a special affinity for him. His canonization in 1165 was, after all, the work of an anti-pope opposed by the French monarch and acting at the instigation of the German emperor. A prophecy created at Saint-Valéry-sur-Somme about 1040 predicted that the Capetians would hold the throne of France for seven generations, when it would return to a descendant of Charlemagne. Early in the twelfth century Hugh of Fleury and Sigebert of Gembloux both stressed the usurpation of the Capetians in their influential histories. Only at the end of the twelfth century did the *reditus ad stirpem Caroli* become a literary theme centering on Philip Augustus.[32]

IXe siècle, que de la royauté française du XIe siècle, dans laquelle le roi n'est qu'un "primus inter pares"'.

[32] Karl F. Werner, 'Die Legitimität der Kapetinger und die Entstehung des *Reditus ad stirpem Karoli*,' *Die Welt als Geschichte*, 12 (1952), 203-225. I agree with Laura Hibbard Loomis that the use of the word *auriflamma* at Saint-Denis under Philip Augustus probably derives from the influence of the *Chanson*, rather than the reverse, for *orie flambe* describes the vexillum given by Leo III to Charlemagne at Rome, whether it means 'notched standard' or 'golden flame'. See L. H. Loomis, 'The Oriflamme of France and the War-Cry "Monjoie" in the Twelfth Century.' *Studies in Art and Literature for Belle da Costa Greene* (Princeton, 1954), pp. 67-82, trans. as 'L"Oriflamme de France et le cri "Munjoie" au XIIe siècle,' *Le Moyen Âge* 65 (1965), 469-499; André Burger,'Oriflamme', *Festchrift Walther von Wartburg zum 80. Geburtstag* (Tübingen, 1968). 2, 357-363; Hans-Erich Keller, 'La Version dionysienne de la *Chanson de Roland*,' *Philologica Romanica, Erhard Lommatzsch gewidmet* (Munich, 1975), 270-275. When Carl Erdmann wrote *Kaiserfahne und Blutfahne*, Sitz. Akad. Berlin. Phil.-hist. Kl., 28 (1932) and 'Kaiserliche und päpstliche Fahnen im hohen Mittelalter,' *Quellen und Forschungen*, 25 (1933-34), 1-48, he had not yet taken account of an eleventh-century forgery (*MGH Const.* 1, 1668), which claims that Charlemagne received the *vexillum b. Petri apostoli* at Rome in 774, and the tenth-century chronicle of Benedict of San Andrea (*MGH* SS, 3, 710), which states that on his alleged trip to Jerusalem Charlemagne presented to the Holy Sepulcher a *vexillum aureum*: see *Entstehung*, pp. 179, n. 47 and 183, n. 60 (Eng. trans. pp. 195, n. 47 and 200, n. 60). M. Berger's etymology of 'notched standard' is a solution to the old problem of the color of St. Peter's standard, which according to the Lateran mosaic was a notched green banner (illustrated in Brault, *Song of Roland*, 1, pl. 60). See also Léon Gautier, *Les Épopées françaises* (Paris, 1880), 3, 124f., n. 2: *cf.* the banner *di fiamma e d'oro* in the Italian *Nerbonesi* (Bk, 1, ch. 2), cited *ibid.*, p. 639 n.

One of the literary merits of the *Roland* is that Charlemagne is a noble figure throughout, ready to become the saint placed in Heaven by Dante, and is not insulted as he is in many other *chansons*, though his comparative impotence at the trial of Ganelon may reflect this tradition.[33] It has been suggested that the *Chanson de Roland* was commissioned by Suger or one of his successors to strengthen the prestige of the Capetian monarchy, but this idea, even if it does not fall on chronological grounds, finds precious little support in the writings of Suger himself. In his student days a distinguished French medievalist set out to write a *diplôme* on 'L'idée de Charlemagne dans la pensée de Suger,' and abandoned the project when he found, as can be seen by anyone who consults the index of the *Oeuvres complètes de Suger*, that the great propagandist of Saint-Denis scarcely mentioned Charlemagne and when he did treated him as simply one more king who had the good sense to make donations to the abbey. The arguments of Professor Hans-Erich Keller, which derive a good deal of rhetorical force from repetition and the cumulation of philological detail, all too often must depend on the concept of *mystification*. 'Mystification' can be useful for a writer of religious allegory or a humorous author, like Geoffrey of Monmouth, who had to deal with split allegiances in a turbulent political setting, but it is a senseless technique for a propagandist trying to strengthen royal power, when direct writing would be so much more effective.[34]

---

[33] Karl-Heinz Bender, 'Les Métamorphoses de la royauté de Charlemagne dans les premières épopées franco-italiennes,' *Cultura Neolatina*, 21 (1961), 164-174; see also Gautier, *Épopées* III, 155-160, who expatiates indignantly on the debased image of Charlemagne in many chansons de geste, blaming the uncomplimentary portraiture on a chronological shift.

[34] Professor Keller's arguments that the Oxford *Roland* was composed about 1150 by a poet writing at Saint-Denis in the circle of Abbot Suger may be found in 'La Version dionysienne' (above, n.32); a shorter paper along the same lines, 'The *Song of Roland*: A Mid-Twelfth-Century Song of Propaganda for the Capetian Kingdom,' *Olifant*, 3 (1976), 242-258; and most recently 'La Chanson de geste et son public,' *Mélanges... offerts à Jeanne Wathelet-Willem, Marche romane* (Liége, 1978), pp. 257-285. These arguments seem to me to be unsound for three reasons: (1) as stated in note 32, there is no compelling reason to asociate the oriflamme with the banner of the Vexin preserved at Saint-Denis; (2) the statements (in *Olifant* 3, 254) that 'during the twelfth century, the Abbey of Saint-Denis was most instrumental in the ascendancy of the cult of Charlemagne in France' and that in 'the period of Suger . . . Charlemagne was used to heighten and strengthen the Capetian kingdom' are unsupported by documentation, doubtless because it is hard to find evidence to show that Suger accorded Charlemagne anything more than the respect appropriate for one of many rulers who had richly endowed his abbey; and (3) the discussion of proper names which make the *Chanson a roman à clef* depends upon 'mystification' and etymological subtleties entirely inappropriate for a work of 'propaganda'. For example, the name Pinabel 'would be a name whose meaning was easily discernible to a twelfth-century man in Southern Italy, "beautiful like a pine tree".' But of course the Oxford *Roland* was not written for an audience in Southern Italy ('this totally different world'), and we are told that the name 'could doubtless have been easily understood in Northern France, though with a different meaning – i.e. with the sense of 'membre viril' (*Olifant* 3,

The reputation of Charlemagne, as far as we can tell, never died. As the *Nota Emilianense* suggests, a *cantar de Rodlane* about Charlemagne and his peers may have existed in Castile in the eleventh century.[35] Scholars have placed the origins of the *Chanson de Roland* in areas of France as widely separated as the Midi and Brittany.[36] The existence of songs about Charlemagne in his native Germanic tongue has been postulated, though textual evidence for an early *Song of Roland* in German is as lacking as evidence for a *Chanson* in Francien dialect. For an historian unable to form an independent judgment about the philological discussions, the arguments about the 'national origin' of the *Chanson* seem analogous to those about the origin of Honorius Augustodunensis, who was born in one place and traveled a lot.[37] What is clear from translations and manuscripts is that after the beginning of the twelfth century the *Chanson de Roland* could find a welcome home in France, England, Germany, Norway, Italy, Spain, and eventually Brazil.

In short, one did not have to be French or a subject of the Capetian monarchy to enjoy and be inspired by the *Song of Roland*. The Anglo-Normanisms of the Oxford *Roland*, combined with other evidence, including the name Turoldus, have suggested to some a Norman or Anglo-Norman origin.[38] A French critic has recently written that if the author of the Oxford *Roland* was Norman or of Norman origin, he did not

---

252). Whatever the basis of Pinabel's beauty, arguments of this sort have nothing to do with whether the *Roland* was written at Saint-Denis.

Much stronger textual arguments have been made that the *Historia Karoli Magni* of Pseudo-Turpin was either written at Saint-Denis or by a cleric who favored that monastery: see the ed. of Meredith-Jones, pp. 323-333, and Ronald N. Walpole, 'Sur la *Chronique du Pseudo-Turpin*,' *Travaux de linguistique et de littérature* 3, 2 (1965), 7-18. If one is willing to accept the idea that the 'final' version of the Oxford text was composed in the 1150s, then one must also consider seriously the hypothesis of Émile Mireaux that the poem was composed not only in Angevin rather than Capetian circles but also by someone who precisely wished to contradict the version of Pseudo-Turpin (see *Chanson de Roland*, pp. 70-78). A certain, 'early' dating of the Oxford text would invalidate the theories of both Mireaux and Keller, but if a mid-twelfth-century date is permissible I find the Angevin hypothesis much more convincing than the Dionysian.

[35] Menéndez Pidal, *Chanson*, pp. 384 ff: *cf* Miquel Coll i Alentorn, 'La introducció de les llegendes epiques franceses a Catalunya,' *Coloquios de Roncesvalles* (Zaragoza, 1956), pp. 133-150.

[36] Rita Lejeune, 'La Naissance du couple littéraire "Roland et Olivier",' *Mélanges Henri Grégoire 2. Annuaire de l'Institut de Philologie et d'Histoire Orientales et Slaves*, 10 (1950), 371-401 (Midi); Gaston Paris, 'Sur la date et la patrie de la *Chanson de Roland*.' *Romania*. 11 (1882), 400-409 (Brittany).

[37] *Cf.* V. I. J. Flint, 'The Career of Honorius Augustodunensis. Some Fresh Evidence,' *Revue bénédictine*, 82 (1972), 63-86. This is only one contribution to a continuing reexamination of Honorius by a number of writers.

[38] Ettore L. Gotti, *La Chanson de Roland e i Normanni*, Bibliotheca del Leonardo 40 (Florence, 1949): Michel de Boüard, 'La Chanson de Roland et la Normandie,' *Annales de Normandie*, 2 (1952), 34-38; David C. Douglas, 'The *Song of Roland* and the Norman Conquest of England,' *French Studies*, 14 (1960), 99-116; for an objection see Thomas S.

reveal 'de véritables partis pris normands,' and that 'son idéal s'élève pourtant au-dessus de tous les particularismes, et apparaît déjà vraiment national.'[39] I would prefer either to consider the ideal of the *Chanson* supranational or to say that the term nationalism has little or no meaning in the period we are considering. In *The Battle of Maldon* Byrhtnoth, who in dying for his king and homeland exhibits much the same fierce pride and loyalty as *Roland*, has been said to show 'un haut sentiment national.'[40] Perhaps so, but it is probably to the England of Byrhtnoth's king, Ethelred II, that we owe our single medieval manuscript of *Beowulf*, a manuscript which shows that the glory of the Danish court stayed alive in an Anglo-Saxon kingdom which had suffered grievously from Danish attacks.[41] If we move forward to the twelfth century we find that the French welcomed Arthur and the 'matter of Britain' without regard for his national origins. In the medieval world we are considering, loyalty and love of homeland were admired and 'nationalism' was not understood in the sense that it is today. With equal justice it could be said that if the author of the text from which the Oxford *Roland* was copied was French, he did not reveal 'any deep French prejudices,' for the Normans, the men of Auvergne, the Bavarians, the Gascons, the Saxons, all the troops of Charlemagne's empire as the author conceived it, are treated with respect.

But what, one is bound to ask, of the special place in *dulce France* given to the *Francs de France*, of the phrase 'nos Franceis'?[42] In the *Chanson* 'France'

Thomov, 'Sur la langue de la version oxonienne de la *Chanson de Roland*,' *Société Rencesvals IVe Congrès international, Heidelberg, 29 août-2 septembre 1967. Actes et mémoires* (Heidelberg, 1969), pp. 179-193.

[39] Pierre Le Gentil, *La Chanson de Roland* (2nd ed., Paris, 1967), p. 34: Eng. trans. by Frances F. Beer, *The Chanson de Roland* (Cambridge, Mass., 1969), p. 26. I am happier with the old textbook formulation (I cite from a pre-World War I edition) of Gustave Lanson, *Histoire de la littérature française* (11th ed. rev., Paris, 1909), p. 31, who refers to 'un profond et encore inconscient patriotisme, qui devance la réalité même d'une patrie.' *Cf.* Robert A LeVine, 'The Internalization of Political Values in Stateless Societies,' *Human Organization* 19 (1960), 51-58.

[40] Quotation from Menéndez Pidal, *Chanson*, p. 321. A distinction between the ideals of Roland and Byrhtnoth is asserted by Frederick Whitehead, '*Ofermod* et *démesure*,' *Cahiers de Civilisation Médiévale*, 3 (1960), 115-117 and Cecily Clark, 'Byrhtnoth and Roland: A Contrast,' *Neophilologus*, 51 (1967), 288-293.

[41] The contents of the codex were probably assembled in the second half of the tenth century; see Dorothy Whitelock, *The Audience of Beowulf* (Oxford, 1961), p. 51. Paleographers have placed the writing of *Beowulf* in the last decades of the tenth century. It should be noted that the codex contains three other works – all written by one of the scribes of *Beowulf* – which other paleographers have placed in the mid-eleventh or even the twelfth century: see Robert L. Reynolds, 'Handwriting Illustrations: Some Problems in Economic-Historical Research,' *Studi in onore di Amintore Fanfani* (Milan, 1962) 3, 433-435.

[42] See Pietro Paulo Trompeo, 'Dulce France', in his *L'Azzurro di Chartres e altri capricci*, Artesusa 5 (Caltanissetta-Rome, 1958), pp. 27-33. Léon Gautier, 'L'Idée politique dans les chanson de geste,' *Revue des questions historiques*, 7 (1869), p. 84, n. 3. calculated that in the *Chanson de Roland* the terms 'France' and 'Franceis' were applied to the entire empire of Charlemagne 170 times. Gautier's view that Bavaria, Normandy, Germany, Brittany,

sometimes indicates all the empire held by the Franks, just as 'Francs', and 'Franceis' are usually interchangeable, but in other places the heartland of *Francia* is more limited. Those limits, as worked out by Ferdinand Lot and René Louis, are enclosed in the territory marked out by the four points Mont-Saint-Michel, Sens, Besançon, Wissant, that is, the ancient Neustria of the late tenth-century Carolingian kingdom.[43] For the *Rolandslied* the territory of *Francia* can be expressed as *Carolingie* (see v. 6930). If any political significance is to be given to the limited 'France', it should be directed not at the Capetian monarchy but at that of the late Carolingians, which had so little significance in the twelfth century that the copyist of the Oxford *Roland* garbled his text. A sense of long past history, which is, after all, what an epic preserves, is a different matter from positive political loyalty. To turn from literature to charters for an example, the Catalans forgot neither their historical relationship nor their nominal ties to the French monarchy, so that well into the twelfth century notaries in obscure villages were still dating charters by the regnal years of the kings of France.[44] But that formal, historical tie does not mean that any Catalan, no matter how moved by epic poetry, made the slightest effort to fight and die for a Capetian monarchy which never led a military expedition to the south until Louis VI's campaign in Auvergne.

Up to this point we have dealt with the way in which the *Chanson* treats warfare itself and the Holy War in particular, as well as the question of French or Capetian loyalty, but for a fourth and final theme we come now to the topic which has interested me most and which lies behind the title of this paper. The *Chanson* teaches not the techniques of fighting but the virtues desired for an ideal warrior. My main example is the condemnation of flight, expressed not only in the title of this paper (v. 1255), but in such warnings as 'Dehet ait ki s'en fuit!' (v. 1047). The idea that it is better to die than to retreat is, of course, a commonplace of

---

Frisia, etc. should be considered dependent or conquered territory was challenged by Carl Theodor Hoefft, *France, Franceis & Franc im Rolandslied* (Strassburg, 1891). Douglas, 'The *Song of Roland* and the Norman Conquest', p. 110, points out that William the Conqueror addressed his continental subjects, Normans and Angevins, as *Franci sui*.

[43] Ferdinand Lot, *Études sur les légendes épiques françaises* (Paris, 1958), pp. 260-279 (first pub. 1928), and René Louis, 'La Grande Douleur pour la mort de Roland', *Cahiers de Civilisation Médiévale*, 3, (1960), 62-67; cf. K. J. Hollyman, 'Wissant and the Empire of Charles le Simple', *Journal of the Australasian Universities Language and Literature Association*, 8 (1958), 24-28. I find the theory of Rita Lejeune that v. 1428 refers to Saint-Michel-Pied-de-Port near Roncevaux reasonable but in the end unconvincing: see her 'Le Mont Saint Michel au-péril-de-la-mer, la *Chanson de Roland* et le pèlerinage de Compostelle' in *Millénaire monastique de Mont Saint-Michel*, 6 vols., (Paris, 1966-1971), II, 411-433.

[44] Though forbidden by the Council of Tarragona in 1180, dating by the regnal years of the kings of France continued in a few instances into the thirteenth century: see Arthur Giry, *Manuel de diplomatique* (2nd ed., Paris, 1925), p. 93.

the chansons de geste, as it is of most epics.[45] But it is not, I should add, an ideal military strategy. Confidence in *cran* or guts rather than prudent concern for tactics or logistics was very nearly disastrous for the French in World War I. In the eleventh and twelfth centuries mutual consent was a necessity before individual combat between mounted warriors could take place, and flight or retreat was common. Sometimes it was a skilfully executed and disciplined feigned or Parthian retreat, as probably occurred at Hastings. Sometimes it was ignominious retreat, like that of Stephen of Blois. And sometimes a retreat followed by a later victory, as in the case of Henry Beauclerc, seemed only to illustrate to chroniclers the prudent wisdom that he who fights and runs away, may live to fight – and win – another day.[46]

Even though disciplined retreat can sometimes be the best strategy every commander wants troops who will risk, indeed sacrifice, their lives if necessary.[47] To ensure such readiness to die, the enculturation of warriors through a code of honor and glory that condemns flight as shameful has great value, and epic poetry plays its part in creating this code. The *Institutiones Disciplinae* on the education of noble youths urged instruction in 'the ancestral songs by which the auditors are spurred to glory,' and in the *Chanson de Roland* no one wants to have bad songs sung about him.[48]

Central to the *Chanson de Roland* is a code of honorable loyalty. Loyalty to one's kin appears, notably in the support Ganelon receives from his

---

[45] *Cf.* the vow of Vivien in the *Chanson de Guillaume*, vv. 580-589, ed. Duncan McMillan, SATF, 2 vols. (Paris, 1949-50). For a moralization of the theme see *Pseudo-Turpin*, ed. Meredith-Jones, ch. 12. pp. 134-135, or Brault, *Song of Roland*, 1, 34-35.

[46] Bernard S. Bachrach, 'The Feigned Retreat at Hastings,' *Mediaeval Studies*, 33, (1971), 264-267. On charges of cowardice leveled against the counts of Blois-Champagne see Michel Bur, *La Formation du comté de Champagne* (Nancy, 1977), pp. 482-485. For a medieval version of the proverb which closes this paragraph see *The Owl and the Nightingale*, v. 176 ('Wel fi₃t þat wel fli₃t'). ed. Eric Gerald Stanley. (London, 1960), with notes on other appearances.

[47] On the 'will to combat' see Keegan, *Face of Battle*, pp. 269-279 and elsewhere: this study of the battles of Agincourt, Waterloo and the Somme is informative and thought-provoking throughout.

[48] See Paul Pascal, 'The Institutionum Disciplinae' of Isidore of Seville', *Traditio*, 13 (1957), 426: 'In ipso autem modulandi usu voce excitata oportet sensim psallere, cantare suaviter nihilque amatorium decantare vel turpe sed magis praecinere carmina maiorum quibus auditores provocati ad gloriam excitentur.' Though its editors have attributed this text to St. Isidore and it is treated as authentic by Menéndez Pidal. *Poesía juglaresca y juglares* (6th ed., Madrid, 1957), p. 348, its authorship is uncertain; Jacques Fontaine, 'Quelques observations sur les *Institutiones disciplinae*', *Ciudad de Dios*, 181 (1968), 617-655, considers that it is not by Isidore and places its probable composition in Carolingian Gaul. In either case, a Visigothic or Carolingian author added a favorable reference to the *carmina maiorum* to St. Ambrose's condemnation of love songs. See also Jean Györy, 'Réflexions sur le jongleur guerrier,' *Annales Universitatis Scientiarum Budapestensis. Sectio Philologica*, 3 (1961), 46-60.

family.[49] But towering far above loyalty to kin are a warrior's loyalties to his companions in arms, to his battlefield commanders, to his *pays* and his ruler, and to the Christian religion, all of which are skilfully combined in the Oxford *Roland*. Examples of such loyalty can be found in the twelfth century, perhaps more commonly in England than in France, but the ideals of the *Chanson* were rarely part of everyday life. The tenacious bond of the Germanic *comitatus* is a commonplace of literature and idealized history, but the military and political realities of eleventh and twelfth-century France were not those of Tacitus, *Beowulf*, or even of the historical Charlemagne, who could enforce ties of dependence with a large amount of traditional *auctoritas*. In the France of the first half of the twelfth century, the king had little control over the great princes, who when well-behaved were more allies than subjects. A warrior-king like Louis VI nearly exhausted himself controlling the minor nobility of the Ile-de-France, territorial princes had to worry about the loyalty of their barons, hereditary castellans could dream of retaining more and more power for themselves, and roving *juvenes* were ready to join the most promising commander. If governments were to reverse the disintegrative forces of localism, family loyalty, and self-interest, they needed above all two things. One was institutions which would distribute political power and benefits sufficiently widely to the military class to convince it that its best interests lay in the stability of principalities and indeed in the building of states.[50] The other was an ideal of loyalty that could bind the entire class, from barons to *bacheliers*, into a group which could conduct war, govern, and administer together in support of its common interests, from defense against foreign invasion to mutual repression, exploitation or control of a dependent peasantry and burghers. The question of whether the chansons de geste should be classed as aristocratic or considered intended for *bacheliers* draws a distinction where none is necessary.[51] The *Chanson de Roland* can be considered an enculturative instrument for an entire warrior class, from the most aristocratic descendants and successors of the heroes named in the text to the lowest *milites* with pretensions to chivalric honor.

---

[49] See John Halverson, 'Ganelon's Trial', *Speculum*, 42 (1967), 661-669. In 'The Character and the Trial of Ganelon: A New Appraisal', *Romania*, 96 (1975), 333-367, John A. Stranges argues well that Thierry is the champion of Charlemagne and of justice, but in my opinion greatly overstates the position that the audience could be expected to feel sympathy (as he seems to) for Ganelon.

[50] Joseph R. Strayer, 'The Two Levels of Feudalism', in his *Medieval Statecraft and the Perspectives of History* (Princeton, 1971), pp. 63-76.

[51] While Brault, like many critics, describes the audience of the *Chanson* primarily as 'aristocratic', he notes that some authors have suggested 'that the chansons de geste were primarily intended for *bacheliers*'; see *Song of Roland*, I, 27-28 and 353, n. 162. The argument that the *Chanson* reflects the ideals of the *bacheliers* or apprentice warriors is presented from a Marxian point of view by R. Constantinescu. 'Aspecte ale reflectării societatii feudale in Cînecul lui Roland', *Studii [de Institut de istorie și filosofie de Romîne]* 16 (1963), 565-589.

To conclude this paper we shall now return to the question of the *Chanson* and its particular audience. The 'traditionalist' school holds, with quite forceful arguments that a *Chanson de Roncevaux* existed from some time after the actual battle in the eighth century in one form or another, having as one purpose the commemoration of the event and the glorification of the fallen, and the 'individualist' school allows that versions of the Roland 'story' circulated before 'Turoldus' wrote. The enculturative values of earlier compositions were presumably the political and military ideals of the Carolingian warrior class, though since the prehistory of the Oxford *Roland* is so uncertain, we have almost no evidence of what specific effects an earlier song might have had on its audience, how much of its emphasis, for example, was on loyalty and treason, how much on Christianity, Holy War, kingship, or the special rôle of the Frankish 'nation'. Early songs or stories presumably traveled about the Frankish empire, perhaps circulated with the royal court or army, were carried along the pilgrimage roads described so evocatively by Bédier, or were even part of the 'baggage' of other itinerants, such as the *rotuligeri* who bore mortuary rolls between churches as widely separated as Ripoll, Pampeluna, Paris, and Aachen.[52] Their language could have been Latin or vernacular, their content surely changed with time and local circumstances, and all that can be said with certainty of them today is that their interest must have been sufficient for some elements to have survived and to have left their mark on written records like the *Nota Emilianense* and the 'fragment' of The Hague.

In the late eleventh and early twelfth centuries in France Carolingian government and its political ideals were only a memory, while 'modern' centralized, 'national' government of the type administered by Henry Plantagenet and Philip Augustus was still *in statu nascendi*. In the absence of centralized, bureaucratic governments the burden of social control and civil cohesion fell upon the institutions of the Peace Movement, in which the episcopacy played such an important rôle, and on those relatively short chains of command, of one man bound to another by fief and homage, which we call 'feudal'. Such 'feudal' hierarchies could and eventually often did strengthen kingship, and they brought a new class of men, the *milites*, into the functions of government. In real life from the middle of the eleventh century on, as in the *Chanson de Roland*, a large group of lesser men began their training in power along with the higher nobility or 'peers'. Surely it was one of the enculturative functions of the *Chanson* to extend the values of the aristocracy to these 'others', the *altres*.[53]

---

[52] On the bearers of mortuary rolls see Jean Dufour, 'Les Rouleaux et encycliques mortuaires de Catalogne (1008-1102)', *Cahiers de Civilisation Médiévale*, 20 (1977), 13-48.

[53] On the institution of peers in the mid-eleventh century see Paul Guilhiermoz, *Essai sur les origines de la noblesse en France au moyen âge* (Paris, 1902), pp. 75-182. But besides the peers, who dominate the 'fragment' of The Hague and the *Nota Emilianense*, the named

Awareness of the importance of the knightly class and of the process by which these 'two levels of feudalism' could be brought to work together has provided increased understanding of the political dynamics of Western Europe in the eleventh and twelfth centuries. Analysis of the process has usually concentrated on the incentives offered by rulers to counter the presumable self-interest (or family and local interest) of the class of *milites*: in the words of a recent study of territorial power in the twelfth century, 'to retain the fidelity of other lineages and of equestrian fighting men, the ruler had to share his power with them.'[54] Administrative records necessarily concentrate attention on the distribution of power and wealth, but literature has the peculiar property of allowing us to see as well the sharing of ideals.

The political ideals of the Oxford *Roland* are precisely those which would cement the structure of the military society of the twelfth century. Its audience could hear of vassals bound by a sense of military brotherhood which transcended lineage, of courage and honor in the face of the enemy which assured the survival not of individuals but of the group, of 'loving' loyalty to a ruler who deferred his more important decisions to a council of his barons. A politically-minded critic might move from the observation that these enculturative values ideally prepared men to take their place in a changing society to the conclusion that a shrewd ruler, be he a William the Conqueror or a Suger, would naturally attempt to propagate literature like the *Roland* as part of a political program, but such an observation would miss two crucial points. In the first place, no twelfth-century ruler had sufficient control over 'communications' to give the *Chanson* the circulation and popularity it did in fact enjoy. Secondly, and perhaps more importantly, the ideals and institutions we have been discussing served the interests of the warrior class at least as well as they did the princes. The popularity of the *Chanson* in the class which provided its major audience was surely not due to imposition or nostalgic tradition but to a form of ideological natural selection, a natural selection of ideals and esthetics passed on with appropriate modifications from generation to generation.

The major point of this paper is that the *Chanson de Roland* filled a need, or many needs, for its medieval audiences, and that it had the power to move men to rethink their self-interest in terms of higher ideals, to the point that in real life as in epic imagination they might actually prefer honorable death to shameful flight, group loyalty to limited personal

---

heroes of the Oxford *Roland* are joined by a host of 'altres', 15,000 *chevaliers* and *bacheliers* in vv. 108-113. Moreover, like the *milites* discussed by Strayer, these 'others' not only fought but took part in judicial functions; the duel of Pinabel and Thierry was to take place 'par jugement des altres' (v. 3855).

[54] Thomas N. Bisson, 'Mediterranean Territorial Power in the Twelfth Century', *Proceedings of the American Philosophical Society*, 123 (1979), 145.

advantage, and in the process build stronger governments and assure peace and stability. Historians examine the structures which helped to shape such ideals and behavior, but they can never read or hear the *Chanson* precisely as medieval men did. In this case, however (and unlike, let us say *Beowulf* or *Maldon*) the *Chanson de Roland* had a repeat performance on the stage of modern European history, and in the Great War was again in the minds or on the lips of men who fought for ideals in battles. In analyzing the affective power of the poem the medievalist can perhaps learn from modern experience. But if a study of the *Chanson* in the twentieth century is written, perhaps the modernist can also make a comparison with the medieval experience and ask if the enculturative values of the *Chanson* were of equal benefit for those Rolands and Olivers who were asked to fight – and die – under its influence.

10

Collaborative Approaches to Fantasy and Reality in the Literature of Champagne

This society has come a long way since the first triennial meeting in Philadelphia in 1974.[*] Indeed, I have for the first time the feeling that the society is truly an international one and not simply a congeries of national groups. "Society" I know and "International" I know now, but from time to time I still have my difficulties with the term "Courtly Literature". Obviously a principle which excludes the subject matter of the Société Rencesvals and the International Arthurian Society is not a useful scientific definition but an organizational treaty. Courtly literature includes a surprising amount of Latin literature and excludes very few genres of vernacular literature, including the fabliaux.[1] This is hardly the time for a discussion of definition, and to avoid any question of arbitrary selection, I shall draw the bulk of my material tonight from a manuscript which I have no doubt must be classified as courtly.

I refer to the famous Guiot collection, Bibl. nat. ms. fr. 794. This huge and handsome manuscript, a sort of reference work once marked with tags (*enseignes*) or location markers, was probably written in the second quarter of the thirteenth century, quite possibly for the countess of Champagne, Blanche de Navarre (regent 1201-1222, died 1229), the mother of Thibaut le Chansonnier (ruled 1222-1253).[2] Its one histori-

---

[*] The International Courtly Literature Society (Ed.).

[1] On Latin authors who wrote for episcopal courts note, among others, Hugh Primas, the Archpoet, and the authors who wrote for Guillaume aux Blanches-Mains, on whom see John R. Williams, 'William of the White Hands and Men of Letters', *Haskins Anniversary Essays*, ed. Charles H. Taylor and John L. La Monte (Boston and New York, 1929), pp.365-89. On the fabliaux see Per Nykrog, *Les fabliaux: étude d'histoire littéraire et de stylistique médiévale* (Copenhagen, 1957), criticized by Charles Muscatine in his paper to this Congress. I agree with Professor Muscatine that the coarseness of the fabliaux does not accord with the courtly ideal, but still consider them literature of the courts in terms of the audience. For a modern analogy, one might argue that the language of the Watergate tapes is not ideally 'presidential'.

[2] The fullest description of the manuscript, now somewhat dated with respect to information about the publication of the works it contains, is that of Mario Roques, 'Le ms. 794 de la Bibliothèque nationale et le scribe Guiot', *Romania*, 73 (1952), 177-99. I am grateful to my friend and colleague Michel Bur for calling my attention to the importance of examining this manuscript and for his remarks in his paper on 'Les comtes de Champagne et la *Normanitas*: Sémiologie d'un tombeau', to be published in the *Acts of the Third Annual Battle Conference on Anglo-Norman Studies* (presented 27 July 1980).

ated initial, the *P* at the beginning of the *Lancelot en charrette*, shows an elegant countess of Champagne enthroned and gesturing in conversation or instruction.

Here we have no *manuscrit portatif*. Leaving aside modern added leaves, it contains 433 folios of parchment, which are about 9¼ inches wide (234mm.) and about 12½ inches tall (317mm.); excluding the cover it is about 3 and a third inches thick (85mm.), and with the modern cover it weighs 12¼ lbs (5·565 kg.). The three parts of the manuscript were written separately and may briefly have been bound separately, but before the end of the thirteenth century, when the location markers were inserted and the table of contents written, the manuscript had become a unified, one-volume compendium of frequently consulted romances and histories. The volume is heavier than one of the tomes of the original edition of the *Gallia Christiana*, invaluable for consultation but not a book a peripatetic countess or count was likely to carry about; it probably had a permanent place in one of the comital palaces, quite possibly at Provins where its scribe Guiot wrote it.

All students of medieval French know the Guiot manuscript from the texts of the works of Chrétien de Troyes, made familiar to us in the editions of the Classiques Français du Moyen Age. The section which contains the first four 'canonical' romances ends with a blank leaf.[3] The second section is devoted exclusively to the *Siège d'Athènes d'Athis et Prophilias*, a romance of over 20,000 lines now thought to have been written in the early thirteenth century; its editor, Hilka, found the Guiot manuscript to contain the fullest and best version of the poem.[4] The third and final section is particularly historical: it contains the *Roman de Troie* of Benoît de Sainte-Maure,[5] Wace's *Roman de Brut* with its extensive Arthurian material,[6] the unique text of the *Empereors de Rome* by "Calendre", an early thirteenth-century

---

3. Mario Roques, ed., *Erec et Enide* (1952), *Le Chevalier de la charrette* (1958), and *Le Chevalier au lion (Yvain)* (1960); and Alexandre Micha, ed., *Cligés* (1957). Guido Favati has seriously criticized the quality of the Guiot manuscript in 'Le *Cligés* de Chrétien de Troyes dans les éditions critiques et dans les manuscrits', *CCMe*, 10 (1967), 385-407.

4. See *Li Romanz d'Athis et Prophilias*, ed. Alfons Hilka, 2 vols, Gesellschaft für romanische Literatur, 29 (Halle, 1912-16); Gilles Roques, 'Fantaisie maritime', *Travaux de Linguistique et de Littérature*, 15 (1977), 1, 245-53.

5. Ed. Léopold Constans, SATF (Paris, 1904-12).

6. Wace's complete *Roman de Brut* was edited by Ivor D.O. Arnold, 2 vols, SATF (Paris, 1938-40). The Guiot ms. was used as the *texte de base* for the convenient student's edition of I.D.O. Arnold and Margaret M. Pelan, *La Partie arthurienne du Roman du Brut* (Paris, 1962).

work to which I will return soon,[7] and Chrétien's *Perceval*[8] (here called, rather curiously, "*Percevax le Viel*") with the First Continuation followed without a break by a fragment of the Second Continuation, both in what William Roach has called the "Short Redaction".[9]

Twenty years ago, when in my youthful enthusiasm I thought the study of the literature and society of the court of Champagne would be a relatively simple matter, to be finished quickly before moving on the other courts, I took a prosopographical approach to the court and its literature.[10] For present purposes the study either of manuscripts or of authors produces a similar result, a realization that courtly audiences found in their literature works of moral instruction and serious history with political overtones, as well as compositions which must have amused and sometimes inspired them, as they can still move and inspire us. Much courtly literature was as accurate, true-to-life, and down-to-earth as the authors' skill and knowledge could make it, but some works clearly contain a generous portion of the miraculous and the fantastic. It is the methodological problem of how to approach the material which does not seem to us realistic which is the central concern of this paper.

Let us begin with a simple passage taken from a little-known work which survives only in the Guiot manuscript, *Les empereors de Rome*, written in the early thirteenth century by someone who called himself "Calendre", who praises the late Duke Ferri II of Lorraine and who, surprisingly, seems either to have translated into French King Alfred's Anglo-Saxon abridgement of Orosius or to have used an otherwise unknown Latin translation of Alfred's work. "Calendre" tells us that at the time of the Social War "bread and wine were transformed

---

7. *Les Empereors de Rome par Calendre*, ed. Galia Millard (Ann Arbor, Mich., 1957).

8. The Guiot text forms the basis of the CFMA edition of *Perceval* published in 1973-75 by Félix Lecoy. Roach used B.N. ms. fr. 12576 for his edition, 2nd ed., (Geneva and Paris, 1959), and this was also the base manuscript for Hilka, whose edition lies behind all modern translations before that of Jacques Ribard (Paris, 1979). While I would not want to make much of what is only a subjective observation, it seems to me that in the case of *Perceval* the Guiot text is artistically inferior to the Picard-north francien version used by Hilka and Roach for their editions, suggesting that Chrétien wrote for Philip of Flanders in a northern rather than a Champenois dialect.

9. William Roach, ed., *The Continuation of the Old French Perceval of Chrétien de Troyes*, 4 vols in 5 (Philadelphia, 1949-71), 1,16-19 (description of manuscript, dated "middle of the thirteenth century"); 3, pt 1. 3-601 (ed. of First Continuation); 4,2-62 (ed. of Second Continuation).

10. 'The Court of Champagne as a Literary Center', *Speculum*, 36 ; above, 3-43. For recent criticism of this paper see June Hall Martin McCash, 'Marie de Champagne and Eleanor of Aquitaine: A Relationship Reexamined', *Speculum*, 54 (1979), 698-711. A German translation of my article of 1961 with an updating *Nachtrag* is to appear in a volume of the series Wege der Forschung, edited by Joachim Bumke.

and blood flowed from bread when it was cut".[11] Without doubt a report of a marvellous, indeed miraculous event, but we should not treat it as fantasy; the author very likely considered that it 'actually happened'. The information appeared in his source, and he lived in an age when one often heard of bleeding hosts and many claimed to have seen them.[12] Why not believe that *tuit li pain coupé sainnierent*?

There is an obvious distinction to be made between fantasy and stories of marvels and miracles. Medieval people believed in marvels and joked about them easily. Walter Map, for example, told an anecdote — a courtly one, for it appears in *De Nugis Curialium* — about the alleged miracle of Bernard of Clairvaux lying down on top of a dead boy — *eiectis omnibus incubuit super puerum* — who was still dead when the holy man arose. Walter's comment was that he had never heard of a case when a monk had lain on a boy and the boy did not get up directly thereafter.[13] That was how Walter dealt with the *virtus miraculorum*, or at least with monks. A clerk of Count Henry of Champagne also told the story to a Cistercian and died with satisfying speed.[14] We may class this story with miracle literature, or dirty jokes, but it was probably less of a fantasy than most such anecdotes.

Fantasy (*fantasia*) was defined in the middle ages as applying to a class of known events or objects which took form in the mind. Sometimes they were of uncertain accuracy, sometimes not, which means that one could never be sure of them, and the lack of trust one could put in them was shown by the fact that in debate a fallacy was called a fantasy "since it appears to be other than what it is". *Fantasia* and *fantasma* were only slightly distinguished (properly *fantasma* applied to unknown objects or events), and both were related to *fantasticus*. The classical example of something known not to exist was a *chimera*, a

11. Ed. Millard, p.63, notably lines 1073-77. On the author's use of Alfred see the introduction, pp.6-8. For both Alfred and "Calendre" the account of the bleeding bread surely was considered historical, for it is told by Orosius, Bk 5, ch. 18. Mireille Schmidt-Chazan, 'Un Lorrain de coeur: le Champenois Calendre', *Les Cahiers Lorrains* (1979), pp.65-75, convincingly dates the composition of the poem to the year 1219 or a month or two earlier or later. I disagree with her, however, in dismissing the author's statement that the translation was based on a manuscript which came from the Emperor Manuel. Many Anglo-Saxons left England for Constantinople after 1066 and one could have taken Alfred's text there. Moreover, Manuel Comnenus knighted Henry I of Champagne and later in 1180 ransomed him from the Turks. I have placed the name "Calendre" in quotation marks because of my suspicion that it may be an anagram.

12. See now Giles Constable's sensitive presidential address to the Medieval Academy, 'Miracles and History in the Twelfth Century', to appear in *Speculum*. Prof. Constable cites Peter Brouwe, *Eucharistic Wonders*.

13. Walter Map, *De Nugis Curialium*, ed. M.R. James (Oxford, 1914), p.39.

14. Helinand de Froidment in PL 212, 1038; see also my 'Court of Champagne', (n.10 above), pp.558-59; above, pp. 10-11.

being imaginatively composed of two real-life elements.[15]

Clearly it is not easy to tell the difference between a 'real' marvel and an 'imaginative' fantasy, as readers of reports about automata know,[16] and the serious researcher who spends time and effort attempting to make such distinctions may end up feeling a bit foolish. Today an unhurried traveller journeying between Rennes and Vannes can plan a route through the forest of Paimpont, the remains of the once vast Armorican forest known in Arthurian legend as Brocéliande. The tourist who does so may end up following the footsteps of the Norman poet Wace, who in the middle of the twelfth century made his own visit to this forest to see its marvels, particularly the fairies who were reputed to inhabit it. "I went there to seek marvels," he reported, "I saw the forest, and I saw the land; I sought for marvels, but I did not find them." Wace concluded that he had wasted his time, and the modern critic or historian who sets out in a spirit of naïve positivism to explore the world of fantasy may deserve the harsh judgement Wace passed on himself: "A fool I went, a fool I returned" — *Fol i alai, fol m'en revinc*.[17] The creations of fantasy can, indeed must, be apprehended by other means than a prosaic visit. Gottfried of Strassburg described Tristan's Minnegrotte in detail and explained its significance, adding:

> I know this well, for I have been there . . .
> I have known that cave since I was eleven,
> And I have never been to Cornwall.[18]

How are we to approach Wace's problem? First of all, I suggest, by accepting that courtly audiences could be acutely aware of disjunctions between fantasy and reality and were probably highly sophisticated, perhaps more sophisticated than those modern audiences and even directors who have trouble with Bertolt Brecht's *Veränderung*. Modern readers have difficulty with courtly literature, particularly beginners limited to translations, but anyone can be baffled by the

---

15. On *fantasia* and *fantasma* see *Summa Britonis*, ed. Lloyd W. and Bernadine A. Daly (Padua, 1975), p.253; DuCange, *s.v. phantasia*, gives a number of interesting references and shows that the two terms were at times interchanged. Note also John of Salisbury, *Policraticus* 429b, influenced by Macrobius, *De Somn. Scip.* 1,3,3-8. Abelard states, quite conventionally, '*Chimera*' *rei non-existentis nomen est ut non-existentis*; see L.M. De Rijk, ed., *Dialectica* (2nd rev. ed., Assen, 1970), p.201.

16. On automata see O. Söhring, 'Werke bildender Kunst in altfranzösischen Epen', *Romanische Forschungen*, 12 (1900), 80ff.

17. *Le Roman de Rou de Wace*, ed. A.J. Holden, SATF (Paris, 1970-73), 2, p.122, ll.6393-98. In *Yvain*, ll.577-78, Calogrenant, who failed to master the marvellous spring, echoes Wace: *Ensi alai, ensi reving;/au revenir por fol me ting*.

18. Gottfried von Strassburg, *Tristan*, ed. Reinhold Bechstein, 5th ed., (Leipzig, 1930), ll.17100-38.

technical vocabulary of some arcane field where it is hard to tell a hawk from a handsel. Moreover, sophisticated readers today have been trained to believe that approaching poetry with a "willing suspension of disbelief" is a sign of advanced literary sensitivity. We may in fact be more credulous in our understanding of medieval literature than were courtly audiences. I remember as a beginning student, as yet unspoiled by instruction, trying to convince Ernst Kantorowicz, a highly sophisticated man, that the *De Amore* of Andreas Capellanus was humorous, and achieving no success at all. Perhaps Alfred Karnein's recent demonstration that Andreas probably wrote at the court of Philip Augustus rather than that of Marie of Champagne would have helped, but I doubt it, and at a literary congress one might well prefer that enlightenment be based on a discussion of wordplay and allusions, rather than on an investigation of whether a *capellanus* could easily become a *cambellanus*.[19]

The *De Amore*, as many scholars have argued, is not a literal-minded instructional handbook but a work of the imagination, and Marie's letter and the decisions of the courts of love are, in my opinion, amusing fantasies. In fact, it is quite possible that the very creative 'free play' which Andreas gave to his imagination created what I see as unconscious ambivalence and what some other readers have taken as ambiguity or the presentation of a "double truth".[20] To write as acutely as he did, Andreas must have been an extremely sharp observer of the social scene, perhaps even at some time a participant. If Andreas was doctrinally correct but psychologically ambivalent, he would not have been the last Christian moralist to find his irony had become inverted and confusing, justifying Bishop Tempier's condemnation not on grounds of his conscious intention but of his failure to control the feeling he brought to the task. Fantasy, the product not only of imagination but of desire, may indeed embarrass an author by moving in defiance of conscious control.[21]

With my interpretation of Andreas as an author marked by both fantasy and ambivalence one may easily disagree, but when we return to Chrétien there is accord that his work is full of imaginative fantasy, sometimes amusing, sometimes, I think, sublimely spiritual. Our scholarly arguments are over where the boundaries between reality and

19. Alfred Karnein, 'Auf der Suche nach einem Autor: Andreas, Verfasser von *De Amore*', *Germanisch-Romanische Monatsschrift*, n.f. 28 (1978), 1-20.

20. Felix Schlösser, *Andreas Capellanus*, 2nd ed., (Bonn, 1962), believes in a *Koexistenz* of two contrasting principles which he sees as normally contradictory; note here the fine review of Bertina Wind in *CCMe*, 7 (1964), 346-50.

21. See Jean La Planche and J.B. Pontalis, *The Language of Psycho-Analysis*, trans. Donald Nicholson-Smith (New York, 1973), pp.314-19 (*s.v.* phantasy), and 26-29 (ambivalence).

fantasy lie, how we can map the limits of the forest of Brocéliande. The artistic and psychological problems of Chrétien's juxtaposition of reality and fantasy are presented to us brilliantly by Eric Rohmer's recent (1978) film of *Perceval le Gallois*.[22] In Rohmer's cinematic adoption of Chrétien's tale, clothing, armour, weapons, horses, food, musical instruments, tools, and in general the objects which the actors touch directly are presented with a realism and attention to detail worthy of a fine historical museum, except that they are surely a bit too clean. But although Perceval realistically washes grease from his fingers and wears authentic armour, Rohmer's horses parade like carnival ponies on pathways of sand, castles appear as painted backdrops or crude cardboard constructions, and trees are stylized metallic baubles reminiscent of manuscript illuminations. The audience of Rohmer's *Perceval* is continually reminded that real people have been placed in a fantastic setting, and that their behaviour can be interpreted neither as the routine of daily life nor as the incomprehensible activity of alien beings. Through his powerful visual discontinuities Rohmer has recreated for a modern audience something of the effect Chrétien's poetry must have had on his twelfth-century listeners. Those who see Rohmer's film laugh when Perceval's horse knocks off Arthur's cap; they gasp at the simple, direct brutality with which Perceval pierces the Crimson Knight's eye with his javelin; and, perhaps depending upon different experiences with life and love, they are either awed or entranced by the scene of the three drops of blood on the snow and Perceval's reflexive defence against his attackers.

I am so impressed by the artistic genius with which Rohmer evokes the mixture of real life and faerie in *Perceval* that I am little concerned to argue whether he has correctly interpreted any given detail, whether the sword play is realistic or the *graal* would have been suitable for holding an eel or a salmon, or whether his own 'continuation' at the conclusion is artistically or thematically sound. I am as little concerned with these details as I believe a medieval audience would have been with whether the so-called epic stroke, an overhand smash which splits an opponent from the point of his helmet to the spine of his horse, would have been effective or ill-advised.[23] A dis-

22. For the text and some pictures of Rohmer's *Perceval le Gallois* see *L'Avant-Scène: Cinéma*, no. 221 (1 February, 1979). See also L. Carasso-Bulow, *The Merveilleux in Chrétien de Troyes' Romances*, Critique littéraire, 153 (Geneva: Droz, 1976).

23. See Benton, ' 'Nostre Franceis n'unt talent de fuïr': *The Song of Roland* and the Enculturation of a Warrior Class', *Olifant*, 6 (1979), p.239. I mention this point only to correct my earlier statement about the Bayeux Tapestry. I have learned from Mr. Ian Peirce of East Sussex that a stroke delivered from one o'clock (or one-thirty) towards the neck is more effective than either a side-stroke (from three o'clock) or the dangerous 'epic stroke' (from twelve o'clock). The Tapestry probably represents a life-like stroke from one o'clock.

puted point on a map is of much less importance than the question of how one can chart and understand the geography of an imaginary forest.

All medievalists, by describing ourselves with the word, accept that our methodology must be multi-disciplinary. No one person can possibly know enough to work at all broadly without help from disciplines where her or his knowledge must be insufficient. This is equally true of the particular case of the court of Champagne — which was of course only one court among many, courts which should be studied in their interrelationships, as Reto Bezzola so clearly recognized.[24]

My second point, therefore, in approaching the problem of fantasy — and perhaps I put the matter second because of my training as an historian — is that the easiest way to delimit the world of fantasy is to start with what can be shown to be real. How much fantasy Chrétien put into the magical portcullis gate in *Yvain* is best determined after one has studied military architecture, including the magnificent Porte de Jouy at Provins, and has seen what Chrétien's audience would have considered 'real'.[25] The student of medieval literature obviously must understand and appreciate a concrete world of weapons and armour and crafts, a world where coins have different values and buy grain or cloth of differing quality. And he or she must also deal comfortably with institutions and emotions, recognizing that a democratic speech by a social-climbing bourgeois resonated differently at courts where an anti-feudal revolution had not yet canonized bourgeois values than it does today, and that the author of a twelfth- or thirteenth-century debate between *Amor* and *Raison* had never read *Civilization and its Discontents*. These points are so simple and I wish obvious that I would not mention them at all if there were not still some critics, including scholars of great distinction, who seem to believe that their literary sensitivity permits them to 'feel' their way back into the middle ages without paying their dues in historical research. At the same time historians must remember that literature often affects the 'real world', that gates or tombs can be designed after literary models and that courts of love apparently did exist by the fifteenth century. As Valéry put it, *Imaginer, c'est se souvenir de ce qui va être*.

But while I admire, indeed revere concern for historical reality, it seems to me particularly important to stress that historical training alone is insufficient for dealing with the world of fantasy which is such an important part of medieval literature. Once we have determined that

24. Reto R. Bezzola, *Les Origines et la Formation de la littérature courtoise en occident*, 3 vols in 5 (Paris, 1958-63).

25. *Yvain*, ll.907-75. On the Porte de Jouy see Jean Mesqui, *Provins, la fortification d'une ville au moyen âge* (Geneva, 1979).

some literary element should be placed in the realm of fantasy, what then are we to do with it? Historians are trained to identify, date, even clamber intelligently through gates like the Porte de Jouy, but they are not prepared to deal with ladies who are bald behind and hairy in front, gigantic men with mossy ears who beat bullocks to make them behave, or sword-bridges.

There is neither space nor need here to dwell on the well-studied techniques of symbolism and allegory. In *Perceval* Fortune is bald behind and hairy in front; she is also described that way by Alain of Lille — one wonders which, if either, influenced the other — and the two-faced *fortuna bifrons*, properly understood, creatively and imaginatively signifies symbolically something we may have experienced in 'real life'.[26] Allegory is even further removed from reality. We know well enough from a work like Evrat's translation of Genesis or the anonymous translation of the 44th Psalm made for Countess Marie that a courtly audience could be familiar with the techniques of religious allegory.[27] *If* one so wishes one may see in the story of the fountain in the forest of Brocéliande visited by Calogrenant and Yvain a brief and effective allegory in which an ugly, violent man, who knows the way to the fountain but not its meaning, represents the Old Law, and the boiling, transforming fountain represents the waters of baptism, which tropologically every Christian must experience to be reborn. "If," I said, and though I am uninterested in attempting to demonstrate such an allegory now, the literary skills taught to clerics at the time, and taught by them to their courtly patrons if the patrons expressed an interest, provide the basis for such an allegorical argument.[28]

But what of sword-bridges? Lancelot enters Gorre by climbing across a sword-bridge, cutting himself on his extremities in the process. One can argue that these wounds, added to other adventures, were used by Chrétien to emphasize a resemblance to Christ, ironically creating an anti-hero, indeed an anti-Christ, whom Chrétien deliberately left in

---

26. See David Burchmore, '*Mutavit vultum*: Fortune and the Wife of Bath's Tale', California Institute of Technology Humanities Working Paper, 33 (1979), citing the *Anticlaudianus* (ca 1182-83), Bk. 8, 31-33: *Ambiguo vultu seducit forma videntem./Nam capitis pars anterior vestita capillis/ Luxuriat, dum caluicem pars altera luget*, and the *Conte del Graal*, ll.4622-23: *Fortune est chauve derriers et devant chevelue*.

27. On Evrat see Frances Anne Henderson, 'A Critical Edition of Evrat's Genesis: Creation to the Flood', Univ. of Toronto dissertation, 1977, available on microfilm from the National Library of Canada; *Eructavit*, ed. T. Atkinson Jenkins, Gesellschaft für romanische Literatur, 20 (Dresden, 1909).

28. See M.S. Luria, 'The Storm-Making Spring and the Meaning of Chrétien's *Yvain*', *SP*, 64 (1967), 564-85 and Tom Artin, *The Allegory of Adventure: Reading Chrétien's Erec and Yvain* (Lewisburg and London, 1974).

a tower in a final inversion: "He saved others; himself he cannot save".[29] One can, but I have brought up sword-bridges precisely because they do not fit the rational, planned creation of allegory. To my knowledge the most dedicated disciple of D.W. Robertson, Jr. (in his former incarnation, when that great master was still a 'Robertsonian') has not found an *in bono* or *in malo* reference to sword-bridges in the *glossa ordinaria*. For sword-bridges we may turn to comparative studies and note the appearances of the theme collected by Laura Hibbard Loomis and Howard Patch. Folklore is one approach which we must bring to the world of fantasy, but we need to remember that our authors could not consult the motif index of Stith Thompson, F. 152. 1..6, "sword-bridge to other world".[30] When all our dusty research has come to its term, we must never forget that for our authors to a very large degree their world of fantasy sprang from their imaginations, leading us to investigate symbolism not only with the skills of Fr. de Lubac but also with the interests of Carl Jung.

An important reminder of the role of the unconscious in the fantasy world of the middle ages comes from the work of Elizabeth Kennan, now president of Mt. Holyoke College, who has been studying Cistercian dreams and visions. The concept of intention was well developed in the twelfth century, and monastic novices were taught that consciously to harbour and meditate upon aggressive thoughts was sinful. On the other hand, one was not responsible or had only diminished responsibility for what one dreamed, and it was therefore acceptable for a young man to tell his novice master that he had dreamed the night before of doing in father-abbot (an event, by the way, which no monastic historian would consider unrealistic, even if presented as a fantasy). The discussion of dreams as a therapeutic device for handling aggression should surprise no one, but what interests me most is that Dr. Kennan tells me she has found in these dreams reference to sword-bridges.[31] Did the Cistercians, who entered their order as relatively mature monks, bring with them memories of literary sword-bridges? Did they, as Dom Jean Leclercq has argued, have an influence on the

29. D.W. Robertson, Jr., *A Preface to Chaucer* (Princeton, 1962), pp.451-52 refers to the "stigmata at the sword-bridge" in developing the role of an inverted Redeemer. I am not aware that anyone has earlier called attention to the applicability of Mark 15:31.

30. Laura Hibbard, 'The Sword Bridge of Chrétien de Troyes and its Celtic Original', *Romanic Review*, 4 (1913). 166-90, reprinted in L.H. Loomis, *Adventures in the Middle Ages* (New York, 1962); Howard R. Patch, *PMLA*, 33 (1918), 635ff.; Patch, *The Other World according to Descriptions in Medieval Literature* (Cambridge, Mass., 1950), pp.73 (Paul the Deacon) and 302-06 (Chrétien); all cited by Stith Thompson, *Motif-Index of Folk-Literature*, rev. ed., 6 vols (Bloomington and London, 1956).

31. Elizabeth T. Kennan, paper delivered at Folger Shakespeare Library in 1977. 'Some uses of Dreams: Learning to Live in a Medieval Monastery'.

secular literature of love and fantasy?[32] The study of the medieval dream world is, as it were, in its infancy, and I would like to see much more evidence before I felt confident that a modern interpretation of medieval dream work was anything more than modern projection.[33] The point remains, however, that psychoanalytic interpretations of courtly literature can be extremely stimulating and at their best provide insights difficult to achieve in any other way. I am thinking in particular of the detailed, associational work of Jean Györy, which casts light both on the individual works of Chrétien de Troyes and on the apparent obsessions of the author.[34]

In moving from the simpleminded collection of charters and measuring of manuscripts to the insights of Jung and Freud, I do not want to suggest by my approach that we have mounted a ladder where psychohistorical and psycholiterary techniques are at the very summit. The great limiting factor about psychoanalysis is its personalism. Sometimes in deconstructing a text we are left with much less than we had before, perhaps with some new but socially uninteresting information about the author of the text, at worst with the irrelevance of increased insight into the critic's psyche. To give an example unlikely to offend anyone here, if Guibert de Nogent had not written a treatise on relics which was otherwise hard to comprehend, would anyone care that I had found in his other works — or thought I had found, which says something about me — evidence of excessive fear of mutilation?

The fantasy world of the middle ages may stimulate our own fantasies, but that is scarcely a reason for society to support, or be asked to support, a scholarly organization devoted to the study of courtly literature. Personally I enjoy Ezra Pound's translations from

---

32. Jean Leclercq, *Monks and Love in Twelfth-Century France: Psycho-Historical Essays* (Oxford, 1979), esp. pp.14, 10, 121-29.

33. Ellen Karnofsky Petrie is now preparing a *catalogue raisonné* of dreams, 1050-1150. Only after we have a motif-index of medieval dreams and can see the context of the various elements will we be able to judge how much applicability modern research on dreams and literature has to the middle ages. The Centre de Recherche sur l'Imaginaire and its journal *Circé* concentrate on modern literature and *psychocritique*. I am struck by the archaic and therefore imaginative associations commonly given to swords depicted in the Thematic Apperception tests on which Yves Durand reports in 'La formulation expérimentale de l'imaginaire et ses modèles', *Circé*, 1 (1969), 151-248. In the middle ages surely sometimes a sword was only a sword.

34. J. Györy, 'Prolégomènes à une imagerie de Chrétien de Troyes', *CCMe*, 10 (1967), 361-84, 11 (1968), 29-39. Roger Dragonetti's *La vie de la lettre au Moyen Age (Le Conte du Graal)*, published this spring in Jacques Lacan's series, Connexions du Champ freudien, is not an example of the kind of psychoanalytic study I would like to see carried forward on the fantasy world of the middle ages; its subject is neither Chrétien's personal unconscious nor in any but the most limited way the *collective mentalité* of his world, but rather the *jeux de mots* an extremely talented reader has found in or created from his texts.

Provençal, about which he knew something, but I like even better the poetry 'translated' from Egyptian, of which language I gather he knew nothing. Our editions, translations, dictionaries, and monographs, and our Society's laboriously compiled bibliography, are not worth the trouble and the cost if they simply allow medievalists to compete with *The Lord of the Rings* and act as advisors to the Society for Creative Anachronism. Our responsibility to the present and the future lies in the skill and honesty with which we explore a world, including a world of fantasy, actually lived and created by men and women in the past who are in some institutional and spiritual sense our ancestors.

However useful we may find personal approaches, literary, psychoanalytic or biographic, eventually scholarly responsibility leads us back to the social matrix in which our literary records were formed and preserved. I began this paper with reference to a manuscript containing 433 leaves and weighing about 12 lb. If that volume had not been written – and preserved – we would have no text of *Les empereors de Rome* and inferior texts of several other works. Why was such a volume written by a scribe who had a shop near the church of Notre-Dame-du-Val in the fair town of Provins?

You know the answer as well as I: because a courtly patron was prepared to invest in such a production. From the political point of view, in the early thirteenth century the balance of power of the French monarch, the Anglo-Norman monarchy, and the house of Champagne was a delicate and changing one. During the reign of Philip Augustus and the regency of Blanche, Champagne was under the control of the French monarchy, but in July 1226 Thibaut IV broke with Louis VIII and was thought by some to have poisoned the young king. In the following year Thibaut was allied with the duke of Brittany, flirting with the English, and in defiance of the regent, Blanche of Castille.[35] Is it possible that the Guiot manuscript was commissioned at this very time? Let us look again at the third portion of the manuscript: the *Roman de Troie* of the Anglo-Norman Benoît de Sainte-Maure, the *Roman de Brut* of his predecessor Wace, a history of Rome by a critic of Blanche of Navarre's opponent, Duke Thibaut I of Lorraine, and then, following on directly as part of the same gathering, Chrétien's Arthurian *Perceval*, dedicated to Count Philip of Flanders, who came close to marrying Marie of Champagne and challenged Philip Augustus. One could hardly pick a better example of a manuscript which seems to place art in the service of political power,[36] though to what end remains

35. Henri d'Arbois de Jubainville, *Histoire des ducs et des comtes de Champagne* (Paris, 1859-67), 4,1,205-14.

36. For recent work on this Burkhardian theme, see the proceedings of the Eleventh Annual Conference of the Center for Medieval and Renaissance Studies at the Ohio State University on 'Court Patronage and the Arts', held in February 1980.

uncertain as long as the date of the manuscript remains unspecified. When we examine the ensemble, we approach an aspect of its reality not easily noted when the works are separately printed and catalogued into different categories.

To modern readers a contest for power between the count or countess palatine of Troyes and the king of St. Denis, or between those who preferred to sing of Arthur and those who rejoiced in a return to the Carolingian line, may resemble too much a conflict between the hats and the caps. Except for a few inflammatory poems, the literature enjoyed at one court could almost always be transferred easily to another, as multiple dedications and copies attest. What is most unifying about courtly literature is the common, or at least restricted, set of values it promoted and its disdain for the common folk, in opposition to whom a courtly society which was becoming increasingly more refined and courteous defined itself. Chrétien stated his own opinion simply and directly in his prologue to *Yvain*:

> A dead man from a court is worth
> much more than a live vilain.
>
> Car molt valt mialz, ce m'est a vis
> uns cortois morz c'uns vilains vis.[37]

The authors of courtly literature taught *corteisie* and *noblesce*, offering advice and models of behaviour to their patrons and in the process enculturating the members of their courts. Here is what Wace had to say about Arthur, as recorded in the Guiot manuscript:

> I'll tell you about Arthur's qualities.... He was a very courageous, very worthy, and very glorious warrior. To the proud he was proud and to the humble he was gentle and sympathetic. He was strong, brave, successful in battle, a generous patron and benefactor. And if someone in need made a request, if he could help him, he didn't refuse. He greatly loved praise and glory and he greatly wanted his deeds to be remembered. He saw to it that he was served in a courtly fashion, and thus he maintained himself most nobly. As long as he reigned and lived he surpassed all other princes in courtliness and nobility, in force and in generosity.[38]

---

37. *Yvain*, ed. Roques, ll.31-32. In *The Origin and Meaning of Courtly Love* (Manchester, 1977), p.113, Roger Boase takes me to task: "Benton might at least have chosen a courtly work, not the *Chanson de Roland*, to illustrate the medieval tendency to think in rigid categories. It is doubtful whether he could have found a quotation to suit his argument." The "rigid" categorization of *cortois* and *vilain* was well-established before Chrétien; see Glyn S. Burgess, *Contribution à l'étude du vocabulaire pré-courtois* (Geneva, 1970), pp.20-43. In fact, a sharp contrast between courtly society and the rest of the world is necessary to give meaning to the concept of 'courtly love': see Joan M. Ferrante, '*Cortes Amor* in Medieval Texts', *Speculum*, 55 (1980), 686-95.

38. Wace, *Roman de Brut*, ed. Arnold and Pelan (n.6 above), p.56, ll.475-92.

> Molt ama pris, molt ama gloire,
> Molt vol ses fez metre an memoire ...
> Tant com il vesqui et regna
> Tos altres princes sormonta
> De corteisie et de noblesse
> et de vertu et de largesce.

Here surely is a passage where Wace has combined what he felt he knew about Arthur from his sources with his own personal fantasy, a royal fantasy which Chrétien did not share, preferring for either political or personal reasons to make the king much more a figure of fun. Wace's fantasy, the wish he hoped would be fulfilled, surely sprang from his dream of how his own king, Henry II, should behave, and his lines, in their simple, elitist, grasping way, are representative of a collective fantasy of courtly authors about courtly patrons, the belief that the praise of power may help render it beneficent, at least for those in the inner circle.

II

MONEY AND POWER IN FRANCE AND CHAMPAGNE

11

The Revenue of Louis VII

THE assessment of the comparative wealth of Louis VII and his son Philip II has been a key, for both mediaeval and modern writers, to an evaluation of the power of the early Capetian monarchy. Contemporaries of Philip II looked back upon his father as a relatively poor monarch, simple and pious. On the other hand, Philip, the king who annexed Vermandois and conquered Normandy for the royal domain, was called Augustus by his biographer Rigord because he had "augmented" the realm, and chroniclers routinely remarked that Philip had increased or enriched the kingdom.[1] Modern historians have generally accepted this contrast. Before 1180 the Capetian kings were the lords of a relatively small domain in the Île-de-France, which Louis VI was able to consolidate and Louis VII used as a base for influencing his great vassals. Philip II, conqueror and financial innovator, raised the actual (as opposed to theoretical) power of the monarchy above that of the neighboring territorial principalities and began a new period of expansion for the French monarchy. This is the traditional view, set forth in classic form by Achille Luchaire, writing of the power of the earliest Capetians, in Lavisse's influential *Histoire de France:* "Le domaine royal, soutien insuffisant de cette majesté théorique, n'est ni la plus vaste, ni la plus riche des seigneuries dont la réunion forme la France."[2]

To measure the increase in royal revenue inaugurated by Philip II, Luchaire found a numerical basis in the *Notæ* of Conan, provost of the cathedral of Lausanne, which had been recently published by Waitz in the *Monumenta Germaniæ historica*. As Luchaire paraphrased the text, Conan noted that he was in Paris at the time of the death of Philip Augustus, and that he heard directly from royal officials that the predecessor of the dead king had scarcely (*à peine*) 19,000 *livres* to spend a month, while Philip's son had almost double that revenue. Luchaire's conclusion about doubling the revenue was based on the calculation that 19,000 pounds a month equals 228,000 a year, while the figure used for comparison was derived from Conan's statement that Philip left his son a revenue of 1,200 *livres parisis* a day (*qualibet die*).[3]

---

[1] *Oeuvres de Rigord et de Guillaume le Breton*, ed. H. François Delaborde (Paris, 1882–1885), I, 6, and 129, where Rigord quotes Philip as saying in 1194, a year of unusual financial exactions, "quod predecessores sui Francorum reges pauperes existentes." For a brief discussion of the two monarchs see Achille Luchaire in *Histoire de France depuis des origines jusqu'à la Révolution*, ed. Ernst Lavisse, 9 vols. in 18 (Paris, 1900–1911), III, part 1; *1137–1226* (1901), pp. 46–47 and 280–284 on character, and 25 and 238–245 on finances.

[2] *Ibid.*, II, part 2: *987–1137*, p. 176.

[3] *Histoire des institutions monarchiques de la France sous les premiers Capétiens, 987–1180* (Paris, 1883), I, 126. The same passage (with modern equivalents eliminated) appears in the 2nd ed. of 1891, I, 131–132. Luchaire used this passage in much the same way in *Histoire de France*, ed. Lavisse, III, part 1, p. 238. He was followed by Williston Walker, *On the Increase of Royal Power in France under Philip Augustus, 1179–1223* (Leipzig, 1888), p. 140. Charles Petit-Dutaillis, *Étude sur la vie et le règne de Louis VIII*, Bibl. de l'École des Hautes Études, fasc. 101 (Paris, 1894), pp. 384–385, cited the text but noted that we have no means to evaluate Conan's testimony exactly; he concluded that the figure given for Philip II was probably too large. Alexander Cartellieri, *Philipp II August* (Leipzig, 1899–

The view that the early Capetians were the *petits seigneurs* of the Île-de-France was vigorously combatted by the late Robert Fawtier in a brilliant popular study written during the dark days of the German occupation of France. He began, with the same text Luchaire used, to show that Philip II had come close to doubling the revenues left him by his father, drawing from it the same calculation that Louis VII had an annual revenue of 228,000 l.p. He then gave a short sketch of early Capetian history, stressing examples of unexpected royal force and wealth and showing how little the royal domain increased from 987 to 1180. He concluded that "there was possibly small difference between the revenues of Hugh Capet and those of Louis VII."[4] M. Fawtier came back again to Conan's figures, which he called the earliest indications we have of the financial resources of the French monarchy in the Middle Ages, in his volume on royal institutions in the current *Histoire des institutions françaises au moyen âge*. Considering the authority of Conan's informants, he stated that the truth of these indications cannot be doubted, and began his chapter on the royal domain with 228,000 l.p. for Louis VII and 438,000 l.p. in 1223. Drawing the natural conclusions from these immense resources, he asserted that even before 1180 the Capetian monarchy was, after the Church, the richest of all the powers in the kingdom.[5]

The extent to which an income of over 200,000 pounds a year exceeded that of other princes is apparent from a few comparisons. Henry II's revenues as king of England, based upon figures from the Pipe Rolls, averaged about 25,000 pounds sterling a year. In Normandy at the time of Philip's conquest of 1204 the fixed revenues have been estimated at about 20,000 Angevin pounds a year. For Flanders the surviving fragments of the recently edited "Gros Brief" of 1187 show that the count had a cash income which was probably well under 10,000 Flemish pounds. For other great French feudal principalities figures are lacking for the twelfth century, but some idea of size is given by estimates for the thirteenth century which show the count of Champagne with a net income of 27,000 l.p. in 1233, the county of Provence with receipts of about 43,000 l. and expenses (outside those of the court) of about 23,000 l. in 1260, and the duchy of Burgundy rendering ordinary receipts of between 20,000 and 30,000 l. at the end of the century.[6]

1922), IV, 597, also cited the text and deplored the lack of sources; he concluded only that Philip far surpassed his predecessors in property and revenues.

[4] *Les Capétiens et la France* (Paris, 1942), pp. 99–107. The translation by Lionel Butler and R. J. Adam, *The Capetian Kings of France* (London, 1960), pp. 100–108, had M. Fawtier's approval and has been quoted in this article.

[5] Ferdinand Lot and Robert Fawtier, Tome II: *Institutions royales* (Paris, 1958), 159.

[6] The sterling coinage of England under Henry II contained about twice as much pure silver as the deniers of France; in the thirteenth century it was exchanged at a rate of 4 deniers of Tours (one of the two standard royal weights) for 1 d. sterling. The other continental coinages mentioned in this paragraph were roughly comparable to those of the French crown. Even allowing for differences of coinage and for a considerable margin of error in calculating the estimates cited here, the disparity between 228,000 l.p. and the other revenues is obvious. England: James H. Ramsay, *A History of the Revenue of the Kings of England, 1066–1399* (Oxford, 1925), I, 191; cf. Fawtier, "L'histoire financière de l'Angleterre au moyen âge," *Le Moyen Âge*, XXXVIII (1928), 63, and Jacques Boussard, "Les institutions

The gap in French historiography left when Luchaire failed to finish his projected biography of Louis VII has now been filled by a major study by Marcel Pacaut, who bases his work upon all the published sources and an impressive number of unpublished royal acts.[7] M. Pacaut deals in great detail with the questions of the extent of the royal domain and the king's financial resources. His procedure for arriving at an estimate of the total royal income is to begin with calculations for those classes of revenue for which we have some documentary indication of figures. For instance, since a document of about 1173 records that the revenues of Senlis were worth a little over 200 l., and since there were in the royal domain twelve other towns about the size of Senlis, he estimates that the royal revenue from these towns as a group was somewhere around 13×200, or 2,600 l.p. Applying this procedure to the various classes for which figures exist, M. Pacaut comes up with the following approximations:

Great estates	4,800
Towns	2,600
Paris	800
Medium and small landed property	1,100
Woods and forests	500
Fairs and markets	1,320
Market tolls and road and river tolls, etc.	2,750
Quitrents, etc.	200
Prévôts (High justice)	5,700
Ecclesiastical domain (*regalia*)	500
	20,270 l.p.

To these revenues, M. Pacaut points out, must be added others for which it is impossible to establish figures. Those which he names under the heading of domain include income from minting, measuring, tolls on wheeled traffic, preferential sales, non-noble military service, labor service, tallage, and low justice; in addition, there is no measure of exactions paid in kind or of the agricultural produce of the royal estates. The second class of revenue for which no figures are available is that of feudal dues, including military service, payments for alienation of property, and especially relief. And, finally, there are exceptional taxes, such as those levied twice by Louis VII for crusading expenses. M. Pacaut concludes that these

---

financières de l'Angleterre au XII⁰ siècle," *Cahiers de civilisation médiévale*, I (1958), 491–492. Normandy: Maurice Powicke, *The Loss of Normandy*, 2nd ed. (Manchester, 1960), p. 234. Flanders: Adriaan Verhulst and M. Gysseling, *Le compte général de 1187* (Brussels, 1962). Champagne: Henri d'Arbois de Jubainville, *Histoire des ducs et des comtes de Champagne* (Paris, 1859–1866), IV, 803. Provence: *Les Bouches-du-Rhône: encyclopédie départementale*, ed. Paul Masson (Marseille, 1924), II, 584–586. Burgundy: Jean Richard, *Les ducs de Bourgogne et la formation du duché du XI⁰ au XIV⁰ siècle* (Paris, 1954), pp. 384–386. It should be noted that mediaeval figures often do not permit us to make the all-important distinction between gross revenue and net revenue. Complete accounts show that many expenditures were made by local officials before calculating the total owed the lord, and that other obligations were paid from the central treasury. Whether these expenditures were made before or after totalling the lord's "income" is crucial to what we see as revenue.

[7] *Louis VII et son royaume* (Paris, 1964). The section on the royal domain and its finances is pp. 119–160.

revenues, for which he cannot establish figures, probably amounted to about twice as much as the more precisely established revenues, or about 40,000 l.p., making a total annual revenue of about 60,000 l.p.

The difficulties which a modern historian has in estimating mediaeval income are in part the result of incomplete documentation, but they also are produced by the uncertainties of some revenues. From year to year there might be great variation in the amount of money produced by the escheat of feudal tenements or from rights of justice over the property of condemned felons. Mediaeval lords and their clerks experienced these uncertainties too, and the difference between reasonably stable and capricious income is reflected by the categories of royal accounts in the early thirteenth century. As is shown by the earliest systematic record of French royal finance, the account of receipts and expenditures in the fiscal year 1202–03, the greatest single differentiation of ordinary income was between those revenues which could be farmed and those which were not. Farmed incomes varied from year to year, but we may presume that they were regular enough for the tax farmers to make competitive bids with the expectation of profit. In 1202–03 something over 30,000 l.p. was paid in by the *prévôts*, who collected their money from such generally stable sources of income as tolls, fairs and markets, town and estate payments, and the profits of low justice. Other income, totalling about 65,000 or 70,000 l.p., from such sources as high justice, fines and confiscations, and escheats, came under the heading of the *bailli*, an administrative official appointed by the king and superior to the *prévôts;* unfarmed revenues were usually classified under this heading even when such revenue actually was collected by the *prévôt*.[8]

In some ways, the accounts of 1202–03 parallel the classifications and approximate figures suggested by M. Pacaut. Although some small categories for which he found figures, such as ecclesiastical revenue, were entered under the heading of the *baillis*, and some farmed revenues were collected from incomes M. Pacaut could not quantify, his assessable revenues generally correspond to those of the *prévôt* and the "uncertain" incomes are generally those of the *bailli*. Without pressing the correspondence too far, it may be said that the accounts of 1202–03 support M. Pacaut's suggestion that "uncertain" income was about twice the size of assessable income. And while stressing that these figures are only very rough approximations, we may reach a conclusion quite different from that to which M. Pacaut eventually comes, and suggest that a total average annual royal income of somewhere around 60,000 l. under Louis VII was increased by his son, in 1202–03 while the conquest of Normandy was still under way, to an ordinary income from both farmed and uncertain sources of over 90,000 l.p. In addition, in 1202–03 Philip received over 26,000 l.p. under the heading *servientes* or sergeants-at-arms. This income may be considered an extraordinary revenue, a *taxe de guerre*, levied because of the war against King John. The sources and figures of this heading are very close to those of the *Prisée des sergents*, another document

[8] Ferdinand Lot and Robert Fawtier, *Le premier budget de la monarchie française: Le compte général de 1202–1203*, Bibl. de l'École des Hautes Études, fasc. 259 (Paris, 1932). The explanation of the table of income on p. 48, revised to eliminate carry-over accounting, is found on pp. 36, 42, and 47.

of Philip's reign which has been dated in its original form to 1194, the year of the beginning of war with Richard Lionheart. The *Prisée* records the monetary payments made by various communities in lieu of providing non-noble soldiers (*sergents*) for the royal army. In 1194 Philip raised over 7,000 men-at-arms and almost 12,000 l., at a rate of three l. for each soldier not provided by the communities to meet their assessments.[9] In 1202–03 he received more money, but presumably fewer soldiers, and since three pounds was about the pay of a foot soldier for three months, the money he received in lieu of soldiers was probably spent immediately on mercenaries. The money paid *pro servientes* in 1194 and 1202–03 must be considered an exceptional military taxation and not part of normal annual income, since there is no evidence that it was collected every year and it varied in inverse proportion to the number of soldiers levied. The fourth heading of the accounts of 1202–03, that of *marchia*, should not properly be considered income at all. This is a section devoted to military expenses, and the "receipts" are almost all transfers of funds from the royal treasury. Most of the money received and spent under this heading (over 60,000 l.p.) should be credited to previous saving, not to the income of the current year.

This comparison of M. Pacaut's figures with the totals and headings of 1202–03 has been given in some detail because, as noted above, he reaches quite different conclusions about total income. After going through the calculation upon which a possible total of around 60,000 l.p. for Louis VII has been suggested here, M. Pacaut inflates his own figures by concluding that Louis no doubt possessed, *grosso modo*, two and a half or three times as much revenue as the surviving texts reveal to us, and that his annual income may be figured at 150,000 to 180,000 l.p. He adds quite realistically that these figures are astonishing, but he calls to mind that they are still less than the 228,000 l.p. given by Conan of Lausanne. My objection to M. Pacaut's multiplication of his totals to account for lost material is that his approximations were already based upon a system of multiplication. The estimate of 2,600 l.p. paid by thirteen towns did not come from the addition of existing figures, but from multiplying the one figure we have, that of 200 l.p. for Senlis in 1173. The average town in an average year may have paid more than 200 l.p., but it may also have paid less. If we had complete accounts for all thirteen major towns of the royal domain (excepting Paris), the total produced by addition of all figures would be more precise than that produced by multiplication of one figure, but not necessarily larger. More documents might show us other classes of revenue or other estates or people paying them, but the great care with which M. Pacaut has done his work of cataloging and the fact that minor sources of income are more likely to be lost from sight than major ones both give confidence that more information would probably not produce great surprises. Complete documentation would hardly show that there were two and a half or three times more major towns in the royal domain than M. Pacaut has found. The margin of error accompanying the figure of 60,000 l.p. is surely large, but it is based on reasonable calculations, and the documents we have give us no reason to replace it by a figure two and a half or three times bigger.

[9] For text and analysis of the *Prisée*, see Édouard Audouin, *Essai sur l'armée royale au temps de Philippe Auguste*, nouv. ed. (Paris, 1913).

M. Pacaut supports these larger figures with other calculations based on the accounts of 1202–03. Comparing the list of *prévôtés* in the two periods, reducing the revenues of *prévôtés* listed in both periods by about one-fourth, and adding villages controlled by Louis VII but omitted from the joint list, he concludes that in 1180 the royal *prévôtés* produced a revenue of about 23,000 l.p., a figure quite in line with his earlier calculations. The comparison of the revenues of the *baillis*, in which he concludes that since Philip received over 82,000 l.p. from his *baillis*, Louis probably received about 60,000 l.p., is less sound. This calculation starts with incorrect figures, since the elimination of carry-over accounting from one term to the next shows that Philip's actual income from the *baillis* was about 70,000 l.p., or perhaps even as low as about 65,000 l.p.[10] A further criticism is that the estimates based upon the revenues collected by both the *prévôts* and the *baillis* assume that Louis received over three-quarters of the revenue which Philip's agents could collect in the same territory. This assumption may be correct, but it would be very difficult to document; it is, in fact, an assumption about just the matter we are trying to investigate, whether Louis was able to collect anywhere near as much money as his son. To these figures M. Pacaut adds 20,000 l.p. as his estimate of the amount Louis received from the 47,000 l.p. Philip collected for sergeants-at-arms. This final calculation treats an extraordinary war tax as an annual revenue, and suggests that Louis was able to collect a large amount of money for default of non-noble military service (when Philip himself levied a cash assessment of only 12,000 l.p. in 1194). The total M. Pacaut derives from this procedure is 103,000 l.p., though the criticisms given above suggest that it should be nearer 75,000 l.p., or even considerably less. He concludes instead that the figures should probably be doubled to about 200,000 l.p., eliminating the great contrast between the revenues of Louis and Philip and bringing Louis' total closer to that cited from the *Notæ* of Conan of Lausanne.

As the preceding discussion demonstrates, the testimony of Conan of Lausanne has figured prominently in estimates of the revenues of Louis and Philip since Waitz published the most widely cited edition of the text in 1879.[11] It is therefore desirable to examine critically the crucial portion of this text:

Sepultus autem fuit com insigniis regalibus, et vixerat annis 59 et regnavit annis 45, et ditavit regnum et auxit ultra quam credi possit; quia com Lodovicus rex, pater suus, non dimiserit ei in redditibus, sicut officiales regni referebant, mense 19 milia librarum, ipse dimisit Lodovico, filio suo, qualibet die 1200 libras Parisiensium in redditibus, et sicut dictus C. prepositus Lausannensis, qui eius interfuit sepulture, audivit a familiaribus regis et a publica fama, dictus rex Philipus in testamento reliquit de pecunia, quam congregaverat ad succurendum terram Ierosolemitanam, 700 milia marcarum ad defendendum regnum Francorum et manutenendum Lodovico, filio suo . . . .

If the reader is disquieted by a reference to a monthly income in a seasonal economy, he receives no reassurance from the apparatus, which indicates that the entire phrase "mense 19 milia librarum" is an expansion of an interlinear abbreviation "m. 19 m. l." This problem and that of the total annual income are resolved by the unique manuscript, probably autograph, in the Bern Burger-

[10] Lot and Fawtier, *Premier budget*, pp. 42 and 48.
[11] *Mon. Germ. hist., Scriptores*, XXIV, 782.

bibliothek. Waitz, surely not realizing the importance which would later be attached to his reading, had carelessly transcribed the interlinear phrase in question, which actually reads, "nisi .ixx. m. librarum," or "except nineteen thousand *livres*."[12] With this correction made, the passage may be rendered thus:

He was buried with royal honors, had lived fifty-nine years and reigned forty-five years, and enriched the kingdom and increased it beyond what can be believed; since, although King Louis, his father, did not leave him an income, as the officials of the kingdom used to relate, except for 19,000 *livres*, he left to Louis, his son, a revenue of 1,200 *livres parisis* a day, and (as the said Conan, provost of Lausanne, who was present at the interment heard from intimates of the king and from common report), the said King Philip left in his will from the money he had collected for the aid of the land of Jerusalem, 700,000 marks for the defense of the kingdom of France and for the maintenance of his son, Louis.

This corrected reading casts an entirely different light on the whole question of the finances of Louis and Philip. If by *redditus* Conan meant the total annual royal income, his figure of 19,000 l. for Louis VII seems extremely small, and we may be tempted to think that little accuracy should be expected from the graveside comments of Philip's intimates about what royal officials used to report about the income of a king dead forty-three years before. If *redditus*, a recurring income, referred to the revenues which Louis could calculate in advance from year to year, as opposed to extraordinary taxes, feudal aids and escheats, or other uncertain revenues, then 19,000 l. comes strikingly close to the 20,270 l.p. of the first stage of M. Pacaut's calculations. The second explanation has some contemporary justification,[13] and is supported by a statement attributed to Boniface VIII in 1302 that Philip II had (presumably at the beginning of his reign) an income of 18,000 l. from established revenues (*de situatis redditibus*).[14] But the ambiguity remains unresolved, for Conan's use of *redditus* with reference to Philip II must surely mean total revenue, and to keep the terms of his contrast consistent he should have used the word the same way about Louis. The figures which Conan gives for Philip's bequests seem high but are, however, in general accord with other contemporary accounts.[15]

Is Conan's assertion that he had heard that Philip left his son a revenue of 1,200 l.p. a day also suspect? *Qualibet die*, "every day," says nothing of the

[12] Dr Christian von Steiger, librarian of the Burgerbibliothek Bern, kindly sent me a microfilm of Codex B 219 (formerly 37bis), f. 107^r, and later verified my reading from direct examination of the manuscript. He also informed me that this reading is in complete agreement with the critical edition of Charles Roth, *Cartulaire du Chapitre de Notre-Dame de Lausanne. Première partie: Texte* (Lausanne, 1948), p. 546 and p. 547, note g. The correct reading is also given by the edition which preceded that of Waitz, *Cartulaire du chapitre de Notre-Dame de Lausanne*, published by the Société d'histoire de la Suisse Romande (Lausanne, 1851), p. 484.

[13] Giraldus Cambrensis, *De instructione principum*, in *Opera*, Rolls Series, XXI (London, 1861–1891), VIII, 316, contrasts "redditus" and "accidentia."

[14] Paris, Bibl. nat. ms lat. 15002, f. 85^r = Pierre Dupuy, *Histoire du differend d'entre le Pape Boniface VIII et Philippes le Bel* (Paris, 1655), p. 77. I am grateful to Professor Richard Rouse for confirming that Dupuy had accurately transcribed his manuscript source, including the statement that Philip IV had a current income of "quadraginta mill. lib. & plus," though "quadringenti" is the number one would expect. Ms lat. 15002, formerly ms M.M.7 of the abbey of St Victor at Paris, was one of Dupuy's major sources and merits further attention.

[15] Cartellieri, *Philipp II*, VI, 566–567.

number of days averaged, and multiplying by 365 to achieve an annual income may be misplaced concreteness. A revenue of 438,000 l.p. a year would be quite large; in fact, it is over seventy percent of the revenue reported for three terms of the year 1286-87, the first full year for which we have a record after 1202-03.[16] But it is still possible that Conan heard and reported his observation correctly. If one divides the total income of the Candlemas term of 1226, a term of exceptional income (including the relief of the county of Flanders), by the ninety-three days in the term, the result is a daily income of 1,735 l.p. This figure is probably unusually high, and it contrasts with the average of 1,012 l.p. per day for the Ascension term of 1238. With all income included, an average daily income of 1,200 l.p. was a possibility at the end of Philip's reign, particularly in a term of unusually high revenue.[17] While Conan's statement about Philip's revenue is not an indisputable base for an estimate of annual income, his figure should not be rejected out of hand. If it is anywhere near accurate, Conan proved prophetic in saying that Philip enriched the kingdom "beyond what can be believed."

The documents left to us do not permit any certainty about the income of Louis VII. If Conan's figure of 19,000 l. could be accepted as total annual revenue, then we could say with confidence that Louis VII was financially weaker than his major vassals, and far weaker than Henry II, who could probably draw that amount of money from Normandy alone. But probably Conan's figure is either far too small, or refers to only part of the total income. Since M. Pacaut's cataloging shows an income of about 20,000 l.p. for which documentary evidence exists in some form or other, it is likely that Louis' revenues were a good deal larger. How much larger it is hard to say. If Philip's "ordinary" income in 1202-03 (not counting extraordinary military receipts) was about 100,000 l.p., Louis' income was probably under 75,000 l.p., and perhaps a good deal less. The suggestion of a gross income of around 60,000 l.p. is a guess, but one which has a reasonable basis.[18] If, year after year, Louis VII could raise as much as 50 or 60,000 l.p., the Île-de-France was producing more than most if not all feudal principalities in the kingdom, though less than the combined estates of Henry Plantagenet. Whatever we may conclude about his predecessors, the monarchy of Louis VII was able to measure up against the territorial principalities about it, and France as a whole was in a position to resist foreign invasion. But Conan of Lausanne provides no basis for arguing that Louis' revenues came anywhere close to those of his son; indeed, he is another witness to the contemporary view that it was Philip Augustus who "augmented" the kingdom.

---

[16] Fawtier, *Institutions royales*, p. 191.

[17] For daily averages see Appendix D II at the end of vol. II of Léon L. Borrelli de Serres, *Recherches sur divers services publics du XIII° au XVII° siècle* (Paris, 1895-1909). Cf. Fawtier's comment on daily averages in *Hist. des inst. fran.*, II, 189.

[18] It may be only a coincidence that the imprecise *Récits d'un Ménestrel de Reims*, ed. Natalis de Wailly (Paris, 1876), p. 9, reports that Louis VII left his son a landed income of only 60,000 l.

12

Philip the Fair and the Jours de Troyes

When Philip the Fair, fortunate in both his marriage and his inheritance, combined the office of count of Champagne with that of the king of France, he extended the control of the monarchy east to the borders of the Empire and presented his officials with the task of assimilating a feudal principality almost as large as the duchy of Normandy. The ease with which Philip swallowed such a large bite is attributable to the long experience of royal administration in Normandy. One of the most efficient ways the French kings had found to control their new duchy was to send men from Paris to be masters of the high court, the Exchequer, and Philip repeated this procedure in Champagne.[1] The purpose of this paper is to investigate how Philip reconstituted and administered the judiciary of Champagne, the precise timing of his changes, and whether his county court was rivaled by a parallel court of the barons of Champagne which embodied provincial opposition to his centralization.

After the middle of the thirteenth century, about the same time the royal court of Parlement became stationary at Paris, the count of Champagne routinely held his judicial assemblies in the city of Troyes. These days of judgment therefore came to be known as the *Jours de Troyes, dies Trecensis,* or as we might say, the sessions of Troyes. In the early fourteenth century popular usage distinguished these sessions from other, lesser days of court (such as those of the foresters) by calling the high court of the county the "Grands Jours," and by the early fifteenth century the adjectives *grand* and *magnus* were routinely used in government documents. In the

---

* The following pages are dedicated to Professor Joseph R. Strayer, in gratitude for his continuing instruction, encouragement, and inspiration. The research upon which this paper is based was greatly facilitated by a Guggenheim Fellowship in 1963–64 and grants from the Johnson fund of the American Philosophical Society and the American Council of Learned Societies, for which I wish to express my appreciation. I am grateful for the special assistance of Mlle Elisabeth Dunan of the Archives Nationales.

1. On the masters of the Exchequer see Joseph R. Strayer, *The Administration of Normandy Under Saint Louis* (Cambridge, Mass., 1932), pp. 92–93. The administrative effects of the acquisition of Normandy and Languedoc are freshly analysed by Strayer in his Presidential Address to the Medieval Academy in 1968, to appear in *Speculum.*

time of Philip the Fair and his predecessors, however, the official name of the court was simply the Jours of Troyes.[2]

In the period before 1284, when the county of Champagne was independent of French control, judicial sessions were held at Troyes as often as three times a year, frequently at the great religious festivals when the count held court in the cathedral city, but our records are too fragmentary to suggest any pattern, and perhaps the Jours had no fixed calendar.[3] The men who attended this court were a mixed lot. The great barons were rarely present, and the idea that the seven peers of Champagne sat in these sessions with the count is a myth.[4] Some of the more important men of the county attended ex officio. In the absence of the count the governor of the county was the president of the court. The marshal came often, as did the seneschal, the lord of Joinville. A few other barons were present at some sessions, but usually the nobles at court were not great lords in their own right. Although they were men of some substance and experience, these lesser nobles were not wealthy or powerful enough to avoid court service. In the period we are considering, attendance at the court of the county, like attendance at the English Parliament, was still more a burden than a privilege. In addition to the nobles, some churchmen were often present, sometimes an abbot or two, and usually a few lesser clerics. The *baillis*, the major administrative officials of the county, appeared regularly, probably both to give advice and to defend their own actions. For

2. For what little is known of the Jours under the independent counts of Champagne see Henri d'Arbois de Jubainville, *Histoire des ducs et des comtes de Champagne*, 6 vols. in 7 (Paris, 1859–67), IV, 576–577, and Félix Bourquelot, *Études sur les foires de Champagne et de Brie*, 2 vols. (Paris, 1865), II, 258–261. The accounts of the commune of Provins refer to the *"Grans Jours a Troies"* in 1306 and 1308 and the phrase *"in diebus Trecensibus magnis"* appears in the accounts of the chapel of Notre-Dame of the cathedral of Troyes in 1333; see Maurice Prou and Jules d'Auriac, *Actes et comptes de la commune de Provins* (Provins, 1933), with an index (Montereau, 1935), pp. 204 and 214, and Bourquelot, *Études*, II, 270 n. 4. *"Les jours du gruyer"* are mentioned in Auguste Longnon (ed.), *Documents relatifs au comté de Champagne et de Brie*, 3 vols. (Paris, 1901–14), III, 451 L.

3. Arbois de Jubainville, *Histoire*, IV, 577. For other dates see Prou and d'Auriac, *Actes et comptes*, pp. 23, 24, 43, 58, and 60.

4. The old story is repeated by Jean Longnon in Ferdinand Lot and Robert Fawtier, *Histoire des institutions françaises au moyen âge*, 3 vols. to date (Paris, 1957——), I, 131, citing Arbois de Jubainville, *Histoire*, II, cxxi–cxxii. The text printed by Arbois de Jubainville is from the collection of a seventeenth-century antiquarian, the Abbé Decamps. Apparently both Decamps and Pithou (cited *ibid.*, p. cxxii n. 4) based their statements on a decree of March 4, 1404, printed in the *Ordonnances des rois de France*, 22 vols. (Paris, 1723–1849), VIII, 636. The text, of value for showing the rights of the peers at the opening sessions of the Jours under Charles VI, of course tells us nothing of the courts of the independent counts. See Bourquelot, *Études*, II, 262–263.

Philip the Fair and the Jours de Troyes

example, twenty-one people are known to have attended a session in 1276: two barons (the marshal and Joinville, the seneschal); five knights, including one of the guards of the fairs of Champagne; two abbots; six clerks; the four *baillis*; a burgess of Provins who was the other guard of the fairs; and an unidentified person.[5]

The men who composed the court of the Jours in the 1270's had long had experience in delivering justice without the oversight of the count. Thibaut IV had become king of Navarre in 1234, and since then the counts of Champagne had often been absent in Spain. After Count Henri III died in 1274, Champagne was held in trust by his widow Blanche of Artois and her second husband Edmund of Lancaster, who found it easier to govern the county by delegation than in person. The role of the count in the proceedings of the court was therefore restricted. A few barons and abbots, aided by a small number of other nobles and clerics and by the administrative officers, were responsible for dispensing justice and declaring the law. The members of this court were not elected, and they could be called representative of the county only in the most generous sense of virtual representation. Except for a few clerics, they had acquired their legal training in the school of experience. We have no grounds for saying that they were not fair or did not do their duty in preserving the customary law. In fact, we know too little of the court to assess its efficiency or its fairness. Presumably, however, the job done ,by the haphazard collection of courtiers who sat in the Jours of Troyes could have been done as well by any group of honest men who knew the local law, and men with more extensive judicial training and experience could have done it better. When Philip the Fair destroyed the provincial autonomy of the court and staffed it from Paris, he probably improved it greatly.

A review of the chronology of Philip's acquisition of Champagne will help make clear the way in which the monarchy changed the composition and function of its high court. Although Champagne was not definitively attached to the royal domain until 1361, the county came under royal control and administration when Philip the Fair married the heiress of Champagne, Jeanne of Navarre. The marriage was assured by a treaty of May, 1275, between Philip III and Blanche of Artois, widow of the last count of Champagne; this agreement stipulated that Blanche's daughter Jeanne should marry one of King Philip's two oldest sons and gave the little girl into the king's care to be raised. Shortly after making

---

5. See Appendix III. Some of the members of other courts before 1284 are recorded in *L'ancien coutumier de Champagne*, ed. Paulette Portejoie (Poitiers, 1956), pp. 165–167 (1270), 171–173 (1270), 174–175 (1271), and 148–150 (1278).

this agreement, Blanche married the only brother of King Edward of England, Edmund of Lancaster, who held the guardianship of the county until 1284. On August 16 of that year Jeanne, not yet twelve, married Prince Philip, who was then sixteen. A little over a year later, on October 6, 1285, Philip III, then forty, died as he was returning from his ill-fated crusade against Aragon, and the young count and countess of Champagne became king and queen of France.[6]

For the next twenty years Philip ruled Champagne directly, but only by virtue of his wife's position as countess. When Jeanne died in April, 1305, her rights to the kingdom of Navarre and the county of Champagne and Brie passed to her eldest son Louis, who was then fifteen years old. After his mother's death Louis could style himself count of Champagne, and in January, 1310, after he had reached nineteen, he bought his brothers' rights in the inheritance of their mother and had them do homage to him.[7] It is not certain, however, to what degree Philip permitted his son to gain experience by exercising authority in Champagne, or how soon Louis assumed complete responsibility for the administration of the county. The death of Jeanne of Navarre also raised the problem of the possible separation of Champagne from direct royal control, a problem which was to trouble the monarchy greatly in the fourteenth century. If—as actually happened—Louis died leaving only a female heir, the succession to the kingdom could pass either to his daughter or to his brothers, but there was no question that unless special arrangements were made the right to Champagne should properly go to his child.[8] With the advantage of hindsight we can see that the last ten years of his reign provided time in which Philip could prepare for the day when once again Champagne might be bound to the monarchy only by ties of vassalage, and we may try to determine whether this consideration actually affected his policy.

This summary shows that before 1314 royal control of the county had passed through four stages. After May, 1275, when an eventual marriage of the heiress to a royal prince was anticipated, authority in the county was held by Blanche of Artois and Edmund of Lancaster. Then came the

6. Arbois de Jubainville, *Histoire*, IV, 440–456.

7. *Registres du Trésor des Chartes: Inventaire analytique*, pub. under the direction of Robert Fawtier (Paris, 1958———), I, No. 1451. According to the customary law of Champagne a boy could inherit at age fifteen; see Portejoie (ed.), *Coutumier*, art. 5, p. 148.

8. Unfortunately, there has been no detailed study of the acquisition of Champagne by the monarchy since that of Denis François Secousse, "Mémoire sur l'union de la Champagne et de la Brie à la couronne de France," *Mémoires de l'Academie des Inscriptions et Belles-lettres*, XVII (1751), 295–315.

period of fourteen months between August, 1284, and October, 1285, when Philip III supervised the administration for his teenage son. The third period, when Philip IV ruled both France and Champagne, began in October, 1285. Finally, after the death of the queen in 1305, Prince Louis was nominally count but acted more or less under his father's direction.

The degree of royal influence on the composition of the high court in the first period is not certain. In theory Edmund of Lancaster or his lieutenants should have been free to choose their own courtiers without any direction from the king. But two clerks closely connected with the Parlement of Paris, Master Anseau de Montaigu and Florent de Roye, are known to have attended a session of the Jours in 1278, and it has therefore been suggested that during the minority of Jeanne of Navarre, Philip III began the practice of sending commissioners from Paris to attend the provincial court.[9] Before concluding that the king regularly or even frequently sent representatives of the Parlement to the Jours, however, we should examine the nature of the case in which the two royal clerks were involved. A vital question at issue between the king and Edmund of Lancaster was the age at which Jeanne would reach her majority, when Edmund would lose his guardianship. Any determination of the age at which girls could inherit property in Champagne was therefore critical to the monarchy. And it was just such a case, in which the court of Champagne declared that a girl's wardship ended when she had reached eleven, that brought the royal clerks to Troyes.[10] Our record tells us only that these men were present, and not whether they acted as judges, advocates, or simple witnesses. We do know that their attendance was later of special importance to the king, for at a hearing on March 11, 1284, they testified about the majority of Jeanne of Navarre.[11] This special case is therefore a poor basis on which to build a theory that Philip III made a practice of sending Parisian masters to the Jours during Jeanne's minority.

Our next question is whether Philip III altered the established relationship between the Parlement and the Jours in some other fashion. Under Louis IX it had been extremely rare for cases from Champagne

9. Emile Chénon, "L'ancien coutumier de Champagne," *Nouvelle revue historique de droit français et étranger* (année 1907), p. 317; see also Chénon, *Histoire générale du droit français public et privé*, 2 vols. (Paris, 1926), I, 691, and Fawtier in Lot and Fawtier, *Histoire*, II, 470. For encapsulated biographies of the two men see Portejoie (ed.), *Coutumier*, p. 149 nn. 4–5. Florent de Roye came to be one of Philip IV's experts on the affairs of Champagne. He probably was not a native of Champagne but came from Picardy, for St. Florentius was the principal patron of the church of Roye (Somme).
10. Portejoie (ed.), *Coutumier*, art. 5, pp. 148–150.
11. *Les établissements de Saint Louis*, ed. Paul Viollet, III (Paris, 1883), 166–168.

to be heard before the Parlement and quite difficult to get a ruling that the royal court had any jurisdiction over cases which belonged in the Jours. In 1267 when the abbot of Saint-Urbain of Joinville brought charges against the lord of Joinville, the Parlement sent the case back to the court of Count Thibaut, who had claimed jurisdiction, and in 1269 the royal court heard charges made against the count of Sancerre by the abbot of St. Germain of Auxerre only because the matter was ruled to be personal and not feudal.[12] Two other cases show that during this period the count of Champagne was well treated in the royal court, for when the count claimed that royal *baillis* had encroached on his jurisdiction, Parlement ruled against the *baillis*.[13]

The court of Philip III appears to have made no radical change in St. Louis' policy of respecting the judicial rights of the count of Champagne. There was, it is true, an increase in the number of cases between the count and royal vassals or religious houses under the king's guard recorded in the *Olim*, those invaluable registers of the early Parlements, but this was probably only a result of a general increase in litigation.[14] In a conflict of 1279 between Count Edmund and the abbey of Sainte-Colombe of Sens, Parlement ruled that it had jurisdiction because the abbey was in the king's guard, but in the same year the court told the monks of Saint-Jean of Laon that if they wanted to bring a case against the lord of Joinville over the priory of Ragecourt, they should complain to the count of Champagne.[15] In fact, Parlement under Philip III remained quite sensitive about usurping the authority of the Jours. In 1283 the dissatisfied children of a certain Jaillart appealed a decision of the *bailli* of Provins to the Parlement on the grounds of denial of justice. Jean of Acre, Count Edmund's lieutenant, in turn demanded that the case should be returned to the court of Champagne. Finally, *with the agreement of the officials of Champagne*, the court decided that the appeal should be settled by the bishop of Dol and the abbot of Saint-Denis, but it clearly stated that no future rights of the heir of Champagne should be prejudiced "and the court of France should through this procedure acquire no new right." The exceptional treatment of this case shows that in the time of the independent

---

12. *Les Olim*, ed. Arthur Beugnot, 4 vols. (Paris, 1839–48), I, 677, vi, and 756, xi. Of course cases between the count and other royal vassals were heard in Parlement; see *ibid.*, I, 657, xix, and 759, xix.

13. *Ibid.*, I, 420, viii, and 639, xiii.

14. *Olim*, II, 103, xviii; 126, lix; 169, xliii; 178, xxiii; 197, iv; and *Essai de restitution d'un volume perdu des Olim*, ed. Léopold Delisle, in Edgard Boutaric, *Actes du Parlement de Paris*, 2 vols. (Paris, 1863–67), I, 338, Nos. 234 and 235; 353, nos. 335 and 339; 370, no. 465; 372, no. 475; 374, no. 487; 375, no. 494; 385, no. 525.

15. Delisle (ed.), *Essai*, p. 358, No. 380, and *Olim*, II, 137, xxiv.

counts there was no regular procedure for appeal to Parlement from Champagne, and that the court of Philip III respected this independence.[16]

The Parlement of Philip III did discuss some matters involving Champagne, not to take up cases which the count claimed as his own, but for administrative purposes and in occasional cases of voluntary jurisdiction. As has been said before, the agreement of 1275 had assured that eventually Champagne would come under royal control, and the king therefore had an interest in the administration of the county. This interest explains why in 1278 the Parlement ordered the marshal of Champagne to pay the money fiefs which he owed (presumably so that arrears would not build up) and to cease excessive exploitation of the woodlands.[17] And in 1281 Edmund's lieutenant Jean of Acre used the Parlement rather than the Jours as the proper setting in which to return the charters which he had confiscated from the commune of Provins.[18] Foreseeing that the monarchy would increase its role in the county, a few litigants voluntarily brought their cases before the royal court for settlement. In 1282 the chief financial officer of the county, Renier Accorre, and some money-changers of the fairs of Champagne by mutual consent moved their conflict from the Jours to the Parlement.[19] And in the following year the burghers of Provins went to Paris as well as to the Jours to complain that the *prévôt* had knocked down their judicial ladder used for displaying criminals.[20] It is noteworthy, however, that the settlement of this second case came from the Jours rather than from Parlement. Philip III appears to have protected his future rights in Champagne without showing any special desire to infringe the judicial autonomy of the county.

For the story up to this point we have only scattered sources of information about the Jours, but starting in the fall of 1284 there is more information, though not nearly enough. The reason for this improvement is that a clerk marked the beginning of Prince Philip's power in Champagne by starting a new register of the proceedings of the Jours of Troyes. This register, which carried the record of the court up to 1295, and a second volume which went up to 1299, did not survive the fire of the Chambre des Comptes in 1737, but before they were lost Nicolas Dongois, Du Cange, Nicolas Brussel, and other antiquarian historians had copied

16. *Olim*, II, 228, vi; cf. Portejoie (ed.), *Coutumier*, art. 39, pp. 193–194. Arbois de Jubainville, *Histoire*, IV, 578–579, in using this case as evidence of the principle of appeal, does not do justice to the hesitations of the royal court.
17. *Olim*, II, 119, xxxvii; see also 223, iii.
18. *Ibid.*, II, 177, xix.
19. *Ibid.*, II, 214, xxxviii. Possibly the changers felt that Renier had too much influence in the county for them to receive a fair hearing in the Jours.
20. Prou and d'Auriac, *Actes et comptes*, pp. 59–60.

extracts which we can use today.[21] If the complete registers had survived, we would know almost as much of the Jours of Troyes under Philip the Fair as we do of the Parlement of Paris.

Brussel's extracts tell us of the composition of the court which gathered at Troyes in early December, 1284.[22] Twenty-five names are recorded, of which many are of men known to have attended the court before. The marshal of Champagne and Joinville, the seneschal, head the list. Abbot Robert of Montiéramey was there, as he had been in 1276, though this time with a different abbot as a colleague. Among the administrative officials were the tax collector of the county, a guard of the fairs, a former chancellor, the *baillis* of Sens and Troyes and the former *bailli* of Vitry, and among the clerks we find the familiar names of Anseau de Montaigu and Florent de Roye. In addition, however, the court contained a number of men new to Champagne but previously associated with the Parlement, including the great noble Simon de Clermont; an experienced royal administrator, Gautier de Chambly, archdeacon of Coutances; the archdeacon of Bayeux; and other men who had worked together in Paris. The influence of the royal court on the Jours of Troyes was not yet paramount, but it had begun.

Whether young Philip the Fair exercised any personal influence in this session is a question which, like so many others concerned with his role in government, is tantalizing.[23] The new count was represented in court by a proctor, and we do not have the evidence to determine if Philip was actually present.[24] It would be hard in any case to see the prince through the crowd who attended the Jours, but we simply cannot tell whether Philip or his father's courtiers should be considered responsible for decisions of unusual severity in two feudal cases.

Pierre de Bourlemont was in trouble with the count for a number of reasons, particularly because he had broken an oath of peace made earlier to the abbot of Mureaux, and he therefore had to make a special petition to do homage for Bourlemont and Rorthey. Philip's proctor at first

21. See Appendix I, pp. 213-14.
22. Appendix II, No. 1.
23. For the most successful effort to date to solve the mystery of Philip's political personality see Joseph R. Strayer, "Philip the Fair—A 'Constitutional' King," *American Historical Review*, LXII (1956), 18–32.
24. The accounts of Provins show that the king (of France or of Navarre?) was at Troyes on Oct. 13, 1284; see Prou and d'Auriac, *Actes et comptes*, p. 65. In November, Philip issued a charter as king of Navarre for the abbey of La Barre (British Museum add. chart. 1391) which was dated at Paris. The fact that the lord of Bourlemont did homage at the Jours does not necessarily mean that Philip was there to receive it.

opposed this petition, and then after the lord of Bourlemont was finally permitted to do homage, his fiefs were taken into the count's possession. Gautier de Chambly, a member of the royal court, and Guillaume de Prunay, a local noble, were then appointed to make an investigation. The final result was that Pierre was condemned to pay a fine to the count of Champagne and damages and expenses to the abbot of Mureaux.[25] The second case is one in which the court exacted an even heavier penalty for what seems like a relatively minor offense. Henri de Grandpré, who held the guard of the abbey of Chéhery along with the rest of the county of Grandpré in fief from the count of Champagne, had been paid by the monks to permit them to abjure his guard and place themselves under the protection of Philip III. Since this increase of the king's power was to the detriment of the county of Champagne, Philip's proctor demanded that all the fiefs of the count of Grandpré should be forfeited. Count Henri sought a delay to take counsel, and after this was denied, he requested a hearing at Chéhery, which was granted. At this point our extract breaks off, but we need not assume that Henri escaped his punishment, for in 1287 the county of Grandpré was in Philip's hands.[26] Rigorous exercise of his legal rights seems to have been a part of Philip's government from the very beginning.

In the spring of 1285 Philip III began his crusade against Aragon, taking Prince Philip with him. He left Champagne in the care of two guardians: Joinville, a native of the county and a trusted adviser of about sixty; and Gautier de Chambly, a courtier who had sat in Parlement as early as 1262, had been St. Louis' chaplain, and was to become bishop of Senlis at the end of the year. When these guardians held a session of the Jours of Troyes after Easter, they were assisted by six men who were paid wages for their attendance. Besides four clerks, including Florent de Roye, there was the abbot of Montiéramey, formerly chaplain to Count Thibaut V, and a distinguished old baron of Champagne, Gilles de Brion, who had been governor of the county in 1261. This court was therefore balanced between men from Champagne and men who owed their primary loyalty to the royal court. In this transitional period the influence of Paris was apparent but men from the county still played a significant part in the court of the Jours.[27]

25. Appendix I, No. 11.
26. *Ibid.*, No. 3. For what little is known of the annexation of Grandpré, see Longnon, *Documents*, III, 54 n. 1.
27. Appendix II, No. 2. On the abbot of Montiéramey and Gilles de Brion see Arbois de Jubainville, *Histoire*, IV, 459 and 531.

Once his father was dead, Philip changed the composition of the court even more. Under Philip III, as we have seen, Joinville had headed the administration of the county, but Philip the Fair did not cherish the advice of his sainted grandfather's old friend, and between 1285 and 1291 Joinville's name does not appear as a member of the Jours. Gilles de Brion died in 1287, so that his disappearance from the court cannot be attributed to Philip. But the systematic exclusion of men of stature from the county is clearly showed by the elimination of the abbots from Champagne. For years under Philip the Fair no major ecclesiastic from the county was included among the "masters holding the Jours of Troyes."[28]

After 1285 almost without exception the new judges came down from Paris, and they were regularly men who sat in the Parlement. Nobles from Champagne were notable by their absence; in the first years of Philip's reign the only noble layman in the court was usually Guillaume de Grancey, the head of the second most important feudal house in Burgundy.[29] The dependence of the Jours on the Parlement of Paris was finally spelled out for all to see by an ordinance issued in 1296, which declared that twice a year at the end of the sessions of Parlement four members of that court should be delegated by the king or the president of Parlement to attend the Jours of Troyes; these four were to be a prelate, a baron, one of those who issued judgments, and one other member of the council.[30]

Under Philip the Fair, the court of the Jours changed not only its membership but its procedure, for there is an obvious difference between a court with a handful of judges and one composed of over twenty people. The earlier practice, which continued through the first session of Prince Philip's Jours, was for a large number of people of differing status to meet together as an undifferentiated court. While the opinion of a minor

---

28. As will be seen later, the abbot of Montiéramey was present at a session of the Jours in 1286, but not as a master. In 1296 Guichard, abbot of Montier-la-Celle (and later the famous bishop of Troyes), was the next ecclesiastic from Champagne known to have a seat at the Jours. See Appendix II, Nos. 14–16.

29. For the genealogy of the family of Grancey see Ernest Petit, *Histoire des ducs de Bourgogne*, VI (Dijon, 1898), 537–546, and the chart following p. 548. Guillaume was a member of the judicial council of Burgundy in 1285 and sat in the Parlement of Paris in the same year; see *ibid.*, p. 330, No. 4737, and Portejoie (ed.), *Coutumier*, pp. 207–209.

30. Charles Victor Langlois, *Textes relatifs à l'histoire du Parlement* (Paris, 1888), pp. 161–167. The date of this ordinance in the spring of 1296 was established by Léon L. Borrelli de Serres, *Recherches sur divers services publics du XIIIe au XVIIe siècle*, 3 vols. (Paris, 1895–1909), I, 339–347.

noble would not carry the weight of that of a baron, all present were thought to have been involved in the common decision. But as early as the spring court of 1285 there was a distinction between the people who were paid to hold the court and others who simply attended the sessions. We cannot be certain that the payment of a few people to be "masters" of the court was an innovation, but it is likely that this practice was newly introduced in Champagne on the model of Parlement and the Exchequer. The difference between the new and the old forms of the Jours is shown by a charter of 1286 which lists five people who held the court for the king, and then names thirteen others who were present, including the abbot of Montiéramey, two *baillis*, the mayor of Provins, and two local lawyers.[31] Those who were "present" might give advice, and they could testify later to what had happened at the session, but they were not responsible for the judgment of the court. Physically this court of 1286 may have appeared no different from its predecessors, but within a few years the status of the masters was enhanced by special furniture, for in 1288 the *bailli* of Troyes paid a little under one *livre* "to make the seats for the masters at the Jours of Troyes."[32]

The new administration changed the Jours from a nonprofessional feudal court to one run by specialists. A few experienced men were paid from the income of the county for their services as a panel of judges and their expenses in making the journey, if they had to come from Paris. Sessions were held on a more orderly schedule, usually with one meeting in September and one in the spring; some lasted for over three weeks, though not all the masters stayed the whole time.[33] Cases were regularly heard *bailliage* by *bailliage*, in a fashion similar to the *dies balliviarum* at Paris. A clerk kept a written register, more informative and detailed than the *Olim* and not divided into separate sections for *arresta* and *inquesta*.[34]

As a professional court the Jours of Troyes, like the Exchequer of Normandy before it, became a delegated branch of the Parlement of Paris. It was no more necessary for a master of the court to be from Champagne than for a *bailli* to come from the region in which he served, and perhaps it was believed that judges from outside the county would be more

31. Appendix II, No. 4.
32. Longnon (ed.), *Documents*, III, 87.
33. The judicial sessions therefore did not coincide with the two accounting terms, which ended the week after Christmas and the Sunday before the feast of St. Mary Magdalen (in July). On the time individual masters spent at the Jours, see Appendix II, Nos. 2, 9, and 19.
34. This summary of procedure in the Jours is based on the reconstruction of the existing fragments of the lost first register in Appendix I.

impartial and render better justice. Others among those present could advise them on the customary law of Champagne, or they could refer to the custumal of the county, which may well have been prepared to meet the needs of the new masters.[35] The law was presumed to be local, but the judges came and went.

Since Philip was both king and lord of Champagne and the same judges sat in the Jours and the Parlement, there was little reason to maintain a rigid separation of the jurisdictions of the two courts. Royal vassals and churches under royal protection had the right to bring their cases to Paris, and in some instances it seems to have been a matter of convenience or timing whether a case was heard in Paris or Troyes. In 1289 the Parisian court referred a dispute between Joinville and the abbey of Saint-Urbain to the court at Troyes, and when the masters of the Jours were unable to reach a decision because Joinville challenged the authenticity of a charter, they adjourned the dispute "to the next Jours of Troyes or to the coming day of the barons [i.e., the time at Parlement reserved for baronial cases]." The matter was finally settled in Paris.[36] Again in 1289, when the count of Bar failed to answer their summons, the master of the Jours ordered him to appear "at the next day of the barons at Paris."[37] These cases concerned barons and therefore might easily be heard at Paris, but lesser people could also bring their complaints about affairs in Champagne directly to Parlement. We have no reason to think that the masters of Parlement wanted to aggrandize their jurisdiction, but once plaintiffs had appeared before them, it probably seemed simpler to settle the matter on the spot than to refer it to Troyes.[38] The masters of the Jours may also have referred difficult cases to the larger and more important court at Paris. Without fuller records it is hard to tell why a matter like the question of the royal right to collect *mainmorte* should have been decided in Paris rather than Troyes.[39] But whatever the reasons for them, cases from Champagne became sufficiently common

---

35. Portejoie argues convincingly (*Coutumier*, pp. 9–11) that the custumal was completed shortly after 1295, and was perhaps prepared by the *bailli* Guillaume du Châtelet.

36. Appendix I, No. 67. The Parlement of St. Martin 1289 decided against Joinville and declared that Saint-Urbain was under the king's guard; see Delisle (ed.), *Essai*, p. 425, No. 720. The monks of Saint-Urbain renounced Joinville's guard in a charter of October, 1288, printed in Jules Simonnet, *Essai sur l'histoire et la généalogie des sires de Joinville* (Langres, 1876), pp. 201–204.

37. Appendix I, Nos. 73–74.

38. For complaints taken to Parlement see *Olim*, III, 91, xxxviii; III, 206, xxxi; Delisle (ed.), *Essai*, p. 455, No. 880.

39. *Olim*, II, 440, xxiv; cf. Delisle (ed.), *Essai*, p. 442, No. 800; p. 446, No. 833.

that the county was allotted a specific time in the schedule of the Parlement along with the *prévôté* of Paris and the *bailliage* of Sens.[40]

The blurring of jurisdictional lines was an encouragement for litigants dissatisfied by their treatment in Troyes to try again in Paris. After the masters of the Jours had judged that the possession of the lepers' hospital of Montmirail belonged to the nunnery of Saint-Jacques of Vitry and not to the bishop of Châlons, the bishop appeared before the Parlement of St. Martin of 1289 and complained that the royal officials had *de facto* and improperly transferred the possession of the hospital. The masters of Parlement then heard the testimony of the royal officials who were present and judged in the bishop's favor, annulling the transfer. In the following Parlement of Pentecost 1290, however, the abbess of Vitry had her turn and testified that the action had been taken following a formal decision of the court of Troyes, and after seeing the judgment of their colleagues, the Parisian masters returned possession to the abbess.[41] About the same time Parlement had to judge a case between the abbey of Saint-Pierre of Oyes and Lord Jean de Châteauvillain concerning his rights of guard over the abbey. Although the *Olim* does not specify who made the complaint, we may presume that the abbey initiated the action in Paris. Jean maintained his rights by claiming that the guard of the abbey had been granted to him by the court of the Jours. Some of those who had held the Jours and were present in the Parlement then stated that Jean had been granted the guard of the abbey on such terms that if the abbey was dissatisfied it should not have recourse to the royal court.[42]

In these two cases the bishop of Châlons and the abbot of Oyes seem to have counted on a certain lack of communication between the masters of the two courts, and during his first hearing the bishop did indeed find that the masters present in Parlement were unaware of what had happened before in the Jours. Both parties hoped for a better judgment than they had received before, but I think it is significant that the *Olim* does not say that either one was making an appeal. In informal terms, they were complaining, rather than asking for a formal reconsideration of the decision reached in Troyes. During this period of the reign of Philip IV the Parlement exercised authority in Champagne, but

40. The schedule for early 1309 is published in Langlois, *Textes*, pp. 181–182, and *Registres du Trésor des Chartes*, I, No. 864. We do not know how early the county of Champagne had a place in the *dies balliviarum*, but it is interesting to see that it was scheduled after Louis became count.

41. *Olim*, II, 292, xii, and 301, viii.

42. *Ibid.*, 289, v.

it does not seem to have reduced the Jours to the position of "a simple court of first instance."[43]

While there is no evidence of formal appeal from the Jours to the Parlement in the period before the death of Jeanne of Navarre,[44] there are several instances recorded in the *Olim* of appeals to Paris from the court of the guards of the fairs. The first of these occurred in 1296, when the decision of the guards was upheld. In 1304 there were two appeals, one of which was denied and the other accepted. And then in 1306 there were four appeals, in three of which the judgments of the guards were reversed. It is possible that this high percentage of reversals in 1306 was associated with the fact that in the same year Parlement found one of the guards guilty of peculation.[45]

The final period of Philip's reign is the one for which we have the least evidence of the working of the Jours. Only one list of the masters of the court of Troyes survives from the period after the death of the queen, but that list fortunately can be dated about 1311, after Louis had bought out his brothers' rights in the county.[46] This precious document shows that even after the heir apparent had become count, masters of Parlement were still sent to Troyes to hold the Jours, and it seems safe to assume that throughout his reign Philip or his officials appointed the masters of the Jours from Paris. In this important matter Philip's practice does not seem to have changed.

But the separation of the offices of king and count did call for some recognition of the judicial distinctiveness of the county.[47] It is hard to be certain which cases should have been tried where, but after about 1306 the number of cases coming to Paris from Champagne without explana-

43. The phrase is Beugnot's in *Olim*, II, p. xiv. Beugnot has, I think, misinterpreted the scope of the order to all the king's *baillis* and guards of the fair which he cites in support of his argument. Such an order was quite properly made in the royal court, since contractual letters agreed to outside the fairs could be made outside the county as well as in Champagne. While on occasion it was convenient for the Parlement rather than the Jours to treat matters from Champagne, at this time there was no advantage in reducing the authority of the Jours. Orders to the guards of the fair or the *baillis* of Champagne could also easily come from the Jours; see Appendix I, Nos. 24, 27, 35, 44, 45, 53.

44. Except for the unusual case of 1283 cited in n. 15.

45. *Olim*, II, 411, xxiii; III, 144, xiii; 154, xxxii; 200, xxii; 204, xxix; 209, xxxvii; 216, xlvii; and for the peculation of the guard Hugues de Chaumont, III, 207, xxxiv.

46. Appendix II, No. 20.

47. One important change was that fines levied in the county now went to Louis and not to his father. See *Olim*, III, 775, lxi (which refers to the earlier time in which "dominus Rex comitatum Campanie ad manum suam immediate tenebat") and *Registres du Trésor des Chartes*, I, No. 653.

tion seems to have declined sharply. In 1308 the king declared expressly that an interminable conflict between the commune of Provins and the nuns of Faremoutiers, an affair which had been heard in both Paris and Troyes, should be settled in his son's court of Champagne.[48] And, as will be seen, appeals from the decisions of the guards of the fairs no longer went directly to Paris but had to be taken to the Jours.

At the same time that a greater effort was made to distinguish between the jurisdiction of the king and the count, a new principle was introduced into the relationship between the Jours and the Parlement—the recognition of a formal right of appeal. In 1307 a case involving the abbey of Saint-Pierre of Bèze and some burgesses of the abbey was taken to the Parlement from the Jours by the mutual consent of the interested parties. In this case the word "appeal" was not used, and the matter seems to have been one of voluntary jurisdiction, perhaps taken to Parlement because the abbey was in the duchy of Burgundy.[49] But finally in 1310 a disappointed litigant, one Jean Cristo, appealed from the guards of the fairs to the Jours and then formally appealed to the Parlement against a judgment he considered "*falsus et pravus.*"[50] In 1312 there were three more cases of formal appeal, including one from the guards to the Jours to Parlement and another from the *bailli* of Vitry to the Jours to Paris. The third appeal is the most interesting, for it is the only one in which the judgment of the lower court was reversed. Erard de Nanteuil had brought suit against some alleged serfs, who produced letters of franchise which convinced the masters of the Jours that the defendants were free. Erard then brought a suit for false judgment to the Parlement, where the Parisian masters reviewed the testimony and declared that the judges of the Jours had made a poor decision and should therefore pay a fine to the Parlement.[51]

This chronological survey permits a more precise answer to the old question of whether the Jours was a court of first instance or had final jurisdiction. No one principle applies to the whole period under study. Louis IX fully respected the judicial autonomy of Champagne, and Philip III permitted only a few cases to come before his court with the consent of those involved. As long as he was both count and king, Philip IV recognized no formal principle of appeal, but in practice he tolerated some confusion of the jurisdiction of his two courts. And finally, when his

48. *Registres du Trésor des Chartes*, I, No. 829.
49. *Olim*, III, 228, viii.
50. *Ibid.*, p. 575, lxx (the case is repeated on p. 615, cviii).
51. *Ibid.*, II, 573, viii; III, 765, li; 784, lxx.

son became count, Philip's masters met the immediate problem of separate courts and the possible eventual separation of Champagne from the crown by permitting (and perhaps even encouraging) appeals from the Jours to Parlement. In the latter part of his reign Philip treated the Jours as a delegation of Parlement by appointing the judges, but also established the right of appeal. In this the practice of Champagne was different from that of Normandy, for appeals from the Exchequer seem to have been quite unusual, and by the charter of 1315 they were finally banned.[52] But Normandy was firmly part of the royal domain and Champagne might possibly be lost to the monarchy. Throughout his kingdom Philip the Fair showed no intention of leaving any of his vassals free from judicial review, even if this supervision meant that for Champagne the officials of King Philip had to reconsider cases they had already settled for his son as count.

The preceding account has shown that royal control of the judicial system was from the start of Philip's reign so strong and pervasive that there was no opportunity for provincial opposition to develop. Most previous writers on the Jours of Troyes have thought differently and have maintained that there was an alternative Court of the Barons which to some degree resisted Philip's centralization and attempted to preserve the old feudal and provincial traditions of Champagne. This concept of two different courts was introduced in 1727 by Nicolas Brussel, who described a *"Cour des Barons"* as the ordinary court of the county and the *"Cour des Grands Jours"* as an extraordinary court.[53] Brussel's view was challenged by his contemporary Lévesque de la Ravallière, but unfortunately La Ravallière's learned history has remained unpublished and has had little influence.[54] The more easily available and seemingly authoritative opinion of Brussel was followed by Arthur Beugnot, Théophile Boutiot, and Arbois de Jubainville, and Félix Bourquelot was exceptional in contradicting it.[55] The dissident view of the distinguished historian from Provins has been either dismissed or ignored by modern authors, however, and Brussel's concept of two separate courts appears today in our legal

---

52. Strayer, *Administration of Normandy*, p. 16 n. 2; Strayer shows (p. 14 n. 2) the same interchange of cases between the provincial court and Parlement that can be seen in Champagne. For the Norman charter see Isambert, *Recueil général des anciennes lois françaises*, 29 vols. (Paris, 1822–33), III, 51, art. 13.

53. Nicolas Brussel, *Nouvel examen de l'usage général des fiefs en France*, 2 vols. (Paris, 1727; reissued with altered title page in 1750), pp. 249–251.

54. B. N., Coll. de Champagne, t. 67, fols. 11–12.

55. *Olim*, II, pp. ix–xiv; Théophile Boutiot, "Recherches sur les Grands Jours de Troyes," *Mémoires de la Societé academique . . . de l'Aube*, XVI (1852), 405–446; Arbois de Jubainville, *Histoire*, IV, 565–566; Bourquelot, *Études*, II, 259–260.

and historical handbooks.[56] Moreover, in her meticulous edition of the custumal of Champagne published in 1956, Paulette Portejoie presents additional evidence in support of the theory of parallel courts, which she describes in this way:

> After the highest court of Champagne had become an outgrowth of Parlement, the barons of Champagne, who had been eliminated, independently formed another court, as if the old Grands Jours had been split apart, forming on the one hand a court composed of masters of Parlement and on the other a court of the barons.[57]

The belief in the existence of separate courts is based on three different arguments. The first, which seemed conclusive to Brussel, is that the register of the Jours in two places referred to the *dies baronum* or "day of the barons," which he thought meant the court of the barons of Champagne.[58] As has been seen, however, the "day of the barons" was the time at Parlement reserved for baronial cases. Brussel knew that the term *dies baronum* had referred to Parlement in the past, but he thought that it no longer had that meaning in the days of Philip IV. In this he erred, for the three examples Du Cange gives for *dies baronum* all refer to a period of time at Parlement, and two are from the reign of Philip the Fair. In addition, in the late thirteenth century the accounts of the commune of Provins tell of sending officials to the *Jours au barons* at Paris. Furthermore, the register of the Jours itself specifically states that the *dies baronum* took place at Paris. This phrase therefore provides no basis for a theory of a baronial court in Champagne.[59]

The second argument, fundamental to the discussion of Portejoie, is based on a set of decisions recorded in the custumal of Champagne. One of these, article 57 of the new edition, is the settlement of a conflict between Hélissande d'Arcis and her brothers over the division of the inheritance of Chacenay. It is dated the week after Pentecost of a year which seven manuscripts give as 1287 and one as 1281, and it concludes with the statement: "A cest jugement faire furent Messire de Joinville senechaux de

56. Chénon, *Histoire générale*, I, 691; Lot and Fawtier, *Histoire*, II, 470.
57. Portejoie (ed.), *Coutumier*, p. 6.
58. Brussel, *Nouvel examen*, pp. 249–251; cf. Appendix I, Nos. 67 and 73.
59. Two of the texts in Du Cange, *Glossarium*, s.v. *dies baronum* (ed. Henschel, II, 846) are edited in Delisle (ed.), *Essai*, p. 413, No. 678, and p. 428, No. 724. See also Langlois, *Textes*, p. 108; *Comptes royaux, 1285–1314*, ed. Robert Fawtier and François Maillard, 3 vols. (Paris, 1953–56), II, 373, No. 20503; and Prou and d'Auriac, *Actes et comptes*, pp. 69 and 76.

Champagne, et tuit li autres qui sont nommé au jugement devant cestue."
There are no names included in the immediately preceding article, but article 55 of Portejoie's edition ends with the names of Joinville and seven other nobles, including the lords of Jully, Chappes, and Broyes, plus Guillaume du Châtelet, a man who served as *bailli* in a number of places and Pierre de la Malmaison, at one time *bailli* of Vitry. Article 55 is undated, but on the basis of the reference to "the preceding judgment" in article 57, Portejoie assigns it to the week after Pentecost of 1287.[60]

If we could trust the date of 1287 given to article 57 and if article 55 were of the same date, then the existence of a separate Court of the Barons, rivaling the Jours of Troyes after Philip came to power, would be established. Bearing in mind that the court of the Jours was convened at Troyes the week after Ascension in 1287, let us try to imagine the circumstances under which this baronial court would have been held. Since it began just ten days after a session of the Jours, Hélissande d'Arcis and the others who brought their cases before it were deliberately avoiding the court favored by the king and his justices. Since Philip had dropped Joinville from the Jours since 1285, we must give the seneschal credit for courage, if not audacity, for presiding over a competing court. And we must note that in laying down this challenge to the king, Joinville did not surround himself with hot-headed young nobles, but called upon some of his oldest friends and companions, for seven of the nine men are known to have sat together in a session of the Jours seventeen years before.[61]

My own conclusion from this evidence is not that a remarkable group of old-timers held court in Troyes concurrently with the Jours or just a few days after its masters had ridden off to Paris, but that the custumal as we have it now contains one or perhaps two errors. The most obvious explanation of the problem is to suggest that we do not have the original arrangement of the articles, and that the reference to "the preceding judgment" refers to article 10, a case concerning Hélissande's brother Erard d'Arcis, which was judged by Joinville *"qui lors gardoit Champagne"* and four other men. The date given in the custumal is 1284, but it is likely that this case is from the spring or summer of 1285. That is also a

---

60. The two articles are printed in Portejoie (ed.), *Coutumier*, pp. 220–222. The editor assigns both to the same date on p. 7. It is hard to date article 55 from its references. The latest reference I have found to Guichard de la Porte, at one time mayor of Bar-sur-Aube, is an act of 1279, Aube, arch. dép., 3 H 41.

61. For the session of the Jours the week after Ascension, 1287, see Appendix II, No. 6. For members of the court in 1270 see Portejoie (ed.), *Coutumier*, pp. 165–167 and 171–173. Article 22 (pp. 175–176) contains a list of members of the court identical to article 55. It is undated, but for unexplained reasons Portejoie assigns it a date of 1271 on p. 7.

likely date for a case involving Hélissande d'Arcis and her brothers to have been tried by the Jours before the question of the succession of Chacenay was taken to Parlement in the winter of 1285. In fact, the dates given in the custumal are so uncertain that no argument should be based on them without supporting evidence. To answer this second argument briefly, it is probable that the date of article 57 is wrong and should be 1285, and in any case, the connection between article 57 and article 55 is tenuous.[62]

The third argument cannot be challenged in such a categorical fashion as the first two, for it is true that there was a place for nobles from Champagne in the judicial administration of the county after 1285. The custumal of Champagne contains the record of four court sessions between 1287 and 1290 held outside of Troyes and independently of the assizes of the *baillis*, and shows that the masters of the Jours were not present at these courts but that some nobles from Champagne were. Although it is accurate to refer to these meetings as baronial courts, it would be misleading to think of them as sessions of an institutionalized Court of the Barons which had split off from the Jours of Troyes.[63]

One of these courts was held at Val-des-Escoliers and two were at Châteauvillain; no location is given for the fourth, but it judged the rights of the chapter of Châteauvillain and very likely took place there. The reason why these cases were heard by nobles from the region of Chaumont, rather than at the Jours of Troyes or the court of the *bailli* of Chaumont, is to be found in the special nature of the two places. To begin with the more certain case, Val-des-Escoliers, or more precisely a meeting place named Les Etaux in a field near the Augustinian priory on the banks of the Marne, was the point on the border at which the count of Champagne customarily did homage to the bishop of Langres and where, "according to the custom of the march," conflicts between the two territories were to be heard. The custumal of Champagne tells of two disputes between the *bailli* of Chaumont and the bishop of Langres which

---

62. The extent to which the articles of the *Coutumier* have been shuffled is shown by the editor's table on pp. 231–232. For the date of article 10 see Appendix I, note 8. Portejoie has shown (p. 207 n. 2) that article 50, in which the Parlement settled the succession of Chacenay, must be of 1285 and not 1283, as the custumal has it. See also Delisle (ed.), *Essai*, p. 400, No. 585. Bourquelot, *Études*, II, 261, used a copy of the custumal which gave the date 1281 to article 57. He was therefore spared this problem. I have not been able to determine that any of the men named in article 55 were actually dead in 1287, but Pierre de la Malmaison had surely retired by that time, for he last appeared as *bailli* of Vitry in 1276.

63. These cases are in Portejoie (ed.), *Coutumier*, pp. 168–170, 187–188, 197–198, 209–214. Portejoie calls these decisions "arrêts de la Cour des barons, fonctionnent concuremment avec les Grands Jours royaux" (p. 7).

were brought before a court of nobles and churchmen of the border region on February 20, 1290. Agreement was reached on one of the issues, but the court divided on the other, which therefore had to be sent to Parlement for settlement. This court was convened simply because neither the Jours nor the court of the bishop of Langres had jurisdiction, and because it was the custom to try to avoid the expense of litigation in Paris by local settlement if possible.[64]

We know less about the other three cases, two of which concerned Châteauvillain, and the other of which involved someone from Arc-en-Barrois. We do know a little, however, about the peculiar feudal position of the seigneury of Châteauvillain and Arc. This once unified fief had split off from the county of Bar-sur-Aube in the eleventh century, and in an unexplained fashion became divided between its two powerful neighbors, with its lord owing homage to the count of Champagne for Châteauvillain and to the duke of Burgundy for Arc.[65] The attempt to settle cases from this seigneury in courts in which men from both Champagne and Burgundy were present probably resulted from this feudal split. In summary, these four courts recorded in the custumal were not sessions of the baronage of Champagne per se, but meetings of the nobles of border regions, in what we might call "courts-in-march," to settle cases in which neither neighboring lord had full jurisdiction. In one particular instance, when no settlement could be reached locally, the case then went to the Parlement at Paris.

Once we are in a position to eliminate from the historical record the phantom court of the baronage of Champagne created by Brussel, the process by which Philip the Fair took over the judicial system of Champagne and subordinated it to the Parlement can be seen as simple, effective, and unchallenged. The jurisdictional barrier which had been maintained scrupulously by Louis IX and somewhat less rigorously by Philip III began to crumble when young Philip brought Parisian courtiers to his first session of the Jours in the fall of 1284, and it was destroyed when Philip made the Jours a professional court with masters sent down from Paris. The people of Champagne came before Philip's justices because there was nowhere else to go, and by the end of Philip's reign the Jours of

---

64. On the location see Jean François Lemarignier, *Recherches sur l'hommage en marche et les frontières féodales* (Lille, 1945), pp. 168, 172–173. The record of the case which was not settled locally and which came before the Parlement of Candlemas 1291 refers to the customary meeting place of *Scella* or *Scallis*, which I take to be a corruption of *Stalla, Stallis*, for *Les Etaux*. For the case, which contains a reference to the custom of the march, see Delisle (ed.), *Essai*, p. 436, No. 770.

65. Eugène Jarry, *Provinces et pays de France, III: Bourgogne* (Paris, 1948), p. 252 n. 50.

Troyes had become even more a branch of Parlement than the Exchequer of Normandy.

One of the paradoxes of French history is that the duchy of Normandy, subject to the monarchy since the early thirteenth century, emerged from the middle ages with stronger provincial institutions than the county of Champagne, which was not definitively attached to the crown until 1361. By the early sixteenth century the old Norman Exchequer had grown into the Parlement of Rouen, while in Champagne the Jours of Troyes withered away and the county remained under the jurisdiction of the Parlement of Paris.[66] Although Rouen and Troyes are about the same distance from Paris, the Norman city became a provincial capital, while Troyes was subject to the influence and administration of the central government and Champagne became a province without a capital.

The reign of Philip the Fair was a turning point in the development of the two provinces, and the explanation of the greater dependence of Champagne contains an ironic element. When Philip Augustus conquered Normandy, its administrative and judicial institutions were independent of the monarchy and there was a clear demarcation between the rights and obligations which were Norman and those which were French. Since the king replaced his predecessor by conquest, the simplest way for him to govern his new territory was to keep the institutions separate but to replace the administrators with men loyal to his court. The feudal history of Champagne before its acquisition was quite different, for its counts never had the independent power of the Norman dukes, and the western frontier of the county was permeable to royal influence. People from Meaux, for instance, could go more easily to nearby Paris than to Troyes, and since the king exercised considerable feudal authority in the county, many religious houses and some lay vassals found it advantageous to invoke the king's power against the count. Even before Philip the Fair became count there were plenty of excuses for royal administrators to act in Champagne, while there was no reason for a royal agent outside Normandy to interfere with another agent of the king inside the duchy.

When Philip became both king and count, there was no longer an independent administration with an interest in opposing royal influence. There was also pressure within Champagne to take cases to the more

66. Sessions of the Grands Jours were held intermittently in Troyes until 1409. Apparently documentation to show what happened to the high court of the county under Isabelle of Bavaria and the Burgundians has not survived. In 1431 representations from Troyes were sent "aux prochains Jours de Sens et de Champagne, à Poitiers." See Théophile Boutiot, "Nouvelles recherches sur la cour des Grands Jours," *Annuaire administratif, statistique et commercial de l'Aube* (1870), p. 83.

powerful court, and litigants on expense accounts (like the communal officials of Provins) undoubtedly preferred to plead in Paris rather than in the moribund city of Troyes. The flow of cases from Champagne to the Parlement could only have been checked if the government of Philip IV had made an effort to prohibit it, as Philip III had earlier attempted to limit the cases coming to Paris from provinces which had royal *baillis*.[67] But Philip the Fair, count only in his wife's name, had no reason to build a strong local judicial system in Champagne. The masters of the Jours were not recruited from the county but sent from the royal court, and cases could be judged in Troyes or Paris as convenience dictated. Finally, when it was apparent that the monarchy might not be able to appoint the masters of the Jours indefinitely, Philip established the right of appeal from the Jours to the Parlement, a principle it was not necessary to impose on Normandy. The great centralizer of medieval France subordinated the Jours but permitted the Exchequer to remain relatively independent because in his day the monarchy had a firmer hold on Normandy than on Champagne.

67. Langlois, *Textes*, p. 95, art. 1.

APPENDIX I
REGISTERS OF THE COURT OF THE JOURS

Two registers of the court of the Jours of Troyes were once kept in the *Chambre des comptes* at Paris. One of these—we do not know which—was described in an inventory of the registers of the *Chambre de Champagne* made in 1489 as a volume of 190 leaves of parchment, bound in white leather on boards, with five nails in each board, and labeled on the cover: "*Arresta antiquitus prolata ad magnos dies Trecenses seu registrum ipsorum arrestorum.*"[1] Later users recorded the dates of the two registers; one went from 1284 to 1295, the second from 1296 to 1299. Du Cange quoted this second volume once,[2] and anonymous antiquarians listed some of the nobles and masters of the Jours named in it, but only the earlier volume was the subject of careful study.

Nicolas Dongois, who wrote a treatise *De l'origine des Grands Jours* in 1666, systematically extracted from the first register in an appendix which he entitled *Jours de Troyes tenus sous Philippe Le Bel depuis 1284 Jusques en 1291*. The treatise is now preserved in the Archives Nationales as U 749, and the appendix exists in two copies in U 749 and U 750. The second copy is more clearly written and is the one cited here as MS D. At the time Dongois used it the register was already badly damaged, and he had to conclude his extracts at 1291 with the comment: "Il est impossible de rien dechifrer de tout le reste du registre." Quite possibly Dongois marked the material he extracted in some way, for the cases he thought interesting were often copied again, particularly by Brussel.

The great scholar Charles du Fresne Du Cange also made use of the registers of the Jours in the seventeenth century, either directly or through the intermediary of his friend Vyon d'Hérouval, auditor of the Chambre des Comptes. Du Cange quoted from the registers in his *Glossarium* and in the *Histoire de S. Louys*. He may also have been responsible for the copying of a list of "Chevaliers Champenois denommez aux Assises de Champagne, qui sont en la Chambre des Comptes de Paris." This list is on fols. 54–55 of B. N., MS fr. 9501, which came from the Du Cange collection and is labeled on the first folio "Mss. duCange 1226." The list for the first volume, which can be checked against the extracts, is incomplete

1. Longnon (ed.), *Documents*, II, 575.
2. *Glossarium*, s.v., *dies magni Trecensis*.

and not entirely accurate, but in turn it provides a check on the folio numbers given elsewhere. It ends at fol. 111 in 1289, and no foliation is given for the names from the second volume. This manuscript also contains on fols. 37–38v a list of the "Maistres des grands Jours de Troie, Envoyes et Deputez par les Comtes de Champagne, et par les Roys de France. Ensemble ceux qui les ont assistez dans les Jugemens. Tirez de deux Vol. des Assises de Champagne de la Chambre des Comptes de Paris, et du vieux Coustumier de Champagne." It is cited hereafter as MS C.

A   The list of the "Maistres des grands Jours de Troie" copied in C also appears on fols. 377–380v of B. N., n. a. fr. 7412. This volume of notes and extracts was formerly MS 82 of the collection of the Abbé Decamps and is cited in Appendix II as MS A.

B   Possibly the second register had disappeared from the Chambre des Comptes by the early eighteenth century, but the first register remained in the *dépôt des Terriers*, where it was used extensively by another auditor of the Chambre des Comptes, Nicolas Brussel. Brussel's *Nouvel examen de l'usage général des fiefs en France*, which was first published in 1727 and reissued with a new title page in 1750, contains our longest extracts from the first register. It is cited hereafter as B. Brussel noted that the manuscript was badly damaged by moisture, forcing him to leave some blanks or to provide tentative readings in parentheses, and his book contains no extracts later than fol. 112v. I have not been able to find the manuscript of Brussel's transcription, but apparently copies not included in his book were available to Lévesque de la Ravallière, who noted:

> Mr Brussel a ecri[t] à la fin des titres qu'il a extraits du registre, f° 119, apres le titre des arrests qui furent rendus en l'an 1289: "Le registre n'est plus susceptible d'extraits pour son grand endommagement de pouriture; il paroit qu'il va jusqu'environ l'an 1295. Il s'y trouve l'ordonance autrefois faite pour tenir les grands jours de Champ^e avec les instructions aux comissaires, mais elle est aussi presqu'entierement mangëe de pourriture."[3]

L   It is not clear whether La Ravallière also had access to the original manuscript before the great fire of the Chambre des Comptes in 1737 or depended on copies, but his work contains material from the register not otherwise available. His essay and notes on the Grands Jours are in B. N., Collection de Champagne, t. 67, fols. 8–18, and t. 133, fols. 420–422, and his notes on Provins are in t. 26. All this material is cited as L.

3. B. N., Coll. de Champagne, t. 67, fol. 12.

These materials and a few other sources of information on the decisions of the court of the Jours permit the very limited reconstruction which follows of the first part of the first register of Philip's court. Most of the material is available in Brussel's book, but since his dating and foliation are not always accurate, a systematic ordering of his extracts provides a useful check and much more precision. Material not available in print has been quoted in full, but otherwise I have given only analyses. Personal names and other information not in the text have been supplied in square brackets at their first appearance in each entry. I have attempted to make the analyses detailed enough for the reader to follow the procedure or significant arguments, but have summarized as much as possible. Place-names in this and the following appendixes are identified in the index.

EXTRACTS FROM THE FIRST REGISTER

Session Beginning November 25, 1284

fol. 4   1. The daughters of the late Jean de Montréal failed to appear against Beatrice, duchess of Burgundy, and were placed in default. Their brothers, who were present and were therefore permitted to submit a new petition, requested that the duchess be summoned to the next session of the Jours of Troyes, which was granted. For the continuation of the case before the Parlement of Paris in 1292, see *Olim*, II, 343, xxii; Jean's daughters were Agnes, wife of Odo Bezors, lord of Villarnoult, and Beatrice, wife of Jacques, lord of La Roche-en-Brenil, and his son was Gui de Montréal.— B, p. 238 n.

fol. 10v   2. Agathes de Damery claimed that her husband held all the property which belonged to her and her children by her first marriage and did not permit them to have any income from it, but made those who administered it for her appear before the church court. The *bailli* of Vitry was ordered to make a settlement between the parties, and if this was not possible to take the property into his possession and administer it for her.

   Dicebat domina Agathes de Damery quod maritus suus tenet omnes hereditates et bona ipsius et liberorum suorum ex primo cubili suo procreatorum, nec permittit quod habeant aliquod commodum de eisdem, et omnes illos qui ex parte dominae praedictae colunt hereditates et bona facit coram judice ecclesiastico conveniri, ipsos fatigando laboribus et expensis. Quare petit quod subveniatur eidem et liberis[1] et quod de bonis predictis eisdem sua necessaria ministrentur. Injunctum est baillivo Vitriaci quod vocet partes et eas inter se concordet, ut maritus uxorem suam et liberos secum revocet et ipsos modo debito tractet, et quod eisdem de bonis praedictis commoda ministret, et si alteratrum istorum nolit facere, capiat baillivus de bonis praedictis et de eisdem ministret sufficienter dictae dominae et liberis suis supradictis.—D, fol. 21v.

fol. 12v 3. The proctor of the count of Champagne charged that although Count [Henri] of Grandpré held his county, including the guard of the abbey of Chéhery, directly from the count of Champagne, the count of Grandpré had sold permission to the abbey of Chéhery to enter the guard of the king of France, to the detriment of Champagne. The proctor therefore requested that all the land of the count of Grandpré be confiscated and adjudged to the count of Champagne. The count of Grandpré requested a delay to take counsel, which was denied, but he was granted a hearing at Chéhery on the following February 11. On this case, see above, p. 289.—B, 808–809 n.

fol. 17 4. Concerning the claim of Lord [Jean] de Chappes that Duke [Robert II] of Burgundy had threatened violence to the village of Essoyes, which he held in fief from the count of Champagne, the *bailli* of Chaumont was ordered to protect the property the lord of Chappes held from the lord of Champagne.—B, p. 238 n.

fol. 17 5. Concerning the request of Lord Jean de Norrois that Duke [Ferri III] of Lorraine, who had announced hostilities with him, should make him an oath of peace (*asseguramentum*), the court agreed that the duke should be told in writing to keep peace with the lord of Norrois.—B, p. 239 n.

1. MS: *libelis*.

fol. 17v   6. Lord Erard de Grand proposed a division through sale of the forest of Grand, which he held in equal shares with the count of Champagne and Duke [Ferri III] of Lorraine. The court ordered that the duke be addressed on this matter, and that if he consented, the forest should be sold.—B, p. 239 n.

fol. 17v   7. The court ordered that whenever the officials of the count of Champagne retained in their villages any serfs of lords who were vassals of the count, the *bailli* should determine why the serfs wished to be in the jurisdiction of the count of Champagne and report what he found to the court.—B, p. 269 n.

fol. 17v   8. Concerning the request of Gui de Virey-sous-Bar, knight, that he be permitted to bear arms for the defense of his home, the court ordered the *bailli* of Troyes to determine if Gui had just cause to bear arms against persons who were not in the jurisdiction of the count of Champagne, and if so, to grant him permission to bear arms.—B, p. 230 n.

December 4, 1284

fol. 17v   9. At the request of Guillaume du Châtelet, formerly *bailli* of Chaumont, the court ordered Lord Pierre de Bourlemont to make an oath of peace to Guillaume in full court at the Jours of Troyes, in the presence of many witnesses (see Appendix II, No. 1).—B, p. 859 n; D, fol. 22.

December 5, 1284

fol. 17v   10. Lord Pierre de Bourlemont renewed his oath of peace to the abbot of Mureaux[2] in full court at the Jours of Troyes in the presence of many witnesses (see Appendix II, No. 1).—B, p. 859–860 n.

fols. 17[v]–18   11. The proctor of the count of Champagne argued that Lord Pierre de Bourlemont should not be received in homage for Bourlemont and Rorthey because, among other reasons, he had broken the oath of peace he had made about five years before to the abbot of Mureaux, and which he had

2. Brussel erroneously modernized *Miroaut* as the name of the abbey of "Mirevaux."

renewed about three years before. It was finally agreed, with Pierre's consent, that he should be received in homage by the count of Champagne, but that this homage would not prejudice the proctor's case against him. After Pierre had done homage, his fiefs were taken into the count's seisin, and Gautier de Chambly and Guillaume de Prunay were named as auditors to make an inquest for the court. Brussel added that Pierre was later condemned to pay a fine to the count and damages to the abbey.—B, pp. 862 and 862–863 n; cf. B, p. 814.

Session Beginning April 8, 1285[?] [3]

fol. 18v 12. Lady Mathilda, wife of Gilo Fuiret, requested the return of her own inheritance, which had been confiscated by the officials of the king of Navarre because of her husband's crime; Count Edmund of Lancaster had granted her this dispensation during his guardianship. The *bailli* replied that according to the customs of Champagne, she should not enjoy her inheritance during her husband's lifetime.[4] The court declared that she should have the same dispensation Edmund had made.—B, pp. 218–221.

fol. 21v 13. Erard de Dinteville, squire, stated that when he began to build a fortified house in some of his allodial land in Champagne, for which he had recently entered the homage of the count of Champagne, he had been prevented by officials of the king of France acting at the request of the bishop of Langres [Gui II], although there were many other such houses held in fief from the count in the same allod. The court declared that the count of Champagne should prosecute his rights concerning this fortified house in the next Parlement of Pentecost, and Erard was ordered to be present to defend his rights against the officials of the king of France and the bishop of Langres.—B, p. 385 n.

fol. 21v 14. The prior and canons of Belroy, of the order of Val-des-Escoliers, complained that they were no longer receiving

---

3. Brussel places case No. 12 in the session of April 8, 1285, but dates Nos. 13 and 14 in 1284. According to C, fol. 54, the year 1285 began somewhere between fol. 21 and 24.

4. On this principle see Portejoie (ed.), *Coutumier*, p. 57.

a *muid* of grain granted them from certain granges, which the count of Champagne had later given to the duke of Lorraine (see below, No. 23). The *bailli* was ordered to make an investigation and to do right.—B, p. 240 n.

Session Beginning April 8, 1285

fol. 23   15. The lady of Saint-Remy [-en-Bouzemont?] requested the return of property taken from her by order of the *bailli* of Vitry for fines imposed by her on some of her men, who claimed to have appealed to the officials of the king [of Navarre] for false judgment and denial of justice. After a hearing the court ordered that the goods be returned and the lady permitted to do justice to her men, unless they pursued their appeal.—B, p. 266 n; D, fols. 22-22v.

fol. 23   16. Lord [Henri] de Hans stated that according to an agreement made between himself and [Thibaut V], king of Navarre–count of Champagne,[5] the burgesses of Hans did not have the right to settle in the towns of the count of Champagne without losing their property in Hans. Although the burgesses of Hans made a contrary claim, the court declared that the king-count did not guarantee the property of burgesses coming to his towns from Hans.—B, pp. 1014–1015 n; Du Cange, *Glossarium*, s.v. *percursus*.

fol. 26[6]   17. Henri de Saint-Benoît-sur-Vanne, knight, requested the return of his serfs held in the royal prison at Troyes for debt, claiming that his men could not make obligations without his special permission. The *bailli* replied that his men and all men of any condition in Champagne could engage in trade and make contracts with their own goods. After hearing these statements, the court declared that it would not hear the knight's case.

Petebat Henrions de Sancto Benedicto miles homines suos de corpore sibi reddi et deliberari qui in prisione regis Trecis detinebantur pro debitis in quibus se obligaverant per litteras balliviae ut dicebatur cum omnibus bonis suis;

---

5. See Arbois de Jubainville, *Histoire*, VI, No. 3453.
6. Folio supplied from C, fol. 54.

dicens dictus miles quod ipsi homines non poterant se obligare nec eorum bona alienare sine ipsius licentia speciale, baillivo pro rege dicente quod tam ipsi quam alii homines cujusque conditionis in toto comitatu Campaniae possunt de bonis suis mercari et contrahere et ratione contractuum se per litteras obligare. Auditis hinc inde propositis, pronunciatum est dictum militem non esse super hoc audiendum. —D, fol. 22v.

fol. 28   18. In a case between the king of Navarre and the lord of Crécy-en-Brie [Gaucher V de Châtillon], by order of the court an inquest was made on the right to collect mainmorte from bastards and on the ownership of servile bastards in the village of Artonges. The inquest showed that these rights belonged to the lord of Crécy, and the *bailli* was ordered to withdraw his injunction.—B, p. 956 n.

Session of August 1285

19. The proctor of the commune of Provins complained that, contrary to the charter granted to the commune by the count of Champagne,[7] the officials of the count were preventing the commune from collecting fines up to 20s. from those coming to Provins from outside the town. After seeing the charter the court ordered the *bailli* of Troyes to permit the commune to collect these fines.—Prou and d'Auriac, *Actes et comptes*, p. 282.

Uncertain Session, Probably in 1285[8]

20. Lord Erard d'Arcis brought suit against Henri l'Armurier and Thibaut de Saint-Antoine, both of Troyes, because they

---

7. This charter of Thibaut V of 1268 was confirmed by Prince Philip and his wife in February, 1285; see Félix Bourquelot, *Histoire de Provins*, 2 vols. (Provins, 1839–40), II, 416–417 and 432.

8. The custumal names the masters and dates this case in 1284. For this date to refer to the old style calendar, there would have had to have been a session of the Jours between March 11, when the masters Joinville and Gautier de Chambly took up their duties as guardians after the king's departure from Orléans, and Easter. Since no such session is recorded in the accounts of Champagne for the first half year of 1285 (see Longnon [ed.], *Documents*, III, 27–28), the date should probably be corrected to 1285 (N.S.). There is no way to tell whether this case was tried in the April or the August session.

Philip the Fair and the Jours de Troyes

had purchased houses and other property at Sacey and Thénnelières from serfs held in fief by Erard. The court declared that the defendants could not make these purchases and that Erard should have them.—Portejoie (ed.), *Coutumier*, art. 10, pp. 155–158.

Session Beginning January 27, 1286[?][9]

fol. 27[?][10] 21. Lord Henri de Hans was ordered to name a guardian (*tutor seu curator*) for his cases, both for and against him, since he claimed to be continually ill. If he failed to do so, his goods were to be administered in justice by the *bailli* of Vitry.—Brief analysis in L, t. 67, fol. 11.

fol. [?][11] 22. The court declared that the woman who married the son of the lord of Hans did not have to pay relief, since the marriage was void because at the time it was constituted the son had entered holy orders.

Curia declaravit quod quaedam femina quae duxerat in virum filium domini de Hans non tenetur ad solvendum rachatum pro eo quod dictum matrimonium nullum fuit ex eo quod dictus filius tempore constituti matrimonii erat in sacris ordinibus constitutus.—D, fols. 22v–23.

Session Beginning April 22, 1286

fol. 33 23. The prior and canons of Belroy declared that Lambert le Bouchu, chamberlain of Champagne, had granted them an annual revenue of two *muids* of grain from the granges of Beaurepaire, La Grange-au-Bois, Arrentières, and Rouvre,[12]

---

9. This date is uncertain and puzzling. D, fol. 22v, places the session "in quindena festi Sancti Remigii 1286" after that "in quindena Pasche 1285" and before that "in crastino octave Pasche anno 1286." Although in Champagne the year normally began at Easter, this position suggests that in this instance the year had already changed. L places this case "aux jours de la S. Remy 86."

10. C, fol. 54, places a case concerning "Henricus dom. de Hans senior" in 1286 on fol. 27. L gives no folio.

11. Dongois records this case "in quindena festi Sancti Remigii 1286." On the problem of dating and placement see the notes to the preceding case.

12. For this charter of January, 1232, see Charles Lalore, "Notice sur le prieuré de Belroy," *Mémoires de la Société academique . . . de l'Aube*, LI (1887), 184.

that three of these granges had come into the possession of Count Henri III of Champagne, and that the count had granted two of them to Duke [Ferri III] of Lorraine in the settlement of the dowry of his sister [Marguerite of Navarre]. They therefore requested that the duke's son Thibaut be ordered to pay them the revenue from the two granges of Arrientières and Rouvre. Thibaut's proctor responded that the granges had been assigned free of obligations. The court ordered that Thibaut should pay the grain to the priory, without prejudice to his right to bring an action against the lord of Champagne (cf. above, No. 14).—B, pp. 241–242 n.

fols. 34–35 24. The court declared that when the guards of the fairs, acting by reason of their office and in conformity with the customs of the fairs, had imprisoned a debtor attached to the fairs (*de corpore nundinarum*) at the request of any merchant, if the debtor left the prison without the assent of the merchant, the guards (and the lord of Champagne whom they represent) should be obliged to pay the merchant the sum for which the debtor had been imprisoned.—Du Cange, *Glossarium*, s.v., *custodes nundinarum Campaniae*.

Uncertain Session in 1286

fol. 39 25. Lord Thibaut de Broyes and the abbot and community of Saint-Pierre of Oyes made mutual oaths of peace in the presence of the court.—B, p. 857 n.

fol. 39 26. Borgine, daughter of Huard Baudier, accused the lady of Chassins of holding her father in prison on suspicion of the murder [of Philippe de Moncel] and of hanging him without proper procedure and sufficient evidence, wherefore she requested that his body be taken down from the gallows and his property be released to her. The lady replied that Huard, her serf, had been judged with the counsel of good men for a murder committed in her jurisdiction. The court decided that Borgine's accusation should not be taken up.—B, p. 222; for details see *ibid.*, pp. 228–229 n.

fol. 39v 27. The *baillis* were ordered to investigate the property acquired by churches in their districts. If they found that grants of real property had been confirmed by the king [of Navarre] and had been held for a sufficiently long time, they were to leave the churches alone. Otherwise, they were to deal with the churches as best they could, and to refer their settlements to the king for approval.—B, p. 666 n.

fol. 39v 28. The proctor of the abbot and community of Saint-Médard of Soissons stated that the church was obliged to pay annually 20 *livres* for the *gîte* of Damery and 10 *livres* for that of Cierges when the king did not stay there in person, but that when the king came to those places, they had to pay all the expenses of his stay. The proctor complained that although the recent visit of the king had cost them 100 *livres tournois*, they were still required in the same year to pay the stated 30 *livres*, which they requested be returned. The court granted the request.—B, p. 566 n.

Session Beginning November 8, 1286

fol. 40 29. In an inquest and local hearing in a case which Oudin Louchat had brought against Perrin Fumon, knight, concerning the plaintiff's status, Oudin had sufficiently proved that Perrin's mother had freed him. The court therefore declared that Oudin was to remain a royal serf in the same fashion as he had been a serf of Perrin.[13]—B, p. 934 n.

November 15, 1286

30. The court declared in favor of the abbey of Jouy in a case concerning its mills.—B. N., MS lat. 5467 (cartulary of Jouy), p. 201; Bourquelot, *Études*, p. 262.

fol. 43 31. After a man had been murdered in the town of Meaux, his widow was charged with the crime and detained in the royal prison. Since she was a serf of Saint-Faron at Meaux, the abbey claimed the right to judge her. The *bailli* replied

13. Presumably Oudin had been freed without royal authorization, thereby reducing the fief Perrin held from the king.

that the king held all the rights of justice in Meaux. The court declared that the woman should be handed over to the monks.—B, p. 223 n.

fol. 43v 32. The proctors of Saint-Quiriace of Provins, of the abbey of Rebais, and of the Temple and its treasurer at Laon and its men at Provins claimed that by grant of the count of Champagne their men at Provins were freed of all exactions, and that the royal officials were unjustly compelling them to pay taxes on cloth and other goods. The royal officials and the mayor and commune of Provins replied that these taxes, established by ordinance,[14] were not placed on persons but on goods, and therefore should be paid by all. The court ruled that in spite of the objections of the churches, the ordinance should remain in effect.—L, t. 26, fol. 115.

Procuratores S. Quiriaci Pruvinensis, abbatis et conventus Resbacensis et Templi ac thesaurarii Laudunensis suo et hominum suorum Pruvini, commorantium nomine, dicebant contra Regem, majorem et communitatem de Pruvino, quod cum homines predicti ipsarum ecclesiarum et thesaurarii sint per privilegia comitum Campaniae sibi concessa liberi et immunes ab omni taillia, et gentes domini Regis ipsos compellant ad solvendum de quolibet panno persico duodecim denarios, de radiato, sex denarios, et quasdam alias redevancias quotiens vendunt pannos seu alias mercaturas contra libertatem suam veniendo, petibant homines suos in sua libertate remanere et gaiges dictorum hominum propter hoc capta.

Sibi reddi, et per jusdici, gentes domini Regis et majorem et communitatem predictam non habere jus talia faciendi, gentibus domini Regis et majore et communitate praedicta in quantum tangit seu tangere potest quemlibet ipsorum e contrario dicentibus, quod olim de voluntate et assensu comitis Campaniae, archiepiscopi et majoris partis burgensium et ministrorum marchandisiorum de Pruvino fuerat ordinatum, quod quilibet (quantumcumque privilegium haberet) de pannis quos venderet et mercaturis quas faceret, solveret redevancias supradictas, quare cum ista onera

---

14. For Henri III's regulations of 1273 see Longnon (ed.), *Documents*, II, 78–79.

fuissent imposita personis sed mercaturis, hoc non erat contra privilegia eorumdem et debebant adsolvendum compelli. Auditis omnibus hinc et inde, pronunciatum est per arrestum quod non obstantibus propositis ex parte procuratorum S. Quiriaci, Resbacensis et Templi et thesaurarii, ordinatio praedictorum comitis et archiepiscopi cum burgensibus de Prŭvino in suo robore remanebit.

fol 44   33. Having seen the letter of manumission at the king's pleasure granted to Henri l'Armurier [of Troyes] by the king, the court declared that his wife [Marie] was free of the *jurée*[15] for as long as the king should please.—B, p. 921, marginal note.

fol. 49   34. Jean Banloquiers, a royal burgess [at Passavant], declared that Geoffroi de Louppy-le-Château had unjustly disseized him of the house and goods left him by his mother. Geoffroi, seconded by the proctor of Count [Thibaut II] of Bar-le-Duc, pleaded that the case should be tried in the court of his lord, the count of Bar. The court declared that the count should not have jurisdiction over the movable goods, and that it would determine the location of the real property and make a later decision concerning it. Consequently Geoffroi contumaciously left without giving a response. The *bailli* of Vitry was ordered to put Banloquiers in possession of his movable goods (cf. No. 60).—B, pp. 937–939 n.

Session Beginning April 14, 1287

fol. 50   35. The court forbade all the *baillis* and *prévôts* of Champagne and Brie to sell the offices of sergeants or mayors, or to permit them to be sold to anyone, until they should receive a special order to the contrary from the king. If they did otherwise, they were to be severely punished.—B, p. 242 n.

fol. 50v   36. The men of Lord Gui de la Neuville-aux-Bois complained of injuries Gui had done them contrary to their charter. Gui responded that he was not bound to reply to

15. At Troyes the *jurée* was a tax of six *deniers* per *livre* on the assessed value of movable property and two *deniers* per *livre* on real estate. In the 1270's it produced a revenue of about 1500 *livres* a year. See Longnon (ed.), *Documents*, II, 13 D.

this charge of his serfs, since it did not concern default of justice or false judgment. The court declared that the case should be returned to Gui's court, and ordered him to do no injury to the plaintiffs and to observe their charter in order to avoid royal action because of his default.—B, p. 267; D, fols. 23–23v; L, t. 67, fol. 12.

fol. 51　　37. The monks of Montier-en-Argonne claimed to be under the guard of the count of Champagne.—B, p. 814.

Uncertain Session in 1287

fol. 53[16]　　38. Lord [André] de Saint-Phal, knight, pleaded that the land of Courgerennes, which had formerly been held by Lord Gautier de Courgerennes, knight, and which had been confiscated by the king for Gautier's crime, should be held in fief from him, but that it had had no vassal or tenant since Gautier's death.[17] The court declared that if the land was held in fee, André should have a vassal, and if it was held in villenage, he should have a tenant.—B, p. 155 n.

fol. 53　　39. Jean du Plessis-lés-Chaast had captured a thief and hanged and condemned him; later the *bailli* of Troyes had the body removed and hanged from the royal gallows. The *bailli* was ordered to determine whether the thief had been captured in the territory of royal justice or in that of Jean's. —B, p. 222; D, fol. 23v.

fol. 54　　40. Lord Jacques Mauferas [of Turgy], knight, complained that a year before he had been beaten and wounded by Jean Boutauz [of Lignières?], knight, and his accomplices, who had also beaten one of his servants and stolen his sword. Jean responded that he was under the jurisdiction of the lady of Lignières and sought to have the case heard in her court; he was seconded in this by the lady of Lignières. The royal proctor replied that the officials of Champagne had juris-

---

16. B gives the folio as 53 and the date as 1286. The folio is confirmed by C, fol. 54.

17. Gautier was condemned and his brother banished as early as Pentecost, 1285. Up to Christmas, 1287, their lands paid the king over 112 *livres*. See Longnon (ed.), *Documents*, III, 35.

diction of all nobles of Champagne with respect to their movables and in criminal cases. The court declared that before going further the matter should be referred to the king, that the *bailli* should seek more information, and that Jean should remain in the royal prison at Troyes.—B, pp. 231–232 n; D, fols. 23v–24.

Session Beginning May 22, 1287

fol. 57   41. The viscount of Bar-sur-Seine complained that the *bailli* of Chaumont had seized a certain serf whose dues he had fixed (*abonaverat*) with the authorization of the lady of Honneriis,[18] from whom he held the serf. The *bailli* stated that since the lady held the serf from the king and the agreement to fix his dues had been made without royal authorization, the serf should belong to the king. The court declared that henceforth the viscount should receive from the serf no more than the sum agreed upon and the king should receive the rest of his payments as the viscount had before.—B, p. 935.

fol. 60   42. Two daughters of Huard Baudier brought the same charges against the lady of Chassins as Borgine had before (No. 26), and the lady made the same defense, requesting that the case not be taken up, particularly since the court had ruled against a similar charge brought by one of the daughters. The court declared that the charge should not be taken up, but ordered the *bailli* of Vitry to free the daughters' maternal inheritance, which had been seized by the lady of Chassins, to seek more information, and to submit a sealed report at the next session of the Jours.—B, p. 224; cf. D, fol. 26.

Session Beginning September 9, 1287

43. The court ordered the *bailli* of Troyes to permit the free entry of wine being taken into Troyes for the use of the

18. I cannot identify any place in Champagne named *Honneriis* or Honnières. Possibly Brussel made an error for *Lyneriis*. The family of Lignières had once held the office of viscount of Bar-sur-Seine; see Alphonse Roserot, *Dictionnaire historique de la Champagne méridionale* (Langres, 1942–48), pp. 114–115.

Hôtel-Dieu-le-Comte of Troyes, since such wine did not have to pay portage. He was also ordered to see that justice was done with respect to the prebend in Saint-Etienne of Troyes, which the brothers of the Hôtel-Dieu claimed belonged to them and had been unjustly retained by the dean and chapter of Saint-Etienne.[19]—Printed by Philippe Guignard, *Les anciens statuts de l'Hôtel-Dieu-le-Comte de Troyes* (Troyes, 1853), pp. 104–105, from an eighteenth-century copy in Aube, arch. dép., Lay. 5. D. 19.

fol. 61   44. The court ordered that all those guarantors of debts (*personarii*) held in prison for debt who wished to hand over their goods, both movables and real property, should be freed, no matter whether the debts had been recorded by the *baillis* or not. This order was made without prejudice to the rights of the fairs of Champagne.—B, pp. 243–244 n; D, fol. 24v.

fol. 66v 45. The court ordered that in every place where there should be a mayor the *baillis* of Champagne and Brie should establish an appropriate person, that no other sergeants should remain in the office of mayor, and that the mayors should engage in no other service except that of their districts, for which each should answer in the assizes of his *bailli*.—B, p. 243.

46. The court recorded an offer of concord made to Lord [Jean] de Chappes by Lord Erard d'Arcis and Lord Guillaume de *Gant*, knight.[20]

Erard d'Arcies pour luy et pour Monsieur Guillaume de Gant, chevaliers, lequel Messire Erars prenoit en main, cet offre que Erars d'Arcies ha faite a Monsieur de Chappes.

Premierement Messire Erars se doit mettre en la prison de Monsieur Guillaume de Juilly, et le terra s'il velt autretant en prison et en telle prison comme il tint Monsieur de

19. In the twelfth century the founder of the Hôtel-Dieu, Count Henry I, had granted it "annualia quoque prebendarum Sancti Stephani quocumquemodo prebenda vacet vel muttetur exceptis prebendis personatuum," Aube, arch. dép., 40 H layette 1.

20. Dongois gives neither date nor folio, but apparently the entry should precede Nos. 47 and 48.

Chappes. Et ce fait, quand il istrera hors de prison, il s'en doit aller outre la mer d'Angleterre au rapport de Monsieur de Juilly, et ce fait, il s'en doit aller à Saint Jacques en Galice et à Nostre Dame de Vauvert et a Saint Nicolas de Varangéville, et de ces choses faire il est à la requeste de Monsieur de Juilly ou son commandement; et ce faisant li ditz Erars et le ditz Guillaume ont bonne paix à Monsieur de Chappes et à tous les siens et quittent de toutes choses dou temps passé jusques aujourdhuy.—D, fols. 24–24v.

fol. 68   47. Through the testimony of Jean de Villeblevin, Gilles de Compiègne, Jean l'Esquallot, and Pierre de Chaource, the court recorded the mutual oaths of peace (*assecuratio*) made by Lord Erard d'Arcis and his party and Lord [Jean] de Chappes and his party. These oaths had been made in full court at the Jours of Troyes a year before.[21]—B, p. 857 n.

48. Lord [Jean] de Chappes maintained that after he had made an oath of peace (*aseurement*) with Lord Erard d'Arcis, the two of them had made a concord (*pais*). Their later hostilities had therefore broken the concord but not the oath. The court ruled in favor of Jean, declaring that he should be fined for breaking the concord [and not punished for the more serious crime of breaking an oath of peace].— Portejoie (ed.), *Coutumier*, art. 30 (dated 1287), pp. 182–185.

fol. 68   49. The court determined that the mayor and counsellors of Provins had sufficiently proved their right to a pillory (*scala*) and declared that one should remain there, without prejudice to the rights of the king.—L, t. 26, fols. 112–112v, giving date and folio; B. N., Coll. Dupuy, t. 761, fol. 49; Grillon entered the text in the "Cartulary" of Provins (Provins, Bibl. mun., MS 89), fol. 45, with the date 1283; printed from this last source in Prou and d'Auriac, *Actes et comptes*, p. 62.

21. Among those of whom the court was to enquire further was the "Senescallus de Biaucaria tunc Baillivus de Calvomonte." This statement indicates a step in the career of Jean de Champrupin not otherwise recorded; see François Maillard, "Mouvements administratifs des baillis et des sénéchaux sous Philippe le Bel," *Bulletin philologique et historique du Comité des travaux historiques et scientifiques* (année 1959), pp. 408–411. Jean l'Esquallot and Pierre de Chaource were guards of the forests of Champagne; see Longnon (ed.), *Documents*, III, 50 and 58.

Visa apprisia facta super hoc quod major et scabini de Pruvino dicebant se esse et fuisse in bona saisina faciendi et habendi scalam a tempore dominorum Campaniae predecessorum domini Regis apud Pruvinum in medio vico ante Domum Dei Pruvinensem ad ponendum ibidem malefactores, jurantes in honesta juramenta, et justiciandi eosdem in scala sive puniendi secundum loci consuetudinem et secundum delictorum quantitatem, inventum fuit et probatum dictos majorem et scabinos vel juratos intentionem suam sufficienter probasse: quare pronunciatum fuit per curiae consilium quod ibidem prout esse consueverat, salvo jure domini Regis, scala fiet et remanebit.

Uncertain Session in 1287 (O. S.)

fol. 69   50. Jean de Fay charged that Jean Raymond [a prominent citizen of Provins] had beaten and threatened him, and he requested that Jean Raymond be fined. Jean Raymond replied that the case should not be taken up, since Jean de Fay had brought similar charges before the court of the *bailli* of Troyes at the assizes of Provins, where Jean Raymond had been released by judgment of the court. Jean de Fay replied that Jean Raymond had broken the judgment of the court, since he was supposed to submit any later grievances to arbitration. The court declared that Jean de Fay's case should not be taken up.—B, p. 237 n.

Session Beginning May 3, 1288

fol. 71   51. The *bailli* of Vitry had not made the investigation into the case of Huard Baudier requested earlier by the court (No. 42) because of a transfer of office.[22] The new *bailli* was directed to make a sealed report at a later session of the Jours.—B, p. 225 n.

fol. 73[?][23]   52. The abbot and community of Saint-Memmie-lés-Châlons stated that although they had made use of their

22. Pierre Saymel was named *prévôt* of Paris and replaced as *bailli* of Vitry by Jean de Champrupin in late 1287 or early 1288; see Maillard, "Mouvements," p. 411.
23. Brussel gives the folio as 37, but the date suggests that the figures were reversed.

burgess rights (*burgesia*) in Châlons and had received burgesses in their tenures since time immemorial, paying 40 *livres tournois* a year to the count of Champagne for this,[24] now the *bailli* of Vitry and the bishop of Châlons were interfering with these burgess rights; they therefore petitioned for relief. The court ordered the *bailli* to permit the abbey to enjoy its burgess rights, notwithstanding the constitution [passed in the Parlement of Pentecost 1287].[25]—B, p. 903 n.

fol. 73v 53. The court ordered that debtors bound by notarial letters and jailed by reason of their personal obligations should be released from prison if they gave the judges a claim on all their forthcoming inheritances for the satisfaction of their debts, that debtors bound by notarial letters should be able to prove through acceptable witnesses that they had paid their debts, that notaries should not do their work outside of castles, and that the *baillis* should prevent notaries from making or receiving obligations which were against the law.—B, pp. 244–245 n.

fol. 74 54. The court recorded the terms of the concord (*paix*) made between the relatives of Raolin d'Argers and the Hermit of Stenay. The Hermit gave the friends of the dead Raolin 100 *livres* to establish a chapel for him, and his son Girard was obliged to go overseas and bring back letters testifying to the journey.—Du Cange, *Dissertations sur l'histoire de Saint Louis* in *Histoire de S. Louys* (Paris, 1668), pp. 337–338, reprinted among other places in *Glossarium*, ed. Henschel, VII, 125.

Uncertain Session in 1288

fol. 79 55. Lord Jean de Bourlemont, knight, and Jean de Gondrecourt-le Château, squire, and their supporters made mutual oaths of peace.—B, p. 857 n.

24. According to the accounts of 1287 and 1288 the abbey paid the count 40 *livres* a year for "garde" or "taille"; see Longnon (ed.), *Documents*, III, 53*E* and 91*H*.
25. For the text of this constitution see César Chabrun, *Les bourgeois du roi* (Paris, 1908), pp. 135–144.

Session Following September 14, 1288

fol. 79v 56. The prior of Gimont was condemned to a fine of 60 *livres tournois* because he had appealed from a judgment made in the assizes of the *bailli* of Chaumont to the masters of the Jours of Troyes, but had then made peace with the *bailli*, renounced his appeal, and approved the judgment.—B, p. 237 n; D, fol. 25.

57. The court ordered that all of the acquisitions made by the church of Saint-Quiriace of Provins more than forty years before should remain in their hands without impediment, but all acquisitions made more recently should remain in the hands of the king.[26]

Auditis rationibus decani et capituli Sancti Quiriaci super acquestibus ab eisdem factis, quos impedium receptores Campaniae, injuste ut asscrum: dictum et ordinatum est per Curiae consilium quod omnes acquestus suos quos fecerunt ultra quadraginta annos, penes ipsos absque impedimento remanebunt; omnes autem alios quos fecerunt quoquomodo infra quadraginta annos, penes dominum regem remanebunt, et de praemissis receptores se informabunt.—D, fols. 25–25v.

fol. 80v 58. Two men of Grand who had made a concord between themselves after arming for a judicial duel, as reported by the *bailli* of Chaumont, were ordered to pay 30 *livres* apiece to the royal tax collectors.—B, p. 989 n.

fol. 87 59. The *bailli* of Vitry made a partial report on the case of Huard Baudier (cf. No. 51), but since the lady of Chassins was ill, as certified by the court, the matter was prorogued until the next session of the Jours. The *bailli* was ordered to hear witnesses from both sides and to submit a complete sealed report.—B, p. 226 n.

fol. 87 60. Geoffroi de Louppy-le-Château, squire, charged that Jean Banloquiers, whom he claimed to be his serf, had made an oath of peace to another man in his presence, that he had

---

26. Dongois gives no folio but places this case in the same term as No. 56.

imprisoned Banloquiers for breaking this oath, and that Banloquiers had escaped from his prison. He therefore requested that Banloquiers, as his serf and subject, be returned to him for examination. Banloquiers replied that for about three years he had been in conflict with Geoffroi over his mother's property (see No. 34), that never before had Geoffroi brought this charge, that he was a royal burgess living at Passavant, and that he was prepared to defend his burgess right against anyone in the king's court. The court ruled that Banloquiers did not have to answer this charge [in Geoffroi's court], but that if Geoffroi wished to have him brought before the *bailli* of Vitry, the *bailli* should render a judgment which might not be appealed to the court of Champagne.—B, pp. 939–940 n.

fol. 89

61. Lady Christine de Bar requested that since Miles de Jaucourt had been found guilty of the murder of her son, as certified by the local *bailli*, Miles should be called before the king's justice and given the appropriate punishment. The court instructed the *bailli* to take Miles, said to be a cleric, outside of Holy Church, to hand him over to the bishop of the place for punishment, to confiscate all the property which Miles possessed at the time of the murder, and not to proceed to a hearing on the disposition of that property without the king's special order.—B, p. 233.

fol. 90v

62. Lord [Jean] de Joinville complained that the *bailli* of Chaumont had taken over the justice of Joinville and had prevented him and his men from exercising justice there. The *bailli* responded that he had done this properly because of a denial of justice, since after two men had made oaths of peace before the royal *prévôt*, one of them with the help of accomplices had beaten and wounded the other in the town of Joinville, and the justice of Joinville had not acted to apprehend the malefactors or to restrain them. The lord of Joinville admitted these facts, but claimed that the *bailli* did not have the right to interfere with his justice, since he was a noble castellan, that the *bailli* had not summoned him to his assizes on the charge of denial of justice, and that the *bailli* could not try his case or interfere with his justice without a

sufficient summons.[27] The court declared that the cognizance of the alleged case of broken oaths of peace should remain with the *bailli*, that he should return the authority to exercise justice in Joinville to its lord, and that he should not permit the lord of Joinville to be molested.—B, pp. 865–866 n.

fol. 91   63. The court ordered the *bailli* of Troyes to permit the lord of Jully [Guillaume I] to collect the *jurée* from his serfs married to female serfs of the lord of Champagne in the same fashion that the lord of Champagne customarily collected it in those places where the men lived. Concerning the request of the lord of Jully to divide their children and to collect *taille à merci* from these men as he had before their marriages, the *bailli* was ordered to determine the local customary practice and to submit a sealed report at the next session of the Jours.—B, 923 n.

Session Beginning March 17, 1289

fol. 93v   64. One of the daughters of Huard Baudier requested that the report of the *bailli* of Vitry on her father's case be considered and a judgment made. The lady of Chassins, who appeared in person, argued that the case should be dropped. The court agreed to consider the case (cf. No. 59).—B, p. 227 n.

fol. 94v   65. Pastorelle de Verdun, who claimed to be a burgess of the lord of Champagne, complained that the Thirteen Justices of Verdun had unjustly confiscated her goods and had refused the request of the *bailli* of Vitry that they return them. The Thirteen Justices, although summoned by the *bailli* to appear at this session of the Jours, had not appeared, and therefore Pastorelle requested restitution of her goods with damages and expenses. The *bailli* was instructed to make restitution to Pastorelle from the goods of people from Verdun staying in Champagne if he could find them, but that if the Thirteen Justices wished to appear in his

27. Portejoie (ed.), *Coutumier*, p. 74, explains that since the oaths were made before a royal *prévôt*, the lord of Joinville could not be blamed for failing to act in a matter in which he did not have competence. But this was not the defense Joinville actually made.

assizes, he was authorized to do justice to the parties as reason dictated.—B, p. 920.

fol. 95   66. In the case between Ermengarde, daughter of Huard Baudier, and the lady of Chassins (cf. No. 64), the court declared that neither the court of Champagne nor anyone else could make any demands on the lady of Chassins for her execution of Huard Baudier, but that if the dead man were alive (*se cieus vesquesit qui est mort*), the court would charge him as guilty of Huard's death.[28] Consequently Huard's body was to be taken down from the gallows publicly and buried in a cemetery, if it was acceptable to the church, and the lady of Chassins was ordered to deliver to Ermengarde all the goods Huard had possessed on the day of his trial.—B, pp. 228–229 n; D, fols. 26v–27.

fol. 97   67. Lord [Jean] de Joinville requested a review of the inquest made on the guard of the abbey of Saint-Urbain of Joinville, which had been referred to the court of Champagne by order of the court of France. The *bailli* of Chaumont replied that the inquest should not be reviewed until a judgment had been made on the authenticity of the charter which the monks had offered in proof and which the lord of Joinville declared false. The court ordered that the matter should be reviewed at the next session of the Jours or at the coming day of the barons [at Parlement], and the proctor of the abbey was ordered to bring the charter with him to that judgment (see above, p. 292 and note 36).—B, pp. 249–250 n; cf. *ibid.*, p. 814.

Unspecified Session in 1288 (O. S.)

68. Pierre de la Ferté was condemned to pay a fine of 10 *livres tournois* for breaking an order of the court.—Brief analysis in L, t. 67, fol. 11.

28. In this amazing decision the court was obviously straining to fit an equitable judgment into the framework of the law. The reason for the argument actually used was not made clear. Nowhere in the previous record was it stated that the plaintiffs had claimed that Huard had acted in self-defense or that the dead man was in any way at fault.

Session Beginning September 9, 1289

fol. 101 69. The mayor and town counsellors of Monthois, who claimed that their charter granted them the customs of Beaumont-en-Argonne, requested the right to try their burgess, Baudier de Donzy, who had been arrested by the *bailli* of Vitry.[29] The *bailli* replied that Baudier had done great injury to the officials of Champagne, and that he had voluntarily accepted the *bailli*'s jurisdiction and then broken away while on the way to prison. Moreover, the burgesses of Monthois offered in proof only an inquest made by the Council of Forty of Beaumont, and not the text of the charter itself. The court deferred the case until the next session of the Jours, when it could see the charter or its authentic transcript, and Baudier was given his choice whether to be delivered on bail to the burgesses of Monthois or kept in the royal prison. The court also declared that a judgment it had rendered earlier in a case between the lady of Corbon and certain men of Monthois concerning their status applied only to those men and was without prejudice to the present case.— B, pp. 926–928 n.

fol. 101 70. The court ordered the *bailli* of Vitry to fine and punish anyone who challenged its earlier judgment in favor of the lady of Corbon against certain men who claimed burgess rights at Monthois.—B, p. 928 n; L, t. 67, fol. 11.

fol. [?][30] 71. After the Thirteen Justices of Verdun agreed to make full restitution of her goods to Pastorelle de Verdun through the agency of the *bailli* of Vitry, on condition that she guarantee the amount, Pastorelle was unable to do so. The court ordered the *bailli* to keep her goods and to administer them to provide for her necessities and the costs of prosecuting her case (cf. No. 65).—B, p. 921 n.

fol. 106[31] 72. Lord Guillaume de Grancey, knight, complained that burgesses from Bar-sur-Aube were occupying servile tenures

29. This charter is not recorded in Edouard Bonvalot, *Le tiers état d'après la charte de Beaumont* (Paris, 1884); on the principle of local trial see p. 398.

30. Brussel dropped a digit and gives the folio as 10v. The session is indicated, however.

31. Although Brussel dates this case in 1288, the folio is confirmed by C, fol. 54v.

in his village of Couvignon. The court ordered the *bailli* of Chaumont to seize the produce of the property held by the burgesses and bring it into Couvignon. The *bailli* was then to ask the burgesses if they wished to submit to his judgment in this matter, and if not, he was to protect the lord of Grancey in doing justice himself.—B, pp. 917–918 n.

fol. 106

73. The court ordered the *bailli* of Chaumont to direct Count [Thibaut] of Bar to return to Balduin de Tour, squire, his house of La Tour-en-Woëvre, which Balduin claimed to hold from the lord of Champagne.[32] And since the count of Bar had been summoned to this session of the Jours and had not come or excused himself, the *bailli* was ordered to summon the count to appear at the next day of the barons at Paris [i.e., the Parlement of Pentecost 1290].[33] —B, p. 250 n.

fol. 106v

74. The *bailli* of Chaumont was ordered to go to Count [Thibaut] of Bar, who had been summoned to this session of the Jours and had not appeared, to request a truce with Hugues Bekait, knight, who had complained to the court of Champagne. If the count alleged a just cause for not keeping peace with Hugues, the *bailli* was to summon him to appear against Hugues at Paris.—B, p. 858.

fol. 106v [?][34]

75. The *bailli* of Chaumont was ordered to direct Duke [Ferri III] of Lorraine to make amends for the injuries done to the sergeants and *prévôts* of Champagne. If he refused, the *bailli* with an armed band was to seize the goods of the duke wherever he could find them and the persons of those who had done the injuries and to take vengeance to maintain the honor of the king.[35]—B, pp. 245–246 n; D, fol. 27v.

32. La Tour-en-Woëvre was a fief of Champagne; see Longnon, *Rôles des fiefs du comté de Champagne* (Paris, 1877), No. 1341.

33. He did not appear there either; see Delisle (ed.), *Essai*, p. 430, No. 744.

34. Brussel gives the folio as 186v, but both he and Dongois place this case in the September term of 1289.

35. In May, 1289, Philip assumed the guard of the possessions of the chapter of Toul on the left side of the Meuse, while Ferri had renewed his safeguard of the chapter two months before. Perhaps these events explain the violence discussed here. See Fritz Kern, *Acta Imperii* (Tübingen, 1910), No. 62, and Jean de Pange, *Catalogue des actes de Ferri III* (Paris, 1930), No. 891.

Session Beginning September 10, 1290

fol. 112v 76. Ermengarde, daughter of the late Huard Baudier, acting with the approval of her husband, stated that her suit for the rehabilitation of her father's memory had cost her 100 *livres tournois*, and she therefore pleaded that the lady of Chassins should pay her this sum (cf. No. 66). She added that her two brothers-in-law had agreed to pay half the expenses of the suit and pleaded that they should be ordered to pay what they owed. The lady of Chassins replied that since the brothers-in-law were her serfs, the case should be tried in her court. The court declared that the lady of Chassins should not have jurisdiction of this case, but should answer the petition. —B, pp. 268–269 n.

Uncertain Session in 1290[?]

fol. 114[36] 77. Jean de Joinville, lord of Reynel, made an agreement with his father Jean de Joinville, concerning the land of Reynel, which he had inherited after the death of his mother Alix de Reynel.—Du Cange, *Généalogie de la maison de Joinville*, p. 22, in *Histoire de S. Louys.*

fol. 115[37] 78. Geoffroi de Joinville came into conflict with the king of Navarre concerning a female serf.—*Ibid.*, p. 14.

36. Du Cange gives the folio as 114 and the date as 1288. Probably the error is in the date. The seneschal and his son endowed candles at Alix's tomb in November, 1290; see H.-François Delaborde, *Jean de Joinville* (Paris, 1894), Nos. 577 and 585.

37. Du Cange gives the folio as 115 and the date as 1288. Presumably the error is again in the date.

APPENDIX II

MEMBERS AND MASTERS OF THE JOURS OF TROYES UNDER PHILIP THE FAIR

The sources of information about the members of the court of the Jours are the two registers which were once in the Chambre des Comptes, the accounts of Champagne, the custumal of the county, a royal ordinance, a memorandum of Parlement, and a few miscellaneous charters. Of all these records only the custumal was written years after the events it relates. The custumal is therefore of lesser authority than the other materials, and where it is in conflict with them or unsupported, it should be considered suspect.

The names of those attending the Jours are given here with the fullest titles which appear in any of the cited sources, and additional information is added in brackets. All dates have been converted to the Gregorian year. The sigla of the manuscripts are explained at the beginning of Appendix I.

1. 1284, term of St. Catherine (November 25)

Hugues [III] de Conflans, marshal of Champagne
Jean de Joinville, seneschal of Champagne
[Simon II de Clermont], lord of Nesle
Lord Gilles de Brion
Matthieu, *vidame* of Chartres
Lord [Guillaume I] de Jully
Lord Jean de Braisne
Lord Guillaume de Villarcel [guard of the fairs of Champagne]
Lord Henri de Saint Benoît-sur-Vanne
Lord [?] of Breuil
Lord Jacques de *Verna* or *Beona*[1]
[Robert], abbot of Montiéramey
[Guillaume ?], abbot of Montiérender
Master [Gautier de Chambly], archdeacon of Coutances
Master Etienne, archdeacon of Bayeux
Master Jean de Vassoigne
Master Jean ... [Baras ?]

1. These are the readings of D and B respectively.

Master Anseau de Montaigu
Master Guillaume d'Outremer
Vincent de Pierrechastel, formerly [chancellor of Champagne]
Florent de Roye
Renier Accorre [tax collector of Champagne]
Oudard de Neuville, *bailli* of Sens
Guillaume d'Alemant [*bailli* of Troyes]
Hugues de Chaumont, formerly *bailli* of Vitry
And many more.

Based on two different lists in the first register, fol. 17v in B, pp. 859–860 n; D, fol. 22; cf. C, fol. 37v, and A, fol. 378.

2. *1285, term of two weeks after Easter (April 8)*

Those paid wages specifically for attending the court are marked with an asterisk, and the number of days of service is noted in parentheses. The two guardians, who presumably presided, were paid separately.

Lord Jean de Joinville, who then guarded the county
Master Gautier de Chambly
*Master Jean de Vassoigne (17 days)
Gilles de Compiègne
*Florent de Roye (19 days)
*[Robert], abbot of Montiéramey (11 days)
*An unnamed clerk [possibly Gilles de Compiègne]
*Master Jean Baras (16 days)
*Lord Gilles de Brion (9 days)

In addition Renier Accorre was paid expenses for his clerks (13 days), and wages were also paid to Count Philip's proctor, Pierre de Beaumont.

The first five names are those recorded in the *Coutumier* for case No. 20, Appendix I. The accounts, printed in Longnon (ed.), *Documents*, III, 27–28, record the wages paid to those attending the session beginning April 8, 1285.

3. *1285, August 3*

No names are recorded except those of the guardians, Jean de Joinville and Gautier de Chambly.

Prou and d'Auriac, *Actes et Comptes*, p. 282.

4. 1286, term of the week after All Saints (November 8)

Taking the place of the king (*tenentes locum domini Regis*):
Brother Arnoul de Wisemale
Master Simon Matiffas, archdeacon of Reims[2]
Master Gautier de Chambly
Master Jean de Vassoigne
Gilles de Compiègne

Present on November 15:
[Robert], abbot of Montiéramey
Guillaume d'Alemant, *bailli* [of Troyes]
Renier Accorre
Chrétien de Provins
Master Guillaume de Beaumont
Lord Jean de Broyes
Lord Guillaume d'Erbloy
Gautier de Durtain, mayor of Provins
Guillaume Raymond
Gautier, viscount of Saint-Florentin
Lord Gilles, his brother
Master Jean de Taillefontaine
Master Jean de Vandeuvre
Guillaume du Châtelet, *bailli* of Sézanne
And many others.

Appendix I, No. 30.

5. 1287, undated session

Jacques de Boulogne, archdeacon of Thérouanne
Robert de Harecourt, treasurer of Poitiers
Gilles de Compiègne

These three names are given a separate listing under 1287 in C, fol. 37v, and A, fol. 378v. They are probably taken from the first register for the sessions beginning April 14, 1287.

6. 1287, Tuesday after Ascension (May 20)

Jacques de Boulogne, archdeacon of Thérouanne
Robert de Harecourt, treasurer of Poitiers

C, fol. 37v, and A, fol. 379.
2. Became bishop of Paris in 1290.

7. 1287, *term of the day following the Nativity of the Virgin (September 9)*

Those paid for their expenses in attending the session are marked with an asterisk.

Lord Gautier de Chambly, bishop of Senlis [?]
Brother Arnoul de Wisemale, of the Knights of the Temple
*Gilles de Compiègne
*Florent de Roye
Lord Jean de Villeblevin, *bailli* of Troyes
Lord Jacques de Boulogne, bishop of Thérouanne [?]
*Lord Guillaume de Grancey
*Lord Robert de Harecourt, treasurer of Poitiers
*Lord Philippe de Givancourt
*[?], chancellor of Meaux[3]
*Master Rich[ier], paid a salary for preparing *arrêts*
*Gencien   ⎫
*Renier Accorre ⎬ tax collectors of Champagne

The first six names are from a case recorded in the *Coutumier*, Appendix I, No. 48. Since Gautier de Chambly and Jacques de Boulogne are not named by other records, it is possible that the custumal is in error on these two names. In its heading for the session, the register names only three masters, Arnoul de Wisemale, Guillaume de Grancey, and Robert de Harecourt. For this record see B, p. 247 n; D, fol. 24*v*; BN, Coll. Dupuy, MS 761, fol. 49; and C, fol. 37*v*, and A, fol. 379. The comparison of the list with the accounts (Longnon, [ed.], *Documents*, III, 51) shows that not every master was paid for his services from the treasury of Champagne, and that on occasion people who were not listed in the register as masters were paid for attending the Jours.

8. 1288, *term of Monday before Ascension (May 3)*

G[autier de Chambly], bishop of Senlis
Master Gilles Lambert[4]
Lord Guillaume de Grancey
Gilles de Compiègne

First register, printed in B, p. 247 n; cf. C, fol. 37*v*, and A, fol. 379.

9. 1288, *term beginning Wednesday of the week after the Nativity of the Virgin (September 14)*

Those paid for their expenses were:

*G[autier de Chambly], bishop of Senlis

3. Quite possibly Simon Caumy; see *Obituaires de la province de Sens*, ed. Auguste Longnon and others, 4 vols. in 5 (Paris, 1902–23), IV, 60 F.
4. Became dean of Saint-Martin of Tours.

*Lord Guillaume de Grancey
*Gilles de Compiègne (23 days)
*Master Richier, his clerk

> Longnon (ed.), *Documents*, III, 88; first register in B, p. 247 n; D, fol. 25; C, fol. 38, and A, fol. 379. Only the first three were listed in the register as holding the Jours.

10. 1289, term of Thursday before mid-Lent (March 17)

Lord and Master Simon Matiffas, archdeacon of Reims
Brother Arnoul de Wisemale, knight of the Temple
Lord Guillaume de Grancey
Gilles de Compiègne
Oudard de la Neuville, *bailli* of Senlis

> First register, fol. 93 in B, pp. 247–248 n, and D, fol. 25v.

11. 1289, term of the day after the Nativity of the Virgin (September 9)

G[autier de Chambly], bishop of Senlis
Master Jean de Vassoigne, archdeacon of Bruges in the church of Tournai [5]
Lord Guillaume de Grancey
Gilles de Compiègne, of the household of the king of France
Oudard de la Neuville, *bailli* of Senlis

> First register in B, p. 248 n; D, fols. 27–27v; C, fol. 38; and A, fols. 379–379v.

12. 1290, term of Sunday after the Nativity of the Virgin (September 10)

Lord Guillaume de Grancey, knight
Master Etienne Becard, dean of Sens
Gilles de Compiègne
Oudard de la Neuville, *bailli* of Senlis
Master Guillaume, chancellor of Champagne

> First register, fol. 111, in B, p. 248 n; D, fols. 27v–28; and C, fol. 38, and A, fol. 380.

> 5. The register read "Magistrum Joannem de Vaissona brugensem Archidiaconum in Ecclesia Carnotensi." The correction was made by Portejoie (ed.), *Coutumier*, p. 158 n. 7. He became bishop of Tournai in 1292.

13. 1291, term of Sunday of the Nativity of the Virgin (September 9)

Lord G[autier de Chambly], bishop of Senlis
Lord Etienne Becard, dean of Sens
Lord Pierre, dean of St. Quentin [6]
Arnoul de Wisemale, brother of the Knights of the Temple
Master Martin, chancellor of Champagne [7]
Jean de Joinville, seneschal of Champagne
Oudard de la Neuville, *bailli* of Senlis
... de Mondidier, clerk of the king of France

> First register in B, p. 248 n; D, fol. 28; C, fol. 38; and A, fol. 380.

14. 1296, Monday before St. Peter (February 20)

G[uichard], abbot of Montier-la-Celle of the diocese of Troyes [8]
Jean [de *Manstrole*], cantor of Bayeux
Denis, cantor of Paris

> These three men issued a charter as "Dies Trecenses pro domino Rege Francie tenentés" in February, 1295 (O. S.); L, t. 67, fol. 10, and Bourquelot, *Études*, II, p. 266 n. 11. For the date see Prou and d'Auriac, *Actes et comptes*, p. 98. All three names appear in the following list.

15. 1296, unspecified term

G[uichard], abbot of Montier-la-Celle of the diocese of Troyes
Master Jean [de *Manstrole*], cantor of Bayeux
[Master ?] Denis, cantor of Paris
Jean de Montigny, sent and commissioned by the king to hold the Jours with:
Lord [Jean] de Joinville
Philippe le Convers ⎫
Jean de Dammartin ⎬ royal clerks
Florent de Roye, *bailli* of Vitry [9]

> Second register in C, fol. 38, and A, fol. 380.

> 6. B: S. Quiriacii; D, C, and A agree that the church is that of St. Quentin. Canon Michel Veissière has kindly informed me that the dean of St. Quiriace of Provins in 1291 was Etienne Paillard.
>
> 7. B: *Camerarius*; D: *Cancellarius*; CA: *Chancelier*. Martin was chancellor in 1288; see Longnon (ed.), *Documents*, III, 83.
>
> 8. Elected bishop of Troyes in 1298.
>
> 9. Possibly an error, for Florent de Roye is not otherwise named as a *bailli*; see Maillard, "Mouvements," p. 430.

16. 1297, Tuesday after the first Sunday of Lent (March 5)

G[uichard], abbot of Montier-la-Celle
J[ean de *Manstrole*], cantor of Bayeux
Etienne, archdeacon of Bruges in the church of Tournai
Lord Gui de Néry
Lord Simon de Marchais, knight of the king
Lord Oudard de la Neuville

From the second register in C, fols. 38–38v, and A, fols. 380–380v.

17. 1298, the twentieth day after Christmas (January 13)

[Guichard], abbot of Montier-la-Celle
*J[ean] de *Manstrole*, cantor of Bayeux
[Etienne], archdeacon of Bruges [in the church of Tournai]
[Master Guillaume Bonnet], treasurer of Angers [10]
Oudard de la Neuville

Second register in C, fol. 38v, and A, fol. 380v.* The accounts of Jean de *Manstrole* for attending the Jours of Christmas, 1297 (O.S.) are noted in Fawtier (ed.), *Comptes royaux*, I, No. 436.

18. 1298, Monday after the Exaltation of the Cross (September 15)

[Guichard], abbot of Montier-la-Celle
[Jean de *Manstrole*], cantor of Bayeux
[Master Guillaume Bonnet], treasurer of Angers

Second register in C, fol. 38v, and A, fol. 380v.

19. 1299, Monday after Ascension (June 1)

Jean [de la Grange], bishop of Meaux
G[uichard], bishop-elect of Troyes
*Master Pierre de Belleperche, canon of Auxerre (18 days) [11]
Master Nicolas de Châlons, canon of Sens ⎫
Master Philippe le Convers, canon of Noyon ⎬ royal clerks
Lord Simon de Marchais, knight of the king

10. Elected bishop of Bayeux in 1306. For the identification of the treasurer of Angers, see Fawtier (ed.), *Comptes royaux*, I, Nos. 3143–3146.
11. Became bishop of Auxerre in 1306.

Master Martin de la Chambre, chancellor of Champagne, archdeacon of Lisieux

Second register in C, fol. 38v, and A, fol. 380v.* The payment to Pierre de Belleperche for the term before Pentecost, 1299, is noted in Fawtier (ed.), *Comptes royaux*, I, Nos. 3148, 3152.

20. *1311 (or possibly 1312), term of two weeks after St. John (September 12)*

[Jean de Savigny], bishop of Nevers
[Gui de la Charité], bishop of Soissons
[Jean d'Auxy], cantor of Orléans [12]
Master Denis de Sens, [dean of Saint-Etienne of Sens]
Lord G[uillaume] de Nogaret
Lord Hugues de la Celle, [lord of Fontaines]
Bernard du Mès
Pierre de Dicy

Langlois, *Textes*, pp. 178–180. For the date see Borrelli de Serres, *Recherches*, II, 320.

12. Bishop of Troyes (1314-17).

APPENDIX III

SESSION OF THE JOURS IN 1276

The record of a court which met in the count's palace at Troyes on February 1, 1276, was entered in thirteenth-century handwriting on the verso of a sheet inserted at the beginning of the *Petit Cartulaire* of the Hôtel-Dieu of Provins. The text does not have the form of a charter and is clearly a copy, since it leaves blanks for several names. It suggests the existence of some sort of register of the decisions and members of the court of the Jours before the accession of Prince Philip, which could have been used by the compiler of the custumal of Champagne. It is noteworthy that this text names twenty-one members of the court; if the compiler of the custumal used records as full as this one, he selected those names most likely to be familiar to his readers and consequently created a distorted picture of the composition of the court.

The cartulary is now at Melun, archives départementales de Seine-et-Marne, H Supplément, Grand Hôtel-Dieu de Provins, A 13*. The text is on fol. 1v.

Anno domini m° cc° lxx° quinto in vigilia purificationis beate Marie, in aula regia Trecensi, recto regali iudicio adiudicaverunt amovere impedimentum quod excellentissimus Theobaldus ultimus quondam rex Navarre, Campanie et Brie comes palatinus, posuerat sua propria voluntate et de facto in annualibus prebendarum capelle sue aule Provini datis et litteratorie concessis ab antecessoribus suis fratribus et pauperibus Domus Dei Pruvini, hiis agentibus et presentibus: domino Hugone de Conflans, marescallo; domino Johanne de Joinville, senescallo; abbate de Altovillari;[1] abbate Monasterii Ariame;[2] domino Radulpho de Toreta, canonico Meldensi; magistro Matheo de . . . ; magistro Ansello . . . ; magistro Rufino; domino Henrico Tuebuef; domino Petro de Vilecer, milite; domino Guillermo, fratre eius;[3] domino Eustachio de Escuri; domino Guillermo pivole de Paciaco; Christiano dicto Ursi; magistro Johanne; Garsie;[4] quatuor ballivis, videlicet domino Petro de

1. Thomas de Moiremont was abbot of Saint-Pierre of Hautvillers in 1276.
2. The abbot of Montiéramey in 1276 was Robert.
3. At this time Guillaume de Villarcel was one of the guards of the fairs; see Elizabeth Chapin, *Les villes de foires de Champagne* (Paris, 1937), p. 255.
4. Probably Garsie Sanchez, notary; see Arbois de Jubainville, *Histoire*, IV, 541.

Maladomo,[5] domino Guillermo de Joiaco,[6] Guillermo dicto Alexandre,[7] Guillermo dicto ... [probably du Châtelet];[8] et Guillermo Remondi dicto.[9] Quorum consilio et mandato predictus magister Matheus dictum impedimentum [sic] in presentia et generali audientia multorum die predicta in aula Trecensi existantium predictum impedimentum in annualibus capelle aule predicte Pruvini positum generali et sententia et generali iudicio amovisse et de predictis annualibus dictis fratribus et pauperibus dicto iudicio licentiam dedit deserviendi et percipiendi quotiensusque fuerit oportuum [sic].

5. *Bailli* of Vitry; see Portejoie (ed.), *Coutumier*, p. 167 n. 6.
6. *Bailli* of either Meaux or Chaumont.
7. *Bailli* of Troyes and Provins; see Roserot, *Dictionnaire*, p. 1525.
8. *Bailli* of either Meaux or Chaumont; see Portejoie (ed.), *Coutumier*, p. 10 n. 28.
9. Guillaume Raymond, a prominent citizen of Provins, was the other guard of the fairs at this time; see Chapin, *Villes*, p. 255. Arbois de Jubainville (*Histoire*, IV, 486) omitted the preceding name and therefore included him as one of the four *baillis*.

INDEX OF PERSONS AND PLACES IN THE APPENDIXES

References to people are given following baptismal names, when these are known. Places in or near Champagne are identified, and cross references given to people from those places; but people from outside Champagne or its environs are not listed under their place of origin or office. Unless the name of a *bailli* is supplied in the text, *baillis* are listed only by the place of office and year. All entries are to items and appendixes and not pages; those not preceded by a Roman numeral refer to Appendix I. (Abbreviations used are as follows: ar., arrondissement; c., canton; cne., commune; ch. l., chef-lieu; dep., department; dioc., diocese.)

Agathes de Damery: 2
Agnes, wife of Odo Bezors, lord of Villarnout: 1
Alix de Reynel, wife of Jean de Joinville: 77
André de Saint-Phal: 38
Anseau, master: III
Anseau de Montaigu: II, 1
Arcis-sur-Aube (Aube, ar. Troyes, ch. l. c.): *v.* Erard d'
Argers (Marne, ar. and c. Sainte-Menehould): *v.* Raolin d'
Arnoul de Wisemale, of the Knights of the Temple: II, 4, 7, 10, 13
Arrientières (Aube, ar. and c. Bar-sur-Aube): 14, 23
Artonges (Aisne, ar. Château-Thierry, c. Condé-en-Brie): 18

Balduin de Tour: 73
Bar [?]: *v.* Christine de
Bar-le-Duc (Meuse, ch. l. dep.): *v.* Thibaut II, count of
Bar-sur-Aube (Aube, ch. l. ar.), burgesses of: 72
Bar-sur-Seine (Aube, ar. Troyes, ch. l. c.), viscount of: 41
Baudier de Donzy, of Monthois: 69
Beatrice, duchess of Burgundy: 1

Beatrice, wife of Jacques, lord of La Roche-en-Brenil: 1
Beaumont-en-Argonne (Ardennes, ar. Sedan, c. Mouzon): 69
Beaurepaire (Aube, ar. Troyes, c. and cne. Piney): 14, 23
Belroy, priory of Val-des-Escoliers (dioc. Troyes): 14, 23
Bernard du Mès: II, 20
Borgine, daughter of Huard Baudier: 26, 42
Bourlemont (Vosges, ar. Neufchâteau, c. Coussey, cne. Frébecourt): 11; *v.* Jean de, Pierre de
Breuil (*Brolium*?), lord of: II, 1
Brion-sur-Ource (Côte-d'Or, ar. Montbard, c. Montigny-sur-Aube): *v.* Gilles de
Broyes (Marne, ar. Epernay, c. Sézanne): *v.* Jean de, Thibaut de
Burgundy: *v.* Beatrice, duchess of; Robert II, duke of

Châlons-sur-Marne (Marne, ch. l. dep.): 52; bishop of, 52; *v.* Nicholas de
Champagne, *baillis* and *prévôts* in general: 7, 27, 35, 44, 45, 53; chamberlain: *v.* Lambert le Bouchu; chancellors: *v.* Guillaume, Martin de la Chambre,

Vincent de Pierrechastel; counts: Henri I, Henri III, Philippe IV of France, Thibaut V; foresters: *v.* Jean l'Esquallot, Pierre de Chaource; guards of fairs: 24, 44, and *v.* Guillaume de Villarcel; marshal: *v.* Hugues de Conflans; proctor of count: 3, 11, 40, and *v.* Pierre de Beaumont; seneschal: *v.* Jean de Joinville; tax collectors: 57, 58, and *v.* Gencien, Renier Accorre.

Chaource (Aube, ar. Troyes, ch. l. c.): *v.* Pierre de

Chappes (Aube, ar. Troyes, c. Bar-sur-Seine): *v.* Jean de

Chassins (Aisne, ar. Château-Thierry, c. Condé-en-Brie, cne. Tréloup), lady of: 26, 42, 51, 59, 64, 66, 76

Châtelet-en-Brie, Le (Seine-et-Marne, ar. Melun, ch. l. c.): *v.* Guillaume de

Chaumont (Haute-Marne, ch. l. dep.), *baillis* of: in 1276, III; in 1284, 4; in 1287, 41, 47 n [?]; in 1288, 56, 58, 62; in 1289, 67, 72, 73, 74, 75; *v.* Guillaume du Châtelet, Guillaume de Jouy, Jean de Champrupin, *baillis*; *v.* Hugues de

Chéhery, Cistercian abbey (dioc. Reims): 3

Chrétien de Provins: II, 4

Chrétien l'Ours: III

Christine de Bar: 61

Cierges (Aisne, ar. Château-Thierry, c. Fère-en-Tardenois): 28

Conflans-sur-Seine (Marne, ar. Epernay, c. Anglure): *v.* Hugues de

Corbon (Ardennes, ar. Vouziers, c. Monthois, cne. Saint-Morel), lady of: 69, 70

Courgerennes (Aube, ar. Troyes, c. Bouilly, cne. Buchères): 38; *v.* Gautier de

Couvignon (Aube, ar. and c. Bar-sur-Aube): 72

Crécy-en-Brie (Seine-et-Marne, ar. Meaux, ch. l. c.): *v.* Gaucher V de Châtillon

Damery (Marne, ar. and c. Epernay): 28; *v.* Agathes de

Denis, cantor of Paris: II, 14, 15

Denis de Sens, dean of Saint-Etienne de Sens: II, 20

Dinteville (Haute-Marne, ar. Chaumont, c. Châteauvillain): *v.* Erard de

Ecury-le-Repos (Marne, ar. Châlons-sur-Marne, c. Vertus): *v.* Eustache d'

Edmund of Lancaster: 12

Erard d'Arcis: 20, 46, 47, 48

Erard de Dinteville: 13

Erard de Grand: 6

Ermengarde, daughter of Huard Baudier: 42, 51, 59, 64, 66, 76

Essoyes (Aube, ar. Troyes, ch. l. c.): 4

Etienne, archdeacon of Bayeux: II, 1

Etienne, archdeacon of Bruges in the church of Tournai: II, 16, 17

Etienne Becard, dean of Sens: II, 12, 13

Eustache d'Ecury-le-Repos: III

Ferri III, duke of Lorraine: 5, 6, 14, 23, 75

Florent de Roye: II, 1, 2, 7, 15

France, king of: *v.* Philippe III, Philippe IV

Gant [?]: *v.* Guillaume de

Garsie [Sanchez]: III

Gaucher V de Châtillon, lord of Crécy-en-Brie: 18

Gautier, viscount of Saint-Florentin: II, 4

Gautier de Chambly, archdeacon of Coutances, bishop of Senlis: 11; II, 1, 2, 3, 4, 7, 8, 9, 11, 13

Gautier de Courgerennes: 38

Gautier de Durtain, mayor of Provins: II, 4

Gencien, tax collector of Champagne: II, 7

Geoffroi de Joinville: 78

Geoffroi de Louppy-le-Château: 34, 60

Gilles, brother of Gautier, viscount of Saint-Florentin: II, 4

Gilles de Brion: II, 1, 2

Gilles de Compiègne, royal clerk: 47; II, 2, 4, 5, 7, 8, 9, 10, 11, 12

Gilles Lambert: II, 8

Gilo Fuiret: 12

Gimont, priory of: 56

Girard, son of the Hermit of Stenay: 54

Gondrecourt-le-Château (Meuse, ar. Commercy, ch. 1. c.): *v.* Jean de
Grancey-sur-Ource (Côte-d'Or, ar. Montbard, c. Montigny-sur-Aube): *v.* Guillaume de
Grand (Vosges, ar. and c. Neufchâteau): forest of, 6; men of, 58; *v.* Erard de
Grandpré (Ardennes, ar. Vouziers, ch. 1. c.): *v.* Henri de
Grange-au-Bois, La (Aube, ar. Bar-sur-Aube, c. Soulaines-Dhuys, cne. Ville-sur-Terre): 14, 23
Gui II, bishop of Langres: 13
Gui de la Charité, bishop of Soissons: II, 20
Gui de la Neuville-aux-Bois: 36
Gui de Montréal: 1
Gui de Néry: II, 16
Gui de Virey-sous-Bar: 8
Guichard, abbot of Montier-la-Celle, bishop-elect of Troyes: II, 14, 15, 16, 17, 18, 19
Guillaume, abbot of Montiérender: II, 1
Guillaume, chancellor of Champagne: II, 12
Guillaume Alexandre, *bailli*: III
Guillaume de Beaumont: II, 4
Guillaume Bonnet, treasurer of Angers: II, 17, 18
Guillaume d'Alemant, *bailli*: II, 1, 4
Guillaume d'Erbloy: II, 4
Guillaume d'Outremer: II, 1
Guillaume du Châtelet, *bailli*: 9; II, 4
Guillaume de *Gant*: 46
Guillaume de Grancey: 72; II, 7, 8, 9, 10, 11, 12
Guillaume de Jouy, *bailli*: III
Guillaume de Jully-sur-Sarce: 46, 63; II, 1
Guillaume de Nogaret: II, 20
Guillaume de Passy-sur-Seine: III
Guillaume de Prunay: 11
Guillaume Raymond, of Provins: II, 4
Guillaume de Villarcel: II, 1; III

Hans (Marne, ar. and c. Saint-Menehould): burgesses of, 16; *v.* Henri de
Hautvillers, Saint-Pierre of, Benedictine abbey (dioc. Reims): *v.* Thomas de Moiremont, abbot of

Henri I, count of Champagne: 43 n
Henri III, count of Champagne, king of Navarre: 23, 32
Henri de Grandpré: 3
Henri de Hans: 16, 21; his son, 22
Henri l'Armurier, of Troyes: 20, 33
Henri de Saint-Benoît-sur-Vanne: 17; II, 1
Henri Tuebuef: III
Hermit of Stenay: 54
Honneriis [?]: 41
Huard Baudier: 26, 42, 51, 59, 64, 66, 76
Hugues Bekait: 74
Hugues de Chaumont: II, 1
Hugues de Conflans, marshal of Champagne: II, 1; III
Hugues de la Celle, lord of Fontaines: II, 20

Jacques de *Beona* or *Verna* (possibly Béon, Yonne, ar. Auxerre, c. Joigny): II, 1
Jacques de Boulogne, archdeacon and bishop of Thérouanne: II, 5, 6, 7
Jacques Mauferas, of Turgy: 40
Jaucourt (Aube, ar. and c. Bar-sur-Aube): *v.* Miles de
Jean, master: III
Jean d'Auxy, cantor of Orléans: II, 20
Jean Banloquiers, of Passavant: 34, 60
Jean Baras: II, 1 [?], 2
Jean de Bourlemont: 55
Jean Boutauz, of Lignières [?]: 40
Jean de Braisne: II, 1
Jean de Broyes: II, 4
Jean de Champrupin, *bailli*: 47 n
Jean de Chappes: 4, 46, 47, 48
Jean de Dammartin, royal clerk: II, 15
Jean de Fay, of Provins: 50
Jean de Gondrecourt-le-Château: 55
Jean de Joinville, lord of Reynel: 77
Jean de Joinville, seneschal of Champagne: 62, 67, 77; II, 1, 2, 3, 13, 15; III
Jean de la Grange, bishop of Meaux: II, 19
Jean l'Esquallot, forester of Champagne: 47
Jean de *Manstrole*, cantor of Bayeux: II, 14, 15, 16, 17, 18
Jean de Montigny: II, 15
Jean de Montréal: 1

Jean de Norrois: 5
Jean du Plessis-lés-Chaast: 39
Jean Raymond, of Provins: 69
Jean de Savigny, bishop of Nevers: II, 20
Jean de Taillefontaine: II, 4
Jean de Vendeuvre: II, 4
Jean de Vassoigne, archdeacon of Bruges in the church of Tournai: II, 1, 2, 4, 11
Jean de Villeblevin, *bailli*: 47; II, 7
Joinville (Haute-Marne, ar. Saint-Dizier, ch. 1. c.): 62; Saint-Urbain of, 67; *v.* Geoffroi de, Jean de
Jouy, Cistercian abbey (dioc. Sens): 30
Jouy-le-Châtel (Seine-et-Marne, ar. Provins, c. Nangis): *v.* Guillaume de
Jully-sur-Sarce (Aube, ar. Troyes, c. Bar-sur-Seine): *v.* Guillaume de

Lambert le Bouchu, chamberlain of Champagne: 23
Langres, bishop of: *v.* Gui II
Laon (Aisne, ch. 1. dep.), Templers of: 32
Lignières (Aube, ar. Troyes, c. Chaource), lady of: 40, 41; *v.* Jean Boutauz
Lorraine, dukes of: *v.* Ferri III, Thibaut II
Louppy-le-Château (Meuse, ar. Bar-le-Duc, c. Vaubecourt): *v.* Geoffroi de

Marguerite of Navarre, daughter of Thibaut IV of Champagne: 23
Marie, wife of Henri l'Armurier, of Troyes: 33
Martin de la Chambre, chancellor of Champagne, archdeacon of Lisieux: II, 13, 19
Mathilda, wife of Gilo Fuiret: 12
Matthieu, master: III
Matthieu, *vidame* of Chartres: II, 1
Meaux (Seine-et-Marne, ch. 1. ar.): 31; Saint-Faron at, 31; chancellor of, II, 7
Miles de Jaucourt: 61
Mondidier, . . . de, royal clerk: II, 13
Monthois (Ardennes, ar. Vouziers, ch. 1. c.): 69
Montier-la-Celle, Benedictine abbey (dioc. Troyes): *v.* Guichard, abbot of
Montiéramey, Benedictine abbey (dioc. Troyes): *v.* Robert, abbot of
Montier-en-Argonne, Cistercian abbey (dioc. Châlons-sur-Marne): 37
Montierender, Benedictine abbey (dioc. Châlons-sur-Marne): *v.* Guillaume, abbot of
Montréal (Yonne, ar. Avallon, c. Guillon): *v.* Gui de, Jean de
Mureaux, Premonstratensian abbey (dioc. Toul): 10, 11

Navarre, king of: *v.* Henri III, Philippe IV of France, Thibaut V
Neuville-aux-Bois, La (Marne, ar. Sainte-Menehould, c. Givry-en-Argonne): *v.* Gui de, [?] Oudard de
Nicolas de Châlons, canon of Sens, royal clerk: II, 19
Norrois (Marne, ar. Vitry-le-François, c. Thiéblemont-Farémont): *v.* Jean de
Notre-Dame de Vauvert: *v.* Vauvert

Oudard de la Neuville, *bailli*: II, 1, 10, 11, 12, 13, 16, 17
Oudin Louchat: 29
Oyes, Saint-Pierre of, abbey (dioc. Troyes): 25

Paris, Parlement of: 1, 13, 52, 67, 73, 74
Passavant-en-Argonne (Marne, ar. and c. Sainte-Menehould): *v.* Jean Banloquiers
Passy-sur-Seine (Seine-et-Marne, ar. Provins, c. Bray-sur-Seine): *v.* Guillaume de
Pastorelle de Verdun: 65, 71
Perrin Fumon: 29
Philippe III, king of France: 3, 13
Philippe IV, king of France, king of Navarre, count of Champagne: 3, 4, 6, 11, 13, 15, 18, 24, 27, 28, 32, 35, 37, 38, 40, 49, 52, 63, 65, 78
Philippe de Givancourt: II, 7
Philippe le Convers, canon of Noyon, royal clerk: II, 15, 19
Philippe de Moncel: 26, 66
Pierre, dean of Saint-Quentin: II, 13
Pierre de Beaumont, proctor of the count of Champagne: II, 2; *v.* also 3, 11, 40

Pierre de Belleperche, canon of Auxerre: II, 19
Pierre de Bourlemont: 9, 10, 11
Pierre de Chaource, forester of Champagne: 47
Pierre de Dicy: II, 20
Pierre de la Ferté: 68
Pierre de la Malmaison, *bailli*: III
Pierre Saymel, *bailli*, prévôt of Paris: 51 n
Pierre de Villarcel: III
Plessis-lés-Chaast (Aube, ar. Troyes, c. Estissac, cne. Bucey-en-Othe): *v*. Jean de
Provins (Seine-et-Marne, ch. 1. ar.): assizes of, 50; commune of, 19, 32, 49; Hôtel-Dieu of, III; Saint-Quiriace of, 32, 57; *v*. Chrétien de
Prunay-Belleville (Aube, ar. Nogent-sur-Seine, c. Marcilly-le-Hayer): *v*. Guillaume de

Raolin d'Argers: 54
Raoul de Thourotte, canon of Meaux: III
Rebais, Benedictine abbey (dioc. Meaux): 32
Renier Accorre, tax collector of Champagne: II, 1, 2, 4, 7
Reynel (Haute-Marne, ar. Chaumont, c. Andelot): 77; *v*. Alix de, and Jean de Joinville, lord of
Richier, clerk of Gilles de Compiègne: II, 7, 9
Robert, abbot of Montiéramey: II, 1, 2, 4; III
Robert II, duke of Burgundy: 4
Robert de Harecourt, treasurer of Poitiers: II, 5, 6, 7
Roche-en-Brenil, La (Côte-d'Or, ar. Montbard, c. Saulieu): *v*. Beatrice, wife of Jacques, lord of
Rorthey (Vosges, ar. Neufchâteau, c. Coussey, cne. Sionne): 11
Rouvre (Aube, ar. and c. Bar-sur-Aube): 14, 23
Roye (Somme, ar. Montdidier, ch. 1. c.): *v*. Florent de
Rufin, master: III

Sacey (Aube, ar. Troyes, c. Piney, cne. Pouilly-sur-Sacey): 20
Saint-Benoît-sur-Vanne (Aube, ar. Troyes, c. Aix-en-Othe): *v*. Henri de
Saint-Etienne of Troyes, collegiate church (dioc. Troyes): 43
Saint-Faron at Meaux, Benedictine abbey (dioc. Meaux): 31
Saint-Florentin (Yonne, ar. Auxerre, ch. 1. c.): *v*. Gautier, viscount of; Gilles, his brother
Saint-Médard of Soissons, Benedictine abbey (dioc. Soissons): 28
Saint-Memmie, Augustinian abbey (dioc. Châlons-sur-Marne): 52
Saint-Nicolas de Varangéville: or Saint-Nicolas-du-Port, Benedictine priory (dioc. Toul): 46
Saint-Phal (Aube, ar. Troyes, c. Ervy-le-Châtel): *v*. André
Saint-Pierre of Hautvillers, Benedictine abbey (dioc. Reims): *v*. Thomas de Moiremont, abbot of
Saint-Pierre of Oyes, abbey (dioc. Troyes): 25
Saint-Quentin: *v*. Pierre, dean of
Saint-Quiriace of Provins, collegiate church (dioc. Sens): 32, 57
Saint-Remy [-en-Bouzemont?] ([?] Marne, ar. Vitry-le-François, ch. 1. c.), lady of: 15
Saint-Urbain of Joinville, collegiate church (dioc. Châlons-sur-Marne): 67
Santiago of Compostella, in Galicia: 46
Senlis, *bailli* of: *v*. Oudard de la Neuville
Sens, *bailli* of: *v*. Oudard de la Neuville
Sezanne, *bailli* of: *v*. Guillaume de Châtelet
Simon Caumy, chancellor of Meaux: II, 7 n
Simon II de Clermont, lord of Nesle: II, 1
Simon de Marchais, royal knight: II, 16, 19
Simon Matiffas, archdeacon of Reims: II, 4, 10
Soissons, abbey of Saint-Médard: 28
Stenay (Meuse, ar. Verdun, ch. 1. c.), Hermit of: 54; *v*. Girard, his son

Templers of Laon: 32
Thénnelières (Aube, ar. Troyes, c. Lusigny): 20
Thibaut II, count of Bar-le-Duc: 34, 73, 74
Thibaut II, son of Ferri III of Lorraine: 23
Thibaut V, count of Champagne, king of Navarre: 16, 19; III
Thibaut de Broyes: 25
Thibaut de Saint-Antoine, of Troyes: 20
Thomas de Moiremont, abbot of Saint-Pierre of Hautvillers: III
Thourotte (Oise, ar. Compiègne, c. Ribécourt): v. Raoul de
Toul, chapter of: 75 n
Tour-en-Woëvre, La (Meuse, ar. Verdun, c. Fresnes-en-Woëvre): 73, v. Balduin de Tour
Troyes (Aube, ch. 1. dep.): Hôtel-Dieu-le-Comte of, 43; prison at, 17, 40; Saint-Etienne of, 43
Troyes, Meaux, and Provins, *baillis* of: in 1276, III; in 1284, 8; in 1285, 14 [?], 17, 18, 19; in 1287, 39, 40, 43, 50; in 1288, 61 [?], 63; v. also Guillaume d'Alemant, Guillaume Alexandre, Guillaume du Châtelet, Guillaume de Jouy, Jean de Villeblevin
Turgy (Aube, ar. Troyes, c. Chaource): v. Jacques Mauferas

Varangéville: v. Saint-Nicolas de
Vauvert (Gard, ar. Nimes, ch. 1. c.), Notre-Dame de: 46
Vendeuvre-sur-Barse (Aube, ar. Bar-sur-Aube, ch. 1. c.): v. Jean de
Verdun, Thirteen Justices of: 65, 71; v. Pastorelle de
Villarcel (now Riancey, Aube, ar. and c. Troyes, cne. Saint-Lyé): v. Guillaume de, Pierre de
Villarnoult (Yonne, ar. Avallon, c. Quarré-les-Tombes, cne. Buissières): v. Agnes, wife of Odo Bezors, lord of
Villeblevin (Yonne, ar. Sens, c. Pont-sur-Yonne): v. Jean de
Vincent de Pierrechastel, formerly chancellor of Champagne: II, 1
Virey-sous-Bar (Aube, ar. Troyes, c. Bar-sur-Seine): v. Gui de
Vitry [-en-Perthois] (Marne, ar. and c. Vitry-le-François), *baillis* of: in 1276, III; in 1284, 2; in 1285, 15; in 1286, 21, 34; in 1287, 42; in 1288, 51, 52, 59, 60; in 1289, 64, 65, 69, 70, 71; v. also Florent de Roye (see II, 15 [?]), Hugues de Chaumont, Pierre de la Malmaison, Pierre Saymel

13

The Accounts of Cepperello da Prato for the Tax on Nouveaux Acquêts in the Bailliage of Troyes[1]

In the opening novella of the *Decameron* Boccaccio tells in colorful detail of the hypocritical deathbed confession of Ser Cepperello da Prato, known in France as Ser Ciapelletto. According to the tale, an unscrupulous Italian notary – a trusted agent of the Florentine banker Musciatto Guidi – died in Burgundy after making a false confession which created an illusion of sanctity.[2] Research in the nineteenth century confirmed the existence of an Italian financial agent in France named Cepperello da Prato, though not the story itself. In 1885 the Florentine historian and archivist Cesare Paoli published four documents which show that Cepperello acted as royal receiver in Auvergne in 1288-1290 and collected taxes in the

---

[1] I am grateful to the American Philosophical Society for a grant from the Penrose Fund which made possible my trip to Florence in April 1972, to Prof. Reinhold C. Mueller for introducing me to the Florentine archives, and to Prof. Christopher Kleinhenz and Prof. Gino Corti for bibliographical and other assistance.

[2] *Il Decameron*, ed. Charles S. Singleton, Scrittori d'Italia, 97 (Bari, 1965), I, 27-39, or ed. Vittore Branca, 4th ed., (Florence, 1960), 46-66. Boccaccio's portrait of the 'Italian Tartuffe' influenced not only the literature of his own country but that of others as well. For instance, late in the sixteenth century Jakob Ayrer continued the *Fastnachtspiele* of Hans Sachs with *Der Falsch Notarius mit seine unwahrhaften Beicht* and Voltaire retold the story, 'Saint Ciappelletto, qui avait été le plus grand fripon de son temps'; on this and other matters see Luigi Fassò, 'La prima novella del *Decameron* e la sua fortuna,' *Annali della Facoltà di Filosofia e Lettere della Università di Cagliari*, III (1931), 15-64, reprinted in his *Saggi e ricerche di storia letteraria* (Milan, 1947), pp. 33-90. For some other examples of the treatment of 'Ser Ciappelletto' see Vittore Branca, *Boccaccio medievale* (Florence, 1956), pp. 71-99; Luigi Russo, *Letture critiche del Decameron* (Bari, 1967), pp. 51-68; and Aldo D. Scaglione, 'Boccaccio, Chaucer, and the Mercantile Ethic', in *Literature and Western Civilization*, ed. David Daiches and A. Throlby (London, 1973), II, 579-600. The best-documented study of the historical Cepperello is a book by a local historian intended to restore the reputation of a fellow-citizen, Giulio Giani's *Cepparello da Prato* (Prato, 1915); I have not seen his *Ancora due parole su Cepparello* (Prato, 1916). Giani was greatly concerned with the literal truth of the story, which must owe much to Boccaccio's imagination and has antecedents which go back to Sulpicius Severus' biography of St. Martin of Tours.

bailliage of Troyes in 1295.[3] In 1295 he also acted as procurator for Musciatto (Mouche) and Albizzo (Biche) Guidi, the heads of the Franzesi banking firm, in collecting the forced loan levied in the bailliage of Chaumont.[4] And somewhere about this time, perhaps in 1295, perhaps a few years later, he held the important position of treasurer of the Comtat-Venaissin, again working in connection with the Guidi brothers.[5]

Boccaccio di Chellino spent years in Paris during the reign of Philip the Fair, so that his son Giovanni had access to reliable information from his father about Italians in France during this period. The author may even have been accurately informed about the character of Cepperello da Prato. Although our dry administrative documents are silent about the shameless immorality which is the point of the novella, they do show that Cepperello worked with the notorious Noffo Dei, the Italian notary who conducted the perjured investigation of Bishop Guichard of Troyes.[6] But whatever Boccaccio's justification for pinning on Cepperello the tale of an Italian rascal dying among strangers far from the Tuscan hills, other documents show that the story as given is false.

Information about Cepperello appears not only in the evidence of his French service, but also in the records of Prato itself. Moved by a pious zeal to clear his countryman's name from defamation, Giulio Giani worked through the municipal archives of Prato and wrote a small book to show that Cepperello, son of Ser Diotaiuti, of the Porta di Travaglio section of Prato, served his native city honorably from 1300 to the end of his life and died in the fall of 1304, to all appearances at Prato. Far from finding his last resting-place in a Burgundian friary, the real Cepperello was probably buried with other members of his family beside the steps of the Pievi di Burgo, which was then the cathedral.[7] Historical documents give no basis for thinking that Cepperello was forced by travel or other reasons to make a fraudulent deathbed confession. As might have been

---

[3] Paoli, 'Documenti di ser Ciappelletto', *Giornale storico della letterature italiana*. V (1885), 329-369.

[4] Robert Mignon, *Inventaire d'anciens comptes royaux*, ed. Charles-Victor Langlois (Paris, 1899), no. 1158. On the famous banker of Philip the Fair see Friedrich Bock, 'Musciatto dei Francesi', *Deutsches Archiv*, VI (1943), 521-544. Cepperello's nephew, 'Jaqueminus Caym' also worked as a tax-collector in Champagne in the 1290s; see Robert Fawtier, *Comptes royaux, 1285-1314* (Paris, 1953-56), II, 98, no. 15288.

[5] Claude Faure, *Étude sur l'administration et l'histoire du Comtat-Venaissin, 1229-1417* (Paris, 1909), p. 181, dates Vatican Instrum. Miscell. 1288-1295, no. 55, the document which mentions Cepperello as treasurer, as after February 1, 1297. Giani, *Cepparello*, pp. 96-100, dates the document to 1295. Faure erred in his assertion (p. 99) that the treasurer was always an ecclesiastic.

[6] Noffo appears in the accounts of 1288-1290, Paoli, 'Documenti', pp. 346-360. On Noffo (Arnolfo Deghi) see Abel Rigault, *Le procès de Guichard, évêque de Troyes* (Paris, 1896), pp. 23-24.

[7] Giani, *Cepparello*, pp. 61-72.

expected, diligent research has demonstrated that Boccaccio mixed imagination with history in his opening tale.

The purpose of this article is not to add to the biographical dossier of Cepperello da Prato. It makes no attempt to deal with the use Philip the Fair made of Italian bankers and administrators, or the weighty problem recently posed by Professor Strayer of why Philip did not squeeze more advantage from his Italians.[8] Its goal is much more limited, to re-edit one of the documents published by Paoli and to comment briefly on its significance.

The survival of Cepperello's accounts is a matter of good luck. Although one of the documents, written in Italian, is a set of Cepperello's personal financial records,[9] the other three have a certain public character. One is a general account rendered by Jean de Trie as bailli of Auvergne for the All Saints' term of 1288, the second records the amounts of Cepperello received from collectors of the clerical tenth in Auvergne in 1288,[10] and the third is the first membrane of the roll from the bailliage of Troyes – which will be discussed in detail. None of these accounts is mentioned in the inventory of royal accounts which Robert Mignon compiled in the 1320s. Most of the documents of the Chambre des Comptes have been destroyed,[11] but since Cepperello either prudently or carelessly took these records of his royal service back to Italy, they still exist today. Perhaps through some accident of inheritance, they became part of the papers of the Regnadori family and were given to the Florentine archives with a batch of other documents by Vincenzo Gondi in 1883.[12] There Paoli transcribed them, and there in 1972, luckily untouched by the ravages of the flood of 1966, they were still available for study.

Whatever the truth of Boccaccio's story, it is fortunate for French administrative historians that he mentioned Cepperello, for if he had not, it is unlikely that Paoli would have singled out these foreign records for publication. Even though they have been in print for almost ninety years,

---

[8] Joseph R. Strayer, 'Italian Bankers and Philip the Fair', in *Economy, Society, and Government in Medieval Italy: Essays in Memory of Robert L. Reynolds* (Kent, Ohio, 1969), pp. 113-121, reprinted in *Medieval Statecraft and the Perspectives of History* (Princeton, 1971), pp. 239-247.

[9] These accounts have been re-edited in an improved form by Alfredo Schiaffini, *Testi fiorentini del Dugento e dei primi del Trecento*, new ed. (Florence, 1954), pp. 244-259.

[10] These accounts from the Auvergne would also benefit from a new edition by someone familiar with local place-names. If a new edition is prepared, note should also be taken of Jean de Trie's accounts from the All Saints' term of 1287, copied in Clermont-Ferrand, Bibl. mun. ms. 623, fol. 110 ff. (which I have not seen) and partly printed by Henri Gravier, *Essai sur les prévôts royaux* (Paris, 1904), pp. 81-82.

[11] For what remains see Michel Nortier, 'Le sort des archives dispersées de la Chambre des Comptes de Paris', *Bibliothèque de l'École des chartes*, CXXIII (1965), 460-537.

[12] Cesare Paoli, 'Le carte dei Gondi donate all'Archivio di Stato di Firenze', *Archivio storico italiano*, ser. 4, t. XII (1884), 296-300.

little use has been made of these French historical documents in an Italian literary journal. The indefatigable Colonel Borrelli de Serres noted them, of course, and historians interested in Italian relations with France have taken account of them.[13] They did not, however, find their proper place in the *Comptes royaux* edited by Robert Fawtier.[14] Paoli made numerous errors of transcription and did not have available the reference books necessary for proper identification of place-names.[15] Before the accounts from Champagne could be used critically, a new edition had to be prepared.

What most interested Paoli in these rolls was Cepperello's relationship to the *Decameron* and his use of Italian. The accounts from the bailliage of Troyes have a different importance, however, both for the study of thirteenth-century French institutions and for the local history of Champagne. The rest of this article will be concerned with these aspects of the document edited in the appendix.

The money Cepperello collected in 1295 was owed because of the alienation of feudal property to ecclesiastics and non-noble persons incapable of performing feudal service. For centuries, when a vassal sold or donated property held in feudal tenure to a church or anyone else who could not continue the full spectrum of dues and services (including *mainmorte*), the normal procedure was for him or the recipient to seek a charter of authorization, called a grant of amortization, from the feudal superior. At the time, if the lord was unwilling to approve a grant by an additional act of charity, he could exact payment before issuing his confirmation or forbid the transfer entirely. During the course of the thirteenth century it became more and more common for vassals, including royal vassals, to alienate property without seeking approval or paying for it. In 1275 Philip III issued an ordinance setting the terms on which feudal property which had been alienated without permission could be held: churches could have a clear title by paying from one to three years' income from the property, and non-nobles who would not fulfil all

---

[13] Léon L. Borrelli de Serres, *Recherches sur divers services publiques du XIIIe au XVIIe siècle* (Paris, 1895-1909), II, 44-45. For other passing references to Cepperello and these accounts, see Rigault, *Procès de Guichard*, p. 24; Camille Piton, *Les Lombards en France et à Paris* (Paris, 1892-93), I, 71; Elizabeth Chapin, *Les villes de foires de Champagne* (Paris, 1937), pp. 93 and 173.

[14] Fawtier, *Comptes royaux*, III, xlviii, no. 40, noted Paoli's edition, but he did not include it in his list of accounts of the *nouveaux acquêts* on pp. lvi-lx. For displaced accounts not included in Fawtier's magnificent survey, reference may be made to T. P. Voronova, 'The accounts of Renaut de Sainte-Beuve for the expenses of his mission to Lyon, Feb.-March 1313' [in Russian], *Srednie Veka*. XXIX (1966), 260-266.

[15] In preparing this edition I have depended heavily on Alphonse Roserot, *Dictionnaire historique de la Champagne méridionale (Aube) des origines à 1790* (Langres, 1942-48) and the indices of Auguste Longnon, *Documents relatifs au comté de Champagne et de Brie, 1172-1362* (Paris, 1901-14).

feudal obligations had to pay two to four years' income.[16]

Philip III's compensatory penalty soon became a revenue-producing tax. As Philip IV reached for more and more ways to increase the royal revenues, he began in 1292 to send commissioners throughout his domains to seek out churches and non-nobles who owed payments for their *nouveaux acquêts*. The accounts of some of these officials have survived, but no full-scale investigation of the tax and its collection has been published.[17] More study of what was in a quite precise sense a tax on ending feudalism would be desirable. Systematic research could show something of where feudal property was being alienated most extensively, who was doing the purchasing, and perhaps even at what rate.

When such a study is made the detailed accounts of Cepperello da Prato should be included. At present, however, the information we have on *nouveaux acquêts* in the bailliage of Troyes is incomplete and lacks the illumination which comparisons could supply. We are not certain how long a period was covered by this survey, or what percentage of alienated property had already been authorized by charters or amortization, so the scale of the operations accounted for here can be calculated only approximately. As we are uncertain of the rates applied to different classes of transfers, it is hard to make satisfactory contrasts between ecclesiastical and lay purchasers.[18] Over 35 percent of the revenue which Cepperello collected in the bailliage came from the castellany of Troyes, but the fragmentary nature of the accounts prevents further conclusions about the areas of most intensive economic activity.

The most critical question about the roll printed here is the significance of its total and its relationship to other accounts for the same tax. The inventory of Robert Mignon lists three accounts for the collection of the tax on *nouveaux acquêts* under the heading of the bailliage of Troyes-Meaux. The first of these was rendered by Guillaume de Nointeau, canon of Tours, on January 8, 1294. A second was rendered by the same Guillaume and Guillaume de Mantes on the feast of St. Barnabas (June 11) in 1295. The third, which Mignon listed second, was rendered by Guillaume de

---

[16] *Ordonnances des roys de France de la troisième race*, ed. Eusèbe de Laurière (Paris, 1723-1849), I, 303-305.

[17] For the published accounts see Fawtier, *Comptes royaux*, II, 315-364 and III, lvi-lx. Marie-Élisabeth Antoine-Carreau submitted a thesis on 'Les commissaires royaux aux amortissements et aux nouveaux acquêts sous les Capétiens (1275-1328)' to the École des chartes in 1953; see *Positions des thèses*, 1953, pp. 19-22. I am grateful to Mme Antoine for sending me an offprint.

[18] The 69 items in the ecclesiastical column of these accounts produced 844 l. of revenue, while 70 items in the lay column produced 603 l. 19s. 6d. Since churches had to pay less than the laity for the same value of property, it appears that ecclesiastical purchases were significantly more substantial. But since the lists are incomplete, no firm conclusions comparing totals can be drawn.

Nointeau in March 1296 (n.s.).[19] Of the accounts with which we are most directly concerned, rendered by Cepperello along with the royal clerks Pierre de Condé and Jean de Dammartin on June 6, 1295, Mignon was unaware.

References to the accounts of 1294 and 1295 appear in a list of the debts of the county of Champagne prepared by Jean Clersens. We learn from this statement that the tax on the alienation of fiefs was turned over to Biche Guidi for collection. The account of January 1294 produced 2154 l. 12s. 6d., while that of June 11, 1295 came to a total of 5810 l. 18s. 2d. Of that second total, 3894 l. 7s. 4d. was accounted for by Biche.[20] From these figures we can see the relationship of Cepperello's roll to that rendered by Guillaume de Nointeau and Guillaume de Mantes in the following week, for Cepperello noted (item 141) that he shipped off 3898 l. Since minor expenses could easily explain the difference from the figure given for Biche's collection, it follows that Cepperello's roll is an accounting of the collection he made for Biche when the Florentine banker was working for the two French administrators. The large amount still uncollected on June 11, 1295 is probably explained by a comment on the dorse of that account that the bishop of Troyes, the chapters of Saint-Pierre and Saint-Etienne, and the abbot of Montier-la-Celle still had to make payment for lands on which they claimed high justice.[21] The roll of March 1296, of which we have no further record, may have settled the matter. If the two accounts of 1294 and 1295 turned up most of the debts owed the crown, the paper total for this tax was in the neighbourhood of 8000 l., reduced somewhat by expenses and uncollected debts.

Eight thousand pounds was worth collecting, of course, for a government at war and eager to tap every possible source of income, though the work involved in tracking down the transfers of land and collecting the money must have made other expedients seem more attractive.[22] In contrast, the forced loan from the non-nobles of the bailliage of Troyes in 1295 produced over 12,600 l.[23]

---

[19] Mignon, *Inventaire*, nos. 1852-1853. Mignon, as edited by Langlois, spells the place-name as *Noycello*. In the entry cited in the following note, the collector is called 'magister G. de Noentello'. In the index to the *Comptes royaux*, François Maillard identified the place as Nointeau in Indre-et Loire, which seems correct for a canon of Tours.

[20] *Comptes royaux*, ed. Fawtier, no. 15293.

[21] Mignon, *Inventaire*, no. 1853.

[22] In 1292 the collector for the *nouveaux acquêts* in the bailliage of Caux took in under 100 l. and spent over 170 l. in the process; see Fawtier, *Comptes royaux*, III, lvii. Prof. Strayer demonstrates the diligent fund-raising of the monarchy in 1294 in *Studies in Early French Taxation* (Cambridge, Mass., 1939), pp. 25-28, 44-46.

[23] Longnon, *Documents*, III, 119-123. The precise total is 12,631 l. if the figure for Jean Acelin of Méry (p. 123 L) is really xi; 12,660 if it should be xl. Fawtier miscalculated in his total of 12,591 l. in *Comptes royaux*, III,lvi. In this roll we can recognize many names which appear in Latin in Cepperello's accounts. Guillaume du Châtelet, the individual who

What we do not know, and in the present state of our knowledge cannot determine precisely, is the relationship of the alienations accounted for in the rolls of 1294 and 1295 to the total amount of feudal property in the bailliage. If the tax assessed by the agents of Philip the Fair was collected at the same rates established by his father in 1275, then those rates varied from a low (for donations to churches) of one year's income to a high (for non-nobles who transformed all feudal payments into *cens*) of four years' income. If we then assume for the purpose of making a very rough calculation that the average rate was two years' income (since acquisitions by churches seem to have outweighed those of the laity), the total annual value of the property alienated would be 4000 l. But I am unaware of any evidence stating the rates charged by Philip the Fair. They may well have been higher than those of 1275; in 1328 the highest rate charged by Philip VI was eight years' income.[24] This possibility makes the 4000 l. just calculated appear to be a maximum figure perhaps far higher than it should be. Under these circumstancess, an estimate of 3000 l. annual income might well be justified.

We are equally unsure of the period covered by this assessment. The full survey presumably applied to all the time Philip the Fair had governed the county – that is, about ten years – but it was probably also intended to be assessed on lands alienated during the time of Philip's predecessors, and perhaps went as far back as thirty years. If 3000 l. is divided by these minimum and maximum periods, we come up with an annual alienation taxed in this survey of land worth from 100 to 300 l. a year.

Philip's assessors in 1310 were instructed to levy the tax on *nouveaux acquêts* on fiefs, rear-fiefs, and even allods.[25] We have as yet no calculation of the value of all feudal property in the bailliage of Troyes, though the work currently being conducted by Dr. Theodore Evergates may establish such a figure. In 1252 the value of 239 fiefs in the bailliage was 6400 l., so that the total value of an estimated 432 fiefs in the bailliage of Troyes would have been about 11,500. In addition, Dr. Evergates calculates the value of the rear-fiefs in the bailliage at about 7500 l., giving a total of about 19,000 l. annual income for all fiefs and rear-fiefs in the bailliage at the middle of the thirteenth century.[26] I know of no way to estimate the

---

owed the largest amount to Cepperello (200 l.), does not appear in the list of those who subscribed to the loan. He is probably to be identified as the former *bailli* of Troyes who was *bailli* of Sézanne in 1295; see Paulette Portejoie, *L'ancien coutumier de Champagne* (Poitiers, 1956), p. 10, n. 28.

[24] Longnon, *Documents*, III, 210.

[25] *Comptes royaux*, ed. Fawtier, II, 345.

[26] These figures have been supplied to me by Dr. Evergates, who is now revising for publication his 1971 Johns Hopkins dissertation, 'Feudal Society: The Bailliage of Troyes under the Counts of Champagne, 1152-1284.' For a study of the aristocracy of the entire county of Champagne and their income see his articles, 'The Aristocracy of Champagne in

value of allods, but it was probably not large. The total annual value of all property held by the noble class in the bailliage was no doubt something over 20,000 l. This figure, uncertain as it is, is large enough so that we may conclude that the lessening of feudal relations through the acquisition of feudal property by churches and non-nobles was probably not a major problem in the bailliage in the later years of the thirteenth century.

In making his collection Cepperello had the help not only of two royal clerks but also of the local *prévôts*. The *prévôt* was the official most likely to be familiar with such petty transactions as the acquisition by a parish church of land worth a few *sous* a year.[27] The roll is arranged by castellanies (which in Champagne were synonymous with *prévôtés*), and this division gives it a special value for local history. For obvious reasons, ecclesiastical records, including *pouillés* and accounts of the collection of the ecclesiastical tenth, were recorded by diocese.[28] On the other hand, such secular records as the late Capetian hearth tax which is the basis of so many demographic estimates, the *extenta* of income and property belonging to the count or king, and the precious estimate of ecclesiastical revenues in the bailliage of Troyes made by royal agents around 1300 were all based on the bailliage or its subdivisions, the castellanies.[29] In order to make proper comparisons between the two classes of records, it is necessary to know which parishes or villages were in which castellany and bailliage. The bailliage of Troyes has presented special problems: one text of the *État des paroisses et des feux* credits it with 274 parishes, the other with 374.[30] The latter number is probably the correct one, but uncertainty over the boundaries of the bailliage have made it difficult to establish a map which would permit a count of the parishes and a determination of which ecclesiastical houses named in the estimate of ecclesiastical revenues were inside the bailliage and which were not. The eastern border of the bailliage, including the castellany of Troyes, has been particularly difficult to map.[31] Fortunately, Cepperello's accounts provide a basis for a

the Mid-Thirteenth Century: A Quantitative Description', *Journal of Interdisciplinary History*, V (1974), 1-18, and 'A Quantitative Analysis of Fiefs in Medieval Champagne', *Computers and the Humanities*, IX (1975), 61-67.

[27] A note to one entry (158) says the *prévôt* ought to give an accounting for it.

[28] The pouillés of all the dioceses which made up the bailliage of Troyes are edited by Auguste Longnon, *Pouillés de la province de Sens* (Paris, 1904). For the value of the clerical tenth in the reign of Philip the Fair see *Recueil des historiens des Gaules et de la France*, ed. Martin Bouquet et al. (Paris, 1738-1904), XXI, 540-545, 557-560.

[29] Ferdinand Lot, 'L'état des paroisses et des feux de 1328', *Bibliothèque de l'École des chartes*, XC (1929), 51-107, 256-315; 'Extenta terre comitatus Campanie et Brie' in Longnon, *Documents*, II, 9-183; 'Estimation des biens ecclésiastiques au bailliage de Troyes', *ibid.*, III, 124-133.

[30] Lot, 'État des paroisses', p. 71.

[31] The map of the bailliage of Troyes in Roserot, *Dictionnaire*, Introduction, facing p. 44, shows Molins as an enclave surrounded by territory in the bailliage of Chaumont. The

reasonably accurate map of the castellany of Troyes in 1295, although absolute certainty is not possible.[32]

The greatest problem for any editor of Ceperello's roll is the transcription of proper nouns. Unfamiliar with the place-names of a foreign territory, Paoli made numerous errors,[33] some of which, however, may have been the responsibility of the scribe. A few of the more difficult words give the impression of deliberate fudging. Where I have been quite uncertain as to what the scribe meant to write (as in the differentiation of n and u/v or t and c), I have given what I think he should have written when I had a basis for such a judgment, and have otherwise included a warning question mark.

Our fragmentary information about the alienation of feudal property in the bailliage of Troyes and about its geography would be greatly increased if we had more than one membrane of a roll which was probably composed of at least five. Athough this one fragment has been separated from its continuation since its donation to the Florentine archives in 1883, it is possible that the other pieces still exist in some unsorted collection of documents and will one day be properly identified.[34] Cepperello da Prato was a minor functionary who owes his fame to the use Boccaccio made of his name rather than to his own achievements in France. He made his greatest contribution to history by preserving the souvenirs of his foreign service. The few remnants of those records which have come down to us can only make us wish that he and his associates had stuffed more documents in their saddlebags. Until the riches of Italian private archives have been fully explored we cannot be sure how much French documentation was taken home by the Italian notaries and financiers who contributed to the toughness and the skill of the administration of Philip the Fair.

---

eastern boundary of the bailliage in Roserot's map differs substantially from that in the map accompanying this article.

[32] The accounts list payments by the location of the property rather than that of the recipient. Nevertheless, unless we have information to the contrary, it is reasonable to assume that most parish churches were acquiring property within their own parishes.

[33] For instance, he read *Antissiodoro* for *Autissiodoro*, *Lenz* for *Leuz*, *Montanigro* for *Montaingone*, and *Unennoy* for *Vriennon*.

[34] Dr. Rudolf Hirsch, who has catalogued those portions of the Gondi papers acquired by the University of Pennsylvania, has kindly informed me that no thirteenth-century French accounts are part of the collection; cf. *The [University of Pennyslvania] Library Chronicle*, XXXVI (1970), 79-104, and XXXVII (1971), 3-23. Prof. Gino Corti of Florence has also kindly informed me that to the best of his knowledge no missing fragments of these accounts are in the private archives of the Gondi family, and that no Regnadori papers are known to exist outside those given to the archives in the nineteenth century.

Appendix

Accounts of Cepperello da Prata for the collection of the tax on the alienation of feudal property in the bailliage of Troyes, 6 June 1295.

A. Florence, Archivio di Stato, Dono Gondi (1883), no. 4. Parchment, 72 × 25 cm. Dry ruling, 2 cols. on face, 1 on dorse. The first membrane of a longer roll; holes from sewing at bottom.

a. Ed. Cesare Paoli, 'Documenti di ser Ciappelletto', *Giornale storico della letteratura italiana*, V (1885), 365-369.

Compotus Chiperelli Dextahit factus in baillivia Trecensi et dotis seu dotalicii illustrissime domine Blance, Dei gratia regine Navarre, super rebus immobilibus acquisitis [ab ecclesiasticis][1] et ignobilibus personis in castellanis sequentibus baillivie supradicte [cum vener][2] abilibus viris magistris P. de Condeto, archidiacono Suessionensi, et Johanne de Donno Martino, illustrissimi regis Francie clericis, anno Domini M°.CC°. nonagesimo quinto, die lune ante festum beati Barnabe apostoli.

[left column]

In castellania Trecensi ab ecclesiasticis personis:

[1]   Curatus ecclesie Sancti Nissecii Trecensis: 9s.
[2]   Curatus Sanctorum Andree et Egidii Trecensis: 20s.
[3]   Prior Sancti Bernardi de Trecis: 19 l. 15s.
[4]   Stephanus de Creni, qui optinet in ecclesia Sancti Petri Trencensis altare fundatum in honore Omnium Sanctorum: 6 l.
[5]   Guillelmus de Carcassone, presbyter beneficiatus ad altare beati Leonardi in ecclesia predicta: 9 l.
[6]   Henricus de Chacenayo, beneficiatus in ecclesia predicta ad altare sancti Augustini: 12 l.
[7]   Humbertus de Meldis et Johannes Allerii, beneficiati in eadem ecclesia ad altaria sanctorum Trinitatis et Bartholomei: 49s.
[8]   Curatus ecclesie Sancti Dyonisii de Trecis: 14s.
[9]   Curatus Sancti Johannis de Foro Trecensi: 10 l. 16s.
[10] Domus Hospitalis Sancti Johannis Jherosolimitani de Trecis: 17 l.
[11] Curatus ecclesie de Sancto Sepulcro: 19s.
[12] Prior eiusdem loci: 29s.
[13] Prior curatis ecclesie de Sancta Mora: 15s. 6d.
[14] Curatus ecclesie de Capella Valon: 5s.
[15] Curatus ecclesie de Sancta Syra: 8s.
[16] Curatus de Monte Suzano: 73s. 6d.
[17] Curatus Sancti Benedicti supra Secanam: 13s.
[18] Curatus ecclesie Pontis sancte Marie: 20s. 11d.
[19] Curatus ecclesie Sancti Stephani super Barbuise: 10s. 6d.

---

[1] These words, demanded by the sense of the passage, were omitted by the copyist.
[2] Ms. torn.

[20] Curatus ecclesie de Villete: 38s.
[21] Curatus ecclesie de Noeroy: 4s.
[22] Curatus ecclesie de Primo Facto: 12s.
[23] Curatus ecclesie de Faiges: 10s.
[24] Curatus ecclesie de Lujeres: 30s.
[25] Curatus ecclesie de Brevgione[3]: 39s. 10d.
[26] Curatus ecclesie de Ruilly: 39s.
[27] Curatus ecclesie de Saciaco: 108s. 3d.
[28] Curatus ecclesie d'Aubrissel: 19s.
[29] Curatus ecclesie de Dosche: 57s.
[30] Curatus ecclesie de Sancto Patrolo: 100s.
[31] Prior curatus ecclesie de Lonsolt: 46s.
[32] Prior curatus d'Auson: 64s.
[33] Curatus ecclesie de Courlaverdey: 40s.
[34] Marricularii eiusdem ecclesie: 20s.
[35] Prior curatus de Lusigny: 24s.
[36] Curatus ecclesie de Tenillieres: 16s.
[37] Curatus ecclesie des Noes: 10s. 6d.
[38] Curatus ecclesie de Sancto Leone: 26s.
[39] Curatus ecclesie Monasterii Arramerensis: 15s.
[40] Curatus ecclesie de Ruvigniaco: 32s.
[41] Curatus ecclesie de Courtrangis: 3s.
[42] Curatus ecclesie d'Avens: 3s. 6d.
[43] Marricularii dicte ecclesie: 3s.
[44] Curatus ecclesie de Molins: 28s. 11d.
[45] Marricularii de Molins: 8s. 9d.
[46] Curatus ecclesie de Lincon: 37s.
[47] Curatus ecclesie d'Aillefo: 105s.
[48] Curatus ecclesie de Borbere sancti Supplicii: 32s.
[49] Curatus ecclesie de Torviller: 6s. 3d.
[50] Curatus ecclesie de Mace: 2s. 9d.
[51] Curatus ecclesie d'Acensieris: 38s. 6d.
[52] Abbas Sancti Luppi Trecensis: 73 l. 12s.
[53] Girardinus, vicarius in ecclesia Sancti Urbani: 24 l.
[54] Abbas Sancti Martini de Areis: 9 l.
[55] Magister Domus Dei Sancti Spiritus Trecensis: 40s.
[56] Abbas monasterii de Arripatorio: 69 l.
[57] Rector domus Templi Trecensis: 6 l. 16s.
[58] Prior de Claro Loco: 4 l.
[59] Capitulum Sancti Stephani Trecensis: 123 l.
[60] Capitulum Sancti Petri Trecensis: 203 l. 14s.
[61] Abbas et conventus Monasterii Arramerensis: 126 l. 6s.
[62] Fratres Trinitatis Trecensis: 37 l. 8s.
[63] Johannes li Mangineus et Jacobus li Flamens, beneficiati ad altare beati Andree apostoli subtus crucifixum in ecclesia Sancti Stephani: 6 l. 15s.
[64] Dominus Petrus le Sauvage, capellanus in dicta ecclesia ad altare sancti Petri: 60s.

[3] It is difficult to tell if the fourth letter is *n* or *u/v*. The geographical context suggests that the word is a corruption of some form of Brevonne.

[65] Capellani altaris sancti Thome martyris: 20s.
[66] Dominus Nicholaus de Montigny, capellanus altaris sancti Johannis Evangeliste in dicta ecclesia: 60s. 4d.
[67] Martinus de Montaulain, capellanus altaris santi Martini in dicta ecclesia: 6 l.
[68] Guillelmus de Sancta Margareta, capellanus altaris sancti Pauli: 50s.
[69] Dominus Stephanus de Sublanis, capellanus altaris sancti Dyonisii: 100s.

[right column]

Ab ignobilibus personis dicte castellanie Trecensis:

[70] Bricius de Champiguion, civis Trecensis: 40s.
[71] Provencel, corretarius equorum, de Trecis: 9 l.
[72] Dyonisius de Prio Facto, civis Trecensis: 20 l.
[73] Gibertus de Chastillon, de Trecis: 36s.
[74] Theobaldus li Lorgnes, de Trecis: 10 l. 10s.
[75] Phelisetus Marescalli, de Trecis: 12s.
[76] Sebilla, filia Ade capellarii Monasterii Cellensis: 8s.
[77] Perrotus Bachelait, de Lanis Barrosis: 8s.
[78] Thiericus, Johnannes l'Orge [or Lorge], Gorgete, Miletus filius Mariete, et Maria la Sourde, de Lanis: 32s.
[79] Jonannes Matons, clericus, gener Mathe de Auberville, et Johannes Burserii, de Trecis: 48s.
[80] Jacobus la Belle, de Trecis: 12s.
[81] Bertholotus Muete et eius gener, Trecenses: 12s.
[82] Garnerus de Villarcel et Perrotus, eius filius: 12 l. 15s.
[83] Heredes Oberti de Villelous, de Trecis: 30 l.
[84] Johannes Berthier, de Trecis: 15 l.
[85] Relicte dicti Guion et Johannes Carbonnellus, parrochie de Sancta Maura: 12 l.
[86] Girardus d'Espinci, parrochie de Savieres: 50s.
[87] Dictus Belliers, de Capella sancti Petri: 7s. 6d.
[88] Agnes la Goullere, de Trecis: 50s.
[89] Liberi defuncti Renaudi de Vitriaco et liberi defuncti Galteri Comitis, parrochie de Creny: 60s.
[90] Galterus, frater Colardis maioris de Crony: 50s.
[91] Heredes Bartholomie dou Doches, parrochie de Pigny: 60s.
[92] Dictus Thierryez, de Pigny: 100s.
[93] Jaquins et Johannes, filii Christiane d'Aubrussel: 3s.
[94] Johannes Garnier minor, civis Trecensis: 14 l.
[95] Johannes Pinons et Michael Pissionarius, parrochie Sancti Remigii de Trecis: 4 l. 4s.
[96] Johannes de Lonsolt, parrochie de Lonsolt: 30s.
[97] Rogerus Generi, de Lonsolt: 3s.
[98] Galterus de Latre, parrochie de Lonsolt: 10s.
[99] Jaqueta la Beresse, parrochie de Montaingone: 6s.
[100] Oudardis, eiusdem parrochie: 6s.
[101] Johannes Notay, de Villevesque: 5s.

[102] Jaquetus Renart, de Trecis: 10 l.
[103] Robinetus Renart, de Trecis: 100s.
[104] Ogerus de Poilli, de Trecis: 15s.
[105] Clemens de Sancto Anthonio, de Trecis: 4 l. 10s.
[106] Galterus le Cornu, parrochie de Capella beati Luce: 30s.
[107] Johannes Normannus, parrochie d'Avens: 9 l.
[108] Katherina la Roiere, de Trecis: 60s.
[109] Flos, relicta Theoberti Lavener.[?], de Trecis: 21s.
[110] Symon Coci, de Barbere: 60s.
[111] Johannes Prepositi, de Barbere: 60s.
[112] Johannes Billons, de Barbere: 40s.
[113] Johannes Margueus, de Barbere: 30s.
[114] Guillelmus Malrex, de Barbere: 12s.
[115] Felisetus Chapon et Alisia dicta la Guillote, de Barbere: 20s.
[116] Johannes li Bouvars, de Barbere: 10s.
[117] Decanus de Villa Mauri:[4] 30s.
[118] Johannes li Reus, civis Trecensis: 20 l. 5s.
[119] Felisotus Mumerus [?], parrochie de Mace: 6s.
[120] Laurentius Durars, eiusdem parrochie: 2s.
[121] Margareta, relicta Petri Durart: 2s.
[122] Johannes Durars: 2s.
[123] Jaquetus Clericus, eiusdem parrochie: 2s.
[124] Radulphus dictus Conchemeille, eiusdem parrochie: 3s.
[125] Jaquardus Conchemaille: 5s.
[126] Perrardus Conchemaille: 4s.
[127] Felisetus Conchemaille: 5s.
[128] Michael, gener Jaqueti Clerici de Mace: 6s.
[129] Giletus Aubert, parrochie Sancte Savine, Robinus filius Au Caoussin, et dictus Riceus du Mesnil, parochie de Assencieris: 24 l.
[130] Giletus de Crassi, Guillelminus, Juliana, Jaquenetus, Colinetus, et Johannes Garnerii minor: 40 l.
[131] Liberi le Monnoier, parrochie de Mace: 7 l. 10s.
[132] Radulphus Cressart: 6 l.
[133] Dictus Johers, Jaquins Boisseres [?], Felisia uxor dicti Folfais, et Jaquenus Bayars: 40s.
[134] Robinus, filius Au Caoursin, de Mesnilio prope Seellieres: 100s.
[135] Petrus de Marnay: 30s.
[136] Stephanus de Lardilli, de parrochie de Ruilly: 18 l.
[137] Heredes Johannis Nicholay: 9 l.
[138] Johannes Quarrez, de Trecis: 60 l.
[139] Guillelmus de Castelleto: 200 l.

---

[4] Although we would not expect to find a cleric in this list of lay people, if *Decanus* is an office rather than an unusual personal name, this is presumably a reference to Jacques, *doyen de chrétienté* of Villemaur.

[on dorsal side]

Expense et missiones facte per Chipperellum Diextahit pro financia.

[140] Primo pro expensis servientum et pro nunciis missis: 4 l. 18s. 6d.
[141] Item pro portagio trium milium octies centum quatuor viginti decem et octo librorum tur., cordis, sacellis,[5] stalaticis,[6] et aliis minutis expensis: 4 l. 15s.
[142] Item pro scriptura rotulorum et aliarum litterarum et cedularum: 53s.
[143] Item pro restauro unius equi: 7 l.

Summa: 19 l. 6s. 6d.

Hec sunt nomina illorum qui non solvunt de financia.

Troyes

[144] Curatus beate Marie: 6 l. 5s.
[145] Curatus de Sancto Aventino: 30s. Nihil habet.
[146] Curatus de Froiz Parez: 26s.

Laici

[147] Guillelmus de Castelleto: 100 l.

Summa: 319 3s.[7]

Apud Insulas

[148] Petrus le Charnigues, de Montalvain: 40s.

Summa: 2 l.

Apud Meriacum supra Secanam

[149] Curatus de Meriaco: 12 l.[8]
[150] Capellanus Sancti Laurentii de Plansiaco:[9] 10 l.

---

[5] The ms. reads *sacè*.

[6] I read the second letter as *t* (*stalat.*); Paoli read it as *c* and expanded to *scalatis*. In a letter Leopold Delisle suggested to him that this might be a stripped cloth used to cover the sacks of money; cf. Du Cange, *s.v. scallatus*. My interpretation is that the word refers to charges for stallage; *cf. scalaticum* in J. F. Niermeyer, *Mediae latinitatis lexicon minus* (Leiden, 1954-76).

[7] The total is inexplicable.

[8] In margin: *sol. .b.*

[9] The ms. reads *Psiaco*. Paoli expanded to *Prisiaco*, but there is no place-name in the region which fits this reading. *Plansiaco* makes sense; it is possible that the canons of the collegiate church of Saint-Laurent de Plancy had a chapel south of the Aube in the territory of the castellany of Méry.

[151]   Liberi dicti Clerici de Mesnilio, de parrochia de Claelles: 7 l. 10.
[152]   Perrinus de Nemore: 4 l. 10s.
                    Summa: 33 l.

A Hervy

[153]   Matricularii de Flogniaco: 5s. 6d.
[154]   Curatus de Montefuoil: 5s.
[155]   Reginaldus capellanus de Donne Marime:[11] 25 l.
[156]   Guiotus et Henrycus Lumbart: 40 l.[12]
[157]   Bernart de Jannoy, baillivus de Tonnerre: 6 l.
                    Summa: 272 l. 14s. 6d.[13]

Apud Sanctum Florentium

[158]   Curatus de Sancto Florentino: 15 l. 13s. 6d.[14]
[159]   Prior monasterii de Leuz: 60s.
[160]   Fratres minores de Trecis: 45 l.[15]
[161]   Capellanus de Vriennon:[16] 36 l.
[162]   Curatus de Chanlot: 20 l. 5s.
[163]   Archiepiscopus Senonensis: 60 l.
[164]   Curatus de Soumentrion: 11s. 6d.
[165]   Monachi de Bello Prato: 15 l. 10s.[17]
[166]   Abbas Sancti Germani de Autissiodoro: 65 l.
[167]   Prior Sancti Nicholai de Ruvillon in dyocesi Nivernensi:[18] 15s.
[168]   Abbas Sancti Marienni de Autissiodoro: 15s.
[169]   Capellanus Beate Marie du Autissiodoro: 12 l.
[170]   Prior curatus de Venousse: 13 l. 8s. 10d.

Laici

[171]   Reginaldus de Chichi: 18 l.
[172]   Heredes Guillelmi Renardi: 6 l.
[173]   Johannes Viarius et eius mater: 15 l.
[174]   Heredes Domenchi Bordos: 16 l.
[175]   Gauvarius de Ferray, lombardus: 181 l.
[176]   Bergeon la Marcheande: 30s.
[177]   Johannes Erart de Wlpiliers et Guillelmus de Coudrayo: 6 l. 18s.
[178]   Oudinus de Ceretollaz [?]:[19] 26s.

[10] In margin: *sol. b.*
[11] Apparently an error for Marine, though a chapel of Sainte-Marine is not known in the region of Ervy.
[12] In margin: *lib.*
[13] Total inexplicable.
[14] In margin in large writing: *Prepositus debet respondere de argento.*
[15] In margin: *lib.*
[16] Bouy-Vieux was a chapel under the care of the curate of Brienon.
[17] In margin *lib.*
[18] The priory of Saint-Nicolas of Réveillon was in fact in the diocese of Auxerre.
[19] The ms. reads cetollaz, with a mark of suspension over the e which I am not sure how to expand. Paoli read *Certollaz.*

Index

Index personarum

Adam, capellarius Monasterii Cellensis 76
Agnes la Goullere, of Troyes 88
Alisia la Guillote, of Barberey-Saint-Sulpice 115

Bartholomeus dou Doches, his heirs, of Piney 91
Belliers, of Chapelle-Saint-Pierre 87
Bergeon la Marcheande 176
Bernart de Jannoy, baillivus de Tonnere 157
Bertholetus Muete, of Troyes 81
Bricius de Champiguion, of Troyes 70

Chipperellus Diextahit: pp. 264, 268
Christiana d'Aubrussel, her sons 93
Clericus de Mesnilio, his children, of Claelles 151
Colinetus 130

Decanus de Villa Mauri 117
Domenchus Bordos, his heirs 174
Dyonisius de Primo Facto, of Troyes 72

Felisetus Chapon, of Barberey-Saint-Sulpice 115
Felisetus Conchemaille 127
Felisetus Marescalli, of Troyes 75
Felisia, uxor Folfais 133
Felisotus Mumerus [?], of Macey 119
Flos, relicta Theoberti Lavener. [?], of Troyes 109

Galterus, frater Colardus maioris, of Creney 90
Galterus Comes, his children, of Creney 89
Galterus le Cornu, of Chapelle-Saint-Luc 106
Galterus de Latre, of Longsols 98
Garnerus de Villarcel 82
Gauvarius de Ferray, Lombard 175
Gibertus de Chastillon, of Troyes 73
Giletus Aubert, of Sainte-Savine 129
Giletus de Crassi 130
Girardinus, vicarius Sancti Urbani Trecensis 53
Girardus d'Espinci, of Savières 86
Gorgete, of Laines-Bourreuses 78
Guillelminus 130
Guillelmus de Carcassone, of Troyes 5
Guillelmus de Castelleto 139, 147
Guillelmus de Coudrayo 177
Guillelmus Malrex, of Barberey-Saint-Sulpice 114
Guillelmus Renardi, his heirs 172
Guillelmus de Sancta Margareta 68
Guion, his widow, of Sainte-Maure 85
Guiotus [Lumbart?] 156

Henricus Chacenayo, of Troyes 6
Henrycus Lumbart 156
Humbertus de Meldis, of Troyes 7

Jacobus, *doyen de chrètienté* of Villemaur [?] 117
Jacobus la Belle, of Troyes 80
Jacobus li Flamens, of Troyes 63
Jaquardus Conchemaille 125
Jaquenetus 130
Jacquenus Bayars 133
Jaqueta la Beresse, of Montangon 99
Jaquetus Clericus, of Macey 123
Jaquetus Renart, of Troyes 102
Jaquins Boisseres [?] 133
Jaquins, filius Christiane d'Aubrussel 93
Johannes, filius Christiane d'Aubrussel 93
Johannes Allerii, of Troyes 7
Johannes Berthier, of Troyes 84
Johannes Billons, of Barberey-Saint-Sulpice 112
Johannes li Bouvars, of Barberey-Saint-Sulpice 116
Johannes Burserii, of Troyes 79
Johannes Carbonnellus, of Sainte-Maure 85
Johannes de Donno Martino, royal clerk: heading p. 264.
Johannes Durars 122
Johannes Erart, of Verpillières 177
Johannes Garneri minor, of Troyes 94, 130
Johannes de Lonsolt, of Longsols 96
Johannes li Mangineus, of Troyes 63
Johannes Margues, of Barberey-Saint-Sulpice 113
Johannes Matons, clericus, of Troyes 79
Johannes Nicholay, his heirs 137
Johannes Normannus, of Avant 107
Johannes Notay, of Villevoque 101
Johannes l'Orge [or Lorge], of Laines-Bourreuses 78
Johannes Pinons, of Troyes 95
Johannes Prepositi, of Barberey-Saint-Sulpice 111
Johannes Quarrez, of Troyes 138
Johannes Viarius 173
Johers 133
Juliana 130

Katherina la Roiere, of Troyes 108

Laurentius Durars, of Macey 120

Margareta, relicta Petri Durart 121
Maria la Sourde, of Laines-Bourreuses 78

Martinus de Montaulain 67
Mathe de Auberville 79
Michael, gener Jaqueti Clerici, of Macey 128
Michael Pissionarius, of Troyes 95
Miletus, fiilius Mariete, of Laines-Bourreuses 78
Monnoier (le), his children, of Macey 131

Nicholaus de Montigny 66

Obertus de Villelous, heirs, of Troyes 83
Ogerus de Poilli, of Troyes 104
Oudardus, of Montangon 100
Oudinus le Ceretollaz [?] 178

Perrardus Conchemaille 126
Perrinus de Nemore 152
Perrotus Bachelait, of Laines-Bourreuses 77
Perrotus de Villarcel 82
Petrus le Charnigues, of Montaulin 148
Petrus de Condeto, archdeacon of Soissons heading, p. 264
Petrus de Marney 135
Petrus le Sauvage 64
Phelisetus Marescalli, of Troyes 75
Provencel, corretarius equorum, of Troyes 71

Radulphus Conchemeille of Macey 124
Radulphus Cressart 132
Reginaldus de Chichi 171
Reginaldus capellanus de Donne Marime [?] 155
Renaudus de Vitriaco, his children, of Creney 89
Riceus de Mesnil of Assencières 129
Robinetus Renart, of Troyes 102
Robinus, filius Au Caoursin, of Mesnil-Seillières 129 134
Rogerus Generi, of Longsols 97

Sebilla, filia Ade capellarii Monasterii Cellensis 76
Stephanus de Creni, of Troyes 4
Stephanus de Lardilli, of Rouilly-Saint-Loup 136
Stephanus de Sublanis, of Troyes 69
Symon Coci, of Barberey-Saint-Sulpice 110

Theolbadus li Lorgnes, of Troyes 74
Thiericus, of Laines-Bourreuses 78
Thierryez, of Piney 92

Index Locorum

[Note: When no department is given, Aube is understood.]

Acensieres, see Assencières
Aillefol (ar. Troyes, can. Piney, com. Géraudot), parish church 47
Arripatorium, see Larrivour
Assencìeres (ar. Troyes, can. Piney), parish church: 51; resident 129
Aubrissel, Aubrussel, see Laubressel
Autissiodorum, see Auxerre
Auxerre (Yonne, ch.-l ar.), Notre-Dame de la Cité, collegiate church: 169; Saint-Germain, abbey (O.S.B.): 166; Saint-Marien, abbey (O. Praem): 168
Auxon (ar. Troyes, can. Ervy-le-Châtel), priory (O.S.B.)-parish church: 32
Avant-lès-Ramerupt (ar. Troyes, can. Ramerupt), parish church: 42, 43, resident: 107
Avens, see Avant

Barbery-Saint-Sulpice (ar. and can. Troyes), parish church: 48; residents: 110-116
Beaupré (Yonne, ar. Avallon, can. Flogny, com. Soumaintrain), priory (Cist.): 165
Bellum Pratum, see Beaupré
Borbere sancti Supplicii, see Barbery-Saint-Sulpice
Bouy-Vieux (Yonne, ar. Auxerre, can. and com. Brienon-sur-Armançon), chapel: 161
Brevgiona, see Brévonnes
Brévonnes (ar. Troyes, can. Piney), parish church: 25
Brienon (Yonne, ar. Auxerre, ch.-l can.), chapel: 161

Capella beati Luce, see Chapelle-Saint-Luc
Capella sancti Petri, see Chapelle-Saint-Pierre
Capella Valon, see Chapelle-Vallon
Carcassonne (Aude, ch.-l dép.), see Guillelmus de Carcassone
Casteletum, see Châtelet-en-Brie
Chacenay (ar. Troyes, can. Essoyes), see Henricus de Chacenayo
Champguyon (Marne, ar. Epernay, can. Esternay), see Bricius de Champiguion
Champiguion, see Champguyon
Champlost (Yonne, ar. Auxerre, can. Brienon-sur-Armançon), parish church: 162
Chanlot, see Champlost
Chapelle-Saint-Luc (ar. and can. Troyes), resident: 106

Chapelle-Saint-Pierre, now Grandes-Chapelles (ar. Nogent-sur-Seine, can. Méry-sur-Seine), resident: 87
Chappelle-Vallon (ar. Nogent-sur-Seine, can. Méry-sur-Seine), parish church: 14
Châtelet-en-Brie (Seine-et-Marne, ar. Melun, ch.-l. can.), see Guillelmus de Casteleto
Châtillon-sur-Marne (Marne, ar. Reims, ch.-l. can.), see Gibertus de Chastillon
Chichey (Marne, ar. Epernay, can. Sézanne), see Reginaldus de Chichi
Claelles, see Clesles
Clairlieu (ar. Nogent-sur-Seine, can. Marcilly-le-Hayer, com. Pâlis), prior (Cist.): 58
Clarus Locus, see Clairlieu
Clesles (Marne, ar. Epernay, can. Anglure), residents: 151
Colaverday, now Charmont-sur-Barbuise (ar. Troyes, can. Arcissur-Aube), parish church: 33, 34
Condé-sur-Aisne (Aisne, ar. Soissons, can. Vailly-sur-Aisne), see Petrus de Condeto
Courleverday, see Colaverday
Courteranges (ar. Troyes, can. Lusigny-sur-Barse), parish church: 41
Creney-près-Troyes (ar. and can. Troyes), residents: 89, 90; see Stephanus de Creni

Donne Marime [?], unidentified, possibly a distorted reading for Sainte-Marine, see Reginaldus capellanus de Donne Marime
Dosches (ar. Troyes, can. Piney), parish church: 29; see Bartholomeus dou Doches

Ervy-le-Châtel (ar. Troyes, ch.-l. can.), castellany: 153-157
Espincey (ar. Nogent-sur-Seine, can. Méry-sur-Seine, com. Savières), see Girardus d'Espinci

Faiges, see Feuges
Feuges (ar. Troyes, can. Arcis-sur-Aube), parish church: 23
Flogny (Yonne, ar. Avallon, ch.-l. can.), parish church: 153
Froides-Parois (ar. Nogent-sur-Seine, can. Méry-sur-Seine, com. Chapelle-Vallon), parish church: 146

Hervy, see Ervy-le-Châtel

Insulae, see Isle-Aumont
Isle-Aumont (ar. Troyes, can. Bouilly), castellany: 148

Jannoy or *Jaunoy*, unidentified, see Bernart de Jannoy

Laines-Bourreuses (ar. can. Troyes, com. Rosières-près-Troyes), residents: 77, 78

Larrivour (ar. Troyes, can. and com. Lusigny-sur-Barse), abbey (Cist.): 56
Laubressel (ar. Troyes, can. Lusigny-sur-Barse), parish church: 28; see Christiana d'Aubrussel
Leuz, see Montlhéu
Linçon (ar. and can. Troyes, com. Saint-Germain), parish church: 46
Longsols (ar. Troyes, can. Ramerupt), priory (O.S.A.)-parish church: 31; residents: 96-98; see Johannes de Lonsolt
Lujeres, see Luyères
Lusigny-sur-Barse (ar. Troyes, ch.-l, can.), priory (O.S.A.)-parish church: 35
Luyères (ar. Troyes, can. Piney), parish church: 24

Macey, (ar. and can. Troyes), parish church: 50; residents: 119-128, 131
Margerie (Marne, ar. Vitry-le-François, can. Saint-Rémy-en-Bouzemont), see Guillelmus de Sancta Margareta
Marney (ar. and can. Troyes, com. Sainte-Maure), see Petrus de Marnay
Meaux (Seine-et-Marne, ch.-l. ar.), see Humbertus de Meldis
Meldis, see Meaux
Méry-sur-Seine (ar. Nogent-sur-Seine, ch.-l. can.), castellany: 149-152; parish church: 149
Mesnil (Marne, ar. Epernay, can. Anglure, com. Clesles), see Clericus de Mesnilio
Mesnil-Seillières (ar. Troyes, can. Piney), residents: 129, 134; see Riceus du Mesnil
Molins-sur-Aube (ar. Bar-sur-Aube, can. Brienne-le-Château), parish church: 44, 45
Monasterium Arremarense, see Montiéramey
Monasterium Cellense, see Troyes
Monasterium de Leuz, see Montlhéu
Mons Suzanus, see Montsuzain
Montaingone, see Montangon
Montalvain, Montaulanus, see Montaulin
Montangon (ar. Troyes, can. Piney), residents: 99, 100
Montaulin (ar. Troyes, can. Lusigny-sur-Barse), resident: 148; see Martinus de Montaulain
Montefuoil, see Montfey
Montfey (ar. Troyes, can. Ervy-le-Châtel), parish church: 154
Montiéramey (ar. Troyes, can. Lusigny-sur-Barse), abbey (O.S.G.): 61; parish church: 39
Montigny-les-Monts (ar. Troyes, can. Ervy-le-Châtel), see Nicholaus de Montigny
Montlhéu (Yonne, ar. Auxerre, can. and com. Saint-Florentin), priory of Saint-Denis (O.S.B.): 159
Montsuzain (ar. Troyes, can. Arcis-sur-Aube), parish church: 16

Noeroy, see Nozay
Noës-près-Troyes (ar. and can. Troyes), parish church: 37
Nozay (ar. Troyes, can. Arcis-sur-Aube), parish church: 21

Piney (ar. Troyes, ch.-l. can.), residents: 91, 92
Plancy (ar. Nogent-sur-Seine, can. Méry-sur-Seine), collegiate church: of Saint-Laurent: 150
Pont-Sainte-Marie (ar. and can. Troyes), parish church: 18
Pouilly, hamlet (ar., can. and com. Troyes), see Ogerus de Poilli
Premierfait (ar. Nogent-sur-Seine, can. Méry-sur-Seine, parish church: 22; see Dyonisius de Primo Facto
Rouilly, now Rouilly-Sacey (ar. Troyes, can. Piney), parish church: 40
Ruvigny (ar. Troyes, can. Lusigny-sur-Barse), parish church: 40

Sacey, now Rouilly-Sacey (ar. Troyes, can. Piney), parish church: 27
Saint-Antoine, commanderie in the parish of Saint-Martin-ès-Vignes of Troyes, see Clemens de Sancto Anthonio
Saint-Aventin (ar. Troyes, can. Lusigny-sur-Barse, com. Verrières), parish church: 145
Saint-Benoît-sur-Seine (ar. and can. Troyes), parish church: 17
Sainte-Maure (ar. and can. Troyes), priory (O.S.A.)-parish church: 13; residents: 85
Saint-Etienne-sous-Barbuise (ar. Troyes, can. Arcis-sur-Aube), parish church: 19
Saint-Florentin (Yonne, ar. Auxerre, ch.-l. can.), castellany: 158-170; parish church: 158; prévôt: 158 note
Saint Lyé (ar. and can. Troyes), parish church: 38
Saint-Parre-au-Tertre (ar. and can. Troyes), parish church: 30
Saint-Sépulcre, now Villacerf (ar. and can. Troyes), parish church: 11; Cluniac priory: 12
Saint-Syre, now Rilly-Saint-Syre (ar. Nogent-sur-Seine, can. Méry-sur-Seine), parish church: 15
Sancta Margareta, see Margerie
Sancta Mora, see Sainte-Maure
Sancta Syra, see Sainte-Syre
Sanctum Sepulcrum, see Saint-Sépulcre
Sanctus Anthonius, see Saint-Antoine
Sanctus Aventinus, see Saint-Aventin
Sanctus Benedictus supra Secanam see Saint-Benoît-sur-Seine
Sanctus Florentinus, see Saint-Florentin
Sanctus Leo, see Saint-Lyé
Sanctus Martinus de Areis, see Troyes
Sanctus Maurus, probably an error for Sancta Maura
Sanctus Patrolus, see Saint-Parre-au-Tertre
Sanctus Stephanus super Barbuise, see Saint-Etienne-sous-Barbuise
Savières (ar. Nogent-sur-Seine, can. Méry-sur-Seine), resident: 86
Sens (Yvonne, ch.-l. ar.), archbishop: 163
Soulaines (ar. Bar-sur-Aube, ch.-l. can.), see Stephanus de Sublanis
Soumaintrain (Yonne, ar. Avallon, can. Flogny), parish church: 164
Sublane, see Soulaines

Thennelières (ar. Troyes, can. Lusigny-sur-Barse), parish church: 36
Tonnerre (Yonne, ar. Avallon, ch.-l. can.), baillivus, see Bernart de Jannot
Torvilliers (ar. and can. Troyes), parish church: 49
Trecensis, Trecis, see Troyes
Troyes (ch.-l. dép.), castellany: 1-139, 144-147
—, Franciscans: 160
—, Knights of the Hospital: 10
—, Knights Templar: 57
—, Montier-la-Celle, abbey (O.S.B.), see Adam, capellarius
—, Saint-Bernard, hospital: 3
—, Saint-Esprit, hospital: 55
—, Saint-Etienne, collegiate church, chapter: 50; chapel of Saint-André: 63; chapel of Saint-Denis: 69; chapel of Saint-Jean-l'Evangéliste: 66; chapel of Saint-Martin: 67; chapel of Saint-Paul: 68; chapel of Saint-Pierre: 64, chapel of Saint-Thomas-de-Cantorbéry: 65
—, Saint-Loup, abbey (O.S.A.): 52
—, Saint-Martin-ès-Aires, abbey (O.S.A.): 54
—, Saint-Pierre, cathedral, chapter: 60; chapel of Saint-Augustin: 6; chapel of Saint-Barthélemy: 7; chapel of Saint-Léonard: 5; chapel of the Trinity: 7
—, Saint-Urbain, collegiate church: 53
—, Trinitarians: 62
—, parishes, Notre-Dame-aux-Nonnains, parish church: 144; Saint-André, parish church: 2; Saint-Denis, parish church: 8; Saint-Gilles, succursal of Saint-André: 2; Saint-Jean-au-Marché, parish church: 9; Saint-Nizier, parish church: 1; Saint-Rémy, residents: 95
—, residents: 70-75, 79-84, 88, 94, 95, 102-105, 108, 109, 118, 138

Venouse (Yonne, ar. Auxerre, can. Ligny-le-Châtel), prior (O.S.A.)-parish church: 170
Verpillières-sur-Ource (ar. Troyes, can. Essoyes), resident: 177
Villecerf (ar. Troyes, can. Estissac, com. Messon), see Garnerus de Villarcel

Villeloup (ar. and can. Troyes), see Obertus de Villelous
Villelous, see Villeloup
Villemaur (ar. Troyes, can. Estissac), see Decanus
Villette-sur-Aube (ar. Troyes, can. Arcis-sur-Aube), parish church: 20

Villevoque (ar. Troyes, can. and com. Piney), resident: 101
Vitry-en-Perthois (Marne, ar. and can. Vitry-le-François), see Renaudus de Vitriaco
Vriennon, see Brienon

Wlpiliers, see Verpillières-sur-Ource

14

*Written Records and the Development of Systematic Feudal Relations**

Though the terms in the title of this chapter have been cautiously chosen, imaginative members of the audience will already have realized that to speak of 'systematic feudal relations' is an elaborate and yet limiting way of referring to what we often casually call 'feudalism'. A less guarded title might have been 'Did writing put the -ism in feudalism?'

I wanted to avoid the terms 'feudalism' or 'feudal system' initially because of the well-known difficulties with their use; as Maitland once wrote about the awesome lack of specificity in references to the 'feudal system': 'The phrase has thus become for us so large and vague that it is quite possible to maintain that of all countries England was the most, or for the matter of that the least, feudalized; that William the Conqueror introduced, or for the matter of that suppressed, the feudal system.'[1] But I also wanted to stress the concept of *system* itself, to emphasize those feudal relations that seem to me to have a clearly discernible structure and indeed to be ordered in such a way that they seemed systematic to contemporaries themselves.[2]

In this essay I will deal concretely and in some detail with feudal institutions and records in the county of Champagne in the twelfth and thirteenth centuries, but before doing so I would like to set a conceptual stage by moving quickly through a long period of medieval history. This I

---

*[The author's revised version of a paper presented to a conference on 'Language and History in the Middle Ages' at Toronto, Centre for Medieval Studies, 6-7 November 1981. – Ed.]

[1] Frederick William Maitland, *The Constitutional History of History*, ed. H. A. L. Fisher (Cambridge, Eng., 1908; rpr. 1931), p. 143, quoted by Elisabeth A. R. Brown, 'The Tyranny of a Construct: Feudalism and Historians of Medieval Europe', *American Historical Review*, 79 (1974), pp. 1065-66, an article which should have led historians to think at least twice before using the term 'feudalism' and yet has had strikingly little effect.

[2] I wish here to dissociate myself from current jargon about 'the system', a term which seems to refer to existing political, economic and social reality, no matter how chaotic and contradictory that reality may be.

have divided into three periods: first, the eighth and ninth centuries, the time of what Ganshof calls 'Carolingian feudalism', a period we might also describe as one combining proto-feudal institutions with the continuing power of monarchy or empire; secondly, the tenth and eleventh centuries, the period which Bloch calls the 'first feudal age'; and lastly, the twelfth and thirteenth centuries, the period in which feudo-vassalic institutions provided the glue which held the county of Champagne (and many other principalities) together. In terms of the power of government, either on the level of kingdom or principality, these three periods are commonly seen as representing first a move from strength to weakness or from centralization to localism, decentralization and indeed 'feudal anarchy', and then a second shift back to centralizing power, a time of construction of principalities as well as of the strengthening of monarchy, the period in which historians most commonly refer to *a* or even *the* 'feudal system'. Bloch's concept of two feudal ages seems to me convenient, but let us not here be overly concerned with terminology or with absolute rather than relative chronology. Historians who use the word 'feudalism' quite differently agree on the historical reality of the two shifts just mentioned.

It is hard to estimate how many documents were actually produced in the Carolingian period to provide a written record of the creation of personal ties or the granting of benefices. We know from the eighth-century Formulary of Tours that it was considered appropriate for both parties to an act of commendation to draw up letters stating the terms of the agreement or contract.[3] Charlemagne for military reasons ordered his *missi* in 811 to ascertain and record what lands those in their jurisdictions held as benefices and how many vassals (*homines casati*) there were on each benefice.[4] As late as 869 Charles the Bald tried to collect lists (*breves* of the benefices held by the counts and great vassals (*vassi dominici*) throughout his realm, though he had to depend on the vassals and counts to report on each other rather than on *missi*.[5] There is therefore quite good evidence that the Carolingians and their subjects were aware of the value of keeping records. Ganshof tells us that 'it was only rarely that a charter would be drawn up as evidence of the rights of the two parties concerned,' but the charter of Charles the Bald of 876 that he cites as 'an example' seems quite routine, the grantee was probably viscount of Limoges and

---

[3] 'Unde convenit, ut duas epistolas uno tenore conscriptas ex hoc inter se facere vel adfirmare deberent, '*Formulae Turonenses*, no. 43, in *Formulae merowingici et karolini aevi*, ed. K. Zeumer, *M.G.H.*, *Formulae* (Hanover, 1886), p. 152, quoted in F. L. Ganshof, *Feudalism*, 3rd English ed., trans. Philip Grierson (New York, 1964), p. 7.

[4] *Capitulare de iusticiis faciendis*, c. 5, in *Capitularia regum Francorum*, ed. Alfred Boretius and Victor Krause, *M.G.H.*, *Capit.*, 2 vols. (Hanover, 1883-97), I, 177, no. 80.

[5] *Annales de Saint-Bertin*, ed Félix Grat, Jeanne Vielliard and Suzanne Clémencet (Paris, 1964), s. a. 869, pp. 152-153.

does not appear to have been a particularly important person, and there is no evidence that a church was involved in the transaction.[6]

We should note at this point that the records just mentioned concern only the identification of vassals or of benefices, not the obligations of vassals. A ninth-century abbot of St.-Remi of Reims had the knowledge and organizational ability to record that a family of peasants at Condé-sur-Marne owed him three chickens and fifteen eggs at Martinmas and had to haul manure as required,[7] but apparently the responsibilities of fighting men were not recorded in the same way. Perhaps this was because ideally the tie between a fighting man and his lord was personal, honourable, and unconstrained, so that putting an agreement in writing would have seemed inappropriate.[8] Although the practice of multiple vassalage (whenever it developed) should have created a need for clearly delimited vassalic agreements, in neither the Carolingian period nor the 'first feudal age' was there an accepted form of written contract in use to create a mechanism for resolving disputes arising from conflicting obligations to different lords.

As we move into the tenth century the surviving documentation decreases and by any measure I can think of, it is clear that in northern France we have entered a less literate world; for example, the number of surviving royal diplomas falls from about 12 per year under Charles the Bald to less than 2 under Lothaire and Louis V.[9] As Bloch wrote of the laity in his first feudal age, 'Almost strangers to writing, they tended to be indifferent to it.'[10] He illustrates his point with a reference to Otto the Great, and what was true of kings, who had chanceries, must have applied even more strongly to their subjects, who did not. The price of the indifference to writing was the absence of that ability to verify memories of a past act which writing supplies. When Duke William V of Aquitaine asked Fulbert of Chartres what obligations were created by an oath of fidelity, Bishop Fulbert replied forcefully in an often-quoted letter of 1020 or so about a vassal's negative responsibilities, saying in various ways that a vassal should avoid injuring his lord, but he was magnificently vague about the positive *auxilium* which a vassal owed.[11] It could not have

---

[6] Ganshof, *Feudalism*, p. 40 and *Recueil des actes de Charles II le Chauve*, ed. Georges Tessier, 3 vols. (Paris, 1943-55), II, no. 411, pp. 419-420.

[7] *Polyptyque de l'abbaye de Saint-Remi de Reims*, ed. B. Guérard (Paris, 1853), p. 99.

[8] For a modern comparison, hourly employees often have to punch a time-clock, while executives (and professors) do not.

[9] Compare Tessier's edition with the *Recueil des actes de Lothaire et de Louis V, rois de France, 954-987*, ed. Louis Halphen (Paris, 1908).

[10] *Feudal Society*, trans. L. A. Manyon (Chicago, 1961), p. 81.

[11] *The Letters and Poems of Fulbert of Chartres*, ed. and trans. Frederick Behrends (Oxford, 1976), no. 51, pp. 90-92. On the circumstances which may have prompted William's question to Fulbert see George Beech, 'A Feudal Document of Early Eleventh Century

occurred to Fulbert to write that a vassal should carry out faithfully the obligations to which he had agreed in a written contract.

Without written records uncertainty and a rough rule of force reigned, creating those conditions that, not so long ago, were commonly called 'feudal anarchy'. To illustrate these conditions I would like to call to mind an anecdote recorded by Ordericus Vitalis about the battle of Mortemer in 1054 in the time of Thibaut I of Blois, Henry I of France and William the Bastard of Normandy. We will look at just one aspect of that battle, and not from the point of view of kings and great princes but of the relatively minor lord, Roger of Mortemer, whose castle, if indeed he actually had one, happened to become the pivotal point on which the French offensive to overrun the region of Rouen turned. Roger was one of the trusted *milites* whom Duke William sent against French forces led by four great lords, including Ralph of Crépy count of Amiens. Roger of Mortemer and his colleagues fought effectively, two of the opposing leaders fled, and a third was taken prisoner. But it was Ralph of Crépy who posed the greatest problem for Roger of Mortemer, because Roger had done homage to Ralph. Although Roger was a leader of Duke William's army, he interpreted his duty to Ralph of Crépy to be such that he sheltered him at Mortemer for three days and then escorted him back to his own side. After Roger had decided how to deal with Ralph, William in his turn had to decide how to deal with Roger. First he banished Roger from the duchy, but since Roger's treatment of Ralph could be called 'handsome and proper' (the words are those Ordericus puts in the mouth of William himself), the duke restored Roger's honor to him, except for Mortemer itself, which he granted to William of Warenne.[12] The point which this story illustrates is, I trust, obvious, that in the first feudal age it was very hard for anyone to know who owed precisely what to whom in any situation in which less than total commitment was expected.

The central question this paper addresses is how written records were used in the shift from the first to the second feudal age, to continue to use Bloch's terms, or from feudal confusion – if not anarchy – to feudal centralization. It seems to us evident that written agreements would have been useful to men like William of Normandy and Roger of Mortemer in clarifying their relationships, and since the second feudal age of the twelfth and thirteenth centuries is a time of increasing documentation, it is reasonable to suspect that the writing of charters and other such records may well have played a significant and perhaps even essential part in

---

Poitou' in *Mélanges offerts à René Crozet* (Poitiers, 1966), pp. 203-213, and Jane Martindale, 'Conventum inter Guillelmum Aquitanorum comes et Hugonem Chiliarchum', *English Historical Review*, 84 (1969), 528-548.

[12] *The Ecclesiastical History of Ordericus Vitalis*, ed. Marjorie Chibnall, 6 vols. (Oxford, 1969-80), 4, 86-88 [ed. Le Prévost, 3, 236-238].

making feudal institutions effective instruments of centralizing governments.

To establish some sense of scale, let us review the production of written records at a number of different courts. Occasional practices became more routine in the eleventh century, and from the end of that century the writing of records in northern France and England grows exponentially, or so it seems. In his intriguing book, *From Memory to Written Record*, Michael Clanchy has graphed the number of extant letters or charters issued by the papacy and the kings of France and England from about 1080 to the end of the twelfth century. From Philip I of France we have about 3.5 a year, while his great-grandson Philip II has left us about 14 times that figure. William the Conqueror has left us about 11.5 charters a year as king of England, a figure to be compared with a ten-fold increase in the time of Henry II. For the papacy, the relatively well-preserved collection of the energetic Gregory VII contains the texts of about 35 letters a year, but Alexander III has left us 180 a year. In the thirteenth century the papal *cacoethes scribendi* became almost uncontrollable. From Innocent III 280 letters a year extant, from Innocent IV 730, and since the chancery of Boniface VIII is estimated to have issued 50,000 letters a year, no one has attempted to count precisely how many survive today.[13]

Let us now turn from these royal and papal chanceries to the principality with which I am most familiar, the county of Champagne, and review the evidence on which this paper is primarily based. My friend and colleague at the Université de Nancy II, Professor Michel Bur, and I are now engaged in preparing for publication several volumes of a *recueil des actes des comtes de Champagne* in accordance with the norms established for the *chartes des princes* by the Académie des Inscriptions et Belles-Lettres. Monsieur Bur is responsible for the period up to the reign of Henry I, which began in 1152. Starting with an act from 943, he has collected 426 charters, notices or references to charters issued by the counts of Champagne or concerning them.[14] For the tenth century these average approximately one-half charter per year, from the eleventh century we have now approximately one act per year, but with the reign of Thibaut II from 1125 to 1152 the number has mounted to an average of seven per year, not so far below the average of almost ten for his contemporary Louis VI. The documentary increase in Champagne continues in the second half of the twelfth century. My collection of extant charters actually issued between 1152 and 1198 by Henry I (died 1181), his wife Marie (died

---

[13] M. T. Clanchy, *From Memory to Written Record: England, 1066-1307* (Cambridge, Mass., 1979), pp. 44-45; his figures are based in part on Alexander Murray, 'Pope Gregory VII and his Letters', *Traditio* 22 (1966), 145-202, esp. pp. 155 and 166, n. 46, Robert Fawtier, *The Capetian Kings of France* (London, 1960), pp. 8-9, and R. W. Southern, *Western Society and the Church in the Middle Ages* (Harmondsworth, 1970), p. 109.

[14] Michel Bur, *La formation du comté de Champagne, v. 950-v. 1150* (Nancy, 1977), p. 6.

1198), and their son Henry II (died 1197), now totals approximately 700, or an average of fifteen charters a year. In the thirteenth century the chancery of Champagne began to collect in registers the texts of many charters either issued by the counts themselves or written by others on matters which interested them. The great archivist and historian Henri d'Arbois de Jubainville used these registers as the basis for his analysis of over 3,400 charters issued by or otherwise concerning the counts from the period from 1197 until the young Philip the Fair assumed control of the county in 1284, or an average of about 40 a year.[15] A resurvey of the departmental archives and of other materials that have become available since d'Arbois worked in the 1860s might well produce perhaps 10 or 15% more if anyone considered it worth the effort to make such a collection, but I doubt that a new total would pass an average of 45 or 50 a year for the whole century, well below the average of almost 60 issued by Philip Augustus and very small as compared to Philip the Fair's average of over 500 a year. In short, the rate of increase in Champagne in the twelfth and thirteenth centuries is markedly lower than the sharply rising curve of the royal and papal chanceries, but the mass of documents produced and carefully preserved in Champagne in this period is still a monument to bureaucratic activity.

Anyone who argues that fewer documents survive from the tenth and eleventh centuries than the twelfth and thirteenth because the older documents were subject to a long period of turbulence in which they could be destroyed is raising a very sensible point: in the unsettled conditions of Bloch's first feudal age it must have been very difficult to maintain archives in any place but the most secure ecclesiastical establishment.[16] Indeed, the difficulties of maintaining archives in northern France (as compared, let us say, to Catalonia) is precisely a reason why few charters should have been issued, particularly to lay recipients, and it must be stressed that issuing charters was not something that the early counts of Blois-Champagne did routinely. They had no chancellor or chaplain regularly assigned to write charters, and we have no mention of a seal before 1107, during the period when countess Adèle, the daughter of William the Conqueror, was introducing a chancery on the English model.[17] In the early years of the reign of Henry I of Champagne that chancery became one of the most professional in France, to the point that charters prepared by the count's notaries commonly included information, not on who had written the charter (which an experienced eye could determine simply from looking at the handwriting), but on who

---

[15] See the catalogue at the end of Henri d'Arbois de Jubainville, *Histoire des ducs et des comtes de Champagne*, 6 vols. (Paris, 1859-67).

[16] That time alone is not determinative is shown by the fact that more ninth than tenth-century royal charters survive today.

[17] Bur, *Formation*, p. 425.

had taken the notes on the actual event and witnesses, notes used later in the preparation of the charter presented to the recipient.[18]

Though I stand ready to be corrected by Michel Bur, until the 1140s all the existing charters of the counts of Champagne of which I know were prepared for ecclesiastical establishments or show in some way that it was a church that benefited from the recording of a given action in writing; we do not find charters issued to record the terms of lay feudal agreements. Bur explains it this way: 'The fief was the business of the laity. It belonged to the social world of word and gesture and left its mark in writing only in the case of alienation for the benefit of a church.'[19] The earliest charter I know recording a purely lay feudal agreement involving the count of Champagne is a notice of the homage which Thibaut II of Blois-Champagne made to the new duke of Burgundy, Odo II, in 1143. This extremely interesting charter, which names important witnesses from both courts, lists the major fiefs which Thibaut held from Odo. The charter was presumably written to serve the interests of the duke, who preserved it in his archives. There is no evidence to show that Thibaut kept a copy for his own records.[20] In 1156, four years after he had become count, Henry I reviewed the privileges granted by his father to the men of Lorraine who settled at Wassy. Probably Thibaut II had never issued a written charter to these settlers, and it is easy to imagine their conflicts with the *prévôt* of Wassy over the amounts they owed him. Eventually they came to the count to complain that the *prévôt* had frequently exceeded the agreement made by Thibaut II (*legem datam sepissime transivit*). Henry then increased their rates of payment (since, his charter noted, very few had brought along a gift in order to receive his grace) and granted a charter of franchise, the earliest I know from his territory. For the purposes of this paper, what is most interesting about this charter is not that it was issued, but that apparently the count did not keep a copy; as far as he and his chancery were concerned, he had no more need of a written record of the agreement than his father had.[21]

---

[18] The concluding annotation 'Nota Guillermi' (or the name of some other notary, often of a man whose writing does not appear on the charter) is a convention I have found only at the court of Champagne.

[19] Bur, *Formation*, p. 399.

[20] The charter was first published by Etienne Pérard, *Recueil de plusieurs pièces curieuses servant à l'histoire de Bourgogne* (Paris, 1664), p. 227. D'Arbois de Jubainville, who never found a copy in the documents of Champagne and did not identify Pérard's source, was uncertain of the authenticity of the charter; see his *Histoire*, 4, 886. This question was put to rest by Jean Richard, who found Pérard's source in the fifteenth-century 'Grand cartulaire des fiefs de la Chambre des comptes de Bourgogne', A.D. Côte-d'Or, B 10423, fol. 67; see his *Les ducs de Bourgogne et la formation du duché du XIe au XIVe siècle* (Paris, 1954), p. 30.

[21] Arbois, *Catalogue*, no. 40, ed. *Ordonnances*, VI, 314. [My catalogue, 1156e.] It was, of course, the beneficiaries of the charter of franchise who preserved it and presented it to Charles V in 1377 so that the king could confirm their then low rates.

Quite a different situation occurred a few years later, in 1158, when the count issued a charter that dealt with a feudal matter concerning a leading vassal. Thibaut II had granted a money-fief of 120 l. to his nephew, Archambaud de Sully, and after Thibaut's death Henry continued to make the annual payments. But Archambaud preferred quick cash to a steady income and mortgaged his fief for 550 l., with the understanding that he or his heirs could redeem the fief, that is, could receive 120 l. a year, anytime the principal was repaid. Henry duly recorded this commercial transaction affecting a vassalic relationship in a charter. The reason is clear. It is because Archambaud and his heirs would no longer receive the income which reminded them annually of their status as vassals. A written record therefore provided useful insurance against the fallible memories of men, though Henry naturally had his charter witnessed by leading men from his own and Archambaud's courts. And this time his clerks apparently kept a copy of the charter, eventually preserving its text in the thirteenth-century registers, where it is the next to oldest charter in that collection.[22]

Charters recording feudal obligations or political agreements that involved the count and his men but not members of the clergy were non-existent, or practically so, before the middle of the century. They became an accepted instrument for conducting affairs during the reigns of Henry I, his wife and sons, though the number of extant lay charters remains quite low. It was during the regency of Countess Blanche of Navarre and the reign of her son, Thibaut IV (Thibaut the Songwriter), that is, in the first half of the thirteenth century, that the writing of what I will call 'feudal charters' became a highly developed administrative form and their recording routine. It seems, in fact, that the chancery now frequently issued or solicited charters precisely in order to be able to place a copy in their own registers, much as bureaucratic memoranda are 'generated' today, and these registers were constructed for ready information retrieval. In the 'Cartulary of Countess Blanche' of about 1220, for

---

[22] D'Arbois, *Catalogue*, no. 53 [my collection 1158c], ed. Louis Chantereau-Le Fèvre, *Traité des fiefs et de leur origine* (Paris, 1662), *preuves*, p. 4. The charter appears in the *Cartulaire de M. de Thou*, B.N. lat. 5992, fol. 199v [written about 1230] and another register of about the same time, A.N. KK 1064, fol. 245. The oldest charter in these registers, the recognition that he could not alienate the guard of Chablis which Henry made very shortly after his father's death in early 1152, supports my point that at this time the count kept no systematic record of the commitments he made in writing. When in the thirteenth century the clerks who assembled the registers made a copy of this charter, which showed that Henry had granted the revenues of Chablis but not the *fidelitas* of its men to one of his leading vassals, Ansèric de Montréal, they transcribed a recent *vidimus* made by Stephen Langton and the archbishop of Tours from a copy kept by the abbey of St.-Martin of Tours; see d'Arbois, *Catalogue*, no. 1 [my catalogue, 1152a].

example, the contents are arranged not chronologically or geographically but according to the vassal concerned and a system of marginal tabs is provided to facilitate the finding of his name.

My concentration on charters has here moved us ahead too quickly in this account of the development of record-keeping. Were there twice the space available I would attempt to deal with the creation of fee-rolls or lists of vassals in the twelfth century, a practice that seems to have begun under Henry I of England (and Normandy) and to have spread more or less quickly to Sicily, Champagne, and the French royal domain. The earliest lists from Champagne, the *Feoda Campanie*, were produced in the 1170s, quite possibly at the end of that decade, when Count Henry was preparing to leave on crusade and needed to leave records in the hands of his wife and the administrators who would stay at home. The first lists are very simple, usually giving only a name or title, the entry *ligius* if the fief-holder was a liege-vassal, and frequently an indication that castle guard was owed. Only rarely is the location or nature of the fief recorded. Over the next fifty years the entries frequently become much more complex, though sometimes only a name is given and the approach seems largely to be retrospective. The next major step in record-keeping came in the 1220s, when it seems to have been common to record acts of homage as they were made, and for the vassal to make a declaration of his holding, an *aveu*, which could be agreed upon and recorded. It is from these thirteenth-century records that we can see the feudal structure of Champagne in all its complicated splendor. By working backwards from the later fee-rolls and by making use of the witness lists of twelfth-century charters and the information recorded in charters preserved in eccelesiastical archives, it is often possible to put some flesh on the bare bones of the primitive *Feoda Campanie* of the 1170s. Without information supplied from other sources, this earliest fee-roll from Champagne is scarcely usable except as a source of numbers and names, and often even the names of the vassals are not given in sufficient detail to make identification easy at a later time.

There is no evidence at all that any fee-roll existed in Champagne before the one prepared in the 1170s, and this one is so rudimentary that it is reasonable to believe that it was the first to be compiled. In short, though the chancery of Champagne had been established in the early twelfth century and was quite professional in what it produced during the reign of Henry I, there does not appear to have been any attempt to keep systematic records before the preparation of the first surviving fee-rolls in the 1170s. Those few lay agreements recorded in charters by the count's notaries seem to have interested them no more than the charters granted at the request of churches. Thus, without any systematic use of written materials, the counts of Champagne in the twelfth century constructed a remarkably complex feudal government, apparently trying to bring as many men of importance as possible into a direct relationship with the count through the granting of fiefs. By the 1170s approximately 1,900 barons and knights held one or more fiefs directly from the count.[23] Without the benefit of the elaborate feudal records used in the south – I am thinking of the *Liber Feudorum Maior* of Catalonia or the cartulary of the Guillem family of Montpellier[24] – the counts of Champagne had been able to build a principality and to construct an effective system of feudal relationships. The first rolls of the *Feoda Campanie* with their lists of hundreds of names were surely produced because the traditional undocumented or barely recorded feudal agreements had multiplied to such an extent that a written aid to memory was needed.

I can think of no good reason to avoid calling the feudal relations existing in Champagne in the 1170s a feudal system. Any ordered set of relationships can properly be called a system. A system may exist, however, without any of the participants knowing how to manipulate it very effectively. The full development of a feudal system came in Champagne in the half-century after the 1170s. The key activity in this development was not the writing of charters and other documents, for that had long been a familiar practice. What was new, what provided the basis for a form of medieval 'systems analysis', was not charter-writing but record-keeping.[25] When the count of Champagne deposited a copy of the *Feoda Campanie* in his church of Saint-Etienne of Troyes, when he added to it and revised it from time to time, and when he then began to collect the documents which provided precise evidence about the agreements he had made with his vassals, he created a new form of feudal system, a rationalized system he could and did manipulate consciously and effectively. Perhaps I should stress that this system, based on the keeping of records, was effective and rational, rational in an economic sense. It is quite the opposite of the opinion expressed by Michael Clancy with reference to the English royal archives of the late twelfth and thirteenth centuries. He says:

---

[23] Theodore Evergates, *Feudal Society in the Baillage of Troyes under the Counts of Champagne, 1152-1284* (Baltimore, 1975), p. 61 and notes.

[24] See *Liber Feudorum Maior*, ed. Francisco Miquel Rosell, 2 vols. (Barcelona, 1945) and *Liber Instrumentorum Memorialium: Cartulaire des Guillems de Montpellier*, ed. A. Germain (Montpellier, 1884-86), both with lay feudal documents going back to the tenth century. The *Liber Feudorum Maior*, compiled about 1195, was the product of a very recent reorganization of the Catalonian archives, made after a great bundle of charters and other documents had been redeemed from a Jewish moneylender in 1178; see Thomas N. Bisson, 'Feudalism in Twelfth-Century Catalonia' in *Structures féodales et féodalisme dans l'occident méditerranéen (Xe-XIIIe siècles)* (Rome, 1980), pp. 189-190.

[25] Thomas N. Bisson makes a similar point in 'The Problem of Feudal Monarchy: Aragon, Catalonia, and France', *Speculum* 53 (1978), 474, suggesting that under Philip Augustus for the first time 'the records of homages and fiefs were being multiplied routinely'.

It would be rash to assume that such archives brought a return of information to the government which balanced the worry and expense of making them. Like Domesday Book, the Chancery and judicial rolls and writ files benefited remote posterity rather than contemporaries... The making of such records is an indicator of the efficiency of the government rather than its cause. They are a notable step in the transition from memory to written record because documents created more documents in their own image, not because they made for more effective government in themselves.[26]

On the contrary, it is my conclusion that record-keeping was of great benefit to the count and his agents in the successful operation of government. The document printed below is an example of both record-keeping and systematic feudal relations as they had developed in Champagne in the early thirteenth century. The act, issued in the name of John of Le Thoult, was surely the result of negotiation but was probably drawn up by the count's chancery and favors the count in some quite subtle ways. It was recorded in at least three cartularies in order to facilitate information retrieval, and it was also listed in summary form in a section of the *Feoda Campanie* for the same reason. All of this record-keeping made it possible for the count to produce the text of the charter if necessary in order to settle a dispute resulting from the fact that John of Le Thoult held a fortified house from the count but was also the vassal of other men who might become the count's opponents. The clear intent of the charter, however, was not simply to provide evidence if a dispute arose, but to avoid conflict by anticipating alternative contingencies and announcing the consequences of various actions in a form that could be understood by those concerned. Indeed, these alternatives are set forth so clearly that they can be used to construct a game-player's contingency matrix or a game in normal form. What has happened here is that on the eve of a potential conflict with his rival Erard of Brienne, the count of Champagne bought up the service of John of Le Thoult and transferred John's primary allegiance from the count of Grandpré to himself, doing so in a way that put the count of Grandpré on notice that it would be to his disadvantage to side with Erard of Brienne in any conflict with Champagne. It would be hard to find a more sophisticated solution to the problem of multiple-vassalage, which is why historians from DuCange to Strayer have fastened on this charter as an illustration. Here clearly is a feudal system, and one cannot imagine this manipulation of it without the use of written records.

A modern analogy may by this time have occurred to my readers. It may reasonably be suggested that the use of written records transformed feudal relations and political and bureaucratic thinking in a way comparable to the computer revolution of today. Let me illustrate this

---

[26] Clanchy, p. 50.

comparison on two levels, one of detail and the other of structure.

On the level of detail, everyone who has coded material for a computer has learned that the implacable machine forces one to think in terms of clearly designated categories. Something is an *a* or a *b* or an 'I don't know', but the coder has to make some choice; at the same time, the process also leads one to see previously unperceived similarities, and at times to group both *a* and *b* into a new class *c*. This process can be seen in the charters and fee-rolls of the twelfth and thirteenth century. In the *Feoda Campanie*, for example, the clerks began to enter 'ligius' if a fief-holder was a liege-vassal and to enter nothing if he was not. Nothing, however, is a difficult coding to use positively, and so when the clerks were faced with the case of three men from the same family who had divided their obligations so that two were liege-vassals and one was not, they introduced a new term, 'planum hominium', to describe a case that had to be categorized positively because their list itself demanded an entry.[27] In the early eighteenth century this usage puzzled Nicolas Brussel, who concluded that there were three types of homage in Champagne, ordinary, *planum*, and liege. The product of a rational age, he considered that *planum* was to be distinguished from 'nothing' because he did not realize he was witnessing an early step in the rationalization of technical vocabulary.[28]

The opposite process of rethinking language and collapsing categories can be seen in a charter of 1225 issued by Pierre de Viry, the lord of Commenchon near Laon. Here the notary was faced with the problem of the proper way to refer to a woman, Heloïse de Maneux, who was one of Pierre's vassals. If she were male he would have used the term *homo* without a second thought. The word *femina* meant a bond-woman and could not be used in this instance. In oral discourse he could have found some circumlocution like 'this person' to avoid his difficulty, but he was composing his written record within a narrow set of coding conventions. And so he referred to Heloïse as *homo* and indicated his internal tension only by using the feminine adjective *mea*: 'Ego Petrus de Viri . . . notum facio . . quod nobilis mulier Helvidis de Manessies, homo mea, vendidit, etc.'[29] Here are two examples of linguistic invention which can fit under the rubric of 'Language and History'. They are details, but they illustrate

[27] 'Hi tres debent duas ligeitates et planum hominium' in *Feoda Campanie*, ed. Longnon, nos. 488-490.

[28] Du Cange, *Glossarium mediae et infimae latinitatis*, cites the *Feoda Campanie* in his discussion *s.v. Homagium Planum*, ed. Henschel, III, 683. His position that *homagium planum* was in simple contrast to liege homage was challenged by Nicolas Brussel, *Nouvel examen de l'usage général des fiefs en France* (Paris, 1727, repr. 1750), pp. 92-123. No one has yet replied to Brussel's argument in the detail which his evidence requires.

[29] Cartulary of Prémontré, Soissons, Bibl. mun., ms. 7. fol. 40, as published by Maximilien Melleville in *Bulletin de la Sociéte académique de Laon*, 4 (1855), 537-540.

the generalization that a new medium, though it is not itself the message, can produce changes in thought.

Let us now consider a much larger process of institutional change produced by the technologies of writing and record-keeping in the twelfth and thirteenth centuries and of computerization and information retrieval in the twentieth. What seems to happen with a new technology is that it is used first to make a familiar task simpler or more effective.[30] If someone wants a written charter instead of an oral promise, at first one issues a charter and forgets the matter. If one thinks a new set of administrators will have trouble remembering the names of hundreds of fief-holders, a written list may be created, but at first the notaries can be expected to use the list only as a supplement to human memory or as a simple substitute for it.[31]

The next stage is the one which makes technology a revolutionary force. As one works with either writing or a computer to do the familiar tasks more effectively, the instrument itself forces the user to think in new ways, and one consequence is that one begins to speculate on what one could now do that could not be done before. We see about us today the first effects of this new stage in computer technology, and in this paper I have been trying to show the same process at work in Champagne and northern France in the twelfth and thirteenth century. That written records create a powerful instrument for producing evidence is a commonplace in our literature. That they permit precision in contingency planning has been a less noticed consequence.[32] It is a consequence worth stressing, for charters of the type printed here below changed the feudal tie from what Strayer calls a mutual non-aggression pact to a contract of precise positive obligations that were treated systematically. The difference between the obligations of Roger of Mortemer and those of Jean of Le Thoult seems to me to exemplify the difference between the first and the second feudal age.

---

[30] 'In general, the more innovative uses of a new technology are likely to come later than the use of it to perform established functions more efficiently. The least innovative use is simply for an institution to transfer its existing information system to computers and exploit the lower access cost, by consulting the data more frequently. It requires some innovation, but not a great deal, for an organization to enter into more extensive sharing arrangements with other organizations possessing related information. What requires the greatest creativity is to uncover new uses of the powers of computerized information systems and the new information that these uses require.' See Roger G. Noll, 'Regulation and Computer Services', in *The Computer Age: A Twenty-Year View*, ed. Michael L. Dertouzos and Joel Moses (Cambridge, Mass., 1979), pp. 264-265.

[31] For example, a list in the *Feoda Campanie* begins, 'Isti milites sunt de feodo Braii juxta testimonium Girardi Eventati', ed. Longnon, p. 99.

[32] This point is perhaps only a gloss on a statement of Marc Bloch's in *Feudal Society*, p. 108: 'It is a significant fact in the history of the relation of thought and practice – still so obscure a subject – that towards the end of the twelfth century men of action had at their disposal a more efficient instrument of mental analysis than that which had been available to their predecessors.'

Appendix

1217, November 28

John of Le Thoult makes known that he is the liege vassal of Blanche, countess of Troyes, and her son, Thibaut [IV], count of Champagne, except for the liege homage he owes the lords of Coucy and Arcis and the count of Grandpré. He also states the terms by which he holds his maison forte *of Herbigny.*

- A. Original lost.
- B. 'Cartulary of Countess Blanche', written about 1220, B.N. ms. lat. 5993. fol. 94-94v.
- C. 'Cartulary of M. de Thou', written about 1230, B.N. ms. lat. 5992, fol. 223-224.
- D. Cartulary called *Liber principum*, written about 1270, lost.
- E. Copy of *D*, 16th cent., B.N., 500 de Colbert, vol. 58, fol. 208-208v.
- F. Another copy of *D*, 16th cent., B.N. n.a.l. 2454, fol. 589-589v.
- a. Louis Chantereau-Le Febvre, *Traité des fiefs* (Paris, 1662), *preuves*, pp. 88-89, after *D*.

Excerpt: DuCange, *Glossarium*, s.v. *ligius*, after *a*.
Partial trans.: Joseph R. Strayer, *Feudalism* (Princeton, 1968), pp. 146-147, after DuCange.
Ind.: Henri d'Arbois de Jubainville, *Catalogue*, no. 1093.

B

Ego Johannes de Tullo universis presentibus et futuris notum facio quod ego ligius homo sum domine B., comitisse Trecen., et karissimi domini mei Th., comitis Campanie, nati eius, contra omnem creaturam que possit vivere et mori, salva ligeitate domini Ingelrandi
5 de Cociaco, domini Johannis de Arceiis, et . . . comitis Grandis Prati.[33] Si autem contingeret comitem Grandis Prati guerram habere in capite et pro querela propria contra comitissam et comitem Campanie, ego in propria persona juvarem comitem Grandis Prati et mitterem comitisse et comiti Campanie, si me submonerent, milites ad deservendum feodum quod
10 teneo de ipsis. Si vero comes Grandis Prati comitissam et comitem Campanie guerriaret pro amicis suis et non pro querela propria, ego juvarem in persona propria comitissam et comitem Campanie, et comiti Grandis Prati mitterem unum militem pro meo feodo deserviendo, sed non irem in terram comitis Grandis Prati ad forefaciendum. Ceterum de
15 comitissa et comite Campanie cepi in feodo et homagio ligio domum meam de Harbignies, jurabilem et reddibilem eis quandocumque voluerunt et ab ipsis vel ab altero eorum aut a mandato eorum fuero requisitus. Et quando erunt extra essonium suum, ipsi tenentur eam michi reddere ita munitam sicut eam invenerunt. Propter hoc autem ipsi comitissa et

---

[33] Henri V was count of Grandpré at this time; the two dots indicate that the statement applies to *any* count of Grandpré.

20 comes Campanie michi et heredibus meis dederunt viginti libratas annui
    redditus, reddendas michi et heredibus meis in perpetuum singulis
    annis in nundinis sancti Aygulfi de Pruvino. Dederunt quoque michi
    ducentas libras de auxilio ad firmandam predictam domum meam. Quod ut
    notum permaneat et firmum teneatur, litteris annotatum sigilli mei
25 munimine roboravi. Actum anno gratie .M°.CC°. septimo decimo, die
    martis ante festum sancti Andree.

I, John of Le Thoult, make known to all present and to come that I am the liege vassal (*ligius homo*) of Madame Blanche, countess of Troyes, and of my most dear lord, Thibaut, count of Champagne, her son, against all creatures capable of life and death [i.e., not against spiritual beings], except for the ligience (*ligietas*) of Lord Enguerrand of Coucy, Lord John of Arcis, and the count of Grandpré. If indeed it should come to pass (*Si autem contingeret*) that the count of Grandpré should be at war with the countess and count of Champagne for his own grievance and when not in another's service (*in capite et pro querela propria*), I should aid the count of Grandpré personally and, if they summon me, should send the countess and count of Champagne knights to perform the service of the fief I hold from them. If, however, the count of Grandpré is at war with the countess and count of Champagne on behalf of his friends and not because of his own grievances, I should serve the countess and count of Champagne and should send the count of Grandpré one knight to perform the service of my fief, but I should not enter the land of the count of Grandpré to attack him.

Moreover I received from the countess and count of Champagne as a fief and by liege homage my house (*domus*) of Herbigny on oath and returnable (*jurabilis et reddibilis*) to them whenever they wish, and I will be answerable to them or to either of them or to their command. And when they have gone beyond the term of their notice (*erunt extra essonium suum*), they shall be held to return it to me equipped and provisioned just as they found it. Because of this fief the said countess and count of Champagne gave to me and my heirs twenty pounds of annual revenue to be paid to me and my heirs annually forever at the fair of Saint-Ayoul of Provins. Also they gave me two hundred pounds of aid to fortify my aforesaid house.

So that this should remain known and be held as established, I have confirmed that which has been set down in writing with the support of my seal. Enacted in the year of grace 1217, Tuesday before the feast of St. Andrew [28 November].

Note: See the rolls of fiefs of Thibaut IV, *Feoda ballivie Meldensis per litteras* (ed. Longnon, no. 5293): 'Lord John of Le Thoult holds the *maison forte* of Herbigny on oath and returnable. Because of this the count gave him 20 pounds income from the fairs of Saint-Ayoul and 200 pounds to fortify the *maison*.' [Herbigny is in the Ardennes, near Novion-Porcien.]

* * *

Contingencies for service of John of Le Thoult
in conflict between counts of Grandpré and Champagne
[John can serve with self and N knights]

	John owes Count of Champagne	Count of Grandpré
When Grandpré is fighting on his own grievance	substitute service (N knights)	personal service (self)
When Grandpré is fighting on behalf of others	personal service (self + N-1 knights)	substitute service (1 knight)
When there is no conflict between the two lords	full service (self + N knights, if needed)	full service (self + N kights, if needed)

III

SELF AND INDIVIDUALITY

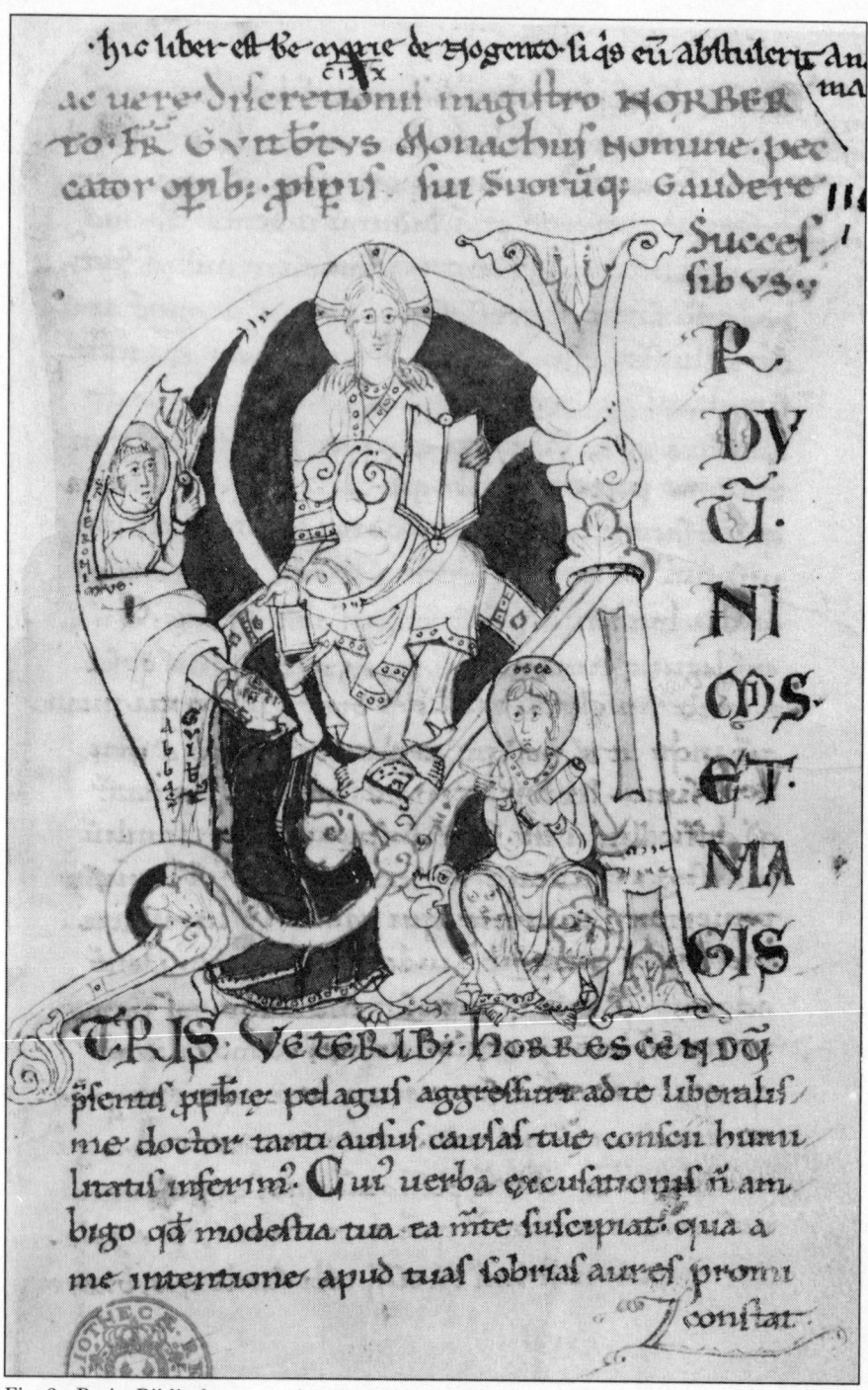

Fig. 3. Paris, Bibliotheque nationale, MS latin 2502, f. 1r

15

The Personality of Guibert de Nogent

In the current collaboration of history and psychoanalysis, Clio benefits more than her partner. The historian for his part can offer material that seems to justify faith in the psychic unity of mankind; a close view of a twelfth-century individual, for example, can support the notion that medieval people were not so different from ourselves as to be incomprehensible. If the material is particularly rich, it may even be possible to test – in an impressionistic way, to be sure – whether a given analytic theory is extensible in time, just as anthropologists test theories in other living cultures. History can greatly increase the range, if not the depth, of case studies.

In this study of the development and personality of Guibert of Nogent, who is unmatched among medieval authors for what he tells of his own childhood and his feelings about his parents, the historical material is arranged in a pattern which owes much to Freud and Erikson. The test of the applicability of this pattern is whether it leads to a richer understanding of the subject's life and works than have previous patterns based on different preconceptions, particularly whether it makes sense of otherwise unrelated details and provides an explanation of uncommon behaviour. Historians have long agreed that this obscure monk, known only because of his writings, was an unusual man, but they have not attempted an explanation of why he struck them as different, or in fact, as peculiarly modern. Economic historians and social psychologists have

---

* This article appears in a slightly different form as the Introduction to *Self and Society in Medieval France: The Memoirs of Abbot Guibert of Nogent (1064?-c. 1125)*, New York: Harper Torchbooks, 1970 – a revision of the translation by C. C. Swinton Bland of the Latin text (entitled *Guibert de Nogent: Histoire de sa vie*), edited by Georges Bourgin (Paris, 1907). Parenthetical references within the following text refer to the book and chapter number of the Latin text, and to the page number of the Torchbook translation.

The preparation of this study was made possible by a grant from the Penrose Fund of the American Philosophical Society.

made major contributions to the understanding of collective behaviour and mentality, but the historian who is concerned with those individuals who stand out from the crowd has the most to gain from the psychoanalyst.

What has struck modern historians as unusual about this Benedictine monk who played only a minor role in his own day and is barely mentioned in the writings of his contemporaries? In the first place, he was the author of what the great historian of autobiographical writing Georg Misch calls the first 'comprehensive' autobiography in medieval Latin.[1] The example of Augustine's *Confessions* lay behind it, but medieval authors seldom followed the demanding example of Augustine's great work of self-examination.[2] When Abelard wanted to write about himself, he wrote a letter (or at least used that form), and we know such men as Bernard of Clairvaux and Peter the Venerable as intimately as we do because of their letter collections. That Guibert was willing to invite a comparison with Augustine by beginning his work with the word *Confiteor* is indicative of the extraordinarily high standard of self-expression he set for himself.

Secondly, Guibert's treatise on relics, *De pignoribus sanctorum*, in which he attacked the alleged tooth of the Saviour venerated at the abbey of Saint-Médard of Soissons and more generally superstition and the cult of relics as practiced in his day, shows that he had marked critical abilities. Abel Lefranc, writing in 1896, was ecstatic about this treatise, which he called 'absolutely unique', and about its author, 'truly enamored with rationalism', whom he compared with Rabelais, Calvin, and Voltaire. 'He was the first who tried to provide a total view, systematic and rational, on the questions of the cult of the saints and their relics.'[3] Bernard Landry joined in calling Guibert's example 'unique', and Charles Haskins said that he 'showed striking skepticism'. Marc Bloch thought that Lefranc had exaggerated Guibert's critical sense, but still called it 'quite sharp, rare indeed in the twelfth century'.[4]

Admiration for Guibert's critical mind has also been based on his

---

[1] *Geschichte der Autobiographie*, III, 2 (Frankfurt am Main, 1959), p. 109.

[2] Pierre Courcelle, *Les confessions de Saint Augustin dans la tradition littéraire* (Paris, 1963), esp. pp. 272-275.

[3] 'Le traité des reliques de Guibert de Nogent et les commencements de la critique historique au moyen âge' in *Etudes d'histoire du moyen âge dédiées à Gabriel Monod* (Paris, 1896), pp. 285, 298, 304. For a modern study which shows Guibert's relationship to other medieval critics of relics, see Klaus Schreiner, 'Discrimen veri ac falsi,' *Archiv für Kulturgeschichte*, XLVIII (1966), 1-53.

[4] Landry, 'Les idées morales du XIIe siècle. VII. Un chroniqueur: Guibert de Nogent,' *Revue des cours et conférences*, année 1938-39, II, 350; Haskins, *The Renaissance of the Twelfth Century* (Cambridge, Mass., 1927), p. 235; Bloch, *Les rois thaumaturges* (new ed., Paris, 1961), pp. 29 and 30, n. 1.

history of the First Crusade, the *Gesta Dei per Francos*.[5] In this book Guibert cites his written sources, discusses the problem of not being an eyewitness, and is methodically critical of the validity (as well as the style) of his predecessors' work, among other things challenging some of the miracles reported by Fulcher of Chartres. Bernard Monod was so impressed by Guibert's historical method that he called him 'the most intellectual man of his century' and came very close to suggesting that Guibert shared the virtues of the contemporary school of scientific history.[6] Lefranc had earlier come to the same conclusion, saying that Guibert was 'better prepared than anyone of his time to glimpse some of the essential rules of historical criticism'.[7] In 1965, Jacques Chaurand swept much of this praise away by arguing that Guibert shows the training not of a critical historian but of a moralizing Biblical exegete.[8] Chaurand's view is preferable, but while the anachronism of Lefranc and Monod should be qualified, still it is true that Guibert showed an unusual desire and ability to dispute with other authors on rational grounds.

A third facet of his thought which has struck historians as unusual or precocious is his patriotism. 'At no time in the twelfth century was the pride of being French expressed so forcefully,' Landry wrote in reference to a spirited defense of the French which Guibert made to the archdeacon of Mainz. Warming up to his subject as he thought later about his conversation with the archdeacon, Guibert had called his people 'noble, wise, warlike, generous, and elegant'. Their very name was a word of praise, so that 'if we see Bretons, Englishmen, or Genoese behaving honorably, we call such men *frank*.'[9] Guibert had an eye for national differences — he was the first to describe for us a Scot wearing a kilt and sporran (II, 5; p. 137)[10] — and he was sure that God had established the French to lead the rest of the world. He was also the first to record unequivocally that a French king could cure scrofula by touch. He added that he knew the English king had never had the audacity to try it.[11] With his patriotism Guibert combined a strong sense of modernity. Joining in the debate over the relative virtues of the ancients and moderns, Guibert stressed the superiority of his own time. Not for him dwarfs sitting on the shoulders of giants; instead he quoted King Roboam: 'Our little fingers

---

[5] Critical edition in *Recueil des historiens des croisades. Historiens occidentaux*, IV (Paris, 1879), 115-263, hearafter cited as *Gesta Dei*, with page references to this edition.

[6] 'De la méthode historique chez Guibert de Nogent,' *Revue historique*, LXXXIV (1904), 51-70, esp. 52.

[7] 'Traité', p. 289.

[8] 'La conception de l'histoire de Guibert de Nogent,' *Cahiers de civilisation médiévale*, VIII (1965), 381-395.

[9] Landry, 'Idées morales,' p. 356; *Gesta Dei*, II, 1, p. 136.

[10] For the kilt, see *Gesta Dei*, I, 1, p. 125.

[11] Bloch, *Rois thaumaturges*, pp. 29-32, 46.

are thicker than the backs of our fathers.'[12]

Nineteenth-century historians were drawn to Guibert by his rationalism, skepticism, and protonationalism. In that condescending fashion with which historians sometimes grant awards, Lefranc called him 'practically a modern man'.[13] But other commentators have noted a dark side to his character, expressed in his violent and scurrilous denunciations of his enemies. In the *Gesta Dei*, he announces that Mohammed preached 'a new license of promiscuous intercourse', and tells a detailed story of his evil life and end. In the process he admits that his sources are questionable, but explains that 'it is safe to speak evil of one whose malignity exceeds whatever ill can be spoken.'[14] Throughout his history Guibert dwells immoderately on the lusts and sexual crimes, both natural and unnatural, of the Moslems. He was also among the first anti-Semitic writers to accuse the Jews of witchcraft and black magic. After relating Guibert's gross story (I, 26; p. 115) of a monk tempted by the Devil, who had been conjured up by a Jewish physician, Joshua Trachtenberg commented in *The Devil and the Jews*: 'To one who is familiar with the later accounts of the witches' and sorcerers' ritual the early appearance of the sperm libation and the act of communion with sperm [in this part of Guibert's book] must provide a particularly revealing insight into the development of witchcraft out of purported heretical practice.'[15] In addition, Guibert provides one of the most vivid descriptions of the unnatural devices of the dualist heretics of his day (III, 17; p. 212). And, besides what he says about Moslems, Jews, and heretics, he is a prime source for stories about the license, depravity, and violence of those with whom he was associated.

This survey of some of the ways Guibert has seemed unusual or precocious or simply interesting has drawn freely upon the words of others to make a point. The traditional comparative approach of intellectual history permits a critic to say that his subject is either 'typical' or 'owes his ideas to some other source', or, as in the case of Guibert, is 'exceptional' or even 'unique'. But medievalists rarely discuss how or why their subjects became typical or unusual people, even when the materials for such an investigation are as readily available as they are in this instance. If we are to have a fuller understanding of this unusual man, our approach must be developmental as well as comparative.

Unfortunately for us, Guibert did not think of his personal reflections as

---

[12] *Gesta Dei*, I, 1, p. 123; cf. III Kings 12:10.
[13] 'Traité', p. 286.
[14] These quotations are noted in Norman Daniel, *Islam and the West: The Making of an Image* (Edinburgh, 1960), p. 145, and Richard W. Southern, *Western Views of Islam in the Middle Ages* (Cambridge, Mass., 1962), p. 31.
[15] New York, 1966, p. 213.

a formal autobiography.[16] He addressed this book to God, Who 'knoweth the secrets of the heart,' and wrote it for the edification of his readers and to provide material for sermons. Modern readers more interested in history or personality than in Guibert's spiritual message may regret that the author buried the story of his life in the religious conclusions that gave it meaning to him. Digging is required, but with application it is possible to put together a reasonably coherent account of the course of his life.

Guibert fails to tell us three pieces of information with which modern biographical statements usually begin: when and where he was born and who his family were. Dom Mabillon, who was once a monk at Guibert's abbey of Nogent and studied him carefully, calculated that he was born in 1053, and, backed by the authority of the great seventeenth-century scholar, that date now appears as an established fact. It really is not soundly based, however, and my conclusion is that a date in the mid-1060's, perhaps 1064, is much more likely. The place of his birth has been disputed. Although Mabillon was confident that he was born in Clermont-en-Beauvaisis, others have argued for Beauvais or other places, or have left the matter up in the air. The weight of the evidence shows, however, that Mabillon was right about his birthplace. As for his family, Guibert gives us tantalizing hints which have suggested to many that he was a scion of the baronage of Picardy. It is more likely, however, that he was descended from a family which guarded the castle of Clermont and who were vassals of the future counts of Clermont, and that he was therefore a member of a family which was noble and influential in a small locality, but was neither wealthy nor highly placed.[17]

What was more important to Guibert than the details of a biographical entry was his personal development. He was born on Holy Saturday, a day which seemed to him and his mother to involve a special dedication. The labor was difficult. Guibert was a tiny baby who seemed unlikely to live, and his mother almost died. The extreme danger of the labor led his father to dedicate the life of his unborn child to God, and Guibert had later to carry with him the knowledge that his birth had almost caused his mother's death.

Some eight months later, his father died. His mother never remarried, and Guibert remained for ever her youngest child and her consolation in her widowhood. Guibert had older siblings, but he tells us so little of them that we do not even know how many were in the family. An elder brother,

---

[16] Although both d'Achery and Bourgin called this book *De vita sua*, Guibert did not use this title or treat the book as an autobiography. He referred to the work as *Monodiae*, which literally means 'songs for one voice' and may be translated as *Memoirs*. For this title, see Migne, *Patrologia latina*, t. 156, col. 622. This volume contains Guibert's collected works; it will be cited hereafter as Migne's edition (ed. Migne).

[17] The evidence for these statements is discussed in Appendix I of *Self and Society*, referred to in the note on the first page of this article.

who was perhaps eight or ten years older, followed his father's military career and held an important position at Clermont as a young man. Guibert mentions in passing that at the time of their mother's death he and a brother had left the abbey of Saint-Germer, where they had been together, and were then busy at the abbey of Nogent (II, 4; p. 133). This passage is our only indication that Guibert shared his monastic life at Saint-Germer with an older brother, who later placed himself under Guibert's authority at Nogent. Guibert expresses neither love nor warm feelings for any member of his family except his mother. Of his relations with his siblings he tells us only that he was his mother's favorite (I, 3; p. 41) and that his brother had earned his punishment in hell (I, 18; p. 95).

From his mother, Guibert received indulgent care if not warm love. The boy in turn loved and admired his mother and saw her as by far the most important human influence on his life. No uncle or other male relative took responsibility for bringing up this orphan, and since he was to be a cleric he was not sent to the court of a relative or feudal superior to be raised. What sort of woman was this widow left to mold her cherished son? From Guibert's description it appears that she was a person of beauty, pride, intelligence, and determination, able to stand up to her husband's relatives and to exercise authority, and vigorous in protecting her child and advancing his interests. But above all Guibert saw her as modest and virtuous, particularly in sexual matters. As a young girl 'she had learned to be terrified of sin, not from experience, but from dread of some sort of blow from on high, and – as she often told me herself – this dread had possessed her mind with the terror of sudden death' (I, 12; p. 64). No doubt her dread affected her young husband, too, for at the beginning of his marriage Guibert's father was afflicted with impotence and could not consummate his marriage for years. During this troubled time, rich neighbors tried to seduce the virgin bride, but she resisted them all. Finally, Guibert's father was able to break the spell of impotence, seen by all as a knot of bewitchment, by conceiving a child with another woman, and and only after this did Guibert's mother begin to have conjugal relations with her husband.

Guibert grew up with a sense of modesty and a determination to strive for absolute sexual self-control. His views can be seen most explicitly in a little statement on 'Why the private parts of the body are covered', which he inserted in the tract on the Incarnation which he directd against the Jews. Here is the beginning of his comment.

> Certain people ask why we clothe those parts of the body so carefully, since we cover no other parts with such attention. Not only do we hide them, but also we scarcely permit the places near them, including the navel and the thighs, to be seen. And why? When my finger, my eyes, my lips move, they move at my direction, by my will, and since they act docilely under my authority, they

occasion me no shame. But since those members we are considering are driven toward unbridled activity by a certain liberty acting against the rules of reason, it is as if there were a separate law in our members, as St. Paul puts it, fighting against the law of our mind and leading us captive in the law of sin that is in our members (Romans 7:23). Therefore quite properly we blush, since whether we like it or not, we appear to be shamefully erected out of passionate desire.[18]

The influence of a censorious mother who had nearly destroyed the potency of her husband and who we are told remained strictly celibate after his death became a part of Guibert's being. His writing abounds with denunciations of the sexual depravity of his male relatives, of nobles whom he disliked, of monks and church officials with whom he came in contact, of practically all women of his own generation in contrast to those of his mother's time. Revulsion from sexuality is also a major theme of his religious writing. His commentary on the first verse of Genesis, written when he was under twenty, took as its theme the struggle of spirit and flesh. Before the Fall, spirit and flesh were in perfect harmony, but now, he says, 'the disobedience of concupiscence is in control, calling us against our wills to indecent movement.'[19]

And so Guibert looked back to his childhood with nostalgia as a time when he was free of the torment of sexuality. As he went on to say in the tract on the Incarnation: 'We see infants and often boys short of puberty displaying themselves naked without shame. If they suffered any excitement, they would surely embarrass themselves or those who happened to meet them. How blessed was the primal condition of Adam and Eve! How happy the ignorance of childhood, since while it is protected by incapacity, it enjoys the security of the angels.'[20]

We may also see the influence of Guibert's childhood in his fastidiousness about bodily cleanliness and his association of excrement with punishment. The reader will note that Guibert goes out of his way to tell stories which involve privies, sewers, and excrement; for instance, he relates a pair of tales in which men who defy religion are struck down with a loosening of the bowels (III, 18; pp. 216-217). In the *Gesta Dei*, we even have a chance to see how Guibert reshaped his sources. The *Gesta Francorum* which Guibert used reported simply that Guillaume of Grandmesnil and his companions deserted from the army at Antioch by

---

[18] Ed. Migne, cols. 496-497. The thought is thoroughly Augustinian: cf. *The City of God*, XIII, 13 and *Marriage and Concupiscence*, I, 6, 7, ed. Corpus Scriptorum Ecclesiasticorum Latinorum XLII (Vienna, 1902), 218-219.

[19] Ed. Migne, col. 33. Guibert's theme is in the tradition of Augustine and Gregory the Great. These comments on Guibert's personal outlook are not meant to minimize the importance of his sources, but to add to our understanding of the vitality of the tradition.

[20] *Ibid.*, col. 497.

climbing down the wall, but Guibert composed a little poem saying that they had crawled out through filthy sewers, after which the skin fell off their hands and feet, leaving the bare bones exposed.[21]

After Guibert had mastered his alphabet, his mother engaged a local grammarian on the striking condition that he give up his other teaching and tutor her son alone. And so as a boy Guibert was denied a chance for rough play or for companionship with other boys in which he could measure himself and his abilities directly against others. Instead, he saw his peers through the moralizing comments of his mother and his tutor. Consider this description of his cousin, whose instruction his teacher had given up to take employment in Guibert's household. He 'was handsome and of good birth, but he was so eager to avoid proper studies and unsteady under all instruction, a liar and a thief, as far as his age would allow, that he never could be found in productive activity and hardly ever in school, but almost every day played truant in the vineyards' (I, 4; p. 46). Nothing in his book suggests that Guibert ever had any close friends.

From six to twelve, his mother and tutor saw to it that his future calling as a monk set Guibert apart. He had to find satisfaction in discipline and virtue, for other pleasures were not permitted. He was forbidden to play childish games, to leave his tutor's company, to eat away from home, to accept presents without permission, or to have a holiday even on Sundays or festivals. 'In everything,' he says, 'I had to show self-control in word, look, and deed' (I 5; p.46).

As was usual at the time, Guibert was severely beaten if he was unable to satisfy his demanding teacher. After an infancy of indulgence came a boyhood which he remembered as a time of frequent and unjustified punishment. How could he bear it? In desperation, he found two lines of internal defense. The first was that his teacher truly loved him and meant the punishment for his own good. The second defense was that his natural endowment and ability were far greater than those of his teacher, and that if he failed it was because of his teacher's failings. This defense was probably strengthened and perhaps encouraged openly by his mother, who had bound up so much of herself in her son's success. But although Guibert could use his sense of his teacher's incompetence as a balm for his outrage, his mother held him to the path of virtue, hard work, and success. Distressed by the beatings her son received and torn by the feeling (surely unrealistic) that his body might suffer less if he trained as a knight rather

---

[21] *Gesta Dei*, V, 14, p. 194; cf. *Gesta Francorum*, ed. Rosalind Hill (London, 1962), pp. 56-57. Since the family of Grandmesnil was bound to his by ties of friendship, Guibert suppressed the name in his account. The anonymous author of the *Gesta Francorum* also informed Guibert in a straightforward manner that the Italians besieged in the castle of Xerigordo were reduced to drinking their urine; Guibert passes on the story, adding that it was 'horrible to relate'. See *Gesta Dei*, II, 10, p. 144, and *Gesta Francorum*, pp. 3-4.

than a clerk, she still rejoiced with his teacher when her little son declared, 'If I had to die on the spot, I would not give up studying my lessons and becoming a clerk' (I, 6; p. 50). The positive result of this experience to Guibert was that he carried over to adult life humane and sensitive ideas about the education of children.

When Guibert was about twelve years old, his mother withdrew from the world and retired to a little house she had built near the abbey of Saint-Germer of Fly, some thirty miles from Clermont, and shortly thereafter his tutor became a monk at the abbey, where he eventually rose to the position of prior. Guibert, now possessing what he called 'a perverted liberty', began 'without any self-control to abuse my power, to mock at churches, to detest school, to try to gain the company of my lay cousins devoted to knightly pursuits'. Free for the first time to amuse himself as he pleased, this boy on the edge of puberty began to wear his clerical clothes 'on wanton pursuits which my age did not permit, to emulate older boys in their juvenile rowdiness, to behave without responsibility or discretion'. But significantly the culmination of his list of misdeeds was that most passive form of pleasure, excessive sleep, in which he indulged so thoroughly 'that my body began to degenerate' (I, 15; p.77).

His mother heard with distress of Guibert's behavior and urged the abbot of Saint-Germer to receive her son into the monastery for training. As soon as Guibert entered the church of Saint-Germer, he conceived a longing for the monastic life which never grew cold. He told his mother of his desire, but at this point both she and his tutor, thinking him not yet ready for permanent vows, opposed his wishes. Finally, after delaying from late spring till Christmas, Guibert defied the immediate preference of his mother and tutor to begin at once the life for which they had prepared him.

In the monastery, control by his mother and master was replaced by that of the abbot and the community as a whole. If Guibert had not learned self-discipline and how to internalize his aggressive feelings before, he had every inducement to do so now. The Benedictine Rule (chs. 24 and 25) provides that if any of the brethren commits a slight fault, he is to be excluded from the common meal and the oratory, and if his offense is more serious, none of his fellows is to associate with him or speak to him till he is repentant. This was the rule of discipline with which Guibert was to live from the age of thirteen until his death.

As a young monk, Guibert plunged into his studies. Many a night he read under a blanket or made compositions when he was supposed to be asleep. His motive, he said, was 'chiefly to win praise, that greater honor in this present world might be mine' (I, 15; p 78). In his fantasies he daydreamed of power and success. Other monks were hostile to him, an emotion which he attributed to jealousy. Guibert denied to himself and to God that he hated his opponents, who declared that 'I was too proud of my little learning' (I, 16; p. 84), though he felt that they hated him. Their envy did not provoke open resentment, but sullenness (*acedia*), and he sought to resolve his problem by withdrawal, hoping 'with the aid of my relatives to be able to transfer to some other monastery' (I, 16; p. 83).

In his literary studies, Guibert was at first caught up in religious works 'and thought my reading vain if I found in it no matter for meditation, nothing leading to repentance' (I, 15; p. 79). But as he grew older he set aside the divine pages for 'worthless vanities' and read Ovid and the *Bucolics* of Virgil. He even wrote love poems in secret, often passing them off as another's work but taking great pleasure in the praise they received, and 'caught by the unrestrained stirring of my flesh through thinking on these things and the like' (I. 17; p. 87). His old tutor censured him severely, however, and the Lord punished him, as he felt, with affliction of the soul and bodily infirmity. Finally, 'the folly of useless learning withered away' (I. 17; p. 88). The rich vocabulary and copious classical allusions of his later writings are a monument, however, to how much Guibert learned from his studies.

As a teen-age writer, Guibert managed to direct much of his energy into a treatise on virginity, quoting Ovid and Terence in the most moral fashion and noting the protection provided by the monastic vocation. In this treatise he revealed his bent for rational criticism by attacking the assertion of Eusebius of Caesarea that St. Paul had been married and by rejecting the alleged letter of Jesus to Abgar which Eusebius included in his *Ecclesiastical History*.[22] He could not subject to rational control the terrors of his dreams, however, and in his sleep he was visited by 'visions of dead men, chiefly those whom I had seen or heard of as slain by swords or some such death' (I,15; p. 79). These dreams were so terrifying that the watchful protection of his master was needed to keep him quietly in bed and to prevent him from losing his wits. That Guibert looked upon his own sexuality with loathing can be seen throughout his writing: in addition, it is possible that an inclination toward homosexuality, violently suppressed on the conscious level, added to his terrors at this time.

Guibert dealt with his twin problems of ambition and carnal itch, which he himself saw as closely associated (I, 16; p. 82), in the most positive way open to him: he applied himself assiduously to the hard work of study. Encouraged and taught by St. Anselm, who frequently visited Saint-Germer while he was at the abbey of Bec, Guibert eventually began to think of writing sermons and scriptural commentary himself. Knowing, as he said, that Abbot Garnier would be annoyed by his efforts at writing, Guibert begged for his permission, managing to suggest that he had only a brief work in mind. He then started on the ambitious project of a commentary on all of Genesis, beginning of course with the Hexameron. When Garnier found that the young monk, then short of twenty, was

---

[22] Ed. Migne, cols. 579-608. For the criticism of Eusebius, see col. 587.

commenting on the story of Creation, a subject traditionally reserved for mature scholars, he ordered him to stop. But Guibert continued to work in secret, and when Garnier retired about 1084, he quickly brought the book to completion and began other writing (I, 17; p. 91).

For the next twenty years, Guibert remained a simple monk at Saint-Germer. His relatives began to seek a higher position for him, hoping, he says, to acquire an abbacy or other post through simony. Guibert's account is that although he was driven by ambition, he did not wish to reveal his 'nakedness' by mounting to office on the steps of simony (I, 19 p. 97). Another limitation is that probably his family could not afford to pay very much. Whatever the reasons, their negotiations produced nothing. And then, when he had finally resigned himself to a humble life, there came the offer of the abbacy of Nogent. The renown of his writing, and not simony, had brought him the post, Guibert reports proudly. By his own efforts he had written himself out of obscurity.

In 1104, at about forty, Guibert left Saint-Germer, and in fact, for the first time in his life, left his mother, who was vexed at his appointment and reminded him that he was not well-trained in legal matters. Nogent was a small abbey, founded in 1059 with an endowment Guibert called sufficient for six monks, and it appears always to have been rather poor. But it provided him with an abbacy, and Guibert made the most of it. Freed from immediate authority, he wrote to his heart's content: his history of the crusade (c. 1108), his memoirs (1115), Biblical commentaries, a tract praising the Virgin and recording some of her miracles, and the treatise on relics (c. 1125). In his twenty years as abbot, we see him involved in ecclesiastical affairs, attending the court of the bishop of Laon and larger councils, and at one time traveling to Langres to see the pope. But we know very little of Guibert's thoughts about life at Nogent. Although the *Memoirs* are quite frank about Saint-Germer, Guibert is very reticent about his position as abbot at Nogent and says nothing about any individual monk. Clearly he thought it neither useful nor edifying for his monks to know too much about their abbot or his feelings toward them. This restraint is illustrated by his brief reference to a crisis at Nogent which became so serious that Guibert retired for a while to his monastery of Saint-Germer, which still drew him even though his mother had been dead for two years. After his eventual return to Nogent, Guibert referred to this flight as 'ignominious', and rather than explaining himself he avoided giving any details about the event (II, 4; p. 133). In order to fill out his section on Nogent, he reverted to stories about life at Saint-Germer.

Characteristically Guibert avoided conflict or direct confrontation by retreat or dissimulation. He was aware of this trait, and illustrated it himself in his treatise on relics. As he told the tale, he was once present at a harangue, where a relicmonger (probably from the cathedral of Laon) was hawking his wares. 'I have here in this little box a piece of the bread

which Our Lord chewed with his own teeth. And if you don't believe me',
he said, pointing at Guibert, 'here is a distinguished man whose vast
learning you all know. He will confirm what I say, if there is any need'.
Guibert blushed and kept silent, he tells us, frightened by the presence of
those supporting the speaker, whom he says he ought to have denounced
on the spot. His defense to himself was to repeat a jingle based on
Boethius:

> Jure insanus judicarer,
> Si contra insanos altercarer.

> (If against the mad I strain,
> I'd be rightly thought insane.)[23]

In his writing, however, Guibert remained a critic to the end. But
although his common sense and his dislike of ignorance and superstition
can be seen throughout his work, Guibert's use of his keen mind did not
lead him to embrace the new rationalism of the early twelfth century. In
his commentary on Hosea, dictated when he could no longer make use of
his own hands or eyes, he denounced those 'who presume to discuss and
examine the dogmas of the church on which they had once been
nourished, treating like something new matters defined by God and the
Fathers . . . We see this today with certain grammarians, who blindly seek
to shine in commenting not only on Holy Scripture but even on any given
heavenly mystery.'[24] Guibert may well have known Abelard at Laon.
Here we have the judgment of the older generation of moral
commentators on the new scholastics.

There is, in fact, a consistent conservatism in Guibert's religious
writing. His tropological commentaries were in the tradition of Gregory
the Great, and he could barely bring himself to differ with that saint.
When he differed with his contemporaries, as often happened, it was not
to rationalize religion but to purify it, to rid the Church of false relics and
superstition. In part, he seems simply to have been expressing his distaste
for the veneration of bones, teeth, hair, and bits of skin. But his turning
from the physical world led to a mystical apprehension of the spiritual.
The conflict of flesh and spirit runs through his works; it is, in fact, the
interpretation he gave to the first verse of Genesis and he carried the
theme through his final work. The fourth book of his treatise on relics,
composed shortly before his death in the mid-1120s, contains a treatment
of visions and the afterlife so finely done that Father Henri de Lubac has

---

[23] Ed. Migne, col. 621. The prose text of Boethius from which the jingle comes is the
Fifth Theological Tractate, ed. H. F. Stewart and E. K. Rand, Loeb Library (London,
1918), p. 74.
[24] Ed. Migne, cols. 377-378.

compared his view of 'transcendental reality' to that of Rudolf Bultmann.[25]

It is rare indeed for a medievalist studying an individual to have so much material on his childhood and his fantasies, reported in his subject's own words. How to use such evidence is a problem, for specialists are far from agreement in explaining the development of personality in living individuals, the application of modern concepts to past cultures is a delicate procedure at best, and 'psycho-historians' have yet to develop a large enough body of evidence to permit satisfactory control, comparison, and generalization. Yet historians and biographers have long agreed with Wordsworth that the child is father of the man. To exclude childhood influences from our understanding of Guibert would be to fail to see him as a whole man.

In a number of ways, Guibert's early life was not typical of that of boys of his class. He was, first of all, an oblate, vowed to the service of God from his birth, and from the age of thirteen on he was subject to the Benedictine Rule in a well-disciplined monastery. Early monastic training must surely have tended to create a 'monastic personality', in which the discipline of the community eventually became self-discipline and monastic values were internalized. Nobles, members of the secular clergy, and those who came late to the monastic profession did not have this training. When Guibert reports the raging violence of the nobility, the hot temper and loose tongue of Bishop Gaudry of Laon, the offenses of monks who came to Saint-Germer late in life, he was looking at people who had a youth radically different from his own.

Oblates commonly grew up in their monasteries, but Guibert spent his first twelve years in the military community of the *oppidum* of Clermont. Boys of the military caste learned early the values of their group: honor, pugnacity, personal loyalty to leader, blood brother, and family, and young nobles spent their 'youth' in gay and violent exploits which prepared them for the hard life of camp and castle ahead.[26] Guibert observed this world of the minor nobility, and he learned ambition, a sense of honor, respect for noble status and family ties. He admits to ambition himself, his history of the crusade condemns those knights who did not live up to the military code, and he takes clear pride in the connections his family had with the higher nobility. How thoroughly Guibert accepted the concept of family solidarity is shown by his

---

[25] *Exégèse médiévale*, II, 2 (Paris, 1964), p. 150. On the conservative character of Guibert's moral commentaries, see Beryl Smalley, 'William of Middleton and Guibert de Nogent'. *Recherches de théologie ancienne et médiévale*, XVI (1949), 281-291.

[26] See Georges Duby, 'Dans la France du Nord-Ouest au XIIe siècle: les 'jeunes' dans la société aristocratique,' *Annales, Economies- Sociétés-Civilisations*, XIX (1964), 835-846, trans. by Frederic L. Cheyette as 'The "Youth" in Twelfth-Century Aristocratic Society,' in *Lordship and Community in Medieval Europe* (New York, 1968), pp. 198-209.

condemnation of those who are 'too eager to secure the advancement of others not only of their own family, which is bad enough, but of those unrelated to them, which is worse' (I, 7; p. 53). But Guibert could never be a part of the rough world of honor and physical achievement. He was not raised with his brothers and cousins, even though an older cousin tried to take over his rearing. His mother and teacher saw to it that he was always the boy on the sidelines, dressed in his clerical garb. His mother even declared that his teacher should have no other students in his class. His father had been a man of violence and lechery, and his mother was determined that her last child should grow up to a different future. Only through the vivid and highly imaginative writing of his crusading history and his *Memoirs* could Guibert express his fascination with slaughter and sexuality.

Guibert's descriptions of noble life and his comments on it reveal the conflict between the values of the male nobility and those he learned from his mother. Men lived in a world of violence, ostentation, sexuality, and irreligion. As a noble, Guibert's mother shared some of the values of her class; Guibert stresses her beauty and refers to her taste for good food and fine clothes, even though she eventually wore a hair shirt under her outer garments. But she differed from the masculine code in her respect for religion and sexual purity. This conflict between masculine and feminine values may have been as common in the middle ages as it is today in southern Italy, an area which in many ways seems peculiarly medieval.[27] What is special about Guibert's boyhood is that he had no father as a model of masculine independence; if he had lived, Guibert says, his father would have broken his vow and have trained him for military rather than monastic life. His closest male influence was his teacher, an asexual figure who was dependent on his mother and who shared her religious values. Guibert was neither encouraged to compete with other boys nor permitted to enjoy their friendship. Without a father to approve violations of his mother's moral code and without playmates to dare him to break rules or admire him for getting away with something, Guibert grew up with little sense that the measure of proper behavior was the approval of his peers or other men; instead he made the values he learned from his mother and tutor, and eventually from his monastic community, a part of himself.

In short, Guibert differed from most members of the noble class, and probably from a great many churchmen, by being more influenced by the internal effect of a sense of guilt than by the external effect of shame. He himself expressed the difference between two ways of life, the one based on a 'conflict between body and spirit', a 'straining after God', the other

---

[27] Medievalists will find very suggestive parallels in Anne Parsons, 'Is the Oedipus Complex Universal? The Jones-Malinowski Debate Revisited and a South Italian "Nuclear Complex."' *The Psychoanalytic Study of Society*, ed. Warner Muensterberger and Sidney Axelrad, III (1964), 278-326.

determined by 'outward honor' and the desire to avoid disgrace. In his mother's youth, he says, her desire was to preserve her worldly honor, and only later in her life did she surrender her desires into the keeping of God (I, 12; p. 67).[28]

One measure of the tension between the old Germanic society and the Christian religion is the conflict between behavior based on the group sanctions of honor and shame and that determined by internalized personal and religious values which may conflict with those of 'society'. Much of the course of medieval history can be seen in the growing influence of monastic and religious reformers who had learned self-control, measured their actions against internal standards rather than group approval, and feared their own sense of guilt more than public censure. In our intimate view of Guibert of Nogent, we can see more deeply than usual into one of the men who supported the Gregorian reform movement.

Guibert was a reformer at heart; he writes as one who wished to reform and purify, and yet he differs greatly from those strong men – the Hildebrands and Anselms of one generation, the Bernards of another – who were actively engaged in changing the church and the world. Guibert was a weaker and less effective man than he wished to be. He shrank from conflict and met challenges by retreat; when forced into difficult situations, he dissimulated to avoid trouble. We have to understand not only his differences with society but his personal weakness.

Guibert did not grow up with the experience of full and healthy parental love. His mother had overwhelming importance to him, and he writes movingly of her and his regard for her. And yet, when one looks carefully at what he says about her, one sees an understratum of bitterness and unhappiness. He stresses her beauty and her virtue rather than her love. She taught him his prayers, he points out, when she had leisure from her household cares (I, 12; p. 68). She spoke continually of his father (I, 13; p. 72). Most notably, when Guibert was about twelve she deserted him to go to Saint-Germer, though 'she knew that I should be utterly an orphan with no one at all on whom to depend . . . I often suffered from the loss of that careful provision for the helplessness of tender years that only a woman can provide . . . She knew for certain that she was a cruel and unnatural mother' (I, 14; p. 74). Guibert can explain her behavior only by saying that God hardened her heart. Her austerity, her religious discipline, her very virtue, and her unending criticism of him made Guibert believe that he could not live up to her standards, that she would have died of mortification if she could look into his heart. And yet he had to trust in her to intercede for him in heaven. The reader may well be

---

[28] George F. Jones stresses the concepts of honor and shame in *The Ethos of the Song of Roland* (Baltimore, 1963). For parallels see Jean G. Péristiany, ed. *Honour and Shame: The Values of Mediterranean Society* (Chicago, 1966).

struck with the similarity of Guibert's feelings toward his mother and those toward the Virgin; at one point he goes so far as to tell the Virgin that if he is damned he will lay the blame on her (I, 3; p. 44).

The death of his father during his infancy doubtless had a powerful effect on Guibert's early development. He says directly that it was fortunate that his father died, and we have no reason to doubt that this was an honest statement of his feelings. Little children find it hard to distinguish between their fantasies and their ability to affect reality. Is it not likely that on some deep level Guibert felt that he himself was responsible for his father's death? If so, that feeling can only have added to his sense of guilt and unworthiness, as well as to his sense that the dead must be cared for and their remains well treated.

After he was six, Guibert's teacher took the place of a father in his life. Perceptively, Guibert saw that his mother and his substitute father were competing to see which he preferred. It was then his mother who gave him rich clothes, his teacher who urged austerity. In these years of pre-adolescence, he was, he says, deeply in love with his teacher; he remembers that in choosing to become a clerk he felt he was following his teacher and opposing his mother. And yet what he says about his teacher contains much openly expressed bitterness. In the first place, he was a harsh, brutal, capricious man who flogged Guibert when he did not deserve it. And secondly, as a man of learning he was incompetent, far less able than Guibert himself. From all he says, it is clear that Guibert did not respect the only male model close to him. Perhaps this lack of respect was compounded by the fact, mentioned before, that his teacher was his mother's employee and servant, a dependent from a lower social class. Guibert's only models of male dominance and self-assurance were his knightly relatives, and the morality of the nobility was consistently disparaged by both his mother and his teacher.

Guibert loved his mother and was dependent upon her, and he tells us that he was driven by some 'innner compulsion' to love his teacher. But he did not have the satisfaction of knowing that his love was returned in full measure; instead, he seems to have felt that he could never be good enough to meet parental standards. In the end, he seems to have turned his love inward upon himself, to have developed what Freud called narcissism. In spite of his professions of sin and weakness (which he does not detail specifically in contrition), the reader will be struck throughout his book by Guibert's high regard for himself. This self-satisfaction is coupled with his continual criticism of others. With the exception of his mother and a few exemplary monks and saints, no one else in the book comes off well.

Compelled as a boy to be rational, self-controlled, and sexually pure, Guibert had trouble dealing with the hostile, aggressive, lustful side of his nature. Again, he seems to have turned these feelings inward. His own internal certification of virtue was constantly threatened by his sense of guilt. His dreams and fantasies reveal his terrors, and we see again and again his irrational fear of punishment, death and mutilation.

Guibert's fear of mutilation requires special attention because it raises the question of whether his relationship to his mother and his fears together fit the Freudian model of a castration complex. While the evidence available is insufficient to warrant any unqualified application of psychoanalytic theory to the culture of medieval Europe, the concurrence of circumstances in this particular case is striking. Guibert's mother was a domineering person with puritanical ideas about sex; it seems reasonable to consider that she was responsible for her husband's impotence during the early years of her marriage. It was also from her, we may presume, that Guibert learned his idea of sexual purity and of the shamefulness of involuntary sexual excitement. Is it not likely that Guibert grew up with a deep-seated fear that the doctrine that 'it is expedient for thee that one of thy members should perish, rather than that thy whole body go into hell' would be applied to him literally? We do know that he dreamed of those who had died by the sword (I, 15; p. 79). He was distressed by the rite of circumcision,[29] and he chronicled stories of Thomas of Marle tearing the male organs off his victims, which may well have been as fantastic as his tale that Thomas pierced the windpipes of his prisoners to make them pull carts (II, 11 and 14; pp. 185 and 201). A particularly striking case of his turn of mind is the way he retold the tale of the man who killed himself on his way to Compostela. In the original poem by Guaiferius of Salerno, the pilgrim simply slit his throat; but as Guibert told the story the licentious man was first induced by the Devil to cut off his offending organ (III, 19; pp.218-220).

In the nineteenth century, Abel Lefranc looked at Guibert's rationality and concluded that he was 'practically a modern man'. In contrast, perhaps we can conclude that Guibert was a medieval man shaped by certain aspects of medieval culture, but that his irrational or unconscious nature was also influenced by the circumstances of his childhood, youth, and immediate family in ways remarkably similar to those observable today.

This view of Guibert's personality provides a new perspective on those aspects of his work which have seemed unusual. Perhaps now we have a fuller understanding of why this inward-turning man wrote about himself. Writing became for him both a retreat and a form of defiance. As he said in the *Gesta Dei*, 'In all things I have written and continue to write, I have banished all else from my mind, thinking only of my own advantage and caring not at all to please others'.[30] Like Augustine's *Confessions*, his *Memoirs* begin as a valiant attempt at introspection. Augustine was far

---

[29] In *Gesta Dei*, I, 3, p. 127, he points out that Mohammed ordained the rite of circumcision.
[30] V, Preface; p. 185.

more successful, however, for his confidence in grace permitted him to look critically at himself without recoiling in horror. Guibert shows much less insight, and may have found it possible to write what he did only because Augustine had done it first. I do not mean that he wrote with the *Confessions* open in front of him or relied on Augustine slavishly, as Einhard did on Suetonius. But he found little in himself which Augustine had not pointed out, and without the support of his guide he could not go on. Georg Misch has called Guibert 'a mighty storyteller before the Lord'.[31] But he was not mighty in self-perception or the ability or concern to write to help others. There is a whining, defiant, and yet self-satisfied tone to much of what Guibert says of himself. Augustine went on from the story of his life to present a testimony of faith; Guibert finished out his book with anecdotes and history.

Secondly, let us consider Guibert's alleged skepticism or rationalism or scientific method. There is much credulous or superstitious material in his writing, and if the spectacle of a medieval monk attacking relics had not seemed so impressive to critics of medieval religion, much less would have been said about his critical intelligence and historical method. In fact, Guibert was only selectively critical and was willing to distort history when it suited his purposes. For instance, he seems to have made up out of some sort of inscription a long, detailed story of how King Quilius of England brought back to Nogent from Palestine a box of holy objects and clothing of the saints but – as we would expect from our author and no other source – absolutely no corporeal relics (II, 1, p. 124). The relics of Nogent he supports; the relics of Saint-Médard he attacks. In the *Gesta Dei*, he challenges Fulcher of Chartres with a rational explanation of some of the miracles Fulcher reports; he also challenges Fulcher by accepting the authenticity of the Holy Lance of Antioch, which Fulcher questioned. What is consistent about Guibert is his quickness to disagree – in writing, not in person – with the opinions of other people. The hallmark of modern critical method is that one applies the same rigorous tests to one's own hypotheses as to those of others. Guibert shared the common human failing of accepting what he liked and finding reasons for discarding what he did not like.

Moreover, his reasons for distrusting relics are sometimes neither particularly modern nor convincing on their own terms. One theoretical argument is in effect a syllogism: the hope of mortals for resurrection depends on the example of the Saviour; if any part of His body remained on earth, the Lord's resurrection would be incomplete; therefore the alleged milk tooth of Jesus preserved at Saint-Médard and other such relics cannot be genuine.[32] Historical arguments are brought in support, such as the assertion that His contemporaries would not have thought to

[31] *Geschichte der Autobiographie*, p. 117.
[32] Ed. Migne, cols. 650-655.

preserve any relics of the young Jesus, since at the time He did not seem out of the ordinary.[33] To take that position, Guibert has to brush aside the argument of the opposition that a birth accompanied by a star, three Magi, and a chorus of angels was an unusual one, and that Mary treasured these things in her heart.

The earlier discussion of Guibert's personality suggests that behind the reasons he gives we should look for the emotional bases of Guibert's dislike of corporeal relics. Marc Bloch suggested rivalry with Saint-Médard,[34] and that may well have been a factor, but there were probably deeper, more influential forces at work. In the first place, Guibert was repelled by the idea of dismembering the human body. 'All the evil of contention [over relics],' he says, 'comes from not permitting the saints to have the quiet of their proper and immutable burial.'[35] Fearful of death and of the power of the dead to affect the living, he understandably urged that the dead be left in peace. A second reason for his distaste may be associated with a particular relic of the Saviour's body which Guibert found offensive. In attacking directly and in detail the milk tooth at Soissons, Guibert was indirectly attacking the veneration of the Holy Prepuce, a relic treasured at Saint John the Lateran at Rome and at the abbey of Charroux near Poitiers, and perhaps at several other churches.[36] After referring to the alleged tooth possessed by his neighbors, Guibert added: 'There are some who claim to have the umbilical cord which is cut off from the newborn, others claim to have the prepuce of the circumcusion of the Lord Himself, concerning which the great Origen wrote, "Avoid those who do not blush to write books about the circumcision of the Lord."'[37] He then addressed himself to a detailed attack on the tooth, concluding: 'What we have said about the tooth applies just as well to the umbilical cord and the other things. Clearly what is said about one covers the rest.'[38] Given Guibert's fear of sexual mutilation, he may well have had the deep motivation – far removed from skepticism – to write a treatise against all the relics of Christ's body, including one he could barely mention.

This comment leads to another of Guibert's characteristic attitudes, his denunciation of the Moslems, Jews, heretics, and others for horrible sexual practices. The question is not whether Guibert made these stories up out of whole cloth, which is unlikely, or passed on, perhaps with embellishments, stories he had heard, but why he promoted these defamations so enthusiastically. It is hard to avoid finding the answer in

---

[33] *Ibid.*, col. 659.

[34] *Rois thaumaturges*, p.29. Note, however, that the abbot of Saint-Médard at the time was the personal friend to whom Guibert had dedicated a volume of his commentaries.

[35] *Gesta Dei*, I, 5, p. 132.

[36] References to this relic are gathered in Henri Denifle, *La désolation des églises en France* (Paris, 1897-99), I, 167.

[37] Ed. Migne, col. 629. The quotation (?) from Origen is unidentified.

[38] *Ibid.*, col. 653.

the theory of projection; that is, of seeing in an enemy those things one most fears and hates in oneself. By an act of will, Guibert had mastered conscious sexual activity, but he had not been able to come to terms with the ferment of desire within him, and so he transferred it to those about him. No doubt many nobles of Picardy were as lustful as Guibert paints them, but he is a poor witness to the objective world. When we try to use him as a window onto medieval life, we look through the eyes of a disturbed man.

And what of the final unusual characteristic of this man, his patriotism? Let us look more closely at his approach to authority. Guibert demanded a highly structured world, one with a strong authoritarian chain. On the other hand, he could not accept his lecherous father as a hero and his tutor was the only individual man for whom he expressed any loyalty – except in the letters of dedication of his works – and even him he calls unjust and incompetent. He disobeyed Abbot Garnier and he criticized his predecessors at Nogent, the bishops of Laon, the pope and the papal court, as well as the nobles of the region and the late King Philippe. The feudal society of his day was built upon the individual loyalty of man to man, and such a personal tie was not congenial to Guibert. But if one is to have authority without honoring individuals, one must support institutions – a strong God-given monarchy even if the king is lecherous and mercenary, a church founded upon a rock even if the pope is corrupt. And if Guibert was to have a sense of political fellowship outside the feudal court, patriotism was a good solution. In shrinking from personal ties and loyalty, Guibert moved toward a more modern concept of government.

These views should be tested by comparison with other in-depth studies of medieval individuals. That task will not be easy. Other autobiographers who tell much about their adult lives – such as Peter Abelard, Margery Kempe, Pius II – say next to nothing of their childhoods. For one who wishes to understand the development of personality in the middle ages, Guibert Nogent is the informant who reveals the most about himself.

16

Individualism and Conformity in Medieval Western Europe

A historian of Western medieval Europe discussing individualism within the context of an ecumenical conference is forced to consider the origin of the term itself and its historiographic development. For far too long the major emphasis in European and American historiography and sociology has been to treat individualism as a particularly Western phenomenon. In the first recorded use of the word *individualisme* the conservative philosopher Joseph de Maistre wrote with horror in 1820 of the revolt of *l'esprit particulier* against religion and the social order, commenting on "this deep and frightening division of minds, this infinite fragmentation of all doctrines, political protestantism carried to the most absolute individualism." But not only reactionaries were opposed to individualism. In the 1820s Claude Henri de Saint-Simon and his followers developed a theory of cyclical historical periods. The Christian Middle Ages was considered by the Saint-Simonians to be a stable and unified "organic" period, which was followed by a modern "critical" period, beginning with the Reformation, which was marked by "disorder, atheism, individualism, and egoism."[1]

Karl Marx, like many Germans, took a more positive view of individualism. In his *Pre-Capitalist Economic Formations*, written over fifteen years and finished in 1858, Marx looked at history in terms of progressive rather than cyclical stages: "man is only individualized (*vereinzelt sich selbst*) through the process of history. He originally appears as a *generic being, a tribal being, a herd animal*."[2] In the final stage foreseen by Marx, Communism will make possible "free individuality, based on the universal development of individuals and on their joint mastery over their communal, social productive powers and

---

[1] A brilliant and well-documented introduction to this subject is Steven Lukes, *Individualism* (New York and London, 1973). The quotations cited in the paragraph above are from pp. 4–7.

[2] Karl Marx, *Pre-Capitalist Economic Formations*, ed. Eric J. Hobsbawm (New York, 1965), p. 96. The German text of Marx's personal notes on stages of development, discovered after the author's death and accessible as *Formen die der Kapitalistischen Produktion vorhergehen* (Berlin, 1953), is so dense that many readers will prefer the interpretative translation by Jack Cohen.

wealth."[3] Most Americans, on the other hand, came to see economic liberalism and capitalism as the high-road to what Herbert Hoover called in a campaign speech the "American system of rugged individualism."[4]

These modern ideas of individualism were crystalized by some of the most influential historians of the nineteenth century into terms that became historical clichés. When Jules Michelet wrote of the Renaissance in the volume on the sixteenth century he published in 1855, he treated it as the period marked by "the discovery of the world and the discovery of man."[5] In *The Civilization of the Renaissance in Italy*, published in 1860, the Swiss historian Jacob Burckhardt placed the shift somewhat earlier and wrote that "the fundamental vice of this [Italian Renaissance] character was at the same time a condition of its greatness, namely, excessive individualism."[6] As Karl Brandi wrote in 1932, "Our conception of the Renaissance is Jacob Burckhardt's creation,"[7] and it is therefore all the more important to remember that the second part of Burckhardt's seminal book was entitled "The Development of the Individual."

With the intellectual constructs already formed by some of the leading theorists of the nineteenth century, it is no wonder that contemporary medievalists have been concerned to investigate "The Discovery of the Individual," a phrase that is the title of a recent book by Colin Morris.[8] On the whole, Professor Morris takes a positive view of individualism and of the Middle Ages and endeavors to show how much interest in the individual was expressed in medieval Europe between 1050 and 1200, particularly in the writing of Christian authors. In *The Individual and Society in the Middle Ages*, Walter Ullmann takes a more political approach, tracing a movement of the later medieval period which he expresses as the shift from subject to citizen.[9]

---

[3] *Grundrisse der Kritik der politischen Ökonomie* (Berlin, 1953), p. 76, quoted in translation by Lukes, *Individualism*, p. 71.

[4] Hoover used the term in a speech on 22 October 1928; while he did not introduce the phrase "rugged individualism" to American political vocabulary, he claimed he would have been "proud to have invented it." See Herbert Hoover, *The Challenge to Liberty* (New York, 1934), p. 54.

[5] *Histoire de France* (Paris, 1833–1862; final ed. 1898), VII, 7.

[6] *Die Cultur der Renaissance in Italien* (Basel, 1860); since Burckhardt turned over the third edition (1877) to a reviser, one had better consult either of the first two editions or that restored by Walter Goetz in 1922. The passage is from the translation of S. G. C. Middlemore, made from the second edition (reprinted London, 1955), p. 279. Cf. Rudolf Stadelmann, "Jacob Burckhardt und das Mittelalter," *Historische Zeitschrift*, CXLII (1930), 457–515.

[7] In *Propyläen Weltgeschichte*, ed. Walter Goetz (Berlin, 1929–1937), IV, 157, cited in Wallace K. Ferguson's valuable interpretative study, *The Renaissance in Historical Thought* (Cambridge, Mass., 1948), p. 179.

[8] *The Discovery of the Individual, 1050–1200* (New York and London, 1972).

[9] *The Individual and Society in the Middle Ages* (Baltimore, 1966). Prof. Ullmann noted (p. 5): "It seems to me—and I would like to stress the point—that the historical recognition of the vital difference between the individual as a mere subject and the individual as a citizen is long overdue." He was unaware, however, that for some years the junior high school course From Subject to Citizen had earlier

It may be worth noting that all the authors I have mentioned treated a shift in attitudes and social arrangements, a phenomenon often labeled as "the growth of individualism" as something that happened in Europe in medieval times or in the later period usually called the Renaissance. There has been a tendency in this historiographic tradition to treat the development of individualism as something comparable with the Industrial Revolution, a tendency based on an underlying assumption that it is something that originated in Europe and then spread to the rest of the world.[10] The primary problem for European historians has been an argument over when it happened, in the Middle Ages as authors such as Ullmann and Morris assert, or in the Renaissance, either in Italy or France, as writers of the persuasion of Burckhardt and Michelet have said. A secondary question has been to determine why this development happened. Ullmann, as one might expect of an historian of political theories, finds the roots of individualism in the practices of feudalism, following ideas about the association of feudalism and liberty already developed by Sidney Painter.[11] Morris, a primarily ecclesiastical historian, traces much of the growth of concern for the individual to developments within Christian thought. Both theories have features that must be treated with respect, though the appearance of two such different books within a few years of each other suggests that one explanation or the other is either incorrect or incomplete and that this comment may perhaps be applied to both books.

That much more concern for the individual than Michelet and Burckhardt and other nineteenth-century thinkers imagined already existed in medieval Europe seems to me adequately established by the two recent books I have mentioned and by a large body of other evidence. Professor S. D. Goitein has argued that something that we may properly consider as individualism existed among the early Arabs,[12] and if this conclusion is correct, we have no reason to

---

been introduced as part of the experimental but successful curriculum of Educational Services Incorporated; see Franklin K. Patterson, *Man and Politics*, Social Studies Curriculum Program Occasional Paper, 4 (Cambridge, Mass., 1965), pp. 42–52.

[10] While historians and anthropologists may note more "individualism" in some societies than in others, the idea that "individualism" is a hallmark of the modern Western world smacks of self-congratulatory ethnocentrism. In *The Cultural Background of Personality* (New York, 1945), p. 17, Ralph Linton long ago put the central issue simply: "The so-called free societies are not really free. They are merely those societies which encourage their members to express their individuality along a few minor and socially acceptable lines. At the same time they condition members to abide by innumerable rules and regulations, doing this so subtly and completely that these members are largely unconscious that the rules exist."

[11] *Feudalism and Liberty*, ed. Fred A. Cazel, Jr. (Baltimore, 1961), p. 253, cited by Ullmann, *Individual and Society*, p. 68. See also Painter's paper of 1942, "Individualism in the Middle Ages," in *Feudalism and Liberty*, pp. 254–259.

[12] See Goitein's brilliant essay above, pp. 3–17,* which should be read along with Gustave E. von Grunebaum's "The Hero in Medieval Arabic Prose" in *Concepts of the Hero in the Middle Ages and the Renaissance*, ed. Norman T. Burns and Christopher Reagan (Albany, 1975), pp. 83–100. Both essays together provide the

Individualism and Conformity in Classical Islam, ed. A. Banani and S. Vryonis (Wiesbaden, 1977), pp. 3-17.

follow the analogy of the Industrial Revolution and to try to explain why individualism developed first in Europe. A far more complex question must attract our attention: Why is more concern for the individual found in certain societies or classes or periods than in others, and what are the reasons for this situation when it appears?

Since social science has the greatest chance to be reasonably objective when subjective factors that can never be eliminated are explicit rather than covert, I should make clear the personal values and definitions that have entered into my treatment of this subject. My personal view is that even though individuals may act either in a fashion harmful to society or to themselves or to both, they may also act with enlightened self-interest which has positive value both to society and to themselves. Often people act in both fashions, but the chances of combining personal happiness and social responsibility are increased when individuals know themselves and have come to terms with their inner conflicts. In other words, I favor heightened self-awareness, which is obviously a form of individualism, and am simply echoing the well-known ethical views of Rabbi Hillel, who wrote some nineteen centuries ago, "If I am not for myself, who will be; if I am for myself alone, what am I?"[13] To quote a Jewish sage who died in the ninth year of the Christian Era is a simple way of asserting that I have not begun my investigation of this subject with the assumption that a high concern for the individual could possibly be the peculiar possession of Christian medieval Europe. As for a definition of individualism, I do not subscribe to the "Great Man" theory which is implicit in Burckhardt's formulations. While it is hard to state a precise definition of individualism, the word has for me associations that lead to the following positions: that each individual has within herself or himself something worthy of respect; that each individual has the possibility of making a positive contribution to society, and (if one accepts a religious viewpoint) the possibility of achieving some form of salvation; and, finally, that there exists a positive responsibility to respect the choices and peculiar characteristics of others, even when they differ from the positions of other individuals of the majority of a given society.

When one applies these three criteria to the Christian society of medieval Western Europe, it is easy enough to demonstrate the presence of the first two positions. The belief that mankind was created in the image of God carried the consequence that each individual has some Godlike quality which is obviously worthy of respect, and this belief led to a large literature on the dignity of man.[14] How far this dignity extended to women was a matter of debate. Peter

---

necessary context for Prof. von Grunebaum's statement (p. 90): "The individual [in medieval Arabic prose] is indeed important, but as a representative of a type."

[13] *Pirke Aboth* (Sayings of the Fathers), I, 14, trans. Joseph H. Hertz (New York, 1945), pp. 24–25.

[14] See, among other important contributions, Robert Javelet, *Image et ressemblance au douzième siècle de St. Anselme à Alain de Lille*, 2 vols. (Strasbourg, 1967); Charles Trinkaus, *In Our Image and Likeness*, 2 vols. (Chicago, 1970); Eugenio Garin, "La 'Dignitas hominis' e la letteratura patristica," *La Rinascita*, I (1938),

Abelard, who wrote eloquently on the dignity of women, noted nonetheless that woman was made not in the image of God but only in His likeness.[15] When a male supporter of women could make a point like this and refer routinely to the "weakness" of women, it is obvious that the literature of antifeminism by more vigorous antifeminists was bound to be intense.[16] This antifeminism is one of the key factors in understanding medieval Christian ideas of the individual, for not only was their Savior born of a woman, but so, of course, were the authors who discoursed on the iniquity of women. As I shall repeat later, failure to make an adequate integration of what every individual took from each parent was mirrored in a larger tension in society itself. But while antifeminism and the attendant tension was powerful, it should not be overestimated. The idea that the Council of Mâcon in 585 actually debated the question of whether or not women had souls is based on a misunderstanding, just as the belief that chastity belts were common medieval contraptions introduced by Crusaders appears to be a myth; these views are to some degree a projection of later antifeminism back onto medieval society.[17] Christian thinkers were agreed that women had souls, and this spark of divinity, if nothing else, made them worthy of respect. Medieval European society could be incredibly brutal to women, children, and the helpless, but it also set up institutions for protecting them.

The second feature of individualism I wish to explore briefly is the possibility of contributing to society and the possibility of salvation. The organic view of society held widely in the Middle Ages had its drawbacks, but it still encouraged

---

102–146. I have profited from Richard C. Dales' unpublished paper, "A Medieval View of Human Dignity," scheduled to appear in the *Journal of the History of Ideas*, which takes special note of developments in the medieval study of natural science.

[15] Abelard, *Expositio in Hexameron*, ed. Migne, *P. L.*, CLXXVIII, 760 D: "Intelligimus virum ad imaginem Dei, feminam vero ad similitudinem." On this passage, and on Abelard's views on women in general, see the excellent article by Mary Martin McLaughlin, "Abelard and the Dignity of Women" in *Pierre Abélard—Pierre le Vénérable*, Colloques internationaux du Centre National de la Recherche Scientifique, 546 (Paris, 1975), pp. 287–333, especially p. 305. Those who know my article on the correspondence of Abelard and Heloise in the same volume, pp. 469–506, may be reassured that I accept all, or almost all, of Abelard's "Ep. VII" as authentic; it may consist of parts of Abelard's lost *Exhortatio ad fratres et commonachos*.

[16] For bibliography and a compelling anthology, see *Not in God's Image*, ed. Julia O'Faolain and Lauro Martines (New York, 1973); the editors have taken their title from a quotation (cited p. 130) from St. Augustine, *De Trinitate* Bk. XII, ch. 7 (9–10) which must have influenced Abelard.

[17] On the alleged debate of the Council of Mâcon see Joseph Hefele and Henri Leclercq, *Histoire des conciles* (Paris, 1907–1938), III, 208 n. 1; 211 n. 7; and p. 1247, addendum. Most of the literature on chastity belts is merely of prurient interest, but there are some striking photographs in an article by Henry Crannach, "Chastity Belts: A Mystification?" in *Olympia: A Monthly Review from Paris*, 1 (January 1962), 19–25. I have never seen a "ceinture de chasteté" with workmanship that can be dated earlier than the Renaissance, and while the argument from silence is usually unconvincing, it is hard to imagine Boccaccio failing to write a story concerning a chastity belt if he had ever heard of one.

the view that any social group had a contribution to make. Prelates and other churchmen, rulers, and nobles, all those in power might be placed higher than other orders of society, but just as one cannot imagine a body operating effectively without arms and legs, so medieval social theorists considered that all workers had a place of respect in contributing to society.[18] In modern societies some advocates of elitism or racial supremacy have been ready to write off whole classes of people as *Untermenschen*, but that view did not gain an effective hold in the medieval West. Without minimizing the antipathy to Jews and the active persecutions which blot medieval history, it must also be said that Christian theorists frequently called attention to the role of the Jewish people in the divine plan.[19] Jews, Muslims, and other non-Christian people were indeed considered by such an author as Saint Thomas Aquinas to be "potentially" members of the *corpus mysticum*.[20] Salvation was open to any living individual, and was in fact the responsibility of the individual. Saint Bernard named four degrees of love, beginning of necessity with love of self, a carnal love which "grows social when it extends to our neighbors," and ending with the fourth degree, "wherein one loves himself only for the sake of God."[21] To paraphrase the abbot of Cîteaux, I hope not unjustly, one cannot love God or one's neighbor unless one first loves one's self, and the final stage is not love of God for the sake of God, but love of self for the sake of God. And medieval commentators often quoted Saint Augustine, "Love, and do what you wish."[22]

Whatever the actual diversity in Christian society, Christianity apparently created more theoretical pressure toward conformity than did Islam—I know of no Christian statement to match the Islamic legal dictum, *ikhtilāf al-umma*

---

[18] Quotations, notably from the *Polycraticus* (Bk. V, ch. 1) of John of Salisbury, and commentary in Ewart Lewis, *Medieval Political Ideas*, 2 vols. (London, 1954), I, 193–240.

[19] In general, see Edward A. Synan, *The Popes and the Jews in the Middle Ages* (New York, 1965), and Solomon Grayzel, *The Church and the Jews in the XIIIth Century*, rev. ed. (New York, 1966). St. Bernard, who called the Jews "bovine" (*Sermo super Cantica*, LX, 5, ed. Jean Leclercq et al., *Opera* [Rome, 1957–], II, 144), nevertheless in his crusading Ep. 363 urged that the lives of Jews be spared, since in his opinion they were *testes nostrae redemptionis* and would be converted in the fullness of time. In spite of a few bright spots, much of the relatively "open" twelfth century was stained by vicious opposition by Christians to Jews and Muslims.

[20] *Summa theologica*, III, q. 8, art. 3, resp.; cf. Ernst H. Kantorowicz, *The King's Two Bodies* (Princeton, 1957), p. 465 n. 41.

[21] *De diligendo Deo*, VIII, 23, and X, 27, in *Sancti Bernardi Opera*, III, 139 and 142.

[22] Augustine, *In Epistolam Joannis ad Parthos tractatus*, VII, 8 (Migne, *P. L.*, XXXV, 2033: "Dilige, et quod vis fac." Cf. *Augustine: Later Works*, trans. John Burnaby, Library of Christian Classics, 8 (Philadelphia, 1955), p. 316 and p. 257, where the editor calls this "the most famous saying in the Homilies." The twelfth-century annotator of a copy of the *In unum ex quatuor* of Zacharias of Besançon now in the library at Camarillo, Calif., wrote in the margin of fol. 88r (opposite the passage given in Migne, *P. L.*, CLXXXVI, 311 A): "Habe," inquit Augustinus, "caritatem et fac quod vis." The epigram probably circulated through *florilegia*.

rahma, "dissension in the commonwealth of Islam is an act of the mercy of God."[23] But in its emphasis on the salvation of the individual soul, orthodox Christian thinkers condemned as heretical the view of Dante's teacher, Remigio de' Girolami, that the citizen must love the city more than himself and be ready to take on his own eternal damnation rather than see his city damned.[24] Another example of the argument that personal sin could be subordinate to collective needs was the conclusion of a late thirteenth-century theorist that adultery with the wife of a man planning to be a tyrant was a lesser evil than the destruction of the *bonum communitatis*.[25] The most common view was the obvious one that a corporate body did not have a soul and was therefore subject neither to damnation nor to excommunication.[26] The Nazi government inscribed on the edges of its most handsome coins "Gemeinnutz geht vor Eigennutz" (the good of the collectivity before the good of the individual), but as those who resisted quickly saw, this doctrine usually meant "Meinnutz geht vor Deinnutz."

It is in the third area of individualism that I mentioned, the acceptance of deviant beliefs and individuals and a respect for choices made on a personal rather than on a group basis, that medieval European society showed its strongest antipathy to individualism. Any discussion of individualism in the medieval West must take account of the drive to demand conformity from members of that society. The epic literature extolling outstanding individuals is one expression of this tendency. It was in his fascination with great men as a measure of individualism in a society that Burckhardt made one of his most significant mistakes. We do not have to wait until the period of the Italian Renaissance to find outstanding, egotistical leaders, tyrants, and military chiefs. Such men, and sometimes women, can also be found throughout the Middle Ages. One has only to think of Constantine (or perhaps I should say Saint Constantine), or Charlemagne (and again I might say Saint Charles the Great), or Richard the Lion-Hearted, or Frederick II or, for that matter, the Senatrix Theodora or Eleanor of Aquitaine, to find ruthless and self-centered individuals well before the period of the Italian Renaissance.[27] Historians have

---

[23] See Joseph Schacht, *An Introduction to Islamic Law* (Oxford, 1964), p. 67. For further bibliography see *The Encyclopaedia of Islam*, new ed. (London and Leiden, 1960–), III, 1061–1062. My knowledge of the dictum is owed to Professor Goitein, whose assistance on numerous occasions it is a pleasure to acknowledge.

[24] See Kantorowicz, *King's Two Bodies*, pp. 478–479. Portions of Remigio's *Tractatus* were published by Richard Egenter, "Gemeinnutz vor Eigennutz: Die sociale Leitidee im *Tractatus de bono communi* des Fr. Remigius von Florenz," *Scholastik*, IX (1934), 79–92.

[25] See Gaines Post, "Ratio Publicae Utilitatis," *Die Welt als Geschichte*, XII (1961), 96 = *Studies in Medieval Legal Thought* (Princeton, 1964), p. 305.

[26] Kantorowicz, *King's Two Bodies*, p. 476, citing, among other places, Otto von Gierke, *Das Deutsche Genossenschaftsrecht*, 4 vols. (Berlin, 1868–1913), III, 363–364.

[27] While the historical individuals named in this and the following sentence are well known, not everyone may be aware that Constantine I is a saint of the Eastern church and that Charlemagne was canonized in 1166 by the anti-pope Victor IV.

often pointed to Peter Abelard as proof of individualism in the Middle Ages,[28] but one could as well single out Saint Bernard, or Gregory VII, or Innocent III, or Boniface VIII as churchmen whose individual biographies are as striking as those of Alexander VI or Julius III. A southern French author, noting that some people considered the elder Simon de Montfort to be a saint, wrote that his epitaph relates that he "is a saint and a martyr, and that he is destined to rise at the last day and to inherit and enjoy the marvellous bliss of heaven... It may well be so: if by killing men, by shedding blood, by destroying souls, by consenting to murders, ... by killing women and destroying children, one can gain Jesus Christ in this world, one should wear a crown and shine in heaven."[29] The same point can be turned around with respect to Burckhardt's famous section on the development of the individual—if bloodthirsty egoism is a mark of individualism, historians are free to issue a great many certificates of individualism to people throughout the Middle Ages and before.

To state this same point not ironically but directly, my own view is that in the period we are considering, military valor, personal bravery, and even the willingness to sacrifice oneself in fighting for a cause (*pro patria mori*) are signs not so much of individualism as of conformity. Medieval warfare, European as well as Arabic, demanded troops who would fight loyally to the death and leaders who could give an example of personal valor. In both *Beowulf* and the *Chanson de Roland* heroes preparing for battle activated their adrenalin by engaging in ritualistic boasting, no different from the warrior who strutted between the Muslim and Meccan armies bearing the sword of the Prophet, of whom Muhammad said, "This is a gait which Allah hates except on an occasion like this."[30] The great medieval military epics—and they are outstanding pieces of literature—may appear to glorify individual heroes, but viewed from a different perspective, they can be seen as compositions intended to instill in their audiences conformity to a particular type of warfare.[31] The epic of Roncevalles had a function when it was written—to bestir men to fight together against those whom they considered their common enemies—and it was still doing so when Charles Scott Moncrieff found it, as he said, "a constant solace" in the

---

[28] See, for example, the incisive remarks of Etienne Gilson, *Héloïse et Abélard*, 3d ed. (Paris, 1964), pp. 147–168. In my opinion the historical individuality of both Abelard and Heloise is well established by other evidence than the *Historia Calamitatum* and the "personal" correspondence attributed to the two lovers. On Abelard as a poet see Peter Dronke, *Poetic Individuality in the Middle Ages* (Oxford, 1970), pp. 114–149; and Joseph Szövérffy, *Peter Abelard's Hymnarius Paraclitensis*, 2 vols. (Albany, N. Y., and Brookline, Mass., 1975).

[29] *Chanson de la croisade contre les Albigeois*, ed. Paul Meyer, 2 vols. (Paris, 1875–1879), I, 354, lines 8683–8696; translated by Palmer A. Throop, *Criticism of the Crusade* (Amsterdam, 1940), p. 40.

[30] Ibn Isḥāq, *Sīra Rasūl Allāh*, ed. Heinrich F. Wüstenfeld, 2 vols. (Göttingen, 1858–1860), I, 561; trans. Alfred Guillaume as *The Life of Muhammad* (Karachi, 1955), p. 374.

[31] George Fenwick Jones, *The Ethos of the Song of Roland* (Baltimore, 1963), esp. pp. 96–158.

summer of 1918 when he began a translation which he dedicated to three friends who fell in battle later that year.[32] *Beowulf* and the *Chanson* are better literature than the *Horst Wessel Lied*, but I am not sure that they differ in function.

Sir Steven Runciman began his book on *The Medieval Manichee* with the succinct statement that "tolerance is a social rather than a religious virtue."[33] He summed up his trilogy on the Crusades by concluding, "There was so much courage and so little honour, so much devotion and so little understanding. High ideals were besmirched by cruelty and greed, enterprise and endurance by a blind and narrow self-righteousness; and the Holy War itself was nothing more than a long act of intolerance in the name of God, which is the sin against the Holy Ghost."[34] People in the Middle Ages found it almost impossible to tolerate those who were different. Heretics might be condemned and reconciled, or they might find their end at the stake, but they were rarely left alone.[35] Homosexuals could not be accepted as supernaturally "stricken" individuals, as Eric Erikson found them to be by the traditionally fierce Sioux Indians whom he visited, but were subject to brutal persecution as a threat to society itself.[36] The belief that God would punish an entire group for what the majority considered to be the sins of individuals was so strong that there was a whole series of devices for the public shaming of those who were caught violating the standards of society. Adulterers were often compelled to parade naked through the streets, and others who misbehaved might be forced to the public humiliation of riding backward in public, to sit in the stocks, or to be dunked in a ritual immersion in a dunking stool.[37] Whether shame or the instillation of guilt was the mechanism, medieval Christian society commonly demanded conformity.

Still, and this is the point of greatest interest, medieval society did not always insist on conformity. When a full-scale history of individualism and

---

[32] C. S. Moncrieff, *The Song of Roland Done into English* (London, 1919), p. xiii.
[33] *The Medieval Manichee* (Cambridge, Eng., 1955), p. 1.
[34] *A History of the Crusades*, 3 vols. (Cambridge, Eng., 1951–1954), III, 480.
[35] An excellent introduction to the immense literature on the subject, with translations and extensive bibliography, is *Heresies of the High Middle Ages*, ed. Walter L. Wakefield and Austin P. Evans, Columbia Records of Civilization, 81 (New York and London, 1969).
[36] See Derrick S. Bailey, *Homosexuality and the Western Christian Tradition* (London, 1955); for Erik Erikson's comments on the Sioux, see *Childhood and Society*, 2d ed. (New York, 1963), p. 153.
[37] There is a wealth of material on the public shaming ordered by ecclesiastical courts in England, Scotland, and New England in *Before the Bawdy Court*, ed. Paul Hair (New York, 1972). Public humiliation is dramatically illustrated in Ruth Mellinkoff, "Riding Backwards: Theme of Humiliation and Symbol of Evil," *Viator*, IV (1973), 153–176 and following plates. The brutality of medieval shaming techniques is obvious; when modern prisons humiliate and "depersonalize" convicts behind their walls, they can be no less brutal, though they have less effect, for good or ill, on the general populace.

conformity in medieval Europe is written, we will need to have ways of testing the balance between these two poles in any given place or time or group. One possibility is to look for examples of antisocial behavior, an approach recently taken by Father Raftis in his study of an English village in Huntingdonshire.[38] It is undoubtedly true that we need to know more about village conformity and deviance, but there are certain difficulties inherent in studying court and jail records. As Father Raftis points out, some families and individuals were "simply unruly by any standards."[39] Moreover, deviance from village standards might also be the product not so much of "individualism," as of conformity to family interests when the interests of one group conflicted with those of another. Unless we know something about motives, we could hardly tell from jail records whether Thoreau was placed behind bars because his individual principles conflicted with those of the state or because he avariciously did not want to pay his taxes. Medieval court records amply show us that many medieval people did not docilely submit to social control, but only very full records allow us to tell the difference between Joan of Arc, who thought of herself as an individual inspired by God to resist laws which she felt did not apply to her, and her contemporary, Giles de Raiz, marshal of France, who was tried for child-murder and became the prototype of the legendary Bluebeard.[40]

Among other possible ways of testing the balance between individualism and conformity in medieval society, I should like to mention three indexes which seem promising. One is the question of the renunciation of worldly values as seen in monasticism and the hermetic life, and particularly the conscious rejection of wealth which played so large a part in the development of the mendicant orders.[41] To some degree, any hermit, monk, or friar was a nonconformist who rejected the way of life of the majority of society. That society found ways to accommodate these nonconformists in the larger order of things should not obscure the fact that men and women who chose to withdraw from the secular world were asserting a particular concern for their own individual salvations, and in the early Middle Ages the most individualistic literature was produced by these people.[42] Of course, communal life created a subculture that carried with it its own conformity, and of course some monasteries and nunneries became quite worldly places indeed. All the same, it is notable that oblates who entered monastic life not of their own volition but by

---

[38] J. Ambrose Raftis, *Warboys* (Toronto, 1974), pp. 241–264.

[39] Ibid., p. 256.

[40] See Frances Winwar, *The Saint and the Devil: Joan of Arc and Gilles de Rais, a Biographical Study in Good and Evil* (New York, 1948).

[41] Lester K. Little, "Pride Goes before Avarice: Social Change and the Vices in Latin Christendom," *American Historical Review*, LXXVI (1971), 16–49 is a good introduction to an extensive literature.

[42] As examples only, one may consider such diverse authors as Otloh of St. Emmeram, Guigues the Carthusian, Bernard of Clarivaux (who, of course, "withdrew from the world" only at times), or Peter Abelard, who, after all, spent a major part of his life as a monk.

the choice of their parents often found that their monastic mentors encouraged their own individual development and self-fulfillment. The study of oblates as compared with children raised in secular society suggests that in the early Middle Ages monks and nuns might well be considered the most nurturing "parents" of their time.[43] And when in the twelfth century the Cistercians decided to refuse admission to anyone under sixteen and accepted only those old enough to make a rational choice of the monastic life, this development too suggests a heightened concern for the individual in monastic circles.[44] As for the "worldliness" of some monastic communities, it must be noted that each successive wave of reform involved a concern for greater rigor and less conformity with majority standards, and that converts tended to flock to those orders and communities which exhibited the greatest rejection of conventional secular society.

Whether one likes him or not, it must be agreed that Saint Bernard was quite an individualist![45] And as for Saint Francis, even when the critical historian cuts through the romantic fog that threatens to obscure him, the story of his rejection of the standards of the mercantile world in which he was raised is one of the most remarkable instances of individualism and nonconformity of all time. What an example he set when during a Lenten retreat he refused to help a companion put out a fire which was burning their cell![46]

A second test of individual choice and of society's acceptance of such choices is the question of the degree to which marriages were arranged to suit the in-

---

[43] See Pierre Riché, "L'enfant dans la société monastique au XIIe siècle," in *Pierre Abélard—Pierre le Vénérable* (cited above, n. 15), pp. 689–701, and Mary Martin McLaughlin, "Survivors and Surrogates: Children and Parents from the Ninth to the Thirteenth Centuries," in *The History of Childhood*, ed. Lloyd deMause (New York, 1974), pp. 129–132.

[44] Although children were accepted at Molesme, the early Cistercian legislation restricted novices to those who were over fifteen years old; see Joseph-Marie Canivez, *Statuta Capitulorum Generalium Ordinis Cisterciensis*, 8 vols. (Louvain, 1933–1941), I, 31, année 1134, no. 78. The limit was later raised to a requirement of eighteen years for admission; ibid., p. 62, année 1157, no. 28. St. Bernard was himself fond of young people; see Jean Leclercq, "Saint Bernard et les jeunes," *Collectanea Cisterciensia*, XXX (1968), 120–127. The practice of oblation was on the wane in the twelfth century, and Pope Alexander III ruled that any monastic profession made before the age of fourteen was not binding; see *Corpus Juris Canonici*, Comp. I, lib. III, tit. XXXI, c. 8 (ed. Friedberg, II, 571).

[45] Jean Leclercq has written a psychological study of the man whose work he has been editing for twenty years in *Nouveau visage de Bernard de Clairvaux* (Paris, 1976). One must wonder at the truth of the report in the *Vita Prima*, cap. 1, that Bernard's mother nursed her children herself, a rare act for a woman of the nobility of her day.

[46] *Scripta Leonis, Rufini et Angeli, Sociorum S. Francisci*, ed. and trans. Rosalind B. Brooke, Oxford Medieval Texts (Oxford, 1970), pp. 176–179. On an eminent historian's influence on our image of St. Francis, see "Paul Sabatier and St. Francis of Assisi" in Christopher Brooke, *Medieval Church and Society* (London, 1971), pp. 197–213. Here too we need a new biography.

terests of the families involved or were the free and undictated choice of the two partners. It is not my purpose to suggest that arranged marriages cannot be happy ones and lead to a high degree of love, or what the canonists sometimes called "marital affection."[47] But I do think there is a major difference between a society in which most people are pushed into marriages not of their own choosing, or even unions that are repugnant to one or both of the partners, and a society in which love and free choice or at least sexual attraction and union commonly precede a contract of marriage.[48] For far too long it has been an accepted tenet of medieval history, and even more, of medieval literary criticism, that no one married for love in medieval Europe.[49] Happily, at last historians are looking to see if the accepted dictum is really true, and when we do, we find that a strikingly large number of marriages began with a commitment based on love rather than parental choice. And while I do not have empirical data to support the generalization, I expect that couples who have entered marriage on the basis of their own free choice are more likely to respect the individuality and free choice of their offspring than are parents who have not experienced freedom to choose in this major step in their own lives.

The subject of marriage brings us to a third way to test the degree of individuality or enforced conformity in medieval society, and that is the fashion in which children are raised. When I stated above that nuns and monks seemed to be the best parents of the early Middle Ages, this judgment was based on the large-scale evidence of infanticide, abandonment, and brutality toward children which exists from this period.[50] The subject of medieval child-rearing is a large one which cannot occupy us here. Let me say at this point only that there is considerable evidence to suggest that as the Middle Ages progressed, the degree of empathy in child-rearing seems also to have increased.[51] Brutality and abandonment still continued to exist in the later Middle Ages, of course, and

---

[47] John T. Noonan, Jr., "Marital Affection in the Canonists," *Studia Gratiana*, XII (1967), Collectanea Stephan Kuttner, 2, pp. 479–509.

[48] See Michael M. Sheehan, "The Formation and Stability of Marriage in Fourteenth-Century England: Evidence of an Ely Register," *Mediaeval Studies*, XXXIII (1971), 228–263, and compare R. H. Helmholz, "Abjuration *sub pena nubendi* in the Church Courts of Medieval England," *The Jurist*, XXXII (1972), 80–90.

[49] See my "Clio and Venus: An Historical View of Medieval Love" in *The Meaning of Courtly Love*, ed. Francis X. Newman; above, chapter 6, pp. 99-121. William D. Paden, Jr., and his collaborators have now made a detailed study of vocabulary in "The Troubadour's Lady: Her Marital Status and Social Rank," *Studies in Philology*, LXXII (1975), 28–50.

[50] See Richard B. Lyman, Jr., "Barbarism and Religion: Late Roman and Early Medieval Childhood," in *The History of Childhood* (cited above, n. 43); Mary McLaughlin, "Survivors and Surrogates," in ibid., pp. 101–181; and, among other works, Barbara A. Kellum, "Infanticide in England in the Later Middle Ages," *History of Childhood Quarterly*, I (1974), 367–388.

[51] See the seminal paper of Lloyd deMause, "The Evolution of Childhood" in *The History of Childhood*, pp. 1–73., also printed with commentary and reaction in *History of Childhood Quarterly*, I (1974), 503–606.

yet we cannot ignore this piece of advice from the thirteenth-century medical guide of Aldobrandino of Sienna: "You ought to know that as soon as the child is seven years old, you ought to make an effort for him to have good habits and see to it that nothing happens to him which angers him too much or makes him lose too much sleep. What he asks for should be given to him and those things which displease him should be removed. One should do this so that his nature may be good humored and full of good behavior, for this is the age when the child retains most and learns good and bad behavior."[52]

The careful reader will already have noted that there is a certain interrelationship between the three measures of individualism I have been discussing. The nurturing care given to oblates, the decision of the Cistercians not to accept children unable to consent rationally to a monastic vocation, and the Franciscan veneration of the Christ child and institution of the crèche as part of the Christmas service[53] all tie together the individualism of those who rejected worldly conformity in their concern for children. Furthermore, I have suggested that there is a connection between the growing acceptance of free choice in marriage with the increased degree of nurturing child care which seems to be a feature of later medieval secular society. William fitz Stephen remarked in passing in his description of twelfth-century London that "we were all boys once," and while he should have said, we were all once children, the major import of his statement still holds:[54] childhood is an experience common to all humanity, and the institutions and attitudes of every society find both their continuity and their change only through the very exacting filter of what is passed from parent to child, from one generation to the next. What is common to Walter Ullmann's association of individualism and political developments and the association with religion made by Colin Morris in his treatment of *The Discovery of the Individual* is that political leaders and ecclesiastics, warriors and churchgoers, and all of the laboring peasants and artisans who supported the rest of society, were all children once. In a significant way, the individualism expressed in a feudal council, a church or monastery, a town or village has something to do with the development of individual people whose sense of self and the world about them was first shaped during childhood.

Psychohistory is a way of looking at the world which is still in its own institutional infancy, and we therefore can hardly expect to find common agreement

---

[52] *Le Régime du corps de maître Aldebrandin de Sienne*, ed. Louis Landouzy and Roger Pépin (Paris, 1911), p. 80.

[53] On the institution of the manger scene created at Greccio by St. Francis in the third year before his death, see Thomas of Celano, *Vita Prima*, chaps. 84–87, ed. *Analecta Franciscana*, X (1895), 63–65. On the earliest known Christ-child statuette, probably of Franciscan origin, see Ursula Schlegel, "The Christchild as Devotional Image in Medieval Italian Sculpture," *Art Bulletin*, LII (1970), 1–10.

[54] William's description, often translated, is a preamble to his *Life of Thomas Becket*, ed. J. C. Robertson and printed in *Materials for the History of Thomas Becket*, 7 vols., Rolls Series, 67 (London, 1875–1885), III, 9; William says "omnes enim pueri fuimus" and means "boys," for he is referring to boys' games.

on the relationship between the findings of modern psychology and the lives and personalities of people in the past.[55] My conclusion must be suggestive rather than didactic. Still, some conclusion to this paper may be drawn from what I have just said. To those versed in psychology I will seem to be stating the obvious when I say that what each child draws, or fails to draw, from both mother and father, or from those people or institutions which take the place of one or both parents, has much to do with the development of that child's individual personality. A child who fails to receive nurturing care from anybody can hardly be expected to treat other people with either trust or respect, and will very likely have a very shaky sense of self-worth.[56] A child who experiences destructive tension or conflict between the most important male and female figures in his or her life can be expected to internalize those conflicts, and perhaps later to project them back on the outside world, leading to hostility and intolerance.[57] As concern for children increased in medieval Europe, so did a sense of self and respect for the individual. But the sorry record of intolerance, rigidity, and the projection of inner doubts and conflicts in antagonism to those who were different or deviated from the norms of society suggest that conflicts felt first within the family and seldom resolved through individual self-awareness were carried on into adult life and continued to trouble both individual and society long after childhood had passed.

---

[55] Besides the exciting work appearing in the *History of Childhood Quarterly*, one should note the warning of Robert E. McClone, "The New Orthodoxy in Psychohistory" in the *Newsletter* of the Group for the Use of Psychology in History, IV, 2 (1975), 4–9.

[56] The discussion of "Anxiety, Dissociation, and the Growth of Self" by Louis Breger, *From Instinct to Identity: The Development of Personality* (Englewood Cliffs, N. J., 1974), pp. 192–238 is pertinent. Surviving medieval children, who so often witnessed the deaths of their siblings and experienced separation from their parents, must commonly have been pushed away from integration and toward dissociation.

[57] Jane Loevinger and R. Wessler, *Measuring Ego Development*, 2 vols. (San Francisco, 1970) have used sentence completion tests to study moral development; their work is compared with that of Lawrence Kohlberg, *Stages in the Development of Moral Thought and Action* (New York, 1972), in Breger's *From Instinct to Identity*, pp. 239–294. I have discussed the combination of moralizing (the "good boy" syndrome) and projective aggression in one medieval monk in the introduction to *Self and Society in Medieval France: The Memoirs of Abbot Guibert of Nogent* (New York, 1970).

17

Consciousness of Self and Perceptions of Individuality

"Consider how, when you recently blundered before the brethren by saying one antiphon for another, your mind sought how it might blame the fault on something else, either on the book itself or on some other thing. For your heart was unwilling to behold itself as it was." So Guigo, prior of the Grande Chartreuse, writing for his own benefit in the desolate and windswept mountains near Grenoble, noted early in the twelfth century.[1] The "you" is Guigo himself, trying to stand apart from his "heart" or "mind" and to be aware of inner drives of which he had not before been conscious. Even an apparently trivial slip in the choice of a liturgical formula was an occasion for self-examination. How far we are here from the barren internal world of the literary Roland and Oliver, who question each other, but who unselfconsciously follow their own imperatives, without reflecting on either the wisdom or the morality of their own acts.

Bernard of Clairvaux, preaching to his monks on the seven steps of confession, explained that the first was expressed in the celestial precept, "Know thyself."[2] The attempt to follow the Delphic command, "Know thyself," had a long and by no means linear evolution from the time of Socrates to the twelfth century.[3] Consciousness of self and of the inner life and motives of

---

For discussion and criticism which have greatly aided the revision of this essay, I am indebted to the members of the Conference on the Renaissance of the Twelfth Century (especially the editors of this volume) and of the Group for Psychology in the Humanities at the California Institute of Technology. Among other friends who have made major contributions to my thinking, I should name in particular Elizabeth Brown, Gerard Caspary, the late Max Delbrück, and S. D. Goitein.

[1] *Meditationes Guigonis prioris Cartusiae: Le recueil des pensées du B. Guigue* no. 282, ed. André Wilmart, EPM 22 (Paris 1936) 114–15; trans. John J. Jolin, *Meditations of Guigo, Prior of the Charterhouse* (Milwaukee 1951) 41 (slightly altered here).

[2] *De diversis*, sermo 40.3, ed. Leclercq 6.1.236.

[3] Pierre Courcelle, *Connais-toi toi-même: De Socrate à saint Bernard* (3 vols. Paris 1974–75). Courcelle states (1.231) that in the West consideration of the topic faltered during the seventh and eighth centuries, and that John the Scot, who translated large portions of Gregory of Nyssa, was the only ninth-century Occidental author to treat the precept at length.

others in the twelfth century differed from what we find in Antiquity, but it would be hard to say that any authors in the Middle Ages understood their subjective world better than Catullus or Augustine of Hippo. Evidence does exist, however, which suggests that the practice of self-examination was deeper and more widespread in twelfth-century Europe than at any time since the fifth century. The twelfth century was not a time of the "discovery of self" or "discovery of the individual."[4] The origin of consciousness as we know it in the human species, the beginning of introspection, of the reflective remembering of the self in relation to things past and imaginative projection into the future, surely occurred in the distant past.[5] In the century and a half which included the lives of Gregory VII and Francis of Assisi there did occur, however, a renewed commitment to the examination of the inner life and a development of modes of thought about the self and others which have profoundly affected our civilization. It was prompted by new values and new forms of material life, rather than being a revival of the self-examination of Antiquity, but in its own way it was a renaissance.

The central matter of this essay is not to demonstrate that a shift in attitudes toward the self and other individuals occurred in the period centering on the twelfth century, for that interpretation of the available evidence has been amply presented elsewhere.[6] Instead, my major concern will be to assess the nature and comparative level of self-awareness, concluding with some theories of why and how the psychology of the twelfth century differed so much from even so stable and wealthy an age as the Carolingian renaissance.

EXAMINING THE SELF

FORMS OF AUTOBIOGRAPHY

Throughout the earlier Middle Ages, clerics continued to read the *Confessions* of St Augustine, a work of such profound self-examination that a "history of

---

[4] I have treated the issue of "individualism" in "Individualism and Conformity in Medieval Western Europe," *Individualism and Conformity in Classical Islam*, ed. Amin Banani and Speros Vryonis, Jr. (Wiesbaden 1977) 145–58. The present essay is intended to complement that lecture, delivered at a conference where the theme and the effort at cross-cultural comparison were determined by an Orientalist, S. D. Goitein. See above, chapter 16, pp. 313-26.

[5] In *The Origin of Consciousness in the Breakdown of the Bicameral Mind* (Boston 1976), Julian Jaynes argues that consciousness is not an inherent attribute of the human condition but has had specific, historical origins in what he calls the breakdown of the bicameral mind, occurring at different times in different cultures ("bicamerality" being a condition in which the right hemisphere of the brain dictates to an "unconscious" left hemisphere). While I have found Jaynes's book heuristically stimulating, his theories that "consciousness" in humans developed relatively recently on the evolutionary scale and is closely related to a highly developed, metaphorical language are not in accord with the findings of current split-brain research; cf. Roger W. Sperry, "Changing Concepts of Consciousness and Free Will," *Perspectives in Biology and Medicine* 20 (1976) 9–19 and "Forebrain Commissurotomy and Conscious Awareness," *Journal of Medicine and Philosophy* 2 (1977) 101–26.

[6] See in particular Colin M. Morris, *The Discovery of the Individual, 1050–1200* (London 1972).

human self-awareness" in Antiquity which concludes with Augustine has been said to end "where it should begin."[7] Until the beginning of the twelfth century no reader of the *Confessions* dared or was moved to write a self-examination in the same mode.[8] About 1115, however, Guibert of Nogent, an ambitious author and abbot of an obscure Benedictine abbey near Laon, began to write in his *Monodiae* or memoirs, "I confess to Thy Majesty, O God, my endless wanderings from Thy paths." In that opening word *confiteor*, Guibert invited a comparison with Augustine, and he starts his work in the confessional mode.[9] But the correspondences between these two confessional autobiographies are verbal, formal, topical; the two books are in no way equivalent in the quality of self-examination. Augustine stripped back the flesh and bared his soul to his God. Though Guibert begins bravely, as the story of his life comes closer to the time of his writing, he hides himself from the monks he knows will be his readers in a mist of anecdotal history about external events. Where Guibert is most openly revealing, in what he writes of his mother, his long-dead father, his dreams and fantasies, he appears to be naive rather than self-aware. He is perhaps most revealing in what he hides, in what he fails or does not dare to tell us about himself.

While the confessional tradition which influenced Guibert had few followers, many medieval authors developed the classical epistolary genre and wrote of themselves and their reflections in letters. From Bernard of Clairvaux and Peter the Venerable to quite obscure correspondents, some of the most revealing authors of the twelfth century expressed themselves in letters.[10] Closely related genres were the *apologia*, like the defense against his detractors Guy of Bazoches dedicated to his mother, and the *otium*, of which a good example is the collection of meditations Hugh Farsit of Soissons sent to his sister.[11] The most famous autobiography since that of Augustine, Abelard's

[7]Arnaldo Momigliano, *The Development of Greek Biography* (Cambridge Mass. 1971) 18, referring to Georg Misch, *Geschichte der Autobiographie* (4 vols. in 8 Frankfurt 1949-69). The first volume of Misch has been translated as *A History of Autobiography in Antiquity* (2 vols. London 1950 and Cambridge Mass. 1951). Misch says (*History* 1.8, *Geschichte* 1.11), "In a certain sense the history of autobiography is a history of human self-awareness" (*menschlichen Selbstbewusstseins*).

[8]Pierre Courcelle, *Les confessions de saint Augustin dans la tradition littéraire* (Paris 1963) esp. 272-75.

[9]My own views on Guibert appear in the introduction to *Self and Society in Medieval France: The Memoirs of Abbot Guibert of Nogent (1064?-c. 1125)* (New York 1970); a slightly different version appears in "The Personality of Guibert of Nogent," *Psychoanalytic Review* 5; above, 293 ff. See also Frederic Amory, "The Confessional Superstructure of Guibert of Nogent's *Vita*," *Classica et Mediaevalia* 25 (1964) 224-40. The most recent edition of the Latin text is *Guibert de Nogent, Histoire de sa vie (1053-1124)*, ed. Georges Bourgin, CTSEEH 40 (Paris 1907).

[10]For a general survey with bibliography, see Giles Constable, *Letters and Letter-Collections*, Typologie des sources du moyen âge occidental 17 (Turnhout 1976). Excellent studies of the collected letters of two major authors are the introduction to *The Letters of Peter the Venerable*, ed. Giles Constable, Harvard Historical Studies 78 (2 vols. Cambridge Mass. 1967) and Jean Leclercq, "Lettres de S. Bernard: Histoire ou littérature?" *Studi medievali* 3rd ser. 12 (1971) 1-74.

[11]On Guy's *apologia*, of which only extracts have been edited, see Wilhelm Wattenbach, "Die Apologie des Guido von Bazoches," SB Berlin (1893) 395-420. Guy's letters have recently

history of his calamities, appears as a letter, overtly of consolation but more accurately of self-criticism and justification. Whether this "letter" was actually sent to an anonymous friend or was composed as the introduction to a unified literary composition, and whether any portion of the work was reworked by another hand, are questions not yet resolved.[12] What is clear is that Abelard did set down for posterity his own errors (or at least some of them), his shame and his glory, as well as recounting the envy and hostility of his critics, the only explanation for opposition he and many other medieval authors were willing to admit. Part of Abelard's genius lies in his literary skill and ability to record evocative detail, part in his awesome sense of the importance of his own feelings and position. But while Abelard's autobiography stands out as an unparalleled masterpiece, it is also important to remember that in their letters many of his contemporaries matched or even exceeded his capacity for self-examination.

History provided a medium for other autobiographical writers, such as Gerald of Wales, who in his third-person account of his exploits revealed much of his fiery and tempestuous personality.[13] Such distancing or reification of the self, writing as if one were one's own biographer rather than autobiographer, was not used to obtain greater objectivity of analysis, but rather made the author appear as an actor in his own account. The *Commentaries* of Pius II are no more personal than the *Commentaries* of Julius Caesar, and the histories of Villehardouin and Joinville tell us little of the authors' subjective awareness of their historical roles. Margery Kempe regularly referred to herself as "this creature," and in all the torrent of words this fifteenth-century woman released upon her harassed secretaries, she never revealed even the nature of the secret sin which she could not confess and which drove her out of her mind.[14] Any reader who expects the frankness of a Rétif de la Bretonne from medieval authors will be sorely disappointed, for a great leap in subjectivity separates medieval Europe from the eighteenth century.[15]

---

been edited by Herbert Adolfsson, *Liber epistularum Guidonis de Basochis*, Studia latina Stockholmiensia 18 (Stockholm 1969). On the largely unpublished *Otium ad Helvidem* of Hugh Farsit in MS Troyes, Bibl. mun. 433, fols. 49–106v, see André Vernet, " 'Loisirs' d'un chanoine de Soissons," *Bulletin de la Société nationale des Antiquaires de France* (année 1959) 108–11.

[12] Since publishing "Fraud, 'Fiction, and Borrowing in the Correspondence of Abelard and Héloïse" in *Pierre–Pierre* 469–511, I am much more willing to accept the view that the *Historia calamitatum* and the other letters in the correspondence attributed to Abelard are indeed his own compositions. My reasons for this change appear in "A Reconsideration of the Authenticity of the Correspondence of Abelard and Heloise," *Petrus Abaelardus: Person, Werk und Wirkung*, ed. Rudolf Thomas, Trierer Theologische Studien 38 (Trier 1980). See below, ch. 21-5, p. 411 ff.

[13] Passages from a number of works in which Gerald wrote about himself, notably *De rebus a se gestis*, have been edited and translated by Harold E. Butler, *The Autobiography of Giraldus Cambrensis* (London 1937).

[14] *The Book of Margery Kempe* c.1, ed. Sanford Brown Meech, EETS 212 (London 1940); modern version by William Butler-Bowdon (New York 1944); cf. Louise Collis, *Memoirs of a Medieval Woman: The Life and Times of Margery of Kempe* (New York 1964).

[15] In *The Value of the Individual: Self and Circumstance in Autobiography* (Chicago and London 1978), Karl Joachim Weintraub states, correctly, I believe, "The full convergence of all the

Dreams are today such a powerful tool for analysis of the self that the modern reader might expect medieval dream reports to be closely tied to autobiography or self-examination. On the whole, they are nothing of the kind. Guibert reports frankly on a few of his dreams or visions, as did Gilbert of Sempringham and Rupert of Deutz. The eleventh-century monk Othloh of St Emmeram relates some in his *Book of Visions*, but in the *Book on the Temptations of a Certain Monk*, Othloh can never bring himself to record the specific content of the vivid, erotic dreams which tormented him from early childhood and made him wish an angel would pluck "from his viscera the fiery tumor" that was inciting his flesh.[16] Most dreams or visions were recorded by others, as Orderic Vitalis reported the vision of the priest Walchelin, who on the night of 1 January 1091 was terrified by a hellish troop of the dead, including women riding on saddles covered with red-hot nails as a punishment for their mortal "obscene delights and seductions" and his own brother with fiery spurs to which he had been condemned because of his eagerness to shed blood in battle.[17] Hundreds of reports of such experiences are extant, providing fascinating, if difficult, material for the psychohistorian. But though dreams may be used to examine the inner life of the dreamer, in the Middle Ages they were normally considered not psychologically creative but imposed experiences, originating from such causes as poor digestion, carnal prompting, irritating anxiety, or demonic or other external influences.[18]

Dreams or visions, sometimes troublesome or indeed terrifying, could also be accepted positively as divine inspirations, as they were for abbess Hildegard of Bingen. Hildegard was an effective administrator as well as an intelligent student of science, a talented poet, and a devout contemplative, though from childhood until her death at 82 she suffered from repeated and protracted illness which has been described as "a functional nervous disorder" or "hystero-

---

factors constituting this modern view of the self [i.e., the emergence of individuality as a self-conscious concern] occurred only at the end of the eighteenth century" (xv). The viewpoint of his survey of autobiographical literature from Augustine to Goethe differs significantly from mine, primarily because his major concern is individuality, not self-awareness. As he says on p. xiv, "St. Augustine produced in the *Confessions* an autobiographical form and a view of the self (though not of individuality) of extraordinary power for the subsequent story."

[16]Othloh, *Liber de tentatione cuiusdam monachi*, PL 146.47C, and *Liber visionum*, ibid. 343-88. The religious rather than the psychological aspects of his life are stressed by Helga Schauwecker, *Otloh von St. Emmeram*, Studien und Mitteilungen zur Geschichte des Benediktiner-Ordens und seiner Zweige 74 (Munich 1964).

[17]Orderic Vitalis, *Ecclesiastical History* 8.17, ed. and trans. Marjorie Chibnall (6 vols. Oxford 1969-80) 4.236-50; cf. xxxviii-xl.

[18]Paul Gerhard Schmidt provides a recent bibliography concerning medieval visions in his edition of the *Visio Thurkilli* (Leipzig 1978) xi-xiv; see also Carolly Erickson, *The Medieval Vision: Essays in History and Perception* (New York 1976). Ellen Karnofsky Petrie is now preparing a *catalogue raisonné* of dreams and visions from the period 1050-1150. In his classification of dreams, in the immensely influential *Commentarii in Somnium Scipionis* 1.3.1-8, ed. James A. Willis (2nd ed. Leipzig 1970) 8-10, Macrobius is interested only in oracles or visions, because they allow one to deal with or foresee future events; dreams which arise *ex habitu mentis* are of no concern because they have "no utility or significance."

epilepsy," or what today might be diagnosed as temporal lobe epilepsy.[19] Hildegard read widely in the best scientific works available—Hugh of St Victor, Bernard Silvester, the translations by Gerard of Cremona. She incorporated this knowledge and then perceived it in visions which seemed to her more "real" than her own thoughts: "From my infancy . . . I have always seen this light in my spirit and not with external eyes, nor with any thoughts of my heart nor with help from the senses."[20] Hildegard, who combined with intelligence and a passion for learning a fascination with deterministic systems and a comparative lack of subjective consciousness, understood herself in terms of *in*spiration rather than personal *ex*pression, and is comparable to Joan of Arc, who believed her life was directed by voices today called "hallucinatory."[21]

Terms like "hystero-epilepsy" or "hallucinatory" may shock when applied to functionally effective people like Hildegard and Joan. They remind the reader that in the application of psychology to history there is an ever-present danger of concentrating only on pathology or imposing modern Western values on another culture. If, as in the Middle Ages, a significant portion of a population sees visions or hears "voices" and is indeed honored for doing so, there is no historical, moral, or psychological value in labeling either the individuals or the society as "sick" or "pathological." Nevertheless, when medical or psychological diagnoses can explain a person's inability to carry out a desired act, or thoughts or behavior which otherwise seem strange, they can be a useful tool for the historian. If Guibert of Nogent's treatise on relics was shaped by an excessive fear of sexual mutilation, if Bernard of Clairvaux suffered from an acute gastritis which interfered with his duties as abbot and may have caused him such pain that when he rode a mule all day along Lake Geneva this unusually observant man did not notice the scenery (a limitation of sight which John Addington Symonds blamed on his monk's cowl, not his physical condition), or if Abelard, after calling for a confrontation at the

---

[19] The quoted diagnosis is that of Charles J. Singer, M.D., "The Visions of Hildegard of Bingen," *From Magic to Science: Essays on the Scientific Twilight* (New York and London 1928) 199-239. Much research on temporal lobe epilepsy, which produces visual hallucinations of structured images, has been done since the time of Singer's essay.

[20] PL 197.18B, quoted by Singer (n. 19 above) 233-34 in his section on "The Pathological Basis of the Visions."

[21] The highly structured, geometric forms revealed to Hildegard suggest the value of comparison with similar figures produced by visionary mystics like Joachim of Fiore (see Marjorie Reeves and Beatrice Hirsch-Reich, *The Figurae of Joachim of Fiore* [Oxford 1972]) and Ramón Lull (see Frances A. Yates, "The Art of Ramon Lull: An Approach to it through Lull's *Theory of the Elements*," JWCI 17 [1954] 115-73), or a "certified" hysterical neurotic like Opicinus de Canistris (see Richard Salomon, *Opicinus de Canistris*, Studies of the Warburg Institute 1A and 1B [1 vol. + atlas London 1936] and Ernst Kris, *Psychoanalytic Explorations in Art* [New York 1952] 118-27). Joan of Arc is mentioned here, not because her well-documented accounts of her voices are particularly unusual, but because she is the only medieval individual named by Jaynes (n. 5 above, 74, 79), who suggests an explanation for those voices as right-hemispheric messages perceived (or "heard") by the left side of the brain.

Council of Sens, failed to defend himself because of either acute depression or Hodgkin's disease, then the accurate diagnosis and understanding of either physiologic or psychogenic conditions can enrich history without turning it into a form of anachronistic autopsy.[22]

BIOGRAPHY

An egocentric logic suggests that greater awareness of the self precedes and permits greater awareness of the individuality, the special characteristics, and indeed the motives of others. Possibly, however, the process works in the opposite direction, or is more likely reciprocal, for greater understanding and more acute observation of others may permit by comparison deeper understanding of the subjective self. Despite the example of Augustine, clearer delineation of individuality appears in twelfth-century biography than autobiography. The limitations of biography in the Carolingian renaissance are demonstrated by the most notable attempt of that period, the *Life of Charlemagne*, in which Einhard follows Suetonius both in what he feels free to record and in his very choice of words.[23] Einhard's sparkling image of Charlemagne is like a mosaic created by rearrangement from tesserae taken from the work of another author, comparable to a *cento* on Christ restricted to phrases from Vergil. The saints' lives of the earlier period—formulaic, didactic, and inspirational—reveal even less of "personality." By contrast, in the renaissance of the twelfth century we see a multicolored flowering of biography. Eadmer's *Life of St Anselm*, "the first intimate portrait of a saint in our history," tells us much more of Anselm than Einhard ever conceived of writing about Charlemagne, and in the process tells us much of the author himself.[24]

One could continue for pages with the great biographies, some but not all of saints: the *Life of Aelred of Rievaulx* by Walter Daniel, the *Chronicle* of Jocelin of Brakelond, which records the life of his abbot Samson of Bury St Edmunds, the *Magna Vita* of St Hugh of Lincoln by Adam of Eynsham, to name

---

[22] On Guibert, see Benton, *Self and Society* (n. 9 above) introduction, esp. 29-30; a psychological problem which troubled Guibert consciously was his inability to speak out in the face of opposition (20). Elphège Vacandard, *Vie de Saint Bernard, abbé de Clairvaux* (4th ed. 2 vols. Paris 1910) 1.76-79 and 232-35 deals with Bernard's illness. The story of the ride along Lake Geneva is told by Alan of Auxerre in the *Vita secunda* c. 16 and is (mis)used by Symonds at the beginning of his *Renaissance in Italy* (3rd ed. 5 vols. in 7 London 1926-29). On Abelard at the Council of Sens see Jean Jeannin, M.D., "La dernière maladie d'Abélard: Une alliée imprévue de Saint Bernard," *Mélanges Saint Bernard*, XXIVe Congrès de l'Association bourguignonne des sociétés savantes (Dijon 1954) 109-14.

[23] Louis Halphen, *Etudes critiques sur l'histoire de Charlemagne* (Paris 1921) 91-95. In the twelfth century, William of Malmesbury avoided the annalistic style by following the structure of Suetonius, but he clearly felt much freer to digress than Einhard had; see Marie Schütt, "The Literary Form of William of Malmesbury's 'Gesta Regum,'" EHR 46 (1931) 255-60.

[24] *The Life of St. Anselm, Archbishop of Canterbury, by Eadmer*, ed. and trans. Richard W. Southern (London 1962) vii. Southern discusses "intimate biography," in contrast to other forms of biography, in *Saint Anselm and His Biographer: A Study of Monastic Life and Thought 1059-c. 1130* (Cambridge 1963) 320-36.

only a few.[25] These books are so untraditional, so personal, that we can even see the individual proclivities of their authors. Jocelin, for example, is humorous and enamored with words: he notes Samson's reputation as a "disputer," praises the abbot's eloquence in Latin, French, and the dialect of Norfolk, himself fakes a Scottish accent as a disguise in Italy, or repeats with bemusement a weak pun on the name of the Muses.[26] Adam, on the other hand, is both more pious and more visually oriented, achieving his best effects through images of actions, showing us Henry II at Woodstock angrily sewing a bandage on his finger in silence "instead of doing nothing" and then, pierced by a daring jest, lying on the ground dissolved in laughter; or an infant, entranced by bishop Hugh, chuckling with delight and stretching out his arms as if to fly. Adam also reveals his own attitude toward "personality" as he explains the baby's pleasure: "What could the infant have seen in the bishop which gave it so much delight, unless it were God in him?"[27]

Both abbot Samson and bishop Hugh were outstanding individuals, but perhaps the most interesting new departure in biography comes in the lives of rather ordinary men who happened to be saintly. Stephen, first abbot of Obazine in the region of Limoges, sprang from a family of modest means and had only a rudimentary education. The verbose author of his *Vita* meets the obligatory hagiographic requirements by telling us of his virtues and miracles, but the anecdotes he reports build up a realistic portrait of a man who laughed vindictively when fire broke out in a house of canons who had turned him away, wandered about the cloister picking up scattered vegetables, could terrify two playful bakers with a cough, punished breaches of discipline severely, was also quick to extend the consoling arm of charity, and criticized "indecent" spitting and showing one's teeth while laughing. Religious zeal and piety aside, Stephen must have been like a great many other rough, emotional, and authoritarian leaders of his day. His biographer showed the everyday side of a man he considered a saint.[28]

---

[25] As an indication of merit and for the convenience of readers of English I have limited these examples to volumes edited and translated in the Nelson-Oxford Medieval Texts, except for *The Life of Christina of Markyate, a Twelfth-Century Recluse*, ed. and trans. Charles H. Talbot (Oxford 1959).

[26] *The Chronicle of Jocelin of Brakelond, concerning the Acts of Samson, Abbot of the Monastery of St. Edmund*, ed. and trans. Harold E. Butler (London 1949) 34, 40, 48, 130; in the final example, to decline *musa, musae* was commonplace, for it was a paradigm in the *Ars minor* of Donatus.

[27] *The Life of St. Hugh of Lincoln* 3.10, 14, ed. and trans. Decima L. Douie and Hugh Farmer (2 vols. Edinburgh 1961-62) 1.117, 130. Discussing contrasts between guilt and shame, Herbert Morris, *On Guilt and Innocence: Essays in Legal Philosophy and Moral Psychology* (Berkeley 1976) 62 states that "shame connects with sight and guilt with hearing." Although this suggested contrast has a certain *a priori* plausibility, it is not supported by the two authors cited here, for the more visual Adam seems to be more concerned with guilt than the verbal Jocelin.

[28] *Vie de saint Étienne d'Obazine* 1.25, 2.11, 53-55, 59, ed. and trans. Michel Aubrun, Publications de l'Institut d'études du Massif Central 6 (Clermont-Ferrand 1970) 80, 110-12, 178-86. For comparable details, see "Le texte complet de la Vie de Chrétien de l'Aumône," ed. Jean Leclercq, *Analecta Bollandiana* 71 (1953) 21-52. For a discussion of "ordinary" characteristics in the

GUILT, SHAME, AND INTENTION

The profundity of spiritual meditations like those of Guigo or Bernard of Clairvaux, the confessional nature of the most revealing autobiography, and the religious function of so much biography lead us to examine with special attention the spiritual climate which nourished these works, particularly by a growing and institutionalized concern with confession and penance.[29] In the setting of examination of conscience, either by private meditation or with the aid of a confessor or spiritual director, we find our clearest evidence of the twelfth-century Church's contribution to the nurturing and propagation of introspection. The term "introspection" as used here does not mean exactly the same thing as "self-awareness," for a person may ruminate compulsively on a thought or fault without learning anything from the experience. For Freud and his followers, guilt is one of the greatest inhibitors of self-awareness, but in the march toward an increased understanding of the subjective self, guilt may be a necessary stage, either culturally or individually. A person who obeys the directions of authoritative internal voices may not feel guilt, nor does one whose actions are determined solely by the shame or honor bestowed by his peers. Examination of conscience and reflection on one's own faults, fostered by both the immediate family and the Church, must have helped to cause the apparent shift which changed medieval Europe from a "shame culture" to a "guilt culture," to use the terms once favored by anthropologists, or more precisely, from a shame-dominated culture to one in which guilt played a rapidly increasing role.[30]

The concepts of "shame" and "guilt" cultures conveniently and attractively summarize many of the differences observable between earlier and later medieval society, and yet there is a danger in their uncritical use, for human societies are not homogeneous and individuals are motivated by both shame and guilt. The aristocratic audience of the *Song of Roland* enjoyed that great

---

lives of twelfth-century saints, see Chrysogonus Waddell, "La simplicité de l'ordinaire: Note dominante de la première hagiographie cistercienne," *Collectanea Cisterciensia* 41 (1979) 3-28.

[29]On the larger subject, see Paul Anciaux, *La théologie du sacrement de pénitence au XIIe siècle* (Louvain 1949) and Jean-Charles Payen, *Le motif du repentir dans la littérature française médiévale (des origines à 1230)*, Publications romanes et françaises 98 (Geneva 1967). A short guide to the new confessional literature which became popular in the later twelfth century is Pierre Michaud-Quantin, *Sommes de casuistique et manuels de confession au moyen âge (XII–XVI siècles)*, Analecta mediaevalia Namurcensia 13 (Louvain 1962). John W. Baldwin shows how these ethical concepts were actually applied in his *Masters*.

[30]The concepts were popularized by Ruth F. Benedict, *The Chrysanthemum and the Sword* (Boston 1946) and have since been subjected to severe criticism, e.g. Gerhart Piers and Milton B. Singer, *Shame and Guilt: A Psychoanalytic and a Cultural Study* (Springfield Ill. 1953; repr. New York 1971). For a sensitive assessment of the strengths and weaknesses of Benedict's theories by a Japanese psychiatrist see Takeo Doi, *The Anatomy of Dependence*, trans. John Bester (Tokyo 1973, New York 1977) 48–57. For a recent application to medieval literature see Josef Szövérffy, "'Artuswelt' und 'Gralwelt': Shame Culture and Guilt Culture in 'Parzival,'" in his *Germanistische Abhandlungen: Mittelalter, Barock und Aufklärung*, Medieval Classics: Texts and Studies 8 (Brookline Mass. and Leiden 1977) 33–46 (= *Paradosis: Studies in Memory of Edwin A. Quain* [New York 1976] 85–96).

epic at the same time that Guigo wrote his meditations and Guibert confessed his sins to God.[31] How many medieval authors, including churchmen, ascribe their misfortunes, not to their own weaknesses, but to the envy of their rivals, to the jealousy of *losengiers*! Honor continues today to challenge moral virtue as a major determinant of human behavior.[32] Nevertheless, in the twelfth century, guilt and its expiation became increasingly dominant themes, and the values and judgments of European society were never again to be as simple as they had been in the shame-conditioned world of Gregory of Tours.

For us, the determination of guilt is closely tied to the concept of intention. Intention was a matter of legal and moral concern to jurists of the late Roman Empire and some Fathers of the Church, but when Germanic culture became dominant, the importance of intention was significantly reduced. In Anglo-Saxon law, a principle of simple behavior modification prevailed: "He who sins unknowingly shall pay for it knowingly."[33] The assessment of early medieval wergeld had been based on both the gravity of the offense and the rank of the injured party. A new attitude can be seen forming in the argument made about 1080 by master Pepo, the legendary founder of the school of law at Bologna, that the punishment for homicide should not be determined by the status of the victim, for what was at stake was the value of a human life. But Pepo, though critical of earlier Germanic practice and fascinated by what could be learned from Roman law, did not make an issue of intention, of a *mens rea*.[34] Throughout the early Middle Ages intention was the concern of authors of penitentials, not of law codes and commentaries, and even in the penitentials far more attention was concentrated on sinful actions than on thoughts. With the Gregorian Reform and the great expansion of penitential literature in the twelfth century, which brought an increased emphasis on penance to ever-widening circles of the laity, intention—the choices and

---

[31]On the "shame" cultural content of the *Song of Roland* see George F. Jones, *The Ethos of the Song of Roland* (Baltimore 1963). The conflict of differing values derived from both parents is discussed by Anne Parsons, "Is the Oedipus Complex Universal? The Jones-Malinowski Debate Revisited and a South Italian 'Nuclear Complex,'" *The Psychoanalytic Study of Society* 3 (1964) 278-328.

[32]See Jean G. Peristiany, ed., *Honour and Shame: The Values of Mediterranean Society* (Chicago 1966).

[33]On intention in ancient (particularly Hebrew and Greek) law see David Daube, *Roman Law: Linguistic, Social and Psychological Aspects* (Edinburgh and Chicago 1969) 163-75; on 173-74 Daube discusses a case of unintentional homicide in *Beowulf*. For the precept "qui inscienter peccat, scienter emendet," see *Leges Henrici primi*, ed. and trans. Leslie J. Downer (Oxford 1972) c. 88.6a (p. 270), c. 90.11a (282), and cf. c. 70.12b (222). King Alfred's well-known ordinance (Alf., c. 36) that a man who killed another while carrying his spear in a "safe" manner over his shoulder owed payment to the victim's family but could purge himself of *wite* owed to the king seems more to be an assessment of a degree of criminal negligence than a judgment of innocence by virtue of an absence of criminal intent. Moreover, Alfred's distinction is most significant because exceptional.

[34]Ludwig Schmugge, "'Codicis Iustiniani et Institutionum baiulus'—Eine neue Quelle zu Magister Pepo von Bologna," *Ius commune* 6 (1977) 1-9, esp. 6. Francis B. Sayre, "Mens Rea," *Harvard Law Review* 45 (1932) 974-1026 at 981 concludes that "up to the twelfth century the conception of *mens rea* in anything like its modern sense was nonexistent."

desires of the conscious self independent of specific actions—again became a central issue.[35]

The way in which one twelfth-century man weighed the ancient literature on intention is laid bare in the dialectical presentation of Gratian's *Concordance of Discordant Canons*, significantly, in the "Treatise on Penance" (= C.33 q. 3). Here the old, conflicting authorities are mustered and called forth, on the one hand "A vow is treated as a deed," on the other the *Digest's* "No one shall suffer punishment for a thought." Midway through his discussion, Gratian states as a provisional conclusion, "It appears clearer than light that sins are remitted not by oral confession but by inner contrition." But such an emphasis on an inner state of mind, revealed only to the subjective self and the deity who knows "the hearts and reins of men," could also be opposed on both practical and theoretical grounds. In the end Gratian left the question of the necessity of oral confession to his readers' judgment, "for both sides are supported by wise and pious men." Within a few years Peter Lombard used many of the same authorities to reach the conclusion that confession to God alone is not sufficient if it is possible to make oral confession to a man, preferably a priest. By the early thirteenth century the role of the priest as confessor was settled and a new style of *Liber penitentialis*, such as that of Robert of Flamborough, specified how penance should be weighted according to the individual characteristics of the penitent.[36]

Gratian's initial emphasis on inner contrition and the primacy of intention accorded with a powerful current of thought in his age. For twelfth-

[35]Charles M. Radding, "Evolution of Medieval Mentalities: A Cognitive-Structural Approach," *American Historical Review* 83 (1978) 577-97 makes stimulating use of modern theories of the stages of moral development in children, as studied by Jean Piaget, Lawrence Kohlberg, Elliot Turiel, and others, but seems to me to underestimate the concern with intention exhibited in early medieval law. Impressed by the fact that penitentials commonly quoted or paraphrased earlier authorities, he also places less emphasis on the importance of penitential literature than I am inclined to do. In contrast, I believe that the availability of patristic and other "authorities" dealing with intention and examination of conscience meant that, unlike children, twelfth-century Europeans did not have to create a *new*, previously unexperienced moral stage, but instead renewed or increased a concern with interiority already known in late Antiquity. Thomas Pollock Oakley's still useful *English Penitential Discipline and Anglo-Saxon Law in their Joint Influence*, Columbia University Studies in History, Economics, and Public Law 107.2 (New York 1923) concludes (200) with an approving quotation from Henry Charles Lea, *A History of Auricular Confession and Indulgences in the Latin Church* (3 vols. Philadelphia 1896) 2.107: "It was no small matter that the uncultured barbarian should be taught that evil thoughts and desires were punishable as well as evil acts."

[36]The citations from Gratian are *De pen*. D.1 c.5 ("Augustine"); c.14 (= *Dig*. 48.19.18); dict. p. cc.30, 89 (Gratian); *Corpus iuris canonici*, ed. Emil A. Friedberg (2 vols. Leipzig 1879-81) 1.1159, 1161, 1165, 1189. Although Gratian wrongly attributes to Augustine "Votum enim pro opere reputatur," the statement is a fair summary of much patristic thought; it is a paraphrase of Cassiodorus, *Expositio psalmorum* 31.5, PL 70.220 or ed. M. Adriaen, CCL 97 (1958) 278. For Peter Lombard see *Sentences*, 4.17.1-4, PL 192.880-82 or ed. Ignatius Brady, Spicilegium Bonaventurianum 4 (2 vols. Grottaferrata 1971-81) 2.342-55. On Gratian, Lombard, and Robert of Flamborough see Anciaux (n. 29 above) 122-26, 196-208, 223-31. Robert of Flamborough's *Liber poenitentialis* has been edited by J.J. Francis Firth, Pontifical Institute of Mediaeval Studies, Studies and Texts 18 (Toronto 1971).

century scholars concerned with either classical or patristic authors, determining the intention of the writer became a powerful tool of literary analysis.[37] In the realm of moral philosophy, conscience and intention were topics of intense debate at Laon and Paris, and the subject found its most daring exposition in Abelard's *Ethics*, called in the manuscripts *Know Thyself*. Abelard went too far, as he often did, and carried an idea of Anselm of Bec beyond the pale in arguing that the crucifiers of Christ were innocent of unjust action (*culpa*), for they knew not what they did.[38] Were Abelard's extreme conclusions the product of his relentless logic alone? We may well ask, for an anonymous twelfth-century poem states that Heloise was innocent of crime, since she did not "consent."[39] We are reminded here of the growing canonistic agreement that consent rather than coitus makes a marriage.[40] Abelard never mentions Heloise in his *Ethics*, but we would see him at his most human if we could think that his doctrine of intention, which earned him an article of condemnation at the Council of Sens, was an extended defense of the innocence of his beloved wife before man and before God. Few Christians could excuse the killers of Christ, but the anonymous poet absolved Heloise on the basis of her intention rather than her actions.

MODES OF INDIVIDUALIZATION

PORTRAITURE

In the visual arts, a similar decline and then reemergence of interest in the individual are apparent, though on the whole artists lagged behind authors in the renewed concern with personal representation. Individualized portraiture had been widespread in Antiquity, in the busts of the Greek philosophers and rulers, the widely disseminated statues of the Roman imperial family, the haunting painted faces of quite common people found on the mummies of Fayum.[41] But as individualization receded from biography with the Germanic

[37]Bernard of Utrecht, writing at the end of the eleventh century, is the earliest author of an *accessus* known to have replaced the seven formal questions mandated by Priscian (*quis, quid, ubi*, etc.) with three new questions, of which one was the intention of the writer; see Conrad of Hirsau, *Dialogus super auctores*, ed. R. B. C. Huygens, Collection Latomus 17 (Brussels 1955) 11. On the treatment of *intentio* by such commentators as Abelard, Honorius Augustodunensis, Gerhoch of Reichersberg, and others, see the study in this volume by Nikolaus M. Häring, 185–87, 196–97.

[38]*Peter Abelard's Ethics*, ed. and trans. David E. Luscombe (Oxford 1971) 56–67 and notes; see also xxxv–xxxvi. On canonistic discussion of Abelard's problem see Stephan Kuttner, *Kanonistische Schuldlehre von Gratian bis auf die Dekretalen Gregors IX.*, Studi e testi 64 (Vatican City 1935) 137–40.

[39]MS Orléans, Bibl. mun. 284 (*olim* 238), p. 183: "Sola tamen Petri coniunx est criminis expers, / Consensus nullus quam facit esse ream." The poem is partially edited and translated with commentary by Peter Dronke, *Abelard and Heloise in Mediaeval Testimonies*, W. P. Ker Memorial Lecture 26 (Glasgow 1976) esp. 45–46.

[40]See Rudolf Weigand, *Die bedingte Eheschliessung im kanonischen Recht* (Munich 1963) 47–58; Piero Rasi, *Consensus facit nuptias* (Milan 1946); and Michael M. Sheehan, "Choice of Marriage Partner in the Middle Ages: Development and Mode of Application of a Theory of Marriage," *Studies in Medieval and Renaissance History* n.s. 1 (1978) 1–33.

[41]I am aware that many of the Egyptian mummy "portraits," particularly from the third century A.D. and beyond, are not actual portraits, but there are some which seem to have been

Consciousness of Self and Perceptions of Individuality 339

invasions, so it was also reduced to a modicum in art. Even the exquisite Carolingian statue of a mounted emperor now in the Louvre cannot be identified with certainty as Charlemagne, so unsure are we of the physical appearance of this preeminent man.[42] In the elongated Romanesque statues of the west façade of Chartres, one king of Israel looks like the next. How radical is the change in style in the differentiated faces of Reims, carved in the early thirteenth century! Here again is a "renaissance" phenomenon, for it is hard to treat as coincidental the resemblance of St Peter at Reims to the official imperial bust of Antoninus Pius.[43] In the visual arts this fascination with individualization becomes evident late in the twelfth century and rushes forward through the thirteenth century, through the awesomely mimetic statues of the long-dead male founders of the cathedral of Naumburg,[44] to the tomb statue of Rudolf of Habsburg at Speyer, carved during his lifetime, whose sculptor was said to have hastened to alter his work after he had noticed a new line in the king's face.[45] But such funerary effigies made from living subjects, which indicate a desire to remember the dead as they actually were, appear only at the end of the thirteenth century.[46]

Change toward individualization was not only slow in the twelfth century, as compared to the thirteenth, but it was also uneven in the work of an individual artist. Just as an early medieval artist could use a late antique style to represent angels and a "Byzantine" style for other figures,[47] so in the later twelfth century Herrad of Landsberg, abbess of Hohenbourg (or her illustrator), drew the faces of the damned at the Last Judgment with more differentiation than she gave to familiar people, herself included. In the "group

---

painted from life. See David L. Thompson, *The Artists of the Mummy Portraits* (Malibu Calif. 1976) 12. On antique portraiture in general see James D. Breckenridge, *Likeness: A Conceptual History of Ancient Portraiture* (Evanston Ill. 1968).

[42] Percy Ernst Schramm, "Karl der Grosse im Lichte seiner Siegel und Bullen sowie der Bild- und Wortzeugnisse über sein Aussehen," *Karl der Grosse*, ed. Wolfgang Braunfels et al. (5 vols. Düsseldorf 1965-68) 1.15-23, esp. 21; and *Charlemagne: Oeuvre, rayonnement et survivances*, ed. Wolfgang Braunfels (Aachen 1965) 39-40.

[43] On the movement toward naturalism and the classicizing tendencies of art toward the end of the period we are considering there is ample illustration in *The Year 1200*, ed. Konrad Hoffmann and Florens Deuchler, Cloisters Studies in Medieval Art 1-2 (2 vols. New York 1970). On St Peter at Reims see Panofsky, *Ren & Ren* 62-63.

[44] Willibald Sauerländer, "Die Naumburger Stifterfiguren: Rückblick und Fragen," *Die Zeit der Staufer: Geschichte, Kunst, Kultur*, ed. Reiner Haussherr et al., Württembergisches Landesmuseum, Katalog der Ausstellung (5 vols. Stuttgart 1977-79) 5.169-245, citing earlier literature. It is worth noting that the male faces in the choir at Naumburg show greater "individuality" than the three women.

[45] *Ottokars Österreichische Reimchronik*, lines 39,125-59, ed. Joseph Seemüller, MGH Deutsche Chroniken 5.1.508-09, cited with literature in Bruno Gebhardt, *Handbuch der deutschen Geschichte*, 9th ed. by Herbert Grundmann (4 vols. in 5 Stuttgart 1970-76) 1.490-91.

[46] It is curious that the tomb of Rudolf of Habsburg is, as far as I know, the earliest for which there is direct, independent evidence of funerary sculpture made from life, since death masks were made at the beginning of the period we are considering; for the death mask of Hildegard of Büren (d. 1094), now in the Musée de l'Oeuvre Notre-Dame at Strasbourg, see *Die Zeit der Staufer* (n. 44 above) 1.270 no. 385 and 3.344.

[47] For example, contrast the "classical" style of the attendant angels with the "Byzantine" style of the Virgin and Child at Santa Maria in Trastevere at Rome, illustrated in this volume, fig. 36.

portrait" of her convent (fig. 4), Herrad represented herself at full length, but her face is similar to the faces of sixty equally similar nuns who stare away from her. Except for two nameless nuns who bracket the congregation like parentheses, each of these women has her name written above her head, her only identifying distinction. Herrad could address her flock as individuals, but she did not choose to portray them as such.[48] Nevertheless, the beginning of medieval "portraiture" appeared in a few isolated instances in the twelfth-century renaissance.

The most famous artistic representation of an individual made in the twelfth century is the gilded bronze head, probably created in the 1160s, which Frederick Barbarossa presented to his godfather, count Otto of Cappenberg. The artist made use of symbolic and unrealistic conventions, but his representation of the emperor accords with the cut of the hair described by Rahewin, and there is no reason to doubt that his contemporaries could recognize his work as a likeness of Frederick. The significance of the Cappenberg head is twofold, or indeed double-edged. It exists, and therefore shows that in the classicizing environment of Frederick's court the antique tradition of imperial portraiture could be revived, providing an example of true *renovatio*. On the other hand, the uniqueness of the head, and our consequent inability to compare it with other "portraits" of even such a prominent figure as Frederick I, emphasize the comparative rarity of naturalistic likeness in twelfth-century art.[49]

To attribute the scarcity of portraiture to the incompetence of artists would be improper, for eleventh- and twelfth-century artists knew perfectly well how to depict recognizable individuals. The proof of this statement is to be found in the representation of certain prominent saints. The convention that St Peter had a short, rounded, curly beard and the balding St Paul a

---

[48]Herrad of Landsberg, abbess of Hohenbourg, *Hortus deliciarum*, ed. Rosalie Green et al., Studies of the Warburg Institute 36 (2 vols. London and Leiden 1979) 2.505 (= fol. 323r of destroyed MS). This plate reproduces a hand-colored copy of Christian Moritz Engelhardt, *Herrad von Landsperg, Aebtissin zu Hohenburg, oder St. Odilien, im Elsasz, im zwölften Jahrhundert; und ihr Werk: Hortus deliciarum* (Stuttgart 1818) plate 12. This same plate was reproduced in the partial edition of the *Hortus* by Alexandre Straub and Gustave Keller (Strasbourg 1901) plate 80, and its English reproduction by Aristide D. Caratzas (New Rochelle N.Y. 1977), the source of the reproduction given here as fig. 4. The fidelity of the Engelhardt plate is attested by the tracing in Paris, BN, Cabinet des Estampes, Coll. Bastard, Ad 144a folio, fol. 323r p. 122 (kindly located for me by Prof. James Greenlee), reproduced by Green, 1 no. 334. For the damned at the Last Judgment see 2.434 (= fol. 253v). On fol. 38r-v the faces of Pharaoh and King David are practically identical. In his introduction Canon Keller remarks (p. vi) that "les physionomies en général se rassemblent et n'ont pas de caractère individuel." The colored reproduction reveals, nevertheless, that in the painted original the variety of colors somewhat mitigated the similarity of the drawing of the faces in the "group portrait."

[49]On this uncommon effigy see Herbert Grundmann, *Der Cappenberger Barbarossakopf und die Anfänge des Stiftes Cappenberg* (Cologne 1959) and Horst Appuhn, "Beobachtungen und Versuche zum Bildnis Kaiser Friedrichs I. Barbarossa in Cappenberg," *Aachener Kunstblätter* 44 (1973) 129-92 (with bibliography), and Willibald Sauerländer's essay in this volume,* at n. 76; the head is reproduced as fig. 73. For Rahewin's description see n. 52 below.

Renaissance and Renewal in the Twelfth Century, ed. R.L. Benson and G. Constable (Cambridge, Ma., 1982).

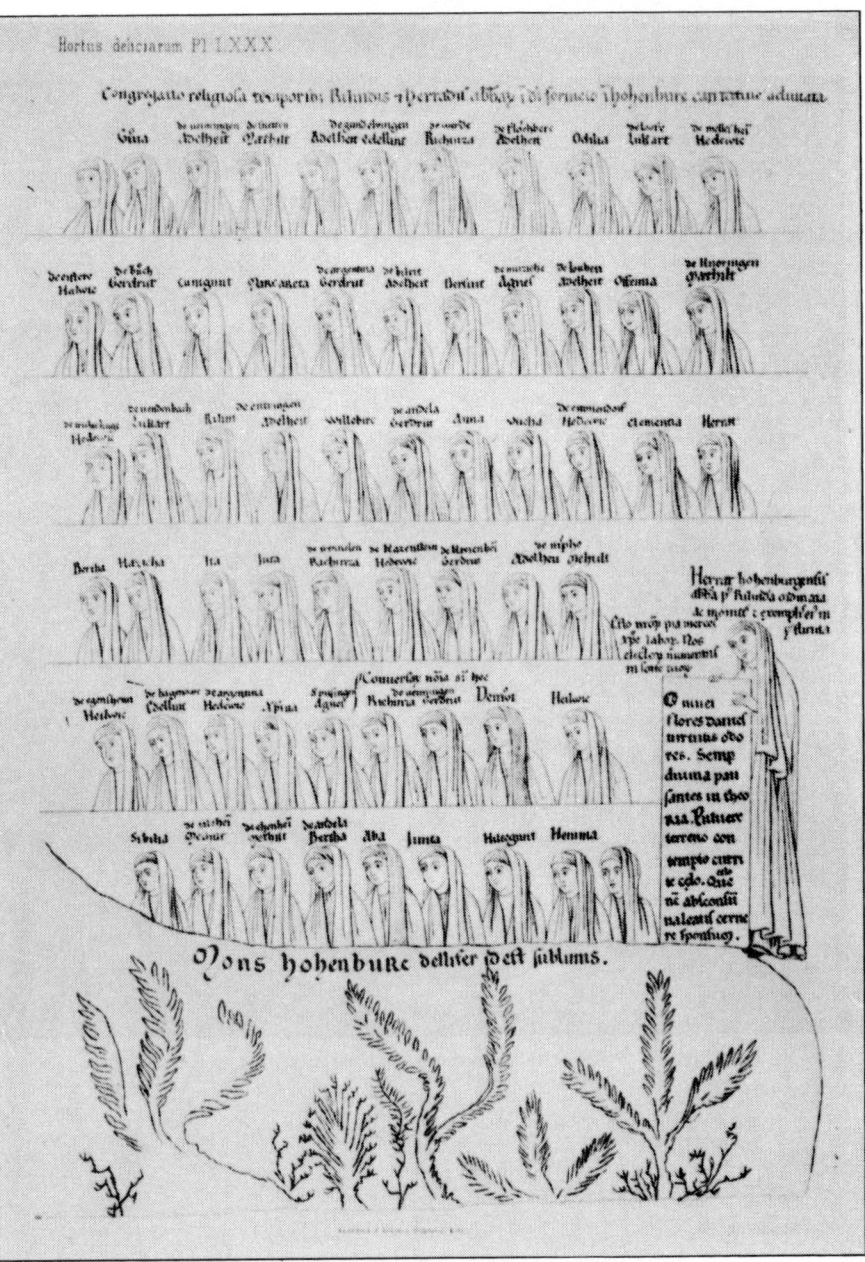

Fig. 4. Herrad of Landsberg, *Hortus deliciarum* (late twelfth century), fol. 323r: 'group portrait' of the Hohenbourg convent under Abbess Herrad. The library and codex were destroyed in the 1870 fire; figure after *Herrad of Landsberg, Hortus deliciarum (Garden of Delights)*, ed. Aristide D. Caratzas (New Rochelle, N.Y., 1976), 323r (= *Hortus deliciarum*, ed. Alexandre Straub and Gustave Keller 'Strasbourg, 1901§, pl. 80). (*Reproduced courtesy of Caratzas Brothers, Publishers, New Rochelle*)

Fig. 5. St. Peter. Mosaic, Cappella Arcivescovile, Ravenna

Fig. 6. St. Paul. Mosaic, Cappella Arcivescovile, Ravenna

Fig. 7. The coronation of Otto III, from the 'Bamberg Apocalypse', fol. 59v

Fig. 8. Papal bulls: (*left*) Pascal II (1103); (*right*) Innocent III (1200)

longer, pointed beard, to pick the most common example, was established in early Christian art and never disappeared (fig. 5).[50] The two saints who crown Otto III in the early eleventh-century Bamberg Apocalypse (fig. 6a) have precisely the same faces as the images of Peter and Paul which unchangingly represent the papacy on the bulls of Pascal II and all his medieval successors (fig. 6b).[51] In short, artists *could* produce "portraits" as instantly recognizable as those of a modern cartoonist when they saw a reason to do so, and their preference for the conventional and symbolic representation of living individuals was a matter of choice. In the twelfth century, historians and other authors frequently described individuals in a detailed, personal, and naturalistic fashion, and though these verbal portraits were heavily influenced by literary sources and sometimes by flattery, they were probably reasonably accurate.[52] That artists of the same period so rarely showed the same concern with individualized depiction of their subjects is apparently due to differences between the traditions and functions of the two forms of expression.

NAMES

Interest in the presentation of character is an outstanding development in twelfth-century imaginative literature.[53] Even a name, a simple phonemic expression, can evoke an individual human being, a specific character. In

---

[50] The medallions illustrated in fig. 9 are from a late fifth-century mosaic in the archiepiscopal chapel at Ravenna, but a wealth of other early representations could have been used, such as the sixth-century Syrian silver vase found at Emesa (now in the Louvre) or the sixth-century ivory diptych from Constantinople (now in the Staatliches Museum in Berlin), both illustrated in *Age of Spirituality: Late Antique and Early Christian Art, Third to Seventh Century*, ed. Kurt Weitzmann (New York 1979) 528-30 no. 474 and 615-17 no. 552.

[51] On the Bamberg Apocalypse see Heinrich Wölfflin, *Die Bamberger Apokalypse: Eine Reichenauer Bilderhandschrift vom Jahre 1000* (Munich 1918). The bulls illustrated in fig. 11 are of popes Pascal II and Innocent III, but the choice is inconsequential, for the representations of Peter and Paul remained practically static from Pascal II (1099-1118) to Pius II (1458-64); see Camillo Serafini, *Le monete e le bolle plumbee pontificie del Medagliere vaticano* (4 vols. Milan 1910; repr. Bologna 1965) 1.25 and 125 and plates H and M.

[52] Most of Rahewin's "portrait" of Frederick I is drawn from the descriptions by Sidonius Apollinaris of Theodoric II, by Einhard of Charlemagne, and by Jordanes of Attila the Hun, with a few words of his own on Frederick's hair; see GF 4.86 (342-44). Far more realistic and concerned with character is Peter of Blois, writing of Henry II, see *Epist.* 66, PL 207.195-210 and the curious dramatic dialogue between the king and the abbot of Bonneval, ibid. 975-88. Erich Kleinschmidt has gathered material on the conventions of the *descriptio personarum* and its application to rulers in *Herrscherdarstellung: Zur Disposition mittelalterlichen Aussageverhaltens, untersucht an Texten über Rudolf I. von Habsburg*, Bibliotheca Germanica 17 (Bern 1974) 11-90. For the highly formalized conventions of personal descriptions in literature see Alice M. Colby, *The Portrait in Twelfth-Century French Literature: An Example of the Stylistic Originality of Chrétien de Troyes* (Geneva 1965).

[53] For a treatment which deals with "inner awareness" as well as individuality, see Robert W. Hanning, *The Individual in Twelfth-Century Romance* (New Haven and London 1977). The change from epic to romance, the growth of "poetic individuality," are subjects both too large and too familiar to be treated here. See, for example, the concluding section, "From Epic to Romance," in Richard W. Southern, *The Making of the Middle Ages* (London 1953) 219-57, and Peter Dronke, *Poetic Individuality in the Middle Ages: New Departures in Poetry, 1000-1150* (Oxford 1970).

literature a prophetic "baptismal" name, a "Tristan," can easily encapsulate character, but real life is not so simple. At first it seems contradictory that as we move forward from the Dark Ages to the twelfth century, the variety of names given at birth decreases. So much diversity exists in the jumble of tongues we find in Gregory of Tours, the combination and recombination of meaningful syllables in Germanic "leading names," and so little in the baptismal names of the twelfth century, when a banquet in Normandy was limited to knights named Guillaume and 110 men of the same name jammed into the hall.[54] We may be reminded of a similar shift in another culture, when under the conformity-producing influence of Islam the onomastic richness of the early desert Arabs was reduced to the routine Muḥammads and ʿAlīs.[55]

In Western Europe the paradoxical shift proves more apparent than real, for the complex names of Germanic Europe were often created to indicate lineage rather than personal characteristics, as today breeders name horses and dogs. As conformity to a relatively restricted list of the names of saints and recognized heroes became more general, the need for accurate individualization produced added appellations, frequently indicating not family or locale (though these too were part of a "person") but recognizable characteristics. In the 1140s three canons of the cathedral of Troyes named Peter sat in the stalls together; their colleagues distinguished them as Peter the Squinter (*Strabo*), Peter the Drinker (*Bibitor* or *Potator*), and Peter the Eater (*Comestor* or *Manducator*).[56] Burghers and peasants too developed highly distinctive, personalized names through the use of *cognomina* or nicknames, often more personalized than those used by the aristocracy: Lipestan Bittecat, Robert Bontens, Herbert Gidi, Godewin Clawecuncte, and William Mordant, to pick a few of the more colorful from the Winton Domesday.[57] As family names for peasants

---

[54] For the Norman banquet see the *Chronicle of Robert of Torigni*, in *Chronicles of the Reigns of Stephen, Henry II, and Richard I*, ed. Richard Howlett, RS 82 (4 vols. London 1884–89) 4.253, and James W. Greenlee and John F. Benton, "Montaigne and the 110 Guillaumes: A Note on the Sources," *Romance Notes* 12 (1970) 177–79. On the earlier diversity of names in Gaul alone see Marie-Thérèse Morlet, *Les noms de personne sur le territoire de l'ancienne Gaule du VIe au XIIe siècle* (2 vols. Paris 1968–72). Karl Ferdinand Werner, "Liens de parenté et noms de personne," *Famille et parenté dans l'Occident médiéval*, ed. Georges Duby and Jacques Le Goff, Collection de l'Ecole française de Rome 30 (Rome 1977) 13–34 at 13–18 and 25–34 provides a succinct survey of current literature and research on given names in relation to lineage.

[55] S. D. Goitein, "Individualism and Conformity in Classical Islam," *Individualism and Conformity* (n. 4 above) 3–17 at 6 and 14.

[56] Jacques Laurent, *Cartulaires de l'abbaye de Molesme* (2 vols. in 4 Paris 1907–11) 2.379 no. 334, incorrectly dated 1125 instead of 1145. Unless we assume that Petrus Potator was known for imbibing knowledge, it is hard to believe that the more famous Petrus Comestor received his name because he devoured books.

[57] See Olof von Feilitzen, "The Personal Names and Bynames of the Winton Domesday," *Winchester in the Early Middle Ages: An Edition and Discussion of the Winton Domesday*, ed. Martin Biddle, Winchester Studies 1 (Oxford 1976) 143–229 at 207–17. Feminine bynames rarely appear here or in the Canterbury rentals published by William Urry, *Canterbury under the Angevin Kings*, University of London Historical Studies 19 (London 1967). For comparison I note, from a thirteenth-century French serf-list (BN lat 5993 A, opening 293–94), Odeline la mignote, Emeline la fadoule, Odeline called Queen (*dicta Regina*), and Isabelle la lardone.

became more routine, characterization in naming was reduced, but we should not forget that it grew in the twelfth century and flourished in the thirteenth.

"What's in a name?" is a question which lies at the heart of the debate over the meaning of universals. That question could rise, inflated with logic and learning, to explode catastrophically against the mystery of the Trinity, but in the schoolroom the most concrete topic for debate was the observable reality of personalized differences between individuals who still had *something* in common. How can the words *homo* or *albus* be predicated of Socrates or Plato? If we take "Socrates is white" to be the locating of the individual (*individuum*) Socrates among other individuals, such as Plato, that are white, the statement makes no sense, for if Socrates is altogether individable, there is nothing that is common to both Socrates and Plato and no ontological basis for locating the two white things in a single group. And if we take "Socrates is white" to be the locating of whiteness in Socrates, we have pulled a thread that leads to the unraveling of the individual to an aggregate of properties, for "he" will turn out to be only an inexplicable congeries of universals. The problem faced by Abelard and his fellows was that the first approach erodes the universal, the second the individual.[58] Though they phrased their arguments with ancient referents, early scholastic philosophers were as deeply concerned with the contemporary problem of understanding the relationship of the individual self to others as was the more mystical Bernard of Clairvaux, preaching to his monks to know themselves.

THE EMERGENT AWARENESS OF SELF

THE MONK IN HIS COMMUNITY

The monasteries fostered humility and obedience and based self-fulfillment on contemplation and community life; the schools of the secular clergy thrived on intellectual pride and questioning. The contrast should not be overstressed, however, for Abelard spent the last and highly productive third of his life as a monk, and the brilliant Benedictine theologian Rupert of Deutz daringly asserted his reliance on his personal talents (*proprium ingenium*).[59] Moreover, one may wonder if the questions of interiority so sharply debated in the twelfth-century schools by such masters as Gratian, Lombard, and Peter the Chanter could have been developed as they were if monastic culture had not prepared the way. The monasteries not only transmitted the learning and literature of Antiquity but had applied themselves to examining the inner life in their own special way. Such profound psychologists as John Cassian and

---

[58]Abelard's investigation of the problems of predication is discussed in detail in Norman Kretzmann's contribution to this volume. The preceding four sentences summarize a memorandum kindly prepared for me by Prof. Kretzmann.

[59]Rupert's introduction to his commentary on the Apocalypse, PL 169.827-28.

Evagrius Ponticus had directed early monastic contemplation to questions of will and the human passions, and the regular reading of these authors, coupled with the discipline of community life, must have had a continuing effect on those prepared to be receptive. In many ways the twelfth-century concern with the self and others can be seen as a spreading of monastic habits of thought to a larger world.[60]

"The first degree of humility is obedience without delay," St Benedict had written in his Rule, citing the Psalmist, "At the hearing of the ear he hath obeyed Me."[61] In a Benedictine community the commands of the abbot could be treated as the voice heard by the Psalmist, and the Rule prescribed instant, unreflective obedience as the first step toward a life of Christian charity. Benedict expected that his monks had renounced their own wills; the authoritative voice of the abbot should ring out louder than the murmuring of monks discussing their interpretations of a written Rule. The Rule of St Benedict is not simply an expression of a sixth-century mentality; it dominated the religious structure of monastic Europe till the twelfth and thirteenth centuries, when it was partially replaced by new forms of organization.

Why did thirteenth-century men and women flock to the new mendicant orders? One reason may be found in simple economic reality, for the religious expansion of the twelfth century had put heavy pressure on the resources of monasteries and collegiate churches, and it was much cheaper to establish a house for urban mendicants than to provide for monks, even hardworking Cistercians, or canons. But while financial considerations may have affected both benefactors and converts to the religious life, the new Rules reveal an altered ideal of the relationship of the individual to a religious community. A comparison of the Rule of St Benedict and the various redactions of the Rule of St Francis shows dramatically how much had changed in the twelfth century. Francis of Assisi stressed vocation rather than organization, and he reveled in an absence of hierarchy in his "order." "Through spiritual charity let them render services willingly and obey each other mutually," he wrote in his first brief precepts. In the more formalized Rule of 1221, when organizational requirements seemed to make "ministers" necessary, he limited their authority: "If any one of the ministers gives to his brothers an order contrary to our rule or to conscience, the brothers are not bound to obey him, for obedience cannot command sin." Francis was readier to accept authority than Peter Waldo, who eventually suffered excommunication for disobedience; he used commands as well as admonitions in his Rule, but he was reluctant to impose

---

[60]Owen Chadwick, *John Cassian* (2nd ed. Cambridge 1968) 82–109; Adalbert de Vogüé, "Les relations fraternelles et le souci de la subjectivité," *La communauté et l'abbé dans la Règle de saint Benoît* (Paris 1961) 438–503; and Leclercq, *Love of Learning*, trans. from *L'Amour des lettres et le désir de Dieu* (Paris 1957).

[61]*La règle de saint Benoît*, text ed. by Jean Neufville, introduction, trans. and notes by Adalbert de Vogüé, Sources chrétiennes 181–86 (6 vols. Paris 1971–72) 1.464 c. 5, citing Ps. 17:45; on obedience and hearing see 4.262–63 and cf. 6.1231.

authority on the consciences of others.[62] The Dominicans, adopting a modified form of the Augustinian Rule, found another, innovative way to limit the authority of superiors, introducing the election by majority vote of officers to serve for specific periods of time.[63]

TWELFTH-CENTURY CONCEPTIONS

The idea of order itself is a human construction—a metaphor—and therefore mutable. Language and metaphor both limit and stimulate the ways we think, even about ourselves. Though there is a perfectly good Latin word for "self," so that Fulbert of Chartres could write a poem *Ad se ipsum de se ipso*,[64] there is no medieval word which has anything like the meaning of "personality," and *persona* was still defined in the twelfth century primarily in its etymological sense as a mask held before an actor.[65] In this essay the word "personality" has always been enclosed in quotation marks as a reminder that a medieval person could never verbalize the idea of having a "personality." Nevertheless, one feature of the renaissance of the twelfth century is the growth of precision in language and definition and the propagation of metaphoric terms like "microcosm" and "macrocosm" which facilitated new conceptualizations, indeed, new forms of consciousness. The treatises *De anima* which were recovered or written in this period encouraged and permitted a collective language of awareness.[66]

Whatever the causes, European authors in the twelfth century had a clearer sense of their own inner life and their relations to others than their Carolingian predecessors. A heightened sense of history is a form of self-consciousness, and in both theology and in the study of *res gestae* the twelfth century was a great age of historical awareness.[67] Investigation of the concept of

[62]See the article by P. Cyprien, "Franciscaine (règle)," in *Dictionnaire de droit canonique* 5 (1953) 884-96, and Lothar Hardick, Josef Terschlüssen, and Kajetan Esser, *La règle des Frères Mineurs*, trans. Jean-Marie Genvo (Paris 1961).
[63]Georgina R. Galbraith, *The Constitution of the Dominican Order, 1216 to 1360* (Manchester 1925) 46-47, 103.
[64]*The Letters and Poems of Fulbert of Chartres*, ed. and trans. Frederick Behrends (Oxford 1976) 242-44.
[65]In his theological dictionary Alan of Lille followed Boethius in his definition of *persona*: "Etiam apud illos qui tractant comoedias vel tragoedias persona dicitur histrio, qui variis modis personando diversos status hominum repraesentat, et dicitur persona a personando" (PL 210.899A), cited by Hans Rheinfelder, *Das Wort "Persona,"* Beihefte zur Zeitschrift für romanische Philologie 77 (Halle 1928) 19.
[66]Harder to evaluate, because linguistic interaction had existed before, is the heightened consciousness of different "selves" which occurs when one speaks different languages, as well as the enrichment of vocabulary created by works like Burgundio of Pisa's translation of *De natura hominis* by Nemesius of Emesa, ed. Gérard Verbeke and J. R. Moncho (Leiden 1975).
[67]See the lucid chapter by Marie-Dominique Chenu, *Théologie* 62-89, "Conscience de l'histoire et théologie," trans. as "Theology and the New Awareness of History" in *Nature* 162-201.

"experience" also forces special consideration of the role of the self.[68] In scientific cosmology, Man self-consciously marked out his place in the universe. Perhaps increased political stability and material wealth encouraged an optimistic humanism, but the self-esteem, the positive view of the powers of human reason which we see in the best scientific and theological writing, may also have helped to create a collective consciousness of human dignity.[69]

These compressed pages have attempted to illustrate from a variety of fields a striking growth of self-awareness in the twelfth century, without suggesting that these people had a sense of subjectivity anywhere nearly as fully developed as our own. Two great limiting restraints in the mentality of the twelfth century are readily apparent.

In the first place, the conceptualization of the nature of self and of what we call "personality" differed from our own. To state the matter in a metaphor of direction, in the Middle Ages the journey inward was a journey toward self for the sake of God; today it is commonly for the sake of self alone.[70] In the modern secular world, when a person sets out to "find himself," his quest is usually conceived of as a stripping away of the layers of conformity and contrived artifice and the psychological defenses which encrust, hide, and even smother the "true self." It is as if each wondrously unique infant were wrapped by its social environment in thick swaddling clothes which must be broken or cut away in order for the individual "personality" to appear most fully. In medieval thought the *persona* was not inner but outer, and looking behind the individualized mask eventually brought one closer to the uniqueness, not of self, but of God. Modern readers more concerned with personality than the soul find Dante's *Inferno* far more interesting than his *Paradiso*, but Dante's own pilgrimage was away from both hell and personality.

A second restriction was the availability of very limited and mechanical theories of what creates individuation or "personality"—and it should be noted that what creates individuality, not conformity, was the major question examined. When Matthew of Vendôme wished to explain why one of his aca-

---

[68] See the works cited by Jean Leclercq in n. 37 of his essay in this volume.*

[69] See Robert Javelet, *Image et ressemblance au douzième siècle: De saint Anselme à Alain de Lille* (2 vols. Strasbourg 1967) and Richard C. Dales, "A Medieval View of Human Dignity," *Journal of the History of Ideas* 38 (1977) 557-72, who cites the important articles of Robert Bultot. For the relationship of developments in medieval science to self-awareness see Lynn White, jr., "Science and the Sense of Self: The Medieval Background of a Modern Confrontation," *Daedalus* 107 (1978) 47-59. Our two essays were written without knowledge of the other's work, and our remarkable agreement therefore provides a form of independent and mutually gratifying confirmation.

[70] Hugh of St Victor, for example, equated "ascent to God" with "entry into oneself" in *De vanitate mundi*, PL 176.715B. On the soul as a mirror of God in patristic literature see Jean Daniélou, *Platonisme et théologie mystique: Doctrine spirituelle de saint Grégoire de Nysse*, Théologie 2 (2nd ed. Paris 1944) 210-22, and Régis Bernard, *L'image de Dieu d'après saint Athanase*, Théologie 25 (Paris 1952) 72-74. A variety of stimulating essays appears in *Images of Man in Ancient and Medieval Thought: Studia Gerardo Verbeke . . . dicata* (Louvain 1976).

Renaissance and Renewal in the Twelfth Century, ed. R.L. Benson and Giles Constable (Cambridge, Ma., 1982).

demic rivals was a treacherous and scandalous scoundrel, the matter was simple: Arnulf of Orléans had red hair.[71] This conclusion had all the authority of proverbial wisdom, "Never trust a redhead" (*In rufa pelle nemo latitat sine felle*). Other differences were created by "national character." Early in the thirteenth century James of Vitry reported the mutual "national" insults exchanged in the schools of Paris: the English were said to be great drinkers and had tails; the French were proud, delicate, and womanizers; the Germans were mad and given to obscenity at social gatherings.[72]

Such simplistic views were too crude for the better scientific minds of people who observed differences among Germans, French, and English or even the redheaded. Physiological theories inherited from Antiquity, which find their modern counterpart in Sheldonian somatotyping, explained differences of character in terms of the balance of the four bodily fluids or cardinal humors, blood, phlegm, and black and yellow bile, which when dominant produced the sanguine, phlegmatic, melancholic, and choleric temperaments. Different balances, and the new combinations in children engendered by men and women of different humoral types, could create quite a sophisticated variety of physiologically determined character traits, as Hildegard of Bingen explained in one of her treatises.[73]

Alternatively, our fates could be found in the stars, as we are reminded by such terms for temperament as mercurial, martial, saturnine, or jovial. Since both humoral theory and astrology were developed in Antiquity and transmitted, often by means of translations, to the twelfth century, this revival of learning must also be considered a "renaissance" phenomenon.[74] Since it was obvious to any reasonably informed scholar that the celestial bodies had an effect on climatic conditions, agriculture, and the movement of the tides, it is not surprising that most people believed that they also influenced mutable human beings, and astrology was simply an attempt to set that belief on a sound theoretical foundation. Nevertheless, though physiological or astrological explanations of character differences satisfied a large percentage of the population, they posed both a social and a spiritual threat, one that was met by recourse either to free will or to the will of God. Hildegard placed her ultimate deterministic faith not in the power of the planets but in the permission and decree of God; and Abelard, more conscious of the element of human choice, criticized humoral prediction and noted that astrologers would foretell on the basis of the stars what others would do, but were unable to predict intention and feared to make such a forecast directly to the person in-

---

[71] See Berthe M. Marti, "Hugh Primas and Arnulf of Orléans," *Speculum* 30 (1955) 233-38.

[72] *The Historia Occidentalis of Jacques de Vitry* c. 7, ed. John Frederick Hinnebusch, Spicilegium Friburgense 17 (Fribourg 1972) 92.

[73] *Causae et curae*, ed. Paul Kaiser (Leipzig 1903) 70-76, 87-89.

[74] Haskins begins his chapter in *Science* on Hugh of Santalla, the translator of Albumasar and Messahala, with a reference to "the renaissance of the twelfth century" (67). He used the same term in the first version of that essay, "The Translations of Hugo Sanctelliensis," *Romanic Review* 2 (1911) 1-15 at 1.

volved because he might prove them wrong by deliberately following an alternative course.[75]

In determining the characteristics and destinies of humans, the concept of free will, which gives the greatest incentive for self-awareness and the choice of one's destiny, lies at one extreme.[76] Mechanistic explanation of individual differences occupies a middle ground, and in its medical form, with its possibility of altering the balance of the humors through diet or other means, it offers the hope of some conscious control of the differentiated self. We must not forget, however, that throughout the renaissance of the twelfth century a dark and ancient substratum persisted, the belief that Fate determines all and can be discovered by magical practices, that individual selves have no meaning in a world where neither choice nor chance exists.

The survival of an ancient, unselfconscious system of belief can be seen in the practice of fortune-telling or sortilege. It was, like witchcraft, condemned repeatedly by the Fathers of the Church, successive church councils, and the medieval canonists, and was eventually forced underground though never eliminated. Its open practice in the twelfth century is clearly revealed in an English scientific miscellany. After illustrating the ancient "sphere of Pythagoras" and other predictive devices, the manuscript continues in a bold hand with a mass for telling fortunes by lot, including an episcopal benediction. The supplicant then casts three dice which determine one of fifty-six "fortunes," the *sortes sanctorum*, apparently derived from texts of the Hellenistic East, including such vague wisdom as "The winds are cruel" or "You have honey and seek vinegar." What is striking is not the banality of the "fortunes," but that in the twelfth century such a denial of conscious decision-making could be considered to have episcopal sanction. That such practices eventually lost their official approval is shown by the same manuscript, since a late fourteenth-century hand has added a new litany and a set of rules for this form of sortilege, beginning with the instruction, "Whoever wishes to administer these fortunes should go into a secret room or a field, so that no one may disturb or come upon him. . . ."[77]

TWENTIETH-CENTURY PERSPECTIVES

The twelfth century was not so brilliantly self-conscious, or even interested in the search for self-awareness, as an isolated reading of Abelard's *Know Thyself*

---

[75] Hildegard, *Causae et curae* (n. 73 above) 19–20, and Abelard, *Expositio in Hexaemeron* (4th day), PL 178.754–55. A new edition of Abelard's commentary is being prepared by Mary Romig.

[76] A fine historical survey, amply supported by quotations from the sources, is given by Odon Lottin, "Libre arbitre et liberté depuis saint Anselm jusqu'à la fin du XIIIe siècle," *Psychologie et morale aux XIIe et XIIIe siècles* (6 vols. in 8 Louvain 1942–60) vol. 1 (2nd ed. 1957) 11–389; cf. vol. 3 (1st ed. 1949) 606–20.

[77] MS Köln, Schnütgen-Museum, Ludwig XIII 5, fols. 48–50; on the practice, see Pierre Courcelle, "Divinatio," in *Reallexikon für Antike und Christentum* 3 (1950) 1235–51 and Richard Ganszyniec, "Les sortes sanctorum," *Congrès d'histoire du christianisme* 3 (Jubilé Alfred Loisy), ed. Paul-Louis Couchoud (Paris 1928) 41–51.

would suggest, but it is unquestionable that changes, dramatic changes, did occur in spite of all the limiting factors. Qualitative judgments about a culture based on the examination of a few individuals are always tentative; if asked whether Augustine understood himself and his feelings better than Guibert of Nogent or Rousseau, we might well answer in the affirmative, but we would have to add that Augustine is a thoroughly unrepresentative figure of his own period, a mountain, as it were, surrounded only by hills. But if we look comparatively at the relative, quantitative indications of self-examination and concern with the inner life of oneself and of others, it is easy to see that there was significantly more of such interest in the twelfth century than in earlier medieval times. A quantitative graph, if one could be constructed accurately, would probably show a decline from the time of Augustine—roughly coincident with the Germanic invasions—only a slight increase in the Carolingian renaissance, a rise in the eleventh century which sharply increases in the twelfth, and then a continuing though perhaps irregular increase up to the present.

Comparison of this sort is relatively easy within one cultural tradition. Comparison between differing cultures is much more difficult, for it is by no means clear what weight and significance to attach to different indications of the awareness of self. We have seen, for example, that twelfth-century Europe produced practically no individualized portraiture and that most evidence of concern with individual differences appears in writing. We have some grounds for comparing the levels of awareness of self and the determinants of individual differences found in Carolingian and twelfth-century Europe, but how could we compare either culture with the Merovingians' contemporaries in Peru? There, Moche artists have left us stunningly differentiated sculptured pots, some of them apparently authentic portraits, but no written records at all.[78] This extreme case is cited only to illustrate the nature of the comparative problem. Even where extensive written records exist, the difficulty of comparing the level and nature of self-awareness of medieval Western Europe with the culture of Islam, Mediterranean Judaism, or even Christian Byzantium seems immense, though perhaps not insurmountable.[79]

Where comparison is difficult, explanation is too, and yet some attempt at explanation should be made. For such complex phenomena as those dis-

---

[78] Although Christopher B. Donnan, *Moche Art of Peru: Pre-Columbian Symbolic Communication* (rev. ed. Los Angeles 1978) is concerned with art as a means of symbolic communication and does not discuss individuation in his catalogue, some of the portrait-head bottles in figs. 1-9 illustrate my point.

[79] The possibilities as well as some of the difficulties of comparative treatment can be seen in the essays collected in *Individualism and Conformity in Classical Islam* (n. 4 above) and *East-West Studies on the Problem of the Self*, ed. Poolla T. Raju and Alburey Castell (The Hague 1968). Alexander Altmann has collected material on "The Delphic Maxim in Medieval Islam and Judaism" in *Biblical and Other Studies* (Cambridge Mass. 1963) 196-232, a study to be compared with that of Pierre Courcelle cited in n. 3 above. For recent literature on Islamic autobiography (and to some extent biography) see Rudolf Sellheim, "Gedanken zur Autobiographie im

cussed here we can scarcely expect a single explanation, for influences must surely have been reciprocal, but it should still be useful to consider explanations under separable headings. A change in psychology invites first a psychological explanation. If twelfth-century Europeans were more interested in themselves, more ready to take the risks of turning inward, then they probably had more self-esteem, or a different sense of self-worth, than their Merovingian and Carolingian predecessors. A sense of self-esteem, we know today, is most easily formed in childhood, and we attribute that process in large part to the role of parents or their surrogates. Was love or "marital affection" between spouses more likely to be found in twelfth-century families than in earlier centuries?[80] Did social restraints on infanticide leave surviving children with a greater sense of security?[81] Were parents or nurses, or at least some of them, more nurturing in the late eleventh and twelfth centuries than they had been in a previous age?[82]

Evidence of an increased concern with family life and the nurturance of children in the twelfth century can be found, though it is scanty and sometimes contradictory. In his discussion of the disadvantages of marriage in his autobiographical letter, Abelard assumed that a child would be a noisy bother precisely because the baby would be cared for by a nurse in his own home and not sent out to a wet-nurse, and in one of his hymns he pointed out that the infant Jesus was more favored than the sons of kings because he was suckled by his own mother.[83] Though the first biographer of Bernard of Clairvaux reported that the saint was nursed by his mother (for William of St Thierry was writing an idealized work of hagiography), he quickly added that Aleth did not pamper her children with delicate food but toughened them with a coarse

---

islamischen Mittelalter," *Zeitschrift der deutschen morgenländischen Gesellschaft* supp. 3.1 (1977) 607–12. The richest treatment of personal life in medieval Mediterranean Judaism is vol. 3 (1978) of S. D. Goitein's *A Mediterranean Society* (4 vols. projected, Berkeley 1967–), which deals with the family; vol. 4 will conclude with a section on "The Mediterranean Mind."

[80] In spite of all that has been written about "courtly love" and adultery, what seems to be most interesting about new developments in the twelfth century is the growing attention paid to love between married spouses; see John T. Noonan, Jr., "Marital Affection in the Canonists," *Collectanea Stephan Kuttner* 2, = *Studia Gratiana* 12 (1967) 479–509, and John F. Benton, "Clio and Venus: An Historical View of Medieval Love," *The Meaning of Courtly Love*, ed. Francis X. Newman; above, ch. 6, 99-121. Literary specialists, who often seem to be surprised that adultery is a relatively minor theme in their sources, should now see William D. Paden, Jr., et al., "The Troubadour's Lady: Her Marital Status and Social Rank," *Studies in Philology* 72 (1975) 28–50.

[81] The idea has been developed by Lloyd deMause, ed., *The History of Childhood* (New York 1974) 1–73 at 25–32, "The Evolution of Childhood"; see also Barbara A. Kellum, "Infanticide in England in the Later Middle Ages," *History of Childhood Quarterly* 1 (1974) 367–88.

[82] On child-rearing practices in the twelfth century see Mary M. McLaughlin, "Survivors and Surrogates: Children and Parents from the Ninth to the Thirteenth Centuries," in deMause (n. 81 above) 101–81.

[83] *Historia calamitatum*, ed. Jacques Monfrin (Paris 1959) 76, and *Hymnarius Paraclitensis*, ed. Josef Szövérffy (2 vols. Albany N.Y. and Brookline Mass. 1975) 88 hymn 32; Abelard underlines the mercenary or even servile character of wet-nurses by the phrase "subacta nutricum ubera."

and common diet.[84] The mother of Guibert of Nogent indulged her son with fine clothes, but he called her "cruel and unnatural" because she abandoned him when he was about twelve. Both men probably absorbed a sense of guilt along with whatever self-esteem they derived from their mothers, and as has been suggested before, guilt rather than shame may be an important stage in the development of introspection. An evolutionary psychogenic theory of the development of personality fits much of the observed evidence and deserves serious attention.[85] Such a theory is hard to test by traditional historical methods, however, for the central issue here may not be "causation" but "function," the question of how cultures in the past "used" childhood "to synthesize their concepts and their ideals in a coherent design for living."[86]

A second theoretical approach is political, tied more, it should be said, to the development of individual liberties, the passage from subject to citizen, than to the growth of self-awareness, though the two phenomena may well have an intimate relationship. If civil society is to remain coherent, recognition of individual differences cannot easily be dissociated from a right for those differences to exist, or at least for individuals to have a certain equality before the law. In twelfth-century Europe a notable increase in codified or customary liberties occurred—the *libertas ecclesie*, the granting of town and communal charters, the rights of free men as they were set down in Magna Carta and other great charters. These political developments had traceable political antecedents in the practices of the Germanic right of resistance and in the contractual aspects of feudal relations, and in the view of at least one theorist they created the conditions for a greater sense of self-worth among certain groups of men.[87] But it does not seem likely that widespread and large-scale changes in attitudes toward the self were solely or even primarily produced by political changes. It is hard to believe that Guigo the Carthusian wrote his meditations because of changes in the political world from which he had fled, or that the sculptures of the façade of Reims differ from those at Chartres because of the communal liberties possessed by the burghers of Reims.

An economic theory for the growth of "individualism" has also been developed.[88] Since specialization of labor provides economic benefits, internal

---

[84] *Vita prima* 1.1, PL 185.277C; on the issue of this report's accuracy Jean Leclercq raises questions rather than answering them in *Nouveau visage de Bernard de Clairvaux: Approches psychohistoriques* (Paris 1976) 20–27.

[85] I am particularly impressed by the approach taken by Lloyd deMause in his introduction to *A History of Childhood* (n. 81 above).

[86] Erik H. Erikson, *Childhood and Society* (2nd ed. New York 1963) 185.

[87] Walter Ullmann, *The Individual and Society in the Middle Ages* (Baltimore 1966), in part developing ideas expressed by Sidney Painter, "Individualism in the Middle Ages," repr. in his *Feudalism and Liberty*, ed. Fred A. Cazel, Jr. (Baltimore 1961) 254–59.

[88] These ideas of the effect of increasing wealth and specialization of labor on "individuation" are presented in my own formulation. They require no special annotation, for they are commonplaces of late nineteenth-century economic and sociological theorists, such as Karl Marx in *Formen, die der kapitalistischen Produktion vorhergehen*, written in 1858, published in Berlin in 1952 and interpretatively translated by Eric J. Hobsbawm and Jack Cohen as *Pre-Capitalist Economic Formations* (London 1964, New York 1965); Emile Durkheim, *De la division du travail*

economic forces produce a growing social differentiation of labor. Not only do some fight, others pray, and others work, but among those who work a growingly differentiated economy supports the smiths, farmers, bakers, fletchers, tanners, weavers, carters, and others whose names, now capitalized, remind us that a specialized occupation is a form of identity. What effect the growing towns of the twelfth century had on the people who lived in them is indeed uncertain. Did they produce urban alienation or urban freedom and self-fulfillment? Probably both, depending on class and personal differences. It is obvious that wealth facilitated the expression of self-awareness in durable form. It is equally clear, however, that great wealth was not essential for psychological development. Iceland was one of the poorest and least urbanized countries of Greater Europe, but by the thirteenth century it was producing literature crammed with finely drawn, highly individualized portraits of great psychological profundity. The first settlers of Iceland knew who they were, as we can see from the *Book of Settlements* or Landnámabók; by the thirteenth century their best authors could perceive and express what manner of people they were in all their multifaceted diversity.

What was the influence of religion over such a luxuriantly diverse economic, political, and cultural area as that which stretched from Iceland to the Mediterranean? Although all the evidence discussed so far has been taken from the dominant Christian culture, in evaluating the role of religion we should avoid the unwarranted assumption that the Christian religion was uniquely capable of fostering the development of consciousness and increased psychological awareness. If by some chance the Jewish Khazars or the Moslem Moors instead of the Catholic Franks had created an empire in early medieval Europe, interest in the examination of the subjective self might have recovered at the same rate, or perhaps even faster. This conclusion is based on the existence of a form of "control group," the small Jewish communities which shared much of the same cultural, economic, and even political environment as their Christian neighbors, though they differed both through the effects of exile, hostility, and persecution and in a greater devotion to learning, which one of Abelard's students observed with envy.[89]

---

social (Paris 1893; 5th ed. 1926), trans. from both editions by George Simpson as *The Division of Labor in Society* (New York 1933; incomplete repr. 1964); and Georg Simmel, *Über sociale Differenzierung*, Staats- und socialwissenschaftliche Forschungen 10.1 (Leipzig 1890).

[89]Detailed, comparative study should be made of self-awareness in medieval Christian, Jewish, and Islamic cultures, with particular attention to points of intercommunication and influence. In a private communication, Professor S. D. Goitein has suggested to me that the Jewish pietists in Germany were influenced by their environment and that in the matter of self-awareness something new really did begin in Western Christendom in the twelfth century. If Jewish introspection and self-awareness was significantly more advanced in northern Europe than in the world revealed by the records of the Cairo Genizah (and in fact Maimonides seems to have had no time for introspection), then the northern European environment, including its particular forms of Christianity, played a determining role in the development of consciousness of self. For the remark of Abelard's student on Jewish learning, see *Commentarius Cantabrigiensis in Epistolas Pauli e Schola Petri Abaelardi*, ed. Artur M. Landgraf (4 vols. Notre Dame Ind. 1937-45) 2.434, cited by Smalley, *Study* 78.

Some four centuries before the time of Christ, the prophet Joel had recorded the Lord's command to "rend your hearts and not your garments." Judaism maintained and developed its own institutions for both inner contrition and public atonement, and twelfth-century Jews, like their Christian contemporaries, practiced examination of conscience and suffered from a sense of guilt. Following traditional liturgical forms, they questioned whether their own faults were the cause of their exile, and even internalized the epithets hurled at them by Christians, as can be seen in a liturgical poem composed by rabbi Eleazar ben Nathan of Mainz for the Sabbath between the New Year and the Day of Atonement:

> Let us return to our God in the sorrow of our exile,
> For Thou art righteous in all that befalls us.
> We have been sent away from Thy face for our sin of avarice.
> Cause us to return and we shall return.
> "Exiles the son of exiles," they call us with enmity,
> "Filthy lucre," they name us in condemnation. . . .[90]

Whatever effect another religion might have had if it had prevailed, in fact Christianity triumphed in medieval Europe, and we must therefore examine its influence on the majority of the population. A central problem, however, is that Christianity is and has been many things to many people. One can find in the Gospels a stress on intention ("who looks at a woman lustfully has already committed adultery with her in his heart"); a private and personal relationship to God ("and when you pray, you must not be like the hypocrites"); a rejection of form and ritual ("this people honors me with their lips, but their heart is far from me"—this last a quotation from Isaiah). And on the other hand, the same Gospels provide an ample and express textual basis for a concern with the power of baptism, salvation by faith, respect for the law, and external miracles.

Emphasis on ritual, sacraments, relics, collective worship, and community life is as much a part of the Christian religion as concern with interiority and individual self-examination.[91] When Gregory of Tours recounts how a priest drove away a demonic fly with a sign of the cross or that oil consecrated at the tomb of St Martin cured a rash of pimples, his *pura credulitas* may today seem rank superstition,[92] but by the standards of his own time he was nonetheless

---

[90]Text in Seligmann Baer, *Die Piutim für alle Sabbathe des Jahres* (Rödelheim 1854) 254–56, trans. rabbi Michael Signer of Hebrew Union College (Los Angeles), who informs me that Baer's German translation avoids much of the self-condemnatory nuance of the Hebrew. For a comprehensive study of Jewish thought see Haim Hillel Ben-Sasson, "The Uniqueness of the Jewish People in Twelfth-Century Thought" (in Hebrew) in *Perakim: Yearbook of the Schocken Institute for Jewish Research of the Jewish Theological Seminary of America* 2 (1969–74) 145–218, and the same author's medieval chapters (in English) in his *History of the Jewish People* (Cambridge Mass. 1976).

[91]On changing attitudes toward liturgy and communal worship see Louis Bouyer, *Liturgical Piety*, Notre Dame University Liturgical Studies 1 (Notre Dame Ind. 1954).

[92]*Liber miraculorum* c. 106, ed. Bruno Krusch, MGH SS rer Mer 1.2.561, and *Historia Francorum* 8.15, 2nd ed. Krusch and Wilhelm Levison, MGH SS rer Mer 1.1 (1951) 380–83. The quite

Christian and could devoutly worship a thaumaturgic Savior who had cured a speech impairment by spitting and touching the tongue of the afflicted man. Paul and even more Augustine stressed the interiority of their religion; many other Christians did not. Augustine readily acknowledged his own personal responsibility—"I, not fate, not fortune, not the devil"—and he put so much trust in informed Christian virtue that he could even advise, "Love, and do what you wish," a statement often quoted in the twelfth century.[93] If Christianity in the renaissance of the twelfth century once more served to foster self-awareness, it must have been because of changes in that religion itself.

We are therefore brought back to a problem of historical change. Why and how did Christianity develop a renewed concern with the interior life? The reasons behind the change require deep examination, but very likely they are associated with other cultural changes already discussed—political, economic, and probably particularly psychological. The means of propagating a change in religion are far clearer, for with the Gregorian Reform the Christian Church became better organized and effective in spreading and indeed enforcing whatever modes of religious thought were then dominant. The effect of that reform was felt most strongly by the clergy in the late eleventh and early twelfth century, and in the course of the twelfth and thirteenth centuries the Christian beliefs and practices of the time were institutionalized and came to have more and more effect on a receptive European populace.

Different readers will weigh these, and perhaps other, explanatory theories differently, and far more must be known about self-awareness and consciousness of others in both medieval European and other cultures before solid statements about the relative importance of various causative influences can be seriously proposed. At this point, however, I may state briefly my own tentative and personal conclusions. Germanic Europe's political tradition of "individualism" provided a fertile ground in which concern with the self and others could grow, though it is hard to see that early Germanic culture as a

---

common view that Gregory's *pura credulitas* (H.F. 1, pref.) should be considered a "system of superstition" is that of one of his translators, Ernest Brehaut, *History of the Franks, by Gregory, Bishop of Tours: Selections*, Columbia University Records of Civilization 2 (New York 1916) xxi. Gregory's story about the fly reported only a simple exorcism, but William of St Thierry records that St Bernard actually excommunicated some flies (*Vita prima* 1.11, PL 185.256B–C), and the debate over the excommunication of animals continued long into the modern period; see, for example, Jules Desnoyers, "Excommunication des insectes et d'autres animaux nuisibles à l'agriculture," *Bulletin du Comité historique des arts et monuments* 4 (1853) 36–54, and Ernest Gelée, "Quelques recherches sur l'excommunication des animaux," *Mémoires de la Société académique . . . de l'Aube* 29 (1865) 131–71.

[93]"Ego, non fatum, non fortuna, non diabolus," in *Enarrationes in psalmos* 31.16, PL 36.268. The Latin text in *Tractatus in Epistolam Iohannis ad Parthos* 7.8, PL 35.2033, is "Dilige, et quod vis fac." The quotation is cited in its original and correct form by Abelard in *Sic et non*, prologue, ed. Blanche B. Boyer and Richard McKeon (Chicago 1977) 98.221. The possible ambiguity of *dilige* was avoided in the version quoted (or created?) by Ivo of Chartres, prologue to *Decretum*, PL 161.48B: "Habe caritatem, et fac quidquid vis." This reworking was preferred by Abelard, Hugh of St Victor, and other twelfth-century authors; see *Sic et non*, prologue, 98.217–18 and notes, and Benton (n. 4 above) 150 n. 22; here p. 318, n. 22.

whole provided an environment favorable to self-awareness. Changing attitudes were nurtured, and in some cases probably produced, by changing economic conditions, particularly specialization of labor, greater wealth, and the growth of towns. Intellectual support was provided by both a "classical renaissance" and "reformed" religion, and while intellectual arguments on the nature of the individual were more likely influenced by other changes in society than their fundamental cause, the development of a richer and more precise vocabulary for the discussion of the self surely had a cumulative effect on European consciousness. A shift from a culture in which shame and worth accorded by peers predominated to one in which a sense of both guilt and self-esteem became far more common profoundly affected the way in which individuals perceived themselves.

Here we should distinguish between childhood and adult influences. For children, changes in family structure, marital love, and maternal nurturance must be considered fundamental; for adults the most important influences encouraging self-awareness and examination were the institutions of the reformed Church. Childhood and adult influences surely were reciprocal, for the institutions of the Church affected family life and child care, and every adult who legislated and enforced changes, exhorted and gave moral instruction, or nurtured children more or less well had been a child subject to the shaping influence of family life. The two stages of life cannot be separated, and as we seek to know more about the growth of self-awareness in the renaissance of the twelfth century we should look most closely at the influence of Mother Church and biological mothers.

Bibliographical Note

For evidence of medieval self-awareness the best large-scale work, which goes beyond the apparent limits of its title, is Georg Misch, *Geschichte der Autobiographie* (4 vols. in 8 Frankfurt 1949–69). Briefer and more recent is Karl Joachim Weintraub, *The Value of the Individual: Self and Circumstance in Autobiography* (Chicago and London 1978), which for its medieval chapters is based on material already treated by Misch.

Pierre Courcelle covers an immense range of philosophical and theological literature in *Connais-toi toi-même: De Socrate à saint Bernard* (3 vols. Paris 1974–75), as does Robert Javelet, *Image et ressemblance au douzième siècle: De Saint Anselm à Alain de Lille* (2 vols. Strasbourg 1967). Particularly important for the theme of this essay are a small gem, Marie-Dominique Chenu, *L'éveil de la conscience dans la civilisation médiévale*, Conférence Albert-le-Grand 1968 (Montreal and Paris 1969) and Paul Anciaux, *La théologie du sacrement de pénitence au XIIe siècle* (Louvain 1949).

A recent cluster of books has treated the theme of the "individual" or "individualism," which should be carefully distinguished from the topic of this essay: Colin M. Morris, *The Discovery of the Individual, 1050–1200* (London 1972); Walter Ullmann, *The Individual and Society in the Middle Ages* (Baltimore 1966); *Individualism and Conformity in Classical Islam* (which also goes beyond its title for comparisons), ed.

Amin Banani and Speros Vryonis, Jr. (Wiesbaden 1977); Peter Dronke, *Poetic Individuality in the Middle Ages: New Departures in Poetry, 1000-1150* (Oxford 1970); Robert W. Hanning, *The Individual in Twelfth-Century Romance* (New Haven and London 1977); and Steven Lukes, *Individualism* (New York and Oxford 1973).

Among the many fine recent contributions to the study of twelfth-century thought two may be cited as stimulating introductions for readers of English: Southern's *Humanism* and Chenu's *Nature*. Two especially stimulating articles are Peter Brown, "Society and the Supernatural: A Medieval Change," *Daedalus* 104 (1975) 133-51 and Lynn White, jr., "Science and the Sense of Self: The Medieval Background of a Modern Confrontation," *Daedalus* 107.2 (1978) 47-59.

Good samples of anthropological papers of value for medievalists are collected by Douglas G. Haring, ed., *Personal Character and Cultural Milieu* (3rd ed. Syracuse N.Y. 1956) and Robert A. LeVine, ed., *Culture and Personality: Contemporary Readings* (Chicago 1974). Psychohistory itself is a new field for medievalists, and a pioneering study of great interest is *A History of Childhood*, ed. Lloyd deMause (New York 1974). Recent developments can be followed in the articles and reviews in *The Journal of Psychohistory* (formerly *The History of Childhood Quarterly*), *The Psychohistory Review*, and *Psychohistory: The Bulletin of the International Psychohistorical Association*.

An introduction to twelfth-century ideas of the self and of others can, however, probably best be gained from careful attention to biographical studies and the work of medieval authors and artists themselves, such as Guigo the Carthusian, Bernard of Clairvaux, Hildegard of Bingen, Guibert of Nogent, Hermannus Judaeus, Peter Abelard, Jocelin of Brakelond, Christina of Markyate, Gerhoch of Reichersberg, Rupert of Deutz, and many, many others. For the visual arts, two fine works by Erwin Panofsky have excellent plates which permit long-range comparisons: *Ren & Ren*, which is particularly recommended, and *Tomb Sculpture* (New York 1964).

18

Les entrées dans la vie: étapes d'une croissance ou rites d'initiation

C'est un grand honneur pour un étranger de prendre la parole à un Congrès de la Société des Historiens médiévistes de l'Enseignement supérieur public français et c'est aussi un grand plaisir d'y présenter une communication sur un sujet aussi neuf et aussi stimulant que les « Entrées dans la vie ». Mon ami Michel Bur m'a demandé d'envisager la problématique du sujet d'un point de vue américain. Comme il me serait difficile de le faire de tout autre point de vue, je suis heureux de pouvoir répondre à sa demande, même si bien des auteurs qui font autorité aux Etats-Unis sont en réalité des Européens.

En sciences humaines la théorie a toujours pour but d'aider à réfléchir sur des problèmes d'actualité et en conséquence son application à l'histoire garde une saveur d'anachronisme. Pour comprendre comment se posent aujourd'hui aux Etats-Unis les problèmes relatifs à l'entrée des jeunes dans la société, à leur insertion dans le marché du travail ou encore celui plus philosophique de la découverte de soi-même et de l'épanouissement de la personnalité, il faut se replacer, en dehors de toute prise de position politique, dans l'ambiance de crainte ou même de crise qui est la nôtre aujourd'hui. L'enseignement secondaire, obligatoire pour les jeunes, est livré à la pagaille. La délinquance dans les lycées est un problème quotidien et si l'usage de la drogue, massif dans les années 60, tend à plafonner, il n'en demeure pas moins très préoccupant. Les adolescents qui pour la première fois abordent le marché du travail sont victimes du chômage. Quand les faits, dont la théorie doit rendre compte, sont à ce point inquiétants, il est difficile de parvenir à un consensus sur la théorie elle-même. Comme l'a dit Joseph Church, l'un des plus éminents spécialistes de la psychologie de l'enfance et de l'adolescence : « Nous ne savons pas ce que nous faisons, et quoi que nous fassions, nous le faisons mal ».

Laissons donc cette agitation du monde contemporain pour nous tourner vers les théoriciens et interroger leur pensée. Qu'il s'agisse du développement des sociétés ou de la transformation des individus, celle-ci s'organise autour de la notion d'étape. Il n'est pas nécessaire d'être marxiste ou freudien pour adopter ce point de vue. Water W. Rostow qui a publié en 1960 *The stages of economic growth* et en 1963 *The economics of take-off into sustained growth* est en économie un déterministe de style libéral bourgeois. Appliquant la théorie des étapes au développement psychohistorique, Lloyd de Mause, éditeur du *Journal of Psychohistory* (antérieurement *History of Childhood Quarterly*) considère l'éducation comme une succession de six manières d'élever les enfants selon qu'elles admettent l'infanticide, l'abandon, l'ambivalence, l'ingérence autoritaire, la socialisation, le soutien. En ce qui concerne l'adolescence et les cycles de la vie, le théoricien le plus influent aux Etats-Unis est actuellement Erik Erikson qui, âgé de 78 ans, vit à Tiburon en Californie. Dans l'essai pionnier qu'il publia en 1950, il défend une conception graduelle de l'existence, caractérisant chacun des huit âges de l'homme compris entre la prime enfance et la maturité par des conflits qui d'abord dressent l'une contre l'autre confiance et défiance dans le sein du nouveau-né et finissent par opposer l'intégrité du moi au désespoir des vieux jours. Chez l'adolescent pubère le conflit se situe entre la personne qui se forme et les personnages qu'elle assume temporairement. Pour Erik Erikson, l'adolescence est l'époque de la crise d'identité. Cette idée qui s'est imposée à tous les psychohistoriens est développée dans un autre ouvrage de 1958, intitulé *Young man Luther,* ouvrage qui fait autorité dans tous les programmes universitaires au point que le livre de Lucien Fèbvre sur le même sujet est pratiquement tombé dans l'oubli. Il est difficile de rencontrer en Amérique un psychohistorien ou un historien des mentalités qui n'ait une dette originelle envers Erik Erikson et ses théories néo-freudiennes.

Erikson a été naturalisé américain. Pour ceux qui là-bas s'intéressent aux enfants, Jean Piaget, grâce à des traductions, est devenu aussi une sorte de citoyen honoraire, comme le prouve la dimension des notices nécrologiques qui lui ont été consacrées dans les journaux américains. Il n'est pas nécessaire que je m'étende ici sur les théories de Piaget relatives au développement de la connaissance ni sur son livre intitulé *The moral judgment of the child* (1932), mais je veux dire que cet auteur a subi une sorte d'américanisation de la part de Lawrence Kohlberg qui l'a utilisé pour créer sa propre théorie des étapes du développement moral. Kohlberg distingue six étapes qui constituent des entités et peuvent théoriquement faire l'objet d'un enseignement. Bel exemple de la confiance que certains placent dans une éducation abstraite, Kohlberg n'a pas manqué de réclamer des crédits gouvernementaux pour enseigner la morale dans les lycées. Ses théories ont eu une certaine influence sur la problématique des médiévistes. Dans un article important paru en 1978 dans l'*American historical Review,* Charles Radding utilise Piaget et Kohlberg pour traiter de « *The evolution of medieval mentalities, a cognitive-structural approach* » (AHR 83 (1978), 577-592 ; voir aussi « *Superstition in Science : Nature, Fortune and the Passing of medieval Ordeal* », AHR 84 (1979), 945-969).

La théorie des étapes est particulièrement séduisante pour tous ceux qui s'occupent de développement économique ou psychologique tandis que l'étude de rites intéresse davantage les anthropologistes. Daté de 1908, le livre d'Arnold Van Gennep sur *Les rites de passage* a été traduit en anglais en 1960. L'anthropologiste américain le plus marqué par ce livre est actuellement Victor Turner. Pour Van Gennep, toute transformation comporte trois étapes : la rupture, le seuil, l'intégration. Dans *The ritual process, structure and antistructure* (1966), Turner a concentré son attention sur le seuil, qui apparaît chez lui, non comme une étape, mais comme le lieu d'un rapport entre le rite et la communauté. Sa théorie a exercé une forte influence sur les historiens. En 1978 par exemple, Ronald Weissman s'en est inspiré dans sa thèse sur les confréries florentines. Etant donné le thème de notre congrès, on notera qu'à la fin du XV siècle, 43 % des nouveaux membres de la confrérie de Saint-Paul avaient entre 15 et 19 ans tandis qu'au début du siècle la confrérie recrutait des hommes sensiblement plus âgés (Weissman, *Community and Piety between Renaissance and Counter Reformation. Florentine confraternities, 1200-1600,* p. 185).

Pour bien comprendre ce que pensent les Américains du passage de l'enfance à l'âge d'homme, il faut être conscient de l'immense prestige dont jouit auprès d'eux le théoricien français Philippe Ariès. Publié en France en 1960, *L'Enfant et la vie familiale sous l'Ancien Régime* a, dès 1962, été brillamment traduit en anglais sous le titre : *Centuries of childhood : a social history of family life.* Aux Etats-Unis, Ph. Ariès est tenu pour un expert auquel, tout en discutant son argumentation, on reconnaît généralement une indiscutable autorité. Dans *Parents and children in History,* David Hunt le place au même rang qu'Erikson, comme l'un des deux penseurs qui ont inspiré son œuvre.

Si elle influence les théoriciens qui empruntent à l'histoire de quoi bâtir leur théorie, l'opinion d'Ariès selon laquelle « Au Moyen

Age, le sentiment de l'enfance n'existait pas » risque d'avoir aussi des répercussions sur notre propre société. Dire qu'il n'y a pas d'enfance, affirmer qu'un jeune prend simplement sa place dans la société quand il est en mesure d'y accomplir sa tâche, revient à supprimer toutes les étapes par lesquelles il sort de l'enfance. En Amérique aujourd'hui, de violentes attaques sont dirigées de la droite et de la gauche contre les écoles publiques et leur rôle traditionnel dans l'éducation populaire. Les ultra-conservateurs veulent se débarrasser d'un système de promotion sociale et d'intégration raciale pour lequel ils refusent de payer. La Gauche radicale estime que les écoles publiques sont des instruments de répression et le Centre leur reproche d'avoir échoué. De tout cela résulte un mouvement de plus en plus puissant en faveur du libre choix assorti de bons de scolarité et aussi d'une réduction de l'obligation scolaire de 16 à 14 ans. Dans un tel contexte, l'idée qu'au Moyen Age la scolarisation était un épiphénomène, que la plupart des gens découvraient le sens de la vie en commençant à travailler dès qu'ils en étaient capables, que l'essentiel de la formation n'était pas donné en classe mais sur le lieu de l'apprentissage, acquiert une redoutable signification.

Les prémisses de mon exposé doivent à présent s'éclairer au cas où ma remarque sur l'utilisation anachronique des théories vous aurait échappé. En tant que médiévistes, nous avons certainement quelque chose à apprendre des théoriciens contemporains qui fixent les conditions dans lesquelles nous communiquons avec le public, mais dans le domaine qui nous est propre, nous avons aussi le moyen de contribuer, sinon à la formulation des problèmes, du moins à leur discussion intelligente. Comme nous le savons tous, la société médiévale a l'avantage d'appartenir au passé. Nous pouvons donc l'aborder dans un autre état d'esprit que la société présente. Avec le recul des siècles, nous croyons sans peine que l'éducation scolaire diffère de l'apprentissage. Nous distinguons aisément les entrées dans la vie qui sont déterminées par une chronologie préétablie fixant l'âge du mariage, de l'ordination, de la chevalerie ou encore de la prise de possession d'un héritage, de celles qui ont un caractère purement fonctionnel. De ces dernières, la loi anglaise donne un bon exemple quand elle déclare qu'un individu peut tenir un bourgage dès qu'il est capable de mesurer un tissu ou de compter des deniers. Nous pouvons aussi, comme l'a fait Georges Duby dans un article fameux des deux côtés de l'Atlantique, nous pencher sur le statut des jeunes qui, en dépit de leur aptitude au combat, étaient contraints d'attendre pour se marier ou posséder un bien foncier. Mais il ne me semble pas opportun de poursuivre dans cette direction puisque les travaux de ce congrès vont traiter de cas concrets et fournir de nouveaux matériaux à la théorie de demain. Permettez-moi donc avant de conclure de soulever un dernier problème à propos des entrées dans la vie au Moyen Age et chez nos contemporains.

La théorie des étapes suppose que si l'une d'entre elles manque, il en résulte une perte ou un trouble sérieux. Il serait ainsi difficile de passer du féodalisme au socialisme sans l'intermédiaire du capitalisme. Un enfant qui apprendrait à marcher sans s'être d'abord traîné par terre risquerait de voir son développement perturbé. Toujours selon cette théorie, alors que le système éducatif moderne, conçu comme une suite de degrés, ne peut que favoriser la croissance de l'individu, celui du Moyen Age, presque entièrement dépourvu de palier, aurait été de nature à engendrer chez les enfants et chez les jeunes des troubles de la personnalité.

Il importe donc de revenir à cette question : le Moyen Age a-t-il vraiment méconnu la notion de palier ? En affirmant que dix siècles ont ignoré le sentiment de l'enfance, Ph. Ariès s'est de toute évidence fourvoyé. Pour s'en convaincre, il suffit de relire Isidore de Séville dont les *Etymologies* n'ont jamais cessé d'être consultées : « *Gradus aetatis sex sunt : infantia, pueritia, adolescentia, juventus, gravitus atque senectus* (XI, 2, 1). Toutefois à cette époque, le besoin d'une progression ordonnée était moins lancinant qu'aujourd'hui. L'éducation avait un but fonctionnel. Elle visait à préparer à une tâche connue d'avance, que ce fût celle d'artisan ou celle de roi. Abstraction faite de l'obligation d'attendre l'héritage (mais les jeunes de Duby étaient peut-être les plus frustrés des garçons de leur âge !), on devenait un homme ou une femme quand on pouvait accomplir le travail d'un adulte. Insister sur les âges théoriques du mariage ou de l'héritage conduirait à une impasse car, en un temps où les dates de naissance demeuraient incertaines, on savait qu'un individu avait atteint la puberté quand il en administrait la preuve. En Angleterre, les *Inquisitiones post mortem* se multiplièrent non dans l'intérêt des héritiers mais parce que le gouvernement était assez fort pour réclamer des preuves avant de renoncer à de profitables droits de garde. L'entrée dans le monde du travail, l'acquisition du statut d'adulte était affaire de pratique. Par opposition, la jeunesse américaine d'aujourd'hui dans son cursus depuis l'école élémentaire jusqu'à l'Université semble toujours boucler ses malles pour un voyage qu'elle n'entreprend jamais complètement. Ph. Ariès avait bien raison d'affirmer que la scolarisation a engendré le concept moderne d'enfance.

Si un jeune au Moyen Age montait moins de degrés pour entrer dans la vie adulte, il y entrait de façon mieux ritualisée qu'aujourd'hui. La confirmation, l'ordination, l'adoubement, le mariage, l'incorporation à un métier ou à une confrérie s'accompagnaient d'un cérémonial dont le but était peut-être moins d'aiguiser le sens de la communauté que de souligner l'acquisition d'un nouveau statut.

Erik Erikson, — qui s'est forgé lui-même un patronyme à partir de son prénom — est un excellent exemple de théoricien dont la théorie — celle de la crise d'identité — prend sa source dans des problèmes personnels, mais à ces problèmes il a su donner une valeur générale en les interprétant comme la recherche d'un statut et d'une place dans le monde des adultes. Au Moyen Age, le sens de l'identité était excité par la relation fonctionnelle entre l'apprentissage et le travail de l'adulte ; il était consolidé par des rites d'initiation sociale qui exaltaient l'individu et marquaient profondément les étapes de son existence. Vues d'Amérique et peut être de France aujourd'hui, l'acquisition d'une fonction et l'initiation rituelle au sein d'une communauté appartiennent peut-être déjà à un monde perdu pour les jeunes ou en train de sombrer.

19

Trotula, Women's Problems, and the Professionalization of Medicine in the Middle Ages

In the course of the twelfth and thirteenth centuries the practice of medicine in the Christian West moved from a skill to a profession, with academic training based on authoritative learned literature, with degrees and licenses, and with sanctions against those who practiced medicine without a license. Traditional folk remedies continued to be used, of course, and the actual delivery of babies was exclusively the domain of midwives and female attendants, but increasingly the health-care of well-to-do women was supervised by academically trained physicians. The universities did not, of course, produce enough graduates to fill the medical marketplace, but medical schools nevertheless provided the standards and the concepts which determined the nature of professional practice. Since they were excluded from university education, women were thereby barred from the formal study of medicine and from professorial positions, as well as from the most lucrative medical practice. There were, naturally enough, regional variations in this development, and these generalizations apply more completely in northern Europe than in the south, particularly southern Italy and Spain.

Once universities had been granted a role in medical licensing, female practitioners could easily be prosecuted as charlatans, and though women provided most of the direct, bedside care of other women, it was to male physicians that wealthy couples turned for consultation on such matters as sterility or care during pregnancy. The theoretical understanding and scientific investigation of women's medicine was therefore a near monopoly of men. Overwhelmingly, the gynecological literature of medieval Europe was written for a male medical audience and was a product of the way men understood women's bodies, functions, illnesses, needs and desires. For

---

* Revised version of a paper presented at the Joint Meeting of the Medieval Association of the Pacific and the Medieval Academy of America, Berkeley, California, 9 April 1983. I am grateful to the Division of Humanities and the Social Sciences of the California Institute of Technology for financial assistance in procuring microfilms and photographs. I have benefited greatly from the corrections and suggestions generously offered by Joan Cadden, Monica Green, Will T. Jones, Luke Demaitre, Paul Oskar Kristeller, Berthe Marti, Michael McVaugh, George Pigman, Irwin J. Pincus, Margaret Schleissner, Eleanor Searle, and Daniel Sheerin. None of these scholars is responsible for the errors which remain. I am particularly grateful to Richard H. Rouse of the University of California at Los Angeles. He does share my responsibility, for I have relied continually on his paleographic skills and judgment for the dating and localization of manuscripts.

those women who could afford professional medical care, the most fundamental questions of their health and illness were defined by men.[1]

The process I have just described as occurring in the Middle Ages was repeated in the United States with remarkable consistency in the early twentieth century, as the country altered its rural and frontier medical practices and incorporated its new immigrants. At the beginning of the century the ratio of physicians to total population was three times what it is now, and many physicians were products of unaccredited medical schools. Midwives delivered approximately half the babies born in the early years of the century, and women were extensively involved in non-professional health-care for their families and neighbors. Women were excluded from many medical schools and were discriminated against in others, so that in 1900 only 5 percent of the students in regular medical schools were women, though 17 percent of those in homeopathic schools were female.

In the light of these facts, it can be seen that the early twentieth-century campaigns against midwives and for "regular" professional medicine practiced by licensed medical school graduates worked against any significant role for women in medicine except nursing, and even obstetrics and gynecology became overwhelmingly male domains. Today, while the percentage of women students in medical school is now approaching 30 percent, still only 12 percent of board-certified gynecologists and obstetricians are women. In the United States as elsewhere the professionalization of medicine has meant that the scientific investigation and treatment of women's bodies has been largely in the hands of men.[2]

I have cited this modern experience not simply as an example of a "structural regularity in history" but because it is difficult to understand much of the secondary literature on the legendary figure of Trotula without appreciating the social context in which historians have written about women in medicine.

Two questions have long dominated discussions about Trotula: did a medieval female physician named Trota or Trotula really exist, and if so, did she write the widely distributed gynecological treatises attributed to her? In this paper I hope not only to answer, but to go beyond, these long-standing

---

[1] For a recent prosopographical study based on references to some 125 women who practiced medicine as midwives, surgeons, *miresses*, etc., see Danielle Jacquart, *Le Milieu Médical en France du XIIe au XVe siècle* (Geneva: Librairie Droz, 1981), pp. 47–55. Pearl Kibre, "The Faculty of Medicine at Paris, charlatanism and unlicensed medical practice in the later Middle Ages," *Bull. Hist. Med.*, 1953, 27: 1–20, remains a fundamental source for the study of the exclusion of women from the practice of medicine. For the larger setting, see Vern L. Bullough, *The Development of Medicine as a Profession: The Contribution of the Medieval University to Modern Medicine* (Basel and New York: S. Karger, 1966).

[2] For a critical review of recent literature see Martha H. Verbrugge, "Women and medicine in nineteenth-century America," *Signs*, 1976, 1: 957–72. For the details in this and the preceding paragraph see also Frances E. Kobrin, "The American midwife controversy: a crisis of professionalization," *Bull. Hist. Med.*, 1966, 40: 350–63; William G. Rothstein, *American Physicians in the Nineteenth Century* (Baltimore and London: The Johns Hopkins University Press, 1972), pp. 300–301, n. 5; and Barbara Ehrenreich and Deirdre English, *Witches, Midwives, and Nurses: A History of Women Healers* (Old Westbury, N.Y.: The Feminist Press, 1973). On the development of male midwifery (unknown in the Middle Ages), see John S. Haller, Jr., *American Medicine in Transition, 1840–1910* (Urbana: University of Illinois Press, 1981), pp. 150–91.

questions. If a re-examination is now appropriate, it is in good part because the intellectual and social climate has been changed by notable women like those with whom I am about to differ.

The modern history of Trotula was shaped by Kate Campbell Hurd-Mead, who took her medical degree at the Women's Medical College of Pennsylvania in 1888. A gynecologist and president of the American Medical Women's Association, she published an article on "Trotula" in *Isis* in 1930 and devoted a major chapter to her in *A History of Women in Medicine from the Earliest Times to the Beginning of the Nineteenth Century*, which she published in 1938. Dr. Mead made a founding heroine of Trotula, whom she called "the most noted woman doctor of the Middle Ages": "To any woman doctor of the twentieth century ... there would seem to be no good reason for denying that a book having such decidedly feminine touches as Trotula's was written by a woman. It bears the gentle hand of a woman doctor on every page."[3]

Dr. Mead's work inspired Elisabeth Mason-Hohl, a Los Angeles surgeon, who in 1940 delivered her presidential address to the American Medical Women's Association on "Trotula: Eleventh-Century Gynecologist" and in the same year published a translation into English of most of the work attributed to her.[4] With such eminent sponsorship as this, there is little wonder that Trotula is one of the honored guests in Judy Chicago's feminist work of art, *The Dinner Party*.

In the later Middle Ages the most popular treatises on the diseases, medical problems and cosmetics of women were attributed to an author generally known as Trotula. Commonly two treatises were distinguished, known as the Greater Trotula or *Trotula major* and the Lesser Trotula or *Trotula minor*, but the situation is more complex than that, for three different units were presented under these names. One tract, beginning *Cum auctor*, is concerned exclusively with medical matters and is often called *Trotula major*. The authorities cited in this work include Galen, Hippocrates, Oribasius, Dioscorides, Paulus, and "Justinus."[5] A second tract, beginning *Ut de*

---

[3] Quotation from Kate Campbell Hurd-Mead, "Trotula," *Isis*, 1930, *14*: 364–65. It is evident that the editor of *Isis*, George Sarton, accepted this seriously flawed article for publication without being convinced by it, for when submitting a revised text, Mead wrote to Sarton on 3 January 1930: "I only hope you will be converted to my theories about Trotula and become one of her champions." See her correspondence in the Sarton collection at Harvard University, 6MS Am 1803 (1022), and George Sarton, *Introduction to the History of Science*, 3 vols. in 5 (Washington, D.C.: Williams & Wilkins, 1927–48), 2: 242–43. The contemporary treatment of Trotula by Dr. Melina Lipinska is more cautious and restrained than Mead's; see her *Les Femmes et le progrès des sciences médicales* (Paris: Masson, 1930), pp. 27–30.

[4] The lecture was published as "Trotula: eleventh century gynecologist," *Med. Woman's J.*, 1940, *47*: 349–56, the translation as *The Diseases of Women by Trotula of Salerno* (Hollywood, Calif.: Ward Ritchie Press, 1940).

[5] Most early manuscripts read Justinus, Justinianus, or something of the sort; Paris, Bibliothèque nationale (B.N.) lat. 7056, ff. 77–86v (= Ms. *A*) cites Copho at this point (f. 78vb), but it is the only early manuscript I know to do so. Perhaps the name of Justus, a contemporary of Galen and the author of a *Gynaecia*, appeared originally, in which case all of the authors cited in *Cum auctor* would have been ancient authorities. In the second chapter of the introduction, the author says the text is based on material from Hippocrates, Galen and Constantine the African (*A*, f. 77rb); other manuscripts frequently replace the name of Constantine with that of Cleopatra. One should not be overly impressed by the author's learning; most of the ancient citations are to be found in the *Viaticum* and *Pantegni* of Constantine the African.

curis, is largely concerned with medicine, though it includes a good deal of cosmetic information too. It repeats a number of topics treated in *Cum auctor* and cites no ancient authorities, but refers to Copho of Salerno, Magister Ferrarius (the name of a family of physicians at Salerno in the twelfth century), the women of Salerno, and Trota or Trotula herself. Both treatises deal predominantly, but not exclusively, with medical matters concerning women. A third tract, called *De ornatu,* deals almost exclusively with cosmetics, beauty aids, dentifrices, depilatories, body odor and so on; it cites no authorities except unnamed "women of Salerno" or "Saracen women." *Ut de curis* and *De ornatu* are often lumped together in the manuscripts as *Trotula minor.* Other manuscripts present all three tracts together as a single, undifferentiated work, and manuscripts of this type appear as early as the second quarter of the thirteenth century.[6]

The contents of these treatises show that all three were either written at Salerno, the most important center for the introduction of Arabic medicine (and therefore Galenism) into Western Europe, or under the influence of Salernitan masters. A survey of the existing manuscripts suggests two further things about their origins. In the first place, no manuscript of any of these texts has been discovered which can be dated much before 1200, a fact which speaks strongly though not conclusively against composition before the latter part of the twelfth century. Secondly, in some of the earliest manuscripts the three tracts appear separately from each other, and commonly anonymously, indicating that they were not thought to have a common author, or even any identifiable author.

In one of the two earliest manuscripts of any of these texts I have studied, which on paleographic grounds may be attributed to the early thirteenth century (or possibly the very end of the twelfth century), *Cum auctor* appears with *De ornatu* but without *Ut de curis.* This manuscript, from southern France, is headed *Liber de sinthomatibus mulierum* and does not mention Trotula in either its text or rubrics.[7] Another manuscript of approximately the same date contains *Ut de curis* without the other two texts; this is the earliest manuscript of these texts I have seen which contains the name of Trotula in its rubrics.[8] In a manuscript of the second quarter of the thirteenth century which once belonged to Richard de Fournival, *Ut de curis* is followed directly by *De ornatu,* creating the usual form of *Trotula minor,* but *Cum*

---

[6] Cambrai, Bibliothèque municipale ms. 916, a northern French collection of medical texts, presents all three tracts as a single unit on ff. 228v–242v, with the rubric: *Incipiunt Cure Trotule.*

[7] Paris, B.N. n.a.l. 603, ff. 55–59v. I have not yet seen Erfurt, Wissenschaftliche Bibliothek, Amplonian Q 204, which contains *De ornatu* on ff. 78v–79v and *Cum auctor* on ff. 95v–97, both in hands described in the catalogue as twelfth century; see Wilhelm Schum, *Beschriebendes Verzeichniss der Amplonian Handschriften-Sammlung zu Erfurt* (Berlin, 1887), pp. 461–63.

[8] London, British Library (B.L.) Sloane 1124, ff. 172–178v; the opening rubric is *Incipiunt capitula Trotule* in the same hand as the rest of the text, though the chapter headings were never added. The manuscript is contemporary with B.N. n.a.l. 603, cited above.

auctor does not appear at all.[9] In some ten manuscripts *De ornatu* appears without the other two treatises. The origins of these three texts are to be found in the separateness of their manuscript histories, not in their eventual unity.

Stylistically *Cum auctor* differs so markedly from *Ut de curis* that I conclude they had different authors. For instance, in *Ut de curis* twenty-five sentences begin with the word *Sunt* (*Sunt quedam mulieres, Sunt quedam, Sunt et alie,* etc.), while in *Cum auctor* no sentence uses this construction. The third treatise, *De ornatu,* begins with a preface, *Ut ait Ypocras,* followed by the main text, *Ut mulier levissima et planissima.* While the first two tracts are written for the use of other physicians, *De ornatu* in its original form addresses a female audience directly; it seems to me clear that it was written by a different author from either of the first two. This author, in fact, refers to himself as a man. The introduction which normally begins *De ornatu* when it appears with other texts is an abbreviated variant of the prologue to the independent treatise which survives in a mid-thirteenth-century manuscript from southern France as well as in later manuscripts. In this prologue the author or compiler refers to himself in the masculine gender, quotes Persius, and says he is publishing his work because women have many times asked him for advice on beauty aids. The rubric of one fifteenth-century manuscript identifies the author as "Ricardus medicus expertus," perhaps meaning Ricardus Anglicus, sometimes known as Richard of Salerno.[10] The edited prologue follows in an appendix.

Most manuscripts of the three tracts make no distinction of authorship. In their rubrics the scribes commonly attribute the texts to "Trotula" or "Trota," treat the author as a woman, and sometimes identify her as a "healer from Salerno" (*sanatrix Salernitana*) or something of the sort. Such information shows us what scribes believed to be the case, but rubrics are a notoriously poor source of biographical information. In the sixteenth century the situation became even more muddled, for the editor of the *editio princeps,* Georg Kraut, created a single work from the three medieval treatises at his disposal, rearranging material from *Cum auctor, Ut de curis* and *De*

---

[9] New York Academy of Medicine ms. SAFE, ff. 77–82. This important manuscript, which once belonged to the Drabkins, is described in Caelius Aurelianus, *Gynaecia,* ed. Miriam F. Drabkin and Israel E. Drabkin, Supplement to the *Bulletin of the History of Medicine,* 13 (Baltimore: The Johns Hopkins Press, 1951), pp. v–vi. Though the Drabkins state that the manuscript "seems to be a copy of the very volume that de Fournival had in mind," Professor Rouse is convinced that it is the manuscript owned by Richard de Fournival (who was licensed to practice surgery) and which he may have inherited from his father, physician to Philip Augustus. For the history of the manuscript and the transmission of the text, see L. D. Reynolds, *Texts and Transmission: A Survey of the Latin Classics* (Oxford: Clarendon Press, 1983), pp. xxxvii and 33–34.

[10] Paris, B.N. lat. 16089, f. 113; Oxford, Exeter College 35, f. 227v; London, B. L. Harley 3542, f. 97v; and Salzburg, Museum Carolino-Augusteum 2171, ff. 180–180v. In the last manuscript the text is headed: *Incipit tractatus brevis et utilis. De decoratione et ornatu mulierum Reichardi medici experti.* In all four manuscripts the text has been badly distorted in transmission, and my edition is conjectural in places. The possibility that Ricardus Anglicus was the author is worth exploring further. Munich, CLM 444, f. 208 also contains this prologue, but I received a microfilm too late to include its readings in this edition.

ornatu under chapter headings he thought appropriate.[11] Practically all of the material which appears in the manuscripts is in the printed text, but in an arrangement of Kraut's creation. He thereby obliterated the stylistic distinctions in the material and for centuries confused readers, who thought they were reading a unified work by a single author. All later editions followed or indeed pirated Kraut's edition of 1544, to which he gave the title *De passionibus mulierum* or *The Diseases of Women.*

The Trotula texts were extremely popular in the thirteenth, fourteenth and fifteenth centuries; in fact, separately or together they became the most widely circulated medical work on gynecology and women's problems. I am aware of nearly one hundred extant manuscripts containing one or (usually) more of these three texts, and there are doubtless others to be found. A Latin verse translation was written in the thirteenth century, an Irish translation in the fourteenth, and in the fifteenth century works attributed to Trotula were translated or rewritten into French (both prose and verse translations), English, German, Flemish and Catalan.[12] By the end of the thirteenth century the name of Trotula had become famous. In the *Dict de l'Herberie* of Rutebeuf, a medical charlatan making his spiel tells his audience that he has been sent by "ma dame Trote de Salerne," "the wisest woman in the whole world."[13] Chaucer put her in distinguished company as one of the authors included along with Tertullian, Heloise, Ovid, Chrysippus, and Sol-

---

[11] Kraut was a physician from Hagenau. His edition appeared as *Trotulae curandarum aegritudinum muliebrum ... liber* in *Experimentarius medicinae* (Strassburg: apud Joannem Schottum, 1544), pp. 3–35. Paulus Manutius labeled his reprinting of this work as *nusquam antea editus,* corrected the chapter numbers of his edition, but otherwise changed little else and used no new manuscripts in *Medici antiqui omnes* (Venice: Aldus, 1547), ff. 71–80v. Other editions, such as those of Benedictus Victorius, *Empirica* (Venice, 1554), pp. 460–525 and Hans Kaspar Wolf, *Harmonia Gynaeciorum* (Basel, 1566), cols. 215–310, and their numerous reprintings, repeat the text of the Kraut edition with occasional misprints or "corrections." I have consulted and compared the copies in the National Library of Medicine, Bethesda.

[12] The Latin verse translation is printed in Salvatore De Renzi, *Collectio Salernitana,* 5 vols. (Naples, 1852–59; rpr. Bologna: Forni Editore, n.d.), 4: 1–24. An Irish translation of *Cum auctor,* preceded by a translation of *De gradibus* dated 1352, has been edited by Winifred Wulff as *A Mediaeval Handbook of Gynaecology and Midwifery* in *Irish Texts: Fasciculus V,* ed. John Fraser, Paul Grosjean, and J. G. O'Keeffe (London: Sheed & Ward, 1934), pp. 12–54. There is a French translation in Paris, Bibliothèque Ste-Geneviève 1057, f. 20ff. (which I have not seen), a literal prose translation in Paris, B.N. ms. fr. 1327, ff. 61–117 (closely related to the Latin of the N.Y. Academy of Medicine ms. cited in n. 10), and a verse translation in Cambridge, Trinity College 0.1.20, cited by Paul Meyer in "Les manuscrits français de Cambridge," *Romania,* 1903, *32:* 87–90. The fifteenth-century German translation by Dr. Johann Hartlieb exists in many manuscripts, including Baltimore, Johns Hopkins Institute of the History of Medicine, ms. 3, ff. 69–109v; see Henry E. Sigerist, "Johannes Hartlieb's Gynaecological Collection," in *Science, Medicine and History: Essays in Honor of Charles Singer,* ed. Edgar A. Underwood, 2 vols. (London: Oxford University Press, 1953), 1: 231–46. There is a Catalan translation of *De ornatu* in a fifteenth-century manuscript, Madrid, Biblioteca Nacional 3356, ff. 1–32v, accompanied by a Catalan translation of a work of erotica, the *Speculum Alfoderi;* see A. Paz y Mélia, "*Trotula,* por Maestre Joan," *Revista de archivos, bibliotecas y museos,* 1897, *1:* 506–12. An English translation appears in two fifteenth-century manuscripts, Oxford, Bodley ms. 483, ff. 82–117 and Douce ms. 37, ff. 1–42. Beryl Rowland's *Medieval Woman's Guide to Health: The First English Gynecological Handbook* (Kent, Ohio: Kent State University Press, 1981) is not an edition of this work, but of another gynecological treatise in B. L. Sloane 2463. I have no idea why she calls that text the "first." The Flemish *Liber Trotula* (Brugge, Stadsbibl. ms. 593), published by Anna Delva, *Vrouwengeneeskunde in Vlaanderen tijdens de late middeleeuwen,* Vlaamse Historische Studies (Brugge: Genootschap voor Gescheidenis, 1983), is a very free translation and adaptation.

[13] "La plus sage dame qui soit enz quatre partie dou monde" in *Oeuvres complètes de Rutebeuf,* ed. Edmond Faral and Julia Bastin, 2 vols. (Paris, A. & J. Picard, 1959–60), 2: 276–77.

omon in the "book of wikked wyves" from which the Wife of Bath's fifth husband used to read.[14]

No one seems to have doubted that the works attributed to Trotula were written by a woman until 1566, when Hans Kaspar Wolf of Basel in his edition declared that *De passionibus mulierum* was the work of Eros Juliae, a Roman freedman of the first century A.D.[15] This particular bit of unsupported nonsense was the first salvo in a continuing attack on Trotula's existence, or at least on her gender. Wolf's position has been frequently criticized, however, and historians of medicine have regularly included Trotula in lists of women physicians.

Today the question of Trotula's identity remains a subject of controversy, with three major positions being championed. The first and most widely repeated is that Trotula is a well-documented historical figure who lived in the eleventh century and who is sometimes cited as a member of the faculty of the medical school of Salerno or the first woman professor of medicine. According to the retrospective *World Who's Who in Science,* she came from the Ruggiero family of Salerno, was born about 1050, and was married to a physician named Joannes Platearius.[16] Other authors say that she flourished around 1050, rather than being born then. Sometimes we are told that she died in 1097, and Mason-Hohl adds that she was followed to her grave by a funeral procession two miles long. One could hardly ask for more precise identification, if in fact these statements are based on solid evidence.

The second position, advanced by Conrad Hiersemann, a student of the great German historian of medicine, Karl Sudhoff, is that there was an eleventh- or twelfth-century physician and author with a name like Trotula, but this author was in fact a man named Trottus. This position is based on a famous manuscript of Salernitan medical texts, once in Wrocław (Breslau) and now apparently destroyed, in which passages from an otherwise unknown author are identified by abbreviations such as *Tt* and most particularly *Trot,* followed by abbreviation marks which Hiersemann interpreted as representing the masculine *-us* ending.[17]

The third position, recently brought forward by Beryl Rowland, is that the name Trotula is not that of a real person but is related to the French verb *trotter,* to run about (as in the proverb *besoin fait vieille trotter*), and is echoed in the names of Trotaconventos, the old procuress in the *Libro de Buen Amor* of Juan Ruiz, and of the Dame Trot of English nursery rhymes.

The widespread use of the word "Trot" and its associations with expertise in feminine matters may explain why a number of manuscripts variously treating

---

[14] Wife of Bath's Prologue, 11. 676–685; of the authors whom Chaucer cites here, the Stoic philosopher Chrysippus alone seems out of place as the author of a work a fourteenth-century student of women might have read.

[15] *Harmonia Gynaeciorum,* cols. 215–216.

[16] *World Who's Who in Science,* ed. Allen G. Debus (Chicago: Marquis-Who's Who, 1968), p. 1688.

[17] Conrad Hiersemann, *Die Abschnitte aus der Practica des Trottus in der Salernitanischen Sammelschrift "De Aegritudinum Curatione,"* Inaug.-Diss. (Leipzig: Institut für Geschichte der Medizin, 1921), p. 6.

of women's diseases came to be ascribed to her. Although women doctors certainly did exist in the Middle Ages, there appears to be no firm evidence that Trotula was one of them.... My own findings do not add another proverbial nail; they tend to deprive her even of her coffin.[18]

Here I will argue that there is something wrong with all three of these positions. First of all, I have to say that the commonly presented biography of an eleventh-century Trotula is a tissue of ill-founded assertions created largely by enthusiastic amateurs and local historians.

With respect to the statement that Trotula came from the Ruggiero family of Salerno, I can find no author who cites a scrap of medieval evidence. The idea may have been based on the assumption that since the Ruggiero family was extremely important, Trotula should have come from it and therefore did. As far as I have been able to determine, the first person to assert that Trotula was a Ruggiero was Enrico or Heinrich Baccus, a German printer in Naples in the early seventeenth century, who wrote a *Nuova descrittione del regno di Napoli* (Naples, 1629). In his list of the leading people produced by Salerno he included "Trotta or Trottola di Ruggiero, who wrote a book concerning the diseases of women (*de morbis mulierum*) and another on the composition of medicines (*de compositione medicamentorum*)."[19] This unsupported assertion by Baccus probably lies behind a similar statement made in 1817 by Fr. Nicolà Columella Onorati in a biographical dictionary of illustrious men of the kingdom of Naples. Columella Onorati needed no more evidence than a handwritten note in his personal copy of the *Diseases of Women* which identified the author as "Trottula of the Roggeri family of Salerno, distinguished equally for its antiquity and its nobility."[20] And so it has gone, with assertions repeated until they became accepted as unquestioned fact.

As for the idea that Trotula was the mother of Matthaeus Platearius (supposedly the author of a twelfth-century herbal named *Circa instans*), and therefore the wife of Joannes Platearius, this was a conjecture, clearly labeled as such, of that prolific but unreliable nineteenth-century historian of the medical school of Salerno, Salvatore De Renzi. De Renzi noted that *Circa instans* (as printed) refers to the mother of Matthaeus and Joannes Platearius

---

[18] "Exhuming Trotula, *Sapiens materna* of Salerno," *Florilegium*, 1979, *1*: 52; the word *materna* in this title is presumably based on a misreading of the word *matrona* in Ordericus Vitalis. Rowland repeats her argument in *Medieval Woman's Guide*, pp. 3–6. In her book, p. 49, n. 14, she cites Edward F. Tuttle, "The *Trotula* and Old Dame Trot: a note on the Lady of Salerno," *Bull. Hist. Med.*, 1976, *50*: 61–72 and says that he "reaches conclusions very similar to my own." In fact, in his intelligent and useful article, Tuttle says that "Trotula" was "in all probability the name of a Salernitan *matrona* or midwife" (p. 68, n. 28) and urges caution "in relating Dame Trot to Trotula" (p. 72).

[19] I quote from the seventh printing, Naples, 1671, p. 156, from a copy kindly supplied by Dr. Thomas Waldman. A somewhat expanded version appears in a Latin translation, *Nova descriptio regni Neapolitani*, reprinted by J. G. Graevius in the *Thesaurus antiquitatum et historiarum Italiae, Neapolis, Siciliae, etc.*, vol. 9, part 1 (Leiden, 1723), col. 42. I have no idea what work on the compounding of medicines Baccus may have had in mind.

[20] *Biografia degli uomini illustri del regno di Napoli*, 10 vols. (Naples, 1813–26), 4: s.v. "Trotola."

Trotula, Women's Problems, and the Professionalization of Medicine 371

as a physician, and assuming that it was unlikely that there would have been two distinguished women physicians in Salerno at the same time, concluded that Trotula and the mother of the Platearius brothers were probably the same person. That supposition could bear no weight unless it was buttressed by other evidence (which it has not been), and it would have no force at all unless it seemed likely that Trotula lived at the same time as the wife of Joannes Platearius. De Renzi, I should add, did not consider that Trotula, in his opinion surely author of the "Trot'" selections in the Wrocław *Codex Salernitanus,* was also the author of the *Trotula major* and *minor.* Those works he considered compilations made by someone about 1200 who used the work of an eleventh-century physician named Trotula.[21] My point here is not that De Renzi was wrong or that his statements are inherently improbable, but that his assertions were not supported by solid evidence. As we shall see, his conclusion that "Trot'" was a female physician of the period of *Hochsalerno* and that the "Trotula" treatises were written around 1200 is probably correct.

And so we come to the third alleged biographical datum, the assertion that Trotula lived in the eleventh century, in fact, in the mid-eleventh century. This idea stems from a passage in the *Ecclesiastical History* of Ordericus Vitalis, who reports that Ralph Mala-Corona, a worldly cleric and skilled physician, visited Salerno some time before 1050 and "found no one there as learned as he in the art of medicine except a certain learned woman" (*sapiens matrona*).[22] Again, the principle of economy has been applied. How many learned women can there have been at Salerno? Knowing the name of but one, historians have assumed without supporting evidence that this *sapiens matrona* was Trotula. And once one felt confident, however unjustifiably, that Trotula lived in the eleventh century, one could then build on this assumption. De Renzi cited as an example of the appearance of the name "Trota" in the eleventh century a reference to an act of 1097 in which Roger (Ruggiero), lord of Castello di Montuori, made a donation to the monastery

---

[21] Salvatore De Renzi, *Storia Documentata della Scuola Medica di Salerno,* 2nd ed. (Naples, 1857; rpt. Milan: Ferro Edizioni, 1967), pp. 194–208; this is a revised version with additions of *Coll. Sal.,* 1: 149–161. There is no modern edition of *Circa instans.* On the passages used by De Renzi to support his argument, see Walter Starkenstein, "Ein Beitrag zur 'Circa instans'-Frage," *Archiv Gesch. Med.,* 1935, *27:* 375–76. The Starkenstein manuscripts have recently been acquired by the Library of the New York Botanical Gardens; see Eugenia D. Robertson, "*Circa Instans* and the Salernitan *materia medica,*" (Ph.D. diss., Bryn Mawr College, 1982), pp. 104–6. I am grateful to Mrs. Lothian Lynas for sending photographs of these manuscripts which allowed me to verify that the mother of the Platearii was not called a *magistra* in these passages.

[22] *The Ecclesiastical History of Ordericus Vitalis,* ed. Marjorie Chibnall, 6 vols. (Oxford: Clarendon Press, 1969–80) 2: 28 and 74–76. Though it is frequently said that Ralph visited Salerno about 1059, the *eodem tempore* which provides that date refers to the year when Ralph left Marmoutier and became a monk at St. Evroul, not to the time of his visit to Salerno. Ordericus gives contradictory information about the date of Ralph's monastic profession at Marmoutier; he probably became a monk somewhere between 1052 and 1055 (see pp. 28 and 76). Ralph's time of study (and also warfare?) in Italy apparently occurred well before he retired from the world, perhaps in the 1030s, when the Normans established their power at Aversa. Charles H. Talbot suggests, probably incorrectly, that *sapiens matrona* should be translated as *sage-femme* in "Dame Trot and her progeny," *Essays and Studies,* 1972, *25:* 1. Michel Salvat, "L'accouchement dans la littérature scientifique médiévale," *Senefiance,* 1983, *9:* 92, shows that the term *sage-femme* only appeared in the later Middle Ages, and so Ordericus could not have had it in mind when he wrote in the twelfth century.

of Cava, releasing the usufruct of his mother Trotta.[23] Mead repeats the reference, adding that Trotta "may have died the same year."[24] This statement in turn appears to be the basis for Mason-Hohl's assertion that Trotula died in 1097. For her colorful detail about the funeral procession two miles long, I can find no evidence whatsoever.

As for the third position, that there never was a female physician named Trotula or Trota and that her myth was a response to the semantic pull of the word *trot* and in association with the traditional figure of the Old Whore who appears in Ovid, the *Roman de la Rose*, etc., this view seems to me quite unnecessary, since it ignores the evidence for the existence of an actual person named Trota or Trotula. Let us now see what we can learn about such a person from reasonably solid evidence.

First of all, the woman's name "Trota" was common in Southern Italy and specifically in Salerno in the period which interests us.[25] The membership rolls of the confraternity of the cathedral of Salerno from the eleventh to the thirteenth century contain references to some seventy women named Trota or Trocta.[26] None of these women, alas, was named as a physician or as the wife of one, though another woman, Berdefolia, was identified as a physician or *medica*.[27] The obituary rolls also mention a man with the intriguing family name of Trotulus.[28] Trotula as a diminutive means "little Trota," "dear Trota" or even "old Trota"; moreover, the form could be used in creating a book title, a point to which we shall return. Given the frequent use of the name Trota, we should not be surprised to find that the physician who interests us bore that name, and there is no reason to think that it is derived from the verb for "trot." In fact, references to Old Trot, etc. may well receive some of their force from the existence of the Trotula texts.

What evidence is there for the existence of a woman physician named Trota or Trotula? The one reasonably solid piece of evidence on which attention has focused up to now appears in *Ut de curis*. In the form of this text given in the two oldest manuscripts known to me, this treatise tells us how a physician named Trota made her reputation. An unnamed girl was supposed to be "cut," we are told, because of misdiagnosed wind or gas in the uterus. "Hence it came about that Trota was called—so to speak—a female master (*Unde contingit quod Trota vocata fuit tanquam magistra*)"; she took the girl into her home, treated her with a bath in which mallows

---

[23] De Renzi, *Storia documentata*, pp. 198 and XXXIX, document 42, citing Arch. Cavense Arca D. no. 152. Document 43 refers to a Trotta in 1105 who was the sister of a physician named Landulfo.

[24] Kate Campbell Hurd-Mead, *A History of Women in Medicine from the Earliest Times to the Beginning of the Nineteenth Century* (Haddam, Conn.: Haddam Press, 1938; rpt. Dover, N.H.: Longwood Press), p. 128.

[25] In late Latin "trocta" means "trout," which is what *trotta* still means in Italian today. "Trout" seems an odd baptismal name for a woman, and as a proper name it may have had some other origin.

[26] *Necrologio del Liber Confratrum di S. Matteo di Salerno*, ed. Carlo Alberto Garufi, Fonti per la storia d'Italia (Rome: Tip. del Senato, 1922).

[27] *Ibid.*, p. 62. George W. Corner, "The rise of medicine at Salerno in the twelfth century," *Ann. Med. Hist.*, n.s., 1931, *3:* 14, is in error in saying: "The Registers and Obituary of the Cathedral, which name many doctors and women of all ranks, do not apply the title *medica* to a single woman."

[28] *Ibid.*, pp. 110, 134. Though it might be imagined that there is some connection between Trotulus and Trotula, it must be stressed that there is no evidence at all that the Trotulus of the necrology was a physician.

Trotula, Women's Problems, and the Professionalization of Medicine 373

and pellitory had been cooked and with a plaster made of radish juice and milled barley, and this cured her.[29] The same story appears in two manuscripts of the second and third quarters of the thirteenth century, where the physician is named "Domina Trotula" and we are told that she was called "*quasi magistra*"—"as if she were a female master."[30]

The point of this story is, of course, that a woman effected a gynecological success not achieved by men. It is evidence of Trota's reputation, but it also reveals how unusual her situation was. *Magistra,* a feminine form of *magister,* is an unexpected word in a medical context, perhaps even a neologism, and *tanquam* calls attention to its rarity; as one dictionary tells us, *tanquam* is "used to introduce the application of a term to something which is not properly so called."[31] In other words, a woman was not properly a master, but Trota's reputation was so great that an unusual term had to be created to express her situation as a female near-equivalent to men who held that position.

From this anecdote we may turn back to the now lost Wrocław codex, which on paleographic grounds can be dated about 1200. This manuscript contained an extremely important compendium of extracts called *De aegritudinum curatione,* made up of the work of a group of well-known Salernitan masters named in rubrics and marginal annotations, Joannes Afflacius, Copho, Petrocellus, Platearius (whichever member of the family wrote the *Practica brevis,* which is excerpted here), Bartholomeus and Ferrarius, plus a series of extracts attributed to an author designated in the rubrics as "Trot'," "Tt," or some similar form. In addition, many passages bear no indication of authorship; some have been shown to come from the *Viaticum* of Constantine. Conrad Hiersemann, who prepared a careful edition of the extracts labeled "Trot'," pointed out that there is no correspondence between the remedies attributed to "Trot' " and those in the Trotula texts known to him, and that except for one prescription for vomiting to induce a woman to expel a still-born fetus, none of the extracts labeled "Trot' " has anything to do with gynecology, obstetrics or the specific interests of women. This observation provides a form of negative support for his conclusion that the Trot' of the Wrocław codex should be considered a male physician.[32]

On the basis of these extracts Hiersemann concluded that the therapy

---

[29] London, B. L. Sloane 1124, f. 173 and N.Y. Academy of Medicine ms. SAFE, f. 77v: "Unde contingit quod Trota vocata fuit tanquam magistra, cum quedam puella propter ventositatem debuit incidi quasi ex ruptura laborasset, et admirata fuit quamplurimum." Cf. Kraut, ed., *Trotulae,* chap. 20.
[30] Leipzig ms. 1215, f. 66v and Ms. A, f. 82ra. Some later manuscripts have "quasi magistra operis" or "quasi magistra huius operis." It seems to me more likely that *tanquam* was the original form, later replaced by *quasi,* which means almost the same thing.
[31] *Oxford Latin Dictionary* (Oxford: Clarendon Press, 1982), s.v. *"tamquam."*
[32] August W. E. Theodor Henschel discovered the codex and published an unfortunately faulty text of *De aegritudinum curatione* in De Renzi, *Coll. Sal.,* 2: 81–386. Hiersemann's edition of the "Trot' " excerpts in his Leipzig dissertation, *Abschnitte aus der Practica des Trottus,* pp. 10–21, is a distinct improvement. See pp. 7–8 for the points made here. For a description and analysis of the manuscript see Karl Sudhoff, "Die Salernitaner Handschrift in Breslau," *Arch. Gesch. Med.,* 1920, *12:* 101–47. Sudhoff dated the manuscript 1160–70, but on the basis of the photographs Sudhoff published, Professor Rouse prefers a slightly later date, in the period 1185–1215, though more likely in the late twelfth century because of the small, compressed size

advocated here was never "senseless" and that the author was a "skilled practitioner who practiced scarification, phlebotomy and physical medicine *lege artis.*" He also noted one curious distinction in the labeling of these extracts.[33] When the scribe of the Wrocław manuscript identified his selected passages with abbreviated names entered in the margin, usually these names were preceded by the initial *M,* meaning *magister.* Thus we have "M.J.A." for "magister Joannes Afflacius," "M. Plat' " for "magister Platearius," "M. Bart' " for "magister Bartolomeus." Once or twice the *M* was omitted, but in practically every case it was there. But for one set of entries an *M* never appeared, and that was for "Trot' ." If we are to judge from this consistent practice in *De aegritudinum curatione,* "Trot'," whoever she or he was, was not a master.

Up to this point, then, the only evidence historians have had testifying to the existence of an actual practitioner named Trota or Trotula or anything of the sort is the passage in *Ut de curis* about Trota acting *tanquam* or *quasi magistra* and the ambiguous Wrocław manuscript. To this material can now be added a previously unnoticed text. It appears in a manuscript, now in Madrid, which was written by a northern French or English scribe about 1200. The Madrid manuscript is therefore contemporary with the Wrocław codex and with the oldest manuscripts which contain *Cum auctor* or *Ut de curis.*

The Madrid manuscript is an easily portable physician's handbook containing a collection of Salernitan medical texts, including several translations by Constantine the African and a treatise by Johannes de Sancto Paulo, a Salernitan physician and author whose work also appeared in the Wrocław manuscript;[34] it closes with a work identified in the margin in the scribe's hand as *Practica secundum Trotam* and in its later (early thirteenth-century) rubric as *Practica secundum Trotulam.* This treatise begins "According to Trota in order to bring on menstruation when a woman cannot conceive because of its retention" (*Secundum Trotam ad menstrua provocanda quorum retentione mulier concipere non potest*) and continues for four folios with remedies and medical advice concerning gynecology, the care of children, beauty, and a large number of topics which concern men as well as women, such as vomiting, insanity, scrofula, piles and snake-bite. In a number of the chapters the masculine gender is used to refer to the patient.[35]

---

of the script. In his opinion the writing is that of northwest France or Norman England. The crude, "Romanesque" style of the miniatures also suggests composition in the twelfth rather than the thirteenth century.

[33] Hiersemann, *Abschnitte,* pp. 7 and 9.

[34] The *Liber de simplicium medicinarum virtutibus* of Johannes de Sancto Paulo, which appears anonymously in the Wrocław manuscript, is edited by Georg Heinrich Kroemer, Inaug.-Diss. (Leipzig: Institut für Geschichte der Medizin, 1920); the text in the Madrid manuscript is his *Flores dietarum,* ed. Hermann J. Ostermuth, Inaug.-Diss. (Leipzig: Institut für Geschichte der Medizin, 1919). Johannes was active as a physician in the twelfth century; see Ernest Wickersheimer, *Dictionnaire biographique des médecins en France au moyen âge,* 2 vols. (Paris: E. Droz, 1936, rpt. Geneva: Librarie Droz, 1979) 2: 480–81.

[35] Madrid, Biblioteca de la Universidad Complutense, ms. 119 (formerly 116-Z-31), ff. 40–44v. I would not have been aware of the existence of this extremely important text if it were not for the reference to it by Guy Beaujouan, "Manuscrits médicaux du moyen âge conservés en Espagne," *Mélanges de la Casa de Velázquez,* 1972, *8:* 199 (here called a copy of the *Trotula minor*). I am grateful to Dr. Cecilia Fernandez

The most remarkable feature of this text is that almost half of the material which appears in the *Practica secundum Trotam* is also to be found in *De aegritudinum curatione*. Two of these chapters are in paragraphs which were labeled "Trot'" in the Wrocław codex. With one exception, the others appear in sections where no author was given, or appear at the end of chapters, after the work of a named author has ended. A comparison of the two texts makes it clear that a large amount of the anonymous matter in *De aegritudinum curatione* is by the author of the Madrid *Practica*. Much of this previously anonymous material is specifically concerned with women and appears under such headings as "Ad menstrua restringenda," "De purgatione mulieris post partum," and "De albificanda facie." Hiersemann's most convincing non-paleographic reason for concluding that "Trot'" was male is therefore eliminated.[36]

A full discussion of the nature of the *Practica secundum Trotam* and its relationship to *De aegritudinum curatione* must await the publication of the new text. On the basis of the comparison I have made, it seems safe to say at this point that since the "Trot'" selections in the Wrocław manuscript and the text in the Madrid manuscript both contain identical passages and yet each contains chapters not in the other manuscript, both were drawn from a larger work, a "Practica" similar in its form to those of Platearius and Bartholomeus. The Madrid manuscript is quite explicit in attributing this work to a woman, Trota, whose name is twice spelled out in full.

The scribe of the Wrocław manuscript always abbreviated this name, but I am not convinced that his abbreviation indicates that he thought the author was a man, and it seems to me likely that Hiersemann was mistaken in interpreting the abbreviation as a masculine *-us* ending. Hiersemann describes the mark which interests us as "sometimes a comma, sometimes a flourish, sometimes a line." I suggest that it was a simple mark of suspension, a common scribal practice to indicate that a familiar name had not been completed, just as the same scribe wrote "Plat'" for Platearius, "Petro'" for Petrocellus, "Ferr'" for Ferrarius, etc.[37] Hiersemann made the mistake of

---

Fernandez for permission to see the manuscript in November 1983 and to have a microfilm prepared. I intend to publish an edition and discussion of the *Practica* and a description of the manuscript elsewhere.

[36] As examples of correspondence between the *Practica* (*P*) and *De aegritudinum curatione* (*DAC*), I will cite here only the passages edited by Hiersemann, *Abschnitte*, with the differences in italics: 1. *P* (fol. 142): "Ad vomitum restringendum, accipe oleum et acetum et simul bullias, *et ibi* spongiam intingas et pectori *ap*ponas, et restringetur." *DAC* (p. 15, ll. 19–20): "Ad vomitum restringendum, accipe oleum et acetum et simul bullias, *deinde* spongiam intingas et pectori *super*ponas, et restringetur"; 2. *P* (fol. 141v): "Ad cancrum, si in gingivis vel labiis fuerit. In principio loca patientia lavabis, et postea fricentur cum albumine *ovi desiccato et* subtiliter pulverizato, *et* hoc assidue fac*ias*, et sanabitur." *DAC* (p. 13, ll. 37–39): "Ad cancrum, si in gingivis vel labiis *vel dentibus* fuerit. In principio loca patientia *bene cum aceto* lavabis, et postea fricentur cum alumine subtiliter pulverizato; hoc assidue fac et sanabitur *cancer*."

[37] *Abschnitte*, p. 6. Unfortunately Sudhoff did not publish a reproduction of the hand which wrote *De aegritudinum curatione* (see Sudhoff, "Salernitaner Handschrift," p. 191) and the lithographic reproductions appended to August Henschel, "Die Salernitanische Handschrift," *Janus*, 1846, *1:* 40–84, 300–68 are also of no help. Henschel had no doubt that "Trot'" should be expanded to Trotula; on this and the abbreviation of the other names see pp. 329–30. When Hiersemann wrote his dissertation, he was not an experienced paleographer or medievalist, but a twenty-eight-year-old medical student. Sudhoff, his dissertation director, accepted the reading of "Trotus" in "Salernitaner Handschrift," p. 128, but seemingly with caution.

concentrating on the abbreviation of one name alone, rather than taking account of the scribe's abbreviation of other names, and he was probably influenced by finding no passage marked "Trot' " which showed a particular concern for women's medicine or appeared in the treatises attributed to Trotula. Faced with the evidence of the Madrid text, the abbreviation used in the Wrocław manuscript does not constitute a sufficient reason to argue that "Trot' " was male.

Three chapters of the *Practica secundum Trotam* provide a problem of attribution. These chapters (*De conceptu, De matricis humiditate,* and *De vicio viri*) appear in *De aegritudinum curatione* as one long chapter ascribed to "M[agister] C[opho]." Stylistically this material differs from the other chapters in the *Practica secundum Trotam;* it is more fully developed and theoretical, and it uses the verb *precipere* three or four times, a word which does not appear elsewhere in Trota's chapters. Since the *Practica* of Copho has not survived, the attribution of the Wrocław manuscript cannot be verified, but it seems reasonable to assume that either Trota or the author of the Madrid summary of her work borrowed this material from Copho.[38] These same three chapters appear as the final three chapters in most manuscripts of *Cum auctor.* Since the author of *Cum auctor* shows no other evidence of familiarity with the *Practica secundum Trotam,* it seems to me likely that these chapters were borrowed from Copho rather than from Trota. The authors or compilers of the three "Trotula" treatises drew upon a number of earlier works, but there is no compelling evidence that the *Practica secundum Trotam* was one of them.[39]

On the whole, the remedies prescribed in the *Practica secundum Trotam* differ from those in the three texts attributed to Trotula which we have considered earlier. When the subject matter in the *Practica* is the same as that in one of the three other treatises, it commonly is less complex and differs in the *materia medica* prescribed, and when the remedies are reasonably close, there is still a distinct difference in wording which suggests the independent repetition of a common prescription. *Cum auctor* and *Ut de curis* are both far more systematic and fully developed gynecological works; they present a more "learned" level of academic medicine than the *Practica,* which on the whole seems to represent the traditions of empirics and midwives.

---

[38] *Coll. Sal.,* 2: 342–43 = *Practica,* fols. 142v–143. The work which De Renzi publishes as that of Copho in *Coll. Sal.,* 4: 415–505 does not correspond to anything attributed to Copho in *De aegritudinum curatione* and was probably written by Archimatheus; see Friedrich Hartmann, *Die Literatur von Früh- und Hochsalerno und der Inhalt des Breslauer Codex Salernitanus,* Inaug.-Diss. (Leipzig: Institut für Geschichte der Medizin, 1919), pp. 14–15.

[39] On the sources of "Trotula" see Hermann Rudolf Spitzner, *Die Salernitanische Gynäkologie und Geburtshilfe unter dem Namen der "Trotula,"* Inaug.-Diss. (Leipzig: Institut für Geschichte der Medizin, 1921), pp. 29–36. The question needs to be re-examined after an edition of the texts has been established. Spitzner (p. 29) cites a couplet from the *Regimen Salernitanum* which appears in chap. 29 of the printed text and which should help to date the work, but this passage does not appear in any of the manuscripts I have collated and must be considered an addition.

It is the evidence of the Madrid manuscript which will allow us for the first time to write with some confidence about Trota as an historical figure in the history of medicine. Rather than citing that text in further detail, here I will only summarize the more general conclusions I have reached from reading the available material. I begin with the evidence that in the eleventh and twelfth centuries there were a number of women healers in Salerno, the frequently cited *mulieres Salernitane,* and that some of them were distinguished for their medical skill. We have already met Berdefolia *medica;* Ordericus Vitalis tells us of an eleventh-century *sapiens matrona* who greatly impressed Ralph Mala-Corona, a noted physician in his own land; Matthaeus Platearius cites his mother as a physician, and we have no reason to think that these references are all to the same person or that they are in any way exhaustive. The methodological error of De Renzi—and even more obviously of others who have gone beyond his lead—was to assume that the scattered evidence which has survived from the past was produced by a very limited cast of characters, so that a fact here and a reference there can all be used to write a biographical sketch, without the necessity of a close demonstration of the relationship of the different parts.

The texts of the *Practica secundum Trotam* and the "Trot'" sections of *De aegritudinum curatione* together establish that Trota produced a larger *Practica,* which is now lost. She very likely was, as Hiersemann said of his masculine "Trottus," a skilled and sensible physician, but the missing *M* in the Wrocław manuscript suggests that she was not accorded the title of master. Since her *Practica* shows some influence from the work of Constantine and incorporates chapters from Copho, she may be considered to have been active in the twelfth rather than in the eleventh century; indeed, she may still have been alive at the end of the twelfth century when the Madrid and Wrocław manuscripts were written. Though her work was obviously valued at that time, as those two manuscripts (as well as the reference in *Ut de curis*) show, it was apparently rarely copied in later centuries and was replaced by more learned, complex and theoretical medicine.

Two pieces of evidence, each uncertain, suggest a relationship between Trota and Johannes Furias, a little known physician who probably lived in the twelfth century. In a section on the care of the eyes in *De aegritudinum curatione* which Hiersemann prints as the work of "Trot'," there is a reference to a cure used for fifteen years by Johannes Furias. This is the only reference to a contemporary in any passages attributed to Trota, and if it is indeed hers, it could help to date her work.[40] Johannes Furias is cited in the "German Bartholomeus," a macaronic German-Latin medical work which has preserved traces of material no longer extant in Latin. Several manuscripts contain a recipe for a depilatory which Johannes Furias is said to have sent

---

[40] Hiersemann, *Abschnitte,* p. 12, lines 39–48; see also p. 22. The passage is in a section on the care of the eyes which is not labeled "Trot'," but which follows another which is.

to "his friend, called Cleopatra." What makes this reference intriguing is that the recipe is a German version of one which appears in Latin in the *Practica secundum Trotam*.[41] With this text in mind one wonders if Johannes and Trota were in fact colleagues and if she was known familiarly by the name claimed by the author of a late antique or early medieval work on gynecology which was attributed to Cleopatra, *medica reginarum*.

The texts which can be attributed to Trota with reasonable security strongly suggest that she did not write the three widely circulated treatises which have so long been attributed to her. These treatises are difficult to date more precisely than to sometime in the twelfth century, or possibly very early in the thirteenth. As stated before, the earliest manuscripts were probably written at the beginning of the thirteenth century, or just possibly in the closing years of the twelfth. *Cum auctor* draws heavily on the work of Constantine, the reference to Ferrarius shows that *Ut de curis* must have been written after the beginning of the twelfth century, and *De ornatu* quotes from the preface to Hippocrates' *Prognostica* in the translation attributed to Constantine and given wide circulation by its inclusion in the *Articella*. It seems to me likely that all three works were composed not long before the time of the earliest existing manuscripts, that is, in the late twelfth century, or possibly at the very beginning of the thirteenth. No manuscripts have been found from the early or mid-twelfth century, and I have found no reference to these treatises in twelfth-century library catalogues.[42] Moreover, no author before the thirteenth century cites "Trotula" or quotes from these texts. For example, Bernard of Provence, who wrote at the end of the twelfth century, cites the *mulieres Salernitane* more than a dozen times, without ever mentioning the name of Trotula, and the recipes he attributes to these women are quite different from those which appear in the treatises.[43]

There may be some significance in the fact that one of the earliest manuscripts seems to come from southern France. Salerno was sacked by Emperor Henry VI in 1194 and in the thirteenth century the university appears to have been in a period of decline. Both Montpellier and Paris ben-

---

[41] Christian Graeter, *Ein Leipziger deutscher Bartholomaeus*, Inaug.-Diss. (Leipzig: Institut für Geschichte der Medizin, 1918), pp. 48–49, quotes this passage: "Ein meister hiez Johannes Furia, der schreip siner friundinne, diu hiez Cheopatra (*sic*) diese erzenie. Er sprach ...." The recipe in the *Practica secundum Trotam* appears in almost precisely the same words in *De aegritudinum curatione* in De Renzi, *Coll. Sal.*, 2: 145.

[42] For example, in the twelfth century the monastery of Saint-Amand owned copies of pseudo-Cleopatra's *Genecea* and of the "liber Muscionis de pessariis," but no "Trotula"; see Gustav Becker, *Catalogi Bibliothecarum Antiqui* (Bonn, 1885; rpt. Brussels: Culture et Civilisation, 1969), p. 233. There is also no reference to her in Karl Sudhoff, "Die medizinischen Schriften, welche Bishof Bruno von Hildesheim 1161 in seiner Bibliothek besass, und die Bedeutung des Konstantin von Afrika im 12. Jahrhundert," *Arch. Gesch. Med.*, 1916, 9: 348–56.

[43] "Commentarium Magistri Bernardi Provincialis super Tabulas Salerni" in De Renzi, *Coll. Sal.*, 5: 269–328. For example, the recipe of feeding asses' dung to their husbands he attributes to the women of Salerno (p. 287) has no parallel in "Trotula." De Renzi found only one parallel passage worth noting (p. 273), a short recipe which does appear almost verbatim in later manuscripts of *De ornatu* and in the printed version, chap. 61. But this recipe is not in B.N. lat. 16089 or B.L. Harley 3542, which I consider to represent the primitive form of the treatise. Many recipes were added to *De ornatu* in later manuscripts, and this one may have been borrowed from Bernard.

efited from the decline of the Italian city as a center for medical education. It would be plausible to imagine that Salernitan masters or students brought these works with them to Montpellier or produced them there, and that from Montpellier they made their way to northern France and to England, the center of their greatest popularity and diffusion in the thirteenth century.[44]

The authors of these three treatises were probably men. Since men controlled the academic medicine of the time, this supposition is a natural one, and it is supported by some evidence in the texts themselves. Though in late manuscripts adjectives referring to the author in the preface to *Cum auctor* use feminine endings, in the earliest manuscripts that preface is written without any grammatical indication of the gender of the author. The distancing implicit in the way the author writes about *their* diseases (*suarum, earum, in eis*) and says that the treatise was composed "largely at the request of a certain woman" (*maxime cuiusdam mulieris gratia*) suggests to me that the author was male, though these points are hardly conclusive. This author has little to say about childbirth itself and comments that it had been concealed from him how the empirical remedies used by midwives (such as a magnet held in the right hand) actually work.[45] If this tract was indeed written by a woman, I can find nothing in the text to indicate it. The longer, original form of the prologue to *De ornatu* shows that the author or compiler of this treatise was a man. Though *Ut de curis* contains no specific phrasing indicating the gender of the author, the fact that Trota was cited in the third person does imply that she was not the author of the tract.

If Trota was not the author, how did these treatises come to bear her name? In his *editio princeps* Georg Kraut noted his belief that the treatise was called *Trotula* because her name appeared in the text.[46] On this basis, however, *Ut de curis* could as well have been named after the better documented Copho or Ferrarius, and one must remember as well that eventually *Trotula major* and *Trotula minor* came to be applied to all three texts, though only one mentions the name of Trota.

"Trota" is the name used in the text of the Madrid *Practica,* and it is apparently the form originally used in the anecdote in *Ut de curis;* "Trotula" is the form used with overwhelming frequency by the scribes and rubricators who wrote the headings and explicits of the Trotula texts. It was common practice to form book titles in this fashion, so that the *Summa* of Angelus Carletti was known as the *Angelica,* that of Roland of Parma as the *Rolandina,* etc. One early thirteenth-century manuscript makes it clear that *Trotula* is the name of the work through its rubric: "Summa que dicitur Trotula."[47]

---

[44] On the rivalry of Salerno and Montpellier and movement between the two see Karl Sudhoff, "Salerno, Montpellier und Paris um 1200," *Arch. Gesch. Med.,* 1928, *20:* 51–62.

[45] "Notanda quedam que sunt phisicalia remedia, quorum nobis virtus est occulta, que ab obstetricibus profuerunt"; ms. A f. 80rb or Kraut, ed., *Trotulae,* chap. 16.

[46] See Kraut's marginal note on p. 27 of the Strassburg edition (chap. 20). This is also the opinion of Tuttle in *"Trotula,"* pp. 65–66.

[47] On the adaptation of authors' names to titles see Paul Lehmann, *Mittelalterliche Büchertitel,* Sitzungsberichte der Bayerischen Akademie der Wissenschaften, Phil.-hist. Kl., 2 vols. (Munich: Verlag der Bayerischen

Though the evidence is sparse and subject to dispute, it appears that the name of a real twelfth-century author, Trota, was applied to a set of texts, the *Trotula major* and *minor,* in the thirteenth, and that by a process of back formation, the diminutive Trotula was then thought to be the proper name of the author.

The evidence of the manuscripts suggests that the name given to these texts was not a simple accident produced by the presence of the name Trota in *Ut de curis.* When these three texts devoted to women's medicine were brought together early in the thirteenth century and the gender-specific prologue to *De ornatu* was dropped in the compilation, it is not unreasonable to conclude that they were deliberately labeled with the name of the best known female physician of the previous century in order to give them greater credibility or acceptance.

Though they bear the name of a female author, I must say that throughout these three treatises I see no evidence of "the gentle hand of a woman" or that the medicine prescribed, as another writer has said, is "remarkable for its humanity."[48] The major sources of *Cum auctor* are the *Viaticum* and *Pantegni* of Constantine, and as we have seen, some material was probably borrowed from Copho; other medical treatments advocated here are similar to those one finds in the work of male doctors such as Platearius and Bartholomeus. The heavy baggage of Galenic theory, which treats women as "imperfect" and deficient in "innate heat" when compared with men, provides a conceptual frame of mind absent from the simple, nontheoretical treatment of the *Practica de Trota.*[49] In *Cum auctor* and *Ut de curis* bleeding is prescribed for such conditions as excessive menstruation, and in this respect those treatises differ significantly from the *Practica secundum Trotam,* where bleeding is not prescribed for any gynecological problem. As had been advocated since the time of the ancient Egyptians, in the *Trotula major* and *minor* (and in the work of Trota) the womb is to be moved about by suffumigation, that is, having the patient sit over the smoke of sweet or foul-smelling substances. Poultices of various sorts of dung, cupping on the groin or pubis, and pessaries and douches made of such substances as pitch, honey, weasel oil, nutmeg and cloves are frequently advocated. As far as I can tell, with a few exceptions it would be a coincidence if a remedy prescribed here did some good, and many were unpleasant or even harmful.

Akademie der Wissenschaften, 1948–1953), 2: 14. The manuscript cited is B.N. lat 7056 (Ms. *A*), f. 77. The same rubricator introduces *De ornatu* on f. 84v as *Alius tractatus qui dicitur minor Trotula* and makes a clear analogy with the *Rogerina* of Roger Baron; see f. 75: *Tractatus qui dicitur minor Rogerina.* Tuttle, however, has argued in *"Trotula,"* pp. 66–67 that "Trotula" was probably the author's name and that *Trotula major* and *minor* are equivalent to the *Priscianus major* and *minor.*

[48] The second quotation is from Susan Mosher Stuard, "Dame Trot," *Signs,* 1975, *1:* 538.

[49] The issue of Galenic theory itself does not, of course, indicate male authorship, since the thought of people of both sexes is normally dominated by the available theory of their times. On the role of Galenic theory in ancient medicine and the treatises of "Trotula," I have benefited from the dissertation on gynecology from Galen to Trotula which Monica H. Green is preparing at Princeton University.

Academic medicine may even have been more harmful than the empiric practices of Salernitan herbalists, since it was more influenced by theory and farther removed from its practical roots by reliance on classroom instruction and the written treatise. To the degree that the *mulieres Salernitane* were skilled in herbal medicine and were the source of treatments advocated in these treatises, their "traditional" and occasionally effective medicine, tested by experience, was deformed and sometimes rendered dangerous by the process of literate transmission by academic physicians and professional scribes writing for an equally academic audience. Surely the best way to learn herbal medicine was from direct instruction. In manuscripts the symbols for ounces, drams, and scruples were confused with careless abandon (thus at times leading to the recommendation of massive overdosing with powerful herbs) and errors in transcription were common. In the copying of these texts, for example, through a misreading *fisalidos* was transformed into *siseleos,* directing later doctors, if they followed their instructions, to prescribe mountain brook-willow rather than drop-wort, a mistake which could not be made by herbalists working directly with the plants.[50]

At the beginning of this paper I said that learned medieval works on gynecology were largely written for men and contained the ideas of male physicians. *Cum auctor* and *Ut de curis* were written specifically for an audience of other physicians, and that audience was overwhelmingly male. The man who wrote *De ornatu* says in his prologue that he composed the work because women had often asked him for advice. He intended that treatise, which by our standards is only marginally medical, for a female audience. In its original form, recorded in the manuscripts which contain the long version of the prologue, the author addresses a female reader directly with such phrases as "ut sudes" and "abluas te optime," but in the text which became standard these second-person forms were changed to the third person.[51] The readers of all three treatises were normally male, for these Latin texts circulated with other works used by medical school graduates, and the owners which have been positively identified were men or (usually) male institutions. In the fifteenth century when vernacular gynecological and obstetrical treatises were written with an audience of women in mind, we find that some of these new texts differ from the Latin *Trotula* and pay more attention to the practical obstetrical problems which concerned female practitioners.[52]

A striking feature of the three treatises which have traditionally been attributed to Trotula is that they were so frequently copied and so widely

---

[50] *Fisalidos* is the reading in ms. A, f. 77vb, *siseleos* that of the Kraut ed., *Trotulae,* chap. 1. On the two plants see *The Herbal of Rufinus,* ed. Lynn Thorndike (Chicago: University of Chicago Press, 1946), pp. 135 and 298.

[51] See B.N. lat 16089, f. 113 and B.L. Harley 3542, f. 97v. In the second fifteenth-century manuscript "ut sudes" remains in its original form, but "ungas" was corrected by the original scribe with a mark of deletion and a superscript *t* and "te" was overwritten to read "se." Ms. A, an early manuscript of the version which brings all three treatises together, has third-person forms throughout.

[52] See the texts published by Delva and Rowland cited in n. 12 above. Delva argues that the Flemish *Liber Trotula* was written for an audience of midwives by a practicing midwife critical of male university masters

disseminated. The existence today of nearly one hundred manuscripts shows that they became the standard gynecological texts of the late medieval medical profession, though I can find no evidence that they were assigned as school texts in any university. Indeed, the multiple reprintings of the sixteenth century demonstrate the continued importance of the works into the early modern period. Though a few of the earliest manuscripts are anonymous, later copyists, owners and readers assumed that they were dealing with texts written by someone named Trotula or Trota, and until Wolf's misguided and unconvincing attribution, no one doubted that these treatises were written by a woman. Trotula was, moreover, cited as an authority by such medical writers as Peter of Spain, better known as Pope John XXI.

This authoritative use of treatises ascribed to a woman occurred at the very time that licensed women physicians were incredible rarities and university masters were prosecuting women for practicing medicine without a license. For example, in 1322 the masters of the Parisian medical faculty argued successfully that just as a woman was disbarred because of her sex from practicing law or testifying in a criminal case, there was all the more reason that she could be prohibited by law from the practice of medicine, "since she does not know through the letter or art of medicine the cause of the illness of the ill."[53] English physicians wanted a blanket prohibition against women in their field and in 1422 petitioned Parliament requesting the enactment of a statute which would bar men from practicing medicine without a university degree, under pain of imprisonment and a fine of forty pounds, and would insure "that no Woman use the practyse of Fisyk undre the same peyne."[54]

(pp. 30–34). The author of the English text Rowland edited (B. L. Sloane 2463, ff. 194–232) states that it was composed for the benefit of women ("and that oon woman may helpe another in her sykenesse & nought diskuren her previtees to such vncurteys men"—p. 58), but Rowland makes far too much of the unusualness of this work, for much of it is a literal translation of Roger of Parma; see J. H. Aveling, "An account of the earliest English work on midwifery and the diseases of women," *Obstet. J. Great Britain Ireland*, 1874, 2: 73, and the severe review by Faye M. Getz in *Med. Hist.*, 1982, 26: 353–54. The Middle English translation of Trotula states that it was written in English because it was intended for women: "Because whomen of oure tonge donne bettyr rede and undyrstande thys langage than eny other and every whoman lettyrde rede hit to other unlettyrd and help hem and conceyle hem in her maledyes, withowtyn shewying here dysese to man, i have thys drauyn and wryttyn in englysh" (Bodley, Douce 37, f. lv, quoted by Rowland, p. 14). The French verse translation of Trotula in Cambridge, Trinity College 0.1.20 is also addressed to women, beginning (fol. 214): "Bien sachiés, femmes ..." It is a quite literal translation. In the fifteenth century Giovanni Michele Savonarola wrote a work in the vernacular specifically for midwives; see *Il trattato ginecologico-pediatrico in volgare "Ad mulieres ferrarienses de regimine pregnantium et noviter natorum usque ad septennium,"* ed. Luigi Belloni (Milan: Società Italiana di ostetricia e ginecologia, 1952).

[53] Henri Denifle and Emile Chatelain, *Chartularium Universitatis Parisiensis*, 4 vols. (Paris, 1889–97), 2: 266: "cum nullam causam infirmitatis infirmorum per litteram vel artem medicine cognoscat"; cf. Kibre, "Faculty of Medicine at Paris" (note 1 above), p. 8. This argument was put forward by John of Padua, surgeon to King Philip IV. Male authorities were most concerned with female practitioners who posed an economic threat to the male medical establishment. Professor Michael McVaugh has kindly called to my attention the case of a Catalan woman from near Sant Cugat del Vallès who had learned from a visiting *medicus* how to examine urine, take the pulse, and give advice. She swore that she sent cases of abscesses and quartan fever "ad medicos maiores." This early fourteenth-century rural nurse was permitted to continue her practice on condition that she not use charms and not give medicine. See Josep Perarnau i Espelt, "Activitats i fórmules supersticioses de guarició a Catalunya en la primera meitat del segle XIV," *Archiu de Textos Catalans Antics*, 1982, 1: 67–72.

[54] *Rotuli Parliamentorum*, 6 vols. [London, 1767–1777], 4: 158. The ordinance against charlatanism which was enacted in response to this petition dealt with qualifications rather than gender; see *ibid.*, p. 130, no. 11.

How did treatises attributed to a female author become accepted and widely diffused texts among male physicians at the same time that those same physicians were attempting to drive women from the practice of medicine on grounds of professional incompetence? In the first place, though we have reason to think that these treatises were produced by men, the idea that they were written by a woman from Salerno was plausible. In its early years as a medical center, Salerno may be thought of as a highly favored health spa where both men and women practiced medicine (probably frequently as members of the same family) and taught it to others, making what use they could of the learning of the Greeks and Arabs. Though some of these early physicians were clerics, this educational activity was not based institutionally in a cathedral or monastic school. In the twelfth century medical licenses were granted by neither the church nor an organization of masters, but by royal officials; as a decree of Roger II in 1140 stated, "henceforth anyone who wishes to practice medicine should appear before our officials and judges, to be evaluated by their judgment." Since no clerical status was required for such licenses, it seems likely that they could be granted to women. Records still extant from the fourteenth century show that at a time when the Parisian doctors mentioned above were arguing that a woman might easily sin by killing a patient through her ministrations, women in the Kingdom of Naples received licenses occasionally. For example, in 1307 a woman with the intriguing name of "Trotta de Troya" was granted a license to practice surgery. From a perspective north of the Alps, if a woman skilled in medicine was to be found anywhere, it would most likely be in southern Italy.[55]

The frequency with which Trotula's gender was stressed by scribes and rubricators suggests that it was not only plausible that a woman should have written these treatises; more important, it was desirable. Men knew little about feminine physiology and some were intensely troubled by their ignorance. In *De secretis mulierum,* a late thirteenth- or early fourteenth-century vulgarization of questions raised by Albertus Magnus, the author deals with the most elementary anatomical questions and tells of a man who confessed to him that once after intercourse he found his abdomen covered with blood, which "frightened him greatly, and he did not know the cause." This basic sexological handbook, which makes use of information to be found in the treatises attributed to Trotula, illustrates something of the nature

---

[55] On the institutional and intellectual history of Salerno, see Paul Oskar Kristeller, "The School of Salerno," *Bull. Hist. Med.,* 1945, *17*: 138–94 [reprinted in Kristeller, *Studies in Renaissance Thought and Letters* (Rome: Edizioni di storia e letteratura, 1956), pp. 495–551], esp. pp. 146n, 148n, 164, 171–72. In "Learned Women of Early Modern Italy: Humanists and University Scholars" in *Beyond Their Sex: Learned Women of the European Past,* ed. Patricia H. Labalme (New York: New York University Press, 1982), p. 102, after questioning the existence of Trotula, Kristeller adds that "in Salerno, Naples, and the rest of Southern Italy, we do find a number of women, beginning in 1307, who received royal licenses to treat specified diseases." Michael McVaugh kindly pointed out to me the license of "Trotta de Troya" in Raffaele Calvanico, *Fonti per la Storia della Medicina e della Chirurgia per il Regno di Napoli nel periodo Angioino (a. 1273–1410)* (Naples: L'Arte tip., 1962), pp. 124–25.

of medieval male curiosity about female sexuality.[56] Since male physicians did not make intimate examinations of female patients and were normally not present at childbirth, their need and desire for information must have been acute.[57] Yet a fellow male, even an older and more experienced physician, could not provide that information with authority. A great advantage of the treatises attributed to "Trotula," even though they reveal nothing that could not be found in other Salernitan works, is that they appeared to be written "from the woman's point of view." This point was made with striking force by the author of a scientific encyclopedia of the second half of the thirteenth century, *Placides et Timéo,* also known as *Les Secrés as philosophes.* The author of this curious dialogue tells us that physicians "who know nothing, derive great authority and much solid information" from Trotula, partly because she could speak of what she had "felt in herself, since she was a woman" and partly "because she was a woman, all women revealed their inner thoughts more readily to her than to any man and told her their natures."[58]

The modern reader who, like the author of *Les Secrés as philosophes,* wants to know the medical views of a medieval woman is more fortunate than the medieval public, for the works of Hildegard of Bingen have now been printed. This twelfth-century Benedictine abbess corresponded with popes, emperors, bishops and abbots, and was a candidate for sainthood in the thirteenth century. She was also the author of two works which deal with medicine in a highly personal way. Though they do not focus exclusively on "female medicine," they do deal with such subjects as sexual relations, childbirth, and prediction of the character and physical characteristics of offspring.

---

[56] On *De secretis mulierum* see Lynn Thorndike, *A History of Magic and Experimental Science,* 8 vols. (New York: Columbia University Press, 1923–1958), 2: 739–45, 749–50: his "Further consideration of the *Experimenta, Speculum Astronomiae,* and *De Secretis Mulierum* ascribed to Albertus Magnus," *Speculum,* 1955, *30:* 427–43; Brigitte Kusche, "Zur 'Secreta Mulierum' Forschung," *Janus,* 1975, *62:* 103–23; and Helen Rodnite Lemay, "Some thirteenth and fourteenth century lectures on female sexuality," *Inter. J. Women's Studies,* 1978, *1:* 391–400. See *Alberti Magni De Secretis Mulierum* (Amsterdam, 1740), p. 17 ("utrum menstruum fluat per anum ... aut per vulvam") and pp. 104–5 for the post-coital blood; material from "Trotula" is cited as being from a "documentum" on pp. 109–11.

[57] In the case of Jacqueline Félicie heard at Paris in 1322 and discussed above, her lawyer argued that "it is better and more decent that a woman who is wise and trained in the art should visit a sick woman and see and inquire into the secrets of nature and her private parts than a man, who is forbidden to touch the hands, breasts, stomach, feet, etc. of women," *Chart. univ. Paris.,* 2: 264 and Kibre, "Faculty of Medicine at Paris," p. 11. Richardus Anglicus makes quite a point of the fact that he was not present when a patient and the attending *obstetrix* attempted to insert a pessary he had prescribed; see Karl Sudhoff, "Der 'Micrologus'– Text der 'Anatomia' Richards des Engländers," *Arch. Gesch. Med.,* 1927, *19:* 232–33.

[58] Claude A. Thomasset, ed., *Placides et Timéo ou Li secrés as philosophes,* Textes Littéraires Français (Geneva: Librairie Droz, 1980), pp. 133–34. Though Thomasset understandably makes much of this passage, which he says reveals "à la lettre ... une attitude capable de bouleverser le monde médiéval" (see his *Une vision du monde à la fin du XIII*ᵉ *siècle: Commentaire du dialogue de Placides et Timéo,* Publications romanes et françaises, 161 [Geneva: Librairie Droz, 1982], pp. 160–61), it is likely that for the author himself these words are empty rhetoric. I can find no evidence that the author of the dialogue actually read any of the works attributed to Trotula. The passage quoted is used to support the statement that women desire intercourse more when they are pregnant than at any other time, an assertion which does not appear in any of the texts of "Trotula." Moreover, later (p. 148) the author of the dialogue refers to that growth which such physicians as "Ypocras, Galien et Trotules" call *molla,* though this term itself is not used in any of the treatises attributed to Trotula.

These books were presumably intended originally for use in Hildegard's own monastery, and their circulation in the Middle Ages was always limited; today three manuscripts of the *Subtilitates* exist, and of the *Causae et curae* only one manuscript remains.[59] It is an ironic fact that the treatises attributed to "Trotula" flourished, while the *Practica* of Trota and the medical works of Hildegard remained practically unknown.

The position I have presented here is that the professionalization of medicine in the twelfth and thirteenth centuries, combined with the virtual exclusion of women from university education, prevented them from entering the best paid and most respected medical positions. Male doctors controlled medical theory, though not the day-to-day practice of women's medicine, and their gynecological literature incorporated male experience and understanding and the academic learning available to males alone. Though it appears that *Cum auctor* and *Ut de curis* first circulated anonymously and that *De ornatu* was prefaced by a prologue written by a male author, by a process which remains obscure these three texts were brought together and attributed to a female author, and once this change had occurred, no reader could know that these works were not authentic. By including in their medical compendia these treatises falsely attributed to Trota, medieval physicians thereby unwittingly excluded women even further from participation in their own medicine. Though the treatises of "Trotula" bear a woman's name, they were the central texts of the gynecological medicine practiced and taught by men.

In the Middle Ages a female medical author seemed a believable figure, though one best imagined in an exotic locale. But in the sixteenth century Wolf considered that such a woman could not have existed and in the 1920s Hiersemann created the phantasm of "Trottus" from the flourish of a pen. Mead and Mason-Hohl, however, knew in their bones that women could practice medicine and teach it to others. A fresh study of the manuscripts, especially of the Madrid *Practica,* provides evidence for the existence of an expert woman physician named Trota, but also shows, ironically, that she was not the author of the three treatises commonly attributed to her. Thus my investigation fully supports Mead and Mason-Hohl in their faith in a historical Trota, even though it rejects their imagined biography. Seen in a fuller historical context, it should come as no surprise that Trota's career was limited by the social forces of her own day, that she produced a *Practica* quite different from the treatises usually attributed to her, and that when the

---

[59] On Hildegard, see Thorndike, *History of Magic and Experimental Science,* 2: 124–54. Hildegard von Bingen, *Heilkunde,* trans. Heinrich Schipperges, 4th ed. (Salzburg: Otto Müller Verlag, 1981) contains corrections to Paul Kaiser's faulty Latin edition of the *Causae et curae* (Leipzig: Teubner, 1903) in its translation. Peter Dronke writes evocatively of Hildegard's life and thought and cites the most recent literature in *Women Writers of the Middle Ages: A Critical Study of Texts from Perpetua (†203) to Marguerite Porete (†1310)* (Cambridge: Cambridge University Press, 1984), pp. 144–201, but a fully satisfactory study of Hildegard's views on sexuality remains to be written. In his translation and discussion of a passage crucial for understanding Hildegard's treatment of intercourse, Dronke mistakes the closing of the womb over the seed which it has just received for contractions which accompany the sexual act before its climax; see *ibid.,* pp. 175–76.

term "master" was applied to her as a woman, it was with a reservation, *tanquam magistra.*

APPENDIX: ORIGINAL PROLOGUE TO *DE ORNATU*

Ut ait Ypocras in libro quem de scientia pronosticorum edidit, "omnis qui medicine artis studio seu gloriam seu delectabilem amicorum copiam consequi desiderat, rationem suam regulis prudentium adeo munire studeat,"[1] ne in singulis ad artem medendi spectantibus inermis reperiatur et rudis. Quod si facere
5   neglexerit, loco glorie et fame dedecus et infamiam, loco amicorum quamplures sibi acquirat inimicos. Sic etiam efficietur, ut a quibus in foro salutari debet et medicus appellari, eis ridiculum fiat in publico, et neque ab eis medicus appelletur. Huius intuitu rationis, ego his regulis mulierum quas in artificiali decore faciendo sapientes inueni, meam adeo in tantum muniui rationem, ut in singulis
10 ad ornamentum faciei et aliorum membrorum muliebrium doctus reperiar. Ita ut cuilibet mulieri nobili uel gregarie de huius artificio aliquid a me querenti, iuxta suam qualitatem et modum conueniens sciam adhibere consilium, ut et ego etiam laudem et ipsa optatum consequi ualeat effectum. Sed quoniam, ut ait Persius, "scire meum nichil est, nisi me scire hoc sciat alter,"[2] ideo, hoc
15 exemplo motus, uolo que de hoc artificio noui et efficaci opere probaui, litteris commendare et in compendiosum scriptum redigere. Quo mediante, quod in mente habeo in aliorum ueniat usum et iuuamen.

1 ait *PL* dicit *OS; post* libro *add.* suo *S;* edidit *om. S* 2 seu[1] *om. S* 3 rationem ... studeat *om. O;* prudencium *L* prudentum *PS; post* prudentium *add.* etiam *L; post* adeo *add.* se *P* 4 inermis ... si *POL* ne rudis reperiatur et si rudis hoc *S* 5 et fame *om. S;* quamplures *POL* plures *S* 6 etiam *PO* quod *L om. S;* debet *OLS* deberet *P* 7–8 eius ridiculum fiet ... appelatur *S* appeletur *scripsi;* eis fiat r. in publico *L;* eis fiat r. in populo et plebis abittio *P;* eis fiat r. in populo et plebis abiectio *O* 8 Huius *OS* hoc *PL;* his regulis *POL* uolens aliquas experiencias *S* 9 sapientes *POL* facetas *S;* adeo *om. S;* in tantum *om. LS; post* singulis *add.* tam *S* 10 ornamentum *POL* ornatum *S;* et aliorum *L* quam ceterorum *S;* faciei ... membrorum *om. PO;* muliebrium *POL* mulierum *S;* reperiar *POL* reperiatur *S;* Ita *S* Ista *L om. PO* 11 ut *PO om. S;* cuilibet *POL* cuiuslibet *S;* uel ... huius *POL* seu gentili et de eius *S;* a me *om. O* 12 suam *S* sui *POL;* sciam *POL* suum *S;* et[2] *om. S* 13 etiam *L om. POS;* ipsa *OLS* ipsam *P;* optatum *POL* exoptatum *S;* ualeat *POL* ualet *S;* Sed *POL* Sit *S* 14 Persius *POL* Proferius *S;* meum *POL* teum *S;* me *POL om. S;* hoc[1] *OL* meum *P* tuum *S;* alter *PO* alterum *L* aliter *S* 14–15 ideo ... motus *POL om. S* 15 que *POL* itaque *S;* et ... probaui *PO om. LS* 16 Quo *S* Quod *POL;* in[2] *om. O* 17 *post* habeo *add.* et *S;* usum et iuuamen *PO* usum *L* notitiam *S*

[N. B.: Differences of word order are not indicated.]

Paris, B. N. lat 16089, fol. 113 (c. 1250) = *P;* Oxford, Exeter College 35, fol. 227v (XIV[1]) = *O;* London, B. L. Harley 3542, fol. 97v (XV[1]) = *L;* and Salzburg, Museum Carolino-Augusteum 2171, fol. 180 (XV med.) = *S*

1. *Prognostica,* trans. attributed to Constantine the African, preface, printed in *Articella* (Venice, 1492), fol. 40.
2. *Sat.* 1.27: scire tuum nihil est nisi te scire hoc sciat alter.

20

Suger's Life and Personality

When Suger died in 1151, his abbey circulated an encyclical letter that contained the following chronological statement:

> He died between the recitation of the Lord's Prayer and the Creed, the ides of the month of January, in his seventieth year, about sixty years after he assumed the monastic habit, in the twenty-ninth year of his prelacy.[1]

From this statement we may calculate the major dates of Suger's life: born in 1081 (or possibly 1080), he became an oblate of Saint-Denis about ten years later, was consecrated abbot in 1122, and died January 13, 1151.[2] These dates are the most essential points of Suger's monastic chronology. Let us try to go beyond them to the man himself.

Though there has been much uncertainty and controversy about Suger's origins, there is evidence that he was related to a family of minor *milites* who held property at Chennevières-lès-Louvres, a village eighteen

---

[1] William, *Enc. Let.* (L.) p. 408. On William of Saint-Denis, who wrote both this letter and the *Vita Sugerii*, see Hubert Glaser, 'Wilhelm von Saint-Denis,' *Historisches Jahrbuch* 85 (1965): 257-322; André Wilmart, 'Le Dialogue apologétique du moine Guillaume, biographe de Suger,' *Revue Mabillon* 32 (1942): 80-118; and Edmond-René Labande, 'Quelques mots à propos d'une lettre de Guillaume de Saint-Denis,' *Mélanges offerts à Rita Lejeune* (Gembloux, 1969), vol. 1, pp. 23-25 and 'Vaux en Châtelleraudis vu par un moine du XIIe siècle: Guillaume de Saint-Denis,' *Cahiers de civilisation médiévale* 12 (1969): 15-24. By specifying that Suger died during the performance of his final prayers, the encyclical letter establishes a comparison with the founder of Benedictine monasticism, who also died while praying, as Fr. Chrysogonus Waddell has pointed out to me. See *Gregorii Magni Dialogi*, Bk. 2, chap. 37, ed. Umberto Moricca (Rome, 1924), p. 132, line 16: *Spiritum inter verba orationis efflavit*; and also Damien Sicard, *La Liturgie de la mort dans l'Eglise latine des origines à la réforme carolingienne* (Munster, 1978), p. 50.

[2] On the date of Suger's death see Achille Luchaire, 'Sur la chronologie des documents et des faits relatifs à l'histoire de Louis VII pendant l'année 1150,' *Annales de la Faculté des Lettres de Bordeaux*, 4 (1882): 284-312; and Cartellieri, *Suger*, pp. 170-74, and for the date of his consecration, pp. 129-30, no. 24.

kilometers from the abbey of Saint-Denis in the plain northeast of Paris, close to the present airport at Roissy. This was territory of relatively recent settlement – Chennevières may well have been established in the eleventh century[3] – where the abbeys of Saint-Denis and Argenteuil were major landholders, and the Montmorency family dominated a dense implantation of minor vassals and vavasors. The knights of Chennevières can be traced back to a Suger *Magnus*, who was born in the late eleventh century and may have been a nephew of Suger's father. Though the evidence is inconclusive, Suger *Magnus* may have been related, by blood or marriage, to the Orphelins of Annet-sur-Marne, who were in turn connected with the Garlandes. For such families of obscure knights in the region close to Paris, the key to success was royal patronage and church office. To place a child in the great royal abbey of Saint-Denis was a career decision that could benefit the entire family.[4]

We know the name of Suger's father, Helinand, and those of a brother and sister-in-law, Ralph and Emeline, from obituary rolls.[5] Nowhere, however, do we learn the name of his mother, nor does he ever mention her in his writings. Or perhaps I should say he never refers to his natural mother, for repeatedly he writes in the most physical terms of his institutional, or spiritual, mother, the *mater ecclesia*, by which he always means the abbey of Saint-Denis.[6]

When Suger traveled to Germany in 1125, he was accompanied by another brother, a cleric named Peter, along with two sons of Suger *Magnus*, Ralph and Suger.[7] Reaching prominence, Abbot Suger did what was expected of a man in his position and advanced the careers of his nephews. One of them Simon, became the royal chancellor and probably a canon of Notre-Dame, and another, William, was established as a canon of the same cathedral. A third, John, died on a mission to Eugene III on behalf of the abbey of Saint-Denis. Of a nephew named Girard we know only that in the 1140s he owed the abbey five *sous* annually from his house

---

[3] Charles Higounet, *La Grange de Vaulerent*, Les Hommes et la terre, 10 (Paris, 1956), p. 11.

[4] On Suger's family, see the Appendix.

[5] Auguste Molinier, ed., *Obituaries de la province de Sens, Tome I (Diocèses de Sens et de Paris)*, 2 vols. (Paris 1902), pp. 332 (Nov. 28) and 349 (Sept. 4), for Helinand see also p. 325 (Sept. 4). The name of Suger's mother may appear in the necrology of Saint-Denis without any further identification, as does that of Helinand, but if it does, we have no way to know.

[6] Suger, *Vita Lud.* (W), pp. 208-10: '*matrem ecclesiam, que a mamilla gratissimo liberalitatis sue gremio dulcissime fovere non destiterat*'; p. 210: '*ad matrem ecclesiam, Deo opitulante, pervenissemus, tam dulciter, tam filialiter, tam nobiliter filium prodigum susepit*'; Suger, *Adm.* (L), p. 156 pr Suger, *Adm.* (P), p. 40: '*a corpore ecclesiae beatissimorum martyrum Dionysii, Rustici et Eleutherii, quae nos quam dulcissime a mamilla usque in senectam fovit*'; Suger, *Adm.* (L), p. 190 or Suger, *Adm.* (P), p. 50; '*matris ecclesiae honorem, quae puerum materno affetu lactaverat.*'

[7] Jules Tardif, *Monuments historiques* (Paris, 1866), pp. 221-22, no. 397. For a discussion of this text and my argument that the sons of Suger *Magnus* were cousins of Abbot Suger, see the Appendix.

and five *sous* from the money collected for the transport of madder.[8] If, as I think likely, the chancellor Simon is the same man as Simon of Saint-Denis, canon of Paris, we can extend the list of Suger's favored relatives even further, for a witness list shows that Master Hilduin, who died as chancellor of Notre-Dame about 1190, was a brother of Simon of Saint-Denis, and Hugh Foucault, who was prior of Saint-Denis and Argenteuil in the 1160s and died as abbot of Saint-Denis in 1197, was an uncle of one of Simon's nephews. To have provided his nephews with the education and connections that produced a chancellor of France, an abbot of Saint-Denis, a chancellor of Notre-Dame, and at least one other canon of Notre-Dame was an achievement in which any twelfth-century man would have taken pride.[9]

At about the age of ten Suger was oblated at the Main Altar of Saint-Denis, an altar he later enriched with gold panels.[10] He then spent approximately a decade at Saint-Denis-de-l'Estrée, a dependency close to the great abbey church.[11] For a period before 1106 he went to school at some distance from Saint-Denis; he tells us that it was near Fontevrault, and Marmoutier is a possible location.[12] His classical training was solid though not unusually deep and stayed with him throughout the rest of his life, so that in his later years he could impress his monks by reciting from memory twenty or even thirty verses of Horace.[13]

---

[8] On Simon see notes 22 and 31 here and the Appendix. William established Suger's anniversary service at Notre-Dame with an endowment of sixty *livres* a solid indication of his gratitude to his uncle; Molinier, *Obituaires*, p. 99 (Jan. 16). The chancellor Simon was probably that Simon of Saint-Denis, deacon and canon of Notre-Dame, who had nephews named Suger, William, and Herlouin,; ibid., pp. 177-78. For Eugene's letter of consolation to Suger, see Martin Bouquet, ed., *Recueil des historiens de Gaules et de la France*, 24 vols. (Paris, 1738-1904), vol. 15 (1878), p. 456. Girard is mentioned in Suger, *Adm.* (L), p. 157.

[9] An act of 1175, in Joseph Depoin, *Recueil de chartes et documents de Saint-Martin-des-Champs*, 5 vols. (Ligugé and Paris, 1913-21), vol. 2, p. 342, no. 426 bis, includes among its witnesses: '*S. Simonis de Sancto Dionisio. S. magistri Hilduini, fratris eius . . . S. Guillelmi de Sancto Dionisio . . . S. Herluini, nepotis prefati Simonis,*' Molinier, *Obituaires*, pp. xxvi-xxvii, notes the probable relationship between Simon of Saint-Denis and Abbot Hugh. As his patronymic shows, Hugh was the son of someone named Foucaldus. Possibly Simon and Hilduin were the sons of Suger's brother Girard, who held a house from Saint-Denis. Panofsky misunderstands both the historical facts and the obligations of a man of influence owed his relatives when he says, 'Suger kept them at a friendly distance and, later on, made them participate, in a small way, in the life of the Abbey' (Panofsky, *Suger*, p.30).

[10] Suger, *Adm.* (L), p. 196 or Suger, *Adm.* (P), p. 60.

[11] Suger, *Ch.* (L), p. 339. On the location of Saint-Denis de l'Estree, see *Oeuvres de Julien Havet*, 2 vols. (Paris, 1896), vol. I, p. 215.

[12] Letter of Suger to Eugene III in Suger, *Let.* (L), p. 264. Waquet, *Vie*, p. vi, suggests Marmoutier, or possibly Saint-Benoît-sur-Loire.

[13] '*Gentilium vero poetarum ob tenacem memoriam oblivisci usquequaque non poterat, ut versus Horatianos utile aliquid continentes usque ad vicenos, saepe etiam ad tricenos, memoriter nobis recitaret*' (William, *Vita Sug.* [L], p. 381). This passage shows us what a monk of the first half of the twelfth century found impressive. While the ability to recite twenty or thirty lines of any

By the time he was twenty-five years old he began to go on missions for his abbey, to a synod at Poitiers in 1106 and to attend Paschal II at La Charité-sur-Loire and at Châlons-sur-Marne in 1107, when the pope met Emperor Henry V. In 1112 he was present at the second Lateran council. Finding favor with Abbot Adam, he also held settled administrative responsiblities, first as provost of Berneval on the Norman coast near Dieppe, then between 1109 and 1111 as provost of the more important priory of Toury. Toury sits strategically on the road from Paris to Orléans just eight kilometers from Le Puiset. In 1112 the priory was attacked first by Hugh of Le Puiset and then by Theobald of Blois, Milo of Montlhéry, Hugh of Crécy, and Guy of Rochefort.[14] Since Suger wrote in *The Life of Louis VI* with considerable detail about the continuing conflict between the king and all these men, one does well to remember that they were important to Suger not only for their opposition to the crown but for their attacks on a domain of Saint-Denis for which he was responsible.

During these years as a monk of Saint-Denis, Suger served his king, Louis VI, as well as Abbot Adam; notably, in 1118, Louis sent him as an emissary to meet Gelasius II in southern France, and in 1121-22 he went to Italy to see Calixtus II on behalf of Louis. It was on his return from Italy in March of 1122 that the forty-one-year-old monk learned that Adam had died and that his brothers at Saint-Denis had elected him abbot. Suger took pride in the fact that he had been absent and had not even known of the election. His fellow monks may have thought that Suger's election would please the king – the two men were approximately the same age and may have known each other at the abbey school, though Louis probably left Saint-Denis a year or two after Suger became an oblate, and there is no evidence to show that they were ever friends in their youth. Before 1122 Louis had already chosen Suger for responsible positions. If the monks reasoned that Suger's royal connection would benefit the abbey, they still made the crucial mistake of failing to consult the king about the election and had to face his anger and even imprisonment when they sought his assent after the fact. Only after negotiation did the king grant Suger his peace and confirmation. On March 11, 1122, Suger was ordained a priest, and the next day consecrated as abbot.

Within a few years Suger advanced to the position of a favorite royal counselor. As abbot of Saint-Denis he enjoyed a triumph of influence and

---

poet is rarely found today, by classical or nineteenth-century standards Suger's achievement was not so great. Marcel Aubert was so little impressed by what he read that in recall he inflated the figures. '*Il était capable de réciter de mémoire des passages entiers – 200 à 300 vers, dit son biographe Guillaume – d'Horace, qui était un de ses auteurs préférés*'; see his *Suger*, Figures monastiques (Abbaye S. Wandrille, 1950), p. 51.

[14] Suger writes of his service at Berneval and Toury in *Adm.* (L), pp. 170, 184-85; for the other events, consult the index of Suger, *Vita Lud.* (W).

prestige when in 1124 the king came to the abbey to take the banner of the Vexin from the altar and to grant privileges to the church of Saint-Denis and then achieved a bloodless victory over the invading Henry V of Germany. In a charter granted to the abbey at that time, Louis referred to Suger (who in fact probably drafted the charter) as 'the venerable abbot ... whom we had in our councils as a loyal dependent and intimate adviser.'[15]

Because Suger had worked effectively and harmoniously with Abbot Adam, whom he called his 'spiritual father and foster parent,'[16] the monks of Saint-Denis presumably expected their new abbot to continue the policies of his predecessor. As abbot, however, Suger was faced with the problem of bringing the discipline of his flock into line with current ideas of reform. If he moved too far or too fast, he would lose the support of his monks, but if he did nothing he faced attack from Bernard of Clairvaux and other partisans of reform.

It is difficult for us to judge the state of the abbey under Adam and in the first year of Suger's rule. Bernard wrote that 'the very cloister of the monastery, they say, was thronged with knights, beset by business affairs, resounded with disputes, and now and then was open to women.' In a bitter memoir Abelard called the abbey 'absolutely worldly and shameful' and said that Abbot Adam surpassed his monks in evil living and notoriety'[17] But Bernard wrote only of 'what I have heard, not what I have seen,' and Abelard was quite unspecific about what he found worldly and shameful. Given his strong views on the impropriety of monks eating meat, Abelard may well have been shocked by no more than Adam's establishment of an annual feast in memory of King Dagobert at which roast meat and claret were served.[18] But, however exaggerated the charges which have come down to us, Suger was faced with a challenge and took steps to reform his abbey.

---

[15] *'Presente itaque venerabili abbate prefate ecclesie Sugerio, quem fidelem et familiarem in consiliis nostris habebamus . . .'* (Tardif, *Monuments*, p. 217, no. 391). On the terms *fidelis* and *familiaris* see Eric Bournazel, *Le Gouvernement capétien au XIIe siecele, 1108-1180*, pp. 147-51; and his essay in this volume, p. 58. For the events discussed in this paragraph, consult the index of Suger, *Vita Lud*, (W).

[16] '*. . . patri spiritali et nutritori meo*' (Suger, *Vita Lud*. [W], p. 208).

[17] Bernard, Ep. 78. 4 in Jean Leclercq and Henri Rochais, eds., *S. Bernardi opera*, 8 vols. (Rome, 1957-77), vol. 7, p. 203; the full letter is on pp. 201-10; Abelard, *Historia calamitatum*, ed. Jacques Monfrin (Paris, 1978), p. 81, ll. 654-57.

[18] The money for the anniversary of Dagobert came from Berneval, and Suger probably played a part in the creation of this festivity. See Robert Barroux, 'L'Anniversaire de la mort de Dagobert à Saint-Denis au XIIe siècle: Charte inédite de l'abbé Adam, *Bulletin philologique et historique*, 1942-43 (1945): 131-51. See Abelard's Ep. 7 to Heloise, ed. Joseph T. Muckle in *Medieval Studies* 17 (1955): 269: 'O brothers and fellow monks, you who each day, contrary to the teaching of the Rule and your [or our] profession, shamefully slaver for meat . . .'

It seems likely that he was guided more by practicality than zeal and found ways to make what moderate reform he introduced acceptable to his monks. When giving God credit for his achievements, he cites first the recovery of old domains, new acquisitions, enlargement of the church, and the restoration or construction of buildings, and then records with pride that the abbey was fully reformed 'peacefully, without scandal and disorder among the brothers, although they were not accustomed to it.'[19] He personally set an example of moderation though not of austerity for his monks, eating meat only when ill, drinking wine diluted with water, and eating food that was 'neither too coarse nor too refined.'[20]

Suger's reform program satisfied, or at least encouraged, Bernard, who wrote a letter of congratulation around 1127, praising him because now 'the vaults of the church echo with spiritual canticles instead of court cases.'[21] According to Bernard, Suger reduced the splendor of his own life and promoted continence, discipline, and spiritual reading. But the purpose of this letter was not simply to praise Suger for amending 'the arrogance of his former way of life' but to enlist the curial abbot's help in Bernard's campaign against the king's powerful chancellor and seneschal, Stephen of Garlande. Bernard noted that Suger was said to have been bound to Stephen in friendship, and he urged him to make the chancellor also a friend of truth. As we have seen, the friendship Bernard mentioned may have been based on a long-standing family connection.

Suger may well have complied with Bernard's request, though if he did his activity went unrecorded, and one must use caution in deducing intention from events. Stephen of Garlande fell, or rather was pushed, from power by early 1128, and it is reasonable to see Suger's hidden hand behind this coup d'etat and to assume that at this point Bernard and Suger had forged a firm political alliance.[22]

---

[19] Suger, *Vita Lud* (W), p. 212. On Suger's reform, see Giles Constable's essay in this volume, pp. 17-32. Constable describes the features of Suger's Saint-Denis as 'an orderly but not uncomfortable life,' 'a long liturgy', and 'a concern for conspicuous display'; see p. 20.

[20] William, *Vita Sug.* (L), p. 389.

[21] Bernard, Ep. 78.6 in *Opera*, vol. 7, p. 205.

[22] Robert-Henri Bautier considers Suger the responsible party in this event and places it in the context of other political struggles of the time in 'Paris au temps d'Abélard', *Abélard en son temps*, Actes du colloque international, 14-19 mai 1979 (Paris, 1983), pp. 68-69. Though in general I find Bautier's innovative reconstruction of the politics of the time compelling, on this point his case is reasonable but not proven. As evidence that Suger benefited directly from Garlande's expulsion from the chancellorship, Bautier states without supporting documentation that the chancellor named Simon who replaced him between 1128 and 1132 was Suger's nephew Simon. Except for the name, I can find nothing to identify this Simon with Suger's nephew, who was chancellor at the end of Suger's life. See Achille Luchaire, *Études sur les actes de Louis VII* (1885; reprint, Brussels, 1964), p. 56 on Simon as chancellor in 1150-51, and Françoise Gasparri, *L'Écriture des actes de Louis VI, Louis VII, et Philippe Auguste* (Geneva, 1973), p. 14 n.3, who says: *'Après 1127, la*

The monastic victors in this power struggle, wrapped in the banner of reform, aggrandized their own authority and property: in 1128 and 1129 monks replaced the nuns of Notre-Dame and Saint-Jean of Laon, Marmoutier took over Saint-Martin-au-Val near Chartres, and Morigny (with Suger's help) established its monks in the church of Saint-Martin of Étampes-les-Vielles. It is in this context that Suger's acquisition of Argenteuil should be placed.[23]

'In my studious adolescence, I used to read through the old charters of our possessions in the archives,' Suger reminisced as he related how he had found Carolingian records that he claimed proved the abbey of Argenteuil properly belonged to Saint-Denis, although, because of the disorder of the kingdom under the sons of Louis the Pious, the monks had not been able to gain possession.[24] Of the charter attributed to Louis the Pious that Suger produced to support his claims, one must say, '*Se non è vero, è molto ben trovato*,' for the historical account given there appears quite unlikely and the charter is probably a skilful fabrication.[25] And in case his historical and documentary argument seemed insufficient, Suger bolstered his claim with charges about the immoral life of the nuns. The dispute was tried before the papal legate, a former prior of Saint-Martin-des-Champs, and the court was persuaded 'both by the justice of our side and the great stench of theirs.'[26] And so Argenteuil was 'restored' to Saint-Denis, and

---

Chancellerie fut dirigée par un certain "Simon." ' If I am correct that Suger's nephew was Simon of Saint-Denis, who died between 1178 and 1180, then he would have had to become chancellor as a very young man to take office in 1128.

[23] The point is developed by Bautier, "Paris", p. 71. On Suger's involvement in the affair of Morigny and Saint-Martin of Étampes-lès-Vielles, see Léon Mirot, ed., *La Chronique de Morigny*, Collection de textes pour servir à l'étude et à l'enseignement de l'histoire, 2d ed. (Paris, 1912), pp. 46-47.

[24] Suger, *Adm.* (L), pp. 160-61; and Suger, *Vita Lud.* (W), pp. 216-18.

[25] The charter and the related documents of 1129 are in the thirteenth-century *Cartulaire blanc de Saint-Denis*, Paris, Archives nationales, LL 1158, fols. 278-79. It is printed in *Gallia Christiana*, vol. 7, inst. 8-9; see Johann Friedrich Böhmer and Engelbert Mühlbacher, *Die Regesten des Kaiserreichs unter den Karolingern, 751-918*, 2d ed. (Innsbruck, 1908), p. 332, no. 848 (822). Diplomatically the text is appropriate for an act of about 828, though the date is omitted. André Lesort, 'Argenteuil', *Dictionnaire d'histoire et de géographie ecclésiastique* 4 (1930): 22-24, shows that no other document from before 1129 gives an indication that Argenteuil ever belonged or should belong to Saint-Denis, though he does not conclude that the text is a forgery, a matter which seems self-evident to Bautier, 'Paris', p. 71. One should compare the charter with the story Suger tells in Suger, *Adm.* (L), p. 160, where the information Suger gives must come either from some other record than the document in the cartulary or from Suger's imagination. Thomas Waldman has made a strong argument that the charter is a forgery in 'Abbot Suger and the Nuns of Argenteuil', to appear in *Traditio* 41 (1985). If he is, as I think, correct, one must wonder how often Suger resorted to such dishonesty. See Robert Barroux, 'L'Abbé Suger et la vassalité du Vexin en 1124. La levée de l'oriflamme, la Chronique du Pseudo-Turpin et la fausse donation de Charlemagne à Saint-Denis de 813', *Le Moyen Age* 64 (1985): 1-26; and the essay by Eric Bournazel in this volume, pp. 61-66.

[26] Suger, *Vita Lud.* (W), p. 218.

the monks found that reform was good business.

Serious scholars have stated that Suger withdrew somewhat from political affairs after 1127 and deferred to Bernard of Clairvaux, but one may doubt this was the case.[27] The abbey bought, for a thousand *sous*, a house near the northern gate of Paris to be used as a lodging for men and horses, as Suger put it, 'because of our frequent participation in the affairs of the kingdom.'[28] Bernard wrote letters, but Suger could advise privately and in person – and we all know which is more effective. For the remainder of the reign of Louis VI, Suger appears to have been his most trusted minister, and in the summer of 1137 he was one of the leaders of the expedition accompanying the king's seventeen-year-old son to Bordeaux for the marriage with Eleanor of Aquitaine.[29]

Louis VI died a few days later, before the wedding party could return to Paris. In the first years of the reign of the young Louis VII, Suger stood out as the most powerful man at court. In a conflict with the queen mother, Adelaide, and the seneschal, Ralph of Vermandois, both of whom proposed to leave court and retire to their estates, Suger reproached his rivals with the taunt that, though France may be repudiated by them, it would never be bereft. 'Both retired in abject fear,' recounted Suger in the history he began to write about the reign of Louis VII.[30]

Shortly thereafter the young monarch asserted his independence from his father's adviser, and Suger's power was diminished. As the abbot of Saint-Denis held no official position in the royal household that would lend special significance to the absence of his name in royal charters, we must follow the shifts of his influence through the fortunes of a surrogate office, the chancellorship. At the beginning of the reign of Louis VII, the old king's vice-chancellor, Algrin, became chancellor. Algrin fell from power in 1140 and entered into open and effective conflict with the king. Suger and Bernard of Clairvaux were among those who mediated an accord, which was eventually reached at the castle of Ralph of Vermandois. One or perhaps two chancellors succeeded Algrin briefly in 1140, but before the end of the year the office was acquired by a powerful rival to Suger, Cadurc, who held the position until the king left on crusade in 1147 and again briefly after the king's return. Cadurc's second term of office was then followed by that of Suger's nephew, Simon. In 1140, too, Suger's rival, Ralph of Vermandois, returned to the office of seneschal,

---

[27] Molinier, *Louis de Gros*, p. vii; Panofsky, *Suger*, p. 11; and Waquet, *Vie*, p. viii-ix. Aubert, *Suger*, p. 83, states more soundly, '*De 1127 à la mort du roi en 1137, Suger ne quitte guère le palais.*'

[28] Suger, *Adm.* (L), p. 158.

[29] Suger, *Vita Lud.* (W), pp. 280-82.

[30] '*Quibus tam pene desperantibus cum ego ipse, velud exprobando, numquam Franciam repudiatam vacasse respondissem, pusillanimitate nimia uterque dicessit*' (Suger, *Frag. Lud.* [M], p.150).

which had been vacant in 1138 and 1139, and held it until his death in 1151.[31]

As he entered his early sixties, Suger was pushed into the unwanted position of elder statesmen in retirement. While Suger was in eclipse, the youthful king further established his independence and involved himself in an attempt to force the election of Cadurc as archbishop of Bourges (an attempt that led Innocent II to place the king under personal interdict), supported Ralph of Vermandois in his contested divorce and attempted marriage to the sister of Queen Eleanor, and led a bloody invasion of the lands of Theobald IV of Champagne.[32]

Posterity benefited from the redirection of Suger's energies. Between July 1140, when the foundation of the chevet was laid at Saint-Denis, and June 1144, when it was consecrated, the aging abbot engaged in that intense supervision of construction he records so vividly in his writings on his administration and on the consecration of the abbey. Though Suger may well have been influenced by a desire for penance as he worked on the church,[33] during this period he presumably also regretted his loss of influence and threw himself into work that would commemorate his power and might impress the king. The *Ordinatio*, which he enacted in 1140 or 1141, has the appearance of an administrative reexamination of his work at Saint-Denis.[34] And it was probably in the first half of the 1140s that he found time to compose his *Life of Louis VI*, a work that attested to the closeness of his relationship with the king's father.[35] Indeed, all his completed books appear to have been written between 1140 and 1147.

In 1144, and even more clearly in 1145, we find Suger involved again in

---

[31] On the offices of chancellor and seneschal, see Luchaire, *Études*, pp. 44-46, 52. John of Salisbury tells us that after Suger's death the king and Odo of Deuil, the new abbot of Saint-Denis, both took steps to humble Suger's relatives, and that his nephew Simon lost his position as chancellor because of his 'hateful name' (*'ex suspicione nominis odiosi cancellariam regis amiserat'*). Playing on the name of Simon, one may suspect a charge of simony. See John of Salisbury, *Historia pontificalis*, ed. and trans., Marjorie Chibnall, Medieval Texts (London, 1956), p. 87. On the crisis of Abbot Odo's first years of rule, see Glaser, 'Wilhelm,' pp. 300-321.

[32] On the king's activities see Marcel Pacaut, *Louis VII et son royaume* (Paris, 1964), pp. 42-46. Cartellieri's register shows how limited the demonstrable contacts were between Suger and the king from late 1140 to 1143 or early 1144. Pacaut admirably clarifies the twists of royal policy by a narrative which shows Suger's loss of power, though he may go too far in saying that 'Suger fût disgracié' (p. 41). Aubert, *Suger* p. 96, also refers to 'une funeste disgrace.' Disgrace is a public matter, and it is striking that no contemporary author refers to the fall from favor and influence discussed here. I do not, however, go as far as Bournazel (p. 59 in his essay in this volume), who asserts that Suger suffered no diminution of power at all.

[33] See Clark Maines's essay in this volume, pp. 77-94.

[34] Suger, *Ord.* (P), pp. 122-37. The engrossment of the present copy of Suger's will may date from the same period; see note 58 here.

[35] *The Life of Louis VI* was written before *De administratione*, which was begun in 1144 but not completed before the end of 1148. See Waquet, *Vie*, p.xi; and Panofsky, *Suger*, p. 142.

a minor way in royal affairs, as Louis planned his crusading expedition and attempted to draw conflicting factions together before his departure. In 1147, when the king was about to leave France on the Second Crusade, Bernard of Clairvaux proposed Suger and the count of Nevers to an assembly of barons at Étampes as the men to be regents during the king's absence. But Suger, it appears, would accept the position only as representative of the pope, the protector of all crusaders. Bernard then recommended Suger fulsomely to the pope, and the matter was settled when Eugene III named the abbot of Saint-Denis to serve as regent, while the king, acting on his own authority and in a delicate balancing act, also named as regents the archbishop of Reims, Samson Mauvoisin, and Ralph of Vermandois, thus forming a nominal triumvirate of regents. For two years Suger was, for all practical purposes, the chief of state: almost all his surviving letters date from this regency. When in 1149 Louis's brother, Robert of Dreux, broke with the king, returned early from the Crusade, and plotted with Ralph of Vermandois and others against him, it was Suger who called an assembly of prelates and barons, threatened the plotters with papal excommunication, forced Robert of Dreux into submission, and earned the title his biographer records as 'father of his fatherland.'[36]

Although, when the occasion demanded it, Suger did not hesitate to appear at the head of armed troops, his greatest victories were bloodless. In 1124 some counseled a strategy of attack, proposing to cut off the German imperial army in order 'to slaughter them without mercy like Saracens,' but Suger's preference was to let Henry V retreat, and when this strategy was followed it gave the French a greater victory, as Suger put it, than one gained in battle.[37] Suger's thwarting of the plot of Robert of Dreux was equally bloodless. Looking back, near the end of his life, Suger claimed that for twenty years no peace was concluded between Henry I of England and Louis VI in which he had not played a leading role, 'as one who held the confidence of both lords.'[38] Indeed, of all the political leaders of the twelfth century, Suger appears preeminently as a man of peace.[39] Nevertheless, his idea of peace was no sentimental

---

[36] '... *tam a populo quam principe pater appellatus est patriae*' (William, *Vita Sug.* [L], p. 398). On Suger's regency and his conflicts with Ralph of Vermandois, Cadurc, and Robert of Dreux, see Pacaut, *Louis VII*, pp. 57-58. Suger's special role as papal representative in overseeing the kingdom during Louis's absence is highlighted by Aryeh Grabois, 'Le Privilège de croisade et la régence de Suger,' *Revue historique de droit français et étranger*; 4th ser., 42 (1964): 458-65.

[37] Suger, *Vita Lud.* (W), pp. 222-26.

[38] In a letter to Geoffrey of Anjou and Empress Matilda: '*Quod si nobis credi dignaretur, non recordamur pacem aliquam viginti annis cum domino rege Francorum eum fecisse, cui fideliter et praecipue inter omnes operam jugem et fidelem non adhibuerimus, sicut ille qui ab utroque domino credebatur*' (Suger, *Let.* [L], p. 265).

[39] Note his own account of urging Louis VII to show clemency to the people of Poitiers in Suger, *Frag. Lud.* (M), pp. 152-54.

pacifism; it provided a justification for royal repression of disorder and 'tyranny'. Identifying the king with the God of Vengeance, he wrote approvingly of Louis VI's revenging himself 'joyfully', and the word 'vengeance' appears over one hundred time in his works.[40] This desire for peace through royal force justified by necessity was combined with a shrewd sense of the realities of power, and though he expressed violent condemnation of petty 'tyrants' like Thomas of Marle and Hugh of Le Puiset (who were, indeed, personal enemies), he maintained a respectful attitude toward such powerful rivals of the French kings as Henry I and Henry's nephew, Theobald of Blois-Champagne.

Looking back, when he was about sixty, on his early career, Suger noted his regret that he had resorted to military force in protecting the abbey's domain in the Vexin and stated that this weighed on his conscience.[41] When he first began reconstruction at the abbey church, he prayed in the chapter that he – a man of blood, like David – might not be barred from the building of the Temple.[42] His histories show that images of blood struck Suger's mind with special force.[43] His policy of peace was stated aphoristically in the salutation in a letter of 1150 to the rebellious bishop, church, and populace of Beauvais wishing them 'peace above and below from the King of kings and the king of the Franks.'[44]

Both Suger and his biographers commented on his humble origins; others, moreover, remarked on his small size, since he was slender as well as short, and not robust, being easily tired by vigorous exertion. As Simon Chèvre d'Or wrote in an epitaph:

> Small of body and family, constrained by twofold smallness,
> He refused in his smallness to be a small man.[45]

---

[40] '... *votivam in hostes parabat ultionem, tanto hylaris, tanto letabundus, quanto eos subita strage, inopinata ultione, inopinatam injuriam strenue ulcisci contingeret*' (Suger, *Vita Lud.* [W], p. 158). For the calculation of the number of appearances of the word *ultio* and an analysis of Suger's thought on the subject, see Claude Aboucaya, 'Politique et répression criminelle dans l'oeuvre de Suger', *Mélanges Roger Aubenas* (Montpellier, 1974), pp.9-24 (number cited on p. 18).

[41] Suger, *Ord.* (P), p. 122. See also the essay by Clark Maines in this volume, pp. 77-94.

[42] Suger, *Adm.* (L), p. 186 or Suger, *Adm.* (P), p. 44.

[43] Suger, *Vita Lud.* (W), p. 58: *laici manibus gladio sanguinolentis;* p. 60: *sanguine fuso ... vias* (quotation from Lucan); p. 62: *corpus et sanguinem Jesu Christi;* p.92: *humani sanguinis sitibundus;* p. 116; *se totam sanguineam contrectans*; p. 118: *uno sanguine involutos, saturatus humano sanguine*; and so forth.

[44] Ep. 23, '... *pacem superiorem et inferiorem a Rege regum et rege Francorum*' (Suger, *Let.* [L], p. 277).

[45] *Corpore, gente brevis, gemina brevitate coactus,*
   In brevitate sua nolit esse brevis.
See Lecoy; *Oeuvres*, p. 422, or *PL*, vol. 185, cols. 1253-54. I have here used Panofsky's translation in *Suger*, p. 33. The poem was commissioned, not by the king, but almost certainly by Count Henry the Liberal, a final mark of Suger's special relationship with the

Physically as well as socially Suger had to look up to others. In order to reach the level of power and achievement he attained, he must have been, like Abelard, a scrambler; but he was not a man who appears to have been rendered brittle by ambition. It is remarkable that, unlike Abelard (to name only one), Suger seems to have been quite free of jealousy. To the best of my knowledge, no contemporary accuses him of *invidia*. Moreover, unless I have read too hurriedly, the very word *invidia* appears nowhere in his writing. People commonly explain the actions of others by emotions with which they are themselves familiar. Suger frequently writes of *superbia*, but not of *invidia*.[46] Of what other medieval authors could this statement be made? Not indeed of Guibert of Nogent, Abelard, or Bernard.

Suger's ideal was probably to possess the qualities of Gelasius II, whom he describes as acting 'with glory and humility, but with vigor.'[47] Pride was surely the sin with which Suger had to wrestle most vigorously. Bernard had criticized Suger for the 'manner and equipment with which you used to travel, which seemed somewhat arrogant.'[48] Suger's writing sings out with self-satisfaction. He gloried in his artistic and administrative achievements, and yet according to his biographer he lived modestly. As Erwin Panofsky puts it, his vanity was more than personal – it was institutional.[49]

In personal relations with those about him, Suger could be vigorous, witty, and charming; his biographer writes of his sitting up till the middle of the night telling stories, 'as he was a man of great good cheer.'[50] And yet there is a hidden side to his character. Much of Suger's activity and even more of his motivation remain obscure, and this is so not only because of a lack of documentary material from the early twelfth century. Suger's surviving letters are dry and unrevealing, nothing like the letters of monastic friendship left by Bernard, Peter the Venerable, and Nicholas of Clairvaux. In his histories he tells his readers what he wants them to know and attenuates or simply omits that which he found troublesome.[51]

---

house of Blois-Champagne. See my 'The Court of Champagne as a Literary Center,' *Speculum* 36 (1961): 570. According to William, '*Erat quidem corpus breve sortitus et gracile, sed et labor assiduus plurimum detraxerat viribus*' (*Vita Sug.* [L], p. 388).

[46] *Emulus* and *emuli* appear often, however. On *superbia* and *effrenis elatio* see Suger, *Vita Lud.* (W), pp. 182-84.

[47] '... *gloriose, humiliter, sed strenue ecclesie jura disponens*' (ibid., pp. 202-4).

[48] '... *tuus ille scilicet habitus et apparatus cum procederes, quod paulo insolentior appareret*' (Bernard, Ep. 78, *Opera*, vol. 7, p. 203). It is often suggested that Bernard had Suger in mind when about 1125 he wrote in the *Apologia ad Guillelmum abbatem*, XI, 27, of an abbot traveling with a retinue of sixty or more horses; *Opera*, vol. 3, p. 103.

[49] Panofsky, *Suger*, p. 35. I have been strongly influenced by Panofsky's brilliant introduction, which nevertheless now seems to me too uncomplicated and positive.

[50] '... *ut erat jocundissimus*' (William, *Vita Sug.* [L], p. 389).

[51] Historians frequently contrast Suger's description of the defeat at Brémule in Suger, *Vita Lud.* (W), pp. 196-98 with that given by Ordericus Vitalis, *Ecclesiastical History*, ed.

We can understand this aspect of his character if we remember that Suger made his career as an administrator and as an intimate adviser, a *familiaris*. He had the talents of a first-rate counsellor: an excellent memory, a strong sense of history and precedent, a shrewd if somewht cynical grasp of human behavior and motivation, great oratorical skill in both French and Latin, and the ability to write almost as quickly as he could speak.[52] Moreover, he knew what not to say and what not to commit to parchment, and as a minister rather than a sovereign he knew how to efface himself behind his king. His *Life of Louis VI* establishes his own importance, but it tells us almost nothing of what he advised the king, and only in the uncompleted *Life of Louis VII*, which he probably composed after his service as regent, do we have long passages on what Suger himself said to the king.

The intimate counselor may give advice that is not taken or be the instigator of policies for which he receives neither credit nor responsibility. We cannot tell how much political or adminstrative ruthlessness was mixed with Suger's bonhomie. His biographer tells us that rivals and the ignorant who did not know him well 'considered him too hard and unyielding and mistook his determination for brutality.'[53] The case of Argenteuil shows that he could act with self-righteous severity, and probably with duplicity and deception as well.

In the introduction to the *Life of Louis VI*, which he addressed to his close personal friend Bishop Josselin of Soissons, Suger declared his intention to raise a monument more lasting than bronze.[54] His extant writings fill a little more than one thick volume: the *Life of Louis VI*, to which should be added portions of a continuation on the reign of Louis VII; the books on his own administration and the consecration of the church of Saint-Denis; under thirty letters; a will and other miscellaneous documents; and, of course, charters. His learning and the influence of both the classics and Scripture are apparent in his writing, but his style is far from classical – though I would not like to join Henri Waquet in the opinion that he lacked taste.[55] The praise that he resembled Cicero verbally – *Erat Caesar animo, sermone Cicero* – surely applies to his oratory rather than his writing.[56]

Marjorie Chibnall, 6 vols. (Oxford, 1969-80), vol. 6, pp. 234-42 (in Le Prévost's edition, vol. 4, pp. 354-56).

[52] William, *Vita Sug.* (L), pp. 381-83, 405. William tells us that Suger explained his reluctance to discharge his agents, except in major cases and for manifest dereliction, by reasoning that 'those who are removed carry off what they can, and their replacements, fearing the same thing, speed up their looting': '*dum et hi qui amoventur quae possunt auferant et substituti, quia idem metuunt, ad rapinas festinent*' (p. 383).

[53] '. . . *durum nimis aestimabant et rigidum, et quod erat constantiae, feritati deputabant*' (William, *Vita Sug.* [L], p. 383).

[54] Suger, *Vita Lud.* (W), p. 4.

[55] '*Suger manque totalement de goût*' (Waquet, *Vie*, p. xvi).

[56] William, *Vita Sug.* (L), p. 388.

Suger left three major monuments: his writings, his adminstrative and financial reform, and his artistic achievements. He was a man of massive accomplishments – and a correspondingly massive sense of self. Collectively, Suger's writings constitute a sort of autobiography.[57] They do not, of course, tell us many of the things we would like to know, about his family and childhood, for instance, but they are highly personal works. The history of Louis VI is not a biography in the Suetonian sense but a political memoir, an account of deeds, *Gesta Francorum*, deeds of Suger as well as of Louis.[58]

Suger left his mark on his administrative reforms in a most personal way. His testament, which bears the date of June 17, 1137, should be read side by side with *De administratione*. In addition to the anniversary service he established for himself at Saint-Denis, Suger wanted Masses for the dead to be celebrated for himself in all the dependencies of his abbey, and he wanted them to be spread throughout the week: on Mondays and Tuesdays at Argenteuil, the wealthiest of the acquisitions he claimed for Saint-Denis; on Wednesdays at Saint-Denis-de-l'Estrée, where he lived for ten years as a youth; on Thursdays at Notre-Dame-des-Champs near Corbeil, where Suger established a priory; on Fridays at Zell, which Suger had acquired in the diocese of Metz; and on Saturdays at Saint-Alexander of Lièpvre in Alsace.[59] Moreover, we learn from another source, at Saint-Denis Suger was paired with Charles the Bald for a commemoration service on the day before the nones eleven months out of the year.[60]

Finally, Suger placed his mark on his church. Four of his images and seven inscriptions containing his name appeared in his church, from the entry portal to the Infancy window in the chevet. It is hard to find a clearer

---

[57] Georg Misch recognized this: see his *Geschichte der Autobiographie*, 4 vols. in 8 (Frankfurt-am-Main, 1949-69), vol. 3, pt. 1, pp. 316-87.

[58] Suger, *Vita Lud.* (W), p. 68. Time and again we find *et nos ipsi interfuimus* (p. 52); *et nos fuimus* (p. 56); *nos autem* (p. 145); *per nos*(p.260); *apud nos* (p. 262); and so forth. Gabrielle Spiegel concludes in *The Chronicle Tradition of Saint-Denis* (Brookline, Mass., 1978), p. 45, that 'from the time of Suger's abbacy royal historiography becomes the central intellectual activity of Saint-Denis in service to the French crown.'

[59] The testament is published in Suger, *Ch.* (L), pp. 333-41. The original is in the Musée des Archives nationales (A.N. K 22, no 9[7] – AE II 145), and there is an excellent photograph in *Mémorial de l'histoire de France* (Paris: Archives nationales, 1980), no. 10. Though it is dated 17 June 1137, when Suger was on the point of leaving for Bordeaux, the document cannot have been written in this form before 1139, or more likely 1140, since Samson of Reims is named as a witness with the title of archbishop. See Achille Luchaire, *Annales de la vie de Louis VI* (1890; reprint, Brussels, 1964), pp. 264-65. Probably Suger wrote a draft of his will before he left on a major expedition and had it engrossed after his return.

[60] Molinier, *Obituaires*, pp. 306, 309, 311, 313, 316, 318, 321, 323, 325, 330, 332. On October 6 Charles the Bald had his anniversary service to himself. '*Ob Karolus imperator tertius et cultor beati pretiosique martyris Dionysii studiosissimus monasterii*' (p. 328). Suger does not mention his own name in his ordinance concerning the reestablishment of the commemoration of Charles the Bald; see Suger, *Ord.* (P), pp. 128-32.

identification between building and patron in ecclesiastical architecture.[61] Suger treated God as author of both Solomon's Temple and his own construction at Saint-Denis when he wrote, 'The identity of the author and the work provides everything needed for the worker.'[62] Though Suger claimed to be satisfied by an identification between his construction and the divine author, it is Suger's own role as 'author' of his works that most impress modern commentators and is the unifying force of this volume.

If Suger's early childhood was like that of such contemporaries as Ordericus Vitalis, then he was raised with the expectation that he would enter a monastery at an early age. As we know, he became an oblate of Saint-Denis when he was about ten. In many ways Suger's adult personality can be related to the Benedictine formation he underwent. His self-discipline and his ability to keep his thoughts and feelings to himself and to act as a loyal subordinate of an established superior were surely fostered by his early experience of the Benedictine Rule. For contrast, one need only think of Abelard, who was raised to be a knight and did not learn to hold his competitive drives in check. Suger's toughness and determination may also be associated with his monastic training, though these qualities were in ample supply among men and women of other backgrounds as well.

Early clerical and monastic training may well have encouraged a sense of fastidiousness. Both Guibert of Nogent and Suger were repelled by excrement.[63] They also both expressed in their writings a horror of bloodshed. But Guibert differs from Suger in his peculiar fascination with sexuality and mutilation, topics of minimal interest for the abbot of Saint-Denis.[64] The two men were similar, however, in their support of monarchy and fatherland. Both found surrogate parents in institutional form and placed the king in something of the role of a natural father.[65] Suger, moreover, treated Saint-Denis as an ever-nourishing, never-failing mother.

The most obvious contrast between Guibert and Suger is in their effectiveness. Both were abbots and prolific authors, but with respect to the affairs of the world Guibert appears as a timid and ineffective neurotic, Suger as a first minister of self-confidence, power and achievement. One

[61] See Misch, *Autobiographie*, vol. 3, pt. 1, pp. 365-76; and Panofsky, *Suger* p. 29. For these inscriptions and their placement, see the essay by Clark Maines in this volume, pp. 85-86.

[62] '*Identitas auctoris et operis sufficientiam facit operantis*' (Suger, *Cons.* [P], p. 90).

[63] Suger, *Vita Lud.* (W), p. 248.

[64] In a matter-of-fact reference to castration and blinding, Suger treats the punishment as 'merciful', since the subject merited death; see ibid., p. 190.

[65] On Guibert's patriotism and personality see my introduction to *Self and Society in Medieval France: The Memoirs of Abbot Guibert of Nogent* (1970; reprint, Toronto, 1984), pp. 9-31.

would be unjustified in saying simply that a secure institutional mother is better than a crippling real one, but we may conclude that either during that childhood of which we know nothing or as an oblate and young monk Suger acquired a healthy dose of self-esteem.[66]

The contrast between Suger and Bernard of Clairvaux is one of attitude and belief rather than of psychological strength. Unlike Bernard, Suger's monastic formation began before he entered puberty and adolescence. To the best of our knowledge he experienced no crisis of sudden conversion from the world. Indeed, he grew up in an environment that taught the importance of penance and instilled an awed respect for the beauty and grandeur of the great abbey church of Saint-Denis. Bernard was troubled by the problems of poverty and misery in the secular world and the expenditure of Church funds on monastic glory and good living; Suger accepted the world in which he had been raised as one that should be embellished and continued. Bernard's mysticism was one of conversion from this world, Suger's one of appreciation of it; in his famous passage on his transport 'from this world below to that above,' Suger tells us that his contemplation began 'from love of the beauty of the house of God.'[67]

Suger's complex personality and interests are better revealed by this volume as a whole than they can be by any single part of it. As it shows, Suger advanced and glorified himself through developing and preserving the power of the monarchy, through his writings and through enriching, rebuilding, and decorating his church at Saint-Denis. In so doing, he left monuments far more lasting than bronze.

---

[66] For one current view of the development of healthy self-esteem, see Heinz Kohut, *The Analysis of the Self* (New York, 1971), pp. 107-9. But it is hard for historians to make practical use of Kohut's insights, since he treats 'a gifted person's ego' as an exception to his rule, and in Suger's case it is precisely the ego of a gifted person we are trying to explain. Moreover, analysts are far from agreement on the explanation of conflicts about self-worth and esteem; see, for example, the pertinent questions raised by Leo Rangell in 'The Self in Psychoanalytic Theory', *Journal of the American Psychoanalytic Association* 30 (1982): 871-72.

[67] Suger, *Adm.* (L), p. 198 or Suger, *Adm.* (P), pp. 62-64. On Suger 'as an architect who *built* theology', see Otto von Simson, *The Gothic Cathedral*, 2d ed. (New York, 1962), p. 124-33.

Appendix: Suger's Relations and Family Background

Charles Higounet was the first to come upon the evidence of a Suger family at Chennevières-lès-Louvres and to suggest that it provided an indication 'of the background and family ties of the abbot of Saint-Denis.' While preparing his thorough study of *La Grange de Vaulerent*, Higounet explored the rich archives of the abbey of Chaalis, now in the Archives départementales de l'Oise, and the unedited cartulary of Chaalis at the Bibliothèque Nationale, Paris. He found that a certain *Sigerius* appeared as a witness to a donation recorded in an act of 1145 (which also recorded another donation witnessed by *Sigerius, abbas Sancti Dyonisii*), that he had a brother Ralph and a son, John Suger (who appeared in an act of 1169), and that other men used the family name Suger in the thirteenth century. To the suggestive character of this name he added a thirteenth-century reference to a *Campus Sugeri* and a document of 1183 citing rights '*in quodam frustro terre que Sugerius magnus excolebat.*'[1]

Since Higounet was studying the grange of Vaulerent and not the abbot of Saint-Denis and his family, he did no more than raise the question of a possible connection between these texts and Abbot Suger. It has not been difficult to find reasons for dismissing Higounet's discovery and his suggestion of a connection with the family of the abbot. The *Sigerius* of the charter of 1145 could have been a godson of the abbot, or the identity of names could be simple coincidence; and the *Sugerius magnus* of the charter of 1183 could be the *Sigerius* of 1145 or any local, otherwise unknown Suger. Historians concerned with Abbot Suger have either ignored Higounet or treated his material as inconclusive.[2]

When examined more closely and placed in a larger context, however, these documents from Chaalis can be seen as more significant than Higounet suggested. I have consulted and cited here those original charters I could find in the Archives de l'Oise at Beauvais, but for the convenience of the reader I have also given references to the late-fourteenth-century cartulary of Chaalis, Paris, Bibliothèque Nationale, ms. lat. 11003, and the eighteenth-century copies of the charters of Chaalis in the Collection Moreau in the same library. From these texts and the charter naming Suger's companions on his trip to Germany in 1125, the genealogy on pp. 407 can be constructed. I will now present these documents in a systematic fashion.

---

[1] Higounet, *La Grange*, p. 12, and see document no. 8 here. I have gratefully made use of the citations given by Higounet and repeat some of them here, but the reader who compares our references will see that I have been able to expand his documentation.

[2] Spiegel, *Chronicle Tradition*, p. 34, no. 80, cites Higounet's evidence and first drew it to my attention, but concludes, 'The most probable hypothesis is that he was born at Saint-Denis or Argenteuil.'

1. Witness on behalf of Suger in a charter of Mainard, count of Mosbach, at Mainz in 1125: '*Ex parte abbatis testes sunt: Bartholomeus capellanus suus, Petrus clericus frater suus, Stephanus miles suus de Balbiniaco, Hugo de Sancto Dionysio, Radulfus filius Sugerii, Petrus de Dommartino, Sugerius miles . . .*' The charter is published by Tardif, *Monuments*, pp. 221-22, no. 397.
2. Undated *pancarte* of Theobald, bishop of Paris, to which a modern archivist has assigned the date of 1145 on the back of the charter. This general confirmation includes notices of a number of donations to Chaalis, with witnesses to those actions. Among the donations are:

    (a) Donation by *Rogerius Escotins de Sancto Dyonisio* and his wife,*Lupa*, of a piece of land in the territory of Vaulerent and Villeron. Witnesses: *Sigerius, abbas Sancti Dyonisii; Stephanus de Balbiniaco*. After Roger's death *Lupa* confirmed this donation. Witnesses: *Sigerius, abbas Sancti Dyonisii; Willelmus, subprior Sancti Dyonisii; Galterius de Pompona; Lethardus de Sancto Dyonisio*.

    (b) *Sigerius, miles de Canaveris (sic)*, gave land in the territory of Chennevières, *laudantibus et concedentibus Johanne, Hugone et Pagone, filiis suis; Radulfo et Balduino, fratribus suis*. There is also a reference to a daughter of *Sigerius* as a nun at Jouarre. *Sigerius* held the land in fief from *Albertus, miles de Canaveris (sic)*, who had a wife named Agnes and sons named Girard, Hugh, and Theobald.

    (c) *Antelmus de Pissicoc, miles*, and his wife, *Comitissa*, and mother, *Adcelina*, made a donation in the territory of Epiais. Among the witnesses were: *Radulfus, miles de Vilers; Sigerius et Johannes filius eius de Canaveris (sic)*. The sealed original of this act is in the Archives de l'Oise, H 5514. It is summarised in the cartulary, no. 635, fols. 188r-88v, and there is an eighteenth-century copy in Paris, Bibliothèque Nationale, Collection Moreau, vol. 60, fols. 256r-67r.

3. An undated *pancarte* of Manasses, bishop of Meaux, makes known the same donation as that recorded in 2a and names the same witnesses, including the two appearances of *Sigerius, abbas Sancti Dionysii*. The original of this charter is in the Archives de l'Oise, H 5515. There is an eighteenth-century copy in the Collection Moreau, vol. 66, fols. 143r-44r.

4. *Pancarte* of Maurice, bishop of Paris, dated 1163.

    (a) *Adam de Claceu (sic)* and *Bartholomeus de Curbarun* made a donation of land in the territory of *Tarentenfossa*. Among the witnesses: *Sigerius de Chanaveriis*.

    (b) *Girardus, miles de Chanaveriis*, on his deathbed made a donation with the approval of his wife, Mathilda, of land at *Hemerias* in the territory of Chennevières. Among the witnesses: *Gautherius Becherel, avunculus suus*. The sealed original is in the Archives de l'Oise, H 5255; it is excerpted in the cartulary no. 621, fols. 185r-85v, and there is an eighteenth-century copy in the Collection Moreau, vol. 72, fols. 116r-17r

5. Maurice, bishop of Paris, makes known in an act of 1169 that *Johannes, filius, Sugerii de Canaveriis* made a donation to Chaalis of 23 *denarii parisienses*. The act is in the cartulary, no. 644, fol. 194v. I have not been able to find the original or a later copy of this act.
6. In a *pancarte* of 1171, Maurice, bishop of Paris, makes known a donation by *Antelmus Scotus*. Witnesses: *Petrus, sacerdos de Villerun; Guido de Vilerun; Raimbertus cementarius; Sigerius de Chanaveriis; Willelmus de Chanaveriis.* Among the witnesses to another donation is *Johannes, filius Sigerii de Chanaveris (sic)*. The original charter is in the Archives de l'Oise, H 5517, and there is an eighteenth-century copy in the Collection Moreau, vol. 77, fol. 108r.
7. In an act of 1172, Maurice, bishop of Paris, settles a conflict between the abbey of Chaalis and two knights of Chennevières, John and his brother Hugh, over land given by *Sigerius de Canaberiis (sic) et Radulfus frater eius*. The sealed original is in the Archives de l'Oise, H 5257; it is excerpted in the cartulary, no. 623, fol. 186v, and there is an eighteenth-century copy in the Collection Moreau, vol. 78, fol. 43r.
8. In an act of 1183, Maurice, bishop of Paris, makes known a donation by *Hugo de Bosco, miles*, in the territory of Vieux-Chennevières, of a '*campipartem et domum in quodam frustro terre quam Sigerius magnus excolebat.*' The act is in the Collection Moreau, vol. 87, fols. 17r-18r [citing Archives de Chaalis, Vaulerent, liasse 2, no. 27 (or 21) al. 3 L] and is excerpted in the cartulary, no. 687, fol. 200v. I was not able to find the original in the Archives de l'Oise or in the Collection de Picardie in the Bibliothèque Nationale.

From these documents we can establish that Suger, *miles* of Chennevières had already produced three sons by 1145, John, Hugh, and Payen, and that he had a daughter who was a nun at Jouarre. Of the three brothers, Ralph, Suger, and Baldwin, only Suger appears to have had children. It seems likely that Baldwin was the youngest brother, but the birth order of Suger and Ralph is not made clear from these charters from Chaalis. Ralph was not named as a witness in any of the documents which can be dated after 1145. He may have died not long after that date, and his name may appear with that of Suger in the later charters only because they had once held land in common. Suger *miles* was alive in 1172 and probably entered Chaalis or died soon thereafter.

It should be noted that these documents provide no evidence to support Higounet's suggestion that Girard and William of Chennevières were members of the same family as the brothers Ralph and Suger.

The information that Higounet needed to clinch the case for a family relationship (but did not note) was that in 1125 Abbot Suger traveled to Germany with his brother and with Ralph, son of Suger, and a knight named Suger. I do not consider it unwarranted to conclude that Ralph and the knight Suger were the two brothers who appear in the charters of

Chaalis, since the name Suger is most extremely rare. If this is the case, then we can extend the genealogy back a further generation to a progenitor named Suger. Ralph was probably the elder son, and his brother Suger would have been quite a young man in 1125, since he lived into the 1170s. The *Sugerius magnus* of the charter of 1183 was probably this first known Suger. If the knight Suger was born about 1100 and was a younger son, his father may have been born about 1070.

This late-eleventh-century Suger, whom we may tentatively call *Magnus*, may be the same man who appeared along with his brother Payen as a witness to a charter of Saint-Martin-des-Champs of about 1105, where both men are identified as nephews of Peter Orphelin.[3] The identification again rests on the extreme rarity of the name Suger, and it is strengthened by the fact that the name Payen appears again in the family among the sons of Suger of Chennevières. If this is the case, then the family that interests us was connected, perhaps by marriage, with the Orphelins of Annet-sur-Marne, who in turn had connections with the Garlandes. Indeed, William of Garlande was one of the witnesses to the charter of about 1105, which was issued by Peter Sanglier.[4]

There are two reasons for considering that Suger of Chennevières was a cousin of Abbot Suger. We know that the abbot had a brother named Ralph (probably an older brother, since he married) and, given the logic of the naming practices, it is likely that he had an ancestor or uncle named Suger after whom he was named. The pairing of the brothers Ralph and Suger (and probably in that order) in the two families strongly suggests that they were related. Secondly, the fact that Abbot Suger travelled to Germany with a Ralph and a Suger, whom we may now associate with Chennevières, adds strongly to the conviction that they were related. Suger had only been abbot for three years, and for his German expedition he needed to take with him men he could count on. One was his brother, Peter, and another was Stephen of Bobigny, *miles suus*, who appeared again with him as a witness to the donation of Roger Scot recorded in 1145 (in 2a and 3 above). That Ralph, son of Suger, and *Sugerius miles* were relatives of Abbot Suger is by far the most likely explanation of their presence.

The same rough calculation that places the birth of Suger *Magnus*, the father of Ralph and Suger *miles*, at about 1070 would place the birth of Abbot Suger's father, Helinand, at about 1050. These two men were presumably related in the male line. Helinand and the elder Suger may have been brothers (possibly with a father named Ralph or Suger), or

---

[3] Depoin, *Recueil*, vol. 1, p. 166, no. 104. Depoin's edition contains helpful prosopographical notes.

[4] The possible connection between the Suger of this charter and the family of Abbot Suger was first pointed out by Bournazel, *Gouvernement capétien*, p. 72. On the connection with the Garlandes, see also pp. 35-36.

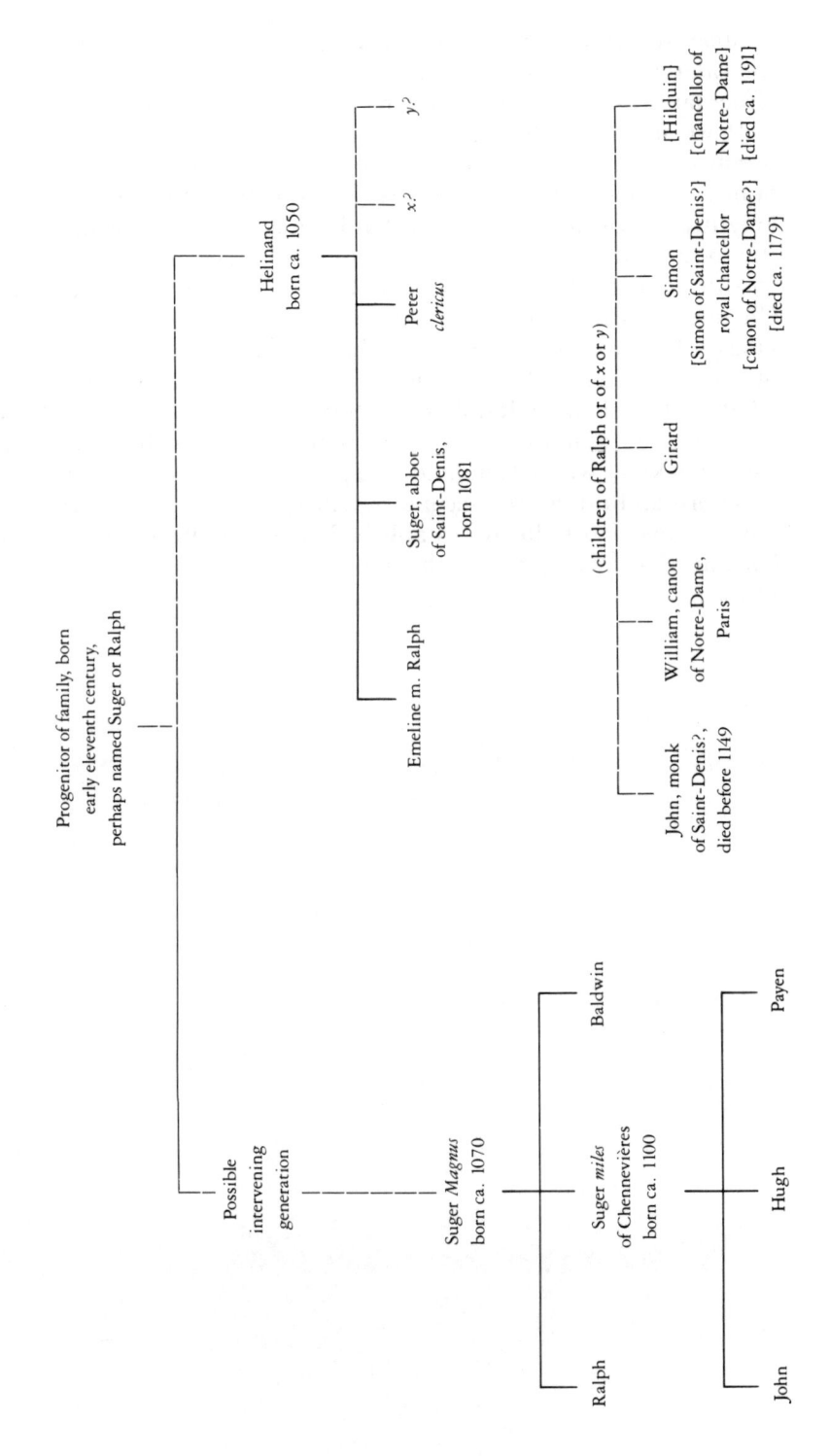

HYPOTHETICAL RECONSTRUCTION OF SUGER'S FAMILY

Progenitor of family, born early eleventh century, perhaps named Suger or Ralph

Possible intervening generation

Suger *Magnus* born ca. 1070

Suger *miles* of Chennevières born ca. 1100

- Ralph
- Baldwin

- John
- Hugh
- Payen

Helinand born ca. 1050

- Emeline m. Ralph
- Suger, abbot of Saint-Denis, born 1081
- Peter *clericus*
- x?
- y?

(children of Ralph or of x or y)

- John, monk of Saint-Denis?, died before 1149
- William, canon of Notre-Dame, Paris
- Girard
- Simon [Simon of Saint-Denis?] royal chancellor [canon of Notre-Dame?] [died ca. 1179]
- [Hilduin] [chancellor of Notre-Dame] [died ca. 1191]

another generation may have intervened, making Helinand the uncle of the elder Suger. Since Helinand is a name that does not appear again in either family, it seems likely that he was a younger son.

If we may consider this relationship between two branches of one family as securely established, we learn two things about the immediate family of Abbot Suger. One is that he came from the lower ranks of the knightly class, since it is unlikely that Helinand was significantly higher in the social scale than his cousins. Ralph and Suger of Chennevières were wealthy enough for both to hold the title of *miles*, but the knights of Chennevières were clearly minor landholders who shared property in a village of no great importance, and the younger Suger was himself a vassal of a minor knight, Albert of Chennevières. It is tantalizing not to be sure what land was held by Ralph, son of Suger. The family may well have held scattered estates in the region immediately to the north of Paris. Though we do not know where Helinand held property and where the future abbot was born and raised, the second conclusion we can draw is that Suger's family was most likely established not far from the cousins of Chennevières, somewhere within ten or fifteen miles of the abbey of Saint-Denis.

IV

ABAELARDIANA

The Paraclete and the Council of Rouen of 1231

The key manuscript in all discussions of the transmission and authenticity of the correspondence of Abelard and Heloise has long been Troyes MS 802, which contains the most accurate and most complete text of the famous letters. Following the correspondence, the rest of the manuscript is devoted to a collection of canon law material related to nuns. Although the Troyes manuscript was written in the latter part of the thirteenth century,[1] most commentators have assumed that it is a copy of a much earlier text. Since the correspondence itself provides no unambiguous clues to its origin, one must turn to the canonistic material to see when the collection was compiled and to try to determine the reason for its existence.

D'Amboise and Duchesne, Abelard's first editors, thought that Heloise might have prepared a portion of the rules and canons concerning the religious life of women and therefore included it in their edition.[2] Victor Cousin noted (incorrectly) that the papal and conciliar passages were to be found in Gratian's *Decretum*, but added accurately that some of the texts seemed to pertain to the Praemonstratensian order.[3] As long as a relatively early date could be assigned to all the material in the manuscript, it was possible to suggest that the whole collection had been prepared under the supervision of Heloise. In 1933 Charlotte Charrier concluded: 'Tous ces extraits semblent appartenir à une epoque antérieure à la mort d'Héloïse (1164). Il n'y a donc pas impossibilité absolue à ce que ce soit la première abbesse qui les ait choisis et transcrits'.[4] As late as 1970, R. W. Southern echoed this opinion: 'Although there is no formal proof that this collection was made at the Paraclete or by Heloïse, we know from the charters that have been preserved that the last years of Heloïse's life were a time of considerable growth and prosperity, for which the rules in the Troyes collection seem well adapted'.[5]

One of the problems about Troyes 802 is that its text is almost precisely the same as that published by d'Amboise and Duchesne from a manuscript procured from the abbess of the Paraclete at the end of the sixteenth century. Minor

---

[1] J. T. Muckle, 'Abelard's Letter of Consolation to a Friend', *Mediaeval Studies* 12 (1950) 164, calls the hand a 'good Gothic of the late thirteenth or early fourteenth century'. Jacques Monfrin, ed. *Historia calamitatum* (3rd ed. Paris 1967) 11, says: 'Il a pu être copié à la fin du xiiie siècle ou plutôt au début du xive, sans qu'on puisse préciser davantage'.

[2] François d'Amboise and André Duchesne, *Petri Abaelardi ... et Heloisae ... opera* (Paris 1616), 198, reprinted in PL 178.313-14.

[3] *Petri Abailardi opera* (Paris 1849-59; repr. 1970) 1.213n.

[4] *Héloïse dans l'histoire et dans la légende* (Paris 1933) 280.

[5] *Medieval Humanism* (New York and Oxford 1970) 104.

textual differences and some information about the ownership and transmission of the manuscript have been enough, however, to make it seem probable that there were once two practically identical manuscripts, that borrowed by d'Amboise and that which is found today in Troyes.[6] This similarity has led Jacques Monfrin, the scholar who has studied the question most closely, to suggest that each of the priories of the Paraclete may once have possessed a manuscript similar to Troyes 802, beginning with the story of the origins of the order given in the correspondence attributed to Abelard and Heloise and the rule provided in Ep. VIII, continuing with the *Institutiones* of the Paraclete, and ending with 'le code traditionnel des moniales d'Occident'.[7] This hypothesis has its greatest strength if all the canonistic material dates from the time of the formation of the order (all the priories were founded during the lifetime of Heloise) and if it is all consistent with the traditional administration of the Paraclete. If some of the canons clash with the accepted liberties of the order, it is hard to see what motive any superior at the Paraclete would have had in transmitting discordant material to the daughter houses, whether multiple exemplars were made in the twelfth century or the thirteenth.

It is time now to look more closely at the contents of Troyes 802, which can be summarized as follows:

> Fol. 1-88v (PL 178.113-314). Letters I-VIII of the correspondence of Abelard and Heloise.
>
> Fol. 89-90v (313-17). *Institutiones nostre*, a set of regulations for the governance of the Paraclete.[8]
>
> Fol. 90v-93 (317-22). Ivo, *Panormia* 3.187-215, the section known in the original as *De virginibus, viduis, et abbatissis*.[9]
>
> Fol. 93 (322-3). Two canons which are the subject of this article.
>
> Fol. 93-94 (323-6). Eleven statutes of chapters general of the Praemonstratensian order. None of these can be dated precisely, but Damien Van den Eynde has concluded that they were issued between 1174 and 1238. He states that two of the statutes were issued before 1198 and that five came after that year, but further chronological precision has not been possible.[10]
>
> Fols. 94v-102v. Canons 7-28 of the *regula sanctimonialium* of the diet of Aix of 816, published from other MSS in MGH, *Concilia Aevi Karolini* 1.1. 422-56, and identified by Monfrin.[11]

In the article which he published on these texts in 1962, Van den Eynde concluded that the compilation of canonistic material must date from the thirteenth

---

[6] Monfrin, *Hist. cal.* 13-17. [7] *Ibid.* 17.

[8] Damien Van den Eynde, 'En marge des écrits d'Abélard: Les "Excerpta ex regulis Paracletensis monasterii",' *Analecta Praemonstratensia* 38 (1962) 72, gives grounds for associating the *Institutiones* with the Paraclete. To what he says may be added the fact that a service-book from the Paraclete specifies that *Veni Sancte* was regularly sung at the entry to the church; see BN MS fr. 14410, fol. 30.

[9] 'En marge' 75. [10] *Ibid.* 76-83.

[11] *Hist. cal.* 12-13.

century, since some of the Praemonstratensian canons were issued between 1198 and 1236-38. On the other hand, although Van den Eynde did not stress this point, *Institutiones nostre*, the excerpts from the *Panormia*, and the Rule of Aix could all have been brought together during the lifetime of Heloise or at least during the twelfth century. For Van den Eynde the unidentified canons on fol. 93, which he called 'deux décisions synodales pour Bénédictines', remained a mystery: 'Comme aucun détail du texte ne permet de préciser ni le temps ni le lieu où ces statuts ont été promulgués, je laisse aux compétences en matière de législation bénédictine le soin de les identifier'.[12]

In 1972 in a paper questioning the authenticity of the correspondence attributed to Abelard and Heloise, I suggested that Troyes 802 (and its apparent double) might have been prepared at the end of the thirteenth century to provide the documentation for settling a dispute over what rule was to be followed at the Paraclete, either that of Ep. viii of the correspondence or that of *Institutiones nostre*. *Institutiones nostre*, which I believe is the primitive rule of the Paraclete, provides for a 'double' monastery in which the monks were subject to the authority of the abbess, who is accorded great authority and independence, while the rule allegedly written by Abelard enhances the position of the head of a community of monks, who is supposed to provide direction for the nuns of the Paraclete. I therefore proposed that Troyes 802 might have been compiled by someone who wished to bring together authorities which would undermine the authority of *Institutiones nostre*. The canons collected by Ivo and the Rule of Aix are both the sort of material someone working at the Paraclete could have found in the library of the monastery to support traditional male authority and the separation of the sexes, for the Rule of Aix (c. 27) says that the priests who celebrate mass should live outside the monastery and *Panormia* 3.215 provides for episcopal control of nuns. The Praemonstratensian statutes, which are notoriously anti-feminist, might possibly have been kept at the Paraclete or could have been borrowed from a neighboring Praemonstratensian house. But since I was no more able to identify the other statues than Van den Eynde, my argument about the composition of Troyes 802 remained incomplete.[13]

When at last I found the source of the unidentified statutes, they turned out to be adaptations of canons of the Council of Rouen of 1231, as can be seen from the following comparison, in which Canon 2 of Rouen, designed for abbeys of men, has been altered to fit the situation of nuns, and Canon 4 of the statutes of 1231 has been carried over directly into the later manuscript.[14]

---

[12] 'En marge' 76.

[13] 'Fraud, Fiction, and Borrowing in the Correspondence of Abelard and Heloise', a paper presented at the Colloque international Pierre Abélard-Pierre le Vénérable held at Cluny in July 1972, published by the C.N.R.S. in the *Actes* of the colloquium ; see below, pp. 417-53.

[14] The statutes of the Council of Rouen exist in a single 13th-century manuscript, Avranches, Bibl. mun. MS 149 (*olim* Mont-Saint-Michel MS 249), fols. 148-149v, and were printed twice in the same year by Guillaume Bessin, *Concilia Rothomagensis provinciae* (Rouen 1717)

Troyes MS 802, fol. 93
De monialibus

Episcopi ut moniales vivant sine proprio curam adhibeant diligentem, ne se possint excusare pretextu alicuius paupertatis.

De sanctimonialibus

Statuimus ut *abbatisse* et *priorisse* et *alie obedienciarie* de singulis proventibus, redditibus et expensis singulis annis computent in capitulo, quater in anno ad minus. Et *ut* status *tam obedientiarum* quam prioratuum a claustralibus cognoscatur, compotus redigatur in scriptis, ita quod conventus penes se retineat unum scriptum et *abbatissa* aliud.

De sanctimonialibus

Propter scandala que ex monialium conversatione *proveniunt*, statuimus de monialibus nigris ne aliquod depositum in domibus suis recipiant ab aliquibus personis, maxime archas clericorum vel laicorum causa custodie apud se minime deponi permittant. Pueri et puelle, qui solent *ibidem* nutriri et instrui penitus *expellantur*. Omnes communiter comedant in refectorio, et in dormitorio solitarie dormiant. Camere monialium omnes destruantur, nisi aliqua per inspectionem episcopi *necessaria* retineatur ad infirmariam faciendam, vel alia de causa, que episcopo *iusta* et necessaria videatur. Item moniales nullatenus exire permittantur, vel extra pernoctare, nisi forte ex magna causa, et raro. Et abbatissis iniungatur, ne aliter permittant egredi moniales. Et si aliquando abbatissa ex iusta causa alicui permittat, eidem iniungat, quod sine mora revertatur. Et det ei sociam, non ad voluntatem suam, sed quam viderit expedire. Ostia suspecta et superflua obstruantur. Circa hoc autem episcopi diligentiam adhibeant, et curam per

Council of Rouen of 1231
Avranches, Bibl. mun. MS 149, fol. 148

[II]

Statuimus *etiam* ut *abbates* et *priores* et *alii obedientiarii* de singulis proventibus *et* redditibus et expensis singulis annis *diligenter* computent in capitulo quater in anno ad minus, et status *abbatiarum* quam prioratuum a claustralibus cognoscatur, *et* compotus redigatur in scriptis, ita quod conventus penes se retineat unum scriptum et *abbas* aliud.

[IV]

Propter scandala que ex monialium [sic] conversatione *perveniunt*, statuimus de monalibus [sic] nigris ne aliquod depositum recipiant in domibus suis ab aliquibus personis, maxime archas clericorum vel *etiam* laicorum causa custodie apud se minime deponi permittant. Pueri et puelle qui *ibi* solent nutriri et instrui penitus *repellantur*. Omnes communiter comedant in refectorio, et in dormitorio dormiant solitarie. Camere monalium [sic] omnes destruantur, nisi aliqua per inspectionem episcopi *intra* retineatur ad infirmariam faciendam vel alia de causa que episcopo et necessaria videatur. Item moniales nullatenus exire permittantur, vel extra pernoctare, nisi forte ex magna causa et raro, et abbatissis iniungatur, ne aliter egredi permittant moniales. Et si aliquando abbatissa ex iusta causa alicui permittat, eidem iniungat, quod sine mora revertatur, et det ei sociam non ad voluntatem suam, sed quam viderit expedire. Hostia suspecta et superflua obstruantur. Circa hoc autem episcopi diligenciam adhibeant, et curam per

---

1.134-138 and Martène and Durand, *Thesaurus novus anecdotorum* 4 (Paris 1717) 175-6. Although Bessin's copy is slightly less accurate, it was the one reprinted by Mansi 23.213-14. The text printed here is taken from a photocopy of the Avranches MS kindly provided by Prof. Stephan Kuttner. Differences between the two texts other than word order and spelling appear in italics. It is worth noting that in several places the Troyes version has preserved a better reading. On the canons of Rouen see Richard Kay, 'Mansi and Rouen', *Catholic Historical Review* 52 (1966) 171.

se et per ministros suos, et vitas et conversationes *ipsarum* taliter *restringant*, quod per eorum diligentiam scandala que de earum vita in presenti *proveniunt*, sopiantur.

se et per ministros suos, et vitas et conversationes *earum* taliter *restringantur*, quod per eorum diligenciam scandala que de earum vita in presenti *perveniunt*, sopiantur.

Up until this point, the more that has been known about Troyes 802, the more likely it has seemed that it was prepared at and for the needs of someone at the Paraclete. But if this is so, one must ask why these canons of a council of Rouen were included, when similar canons were promulgated by the Council of Sens in 1239, the Council of Paris in 1248, and a synod held at Provins in 1251.[15] The language of those canons is sufficiently different for us to see that the Troyes manuscript has indeed adapted those of Rouen and not some other council,[16] and at first glance it seems strange that a manuscript which in many ways is tied to the Paraclete should contain canons from an alien archdiocese.

While no certain answer can be given to this question, there is a least a possible explanation provided by the fact that the brother of Abbess Marie, who took office at the Paraclete in 1249, was the famous Eudes Rigaud. In the year after he became archbishop of Rouen, Eudes made a visit to the Paraclete to visit his newly elected sister.[17] While he was there one of his occupations was to join his sister and a group of the more responsible nuns in overseeing the accounting presented by Pierre des Bordes, a bourgeois of Troyes who was *bailli* and guardian of the goods of the Paraclete.[18] It seems reasonable that he could have left with his sister a copy of the canons he was himself expected to enforce, including one providing for accounting in chapter meetings. Eudes was zealous in demanding proper accounting from the churches under his supervision, and it would have been in character for him to have urged similar practices on his sister. Though it cannot be demonstrated that Eudes presented such a text to the abbey, it is at least sufficiently likely that we should not be surprised to find canons from the Council of Rouen in a manuscript from the Paraclete.

---

[15] Mansi 23.509-12 (Sens), 765-8 (Paris), 793-4 (Provins).

[16] Hefele-Leclercq 5.1524 says that the Council of Rouen repeated texts of a synod of Sens of 912, and if this were so it would of course invalidate the point of this article. But the canons which Mansi 18.323-4 attributes to a tenth-century council of Sens are really those of the Council of 1239; cf. Robert Génestal, *Le privilegium fori en France du décret de Gratien à la fin du XIVe siècle* (Bibliothèque de l'École des hautes études, sciences religieuses 35 and 39; Paris 1921-24) 1.165. James Westfall Thompson, 'The Origin of the Word "Goliardi",' *Studies in Philology* 20 (1923) 84-6 and Boris I. Jarcho, 'Die Vorläufer des Golias', *Speculum* 3 (1928) 524-5, were unfamiliar with Génestal's work and accepted an early date for these statutes. Helen Waddell, *The Wandering Scholars* (London 1927) 254, followed Génestal in treating the canons attributed to a council of 913 as 'spurious'.

[17] Theodore Bonnin, *Registrum visitationum Odonis Rigaldi* (Rouen 1852) 39 [trans. Sydney M. Brown, *The Register of Eudes of Rouen* (New York 1964) 42] shows that Eudes was at the Paraclete 10-12 June 1249.

[18] *Cartulaire de l'abbaye du Paraclet*, ed. Charles Lalore (Paris 1878) 222-4.

What do we learn from these canons and their identification? In the first place, they can be dated precisely, and that date is later than any other datable material in the manuscript. Further evidence can therefore be added to that brought forward by Van den Eynde to show that the canonical collection in Troyes 802 cannot have been made during the lifetime of Heloise or any time during the twelfth century. Even more significantly, these canons help us to understand better the motive of the compiler. As long as these statutes remained unidentified, it might be thought that they were part of the legislation imposed on all Benedictine nuns or that they were canons promulgated in the diocese of Troyes and therefore applicable to the Paraclete. Now, however, we can see that the compiler was not forced by tradition or local necessity to include these canons, which run counter to the established liberties of the order.

When compared with the privileges of the Paraclete, the most striking aspect of these two canons is that they provide for episcopal supervision of nuns. Bishops are charged with seeing that nuns follow proper fiscal procedures, that they refrain from educating children, that they eat and sleep in common and remain in their monastery; bishops are even given the authority to enter a convent, destroy private rooms occupied by nuns, and wall up doors which in the episcopal judgment are suspect or unnecessary. In contrast, the oldest surviving muniment of the Paraclete, a bull of Innocent II of 28 November 1131, provides that the monastery is to be under the direct protection of the Apostolic See and states, 'Nulli ergo omnino hominum fas sit prefatum monasterium temere perturbare, aut eius possessiones auferre, vel ablatas retinere, minuere, aut aliquibus vexationibus fatigare, sed omnia integra conserventur, vestris usibus perpetuo profutura'; moreover, anyone, ecclesiastic or layman, who knowingly violated these liberties, was subject to excommunication.[19]

In short, the two paragraphs introduced into Troyes 802 from the canons of an alien council are a direct affront to the liberties established during the time of Abelard and Heloise. Since they are neither universal legislation applying to all Benedictine nuns nor local legislation applicable to the Paraclete, they appear in the collection by the choice of the compiler. These canons do not accord with the theory that the Troyes MS and any similar to it were compiled for the use and benefit of the nuns of the Paraclete and its priories. They do support the view that the most complete manuscript containing the correspondence of Abelard and Heloise was compiled by someone hostile to the traditional independence of the nuns of the Paraclete.

---

[19] Châlons-sur-Marne, Bibl. mun. MS 583, pièce 31 (orig.), printed with some errors from the cartulary by Lalore, *Cart.* pp. 1-3.

22

Fraud, Fiction and Borrowing in the Correspondence of Abelard and Heloise

> « Il est impossible que cela ne soit pas authentique : *c'est trop beau* ». — Anonymous Benedictine quoted by Étienne Gilson in *Héloïse et Abélard.*

> « Il est bien connu que les plus belles lettres d'amour sont celles qui n'ont pas été écrites sincèrement. Rien n'est moins éloquent que l'amour véritable ». — Henri de Montherlant in *Les lépreuses.*

ABBREVIATIONS

Hist. Cal. — *Historia Calamitatum*, ed. Jacques MONFRIN, 3rd ed. Paris, 1967.

Ep(istola) II — « Heloisae suae ad ipsum deprecatoria, » ed. J.T. MUCKLE in *Mediaeval Studies*, 15 (1953), 68-73, and MONFRIN, *op. cit.*, p. 111-117. Note that the numbering of the letters given by Duchesne-d'Amboise and Migne is followed here, not that of Muckle.

Ep. III — « Rescriptum ipsius ad ipsam, » ed. MUCKLE, *ibid.*, p. 73-77.

Ep. IV — « Rescriptum ipsius ad ipsum, » ed. MUCKLE, *ibid.*, p. 77-82, and MONFRIN, *op. cit.*, p. 117-124.

Ep. V — « Ipse rursus ad ipsam, » ed. MUCKLE, *ibid.*, p. 82-94.

Ep. VI — « Item eadem ad eundem, » ed. MUCKLE, in *Mediaeval Studies*, 17 (1955), p. 241-253.

Ep. VII — « Rescriptum ad ipsam de auctoritate vel dignitate ordinis sanctimonialium, » ed. MUCKLE, *ibid.*, p. 253-281.

Ep. VIII (or *Rule*) — « Institutio seu Regula Sanctimonialium, » ed. Terence P. MC-LAUGHLIN, in *Mediaeval Studies*, 18 (1956), p. 242-292.

Serm. — *Sermones*, ed. MIGNE, *Patrologia latina*, 178, cols. 379-610.

Comm. Rom. — *Commentaria in Epistolam Pauli ad Romanos*, ed. Eligius M. BUYTAERT, in *Petri Abaelardi Opera theologica*, 2 vol., Corpus Christianorum, Continuatio Mediaevalis, 11-12 (Turnholt, 1969), 1, p. 1-340.

Theol. Christ. — *Theologia Christiana, ibid.*, 2, p. 1-372.

Almost seven centuries after the *Roman de la Rose* first introduced the ill-fated lovers to a wide audience, Abelard and Heloise continue to fascinate both medieval scholars and the literate public. Modern readers base their image of these two great figures on the same correspondence read by Jean de Meun and Petrarch; moreover, scholars today derive much of their understanding of early twelfth-century educational and ecclesiastical institutions, passionate love, and the self-image of the individual from the seemingly autobiographical *Historia Calamitatum* and the seven letters which follow it in Troyes ms. 802 (ms. T). The question of the authenticity of these letters must therefore interest everyone attracted to the history of the middle ages; as Étienne Gilson remarked: "Non seulement Héloïse et Abélard, mais le XIIe siècle même changent d'aspect selon que l'on admet ou que l'on nie l'authenticité de ce remarquable document."[1]

Considering the importance of the topic, scholars have been strikingly inactive. We have no history of the Paraclet, no archeological exploration of its site, no edition of the unusually detailed thirteenth-century service book (B.N. ms. fr. 14410) which reveals the liturgical program of the

---

1. *Héloïse et Abélard*, 3rd éd. (Paris, 1964), p. 171. Besides this book the most important discussions of the authenticity of the correspondence are to be found in Ludovic LALANNE, « Quelques doutes sur l'authenticité de la correspondance amoureuse d'Héloïse et d'Abélard, » *La correspondance littéraire*, 1, no. 2 (1857), 27-33 ; E.D. PETRELLA, « Sull'autenticità delle lettere d'Abelardo e Eloisa, » *Rendiconti del Reale Istituto Lombardo de scienze e lettere*, 2nd ser., 44 (1911), 554-567, 606-618 ; Bernhard SCHMEIDLER, « Der Briefwechsel zwischen Abälard und Heloise eine Fälschung ?» *Archiv für Kulturgeschichte*, 11 (1913), 1-30, « Der Briefwechsel zwischen Abälard und Heloise als eine literarische Fiktion Abälards, » *Zeitschrift für Kirchengeschichte*, 54 (1935), 323-338, and « Der Briefwechsel zwischen Abaelard und Heloise dennoch eine literarische Fiction Abaelards, » *Revue bénédictine*, 52 (1940), 85-95 ; Charlotte CHARRIER, *Héloïse dans l'histoire et dans la légende* (Paris, 1933), p. 12-23 ; J.T. MUCKLE, « The Personal Letters between Abelard and Heloise, » *Mediaeval Studies*, 15 (1953), 59-67.

Paraclet, no edition or critique of the charters of the Paraclet since the century-old and careless publication of Abbé Charles Lalore, and no study of the correspondence itself which systematically compares its assertions with all other known evidence about Abelard, Heloise, and their monastery. Medievalists today commonly accept the authenticity of the correspondence either on grounds of style, which has not yet been studied in depth, or on the authority of Monsieur Gilson, who conceived the problem in learned but overly-narrow terms, or because it "feels" genuine.[2] But as the second quotation at the head of this paper suggests, the literary quality of the correspondence does not guarantee its authenticity and may in fact indicate calculating composition. What the study of the correspondence of Abelard and Heloise needs is what it has not yet received, a full-scale investigation of every detail in the letters evaluated on the basis of the objective criteria of accuracy, anachronism, and sources.

As a step toward such an investigation, which will have to call upon the learning of scholars skilled in various disciplines and areas of knowledge, this paper presents an hypothesis intended to stimulate further research, following Abelard's own dictum: "Through doubting we arrive at inquiry, and through inquiry we perceive the truth."[3] Simply put, the hypothesis offered here is that sometime in the thirteenth century a forger, or a pair of forgers, motivated by a desire to modify the institutions of the Paraclet, compiled and reworked the eight letters we can read today in ms. T, making use of both authentic writings of Abelard (including the lost *Exhortatio ad fratres et commonachos*) and a twelfth-century "autobiographical" letter which was itself a work of imaginative fiction, produced perhaps by some skilled student of the *ars dictaminis*. The hypothesis that the text we have now is composed of at least three different elements, authentic but otherwise unrecovered writing of Abelard, inauthentic twelfth-century material, and inauthentic thirteenth-century additions, may seem unduly complicated, but it is the best explanation I can find for the heterogeneous character of the letters, in which some passages must have been written in the twelfth century and others seem to date from the thirteenth, and in which some portions have the ring of the genuine Abelard and others contain errors which presumably would not

---

2. The stylistic elements studied by Schmeidler, Charrier, and Muckle are the use of *tanto ... quanto* and *obsecro* ; as M. Monfrin has suggested in his paper at this colloquium, we need a far more detailed and better controlled analysis of stylistic elements. When, as noted in *Héloïse et Abélard*, p. 14, M. Gilson queried his informant in the Bibliothèque Nationale about the meaning of *conversatio* and *conversio*, he explained, « Du sens de ces mots dépend l'authenticité de la correspondance d'Héloïse et d'Abélard». Most medievalists cite the correspondence as authentic with no further explanation.

3. *Sic et non*, in PL. 178, 1349.

have been written by Abelard, Heloise, or anyone familiar with the early history of the Paraclet.

Let us begin our current investigation with a consideration of the goals of the author or compiler of the text in ms. T. If we think of the correspondence as a series of separate letters, we do not have to be concerned with why they were written. But if we ask why this book of 88 folios was written, or to put the question another way, why this exchange of letters, in its continuity unique in the correspondence of the twelfth-century, was preserved in the form in which we have it, we must think seriously about goals. In reading the correspondence as a whole, for me two are apparent. One is to tell the story of two instances of spiritual conversion. First Abelard, a figure of pride and lust at the beginning of his letter to his friend, is chastened by his misfortunes and through them becomes a devout monk and a sage counselor.[4] Then Heloise, held longer by the fleshly ties of this world, years after her loss of Abelard still preferring to be his mistress rather than the wife of Augustus or a true bride of Christ, is eventually brought by the spiritual counsel of Abelard to the point where she accepts her office in life as nun and abbess. A pair of spiritual adventures to be summarized by Milton's phrase about the primal couple, "He for God only, she for God in him."

There is, however, a second major goal which the compiler or authors of the correspondence had in mind, and that was to provide a rule for the Paraclet. A distinguished historian has written of the treatise on religious women and the rule which end the collection: "They are by no means readable, and they are seldom read. They have no personal interest."[5] I am afraid Professor Southern is right that they are seldom read, which is a pity, for in my opinion a program for the religious life of nuns is a central issue in the correspondence, if not the most important matter. The topic is introduced in the *Historia Calamitatum*, where Abelard confides to his anonymous friend: "I am very much surprised at the long established monastic customs by which abbesses are placed over women in the same way that abbots are placed over men, and both men and women are bound by the profession of the same rule, though it contains many matters which women, whether in authority or not, can in no way

---

4. For a treatment of this literary theme see D.W. ROBERTSON, Jr., *Abelard and Heloise* (New York, 1972), part I. Though I have gone beyond its conclusions, which are generally in accord with those of Schmeidler and Charrier, it was this stimulating book which launched me on an investigation of the authenticity of the correspondence. The fullest and most perceptive literary analysis of the correspondence is now that of Peter von Moos presented at this colloquium.

5. « The Letters of Abelard and Heloise, » in *Medieval Humanism and Other Studies* (Oxford, 1970), p. 101.

fulfill. Moreover, following a reversal of the natural relationship, in many places we find that the more authority these women have over the clergy, to whom the populace is subject, the more power they have to lead them on to their evil desires, and that they lay this most heavy yoke on them."[6]

This passage, seemingly a direct attack on the customs of the Order of Fontevrault, is crucial; it shows that the topic of a rule for women was not an afterthought or shift in the direction of the correspondence when it was reintroduced in the third letter of Heloise. In that letter, which is incidentally her longest, Heloise requests a rule from Abelard: "You with God shall be the institutor of our religious life. Perhaps after you we will have another preceptor who may build something on another foundation and, we fear, be less solicitous of us."[7] Letter VIII, the rule which Abelard provides in response, is almost 30 folios long, a third of the whole collection. If the correspondence is genuine, Heloise made a detailed request for this rule and Abelard spent long hours preparing it. It deserves our careful attention.

Now the most striking feature of the rule in the correspondence is that it was not followed at the Paraclet. This statement can only be demonstrated with texts in hand, and the reader will find in an appendix a list of crucial passages, including extracts from documents from the Paraclet and a rule for nuns of which the opening words are *Institutiones nostre*.[8] We owe our closest study of the *Institutiones* to Father Damien Van den Eynde, who found little reason to doubt that these regulations are a rule from the Paraclet.[9] They were preserved in a manuscript which came from the Paraclet. They establish a rule to be followed by a mother abbey and its daughters. Most notably, they apply to a community where each office began with the singing of *Veni Sancte Spiritus*. Father Van den Eynde conjectured that the singing of this antiphon was a local custom at the Paraclet; his intuition is strikingly confirmed by the thirteenth-century service book from the Paraclet, which specifies: "Et a l'antree dou

---

6. *Hist. Cal.*, p. 105. Text in appendix, no. 8a. Also ed. J.T. Muckle, «Abelard's Letter of Consolation to a Friend,» *Mediaeval Studies*, 12 (1950), 208-209. Although Muckle's edition is competent and his annotations very useful, Monfrin's text is closer to the Troyes ms. and is to be preferred.

7. *Ep. VI*, p. 253.

8. Troyes, Bibl. mun. ms. 802, fol. 89-90v, published most recently in PL. 178, 313-317. The first word of the text is not *Instructiones*, as printed by Duchesne-d'Amboise and Migne. Quotations given in this paper follow the manuscript.

9. « En marge des écrits d'Abélard : Les 'Excerpta ex regulis Paracletensis monasterii',» *Analecta Praemonstratensia*, 38 (1962), 70-84. The author points out that the reference to the *Veni Sancte Spiritus* accords better with the antiphon, well attested in the 12th cent., than with the 13th-cent. sequence.

moustier *Veni Sancte* si com il est acoustumé."[10] He also pointed out that the *Institutiones* were drawn up because of a new foundation, and since all the priories of the Paraclet were established before 1163, it would be reasonable to date the text to the lifetime of Heloise. The objection to this dating which troubled Father Van den Eynde is that the *Institutiones* are in manifest discord with the rule given in the correspondence.

The priority of one of these rules over the other cannot be established simply by comparing them. Fortunately, there is other evidence which can be brought to bear. And in every case where the two rules can be checked against documents from the Paraclet, it is the rule in the correspondence which does not stand up to scrutiny, while *Institutiones nostre* rests confirmed.

Since the reader can examine the texts in the appendix, I need only summarize the differences in general terms. *Institutiones nostre* and the practices of the Paraclet accord with the customs of the Order of Fontevrault, the largest and most important double monastery in France. The *Institutiones* do not mention a male religious superior, and in fact authorize the abbess to correct delinquent brothers in the chapter meetings. The nuns were not strictly cloistered; under proper conditions they could leave the monastery to conduct their own business. As at Fontevrault, a series of papal bulls, beginning during the lifetime of the founder, established the exemption of the Paraclet from local authority and its direct protection by the Holy See. These privileges were summed up by a certificate of 1620 which recorded: "Que l'abbesse du Paraclit est chef d'ordre, qu'elle est exempte de toute cognoissance et jurisdiction épiscopale, qu'elle ne recognoist que le Saint-Siège, ... qu'elle a soub soy non seulement des religieuses, mais aussi des religieux (tant profès que novices et oblats ou frères et sœurs donnés), des abbayes, des prieurés, voire mesme des cures..."[11]

The practices of the Order of the Paraclet differed from the male-dominated monasticism to be found in Champagne and Burgundy in the feminine houses which were dependencies of the abbey of Molesme. When Milo, count of Bar-sur-Seine, granted his castle of Jully as the site of a convent about 1113, he placed the house directly under the

---

10. B.N. ms. fr. 14410, fol. 30.

11. For a modern survey of the institutions of Fontevrault see Micheline DE FONTETTE, *Les religieuses à l'âge classique du droit canon* (Paris, 1967), p. 65-80. We lack a good history of the Paraclet; for its privileges see the faulty but indispensable edition of Charles LALORE, *Cartulaire de l'abbaye du Paraclet*, Collection des principaux cartulaires du diocèse de Troyes, 2 (Paris, 1878). The certificate of 1620 is in Aube 24 H 5 and is quoted with numerous errors by Lalore, p. IX. All the elements in the certificate were based on charters of the 12th and 13th cents.

authority of the abbot of Molesme. At Jully, and at other convents of its lineage, the nuns were required to remain strictly cloistered, and a male prior named by the abbot of Molesme governed the house.[12] The author of letter VIII advocated, not the practices actually established at the Paraclet, but a system similar to the relationship between Jully and Molesme. As he put it, "We wish monasteries of women to be subject to monasteries of men in such fashion that the brothers may care for the sisters and one man may preside as father over both." According to letter VIII, the nuns of the Paraclet were to remain perpetually cloistered, men were to care for their business affairs, and the *prepositus monachorum*, "whom they call abbot," was to have practical direction of the community.[13] If we are to believe the correspondence authentic, we must conclude that Abelard conveyed to Heloise, and had confirmed by papal and episcopal charters, a monastery which from its origin till the Revolution maintained a basic structure the opposite of that which its founder considered proper.

A second way in which letter VIII and the *Institutiones* differ is in the degree of rigor and abstinence. On one alimentary issue the rule attributed to Abelard is more ascetic. *Institutiones nostre* says that if the nuns have wheat to eat, they will eat wheat, and if they have none, then they will eat what is available. Letter VIII, inconsistently with respect to its general argument about dietary liberty, says that the nuns shall never eat bread of pure wheat, but shall mix their wheat with a third of coarser grain.[14] In contrast to this relatively small matter, however, letter VIII contains a truly shocking divergence from normal twelfth-century practices. I refer to Abelard's supposed authorization to the nuns of the Paraclet to eat meat three times a week throughout the year. This authorization must be seen in the context of its day. I am aware of no other twelfth-century monastic rule which permitted meat, except in the infirmary. The nuns of the Order of Fontevrault were not permitted to eat meat, nor were the Norbertines, nor the female Cistercians or Benedictines.[15] It is no surprise to find that *Institutiones nostre* states "In our refectory our meals

---

12. Milon's charter is in *Cartulaires de l'abbaye de Molesme*, ed. Jacques LAURENT (Paris, 1907-11), 2, 225-226. Laurent's introduction (1, 253-266) supplements and corrects Abbé JOBIN, *Histoire du prieuré de Jully-les-Nonnains* (Paris, 1881). For the institutions of Jully at the time of St. Bernard, see Jean LECLERCQ, *Etudes sur S. Bernard*, Analecta S. Ordinis Cisterciensis, 9, 1-2 (1953), p. 192-194.

13. *Ep. VIII*, p. 258-260. Texts in appendix, nos. 7 and 9.

14. *Ibid.*, p. 277; *Institutiones*, ms. T, fol. 89, and PL. 178, 314. Texts in appendix, no. 10.

15. *Ep. VIII*, p. 279 (appendix, no. 11a); FONTETTE, *Religieuses*, p. 15 (note 18), 58, 76.

are vegetables without meat and what is grown in the garden. Milk, eggs, and cheese are partaken of rarely, and fish if they are gifts."[16] Twelfth-century monastic reformers, taking note of the physiological theory that meat increases the heat of carnal desire and remembering that St. Jerome had attacked Jovinian for advocating meat-eating as well as marriage, did not treat casually dietary departures from the Benedictine Rule.[17] St. Bernard mocked the monks of Cluny for the zest with which they ate their eggs. If, when he visited the Paraclet, he had found the nuns dining on meat three times a week, it is hard to believe that his only recorded criticism would have been of the phraseology of the Lord's Prayer.[18]

In the thirteenth century meat became the subject of more open controversy and debate than it had been in the twelfth. The Canons Regular of Saint-Victor of Paris removed dietary restrictions for major feasts, and in the Praemonstratensian Order fulminations against the "scandal" of meat-eating suggest that by the middle of the thirteenth century the practice had become quite widespread. In 1269 the chapter general of the nuns of the Cistercian Order renewed the prohibition against meat.[19] The friars too held the line against meat-eating, and were attacked for their abstinence in that same year of 1269 by a disciple of Guillaume de Saint-Amour. St. Bonaventure and St. Thomas counterattacked with vigor, so that in the period following 1270 arguments for and against meat must have been common in clerical circles.[20] As far as we can tell, however, in the thirteenth century the Paraclet remained faithful to its *Institutiones* and the Benedictine Rule. A set of accounts from the period around 1288 contains a detailed record of the money spent at the Paraclet for grain and wine, quite a lot for wine, in fact, but nothing at all for

---

16. Ms. T, fol. 89, and PL. 178, 314 (text in appendix, no. 11b).

17. *Contra Jovinianum*, PL. 23, 290-312. Note Abelard's approving use of the quotation cited by Jerome (col. 297), « Esus carnium et potus vini ventrisque satietas seminarium libidinis est,» in *Theol. Christ.*, II, 61, p. 156 (PL. 178, 1184). Those who knew Jerome well would recognize the relationship of this passage to its continuation in *Hist. Cal.*, p. 93. It is noteworthy that the text in *Hist. Cal.* has exactly the same omissions as when it is quoted in *Theol. Christ*. Close study of the quotations in the correspondence suggests that almost all were taken from an Abelardian source.

18. For Bernard's visit to the Paraclet see Abelard's letter in PL. 178, 335-340.

19. Fourier BONNARD, *Histoire de l'Abbaye royale de Saint-Victor de Paris* (Paris, 1904-08), I, 78-79 note; Placide F. LEFÈVRE, *Les Statuts de Prémontré réformés sur les ordres de Grégoire IX et d'Innocent IV* (Louvain, 1946), p. 34-35 note; Philippe GUIGNARD, *Les monuments primitifs de la règle cistercienne* (Dijon, 1878), p. 645; cf. Joseph-Marie CANIVEZ, *Statuta Capitulorum Generalium Ordinis Cisterciensis* (Louvain, 1935), III, p. 230 (1283, no. 7) and p. 233 (1285, no. 8).

20. The treatise of GERARD D'ABBEVILLE, *Contra adversarium perfectionis christianae*, is edited, with references to other literature, in *Archivum Franciscanum Historicum*, 31 (1938), 276-329; 32 (1939), 89-200.

meat except for six pigs bought for distribution at Mardi Gras and meat purchased for "hôtes et ouvriers."[21]

The authorization to eat meat is part of a tendency in the letter attributed to Heloise requesting a rule and in the rule itself to avoid the rigor which so many pious women were seeking in the new monastic orders of the twelfth century. The letter of Heloise asks for a rule which protects sleep, which frees the nuns from repeating psalms in the same week, which in the matter of abstinence is no more demanding than the practices of the Canons Regular.[22] If a first motivation for writing the correspondence was to provide a rule which enhanced male authority, a second was to offer regulations which would be laxer than the *Institutiones*. The statement in the letter of Heloise that some second preceptor might introduce a rule which would be more demanding than that which the nuns had received initially from Abelard is the opposite of what our study of the institutions of the Paraclet reveals.

Another curious feature of letter VIII is the advice on the election of an abbess, advice which is not contradicted by *Institutiones nostre* and may in fact contain some elements of Abelard's own thought, but which nevertheless seems strange. Following a twist of the discussion of a text of St. Epiphanius in Abelard's *Commentary on Romans* — "Those women formerly called deaconesses, that is servants, we now call abbesses, that is mothers" — the rule equates the qualifications for abbess with those for a deaconess given by St. Paul.[23] As the equivalent of a deaconess, the abbess of the Paraclet should be an older woman (over 60 if one follows the text of the New Testament, over 40 if one follows the reduction of the Council of Chalcedon), although according to the accepted dating

---

21. The accounts of 1288 are in a register, Aube 24 H 6* (all references to the Archives de l'Aube which are not marked by an asterisk are to liasses) : « pour 6 pors pour la pittance de quaresme prenant » (fol. 4v); « pour... ouvriers et hostes pour vin et poisson pris à Nogent et char fresche achetée » (fol. 5v); « pour vin et viande pour Guimard et li bailli » (fol. 8). Meat was probably eaten at the Paraclet before the reform of 1627, but the earliest reference to the practice I have noted is in a papal bull of 1666 (Aube 24 H 6; LALORE, *Cart.*, p. XXXII) which says that though it is contrary to the Benedictine Rule, the eating of meat had been a custom at the Paraclet since time immemorial. In the early eighteenth century the nuns were spending 2,500 *livres* annually, 17 % of their total expenditures, for meat to be dressed by a resident butcher; see the accounts of 1725 in Aube 24 H 1, and LALORE, *Cart.*, p. XXXIV.

22. *Ep. VI*, p. 245-246, 252-253. According to the Rule of Aix of 816, ch. 115 (*MGH*, *Concilia*, 2, 397), canons were permitted to wear linen, eat meat, own property, and possess churches. What Abelard himself thought of the canons regular appears in *Ep. XII* in PL, 178, 351.

23. *Comm. Rom.*, p. 327 (PL, 178, 971); almost the same words appear in *Ep. VII*, p. 264. The passage is imbedded in a series of quotations which also appear in *Serm. 31*, col. 572-573.

Heloise was only in her mid-thirties when Abelard was supposedly writing. Moreover, the abbess-deaconess should not be a virgin but one who had known men, by preference she should not be a noble or come from the neighborhood of the monastery, and she need not be learned, for as the *Vitae Patrum* said, "He is truly wise who teaches others by his deeds, not by his words."[24] This final comment sounds strange coming from an author who exhorted the study of Latin, Hebrew, and Greek at the Paraclet.[25] The advice seems more appropriate for someone promoting the election of an older nun, formerly married, not noble and not from the neighborhood, not well educated, and quite possibly not overly scrupulous about benefitting from a forgery.

Stating the qualifications for abbess in this way should lead us to look for a disputed election at the Paraclet. The one contested election of which we are informed is described by a bull of Nicolas IV of 30 September 1289, and since that document refers to a timeconsuming series of actions, we can conclude that the conflict began some time before, perhaps as much as two or three years earlier.[26] According to the papal letter, following the death of the previous abbess, Marie, a majority of the nuns, led by a woman from the upper nobility, Isabelle de Grancey, chose as abbess Catherine des Barres, while a minority of seven elected Agnès de Mécringes. Of Agnès we know very little, except that she was the beneficiary of a legacy in 1279 and was therefore quite likely a person of some age. Mécringes is near Montmirail, 45 km north of the Paraclet, and the family which held the village as a fief was of the minor nobility. We do not know if Agnès was a member of that family, whether she was noble at all, or whether she was formerly married. It can be said that she was from a relatively modest background and that as far as we can tell she fits the specifications noted in the rule better than her opponent.[27]

Catherine des Barres, who was eventually confirmed as abbess, led a better documented life. She was alive as late as October 1320, so she must have been fairly young in the 1280s. Her family held the fief of Chaumont-sur-Yonne, 37 km. from the Paraclet, and can be counted among the magnates of France; Jean des Barres, who was involved in

---

24. *Ep. VIII*, p. 252-254.

25. PL. 178, 325-336.

26. *Les registres de Nicolas IV*, ed. Ernest LANGLOIS, (Paris, 1886-1893), 1, 290, n° 1483. Since the preceding abbess, Marie, issued a charter dated 28 July 1286 (LALORE, *Cartulaire*, p. 263-264), the disputed election must have taken place after that date.

27. The will of Marie d'Epernay is printed in LALORE, *Cartulaire*, p. 259-60. Mahieus de Mécringes held a house in fief in 1275; see *Documents relatifs au comté de Champagne et de Brie*, ed. Auguste LONGNON (Paris, 1901-14), 1, n° 6789.

the affairs of the Paraclet, was marshal of France under Philip V. If, as seems likely, Catherine des Barres was his sister, the family name suggests that she entered the monastery unmarried, had the chance for an excellent education, and came from a family of over-mighty neighbors of the Paraclet. Catherine was succeeded as abbess by Alix des Barres, Hélissent des Barres, and Jeanne des Barres, so that from the late thirteenth century to the early fifteenth century the abbey was for all practical purposes a family fief.[28] The seven nuns who opposed Catherine's election may well have realized that they were resisting the feudalization of their monastery. In any case, they fought hard and tenaciously. After they had appealed to the Holy See, Cardinal Giacomo Colonna, the pope's judge delegate, declared that the election of Agnès was not canonical. But then since some people still objected to Catherine as an individual or to the method of her election, Pope Nicolas had to ask the bishop of Paris to investigate further; this was the burden of his letter of 1289. Apparently the case was still not settled quickly, for in 1294 an ecclesiastical lawyer from Troyes paid 10 *livres* to two other lawyers for their salary earned for service on behalf of the abbess and the convent of the Paraclet at the Roman curia.[29] An election which was contested for years must have been the occasion for bitter conflicts involving both the nuns and the monks of the monastery.

The relationship of the passage in the rule on the qualifications for an abbess and this disputed election may well be only coincidental.[30]

---

28. For charters of the Paraclet involving Catherine des Barres or Jean des Barres, see LALORE, *Cartulaire*, p. 272-275 and 279 (Aube 24 H 29). Alix des Barres was elected in January 1323 (n. st.); see LALORE, *Cartulaire*, p. 279-280 (Aube 24 H 18). On the family see Eugène GRÉSY, « Notice généalogique sur Jean des Barres, » *Mémoires de la Société des Antiquaires de France*, 20 (1850).

29. A charter in LALORE, *Cartulaire*, p. 266-267, records that Master Pierre *Theatinus* and his uncle Mathieu, canon of Thérouanne, were paid by Master Etienne Trotin. The latter was an advocate in the archdeacon's court at Troyes; see *Documents*, ed. LONGNON, III, 29 N, 51 A, 87 Q, and 119 E.

30. The *Historia Calamitatum* and the personal letters of Heloise must have been written before Jean de Meun's continuation of the *Roman de la Rose*, since Jean makes use of that material. Scholars generally agree that the *Roman* was written in the 1270s, and in any case, before the death of Charles of Anjou in 1285. Since the rule appears in only one family of manuscripts, and the text which Jean de Meun translated (J) did not contain the rule, it might be argued that J and the *Roman* were written before 1285, while the rule was written independently in connection with an election which took place after 1286. I consider this hypothesis highly unlikely, and will instead argue in an article to be published elsewhere that the *Roman* may well have been written after the death of Charles of Anjou. These questions are intriguing, but they are not central to the issue at hand. The case against the authenticity of the correspondence is substantive, and is based on inaccuracies and anachronisms in the text; the case against the *prepositus monachorum* of the Paraclet is circumstantial, and is meant only to suggest a *possible* motive and circumstances for a fraud. A refutation of the circum-→

Even if the permission to eat meat suggests that the rule was written in the thirteenth century, nothing places it before or after the death of Abbess Marie about 1287. The most we can say is that a conflict like the one which split the community in the 1280s could have provided the occasion and motivation for a forgery. The rule could have been written to favor one candidate over another. The permission to eat meat could have been offered in an attempt to make an otherwise unattractive rule palatable to the nuns. And as the primary beneficiary of such a fraud we should look beyond an old and poorly educated nun in conflict with her more noble sisters to suspect the operations of the *prepositus monachorum*, the male cleric who would have acquired administrative power in no way authorized by *Institutiones nostre* or anything we know of the early history of the Paraclet. The accounts of the Paraclet from the year 1288 refer to the expenses of the *magister* of the community, showing that there was still a leading male cleric at the end of the thirteenth century.[31] Reference to such a monk stresses the importance of the fact that the Paraclet was a true double monastery, smaller than Fontevrault but similar to it. The church of the men was almost certainly the "Petit Moustier," in which Abelard and his relatives as well as Heloise were buried. The location of the "Petit Moustier" is uncertain, but if it was as far removed from the women's church as a monument known as the "Croix au maistre" (which was about 800 meters due south of the main church), then it was a decent distance from the female community which would permit it to have been called a "neighboring monastery."[32]

---

stantial case against some *magister* of the Paraclet in the thirteenth century would destroy an interesting explanation of why a forgery might have been committed, but it would not in itself demonstrate that the correspondence is genuine. On the other hand, proof that the correspondence was written in the twelfth century (perhaps by the discovery of a contemporary manuscript) would render my discussion of the Paraclet in the thirteenth century irrelevant.

31. Aube 24 H 6*, fol. 10.

32. The location of the Petit Moustier has never been firmly established. In the only study of the archeology of the Paraclet, René Louis argued that Abelard's original church was built to the north of the main church, right beside the banks of the Ardusson; see « Pierre Abélard et l'architecture monastique : l'abbaye du Paraclet au diocèse de Troyes » in *L'architecture monastique*, special issue of the *Bulletin des relations artistiques France-Allemagne* (Mainz, May 1951). In this conclusion he adhered to the traditional view at the Paraclet; when Quentin Craufurd visited the monastery in 1787 he learned that : « Il existe dans les jardins de ce monastère, sur le bord d'un ruisseau, un vieux bâtiment de pierre de taille, très-villain et fort petit, qui n'étoit pas autrefois compris dans la clôture, et où Abeillard logea; » see his *Mélanges d'histoire et de littérature*, 2nd ed. (Paris, 1817), p. 24. But as Craufurd noted, « Ce fut depuis un moulin : actuellement on y fait la lessive ». The building which tradition identified with the Petit Moustier is therefore none other than the old mill which is still standing on the banks of the Ardusson, and which cannot be considered the remains of a twelfth-century church and cloister. Indeed, it is hard to believe that before the modern drainage system was →

If we can imagine both a forger and a community which resisted the new rule he proposed, we should probably also conjecture that the rule was contested in an ecclesiastical court. Such a supposition would explain the manuscript tradition of our text. The earliest and best manuscript of the full correspondence, ms. T, is a uniform, carefully copied collection of rules and regulations governing the monastic life of women. After the letters we are considering come the *Institutiones* of the Paraclet, the section on nuns, widows and abbesses from the *Panormia* of Ivo of Chartres, two or three unidentified statutes instructing bishops on the proper oversight of Benedictine nuns (although the Paraclet was exempt), a collection of statutes of Praemonstratensian chapters general concerning the nuns of the order, and in conclusion the legislation concerning the religious life of women elaborated at the Council of Aix in 816.[33] This table of contents suggests that in its earliest appearance known to us the rule and the preceding correspondence were part of a lawyer's dossier. Moreover, the copyist was especially interested in justifying letter VIII; all seven of the contemporary marginal annotations in the correspondence appear in the rule and most call attention to its more rigorous points.[34] Monsieur Monfrin has suggested that ms. T and the

---

created any substantial building could or would have been erected in the marshy area to the north of the main church; we ought therefore to turn our attention to the area south of the main building complex where old maps indicate the fields of the « Petit Couvent. » In 1499 Jacques Raguier, bishop of Troyes, ordered the nuns of the Paraclet to cease their practice of making a procession on the eve of Ascension to the « Croix au Maistre, » where they joined neighborhood girls in singing immodest songs; Aube G 1344*, fol. 354v-355, printed by Henri d'Arbois de Jubainville in *Revue des sociétés savantes*, année 1872, I, 660-661. The procession to the Croix au Maistre is attested in the 13th cent. in B. N. ms. fr. 14410, fol. 60-60v. The Croix au Maistre is shown on a map of 1693 in Aube 24 H 387 at the southern extremity of the « bois de la Garenne. » This location, which is on top of a hill and may have been the place where Abelard taught, is probably not the same as that of « la Croix du Petit-Couvent » cited by Alphonse ROSEROT, *Dictionnaire historique de la Champagne méridionale* (Langres, 1942-48), since the « Petit Moustier » was described in 1497 as a « locus humidus et aquosus » and was probably on low ground; Aube 24 H 18 (cf. LALORE, *Cartulaire*, p. xxiv).

33. M. MONFRIN identified and gives references to the Carolingian material in *Hist. Cal.*, p. 12 ; for the other texts see Van den Eynde in the article cited above, note 9, On the unidentified statutes see below, note 72.

34. In his edition of *Ep. VIII* McLaughlin noted six of the seven annotations in T : p. 256, n. 96; p. 273, n. 7; p. 278, n. 90; p. 279, nn. 8 and 19; p. 282, n. 67. To this list should be added a reference at p. 257, 14 lines from the bottom, to « Contra prelatos austeros. » These marginal annotations are another indication of the amazing similarity of ms. T to the one d'Amboise borrowed from the Paraclet and used for the first printed edition of the correspondence, for Duchesne-d'Amboise printed five of the seven annotations, and the two which they omitted are in inner margins of ms. T where they can easily be missed if the manuscript is not opened wide. If the first editors did not use T, their manuscript was identical even to the point of the placement of marginal notes. And yet I agree with M. Monfrin that T was probably not the ma-→

apparent double which d'Amboise borrowed from the Paraclet and from which he prepared the first edition were both written for use in the administration of the Paraclet or one of its priories. The objection to this theory is that these rules are a collection of discordant documents which a community could not easily follow at the same time; the texts from the *Panormia* and the Rule of Aix envisage the institutions of early Benedictine monasticism, the Praemonstratensian statutes were written for female communities thoroughly dominated by men and which the men eventually eliminated, and only the *Institutiones* give rules for a female-superior double monastery.[35]

To suggest motives for a forgery or call the rule into question is not evidence that the *Historia Calamitatum* and the other letters attributed to Abelard and Heloise are fraudulent. It is possible (though the possibility seems to me highly unlikely) that Abelard wrote a rule which was never put into effect. Or a forger could have introduced a fraudulent rule and some supporting interpolations into an otherwise genuine correspondence. To establish the likelihood of this possibility would have serious consequences for our use of the letters as historical documents, for the difficult distinction between what an innovator found in his materials and what he added would then have to be made. Our interest in this distinction will be reduced, however, if we conclude that there are so many and such fundamental historical errors in the *Historia Calamitatum* that it cannot possibly have been written by Abelard, for if the story of Abelard's adversities is an imaginative work of fiction, then the letters which follow and respond to it cannot be genuine, and we must accept that the most personal parts of the correspondence are not authentic, whether they were written in the thirteenth century or the twelfth.

---

nuscript borrowed by d'Amboise, for an owner's note on fol. 103v shows that T belonged to the chapter of Paris in the early 14th cent., and one must ask how it returned to the Paraclet in the 16th. It is important to note that contrary to what the reference to « 6 fol. cousus » in M. Monfrin's description (p. 10) might lead one to suspect, fol. 103 is unquestionably a part of the original manuscript, since it is part of the same skin as fol. 98. In addition, McLaughlin notes in his edition of *Ep. VIII*, p. 242, that there are several passages where d'Amboise-Duchesne printed a corrupt version of a passage omitted by C and D for which T gives a correct reading. Apparently at the end of the 13th cent. the Paraclet possessed two practically identical manuscripts of the correspondence and of the associated legal material, of which one copy soon made its way to Paris.

35. The best survey of early legislation concerning nuns is the article by Jacqueline RAMBAUD-BUHOT, « Le statut des moniales chez les Pères de l'Eglise, dans les règles monastiques et les collections canoniques, jusqu'au XIIe siècle, » in *Sainte Fare et Faremoutiers* (Abbaye de Faremoutiers, 1957), p. 149-174. The statute « De sororibus non recipiendis » (PL. 178, 323) was written after 1174 and shows that the collection can have been of no use in the governance of the abbey or its priories in their early years; see VAN DEN EYNDE, « En marge », p. 77.

A full demonstration of errors in the *Historia Calamitatum* would have to go far beyond the limits of this paper. All I will attempt here is to call attention to a few short questions worthy of further investigation before turning to a longer discussion of the early history of the Paraclet and its relations with the abbey of Saint-Denis. No one of the possible errors or discrepancies which follow is in itself determinative, though taken together they suggest that the author of the *Historia Calamitatum* knew less about Abelard and his intellectual milieu than we would expect of an autobiographer.

In the *Historia Calamitatum* the author develops some material fully and is maddeningly vague in other areas. Too often we have given him the benefit of the doubt in the interpretation of statements which may well be simple errors. For instance, he asserts that before the Council of Soissons the people were aroused by a charge of tritheism, though Roscelin of Compiègne and Otto of Freising agree in ascribing to Abelard the opposite heresy of Sabellianism.[36] Moreover, his report of the judgment of the Council contains an apparently anachronistic point, for we are told that Abelard was condemned for teaching from a book which had not received prior approval, though precensorship of books does not seem to have been established as a requirement (rather than as a useful form of insurance) until the second half of the thirteenth century.[37] The reference to Abelard's persecution by two "new Apostles," "one of whom prided himself in having restored the life of the canons regular, the other that of the monks," may also be anachronistic. The descriptive phrases do not seem appropriate for the 1130s, and it is also unlikely that a hostile contemporary would have used the imperfect tense in referring to the pride of Bernard and Norbert.[38]

---

36. For the texts of *Hist. Cal.*, Roscelin and Otto concerning the heresy at issue, see Jean JOLIVET, « Sur quelques critiques de la théologie d'Abélard, » *Archives d'histoire doctrinale et littéraire du Moyen Age*, 30 (1963), 8-16.

37. G.B. FLAHIFF, « The Censorship of Books in the Twelfth Century, » *Mediaeval Studies*, 4 (1942), p. 4, n. 18, states : « I have met with no text in the twelfth century, other than the one in Abelard, to even suggest a compulsory preventive censorship. » Donald H. WIEST, *The Precensorship of Books*, Catholic Univ. of America, Canon Law Studies, 329 (Washington, D.C., 1953), p. 15-16, places the beginning of the institution in the 2nd half of the 13th cent. My friend Peter Classen has kindly sent me the text of his forth-coming edition of Burgundio of Pisa's introduction to his translation of St. John Chrysostom's commentary on the gospel of St. John. I believe that this text is an example of *voluntary* precensorship, of which Flahiff found other examples in the 12th cent.; the judgment in *Hist. Cal.* is a case where prior approval was not only desirable but necessary.

38. The passage in *Hist. Cal.*, p. 97, is discussed by MUCKLE in *Med. Studies*, 12, 212-213 and VAN DEN EYNDE, « Détails biographiques sur Pierre Abélard, » *Antonianum*, 38 (1963), 220-223. Since Norbert was living in the region of Laon in 1121, it is likely →

Points of divergence between the *Historia Calamitatum* and other texts could be multiplied, and I will limit myself to a few more brief points which apply directly to Abelard himself. Although the *Historia Calamitatum* tells us that Abelard's first work in theology, in which he took great pride, was a commentary on Ezechiel, it is doubtful whether Abelard ever wrote such a book; he never refers to a commentary on Ezechiel in his other writing, and in the introduction to his *Commentary on the Hexameron* he even mentions the difficulty of Eziechiel without taking the opportunity to note that he had once risen to that challenge.[39] That the author was ignorant of a significant phase of Abelard's career also appears to be the best explanation of why the letter contains no mention of his conflict with Roscelin, even though Roscelin seems to have played a major role in bringing his former student before the Council of Soissons and in his *Dialectica* Abelard writes with more virulence of the ideas of Roscelin than he does about William of Champeaux.[40]

Questions about the early history of the Paraclet which cast doubt on the *Historia Calamitatum* need to be presented at greater length. Three dates are fundamental to the traditional chronology of the foundation

---

that he was present at the Council of Soissons; Abelard might therefore have had excellent reasons for expressing the dislike for Norbert which is to be seen in *Serm. 33*, col. 605. But at the time Abelard supposedly wrote *Hist. Cal.* in the early or mid 1130s was Norbert going up and down the countryside preaching against Abelard? As archbp. of Magdeburg he presumably had more important matters on his mind. It is likely that the author of *Hist. Cal.* knew that Norbert and Bernard were among Abelard's major critics, but was uncertain as to when they assaulted him. It is also possible that this passage has nothing to do with St. Norbert, who died in 1134. The enigmatic comment might also apply to some such reformer of the canons regular as Gerhoch von Reichersberg, who was one of Abelard's theological opponents.

39. *Hist. Cal.*, p. 69-70 and *Expositio in Hexameron*, PL. 178, 731.

40. From Roscelin's attack on Abelard's Sabellianism it appears that he had a major share in the proceedings which led to the condemnation at Soissons. Roscelin's letter is published from the unique manuscript by J. REINERS, *Der Nominalismus in der Frühgeschichte*, Beiträge zur Geschichte der Philosophie und Theologie des Mittelalters, Bd. 8, Heft. 5 (Münster, 1910), p. 62-80; there is a less accurate text in PL. 178, 357-372. In the *Dialectica*, ed. L.M. DE RIJK, 2nd ed. (Assen, 1970), p. 554-555, Abelard refers to Roscelin's *insana sententia*. His differences with « W. magister noster » on p. 541 and with the otherwise unidentified « magister noster » cited in the *Dialectica* who is presumably William of Champeaux are much more restrained. It appears that in an early period of his teaching (that of the *Logica Ingredientibus*) Abelard shared with his master the identity theory of the copula in an affirmative proposition, but that in the *Dialectica* he had moved to the inherence theory. The picture of William as a radically extreme realist presented in *Hist. Cal.*, p. 65-66 is not supported by other texts, and it might be useful for an historian of philosophy to compare two presentations of William's thought, one treating *Hist. Cal.* as a forgery, that other assuming it is not.

of the Paraclet. The first is the Council of Soissons in 1121.[41] The second is the decision to expel the nuns of Argenteuil and to hand that property over to Suger, a decision to which Louis VI and Honorius II agreed in April 1129. The third is 28 November 1131, the date of the papal bull granted to Heloise, prioress, and the sisters of the Oratory of the Holy Trinity, confirming their monastery in the possession of its property.[42] The chronology imposed by the *Historia Calamitatum* is that Abelard became a monk before 1121, established an oratory in the parish of Quincey after that date, left the Paraclet without revenues when he became abbot of Saint-Gildas, brought Heloise to the oratory after the expulsion from Argenteuil, and granted it to the nuns in a donation approved by the bishop of Troyes and confirmed by Pope Innocent II. In other words, Heloise and the other nuns came to the Paraclet between April 1129 and November 1131.

It is my contention that the story of Heloise coming to the Paraclet from Argenteuil after 1129 is an invention. No known document outside the correspondence connects Heloise with Argenteuil or says that nuns from Argenteuil migrated to the Paraclet.[43] The little we know of the expulsion from other records is that a group of nuns from Argenteuil settled at Malnoüe-en-Brie, from which house they were still appealing against Saint-Denis in the early thirteenth century.[44]

---

41. The date of the Council of Soissons has been disputed, but in any case it took place before the death of Conon of Praeneste in August 1122; see Charles DEREINE in *Dict. d'hist. et de géog. eccl.*, 13 (1956), 467. Support for the traditional date is provided by a charter which records a settlement made in the presence of the legate Conon at Soissons in 1121 by Geoffroi, bishop of Chartres, Geoffroi, abbot of Saint-Médard of Soissons, William, abbot of Saint-Thierry and others. This important document, which establishes a basis for conflict between Abelard and William of Saint-Thierry twenty years before the Council of Sens, is copied in Bibl. Nat., Coll. Moreau, t. 50, fol. 149-149v, and has been edited by William Mendel NEWMAN in his as yet unpublished *Cartulary of Mont-Saint-Quentin*, no. 41.

42. The expulsion from the Paraclet is discussed by CHARRIER, *Héloïse*, p. 154-165. The original of the bull of Innocent II is at Châlons-sur-Marne, Bibl. mun. ms. 583, pièce 31; it is published with minor errors in LALORE, *Cartulaire*, p. 1-3, after the copy in the manuscript cartulary of the Paraclet.

43. In spite of claims that Heloise was the author of the *titulus* of Argenteuil in the *rouleau mortuaire* of Vital of Savigny, published by Léopold DELISLE, *Rouleaux des morts du IXe au XVe siècle* (Paris, 1866), p. 299, nothing in the text supports this view; cf. CHARRIER, *Héloïse*, p. 146-154. The presence of the name « Helvidis, monacha » in the *titulus* is not relevant; the usual practice was to enter the names of people dead at the time a church added its section to the role. Many secondary publications refer to Heloise as prioress of Argenteuil, but as far as I can tell, none bases its conclusions on any other document than the correspondence. Heloise's name does not appear in the necrology of Argenteuil, though that of Abelard does; see *Obituaires de la province de Sens : I. Diocèses de Sens et de Paris*, ed. Auguste MOLINIER (Paris, 1902), p. 346.

44. See *Gallia Christiana*, 7, inst. 84-85, and André LESORT, « Argenteuil, » *DHGE*, 4 (1930), 22-34.

We have a clue to how the Paraclet was actually founded in the letter of abuse which Roscelin wrote to Abelard, in response to a letter of criticism which Abelard had addressed to the church of Saint-Martin of Tours about Roscelin. This letter must be dated before the Council of Soissons, for if Roscelin had written after Abelard's theological humiliation it is inconceivable that he would not have waved that condemnation in Abelard's face in the same fashion that he taunted him for his castration. And where was Abelard when Roscelin wrote? He was a monk of Saint-Denis (or seemed to be, said Roscelin) who had accepted a church, called an obedience, from his brothers. There he had brought together a barbarous multitude of students; the money he collected for the error he was teaching he handed over to his whore *(scortum tuum, meretrix)*. The letter moreover provides two interesting sidelights. Abelard had attacked Roscelin for his criticism of Robert of Arbrissel, to which Roscelin replied that his criticism of Robert had been for accepting as nuns at Fontevrault women who had left their husbands. In conclusion, Roscelin noted that Abelard had authenticated his letter with a seal showing the image of two heads, one of a man, the other of a woman.[45]

To what conclusion does this letter lead us? The most reasonable, it seems to me, is that after becoming a monk of Saint-Denis, but before 1121, Abelard withdrew to an obedience of Saint-Denis, where he established a school and where he provided for Heloise. If it were not for the account in the correspondence, we would have no difficulty in seeing in Roscelin's letter a reference to the foundation of the Paraclet. The region of Nogent in which the Paraclet was established was at that time a fief of the abbey of Saint-Denis held by Milon of Nogent. Saint-Denis owned a *villa* at Nogent as early as the ninth century, and was a major landholder in the area; the priory of Marnay (5 km. to the north of the Paraclet), the church of Fontaine-Macon (5 km. to the west), and the grange of Aulne (about 5 km. to the northwest) were among its possessions.[46] Abelard's defense of Robert of Arbrissel and his use of a seal bearing both a male and a female head suggest that he had established a double monastery similar to Fontevrault in its early days. It should be noted that Robert was not called abbot of Fontevrault but *dominus* or *magister*, and until 1115 the female head of the community was not *abbatissa* but *priorissa*.[47] Similarly,

---

45. See the letter as published by REINERS, *Nominalismus*, p. 67, 79-80. I am in accord with M. GILSON, *Héloïse et Abélard*, p. 63, n. 2, that Roscelin's letter applies to Abelard's relations with Heloise at the Paraclet. Where we differ is on the date. Was Roscelin still alive after 1129 ?.

46. On the possessions of Saint-Denis see ROSEROT, *Dictionnaire*, pp. 1031-1032 (Nogent), 867 (Marnay), 596-597 (Fontaine-Mâcon), 46 (Aulne).

47. René NIDERST, *Robert d'Arbrissel et les origines de l'Ordre de Fontevrault* (Rodez), 1952), pp. 54-55.

Abelard was known at the Paraclet as the *magister* or *mestre*, a title used by the head of the chaplains of the Paraclet in the twelfth and thirteenth century, and the earliest surviving document from the Paraclet, the papal privilege of 1131, addresses Heloise as *priorissa*.[48] The hymns and sermons which Abelard wrote for the Paraclet show that he conceived of it as a double monastery and wanted the monks there to fill the role of deacons in serving the sisters. The altars of the church were dedicated to the Holy Spirit, Notre Dame, and Saint Jean l'Evangeliste, the protector of the Virgin, and the carefully planned calendar of the liturgical year gave special honor to women and to deacons.[49] The shadow cast by the correspondence has kept many people from realizing that Abelard was not only a great teacher but that, as Miss McLaughlin has demonstrated at this colloquium, within the system of values of his day he worked mightily to enhance the position of women in the Church. It was, however, both as a teacher and as a companion of women that St. Bernard described him, though not with admiration: "Peter Abelard, who argues with youths and associates with women."[50]

The idea that Abelard established the Paraclet at or near an obedience of Saint-Denis entrusted to his care, is supported by the evidence of Abelard's high regard for St. Denis. This statement, that Abelard honored the Areopagite, may sound strange, since everyone knows from the *Historia Calamitatum* that after the Council of Soissons Abelard came across the statement in Bede's commentary on Acts that Dionysius the Areopagite was bishop of Corinth, not of Athens, that when he jested about this passage the monks of Saint-Denis were infuriated with him,

---

48. Heloise refers to the « magistri absolutio » in her letter to Peter the Venerable, published by Giles Constable, *The Letters of Peter the Venerable* (Cambridge, Mass., 1967), 1, 401, and the refrain of the poem of Hilary, « Tort a vers nos li mestre » (PL., 178, 1855-56), shows the title by which Abelard was known by his students at the Paraclet. The same title appears in B.N. ms. fr. 14410, fol. 47v, 76, 99v, etc. « Guillelmus, presbiter, magister de Paraclito » is named in a charter of 1179 and « Fulcho, magister » is among the chaplains who witnessed a charter about the same time ; see Lalore, *Cartulaire*, pp. 85 and 87, and also above, note 31. The bull of 1131 cited above (note 42) addresses Heloise as « priorissa. » But Lalore has scrambled the chronology of her title by omitting the word « abbatisse » from his edition of a bull of 1135 (*Cartulaire*, p. 3) and printing « priorisse » in place of « abbatisse » in the bull of 1143 (*ibid.*, p. 6) ; both originals are in Aube 24 H 6.

49. A number of sermons are addressed to both « fratres » and « sorores » ; references are collected by Van den Eynde, « Le recueil des sermons de Pierre Abélard, » *Antonianum*, 37 (1962), 17-54. Among the hymns note « Omnis sexus et quelibet, » ed. Guido Maria Dreves, *Lateinische Hymnendichter des Mittelalters*, Erste Folge, Analecta hymnica, 48 (Leipzig, 1905), p. 170-171, (PL., 178, 1794). The clearest statement of the liturgical program of the Paraclet, including the use of the « grand chant » of Abelard, appears in B.N. ms. fr. 14410.

50. Letter 332, PL. 182, 537C.

that Abelard riposted that he preferred the authority of Bede to Abbot Hilduin of Saint-Denis, and that it made no difference to him whether the patron of the abbey was the Areopagite or someone else, so long as he had won a crown with the Lord. This quarrel, as the *Historia Calamitatum* goes on to report, led him to flee to Count Thibaut at Provins, to break with Saint-Denis, and soon to settle in a deserted spot at the future site of the Paraclet.[51]

This story of Abelard's lack of interest in the identity of the Areopagite and his preference for Bede over Hilduin is flatly contradicted by a letter Abelard wrote to Abbot Adam of Saint-Denis (therefore before Adam's death on 19 February 1122), in which he calmly and learnedly argued, with no hint that he was writing either an apology or a retraction, that in this particular case Bede had quite likely been misinformed, and that the patron of the abbey was indeed the bishop of Athens.[52] Seemingly the author of the *Historia Calamitatum* knew that Abelard had been involved in a dispute about St. Denis, but did not know which side he had taken.

To the evidence of this letter may be added the facts that the Petit Moustier at the Paraclet was dedicated to St. Denis and that the anniversary of the dedication of the monastery as a whole was celebrated on the eve of the feast of St. Denis.[53] From the *Historia Calamitatum* one would never guess that Abelard had established his oratory in the heart of a fief of Saint-Denis, a short distance from a priory, a church, and a grange of Saint-Denis, and that one of the original buildings was dedicated to St. Denis. Aside from the correspondence, we have no evidence that Abelard was on poor terms with the abbey in which he made his profession.

The revised chronology offered here places the foundation of the double monastery before 1121. It must be admitted that no known charter refers to the presence of women at the oratory before 1131. The absence of

---

51. *Hist. Cal.*, p. 89-92. It is worth noting that the monks of Saint-Denis included Abelard in their necrology as one of their community : « mon[achus] B[eati] D[ionysii] »; Heloise appears in the same necrology identified only as « abbatissa ». See *Obituaires de Paris*, p. 315 and 317.

52. PL. 178, 341-344. Jürgen MIETHKE, « Abaelards Stellung zur Kirchenreform. Eine biographische Studie, » *Francia*, 1 (1972), p. 164, n. 33, cites three mss. of *Ep. XI*, B.N. ms. lat. 2447 and n.a.l. 1509 (both from Saint-Denis) and ms. lat. 2445, which dates from the end of the 12th cent. To me the great care with which Prof. MIETHKE has documented his study shows how few of the assertions in *Hist. Cal.* can be verified from other sources.

53. In 1497 the abbess of the Paraclet moved the bodies of Heloise and Abelard, which were then « in quadam capella in dicto monasterio in honore sancti Dionisii fundata qui vulgariter appelatur *le petit moustier* »; Aube 24 H 18 (cf. LALORE, *Cartulaire*, p. XXIV). In the 13th cent. the nuns celebrated the anniversary of the dedication of their abbey by singing the vespers of the feast of St. Denis in the Petit Moustier; see B.N. ms. fr. 14410, fol. 103v-104v.

references in charters of other houses than the Paraclet is not at all surprising; the region of Nogent in this period is a documentary wasteland, and not even the genealogy of the lords of Nogent can be established with any certainty. The situation at the Paraclet is more complex. The abbey's fourteenth-century manuscript cartulary contains the text of nine papal bulls before 1160, and in spite of the dispersion of its archives, seven of these still exist and appear to be genuine. For the same period the cartulary contains the text of nine charters; the originals of none of these exist today, though there is a thirteenth-century false original for one. Apparently the bulls were stored separately from the charters and at some time in the twelfth century the non-papal section of the muniment collection was destroyed, leaving the abbey with the task of restoring its titles of foundation from what it could retrieve from its priories, from copies, and from forgeries.[54]

A papal confirmation of 1147 lists the possessions of the Paraclet, but it does not name any donors, leaving one to think that Abelard might have given the original church to Heloise, as the *Historia Calamitatum* states that he did. This thought cannot survive the reading of an original charter of 1194 of Bishop Garnier of Troyes which goes through the same list of possessions and names the donors.[55] Abelard is not included. Instead we find that Simon of Nogent gave a cultivated field in which the oratory was constructed (scarcely the "solitude" inhabited only by wild beasts and robbers to which the first letter of Heloise refers);[56] Milon of Nogent, lord of the territory, gave three fields, and so on. Not enough evidence from the region of Nogent has survived to make it easy to date any of these donations, though it seems a hopeful area for future investigations. One sure date before 1129 would settle the matter. But even without such corroboration, the letter of Roscelin, the letter of Abelard concerning St. Denis, and the evidence showing that Abelard established a double monastery where St. Denis was venerated strongly suggest that the early history of the Paraclet told with such verve in the *Historia Calamitatum* is a tissue of errors which might have seemed possible

---

54. Besides the bulls in Aube 24 H 6 and the one at Châlons, note may now be taken of four in the archives of the city of Metz, published by Henri TRIBOUT DE MOREMBERT, « Quatre bulles pour l'abbaye du Paraclet (1158-1208), » *Annuaire de la Société d'histoire et d'archéologie de la Lorraine*, 69 (1969), 103-106. He shows that the bull attribued by LALORE, p. 4-5, to Innocent II was actually issued by Innocent III. Aube 24 H 24 contains a false original, in a late 12th — or early 13th — cent. hand, of the charter of H., bishop of Troyes, printed by LALORE, p. 69.

55. Aube 24 H 19, printed with minor errors by LALORE, *Cartulaire*, p. 98-105, and *Gallia Christiana*, 12, instr., 278-281. Cf. *Hist. Cal.*, p. 100.

56. Ed. MONFRIN, p. 113, or MUCKLE, p. 69.

to someone unfamiliar with the actual events, but which could not have been written by Abelard or revised at the Paraclet by Heloise.

In spite of the evidence which indicates that the correspondence is either fraudulent or fictitious, one powerful argument for authenticity has convinced many learned and sensitive readers that the letters are genuine. To those familiar with Abelard's works, much of the correspondence sounds like the master. The reader of that collection of patristic and classical texts with which the Heloise of the *Historia Calamitatum* opposes their marriage may well exclaim "Aut Abaelardus aut nullus!" Who but Abelard could have cited his own rare quotation from Sidonius or the texts on the Sibyl which also appear in the *Theologia Christiana*?[57] Who else could have written the defense of the religious role of women, at once moving, profound, and learned, which we have in the letter-treatise on the dignity of nuns?

The answer, I believe, is that much in the correspondence genuinely came from Abelard's pen, that a forger both covered his tracks and lightened the load of the amount he had to create by filling as much as a half of his book with extracts from the writings of Abelard. We know that the sermons of the "mestre" were available at the Paraclet in the thirteenth century, and a long set of quotations found in one sermon does appear in the correspondence. As Bernhard Schmeidler pointed out long ago, a number of other passages, including most of the texts against marriage cited in the *Historia Calamitatum*, also appear in the *Theologia Christiana*.[58] It is, however, quite difficult to identify the work from which any given quotation might have been taken, because once Abelard had found some useful authority or created a turn of phrase which pleased him, he was likely to repeat or quote himself in one book after another. Since we have lost some of the works Abelard is known to have written, it is presently impossible to be sure if a quotation was taken directly from known writing like the *Theologia Christiana* or from a lost work in which Abelard had written the same thing.

A forger working at the Paraclet or commissioned by someone there could have used Abelard's sermons and such books as the *Theologia Christiana* and the *Commentary on Romans*. But presumably there was also available at the Paraclet a work by Abelard now lost to us which

---

57. *Ep. VII*, p. 271-272 = *Theol. Christ.*, I, 126, p. 125-127 (PL. 178, 1162); *Ep. VII*, p. 276 = *Theol. Christ.*, II, 104 and 106, p. 178-179 (PL. 178, 1201-1202). For other correspondences, see SCHMEIDLER, *Archiv für Kulturgeschichte*, 11 (1913), 21-25.

58. The « livre qu'en apelle les sermons au mestre » is cited in B.N. ms. fr. 14410, fol. 47v and 76; the identity with the volume which d'Amboise consulted at the Paraclet is shown by the fact that at the Annunciation the sermon read was « Exordium nostre » (PL. 178, 379). *Ep. VII*, p. 264-265 = *Serm. 31*, col. 572.

probably contained some passages also to be found in books still surviving. The passages in the correspondence which seem most characteristically the work of Abelard, the arguments from authority that a philosopher should remain unmarried, all or practically all of the treatise on the dignity of nuns, the discussion of silence and of learning which we find in the rule, and the scorn for dietary excess, particularly drunkenness, which appears in both the rule and the third letter of Heloise, could all have been taken from a lost work of Abelard. In his *Soliloquium* Abelard states: "Concerning the faith of the philosophers and also their life or code of behavior, I believe we have made a sufficient exposition in our exhortation to our brothers and fellow monks." Father Van den Eynde has demonstrated, I believe, that this *Exhortatio ad fratres et commonachos* cannot be identified with any known text, such as the sermon on St. John the Baptist or the *Theologia Christiana*. Instead, he suggested that portions of the *Theologia Christiana* were drawn from the *Exhortatio*, because in the *Theologia* Abelard "multiplie les allusions aux *fratres*, aux *monachi*, aux *monachi nostri temporis*, à leurs *conventus monasteriorum*, à leur façon de vivre, à leurs vertus et à leurs vices ; en un endroit, il s'en prend même aux excès de table des abbés."[59]

An indication that the author of the correspondence made use of this lost exhortation appears in letter VII. After lauding the virtue of the mother in Maccabees who died rather than eat the meat of pigs, this letter to Heloise continues: "O brothers and fellow monks *(O fratres et commonachi)*, you who each day, contrary to the teaching of the Rule and your [or our] profession, shamefully slaver for meat, what have you to say about the constancy of this woman?"[60] At this point the author of the letter, apparently copying rapidly from an Abelardian work addressed to monks, failed to remove this and a following reference to *fratres*, which have remained as identifying brands marking the source of the material. Must we imagine Abelard addressing his wife, in a moment of inattention, as one of his brothers and fellow monks? Here we surely have genuine Abelard, in a passage written for male religious, lauding the virtue and constancy of women, and incidentally showing his true attitude toward the eating of meat in a monastery.[61]

---

59. « Les écrits perdus d'Abélard, » *Antonianum*, 37 (1962), 469-473.
60. *Ep. VII*, p. 269.
61. Schmeidler, Charrier and Gilson (see *Héloïse et Abélard*, p. 184) have all had to argue that Abelard was here addressing his « fellow-monks » at Saint-Gildas, though the egalitarian tone of this address is not what we would expect of a father-abbot in bitter conflict with his spiritual sons. Elsewhere in *Ep. VII* (p. 264) Abelard echoed Jerome's searing condemnation of the title of « abbot. » Note that in *Ep. VIII*, p. 257, Abelard cites Matt. 23, 8-9, « Vos autem nolite vocari Rabbi. Et patrem vocari [sic in T] vobis [om. Amb.] super terram, » but not the continuation, « Nec vocemini magistri... »

At the same time that this discussion leads us to drop the correspondence from the genuine works of Abelard, it helps us to gain portions of the lost *Exhortatio*. If we can consider major portions of letter VII as part of an exhortation addressed to monks, for whom and under what conditions was it written? It might have been written for the monks of Saint-Denis, as was the letter on the Areopagite, or for the monks of Saint-Gildas, though it does not seem particularly appropriate for either group. But it is more likely that it was written for the Paraclet when Abelard was acting as *magister* of the budding double monastery. Robert of Arbrissel had to take precautions to assure that the brothers of Fontevrault would continue to accept female authority, and it is reasonable to think that besides his sermons Abelard gave the brothers of the Paraclet other good advice on their behavior, in particular exhorting his fellow-monks on the respect they should pay to the religious virtue of the women they were there to serve. This theory explains the curious schizophrenic character of the correspondence which has troubled commentators on the feminism of Abelard, the opposition between theory and apparent practice which we find in comparing letter VII with the institutions of the rule: the first was written to reinforce a female-superior double monastery, the second to overthrow it. One bit of evidence supports this association with the Paraclet. In the *Problemata* Heloise cites a passage on learning which we find now in letter VIII and says that Abelard had written it "ad exhortationem nostram."[62] Since the Paraclet was a double monastery, Abelard may have written two exhortations, one "ad fratres" and the other "ad sorores." If so, the first was probably the source of letter VII, the second of major parts of letters VI and VIII.

Up to this point I have avoided facing squarely the problem of the time of composition of the correspondence, or of its component parts. Extracts from genuine works of Abelard pose no problem; they must have been written in the first half of the twelfth century, and their apparent use gives a twelfth-century flavor to the correspondence. On the other hand, I suspect that the innovative provisions of the rule, notably the authorization to eat meat, were introduced in the thirteenth century. The idea that toward the end of the thirteenth century a scheming author compiled a fraudulent correspondence, making use of some authentic materials, would explain why the earliest manuscripts date from that period, why there is so little variation in the texts preserved by those thirteenth (or early fourteenth-century) manuscripts, and why no earlier authors even mention a correspondence which Jean de Meun found

---

62. *Problemata*, PL. 178, 678 A = *Ep. VIII*, p. 285; cf. VAN DEN EYNDE, « Chronologie des écrits d'Abélard à Héloïse, » *Antonianum*, 37 (1962), 341.

fascinating. The greatest objection to this simple solution lies in the text of the *Historia Calamitatum*. If it contains such fundamental errors that it cannot be considered a genuine work of Abelard, then it cannot be paired with the *Exhortatio* as authentic twelfth-century material used by a thirteenth-century forger. And yet it is hard to imagine that a thirteenth-century author had enough historical sense to write a letter which shows so many marks of twelfth-century composition.

Practically all knowledgeable readers of the *Historia Calamitatum* place it in the twelfth century. In spite of the errors I have noted, the author had at his command a great deal of accurate information about Abelard and about twelfth-century conditions, and moreover he avoided anachronisms which would have trapped a thirteenth-century writer. Most notably, the author held to the language of the twelfth-century schools, and did not use the vocabulary of the thirteenth-century *studium generale*. If one wants an institutional point to demonstrate the avoidance of anachronism, one I have found decisive is that the text says that Abelard returned to Mont Sainte-Geneviève "extra civitatem." This is just what one would expect in the twelfth century, but once Philip Augustus had built the extended walls around Paris, the mount was within the limits of the city.[63]

If the *Historia Calamitatum* is a twelfth-century fiction and was not written by the forger who, according to our earlier hypothesis, falsified the rule of the Paraclet and was most probably active in the thirteenth century, then under what circumstances was it created? In an age when the *ars dictaminis* was a major part of the academic curriculum, fictional letters written under the name of famous people were a common form of literary activity. The *Historia Calamitatum* is a self-contained piece of literature which an imaginative author familiar with Abelard through the *Theologia Christiana*, *Logica Ingredientibus*, and academic gossip could

---

63. *Hist. Cal.*, p. 66. Pierre Couperie gives fine maps illustrating this point in *Paris au fil du temps : atlas historique d'urbanisme et d'architecture* (Paris, 1968). At the colloquium at Cluny I argued, I now think mistakenly, that probably *Hist. Cal.* was written by the same author and at the same time as the rest of the correspondence, that is, most likely in the 13th cent.; to account for the large amount of reasonably accurate information in that letter I offered the hypothesis that the author might have made use of a short *Vita magistri* such as one might expect to find at the Paraclet. Abbé Bernard Merlette quite properly observed that the reference in *Hist. Cal.*, p. 69 to the use of an « expositor » rather than a gloss was evidence of 12th cent. authorship, and various people present noted that the suggestion that the bulk of *Hist. Cal.* was written in the 13th cent. was the weakest point in my hypothesis. While I accept these arguments that most of *Hist. Cal.* was written in the 12th cent., I have not been convinced that the author was Abelard. This paper discusses more inaccuracies in *Hist. Cal.* than I did at Cluny.

have been proud to have created. Medieval epistolary formularies commonly contain fictional letters, as Charles-Victor Langlois put it, "du genre de celles que l'on aimait à fabriquer au Moyen Age afin de condenser en quelques lignes les sentiments ou les prétentions des grands personnages."[64] The *Historia Calamitatum* is longer and better written than most such fabrications, but the errors of fact which it contains suggest that it is all the same fictional, and that its author knew only the broad outlines of Abelard's life and was more familiar with the schools of Paris than with the early history of the Paraclet. If the *Historia Calamitatum* stood alone without the support of the following letters, it is likely that its inauthenticity would have been recognized long ago.

But of course it does not stand alone. It is part of my hypothesis that a forger who falsified the correspondence in the thirteenth century also added to the *Historia Calamitatum*. The most marked case of an addition occurs in the references to the Mosaic law on eunuchs and acceptable sacrifices, where the author cites two Biblical passages, "Book of Numbers, chapter LXXIII," which is Leviticus 22:24 of our modern Bible, and "Deuteronomy, chapter XXI," which is actually Deuteronomy 23:1. These errors derive from different systems of Biblical citation. Numbers ("ad Levitas") was easily confused with Leviticus, and if one checks a twelfth-century Bible of the type Abelard used, one finds in chapter 74 of Leviticus the sentence which is now in chapter 22 of the modern system. But in that same patristic Bible, in which Deuteronomy contains 155 chapters, the quotation from Deuteronomy which interests us is chapter 107. The reference to Deuteronomy XXI is not easily explained as an error for chapter CVII, but it is a simple error for chapter XXIII. In all this discussion the matter of primary importance is that chapter 107 of Deuteronomy was not renumbered as chapter 23 until the early thirteenth century, when Stephen Langton at the University of Paris devised the new system of the so-called "Parisian Bible," which became standard after about 1225.[65] Apparently the original twelfth-century text contained

---

64. « Formulaires de lettres du XIIe, du XIIIe et du XIVe siècle, » *Notices et extraits des mss. de la B.N. et autres bibliothèques*, 35, part 2 (1896), 415.

65. *Hist. Cal.*, p. 80. There is a good survey on « Chapitres de la Bible » by E. MANGENOT in *Dictionnaire de la Bible*, 2 (1926), 559-565. That Abelard used a Bible in which Levit. had 89 chapters and Deut. had 155 can be seen in *Comm. Rom.*, p. 234 (incompletely printed in MIGNE) and *Theol. Christ.*, II, 18, p. 140 (PL. 178, 1172). There is a confusion between Levit. and Num. in *Comm. Rom.*, p. 88 (PL. 178, 817). Abelard himself would presumably have been content to ignore these Biblical passages, since he surely knew better than anyone else of his time that one of the Canons of the Apostles (no. 21) provided that a eunuch who had suffered « per insidias hominum » could become a bishop. See A. VILLIEN, « Eunuque, » in *Dictionnaire de théologie catholique*, 5 (1924), 1515-1516. The popular theory that Abelard was castrated in order to prevent him from advancing in the ecclesiastical hierarchy is baseless.

a citation of Leviticus based on a patristic Bible, and a thirteenth-century interpolator, perhaps quoting from a reference work like the concordance of Hugh of Saint-Cher, added a second citation based on the later system. I think we must reject the explanation that a fastidious scribe modernized a pre-existing reference, for it is hard to imagine why he would change one reference and not the other, and then change that one incorrectly.

We now have a theory of the composition of ms. T which involves two different authors, a twelfth-century imaginative writer who may have composed the *Historia Calamitatum* as a literary exercise with no further fraudulent intent, and a thirteenth-century author who wanted to change the institutions of the Paraclet and who introduced innovative passages into the genuine Abelardian material we find in letters VI, VII, and VIII. Those who accept this theory of multiple authorship are still left with the problem of who wrote the relatively short "personal" letters between Abelard and Heloise, the twelfth-century epistolary "novelist" or the thirteenth-century institutional scoundrel. There are grounds for making a decision either way, either that the letters are such effective literary documents that they should be attributed to the "literary genius" who wrote the *Historia*, or that their emphasis on the need for a rule and the exemplary submissiveness of Heloise to Abelard associates them with the forged rule of the Paraclet. Though I favor the second choice, I know of no way to settle the matter, and it is possible that these letters too contain elements by authors writing in different centuries and with different motives. Unfortunately these letters contain few citations or institutional references which have a potential for precise dating. The section which may be most fruitful in this regard is a passage in letter V which seems to be based on a commentary on the verse of Canticles, *Nigra sum sed formosa*. It seems worth asking what text provided information on Africans comparable to that in Aristotle's *De animalibus*, and says that as the flesh of black women is less attractive to the sight, it is sweeter to the touch, so that their husbands prefer to lead them to the bed-chamber rather than to take them out in public. Can anyone identify the source for this example of medieval racism?[66]

---

66. Ep. V, p. 83-85; nothing like this appears in Frank SNOWDON, *Blacks in Antiquity* (Cambridge, Mass., 1970). The characteristics of a hypothetical commentary on Canticles are these : (*a*) it cites the passage *Nigra sum sed formosa, filiae Hierusalem. Ideo dilexit me rex et introduxit me in cubiculum suum* (p. 83, note 30, and p. 85, note 70), which is Antiphon 3 at vespers and lauds for feasts of the Virgin throughout the year; (*b*) the Bride makes a statement not found in Canticles, « Nolite mirari cur id faciam » (p. 84, note 63); (*c*) there is a passage on the whiteness of the bones and teeth of Africans which Muckle (p. 84, note 44) compares to Aristotle, *De animalibus*, III, ch. 9; (*d*) in commenting on Cant. 3: 1 (In lectulo meo) the commentary may have provided the source for this statement, « Et frequenter accidit ut nigrarum caro feminarum quanto est in aspectu deformior, tanto sit in tactu suavior; atque ideo earum viri, ut illis oblectentur, magis eas in cubiculum introducunt quam ad publicum educunt » (p. 85, note 68). *De animalibus* was first translated into Latin by Michael Scot in the 13th cent.

The reader who accepts the idea that a later author introduced the reference to Deuteronomy in the *Historia Calamitatum* may also conclude that the passage concerning precensorship was added at the same time. It is also possible that the passage quoted at the beginning of this paper about the proper governance of nuns or the extended discussion on marriage attributed to Heloise and based on texts to be found in the *Theologia Christiana* (or perhaps the *Exhortatio*) were added in the thirteenth century by an author who wanted to emphasize the subordinate position of women. In the present state of our knowledge there seems to be no way to go beyond the Biblical references and the allusion to precensorship to say what other portions may have been interpolated in the thirteenth-century. The stylistic and thematic unity of the *Historia Calamitatum* suggests to me that later additions cannot make up more than a small fraction of the whole letter.[67] If that is the case, and if the *Historia Calamitatum* contains significant historical errors in various sections, then the whole letter must be considered inauthentic, and that is the central issue.

Into this reconstruction of the possible composition of the correspondence there is one further complication to be introduced. Close students of this correspondence know that current theories of the origin and nature of the letters are subject to multiple objections, and none has proved fully convincing. The hypothesis offered here may seem overly complicated, and important parts rest on slender pieces of evidence, but it has the advantage of explaining more of the difficulties in the text and the manuscript tradition than any previous theory. Real life is rarely straight-forward and uncomplicated, and simple explanations of complex phenomena are most easily maintained when we know very little about the matters in question.

The reader who accepts the authenticity of the correspondence is bound to ask why in letter VIII Abelard repeats, without so much as an "ut dicis," two fairly extended passages which Heloise had earlier written to him.[68] This question is no less bothersome for someone who attributes the letters to a forger, since one has to ask why a forger should repeat himself in this awkward way. A clue to an answer may lie in the fact that although there are no divisions in letter VII, letter VIII is written in two parts: a short and quite literate introductory epistle ending with "Valete" is followed by the long and quite badly organized "rule," which begins with the word *Tripertitum*. No great literary skill would be required to

---

67. As M. Monfrin argued in the discussion at Cluny and Donald K. Frank has written in « Abelard as Imitator of Christ, » in *Viator* 1 (1970), 107-113, allusions throughout *Hist. Cal.* suggest parallels between the life of Christ and that of Abelard. While there are probably interpolations in the letter, it is hard to believe that most of it was not written by one author.

68. *Ep. VI*, p. 245 = *Ep. VIII*, p. 269; *Ep. VI*, p. 247 = *Ep. VIII*, p. 270.

forge this rule. An author at the Paraclet who had access to an *Exhortatio ad sorores* written by Abelard would only need to introduce his institutional changes, plus perhaps a few banal passages on the officers of a monastery intended to make an exhortation sound more like an administrative document. This theory would explain why letter VIII is the most confusingly organized "rule" in the history of monasticism. If the question of its authenticity occurs to us, it could also have been raised by nuns at the Paraclet, particularly if the rule changed established institutional relationships. A monk at the Paraclet capable of creating a falsified rule might have been unable to write the supporting letters needed to authenticate it. In the search for an explanation of all the anomalies in our text, we may be forced to look for yet another author.

My hypothesis is that Abelard established the Paraclet as a double monastery similar to Fontevrault, and wrote for its use not only an *Exhortatio ad fratres et commonachos* but also an *Exhortatio ad sorores*. Sometime in the thirteenth century, perhaps at the time of the electoral crisis in the later 1280s, one of the monks attempted to overthrow the authority of the nuns who ruled the double monastery. To this end he (or someone working for him) created a forged rule by inserting some institutional changes into this hypothetical, tripartite *Exhortatio ad sorores*. The forged rule, probably identical with the text we have now in letter VIII beginning with *Tripertitum*, was not readily accepted, and so the forger at the Paraclet commissioned a confederate outside the monastery to fabricate supporting documentation, giving him some texts, including Abelard's *Exhortationes*, to simplify his task and lend authenticity. The second author, who may well have been part of the university milieu at Paris, had access to a fictional autobiographical letter attributed to Abelard and written in the twelfth century; taking this fictional letter and making use of genuine works of Abelard written for monastic use, this hypothetical "Parisian" author wrote a manuscript very similar to the text we have today in ms. A or to that translated by Jean de Meun (ms. J of Monsieur Monfrin's schema), a text which began with the *Historia Calamitatum* and ended with the introductory epistle of letter VIII.[69] The forger at the Paraclet

---

69. M. Monfrin's demonstration in his critical edition of *Hist. Cal.* that although A and J are less complete than T, they are independent manuscripts which sometimes give better readings, raises tremendous problems for anyone attempting to construct the history of the text. As C. K. Scott Moncrieff noted in the introduction to his translation of *The Letters of Abelard and Heloise* (New York, 1926), p. ix, George Moore once suggested to him that Jean de Meun was the author of *Hist Cal*. The idea that Jean not only translated the text of J but actually wrote it is attractive, but it cannot be maintained, for the French translation preserved in B.N. ms. fr. 920 contains errors which could not have been made by the author of the Latin text. The one I find most telling is *sanctorum* for *scortorum*, cited by Charlotte Charrier in her edition of the *Traduction de la première épitre de Pierre Abélard* (Paris, 1934), p. 36. The Latin text translated by Jean could, however, have been written by someone who shared his interests and was a member of his literary circle.

then added his rule and prepared a fair copy of his composite document which was equivalent to our ms. T; in fact, T may actually be that fair copy. The result of this dual thirteenth-century composition was two versions of the correspondence, a *versio Paracletensis* which included the full text of the rule, and what we may call a *versio Parisiensis* which ended with the introductory epistle of letter VIII.

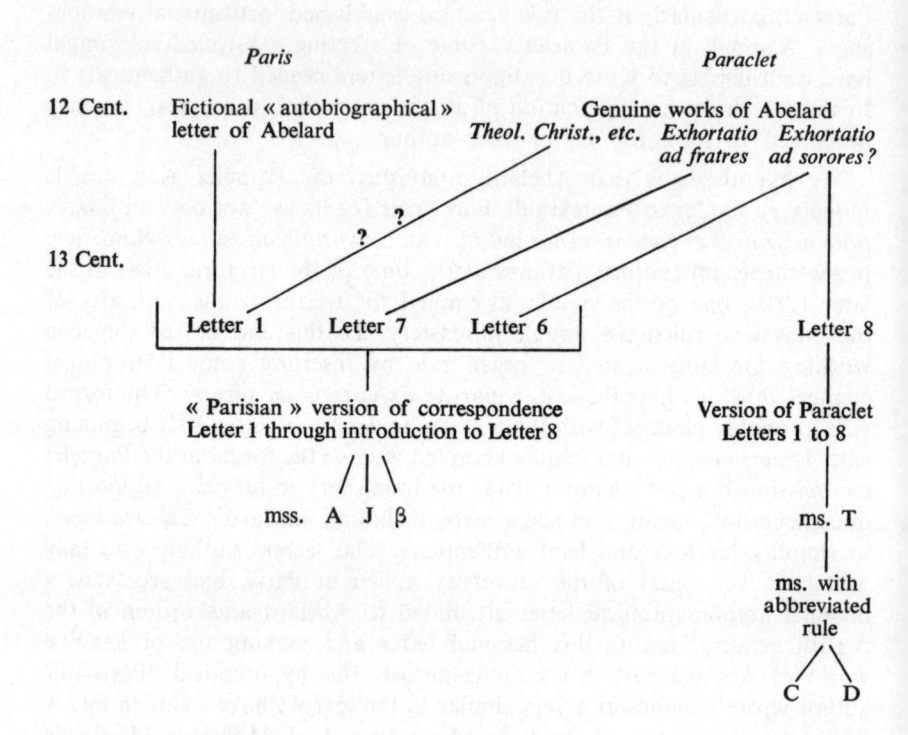

```
                        Paris                                    Paraclet

12 Cent.     Fictional « autobiographical »      Genuine works of Abelard
             letter of Abelard                   Theol. Christ., etc.  Exhortatio   Exhortatio
                                                                       ad fratres   ad sorores ?

                                         ?  ?
13 Cent.

             | Letter 1    Letter 7    Letter 6 |                             Letter 8

             « Parisian » version of correspondence              Version of Paraclet
             Letter 1 through introduction to Letter 8           Letters 1 to 8

                      / | \
                   mss. A J β                                         ms. T

                                                                      ms. with
                                                                      abbreviated
                                                                      rule
                                                                       / \
                                                                      C   D
```

This complicated theory rather neatly explains the manuscript tradition of the letters. There are no twelfth-century manuscripts of the correspondence because there never were any twelfth-century texts, except for the (fictional) *Historia Calamitatum*, which may have been followed by some short and equally fictional personal letters, and the genuine *Exhortationes* and other works of Abelard. The copy of the exhortation which was sent to the hypothetical Parisian author, we may surmise, was never returned to the Paraclet; this would explain why d'Amboise did not find a copy when he visited the abbey at the end of the sixteenth century, and why there was a copy in the library of a canon of Paris, Nicholas de

Baye.[70] The version of the correspondence which was of interest at the Paraclet contained the rule, and probably the two manuscripts which include any portion of the rule, C and D, were copied from an exemplar of this type, perhaps from T itself (or its double). It should be noted that the abbreviated text of the rule preserved in C and D has been cut in a self-serving way: the portions of the rule which place unusual limitations on the nuns, such as the oversight of the *prepositus monachorum* and the prohibition against eating bread of pure wheat, have been eliminated, while the striking privileges, including the permission to eat meat three times a week, have been retained. Ironically, the short form of the rule found in C and D is probably the version used at the Paraclet in the later middle ages, and quite likely the only version ever actually put into effect.

The *versio Parisiensis* had a quite different history. As the text most easily available outside the Paraclet, it was read and enjoyed by Jean de Meun and Petrarch. It is commonly suggested that the scribes of manuscripts which omit the rule grew tired of copying and simply dropped the dull material at the end. This theory is unsatisfactory, for the rule is not really any duller than the bulk of the text in letters VI and VII, and it seems very strange indeed to copy the text of the introductory epistle of letter VIII and not give the rule which followed if it were available. Several excellent manuscripts of the correspondence which omitted the rule circulated at Paris at the end of the thirteenth century, even though the rule is central to the theme of the whole unified correspondence. The hypothesis of double thirteenth-century authorship explains not only why letters VI and VIII contain identical passages, both presumably drawn from an *Exhortatio ad sorores*, but also how mss. A, J, and possibly β could be more accurate and less complete than T.

The practical conclusions to be drawn from this long analysis of the possible, though not surely established, composition of the text preserved in Troyes ms. 802 are both negative and positive. First of all, we can have no assurance that we have here any record of the thoughts or writing of

---

70. As M. Vernet point out in his communication to this colloquium, the *Journal de Nicolas de Baye*, éd. Alexandre TUETEY (Paris, 1888), II, xcv, no. 179 contains a reference to « la Exortacion Pierre Abalard. » A following item (no. 181) is « les Epistres de Pierre Abalard et viij cayers de luy mesmes, tenans ensemble, le premier commençant *tripertite*. » A volume of the letters in 8 gatherings and beginning with the word *tripertite* could very well have been one in which the rule was bound ahead of a text similar to A or J, rather than behind it. Although Tuetey printed the text exactly as it appears in Arch. nat. S 1822, fol. 16v, it is still possible that *et* should be *en* and *tripertite* should be *tripertitum*, for the manuscript is a fair copy of the reports of a number of estimators and not the text written on the spot.

Heloise. The questions posed in the *Problemata*, her long and successful administration of the Paraclet, and the testimony of admiring contemporaries show that Heloise must have been an outstanding person, but since the arguments against marriage in the *Historia Calamitatum* were probably taken by a man from a treatise by Abelard, and her letters in the correspondence may have been composed by a thirteenth-century author who wanted to put women in their place, we need not imagine her as so submissive or as so tortured by sensuality as she appears in the correspondence. Secondly, if the *Historia Calamitatum* is in large part a twelfth-century fiction, it indicates the image which contemporaries or near-contemporaries could hold of Abelard, but it cannot be used as a source of precise information except where it is confirmed by other texts. And thirdly, while much of the monastic and theological writing in the letters is probably genuine, the greatest care must be used in winnowing Abelardian passages from the perversions introduced by an interpolator.

For those who are prepared to judge Heloise and Abelard by standards which they themselves would have considered valid, we are now free to see these two great figures in more positive terms. We can more readily understand why Peter the Venerable wished that Heloise were a nun of Marcigny. If my hypothesis is valid, we can see that Abelard loved his wife deeply and supported her personally and spiritually for far longer than we had realized. In fact, *Institutiones nostre*, the liturgical program of the Paraclet, and letter VII (uncontradicted by the "rule") show that in his relations with women Abelard was not the Origen but the Jerome of his day, more willing even than Robert of Arbrissel to treat women as beings of spiritual worth.[71] His other writings show that Abelard was a proud and aggressive scholar who sometimes fought his theological opponents with no more personal consideration than they accorded him, but we can strike from the historical record the image of Abelard as a calculating seducer or as an arrogant and ungrateful student who could dismiss Anselm of Laon as a sterile and obfuscating teacher years after the death of that great scholar.

For my part, I am happier with the new picture of Abelard and Heloise we may have before us than with the old. Neither picture, however, should be accepted on the basis of likes or dislikes. The hypothesis of fraud, fiction and borrowing offered here as a possible explanation of the puzzles in the correspondence can only be supported or rejected by the objective

---

71. In the great church at Fontevrault the nuns were separated from the officating priests by thick walls and a grill; at the Paraclet, as B.N. ms. fr. 14410 shows, priests and deacons entered the sanctuary with the nuns.

evaluation of as much evidence as we can find the techniques to examine. The collaborative investigation undertaken at the colloquium at Cluny demonstrates the spirit necessary for that future inquiry: "Petrus amicus, sed magis amica veritas."[72]

ACKNOWLEDGMENTS

The paper printed here is an extensive revision of the text delivered at Cluny on July 4, 1972. It incorporates material presented during the discussion of the original paper and revisions and comments suggested by a number of colleagues at the colloquium, including M. Jacques Monfrin, Prof. Jürgen Miethke, Abbé Bernard Merlette, Prof. Peter von Moos, and M. Jean Jolivet. Since on one major point (see below, note 63) I have been led by that discussion to change my position, this paper represents my thought as of October 1972; if it is closer to the truth than my original paper, that progress is due to the collective exchange of ideas made possible by an international colloquium. I wish also to thank Dom Jean Leclercq, Fr. Gaetano Raciti, and Prof. Richard Rouse for their advice and encouragement in the preparation of the original paper, the Walckenaer family for their cordial reception at the Paraclet, and Fr. Nikolaus Häring for later assistance. The support of the California Institute of Technology made possible a period of extended research in France in the spring of 1972, permitting me to work at the archives and municipal library of Troyes, the municipal library of Reims, and the Bibliothèque nationale and the Archives nationales.

---

72. After this paper went to press I found the « unidentified statutes » which are part of the canon law portion of ms. T (PL. 178, 232-323). The first, « Statuimus ut abbatisse et priorisse ... et abbatissa aliud, » is an adaptation with a transformation of gender of the second canon of the Council of Rouen of 1231. In ms. T, though not in the printed text, there is a paragraph break at this point, with a rubricated heading « De sanctimonialibus. » The following text « Propter scandala ... sopiantiur » is a repetition, with only the slightest changes, of canon 4 of that same council; see J.D. MANSI, *Sacrorum conciliorum nova et amplissima collectio* (Florence and Venice, 1759-90), 23, 213-214. These canons are further evidence that the texts in ms. T were not brought together for the use of the nuns of the Paraclet or its priories during the formative period. On this point see « The Paraclete and the Council of Rouen of 1231, » to appear in the *Bulletin of Medieval Canon Law*, n.s. 4 (1974).

CONTRASTS BETWEEN THE CORRESPONDENCE AND OTHER TEXTS WITH RESPECT TO THE INSTITUTIONS OF THE PARACLET

1. The nature of the rule gouverning the Paraclet.

(*a*) Heloise in her last letter to Abelard: Tibi nunc, domine, dum vivis incumbit instituere de nobis quid in perpetuum tenendum sit nobis. Tu quippe post Deum hujus loci fundator, tu per Deum nostre congregationis es plantator, tu cum Deo nostre sis religionis institutor. Preceptorem alium post te fortassis habiture sumus et qui super alienum aliquid edificet fundamentum, ideoque, veremur, de nobis minus futurus sollicitus, vel a nobis minus audiendus, et qui denique, si eque velit, non eque possit. — *Med. Studies*, 17 (1955), 253.

(*b*) Charter of Hugh, archbp. of Sens, for La Pommeraie, 1147 at latest: Alium ordinem, nisi Paraclitensem, non licebit eis observare. — Orig. Aube 24 H 19; LALORE, *Cartulaire*, p. 72.

(*c*) Bull of Alexander III for La Pommeraie, 21 March 1164: Imprimis siquidem statuentes ut ordo monasticus, qui secundum Deum et beati Benedicti regulam in vestro monasterio noscitur institutus, perpetuis ibidem temporibus inviolabiter observetur. — Vidimus of 1442, Aube 24 H 20; LALORE, *Cart.*, p. 23.

(*d*) Institutiones nostre: Institutiones nostre sumunt exordium a doctrina Christi predicantis, et tenentis paupertatem, humilitatem et obedientiam... Domino super nos prospiciente, et aliqua loca nobis largiente, misimus quasdam ex nostris ad religionem tenendam numero sufficiente. Annotamus autem boni propositi nostri consuetudines, ut quod tenuit mater incommutabiliter, teneant et filie uniformiter. — Ms. T, fol. 89; *PL.* 178, 313.

2. The dignitaries of the abbey. The correspondence limits itself to seven dignitaries. Other documents show that the prioress was an important officer of the abbey, and that there was also a subprioress.

(*a*) Regula: Septem vero personas ex vobis ad omnem monasterii administrationem necessarias esse credimus atque sufficere: portariam scilicet, cellerariam, vestiariam, infirmariam, cantricem, sacristam et ad extremum diaconissam, quam nunc abbatissam nominant. — *Med. Studies*, 18 (1956), 252.

(*b*) The prioress shares many functions with the abbess in *Institutiones nostre*.
(*c*) Livre des sépultures du Paraclet: Agnes, prieuse, gist ou petit cloistre, a l'uis dou petit moustier (Agnes, priorissa, neptis magistri nostri Petri...). — *Obituaires des diocèses de Meaux et de Troyes*, p. 390 C.
(*d*) Witnesses to 12th cent. charter of Rainald, abbot of St. Jacques of Provins: Agnes, priorissa; Constantia, subpriorissa. — LALORE, *Cart.*, 87.

3. The title of abbess or deaconess.

(*a*) Not only is the title of deaconess used throughout the Regula, but « Heloise » applies the word to herself in her second letter: Miror... quod... in ipsa fronte salutationis epistolaris me tibi preponere presumpsiti, feminam videlicet viro, ...diaconissam abbati. — Ed. MONFRIN, p. 118, following ms. T, fol. 23v.

(*b*) Nowhere else in medieval materials concerning the Paraclet have I found the term « diaconissa » applied to the head of the abbey. In *Ep. X* (*PL.* 178, 335) Abelard specifically notes that Heloise « illius loci abbatissa dicitur. »

4. The importance of a learned abbess.

(*a*) Regula : Que [diaconissa] si litterata non fuerit, sciat se non ad philosophicas scholas vel disputationes dialecticas sed ad doctrinam vite et operum exhibitione accommodari... Quod diligenter attendamus ut scriptum est : Dixit abbas Ipitius, « Ille est vere sapiens qui facto suo alios docet, non qui verbis. » — *Med. Studies,* 18 (1956), 253.

(*b*) Letter of Abelard to the nuns of the Paraclet, « De studio litterarum » : Magisterium habetis in matre, quod ad omnia vobis sufficere, tam ad exemplum scilicet virtutum, quam ad doctrinam litterarum potest : que non solum Latine, verum etiam tam Hebraice quam Grece non expers litterature, sola hoc tempore illam trium linguarum adepta peritiam videtur, que ab omnibus in beato Hieronymo, tanquam singularis gratia, predicatur, et ab ipso in supradictis venerabilibus feminis maxime commendatur... Quod in viris amisimus, in feminis recuperemus : et ad virorum condemnationem, et fortioris sexus judicium, rursum regina austri sapientiam veri Salomonis in vobis exquirat. — *PL.* 178, 333 and 336.

5. The authorization of the abbess to leave the abbey.

(*a*) Regula : Statuimus itaque ut diaconissa magis spiritualibus quam corporalibus intendens nulla exteriore cura monasterium deserat. — *Ibid.*, p. 258.

(*b*) Charter of Hugh, archbp. of Sens, for La Pommeraie, 1147 at latest : Abbatissa Parracliti semel in anno ibit Pomerium, et sedens in capitulo emendabit, si quid fuerat emendandum de ordine, vel de aliqua re ad ordinem pertinente. — Orig. charter, cited above, No. 1 (*b*).

6. The question of whether the nuns must remain strictly cloistered and have men conduct all their business for them, or whether they may on occasion leave the Paraclet for their affairs.

(*a*) Regula : Si qua vero legatione monasterium egeat, monachi vel eorum conversi ea fungantur. Semper enim viros mulierum necessitudinibus oportet providere... Decrevimus monachos et eorum conversos more Apostolorum et diaconorum in iis que ad exteriorem pertinent curam monasteriis feminarum providere... Nulla umquam sororum septa monasterii egredietur sed omnia exterius, sicut dictum est, fratres procurabunt. — *Ibid.*, p. 258 and 260.

(*b*) Institutiones nostre : Ad familiaria vero negotia et ad custodiam rerum nostrarum mittimus in domos nostras probatas tam etate quam vita et moniales et conversas. — Ms. T, fol. 89; *PL.* 178, 315.

(*c*) In 1237 the abbess of the Paraclet and a number of nuns went to Fontevrault to establish an association of prayers. — LALORE, *Cart.*, p. 196-197.

7. The exemption of the Paraclet from any local control.

(a) Regula : Oportet... ut monasteriis feminarum monasteria non desint virorum et per ejusdem religionis viros omnia extrinsecus feminis administrentur. Illustrated by a canon of the Council of Seville of 619, can. 11 (cf. *PL*. 88, 1071). — *Ibid.*, p. 258.

(b) Regula : Hanc nos itaque providentiam sequentes monasteria feminarum monasteriis virorum ita semper esse subjecta volumus ut sororum curam fratres agant et unus utriusque tamquam pater presideat ad cujus providentiam utraque spectent monasteria. *Ibid.*, p. 259.

(c) Bull of Innocent II for the Paraclet, 28 Nov. 1131 : Vestris justis postulationibus assensum prebentes, monasterium Sancte Trinitatis... sub Apostolice Sedis protectione suscipimus. — Orig., Châlons-sur-Marne, bibl. mun. ms. 583, piece 31; LALORE, *Cart.*, p. 1.

(d) Bull of Innocent II for the Paraclet 17 June 1135 : Ad hec aditientes statuimus, ne propter benedictionem et consecrationem percipiendam de monasterio exire cogamini; nec pro electione abbatisse, aut alia qualibet occasione episcopus, vel alia quelibet persona, ullum vobis gravamen vel molestiam inferre presumat. — Orig., Aube 24 H 6; LALORE, *Cart.*, p. 3.

8. The exercise of authority over men by women.

(a) Historia Calamitatum : Unde non mediocriter miror consuetudines has in monasteriis dudum inolevisse, quod quemadmodum viris abbates, ita et feminis abbatisse preponantur... In plerisque etiam locis, ordine perturbato naturali, ipsas abbatissas atque moniales clericis quoque ipsis, quibus subest populus, dominari conspicimus, et tanto facilius eos ad prava desideria inducere posse quanto eis amplius habent preesse, et jugum illud in eos gravissimum exercere. — Ed. MONFRIN, p. 105.

(b) Institutiones nostre : Soli abbatisse et priorisse debitum exhibetur obedientie. — Ms. T, fol. 89; *PL*. 178, 314.

(c) Institutiones nostre : Quocienscunque autem fratres graviter delinquunt, vocantur in capitulum, et coram communi capitulo corriguntur, ut majori confundantur erubescentia. — *Ibid.*, fol. 89v and col. 315.

9. Office of the head of the monks at the Paraclet.

(a) Regula : Prepositum autem monachorum quem abbatem nominant sic etiam monialibus preesse volumus ut eas que Domini sponse sunt cujus ipse servus est proprias recognoscat dominas nec eis preesse sed prodesse gaudeat. — *Med. Studies*, 18 (1956), 259.

(b) In the 12th and 13th centuries the head of the male clergy at the Paraclet was known as the « magister. » I can find no indication that any man at the Paraclet was ever known as abbot or given the administrative functions of an abbot.

10. Authorization to eat bread of pure wheat.

(a) Regula : Triticee quoque medulle similaginem omnino prohibemus, sed semper cum habuerint triticum, tertia pars ad minus grossioris annone misceatur. — *Ibid.*, 277.

(b) Institutiones nostre : Pane quolibet vescimur; si fuerit triticum, triticeo; si defuerit, pane cujuslibet annone. — Ms. T, fol. 89; *PL*. 178, 314.

11. Authorization to eat meat.

(a) Regula : Ipsumque ita carnium sive ceterorum esum temperamus ut, omnibus concessis, major sit abstinentia monialium quam, quibusdam interdictis, modo sit monachorum. Igitur ipsum quoque car-

(b) Institutiones nostre : In refectorio nostro cibi sine carnibus sunt legumina, et ea que nutrit ortus. Lac, ova et caseus rarius apponuntur, et pisces, si dati fuerint. — *Ibid.*

nium esum ita temperari volumus ut non amplius quam semel in die sumant, nec diversa inde fercula eidem persone parentur, nec seorsum aliqua superaddantur pulmenta, nec ullatenus ei vesci liceat plusquam ter in hebdomada, prima videlicet feria, tertia et quinta feria, quantecumque etiam festivitates intercurrant. — *Ibid.*, p. 279.

(c) Expositio in Hexaemeron, written for Heloise : Ex quo liquidum est tam pisces quam volucres ex aquis procreatos habere corpora ejusdem naturae, nec tantam vim humanis corporibus ad lasciviendum carnes eorum ministrare, quantam carnes terrestrium animantium, quae cum nostris corporibus ejusdem sunt naturae. Unde nec monachis beati Benedicti Regula ita carnes illas sicut has interdicit, cum videlicet a carnibus tantum quadrupedum, non aliarum abstinere praecipit. — PL. 178, 756.

12. Whether the winter is the time of a true fast or simply the elimination of a meal.

(a) Regula : Ab equinoctio vero autumnali usque ad Pascha propter dierum brevitatem unam in die comestionem sufficere credimus. Quod quia non pro abstinentia religionis, sed pro brevitate dicimus temporis, nulla hic ciborum genera distinguimus. — *Ibid.*, p. 280.

(b) Institutiones nostre : In litania majore, tribus diebus Rogationum, sexta feria et sabbato [precedentibus diem Pentecostes?], vigilia sancti Johannis Baptiste, vigilia apostolorum Petri et Pauli, vigilia sancti Laurentii, vigilia Assumptionis, et ab Ydibus Septembris usque ad Pascha jejunamus. — Ms. T, fol. 90-90v; *PL.* 178, 317.

13. Whether newly composed hymns may be sung in the church.

(a) Regula : Nihil in ecclesia legatur aut cantetur nisi de authentica sumptum scriptura, maxime autem de novo vel veteri testamento. *Ibid.*, p. 263.

(b) Abelard was the author of a book of hymns and other chants to be sung at the Paraclet.

23

Philology's Search for Abelard in the Metamorphosis Goliae

> Nupta querit ubi sit suus Palatinus,
> cuius totus extitit spiritus divinus,
> querit cur se subtrahat quasi peregrinus,
> quem ad sua ubera foverat et sinus.   (lines 213–216)

THE public, dramatic, and eventually calamitous love affair of Abelard and Heloise must have had a powerful effect on their contemporaries.[1] In one form

---

[1] This article deals with one small issue which is part of the larger and more important question of the authenticity of the correspondence of Abelard and Heloise. Debate over this question goes back to the early 19th century and still continues. For an historiographical analysis of the literature on this subject see Peter von Moos, *Mittelalterforschung und Ideologiekritik: Der Gelehrtenstreit um Heloise* (Munich, 1974). In July 1972 at the Colloque international Pierre Abélard-Pierre le Vénérable held at Cluny, I presented a paper, "Fraud, Fiction, and Borrowing in the Correspondence of Abelard and Heloise,"*which on historical grounds questioned the authenticity of the correspondence, while at the same session Peter von Moos in "Le silence d'Héloïse et les idéologies modernes" pointed to a number of literary problems in the correspondence. In her paper for the same volume, "Peter Abelard and the Dignity of Women: Twelfth-Century 'Feminism' in Theory and Practice," Mary Martin McLaughlin has challenged some of my assumptions, and the printed volume of the *Actes* of the colloquium, published by the C.N.R.S. (Paris, 1975) contains critical comments by other scholars. I have discussed other aspects of this question in "The Paraclete and the Council of Rouen of 1231," to appear in the *Bulletin of Medieval Canon Law,*†n.s. 4 (1974) and in "The Style of the Historia Calamitatum: A Preliminary Test of the Authenticity of the Correspondence Attributed to Abelard and Heloise," (written jointly with Fiorella Prosperetti Ercoli) to appear in *Viator* 6 (1975). A recent and important publication is *Peter Abelard*, ed. Eligius M. Buytaert, Mediaevalia Lovaniensia, 1,2 (The Hague, 1974), which contains an important essay on style, "Abélard écrivain," by Louk Engels, pp. 12–37. Further discussion of the role of Heloise is also to be found in an article by Peter von Moos, "Palatini quaestio quasi peregrini: Ein gestriger Streitpunkt aus der Abaelard-Heloise-Kontroverse nochmals überprüft," *Mittellateinisches Jahrbuch* 9 (1974), 124–158. In spite of the title this article is not especially concerned with the poem which is the subject of this present study; on this point see the final note on p. 158. Whether the *Epistolae duorum amantium: Briefe Abaelards und Heloises?*, ed. Ewald Könsgen, Mittellateinische Studien und Texte, 7 (Leiden, 1974) were actually written by Abelard and Heloise early in their

* See above, chapter 22, pp. 417-53.   † See above, chapter 21, pp. 411-16.

or another, the story was known far and wide. While he was still in a position to joke about it, Abelard himself made humorous references about his "amica" in the lectures he prepared for his students.[2] After his castration he was the subject of a taunting and probably widely circulated letter by his former teacher Roscelin, as well as of a more sympathetic letter of "consolation" by his fellow monk, Fulk of Deuil.[3] At some unknown time an anonymous poet linked Abelard's castration to that of a Count Mathias, who suffered a similar fate because of a charge of adultery:

> Ornavere due te quondam, Gallia, gemme,
>   Mathias consul philosophusque Petrus,
> Militie decus hic, cleri lux extitit ille.
>   Plaga tibi gemmas abstulit una duas.
> Invida sors summis privat genitalibus ambo.
>   Dispar causa pares vulnere fecit eos.
> Consul adulterii damnatur crimine iusto;
>   Philosophus summa proditione ruit . . . .[4]

Writing in the 1150s, Otto of Freising was more discreet and did not feel it necessary to give any details when he referred in passing to an "occasio quaedam satis nota."[5] The chronicle which has commonly but incorrectly been

---

relationship — and on this question I have serious doubts — these newly edited letters do not help to establish the authenticity of the primary and long-known correspondence.

[2] In his *Dialectica*, ed. Lambert-Marie de Rijk, 2nd ed. (Assen, 1970), Abelard illustrated the desiderative mood by "Osculetur me amica" (p. 151) and explained the logic of grammar with such sentences as "Petrum diligit sua puella" and "Petrus diligit suam puellam." Significantly enough, the succeeding illustrative sentence in this section was "Si aliquis est homo, ipse est risibilis" (p. 319).

[3] Roscelin's letter is published not only in PL 178:357-372 and Victor Cousin, ed., *Petri Abaelardi Opera* (Paris, 1849-59; reprint 1970), 2:792-803, but in a better edition by Jos. Reiners, *Der Nominalismus in der Frühgeschichte*, Beiträge sur Geschihte der Philosophie und Theologie des Mittelalters 8, Heft 5 (Münster, 1910), 62-80. The unique surviving manuscript is German, Munich, Bayerische Staatsbibl. Clm 4643. For Fulk's letter one may consult PL 178:371-376 and the omitted fragment published by Damien Van den Eynde, "Détails biographiques sur Pierre Abélard," *Antonianum* 38 (1963), 219; apparently Van den Eynde did not realize that the complete text was published by Cousin, *Opera*, 1:706-707.

[4] This mysterious poem is preserved in a late 12th or early 13th-cent. copy in Orléans, Bibl. mun. MS 284 (olim 238), pp. 183-184. Charles Cuissard attempted a transcription of this miserably written text in *Documents inédits sur Abélard tirés des manuscrits de Fleury conservés à la bibliothèque publique d'Orléans* (Orléans, 1880), pp. 33-36, but was able to make out even less than I have been able to read from the photographs kindly supplied by the municipal library of Orléans. The poem needs a thorough study and a new edition. Its author had quite likely read the *Historia Calamitatum*, for he refers to Abelard's going to Paris after his mother had taken the veil (cf. the edition published by Jacques Monfrin, 3rd ed. [Paris, 1967], p. 67); it may be worth noting that he expresses greater sympathy for Heloise than for Abelard:

> Deseruisse tamen tulit hanc crudelis amicus —
> Si quis non quia amet sed ametur dicat 'amicus.' (lines 39-40)

If the unfortunate Count Mathias mentioned in the lines quoted in the text (lines 43-50) can be identified, we might have a clue as to when this poem was written.

[5] *Gesta Friderici* 1.48, ed. Georg Waitz and Bernhard von Simson, MGH SS in us. schol. (Hanover and Leipzig, 1912), p. 69.

attributed to Guillaume Godel, probably written in the 1170s, notes that after the death of Abelard he was favored by the repeated prayers of Heloise, "quae vere ipsius amica."[6] Epitaphs which were probably written not long after the death of the *magister* and the first abbess of the Paraclete preserve what Peter Dronke has called "a remarkable conception of the two lovers, of a love-union holding through life and beyond life."[7] By the early thirteenth century a pretty story had been invented that on her death-bed Heloise ordered that she be placed in the same tomb as her husband, who had died some twenty years before, and that when the tomb was opened, Abelard reached out his arms to receive his wife.[8] The absence of other evidence that Abelard and Heloise were

---

[6] This frequently quoted chronicle is printed by Dom Bouquet et al., *Recueil des historiens* 13 (1786), 675, following the text of Bibl. nat. MS lat. 4893, fol. 56v; the editors have there misread a difficult abbreviation to say that Abelard founded his abbey "epistolari auctoritate," thereby creating a problem for later translators, e.g., Charlotte Charrier, *Héloïse dans l'histoire et dans la légende* (Paris, 1933), p. 374. The text should read "episcopali auctoritate," as Robert of Saint-Marien of Auxerre gave it when he copied this passage in his chronicle; see the edition of Oswald Holder-Egger, MGH SS 26 (1882):235.

[7] Dronke, *Medieval Latin and the Rise of European Love-Lyric*, 2nd ed. (Oxford, 1968), 2:469-471. For the epitaph of Heloise it is especially important to consult this edition, for as Dronke points out in *Mittellateinisches Jahrbuch* 5 (1968), 17, a line was unfortunately lost in the first edition because of a faulty transmission through a microfilm, a matter which the author was able to correct through direct consultation of the manuscript. While I do not wish to diminish the importance of these epitaphs as evidence of attitudes towards Abelard and Heloise, Bern MS 211, which contains the epitaph of Heloise, dates from the 15th cent. Dronke commented in his first edition that the "epitaph for Héloïse is clearly by the same author as the two for Abelard or a copy (or source) of one or both of these." While the epitaph of Heloise may indeed be related to or influenced by one or both of the epitaphs of Abelard (which appear in Zürich C 58/275, which has been dated to the 12th cent.), a truly close relationship does not seem so certain after the discovery of the 5th line of the epitaph of Heloise, since the editor's first conclusion of a clear relationship was influenced by the unfortunate textual omission which led him to write, "The unusual form, seven lines in which the fourth and fifth are both pentameters, is the same as in two epitaphs for Abelard." I may add that I am not convinced by the editor's conjectured expansion in the line "V[enereum] studium coniunxit philosophie." Not only is the idea contrary to Abelard's teaching in the *Theologia Christiana* (see below, p. 213), but as Dronke notes, "My completion assumes a metrical irregularity." The first editor, Jakob Werner, prudently left the *V* unexpanded. As Berthe Marti and Daniel Sheerin have suggested to me, *verborum studium* or possibly even *vitale studium* (meaning theology) are good alternatives, and without the evidence of a text, no theories should be built on the suggestion of *venereum*. For the frequently quoted epitaph of Abelard: "Est satis in tumulo, Petrus hic jacet Abaelardus, / Cui soli patuit scibili quidquid erat," see David E. Luscombe, *The School of Peter Abelard* (Cambridge, Eng., 1969), p. 10, n. 2.

[8] *Petri Abaelardi . . . et Heloisae . . . Opera*, ed. François d'Amboise and André Duchesne (Paris, 1616), p. 1195 (cf. PL 178:176, note). The first editors took this story from a *Chronicon turonense* which was once in the Collège de Clermont at Paris and was written between 1224-27; it is now in the Deutsche Staatsbibliothek, MS Phillipps 1852 (see fols. 204v-205 for the story) and is described by Valentin Rose, *Verzeichnis der lateinischen Handschriften der kgl. Bibliothek zu Berlin, 1, Die Meerman-Handschriften des Sir Thomas Phillipps* (Berlin, 1893), pp. 329-331. Since Charlotte Charrier could not find the story in earlier manuscripts of the Chronicle of Tours (see her *Héloïse*, p. 300, n. 4), it is likely that it is a creation of the early 13th century. The identification of the source was made by Enid McLeod, *Héloïse* (London, 1938), pp. 226 and 290-291 (n. 224).

actually buried in the same tomb takes nothing away from the charm of a story which Mlle Charlotte Charrier called a "légende émouvante qui prouve, au moins, que le secret de l'amour invincible de l'abbesse avait franchi les murs du Paraclet."[9]

That Heloise loved Abelard was of course no secret, in the twelfth century or later. The matter of great interest for students of Abelard and Heloise, and for those concerned with the values and mores of the world in which they lived, is the question of *how* she loved him. She may have loved Abelard as a dutiful wife and proper abbess who prayed for her husband after his death, convinced that her prayers could be of value and sharing Abelard's belief that the Christian calling of monk or nun was higher than the sensual life of lovers, whether married or not. In the famous correspondence attributed to Abelard and Heloise, the abbess of the Paraclete is presented, however, as a sensual woman who wrote that the voluptuous delights she had shared with Abelard as a lover were so sweet to her that they remained fixed in her memory and that "obscene fantasies" held her captive during mass; in these letters she even confessed that all her life she had sought to please Abelard rather than God.[10] This same image is presented in the *Carmen ad Astralabium,* a curious collection of proverbial wisdom which Abelard supposedly wrote for his son and in which he informed the young man that Heloise had "often" told him that she preferred sexual satisfaction with Abelard to salvation:

> Imo voluptatis dulcedo tanta sit hujus
> Ne gravet ulla satisfactio propter eam.
> Est nostrae super hoc Eloysae crebra querela,
> Quae mihi quae secum dicere saepe solet:
> "Si, nisi poeniteat me commisisse priora,
> Salvari nequeam, spes mihi nulla foret.
> Dulcia sunt adeo commissi gaudia nostri
> Ut memorata juvent quae placuere nimis."[11]

The romantic image of Heloise as a sensual woman still longing for Abelard as her lover years after his castration had changed both their lives is familiar not only to scholars who have read the correspondence and the *Carmen,* but also to a much larger audience which has been influenced by novels, plays, poems, and popular histories and translations which have made use of these medieval documents.[12] Ultimately our understanding of how the historical Heloise actu-

---

[9] McLeod, *Héloïse,* p. 301.

[10] Ep. IV, ed. Muckle, *Mediaeval Studies* 15 (1953), p. 81, or ed. Monfrin, appendix to *Historia Calamitatum,* p. 123.

[11] Barthélemy Hauréau, "Le poème addressé par Abélard à son fils Astralabe," *Notices et extraits des manuscrits de la Bibl. nat.* 34, pt. 2 (1893), pp. 153–187; the lines quoted are 375–382 on p. 167. Hennig Brinkmann has made a beginning at a critical study of the poem in "Astrolabius," *Münchener Museum für Philologie des Mittelelters und der Renaissance* 5 (1932), 168–201. R. James Long presented an as yet unpublished paper on "The Concept of Love in Abelard's *Monitum ad Astralabium*" at the 8th Conference on Medieval Studies at Kalamazoo in 1973 (see *Abstracts,* no. 2, p. 87).

[12] For the popular image of Heloise one should see not only Charrier's *Héloïse* but also Durant

ally loved Abelard will depend upon whether or not we accept the authenticity of the *Historia Calamitatum* and the seven letters attributed to Abelard and Heloise which follow it in the best manuscripts, but this complex and controversial question has been discussed elsewhere and doubtless will be treated further; it is not the subject of this present article. Nor will this article discuss further the authenticity of the *Carmen ad Astralabium*, a work which still awaits a critical edition, except to say in passing that the crucial passage concerning Heloise quoted above does not appear in at least three manuscripts of the *Carmen*, so that until a thorough study of that poem has been made, the *Carmen ad Astralabium* must be considered an uncertain witness to the authenticity of the correspondence and the image of Heloise which it presents.[13] Leaving the correspondence and the *Carmen* aside, this article deals with a third text, one which on sure grounds can be considered contemporary with Abelard, the *Metamorphosis Goliae*, which must hold our attention because one quatrain, quoted at the beginning of this article, has been called by Father J.T. Muckle, the learned editor of the controversial correspondence, "the earliest Latin document apart from the text itself [that is, the correspondence] which portrays Heloise yearning for Abelard."[14]

When Thomas Wright published the *editio princeps* of the *Metamorphosis* in 1841, he identified the Palatinus of the stanza printed above as Abelard.[15] As we shall see, this identification fits both the poem and what we know about Abelard. Four years later, in one of the most influential books ever written about Abelard, Charles de Rémusat brought Heloise into the picture when he asserted that by *nupta* the author of the poem meant Heloise: "C'est par ce quatrain et sans autre explication qu'il indique Héloïse, que l'on reconnaissait alors à ce nom *nupta, l'abbesse mariée.*"[16] Since that time, a series of skilled

---

W. Robertson, Jr., *Abelard and Heloise* (New York, 1972). The most recently published translation of the correspondence is by Betty Radice, *The Letters of Abelard and Heloise*, Penguin Classics (Harmondsworth, 1974).

[13] The crucial lines about Heloise printed above do not appear in the edition printed by Thomas Wright and James O. Halliwell in *Reliquiae Antiquae*, 1 (London, 1845), 15–21, based on Brit. Mus., Burney MS 216, fol. 100v ff. and Cotton Vitellus C VIII, fol. 18 ff. Only the last two of the lines quoted appear in the edition of Rodolphe Dareste, "Vers d'Abailard à son fils Astralabe, *Bibliothèque de l'Ecole des chartes* 7 (1845–46), 406–421; the lines in question are 235–236 on p. 414. Dr. Mary McLaughlin has informed me that Mrs. J. M. A. Rubingh-Bossche has begun work on a new critical edition of the *Carmen* from which we may hope to have an answer to the question of whether this strange passage concerning Heloise was added to the earliest version of the *Carmen*, or on the other hand, was perhaps suppressed.

[14] "The Personal Letters between Abelard and Heloise," *Mediaeval Studies* 15 (1953), 49.

[15] *The Latin Poems Commonly Attributed to Walter Mapes*, Camden Society (London, 1841), pp. 21–30, and esp. p. 29, note to line 213. Wright knew only Harley MS 978 (XIII s.) which is the better of the two surviving texts, but unfortunately he made so many errors of transcription that his edition is not satisfactory even for the English MS, and a number of false readings thoroughly obscured the text. R.B.C. Huygens, "Mitteilungen aus Handschriften: III. Die Metamorphose des Golias," *Studi medievali*, 3rd ser., 3 (1962), 764–772, has prepared a careful new edition from the Harley MS and Saint-Omer, Bibl. mun. MS 710 (XIV s.) which is now the only text worth citing. It is a pleasure to have this opportunity to record my gratitude to Professor Huygens for his many kindnesses.

[16] *Abélard*, 1st ed. (Paris, 1845), 1:168.

medievalists — Haureau, Brinkmann, Charrier, Raby, Muckle, and Häring — has accepted this identification, thereby demonstrating the strength of the romantic image of Heloise and the danger of analysing one stanza of a poem without reference to the larger context.[17] Only one critic, Winthrop Wetherbee, has had sufficient understanding of the background of the poem to explain who the *nupta* really is. His innovative exposition of the poem places it in the context of Chartrian humanism and shows its deep dependence on *De nuptiis Philologiae et Mercurii* of Martianus Capella.[18]

Wetherbee's fresh treatment is a needed corrective, for the *Metamorphosis Goliae* suffered badly from its early commentators. Wright considered it "in some parts rather obscure," and Brinkmann, who also failed to understand the poem, charged that it did not hang together and noted that "ein grosses Kunstwerk kann ich in der Metamorphosis nicht bewundern."[19] Nevertheless, the poem is really a thoughtfully organized and effective composition, a Chartrian fable in Goliardic meter, in which the mythological setting is used to make a topical point of meaning to academic readers at the time of composition in the 1140s. Wetherbee's discussion dispenses with the need to summarize the mythological portions of the poem, but since his conclusions differ somewhat from my own and his interest in the work is more literary than historical, it may be useful to consider the poem one more time.

Harley MS 978 is an English collection of verse in which the "Metamorphosis Golye episcopi," as it is called in the incipit, appears along with the *Apocalypsis Goliae*, the *Confessio Goliae,* and other poems associated with the legendary Bishop Golias.[20] The *Apocalypse of Golias* is well named, for that poem is a

---

[17] Hauréau, "Mémoire sur quelques maîtres du XIIe siècle," *Mémoires de l'Académie des Inscriptions* 28, pt. 2, (1876), 224; Brinkmann, "Die Metamorphosis Goliae und das Streitgedicht Phyllis und Flora," *Zeitschrift für deutsches Altertum und deutsche Literatur* 62 (1925), 27–36, esp. p. 32; Charrier, *Héloïse,* pp. 376–377; F. J. E. Raby, *A History of Secular Latin Poetry in the Middle Ages,* 2nd ed. (Oxford, 1957), 2:219–221; Muckle, as above, n. 14. Max Manitius, *Geschichte der lateinischen Literatur des Mittelalters* (Munich, 1911–31), 3:269–270 discusses the poem without commenting on the *nupta* at all. In the introduction to her translation of *The Letters of Abelard and Heloise,* p. 46, Betty Radice says that "Walter Map . . . is generally credited with a touching quatrain on the young bride's dismay when her husband leaves her for the monastery." The most recent work to cite the *nupta* as "Héloise in search of Abelard" is Nikolaus Häring, "Chartres and Paris Revisited," in *Essays in Honor of Anton Charles Pegis,* ed. J. Reginald O'Donnell (Toronto, 1974), p. 323. Although Fr. Häring and I differ in our interpretation of the *Metamorphosis Goliae,* I consider his learned article a major contribution to the study of the twelfth-century masters of Paris and Chartres; the reader will find in it references to all the scholars discussed in the present essay.

[18] Winthrop Wetherbee, *Platonism and Poetry in the Twelfth Century: The Literary Influence of the School of Chartres* (Princeton, 1972), pp. 127–134. In "Philologia et son mariage avec Mercure jusqu'à la fin du XIIe siècle," *Latomus* 16 (1957), 105, Gabriel Nuchelmans notes that in the *Metamorphosis* "Philologia y est désignée sous le nom de *nupta,*" but he does not make clear whether this comment applies to lines 213–216 as well as to the earlier appearance of the *nupta.*

[19] Wright, *Latin Poems,* p. 21; Brinkmann, "Metamorphosis Goliae," p. 28.

[20] Wright printed many of these texts for the first time in his *Latin Poems.* For the *Confessio* see *Die Gedichte des Archipoeta,* ed. Max Manitius, 2nd ed. (Munich, 1929), pp. 23–28, and also George F. Whicher, *The Goliard Poets* (Cambridge, Mass., 1949), pp. 106–119. The *Apocalypse* has

parody of the Apocalypse of St. John. It is possible, however, that the thirteenth-century scribe of the Harley manuscript was one of the first readers who misunderstood the literary background of the poem he called a "Metamorphosis," for it bears little relationship to the *Metamorphoses* of Ovid.[21] Instead, its model is Martianus Capella's fifth-century handbook of the liberal arts, which as almost every twelfth-century schoolboy knew, begins with a poetic flight of fancy on the marriage of the learned and beautiful Philology, a personification of wisdom, to Mercury, the divinity of eloquence.[22] So much of the thought, imagery, and even actual phraseology of the *Metamorphosis Goliae* was taken over from the work of Martianus that the later poem might more accurately have been called *De nuptiis Goliae* or *De nuptiis redivivis*.

The *Metamorphosis Goliae*, to hold to the one medieval title we have, begins with a springtime dream in which the author enters a wood which resounds with harmonious music. This wood in the twelfth-century poem is described in terms which would remind a knowing reader of the grove of Apollo in *De nuptiis* 1.11, for such phrases as "nam eminentiora prolixarum arborum culmina perindeque distenta acuto sonitu resultabant" and "gravitas rauca quatiebat" (ed. Dick, p. 11) are transformed into "Set in parte nemoris eminentiore / resonabat sonitu vox acutiore" (lines 25–26) and "gravitas rauca crepitabat" (line 11). Presumably the author of the *Metamorphosis* had studied *De nuptiis* from a glossed version, for his explanation that "illa diversitas consonantiarum / prefigurat ordinem septem planetarum" (lines 31–32) appears to be an echo of a gloss like that of John the Scot: "SUPERUM CARMEN hoc est divinam melodiam ad similitudinem videlicet caelestis armoniae."[23]

It would be tiresome to indicate all the images and phrases which the twelfth-century author took from *De nuptiis;* a reader who cares to compare the *Metamorphosis* with Martianus's first two books can easily find over two dozen instances where the fifth-century author has influenced his successor.[24] Instead, a simple summary of the *Metamorphosis* can take account

---

been edited by Karl Strecker, *Die Apokalypse des Golias* (Rome-Leipzig, 1928); there is an excellent translation by Francis X. Newman in *The Literature of Medieval England*, ed. D. W. Robertson, Jr. (New York, 1970), pp. 253–261.

[21] There is no title at all in the Saint-Omer MS. Karl Strecker, "Kritisches zu mittellateinischen Texten," *Zeitschrift für deutsches Altertum* 63 (1926), 113, notes that lines 37 ff. and 47 show the influence of the *Metamorphoses*, though his major point is the dependence of the poem on Martianus.

[22] In this paper all quotations from Martianus are from the Teubner text, ed. Adolf Dick (Leipzig, 1925; reprinted with additions and corrections by Jean Préaux in 1969). The introductory volume to an English translation by William H. Stahl and Richard Johnson in the Columbia Records of Civilization series has been published as *Martianus Capella and the Seven Liberal Arts* (New York, 1971). See also Stahl, "To a Better Understanding of Martianus Capella," *Speculum* 40 (1965), 102–115. There is a good summary of *De nuptis* by Wetherbee in *Platonism and Poetry*, pp. 83–91.

[23] *Iohannis Scotti Annotationes in Marcianum*, ed. Cora E. Lutz (Cambridge, Mass., 1939), p. 19.

[24] Strecker, "Kritisches zu mittellateinischen Texten," pp. 111–115, notes most but not all of these passages.

of the most important resemblances as well as some rearranging which has taken place. In the wood the dreamer comes upon the palace of Jove (which Martianus had placed in the heavens). It had been built and decorated by Vulcan and here symbolizes the universe of both ideal forms and their actuality: "Ista domus locus est universitatis, / res et rerum continens formas cum formatis" (lines 49–50). Here he finds the king (Jove) and queen (Juno), as well as Pallas and Mercury (called Cyllenius in the *Metamorphosis*, as he usually is in *De nuptiis*); the meaning of these figures is explained in a glossing fashion, and we are specifically told that Mercury stands for eloquence. Only at line 80 do we at last meet Philology, who is never named but is introduced only as the *nupta* and is presented as a figure of wisdom: "Nupta sibi comes est de stirpe divina" (line 85). As in *De nuptiis*, Phronesis presents her daughter with a bridal wreath, and the poet refers to the urns of the four Seasons, described at much greater length by Martianus, as well as to the nine Muses, the gifts of Psyche, and the three Graces.

Slightly over half-way through the poem there is a burst of noise and Silenus leads in a line of satyrs, thus introducing a large party under the domination of Venus. This interjection is a reminder of the opening of Book Eight of *De nuptiis*, where Silenus disrupts the wedding party with an immense belch, and also serves to introduce Venus, Cupid, and a group of gods into the poem. The poet comments on the unending conflict of Pallas and Venus, which is still undécided and is here continued by their supporters: "an plus valeat Pallas Afrodite / adhuc est sub pendulo, adhuc est sub lite" (lines 159–160), and goes on to name four instances of the loves of the gods. Then we are told of the presence of a group of philosophers and of the major Roman love poets, each accompanied by his lover. We should not be surprised by the presence of these humans at the marriage party, for Martianus had also introduced the major philosophers (shown disputing in 2.213) and Linus, Homer, and Virgil (2.212).

Martianus's reference to philosophers and poets provided the author of the *Metamorphosis* with the basis of the most interesting and most original part of his poem, for he included a list of scholars of his own day, most of whom can be easily recognized. There are some problems, however, and the dating of the poem itself depends upon the identification of one man whose office is given rather than his name:

> Et hic presul presulum stat Pictaviensis,
> prius et nubentium miles et castrensis.   (lines 191–192)

One bishop of Poitiers stands out as an intellectual giant among twelfth-century scholars: Gilbert de la Porrée, who was bishop of Poitiers from 1142 till his death in 1154. Hauréau argued for this identification, interpreting line 192 as "il était né chevalier et seigneur châtelain."[25] In an influential

---

[25] Hauréau, "Mémoire sur quelques maîtres," pp. 227–228. H.C. Van Elswijk, *Gilbert Porreta: Sa vie, son oeuvre, sa pensée,* Spicilegium sacrum Lovaniense, études et documents 33 (Louvain, 1966), pp. 13–14, rejects this interpretation and introduces Bernhard Geyer's proposed emen-

article Brinkmann maintained, however, that the reference to *nubentes* indicated that the bishop was someone who resisted the reforming decrees of Gregory VII and supported the married clergy.[26] These comments show how badly both authors misunderstood the poem, for in a work about the marriage of Mercury and Philology, the present participle *nubentes* must surely refer to that married couple. In my opinion, line 192 means that before he became bishop the man in question was a champion of Mercury and Philology, or more generally, of eloquence and wisdom. This delicate compliment aptly fits Gilbert de la Porrée, who was a teacher at Chartres and Paris before he became a bishop, and it permits the poem to be dated to the period following his election in 1142.

Considering the period shortly after Gilbert left Paris to become bishop of Poitiers, it is not hard to recognize most of the other scholars. "Doctor ille Carnotensis" is almost certainly Thierry of Chartres, who was archdeacon of Dreux and chancellor at Chartres.[27] In linking Thierry and Gilbert in the

---

dation of *studentium* for *nubentium;* cf. Geyer, *Die patristische und Scholastische Philosophie* (Berlin, 1928), p. 239. The interpretation of the *Metamorphosis* offered in this article should, if accepted, eliminate this passage from the discussion of whether Gilbert was of noble birth.

[26] "Metamorphosis Goliae," pp. 31-32.

[27] The degree to which Thierry should be associated with Chartres rather than Paris is uncertain. Peter Dronke, *Fabula: Explorations into the uses of myth in medieval Platonism* (Leiden, 1974), p. 58, n. 4, notes the following important comment: "Moreover, as Edouard Jeauneau recently remarked to the present writer, we have no evidence that Thierry ever taught at Paris (an assumption which Southern regarded as proven)." R. W. Southern, *Medieval Humanism* (New York and Oxford, 1970), pp. 69-70, on the other hand, suggests that Thierry may not have taught at Chartres after he became chancellor, an event which he places in 1141, and adds firmly, "The only place where he is *known* to have taught is Paris, and it was certainly there that he spent the main part of his teaching life." When such eminent scholars as these disagree over a question of fact, one must search for the source of the statement that Thierry taught at Paris up to 1141 and became chancellor thereafter. As far as I can tell, the source followed trustingly by Professor Southern is Abbé Alexandre Clerval, *Les écoles de Chartres au moyen-âge* (Paris, 1895, repr. 1965), p. 171, which says of Thierry, "L'auteur de la *Metamorphosis Goliae* le voyait encore en 1041 [sic, obviously an error for 1141], parmi les maîtres fameux de Paris . . . Il revint à Chartres pour y être chancelier, peu après le départ de Gilbert [de la Porrée], sans doute en 1141. . . ." At this point Clerval's only apparent evidence is the *Metamorphosis Goliae,* which he dated as a product of 1141; taking *ibi* in the poem as Paris rather than as the scene of the celestial marriage, he placed Thierry in Paris in that year. The reading of the poem offered here gives us no evidence that Thierry taught at Paris and leaves the date of his chancellorship uncertain. Although Southern's study was published in 1970, it was prepared some years before and takes no account of Edouard Jeauneau, "Note sur l'Ecole de Chartres," *Studi medievali,* 3rd ser. 5 (1964), 821-865. Professor Southern's lively article has stirred up further investigation of scholars active in northern France, including important articles by Peter Dronke, "New Approaches to the School of Chartres," *Anuario de estudios medievales* 6 (1969) [publ. 1971], 117-140, and Nikolaus Häring, "Paris and Chartres Revisited," (see above, n. 17), pp. 268-329. On the particular point of whether Thierry taught at Paris, Fr. Häring supports Southern's position by noting that Clarembald of Arras studied under both Hugh of St. Victor and Thierry and concluding that this work was probably done "at the same time and in the same city," though Clarembald does not say so specifically. Even more telling is the account Fr. Häring cites (p. 283) of Adalbert II of Mainz studying under Thierry at Paris in the early 1130s. The author also concludes (pp. 286-287) that others probably studied with Thierry at Paris "as early as the

first stanza devoted to the modern masters, the poet thereby cited two of the leading scholars of his day at Paris and Chartres. Insofar as the rest of the men can be identified, they all appear to have been members of the Parisian teaching corps in the 1140s. These teachers are known from the reports of John of Salisbury, who was studying at Paris under Gilbert de la Porrée at the time when his master left to become bishop of Poitiers, and William of Tyre, who arrived in France as an adolescent student about 1145.[28] Both John of Salisbury and William of Tyre studied under the Englishman Adam du Petit Pont and Peter Helias, who like Gilbert de la Porrée came from Poitiers. It is interesting that the grammarian Peter Helias here receives the poet's praise, while the dialectician Adam is presented as a disputatious orator who considered his own ideas self-evident:

> disputabat digitis directis in iota
> et quecumque dixerat erant per se nota.[29]   (lines 195–96)

Like Martianus, the later poet shows his philosophers disputing, and presence in his poem is not evidence that the author favored all the men included.

When we come to Peter Lombard, there is a bit of a chronological problem, for if the poem is to be placed as early as 1142, this is the earliest known reference to the Lombard as teaching at Paris; he must, in fact, have achieved a distinguished reputation by the time of writing to merit the epithet of "celeber theologus" (line 197). Nevertheless, it is clear that Peter Lombard was a subdeacon and canon of Notre-Dame of Paris at the end of the decade, and he may well have been as early as 1142; if Gerhoch von Reichersberg's denunciation in his *Libellus de ordine donorum Sancti Spiritus* is not a later addition, the reference to Peter Lombard in that work shows that he already had some celebrity in 1142.[30] In the *Metamorphosis* Peter Lombard

---

late twenties." Like Gilbert de la Porrée, Thierry may well have taught at both Paris and Chartres. I cannot agree with Fr. Häring (p. 285) that the *Metamorphosis Goliae* shows that Thierry was at Paris at the time of composition, since *ibi* refers to the dream-world setting of the poem and Gilbert de la Porrée (who was then at Poitiers) appears in the same stanza.

[28] John of Salisbury's comments on his masters in his *Metalogicon* 2.10, ed. Clemens C. I. Webb (Oxford, 1929), pp. 77–83, are discussed with reference to the *Metamorphosis* by Reginald L. Poole, "The Masters of the Schools of Paris and Chartres in John of Salisbury's Time," *English Historical Review* 35 (1920), 321–42, reprinted in his *Studies in Chronology and History* (Oxford, 1934), pp. 223–247. The long-lost chapter from his *Historia* in which William of Tyre comments on his teachers has been recovered and learnedly annotated by R. B. C. Huygens, "Guillaume de Tyr étudiant: Un chapitre (XIX, 12) de son 'Histoire' retrouvé," *Latomus* 21 (1962), 811–829. This text provides valuable new information on the masters named in the *Metamorphosis*.

[29] For recent work on Petrus Helias see two important articles by Karin M. Fredborg, "The Dependence of Petrus Helias' *Summa super Priscianum* on William of Conches' *Glose super Priscianum*," *Cahiers de l'Institut du moyen-âge grec et latin de l'Université de Copenhague* 11 (1973), 1–57, and "Petrus Helias on Rhetoric," ibid., 13 (1974), 31–41. For references on Adam du Petit Pont, an Englishman who was probably not identical with the later bishop of St. Asaph in Wales, see Huygens, "Guillaume de Tyr étudiant," pp. 827–28.

[30] For Peter Lombard's biography see the *Prologomena* to the third edition of his *Sententiae in*

and Peter Helias are associated in a complimentary fashion with two other men, identified only as Yvo and Bernard.[31] From the discussion of William of Tyre it is now possible to identify these two masters as Bernard de Moëlan, later bishop of Cornouaille in Britanny, and the younger Ivo of Chartres, who was dean of Chartres when he died, probably in 1165 or shortly before. Clerval suggested that Bernard de Moëlan may have been identical with Bernard Sylvestris, but this conjecture has in no way been demonstrated. It is possible that in the 1140s Bernard and Ivo were both archdeacons of Paris; archdeacons with these names appear along with a subdeacon Peter (Lombard?) in a Parisian charter of 1147. Peter Helias, Bernard, and Ivo had all been students of Thierry of Chartres, and Ivo had also studied under Gilbert de la Porrée.[32] The final line of the quatrain which names them states, "et professi plurimi sunt Abaielardum" (line 200), which I take to mean "and many taught [the doctrine of] Abelard."

The next member of the group is a monk named Reginaldus, who is cited in an uncomplimentary fashion and is said to have suspended "noster Porphirius" in a noose. This is little information indeed and gives no sound basis for identifying Reginaldus as the Cornificius denounced by John of Salisbury, but if anyone named Renaud who taught in one of the monastic schools of Paris could be shown to have opposed Abelard, he would have a strong claim on a place in the poetic gathering.[33] Following him are "Robertus theologus," who may well be Robert of Melun, another Englishman, who taught on Mont-Sainte-Geneviève and developed and defended some of Abelard's ideas,[34] and Manerius, who long held a reputation as one of

---

iv libris distinctae (Grottaferrata, 1971), pp. 8*–45*; on pp. 23*–24* the editors suggest that *Petrus puer* who signed charters of the chapter of Paris in 1145–1147 may well have been Lombard. His full title of *Magister Petrus subdiaconus, Parisiensis canonicus* is given in a charter of 1150 in Robert de Lasteyrie, *Cartulaire général de Paris* (Paris, 1887), 1 (all published), 322–323. Cf. Peter Classen, *Gerhoch von Reichersberg* (Wiesbaden, 1960), p. 412.

[31] The Saint-Omer MS reads Ernaldum rather than Bernardum, but it is a distinctly inferior witness.

[32] On these masters see Huygens, "Guillaume de Tyr," pp. 822 and 825–826. The full witness list of the charter of 1147 is given in the *Prolegomena*, p. 24* from Arch. nat. LL 76, no. 15, p. 489. Archdeacon Bernard was named in charters as early as 1142 and was occasionally called *magister*; see de Lasteyrie, *Cartulaire*, pp. 278–281 and 318–319 and *Prolegomena*, p. 11*, note 2. Archdeacon Ivo appears in a charter of 1144 along with Robert Pullen; see de Lasteyrie, *Cartulaire*, pp. 292–293. The most complete study on the younger Ivo of Chartres is Beryl Smalley, "Master Ivo of Chartres," *English Historical Review* 50 (1935), 680–686. On all of these students of Thierry and Gilbert see Häring, "Paris and Chartres Revisited," *passim*.

[33] Carl Prantl, *Geschichte der Logik im Abendlände* (Leipzig, 1855–1870), 2:230–231, first suggested that Reginaldus should be identified with Cornificus. It is possible, if one steps outside the circle of Parisian masters, to see here a reference to Abbott Rainaud of Cîteaux, who arranged for the reconciliation of Abelard and St. Bernard; see *The Letters of Peter the Venerable*, ed. Giles Constable (Cambridge, Mass., 1967), ep. 98, 1:258–259. While there are enough congruences to make this idea worth noting, I am not myself convinced of it.

[34] On Robert see Raymond M. Martin, "Pro Petro Abaelardo, un plaidoyer de Robert de Melun contre S. Bernard," *Revue des sciences philosophiques et théologiques* 12 (1923), 308–333; Ulrich Horst, "Beiträge zum Einfluss Abaelards auf Robert von Melun," *Recherches de théologie*

Abelard's best students. Manerius witnessed a charter at Paris in 1154, is known to have taught there in the 1160s, and held a prebend there as late as 1174. Those dates suggest that he probably studied under Abelard during the Master's last teaching on Mont-Sainte-Geneviève before the condemnation at Sens in 1140; he may have remained at Paris as a teacher, and he eventually became a clerk of Bishop Maurice de Sully. William of Tyre heard him lecture in the 1140s or 1150s.[35] After Manerius comes a rhetorician and dialectician named Bartholomeus, who has not yet been identified with certainty.[36] The final member of the group, Robert Amiclas ("the poor man"), has been identified as Robert Pullen, who left Paris to become a cardinal in 1144, but since William of Tyre heard his lectures, he must have been a Parisian master distinct from both Robert of Melun and Robert Pullen. Perhaps he was that "magister Robertus, praepositus scolae magistri Ivonis" who sent his greetings to Peter Lombard at the end of a letter probably written in 1151.[37]

What this group has in common is not immediately obvious. Thierry of Chartres and Gilbert de la Porrée, two of the most distinguished representatives of the School of Chartres (whether that term is taken ideologically or geographically), are given pride of place among the modern masters, but a third major Chartrian, William of Conches, does not appear at all. It is not a list of the outstanding Parisian masters, living or dead, who might have

---

ancienne et médiévale 26 (1959), 314-326; and Luscombe, *School of Peter Abelard*, pp. 281-298. William of Tyre also heard his lectures; see Huygens, "Guillaume de Tyr," pp. 823 and 826.

[35] Gerald of Wales called Manerius "principalis Petri Abalardi discipulus et rhetor incomparabiliter eximius"; see Luscombe, *School of Peter Abelard*, pp. 55-56. For the charter of 1154 (a reference which I owe to Fr. Häring) see Johannes Ramackers, *Papsturkunden in Frankreich. II. Normandie*, Abhandlungen der Gesellschaft der Wissenschaften zu Göttingen, Phil.-hist. Klasse, 3rd ser., 21 (Göttingen, 1937), no. 79, pp. 163-165. Prof. John Baldwin has informed me that he has found Manerius in 13 charters between 1154 and 1174, and that in one he is designated as "de Sarceio" (Saclay, Essonne, ar. Palaiseau, c. Bièvres); cf. the cartulary of Sainte-Geneviève, Paris, Sainte-Geneviève MS 356, p. 105. On Manerius see also Huygens, "Guillaume de Tyr," pp. 823 and 826-827.

[36] Poole, "Masters of the Schools of Paris," p. 339, followed Wright in identifying this Bartholomeus as the Breton scholar who became bishop of Exeter in 1162, but I am not aware of the evidence that he was a rhetorician and dialectician, nor has it been shown that he taught at Paris. Barthélemy de Senlis, nephew of Bishop Etienne of Paris, became dean of the cathedral chapter in 1142 and bishop of Châlons in 1147. He appears in many charters in de Lasteyrie's *Cartulaire*, and was clearly an important figure in Paris at the time, but there is no evidence to show that he was a scholar. No master of this name was mentioned by either John of Salisbury or William of Tyre.

[37] Poole, "Masters," pp. 339-341, found the proper meaning of Amyclas, but was of course unaware of William of Tyre's text; see Huygens, "Guillaume de Tyr," pp. 823 and 827. Francis Courtney, *Cardinal Robert Pullen: An English Theologian of the Twelfth Century*, Analecta Gregoriana 64 (Rome, 1964), pp. 1-19, also needs to be corrected in light of this new information. The text of the letter which included Robert's greetings was printed both by B. Barth, "Ein neues Dokument zur Geschichte der frühscholastichen Christologie," *Theologische Quartalschrift* 100 (1919), 409-426, and again by Germain Morin, "Lettre inédite d'un étudiant en théologie de l'Université de Paris vers la fin du XIIe siècle," *Recherches de théologie ancienne et médiévale* 6 (1934), 412-416. I have been convinced by the identification of Peter Lombard and the date proposed by Palémon Glorieux, "Autour d'une lettre," ibid., 21 (1954), 137-144.

been remembered around 1142, for Hugh of Saint-Victor, one of the most famous teachers of his day, does not appear; perhaps this omission indicates that only living masters are named and that the poem was written after Hugh's death.[38] But what all the scholars who can be identified with certainty have in common is that they taught at Paris or Chartres early in the 1140s. Perhaps some quite subjective factor led to this choice of names; it is possible, for example, that the poet has here listed those masters whose lectures he attended over a period of years. What is clear is that the author had good things to say about two groups of people, Gilbert de la Porrée and Thierry of Chartres and his pupils (Bernard, Yvo, and Peter Helias) and those who continued the teaching of Peter Abelard (Robert of Melun, Manerius, and to some degree Peter Lombard). Too little is known of the poet's relationship to Adam du Petit Pont, who opposed Gilbert de la Porrée in 1147, to be sure why he was set aside and treated somewhat mockingly. The one thing that can be said about the scorned monk Reginaldus is that he was an opponent of "our Porphry," that is, presumably, Abelard.

This attention to those who were present at the wedding of Mercury and Philology highlights the fact that Abelard was not included, though his name was mentioned in the accusative case as the subject of the teaching of others. This omission may at first seem strange in a poem full of praise for some of his followers, but upon reflection it appears that his absence is the major point of the poem. Just when the reader wonders why Abelard is not among the wedding guests, Philology poses the same question. The quatrain at the beginning of this paper may, in the light of the whole poem, be translated literally as: "The bride seeks for her courtier (*palatinus*), whose whole spirit was divine; she wonders why he whom she had cherished at her breasts and bosom has withdrawn himself like a stranger." In these verses *Palatinus* is a skillful pun, for we know from John of Salisbury's *Metalogicon* (2.10) that it was an epithet applied to Abelard, and at the same time it indicates the philosopher's status as a member of Philology's court, placing him higher than Gilbert de la Porrée, who was only *miles et castrensis*.[39]

Abelard's absence from the wedding party is quickly explained by the poet; he has been silenced by the hooded primate of a crowd of monks, a reference which brings to mind the judgment pronounced on Abelard at the Council of Sens in 1140 under the leadership of Bernard of Clairvaux.[40] The poet then comments on this evil crowd, calling them the heirs of

---

[38] The chronicle of Richard of Poitiers links the deaths of Hugh and Peter Abelard by calling them "duo Latinorum luminaria"; see Bouquet, *Recueil des historiens*, 12:415. For Hugh's death on 11 Feb. 1141 see Roger Baron, "Notes biographiques sur Hugues de Saint-Victor," *Revue d'histoire ecclésiastique* 51 (1956), 933.

[39] According to the *Historia Calamitatum*, ed. Monfrin, p. 63, Abelard was born at Le Pallet near Nantes in Britanny. If this information is true, then Palatinus is a pun which also brings to mind Abelard's birthplace. The word had clearly developed the meaning of royal courtier by the twelfth century; see J. F. Niermeyer, *Mediae latinitatis lexicon minus* (Leiden, 1954 ff.), s. v. palatinus.

[40] On the much disputed date of the Council of Sens see Constable, *Letters of Peter the Venerable*, 2:318–320.

Pharaoh, religious on the outside but superstitious within. He is joined in this evaluation by the gods gathered at the wedding party, who conclude the poem by making a solemn judgment that the monks should be denounced and expelled from the schools.

The *Metamorphosis* was a poem with a purpose. In it a supporter of Abelard could bring all the force of an established literary tradition against the monks who had interfered in the affairs of the schools and had destroyed the career and broken the spirit of a great teacher. The choice of *De nuptiis* as a vehicle for a counter-attack on the monks was not only an artful but a defiant stroke, for some of the same men who opposed Abelard's theological positions were also critical of the use of authors like Plato, Macrobius, and Martianus, who were favored by the Chartrian school.[41] In a contest which found Abelard and members of the "School of Chartres" on one side and Bernard of Clairvaux, Guillaume de Saint-Thierry, and Hugh of Saint-Victor on the other, the author of the *Metamorphosis* suited his means to his doctrine.

In this analysis I have differed somewhat with Wetherbee, though we are in complete accord in identifying the *nupta* as Philology. For him a major theme of the poem is love. After the poet has presented in the first 34 stanzas "an ideal view of the elements of philosophical study," the scene is disrupted by Silenus, the satyrs, Venus, and Cupid, "as if to offer a reminder of the practical unattainability of such intellectual perfection." Wetherbee goes on to associate the four instances given by the poet of gods dominated by Venus with "the ambiguity with which any attempt to evolve a consistent system from the myths of the *auctores* must deal." Although modestly commenting that his ideas are offered "at the risk of overinterpretation," he suggests that "we may see in the juxtaposition of the death of Adonis with the adultery of Venus and Mars a delineation of two phases of human existence. The first, represented by the thwarted idyll of the love of Venus and Adonis seems to stand for a lost ideal, a primordially pure union sundered by violence and death. The second is love in a fallen world, and is crystallized as an archetype of human folly, first by the *vincula* of Vulcan, and now by his art." In Wetherbee's opinion, this opposition is presented as "a case to be tried." He sees the philosophers, poets, and scholars as "a host of witnesses"; at the end of this group "the poet then introduces one who is both philosopher and lover, Abelard. . . . The fate of Abelard, whose 'martyrdom' was due both to love and to his insistence on intellectual freedom, is a particularly appropriate illustration of the problem posed by the debate. . . . Venus and Pallas have been set at odds in Abelard's own life, but

---

[41] Wetherbee, *Platonism and Poetry*, pp. 67–68, refers to a traditionalist reaction to Chartrain thought which he says began about the middle of the century and was "generated largely by the Cistercians," though Hugh of Saint-Victor was included in the movement. Brian Stock, *Myth and Science in the Twelfth Century: A Study of Bernard Sylvester* (Princeton, 1972), pp. 180–182, discusses the possibility that Bernard Sylvestris's bitter description of Saturn in the *Cosmographia* 2.9 may be a veiled portrait of St. Bernard. On Abelard's relationship to the School of Chartres and the use of Platonic mythology, see Wetherbee, pp. 38–43, and Dronke, *Fabula*, pp. 55–68.

the allegory of the poem's earlier portions has offered a rich natural and humanistic context for the debate between them. . . ."[42]

This analysis is intriguing and it would be rash to deny the suggestiveness of the rich mythological detail the poet provides, and yet it seems to me that Wetherbee has seen far more in the poem than it actually says. In my opinion a simpler reading would be closer to both the text and the values Abelard himself espoused. The setting of the poem, as Wetherbee has shown, is the marriage of Mercury and Philology, that is, the joining of eloquence and wisdom which is the proper end of a liberal education. In his *Heptateuchon,* Thierry of Chartres compared the joining of the trivium and the quadrivium, which he intended to integrate in his book, to the marriage of Mercury and Philology.[43] The poetic conception of the author of the *Metamorphosis* was to show this celestial marriage as a timeless act continuing up to the present, a celebration in which modern scholars could take part alongside of the ancient poets and philosophers whose works were still honored and taught in the schools. The interruption of Silenus and his noisy band would be more likely to strike twelfth-century readers as a danger rather than an ambiguity. In his *Theologia Christiana* Abelard discoursed at length on the danger which sexuality and marriage presented for a philosopher, and praised the pagan philosophers for their continence: "Quarum impudentiae petulantiam et Socrates expertus satis est, ceteris in exemplo, quantum oporteat philosophum vitae munditiam observare, nec philosophiae, cui se copulat, alterius quasi adulterae copulam superinducere."[44] For any student of Abelard who took the *Theologica Christiana* seriously, there should have been no doubt that it was better to reject Venus and embrace Pallas, who stood, as the *Metamorphosis* explained, for "mens divinitatis" (line 73).

Is it really likely that a supporter of Abelard in the 1140s would have thought of him as both "philosopher and lover," or would have considered that he had suffered a martyrdom for love? In 1142 Abelard was over 60 years old, and his love affair with Heloise and his castration were both some 25 years in the past. The *Historia Calamitatum,* whether written by Abelard or someone else, makes clear that the brutal attack which he suffered was the result not of love, in some favorable sense of the word, but of lust. Not long after the assault Fulk of Deuil wrote to Abelard to congratulate him on a blessing in disguise which would allow him to come closer to the things of the spirit. A vicious opponent like Roscellin mocked at Abelard for his castration, while a more charitable critic like St. Bernard chose not to

---

[42] *Platonism and Poetry,* pp. 130-134. It should perhaps be noted that all four instances of gods subject to the power of Venus were mentioned at the beginning of *De nuptis.* The conflict between Venus and Pallas also appears in two poems printed by Dronke, *Medieval Latin,* 2:367-373.

[43] The most recent publication of the prologue to the *Heptateuchon* is by Jeauneau in "Note sur l'Ecole de Chartres," pp. 854-855 (cited above, n. 27).

[44] *Petri Abaelardi Opera Theologica,* ed. Eligius M. Buytaert, Corpus Christianorum, Cont. med. 11-12 (Turnholt, 1969), 2:173 (*Theol. Christ.* 2.96 = PL 178:1198).

mention the incident, but there is no evidence that any twelfth-century observer thought of Abelard as a martyr for love.[45] In contrast to his early lectures on dialectic, Abelard's later writings take a hard line against the snares of sexuality. Seen from the viewpoint of an Abelardian of the 1140s, it seems to me more likely that the *Metamorphosis* would be considered to be about education in its highest sense, to which Venus can be disruptive, rather than about the ambiguities of love. Venus and Pallas are in conflict in the poem, but that conflict is not on trial before the gods, nor are the philosophers, poets, and scholars present as witnesses at a trial. The marriage of Mercury and Philology was a wedding of eloquence and wisdom, the goal of liberal education. Poets, philosophers, and scholars, past and present, were all members of the wedding party, but as the bride noted, although Abelard should have been present, he was not there. The reason for his absence was that he had been silenced by a party of monks, and the only trial in the poem is the one in which the gods then decided that the monks should be expelled from the schools. From beginning to end the poem is focused on the proper education of a philosopher; Venus appears as one block to such an education, the monks as another.

Although Professor Wetherbee identifies the *nupta* as Philology, he notes that "one thinks inevitably also of Heloise, and the poet's deep sympathy with her complaint is clear" (p. 133). Here we have the difficult problem of discriminating between what the author put into the poem and what we as readers bring to it. Not one line in the poem refers to Heloise directly. Catullus has his Lesbia, Cicero his Terentia, and Pliny his Calpurnia, but the only female figure linked to Abelard is a bride who throughout the poem is Philology. If she reminds us of Heloise, that is a result of how we see Abelard, not how the poet presents him. After they had both entered the monastic life, Heloise knew perfectly well where Abelard was. After founding a monastery for her, he had become an abbot in Britanny and then a teacher at Paris. When no longer in residence at the Paraclete, he continued to write to Heloise and to compose hymns, sermons, exhortations, and scriptural explanations for her use, and from time to time he was a visitor at the monastery. As his sister in the Lord, Heloise was in frequent communication with Abelard, and if it were not for the correspondence attributed to them, Abelard's reputation would be that of a remarkably considerate monastic husband, granted the limitations of his situation. After 1140, following the condemnation at Sens, Abelard withdrew ("quasi peregrinus") more sharply from education at Paris than he had before from Heloise. The lines about the *nupta* fit Philology more accurately than Heloise, and it is quite likely that they apply to Philology alone. We need not conclude from the imagery of the line which says she had cherished her "Palatinus" at her breasts and bosom that a human figure must be meant. Such a conceit could easily be applied to a mythological figure; an epitaph of Thierry of Chartres

---

[45] Cf. *Historia Calamitatum*, pp. 72–74. For the letters of Fulk and Roscellin, see above, n. 3.

presents Philosophy as undressing and coupling with Thierry to produce an illustrious lineage.[46] The phrasing of the line "quem ad sua ubera foverat et sinus" can, moreover, apply as easily to a *nutrix* as a lover, so that the poet may be suggesting that Philology held the same relationship to Abelard as Philosophy did to Boethius in the *Philosophiae Consolatio* (Bk. 1, prose 2).

Probably there is no way within the terms of the poem to settle my difference with Wetherbee. When he read it, he "inevitably" saw Heloise behind the figure of Philology, while I believe the poem makes excellent sense without reference to Heloise at all. He says that "the poet's deep sympathy with her complaint is clear," while I expect that none of us would think of Heloise's "complaint" if we were not already familiar with it from the correspondence and the *Carmen* and the literature influenced by these works. It would be unrealistic to be too rigid in denying the possibility of meanings in a mythological poem in which some reference to the present is intended. Let me recommend, however, that such a doubtful interpretation should not be used to buttress the genuineness of the correspondence and the *Carmen*, and that the conclusions of de Rémusat, Charrier, and Muckle should be withdrawn. If further research demonstrates the inauthenticity of the correspondence and the *Carmen*, then it may at some later time be possible to read the *Metamorphosis* without inevitably thinking of Heloise and her complaint.

Whatever one's conclusions about the meaning of the *Metamorphosis*, a re-examination permits a new consideration of its author and date. For some time it has been the accepted theory that the author was an Englishman and probably a married clerk, or at least someone who sympathized with the married clergy.[47] Wright found the poem in an English manuscript and was unaware of a second text in a Saint-Omer manuscript; he assumed that the poet was English and suggested that scholars in the poem who were not easily identified — Reginaldus and Bartholomeus — were perhaps Englishmen. The preceding analysis indicates that the author was a supporter of Abelard for whom the schools of Paris and Chartres were sufficient to supply all the modern masters needed at a celestial wedding. The known Englishmen in the poem — Adam du Petit Pont and Robert of Melun — were only two of the many English scholars who came to Paris.[48] The only reason for thinking that the author was a married clerk was Brinkmann's interpretation of "prius et nubentium miles et castrensis," an

[46] André Vernet, "Une épitaphe inédite de Thierry de Chartres," *Recueil de travaux offerts à M. Clovis Brunel* (Paris, 1955), 2:670, lines 29–34.

[47] Hauréau, "Mémoire sur quelques maîtres," pp. 224–225, thought (wrongly) that the *Metamorphosis* gave preference to English masters and therefore concluded that the author was an Englishman. Brinkmann, "Metamorphosis Goliae," argued that the author was an English student of Manerius and a married clerk (see above, note 26). Raby, *Secular Latin Poetry*, 2:211, n. 1, repeated these suggestions, as did Manitius, *Geschichte der lateinischen Literatur*, 3:269.

[48] On the large group of Englishmen who came to Paris, see Astrik L. Gabriel, "English Masters and Students in Paris during the Twelfth Century," in *Garlandiana: Studies in the History of the Mediaeval University* (Frankfurt am Main, 1969), pp. 1–37.

interpretation which ignores the rest of the poem. The poem gives no support to sexuality or marriage, and presents Pallas in far more favorable terms than Venus.

The very large amount of topical information in the poem should make it possible to date the work rather precisely, and yet there are difficulties in the information we have. The reference to the bishop of Poitiers places the composition after Gilbert de la Porrée became bishop of Poitiers, and since his predecessor appears in a charter dated 1142 and is recorded as dying on 27 July, it seems most likely that Gilbert's election took place sometime after the end of July 1142.[49] There is, however, another limit which probably should be applied, that is, the death of Abelard, for if Abelard was dead at the time of writing, Philology might have regretted his banishment and absence, but she would have had no reason to wonder where he was.[50] The problem about this dating is that ever since d'Amboise and Duchesne published the *editio princeps* of Abelard's works in 1616, most scholars have placed the date of his death on 21 April 1142, some months before the time when Gilbert was probably elected.[51]

The day of the month of Abelard's death is securely based, among other sources, on the necrologies of the Paraclete itself and the abbeys of Saint-Denis, Lagny, and Montiéramey.[52] The year, however, is a far less certain matter. Duchesne published the statement "Anno MCXLII obijt Petrus Abaelardus Peripateticus" from an otherwise unidentified "incertus auctor, sed antiquus," and added a reference to a chronicle of Saint-Pierre-le-Vif of Sens which also gave the date as 1142.[53] There are other chronicles which also give the date as 1142, or say that Abelard died in the year after Hugh of Saint-Victor,[54] but there are three important and independent sources which

---

[49] Poole, "Masters of the Schools," p. 333, discusses this question of dating. The same evidence is noted by Van Elswijk, *Gilbert Porreta*, p. 28, who thinks 1141 is also a possible date for Gilbert's election. It is clear that more evidence needs to be sought.

[50] The phrase "Nupta querit ubi sit suus Palatinus" may bring to mind the theme of "ubi sunt qui ante nos fuerunt" and so suggest that Philology is lamenting Abelard's death rather than questioning his banishment from the schools of Paris. The line which states that the leader of the monks "imponi silencium fecit tanto vati" (line 220) leads me to believe that the main issue of conflict in the poem, the one which brings the poem to a conclusion with the celestial judgment that the crowd of monks "a philosophicis scolis expellatur" (line 236), was the silencing of Abelard at the instigation of St. Bernard. After Bernard and Abelard had been reconciled and Abelard had died (as a monk of Cluny) this conflict would have lost a good deal of its force.

[51] Hauréau, "Mémoire sur quelques maîtres," placed the composition before the death of Abelard (p. 224) and after the election of Gilbert (p. 227) without noting any chronological problem. Wetherbee, *Platonism and Poetry*, p. 9, says the *Metamorphosis* was "written shortly after the death of Abelard."

[52] *Obituaires de la Province de Sens: Diocèses de Sens et de Paris*, ed. Auguste Molinier (Paris, 1902), 1:315, 387; and *Diocèses de Meaux et de Troyes* (Paris, 1923), pp. 323 B, 393 A, and 412 F.

[53] The supplementary documents are printed in the unpaginated introduction to the version of *Petri Abaelardi . . . et Heloisae . . . Opera* (Paris, 1616) which bears Duchesne's name on the title page but not in the d'Amboise version. References to the chronicles of the archbishops of Sens and of Saint-Pierre-le-Vif which do appear in the d'Amboise text are reprinted in PL 178:93.

[54] *Recueil des historiens*, 12:120 BC, 284 A, and 415 CD; 13:675 D.

state that the year was 1143. One of these is a chronicle from Britanny, the second is the annals of Lagny (which were apparently written year by year), and the third is a late manuscript from the Paraclete.[55] This is not the place to attempt a full evaluation of these sources, and all that need be said here is that though Abelard may have died in the spring of 1142, there is a good chance that he died on 21 April 1143. If so, the *Metamorphosis Goliae* could have been written in late 1142 or early 1143 after the election of Gilbert and before the death of Abelard. Such a dating would make the composition contemporary with Berengar's defense of Abelard and mocking attack on Bernard, written after the Council of Sens and probably before Abelard's death.[56]

The investigation which lies behind this article began as a search for twelfth-century material which would show whether the image of Heloise presented in the correspondence and the *Carmen ad Astralabium* accords with other contemporary evidence. Pope Adrian IV, Peter the Venerable, and that curious correspondent, Hugh Metel, were prepared to write in glowing terms about her character.[57] If the famous love-letters of Heloise to Abelard and the *Carmen* are genuine, we know something about her innermost thoughts which was hidden from the world of her day. The *Metamorphosis Goliae* tells us something of Abelard's reputation in the schools of Paris, but it provides us with no information at all about Heloise. Whatever we conclude about Heloise and her longing for Abelard will have to be based on other evidence.[58]

---

[55] Ibid., 12:564 A; *Obituaires du diocèse de Paris*, p. 387 (cf. *Bibliothèque de l'Ecole des chartes* 38 [1877], 477–482); *Obituaires du diocèse de Troyes*, p. 412, n. 4.

[56] Luscombe, *School of Peter Abelard*, p. 32.

[57] In a bull of 13 February 1156 Adrian IV wrote to Heloise of "bonae vestrae conversationis odor." The bull, now preserved in the municipal archives of Metz, II, 164, piece 9, has most recently been printed from the original by Henri Tribout de Morembert, "Quatre bulles pour l'abbaye du Paraclet," *Annuaire de la Société d'Histoire et d'Archéologie de la Lorraine* 69 (1969), 104. For monastic letters to Heloise see *Letters of Peter the Venerable*, ep. 115, ed. Constable, 2:303–308, and Charles-Louis Hugo, *Sacrae antiquitatis monumenta historica, dogmatica, diplomatica* (Etival, and Saint-Dié, 1725–1731), 2:348–349; cf. Charrier, *Héloïse*, pp. 281–285, and McLeod, *Héloïse*, pp. 124–127. St. Bernard, ep. 278, recommended a request of Heloise to Eugenius III in the most guarded terms. Fr. Muckle discussed this question of Heloise's reputation with her contemporaries in "Personal Letters," pp. 60–66.

[58] This article has benefited from the comments of a number of readers of earlier drafts, many of whom have been both helpful and unconvinced by my arguments about the authenticity of the correspondence of Abelard and Heloise. Among others I would like to thank Professors John Baldwin, Peter Dronke, Nikolas Häring, R.B.C. Huygens, Berthe M. Marti, and the anonymous referees of *Speculum*. I should also acknowledge with thanks the financial assistance of the California Institute of Technology and the time for research provided by a Continental Oil Faculty Fellowship.

24

A Reconsideration of the Authenticity of the Correspondence of Abelard and Heloise

Three major theories about the nature of the famous eight letters of Abelard and Heloise preserved in Troyes ms. 802 remain in one form or another in the public eye*. The first, that of 'historical authenticity,' is that Abelard wrote the *Historia calamitatum*, that there was an actual exchange of letters between Heloise and Abelard, that each party wrote the letters which bear their names, and that the letters expose the state of mind of their authors, though the texts may have been somewhat edited when they were brought together, perhaps by Heloise. This view was most eloquently expressed by the late and regretted Etienne Gilson, and it is, I believe, the position held by most scholars who cite the letters and do not comment further on the question of authenticity. The second view, first presented with detailed arguments by Bernhard Schmeidler in 1913, is that the letters are a 'literary fiction' written by Abelard, that is to say, Abelard was the author of the letters attributed to Heloise, though he may have based his 'fictional' correspondence on some actual, historical exchange of letters. Schmeidler's position was supported in the 1930s by Charlotte Charrier, who seemed to think, if I may put it bluntly, that anything she liked in the letters attributed to Heloise was probably authentic and anything she did not like was a self-serving interpolation by Abelard. In 1972 the theory of literary fiction was put forward again by D. W. Robertson, Jr., who stressed ironic and moralizing elements in Abelard's presentation of himself. Since no one has suggested that the whole correspondence is a literary fiction created by Heloise, the third, remaining theory has been that the letters were composed by some 'third party,' who may or may not have made use of authentic material. Orelli thought that the letters were composed by a friendly monk shortly after the death of Abelard; Petrella argued that they were the product of the school of Orléans later in the twelfth century; and in 1972 at Cluny I suggested that a falsifying anti-feminist at the Paraclete in the thirteenth century might have concocted the correspondence from both authentic and inauthentic materials in an attempt to change the traditional administrative structure of the abbey.

* Unfortunately events largely outside my control have prevented me from completing the annotation and turning a paper prepared for conference delivery into a form appropriate for publication. I have therefore presumed upon both the goodwill and the knowledge of the readers of this volume and have included only the most basic references, reproducing in a slightly edited form the bare text distributed to the participants at the colloquium at Trier. Those friends and colleagues who provided advice and criticism during the preparation of this paper are thanked either in the text itself or *in petto*, no reference is made to suggestions communicated to me during or after the conference, and if a more fully developed exposition of my argument appears to be needed, it will have to be presented elsewhere in the future. It remains, however, for me to thank Pastor Rudolf Thomas and the other organizers of the *Studientage* for their hospitality, generosity and support.

The complex hypothesis I presented at Cluny in 1972 was the best explanation I could then find to account for differences between the prescriptions of Abelard's Rule and documented practices at the Paraclete, as well as certain difficult passages in the text. I wish I could say now either that significant new evidence supported that hypothesis and raised it to a higher level of certainty, or that on the other hand it had been refuted so thoroughly that it could now be safely ignored. Unfortunately, it does not yet seem to me possible to declare with confidence either that the correspondence is a blatant fraud or that it is unquestionably authentic. In certain significant respects, largely because of the work of Fr. Chrysogonus Waddell which, with his permission, I will present to the public for the first time in this paper, my hypothesis of 1972 now seems to me weaker than it did seven years ago. On the other hand, we still do not have a determinative stylistic analysis of the text and a few of my earlier points remain unrefuted, so that at present it now seems prudent to maintain some doubts about authenticity. In this paper I shall try to present an assessment of the current situation, hoping that further research will resolve our problems before another seven years have passed.

Before discussing matters of detail, it may be useful to distinguish between two different types of forgeries or fraudulent compositions produced in the twelfth and thirteenth centuries. The first class may be labelled 'literary fictions,' including fictitious dictamenal letters attributed to historical figures or such independent treatises as the pseudo-Boethian *De disciplina scolarium*. If the fabricator of a fictitious letter wrote at approximately the same time as the supposed author, there is naturally no reason for anachronism to betray his work, but the author of *De disciplina scolarium* wrote casually of a master of the school of Mont-Sainte-Geneviève and used thirteenth-century terms like *intitulari* without leading any of his medieval readers to charge fraud by reason of anachronism. When we are dealing with literary texts, it is reasonable to state that the concept of anachronism was a discovery of the Renaissance. Medieval critics could be conscious of style in commenting on authenticity – Bovo II of Corbie referred to style in attributing the theological tractates to Boethius – but it is hard to find clear evidence of individualized style in the work of medieval secretaries; Nicholas of Clairvaux learned to imitate the style of St. Bernard very well, but he used many of the same forms and phrases in letters which he wrote in the *persona* of other members of the community at Clairvaux. In short, it is reasonable to imagine a twelfth-century forger imitating the more obvious elements of Abelard's style with some chance of success, but to suppose that a thirteenth-century forger would either attempt to avoid anachronism or could do so successfully in writing a long literary work is a thought which is in itself anachronistic.

The authors of another class of forgeries or frauds did often avoid glaring evidence of anachronism, however. I refer to forged legal documents or works intended to support specific privileges or rights of priority, charters in most cases or accounts of the discovery or translation of relics or of the foundation of religious houses. Here the method by which the forger covered his tracks, if it was at all successful, was to use an authentic document as far as possible or to borrow or build on a genuine historical account, adding only a limited amount of spurious material to suit the fabricator's needs. Such forgeries are commonly suspected when a document supports contested or unusual rights, and they are normally detected by the presence of anachronistic elements, such as a witness who was not alive at the time of the event reported or a technical term or reference to an institution not yet attested by other, authentic documents. When properly identified, such altered documents are labeled forgeries, but if used cautiously the authentic matrix in which the alterations or interpolations are embedded can still have value as historical evidence. Following these distinctions, if the correspondence attributed to Abelard and Heloise contains at most only a few anachronisms, errors, or passages which diverge from the normal style of the supposed authors, it may be safe to consider major portions of the work authentic, though great care must be taken to determine if any given passage is genuine or interpolated. On the other hand, if major portions of the correspondence can be shown to be marred by errors or anachronism, or if substantial units of the text attributed to Abelard do not accord with his known style, then we should treat apparently authentic passages as interpolations in a composition which is fundamentally fraudulent. Let us therefore review the number, nature and magnitude of the passages which have suggested falsification.

In 1972 I called attention to two passages in the *Historia calamitatum* which seemed to me anachronistic and which suggested thirteenth-century fabrication. The first was the issue of the condemnation of Abelard's book at Soissons, which led George Cardinal Flahiff to write. 'I have met with no text in the twelfth century, other than the one in Abelard, to even suggest a compulsory preventive censorship[1].' This passage raises difficulties of interpretation, but it is not necessarily anachronistic. If the procedure followed at Soissons is unattested elsewhere in the twelfth century, it may have been cited for the very purpose of showing that Abelard's judges behaved with outrageous disregard for law and custom. On the other hand, the issue may not be 'precensorship' at all, but Abelard's presumption in lecturing on his own *De Trinitate et Unitate*, rather than Scripture or some other *auctoritas*. In normal twelfth-century practice Abelard's book should have been treated as an aid to study rather than the subject of a *lectio*; Peter Lombard's *Sentences* did not become the subject of formal lectures at Paris until the 1220s.

One instance of apparent anachronism discussed at Cluny has, however, remained unchallenged. I refer to the passage where a quotation from Deuteronomy is cited not as ch. CVII, as it should have been according to the chapter system in use in the time of Abelard, but as ch. XXI, strikingly close to the ch. XXIII which would be the correct number in the thirteenth-century Bible of Stephen Langton. This passage gives us strong reason to think that a thirteenth-century scribe or author made at least one change in the material he had at hand, and if he made one, can we be sure that he did not make more? There is, of course, no question that our oldest manuscripts of the correspondence were written no earlier than the later part of the thirteenth century, and it has recently been shown that the compilation represented by Troyes ms. 802 must have been brought together after 1231, the date of a council of Rouen whose canons are adapted in the collection, and probably after 1249, when the sister of Archbishop Eudes Rigaud became abbess at the Paraclete. At the very least it does seem possible that a thirteenth-century editor reworked the text of the correspondence. In 1972 I argued that much (though not necessarily all) of Ep. VIII was composed by Abelard. But this very long letter, or indeed treatise, may have been shortened by a *remanieur*, for Fr. Chrysogonus has perceptively suggested that the so-called letter *De studio litterarum* (Ep. IX), which does not appear in Troyes ms. 802 and was separately edited by D'Amboise and Duchesne, would fit very well as a termination of Ep. VIII.

Whether or not the text of the correspondence was reworked to some degree in the thirteenth century, practically all readers agree that the bulk of the work was written in

---

[1] George B. Flahiff, 'The Censorship of Books in the Twelfth Century,' *Mediaeval Studies* 4 (1942), 4, note 18, and *Pierre Abélard – Pierre le Vénérable*, p. 484, note 37.

the twelfth century. By whom? The documentation is too sparse to reveal much of the style of Heloise, but in recent years renewed attention has been paid to Abelard's style, notably by Professor Louk Engels, and we shall learn more at this conference. To the best of my knowledge, however, not enough is yet known about Abelard's style for one to declare with statistical certainty that he wrote the letters attributed to him in the correspondence. As long ago as 1914 Bernhard Schmeidler called for a serious critical analysis of Abelard's style, but the full, computer-assisted study which M. Jacques Monfrin advocated at Cluny in 1972 has still not been undertaken. A number of words or phrases have been used in an impressionistic fashion as markers of Abelard's authorship of the correspondence, but the first controlled statistical investigation was that of which Dr. Fiorella Prosperetti and I published the results in 1975. Since we had no machine-readable text of Abelard, we limited our study to nine words and constructions in an attempt to see if a computerized study of the authenticity of the *Historia calamitatum* and the rest of the correspondence would be worth the cost and effort. The word *saltem* appeared too seldom to have statistical significance, *quasi* proved to be too much affected by its context to be a useful marker of individual style, and we did not make sufficient comparison of Abelard's use of *ut* plus the subjunctive with the practices of other authors to be sure that the construction is a good indicator of authorship. The frequency of use of the other six words in the *Historia calamitatum* is so great, however, that all six have statistical significance as indicating that Abelard did *not* write the *Historia*. If one could determine disputed authorship on the basis of six words alone (and it must be stressed that the number is far too low to be in any way probative), the statistical evidence exists to show that it is more likely that Bernard of Clairvaux wrote the passages we tested from the *Dialogus inter Philosophum, Iudaeum et Christianum, Theologia Christiana*, letters, and sermons of Abelard (which is, of course, not at all possible) than that either one of them wrote the *Historia calamitatum*. The article which reported on this work has been in print for over three years, and to the best of my knowledge, no one has yet challenged either our procedures of sampling and counting or our statistical method. Perhaps no one felt a need to do so, for as we readily admitted, six words, not even chosen at random, are insufficient evidence on which to determine authorship – the attributions of authorship of the *Federalist* papers were based on over 160 words and in that test one had only to distinguish between the writing of two possible authors. Nevertheless, the frequencies of the six words we discussed do individually have statistical significance and they all point in the same direction. If one places reliance on stylistic determinations of authorship, the only way to decide with reasonable statistical certainty whether the *Historia calamitatum* was written by Abelard or by a knowledgeable forger who borrowed heavily from Abelard's *fichier* of quotations is to conduct a full-scale study of vocabulary and other indicators of personal style which goes well beyond what is practical with the methods of hand-counting. Our study has not proved that Abelard was not the author of the *Historia*, but it has shown that all earlier demonstrations of Abelardian authorship based on the frequency of vocabulary have no statistical significance and are in fact contradicted by a controlled investigation.

Though statistical studies avoid the dangers of fastening in an impressionistic fashion on a few words, turns of phrase or concepts which might be imitated by an extremely shrewd forger, attention to particular instances of stylistic peculiarities can have value in determining authorship. The most interesting piece of new information about style of which I am aware is a peculiarity unearthed by Fr. Chrysogonus, which he has encouraged me to present here. The 'Breviary' of the Paraclete, or more properly the Diurnal (Chaumont, Bibl. mun. ms. 31), contains eight collects for the eight daily offices which are unique to the Paraclete, as well as a special collect for St. Philip the Deacon, to whom Abelard gave special veneration. All of these collects are built on the structure: *'Deus, qui . . . te quaesumus ut . . .'* Fr. Chrysogonus points out that in liturgical prayer formulas *quaesumus* is normally enclitic, and when more rarely it is used as a main verb, it takes an object such as *bonitatem tuam;* the form *te quaesumus* is so rare as to be practically unique. It is reasonable to assume that the author of the collects used only at the Paraclete was its liturgically creative founder, Abelard himself, and to consider that the innovative formula *'Deus, qui . . . te quaesumus ut . . .'* is a 'marker' of his euchological style. Now the point of importance for the study of the correspondence is that the two prayer formularies which appear in Ep. III, the first as the prayer which the convent was accustomed to offer when Abelard was present, the second as what he requested be prayed when he was absent and in danger, both use the structure *'Deus, qui . . . te quaesumus ut . . .'* In addition, the unusual phrase *'per servulum tuum'* in the first formulary suggests so well the arrogant humility with which Abelard was afflicted that we must think it the work either of the Master or of someone who knew his mentality extremely well.

The simplest explanation of the appearance of an Abelardian 'marker' in these formularies is that Abelard wrote both prayers in his 'personal' style as part of a letter of his own composition. A second, possible explanation is that a forger well acquainted with the Paraclete made use of a traditional formulary in continuing use at the convent for times when the *magister* was present, and modeled the second, more banal formulary on the first. This suggestion has no documentary support, for none of the existing liturgical manuscripts of the abbey contains the text of an *oratio pro magistro* which would have conveyed a precise wording from the time of Abelard to a later forger. A third explanation, in my opinion the least likely, is that a forger had studied and mastered Abelard's style so thoroughly that he — or she, for Heloise is the person most likely to have known Abelard so intimately — could imitate a peculiarity of Abelard's phraseology so minute that no one else had noted or copied the form until Fr. Chrysogonus investigated the unattributed collects.

Others have noted Abelardian phraseology or concepts in the correspondence (besides the use of quotations) and in unpublished work Professor Stephen Jaeger has recently added to that dossier a few more examples from the *Historia calamitatum*. Most readers have concluded that the information, quotations, and phraseology in the *Historia* all indicate that Abelard wrote it, and if it is not supported by evidence of historical inaccuracies which Abelard could not have written, the evidence of the statistical peculiarity of the six words Dr. Prosperetti and I counted or of the citation of Deuteronomy XXI should not be considered of sufficient weight to deny Abelard the authorship of at least major portions of the letter of consolation. In the published version of my Cluny paper I argued that even if the correspondence as we have it is a thirteenth-century fraud, the bulk of the *Historia* must have been written in the twelfth century. That hypothesis of a thirteenth-century fraud could still stand even if the *Historia* is accepted as authentic, though the need to hypothesize a forger for the correspondence as a whole rather than an interpolator would be reduced. At Cluny I argued that all or most of the last three letters was taken from or incorporated authentic writing of Abelard. What is particularly important about Fr. Chrysogonus' discovery is that he has found an Abelardian stylistic marker of a highly unusual sort in one of the 'personal' letters, a letter which according to a theory of forgery should surely be an imaginative fiction or there is no need to imagine a forger at all. The matter of euchological style may not be an absolute indication of authenticity, but it provides a serious stumbling block for a theory of 'third-party' authorship.

Let us turn now to the current status of the arguments about historical inaccuracies which I raised in 1972. The first point to state is that neither I nor, to my knowledge, anyone else has found any new *historical* evidence to support the hypothesis of a thirteenth-century fraud, though for my part I have been looking as diligently and vigorously as I could. This failure to find new evidence has been both a disappointment and a surprise to me. It is a surprise because I began work on my Cluny paper in December 1971 and found almost all the material which seemed striking to me at the time within six months. If six months' work with a new idea could produce a fairly large body of information which raised trouble for the theory of authenticity, how much, I wondered, could be found in six years? New historical evidence has been discovered, particularly about the use of a Cistercian liturgy at the Paraclete and the number of men active (and buried) there – a ratio of about one priest or deacon to every ten nuns for about a century and a half – as well as about the families, notably that of Traînel, who patronized the convent and are named in its necrologies. A possible location for the *Petit Moutier* has been pinpointed by aerial photography and it now seems reasonable to believe that it was the earliest stone church built on the property and was not replaced until after the death of Abelard by the church destroyed after the Revolution. All of this new information has its value, but it is not evidence of fraud or misrepresentation and it does not affect our assessment of the veracity and authenticity of the correspondence.

The hypothesis I presented in 1972 included the suggestion, based largely on the famous letter of Roscelin, that Abelard may have established Heloise and other nuns at the Paraclete before 1121. In a confirmation of the property of the abbey, issued in 1194 but based on earlier charters, Bishop Garnier of Troyes states that Milon, lord of Nogent, confirmed a number of donations in the presence of four named witnesses at the time of the episcopal dedication of the Oratory, and that his son Hugh was later buried at the Oratory, also in the presence of witnesses[2]. If proof existed that Hugh or any of the named witnesses had died before 1129, then a significant error in the account of the *Historia calamitatum* would be demonstrated. The documentation of the region of Nogent is sparse, not all the witnesses can be identified, and I can find no record of the death of Milon's son Hugh, but it must be said that I have found no evidence in the documents of the region which indicates that the convent of the Paraclete was founded before 1129. Moreover, my original suggestion is not even supported by a more careful reading of the letter of Roscelin. The text as I read it suggested that Abelard had accepted an 'obedience' (that is, an *ecclesia* dependent on his abbey and lower in status than a priory; in other words, a *cella*) from the abbot of St. Denis with the consent of this brothers at the abbey, that he moved to a second church, and that at the second *ecclesia* he taught, collected money from his students, and carried it away from the church to Heloise. That Heloise was close by, as it were just over a nearby wall, I deduced from Roscelin's statement that he had heard from Abelard's fellow monks that he returned to his monastery in the evening and then rushed off *(transvolans)* to carry the money away from there to his former lover.

This deduction now seems to me erroneous, based as it was on the identification of the monastery from which Abelard carried his teaching fees with the church where he did the teaching. But in the passage under discussion Roscelin initially uses the word *monasterium* to refer to the abbey of St. Denis, which he contrasts with the *ecclesia*

---

[2] Original charter, Aube 24 H 19, published by Charles Lalore, *Cartulaire de l'abbaye du Paraclet* (Paris, 1878), p. 99.

called an obedience. Abelard taught at the second church (*alia ecclesia*), quite possibly in the region of Nogent or the territory of Count Thibaut of Blois and then carried the money away – to the abbey of St. Denis, for it is likely that the fellow-monks who told the tale to Roscelin were monks of the great royal abbey and the *monasterium* where Abelard stopped briefly in the evening was the abbey near Paris from which he could then go on (*transvolans*) to Heloise, who according to the correspondence was at Argenteuil, about 7 km. from St. Denis. Rather than contradicting the account of Abelard's activities as given in the correspondence, Roscelin's letter serves in a small way to confirm it. And if Abelard was teaching a good 100 km. from St. Denis and Argenteuil, we have no reason to see in Roscelin's reference to a seal showing the heads of a man and a woman an indication of a 'double monastery.' We have no idea what the personal seals of monks of St. Denis looked like in the early twelfth century, but a possible explanation of the two-headed seal is that the spiteful Roscelin had maliciously interpreted a smudged image of the heads of Sts. Rusticus and Eleutherius, who appear on the counter-seal of the abbot of St. Denis in the early thirteenth century[3].

A second issue of an apparent contradiction between the *Historia calamitatum* and other evidence which I discussed at Cluny and which now seems to me to create no difficulty at all for Abelardian authorship is the matter of Abelard's views on St. Denis, Bede and Hilduin. The matter is too complex to be treated both briefly and convincingly, and since it has been explained with insight and persuasiveness by Fr. Chrysogonus, I would prefer, with his permission, to leave the exposition to him, noting only that in my opinion his explanation indicates that the passage on Bede in the *Historia calamitatum* is so personal that a host of skilled translators and commentators has missed its meaning not so much from a failure to read the Latin correctly as to enter properly into the working of Abelard's mind; if Fr. Chrysogonus' interpretation is correct, not only has a difficulty been removed, but the case for stating that only Abelard could have written the *Historia calamitatum* has been strengthened.

Apparent contradictions or errors in a text can result not only from overly subtle expression but also from blunt irony or satire. It is possible that Abelard was himself being ironic when the *Historia* states that the *populus* at Soissons accused him of preaching tritheism, though other sources tell us that the charge at Soissons was actually Sabellianism. Explanations which depend upon ironic readings are always dangerous, but it seems as reasonable to think that Abelard was commenting bitterly and elliptically that the ignorant crowd at Soissons had the charges reversed as to believe that a forger who had mastered a large amount of personal information about Abelard would make a silly error about a public accusation. Personal considerations could also have kept Abelard from writing of his teacher Roscelin in the *Historia calamitatum*, and it is also possible that he chose to over-simplify and exaggerate the nature of his dispute with William of Champeaux. On reconsideration, my earlier treatment of the reference to the two 'new Apostles' seems weak and unconvincing. The author is referring to the period before Abelard became abbot of St. Gildas, so that the imperfect tense would be appropriate, and the two men are not necessarily Norbert and Bernard. Supporters of the authenticity of the *Historia calamitatum* do not need to identify two enemies whom the author does not name, but the men in question may be Norbert and Hugh Farsit, a canon of Saint-Jean-des-Vignes of Soissons, who were both denounced in similar terms in Sermon 33.

---

[3] Counter-seal of Henri de Saint-Denis in 1217 in L.-Cl. Douët d'Arcq, *Inventaires et documents . . . Collection de sceaux*, 3 vols. (Paris, 1863–68), 3, n° 8370 bis.

Aside from the matter of the institutions of the Paraclete, the only remaining question of a possible historical inaccuracy which I discussed at Cluny is whether Abelard ever wrote a commentary on Ezechiel, a work which figures prominently in the *Historia calamitatum* but which Abelard does not mention when he refers to the difficulty of Ezechiel in his *Commentary on the Hexameron*. An argument *ex silentio* should never carry much weight in our field, and with respect to the gloss or commentary on Ezechiel the veracity of the *Historia calamitatum* would indeed be confirmed if it can be shown that the *Expositions Ezechiel* which the nuns of the Paraclete read in their refectory from *un livre velu petit* were indeed the work of Abelard[4].

To summarize the question of the *Historia calamitatum* alone, the reference to Deuteronomy XXI remains a problem, but one which can indicate an interpolator as easily as a forger. Not all the details in the historical account are completely understood, but I can demonstrate no historical errors which by themselves would place the authenticity of the work in doubt; our questions are raised more by omissions, possible exaggerations or other rhetorical devices, and self-serving statements which may conceal the truth. These are all problems we would expect in an authentic autobiography by Abelard. Our statistical analysis of the frequency of use of a short list of words and constructions shows that the style of the *Historia calamitatum* is not as 'typically Abelardian' as some commentators have thought, and it suggests the need for a full, computer-assisted analysis, but it does not prove inauthenticity at any satisfactory level of statistical certainty. No scholar ever questioned the authenticity of the *Historia calamitatum* on stylistic grounds before Dr. Prosperetti and I wrote our article, and our article raised questions about the author's style without claiming to have demonstrated anything about authenticity. There may be other reasons to doubt the authenticity of the *Historia calamitatum*, but our study of style and the issues of possible errors or anachronisms which I discussed at Cluny do not seem to me now to provide grounds for rejecting the document.

The hypothesis presented at Cluny treated the *Historia calamitatum* as a twelfth-century fiction used by a thirteenth-century forger in compiling a fraudulent composition. If the introductory letter is indeed substantially authentic, where does this leave the larger hypothesis? Such matters as meat-eating nuns, the *prepositus monachorum* of a neighboring abbey which does not appear to have existed, the repetition of passages in Epp. VI and VIII, and the odd exhortation to Abelard's *fratres et commonachi* in a letter addressed to Heloise remain troublesome. In theory a fraudulent compiler in the thirteenth century could have made use of an authentic *Historia calamitatum* as well as a fictional one. A theory of thirteenth-century fraud would be most attractive if it could be shown that the correspondence as a whole (or at least including the 'personal' letters) was not known to Jean de Meung or anyone else until after the disputed election which took place at the Paraclete between 1286 and 1289. Whether the *Roman de la Rose* was written before or after the death of Charles of Anjou in 1285 is therefore relevant to our need to hypothesize a thirteenth-century forger rather than simply a thirteenth-century interpolator or editor.

The question of the date of the *Roman de la Rose* is too complex to be treated in detail here. I believe that the view that Jean must have completed his continuation before 1274 should be rejected, that it is likely that he was working on his poem in the 1280s, and that it was not in general circulation before 1291, when Gui de Mori finished writing a revision of Guillaume de Lorris' portion of the *Roman*. It is possible

---

[4] B. N. ms. fr. 14410, fols. 64v and 110.

that Jean himself wrote the B version of the poem (in Langlois' classification) first and then later made a revision which we know as the A family of the text. Gui de Mori apparently omitted the material on Abelard and Heloise from his first edition of Jean's continuation for it is marked as a 'subtraction reprise' in his second edition[5], but Jean's account of the two lovers appears in good manuscripts of both the A and B families. If Jean wrote after the death of Charles of Anjou in 1285 – and this is a proposition many specialists would reject – it still seems highly likely that the work was completed in either the A or B form (or both) by 1290, and that the bulk of the composition was written in the 1280s. If the clerical world had nothing else on which to concentrate than the story of Abelard and Heloise, it is just possible that a fraudulent version of the correspondence could have been fabricated at the Paraclete between 1286 and 1289, have reached Paris or Orléans with post-haste, been read and enjoyed and perhaps translated by Jean de Meung, and then incorporated by him in his current 'best-seller' before 1290 when Cardinal Benedict Gaetani (the future Boniface VIII) visited Paris and ordered the seculars to stop their fussing and complaints. It is possible, but it is not likely, and the odds are on the side of those who would argue that the work of Jean de Meung shows that the Latin text of the correspondence was known before the disputed election at the Paraclete in the 1280s. While I cannot prove that the letters were known to any reader before the time of Jean de Meung, the reference to Deuteronomy XXI is the only evidence which forces us to think of the thirteenth century as the probable time of composition for any portion of the correspondence.

Since the case for thirteenth-century fraud or indeed for 'third-party' authorship now seems to me much weaker than it did in 1972 and I must admit that I cannot raise any arguments I consider significant to show that the *Historia calamitatum* was not written by Abelard, does that mean that the historical authenticity of the entire correspondence (with perhaps the exception of a few small interpolations) has been established by default? If my paper at Cluny had one positive consequence, it was to focus attention on the Rule and the institutions and practices of the Paraclete. A significant decade has passed since Sir Richard Southern could write of the last two letters in the collection. 'They are by no means readable, and they are seldom read. They have no personal interest[6].' After seven years it now seems much clearer to me than before that the most serious problems for accepting the correspondence as authentic are the questions raised by the existence of the Rule and its supporting material and by the evidence which indicates that a Rule which Heloise supposedly requested in a detailed letter was apparently not put into practice in the twelfth or thirteenth centuries. If the Rule and the institutional situation at the Paraclete are not evidence that the correspondence is a third-party fabrication, they may still suggest strongly that the letters as we have them are a fiction – a fiction composed by Abelard to justify a Rule which departed from the normal practices of Benedictine nuns and even from the *Institutiones* of the convent he had founded.

Though I remain dissatisfied with the theory of 'historical authenticity' and no longer feel justified in arguing the case for the theory of 'third party' composition, it would be presumptuous for me now to come forward as a champion of a theory of a literary fiction created by Abelard as an introduction to two of his treatises written for the Paraclete, comparable in some way to the letters with which he introduced his hymnal. If a decision must be made between the theories of authenticity and Abelardian fiction, however, very careful attention must be paid to Ep. VI, attributed to Heloise.

---

[5] Tournai, Bibl. mun.ms. 101, fol. 87v.
[6] *Medieval Humanism* (Oxford and New York, 1970), p. 101.

In 1972 I argued that Abelard was the author of Ep. VI, or of at least large portions of it. On this point evidence produced by the excellent new edition of the *Sic et Non* by Boyer and McKeon supports the theory of Abelardian authorship. Ep. VI contains a long excerpt (over 275 words) from St. Augustine's *De Bono Coniugali* which is with one exception word for word the same as that which appears in the *Sic et Non* (q. 130, cc. 6–9)[7]. The omissions are the same, the placement of *item* is identical, and the texts agree in reproducing a notable error in the transmission of what Augustine wrote. At the beginning of the passage Augustine wrote 'Virtutes autem animi aliquando in opere manifestantur,' and consequently Fr. Muckle amended the text of 'Heloise' to read *opere* rather than the *corpore* given by all the manuscripts. The emendation should be rejected, however, for all the manuscripts of *Sic et Non* which give the extract also read *corpore*. The only difference between the text of Ep. VI and the *Sic et Non* is that toward the end the letter reads 'qui non poterat non promebat,' rather than 'qui poterat non promebat,' an error which remains inexplicable. But this second error, rather than creating a stumbling block, has its value, for it demonstrates, should anyone want a demonstration, that the *Sic et Non* or the Abelardian *fichier* from which it was drawn was the source of Ep. VI, rather than that a letter sent by Heloise or a common source lay behind the passage in *Sic et Non*.

In considering the use of 'Abelardian' quotations, three observations should be noted. The first is that Abelard regularly 'quoted himself' or transferred favored individual quotations or blocks of quotations from one work to another; this is, in fact, one of the surest marks of his compositional style. Secondly, the author of the letter gives no indication that the passage is borrowed from another work. Such a procedure is common for Abelard, who presumably felt that authorities he had collected were 'his,' to be used as he wished, though if Heloise were writing with her finger running down the page of *Sic et Non*, we might expect her to acknowledge her borrowing. And thirdly, there can be absolutely no doubt that this and several other passages in the correspondence are taken word for word, omission for omission, from the *Sic et Non* or Abelard's *fichier* of quotations, for the variants can be accounted for in no other way. Fr. Muckle commented: 'There are several instances where Heloise quotes a text of Scripture or a well-known statement of St. Jerome or St. Augustine to support her argument, which are also quoted by Abelard. This fact is of little importance; one could find repetition of quotations in any two authors of the Middle Ages who are writing on germane subjects[8].' Given the fact that the distinguished editor had no critical edition of the *Sic et Non* available, his judgment of 'little importance' can be easily understood, but with excellent comparative texts in hand (his own and that of Boyer and McKeon), the importance of the identity cannot be dismissed. Etienne Gilson has written that 'Heloise empruntait des citations à Abelard aussi facilement que son style[9].' But while style can be imitated unconsciously, copying long citations word for word from another's writing must be done consciously, and one must ask why it has not been acknowledged.

If Abelard did write Ep. VI, putting words into the mouth of Heloise, is there any reason to suppose that he did not write Ep. II and IV as well? This question is harder to answer conclusively, given the style and the nature of the letters. The issue of Heloise's complaint of a lack of communication or consolation has been long debated, as has the

---

[7] Ed. J. T. Muckle in *Mediaeval Studies* 17 (1955), p. 250.

[8] 'The Personal Letters Between Abelard and Heloise,' *Mediaeval Studies* 15 (1953), p. 56.

[9] *Héloïse et Abélard* (3rd ed., Paris, 1964) p. 189.

matter of the references to Abelard's doctrine of intention, phrased in language strikingly similar to phrases used by Abelard elsewhere[10]. Though I have searched as hard as I could, I can find no phrase or fact in either the personal letters or Ep. VI which stands out as evidence that Heloise rather than Abelard wrote the letters. What would be most convincing to me as an historian would be if the letters of Heloise could be correlated in any way with institutional practices or liturgical usages we can find documented at the Paraclete. But no, 'Heloise' indicates that the nuns were governed at the time of writing by an unmodified Benedictine Rule and asks for a new, less restrictive rule, a rule which, as far as our evidence goes, does not appear to have been adopted under her administration. The meat-eating authorized by Abelard is contrary to the *Institutiones* of the Paraclete, and the provision for oversight by the *prepositus monachorum (quem abbatem nominant)* of a neighboring monastery seems never to have been practiced at the Paraclete, where a group of priests and deacons, headed by a *magister,* served under the direction of the abbess.

To understand this discrepancy between Abelard's *Regula* and practice at the Paraclete we need to know much more about the early history of the Paraclete, including the intriguing question of when a Cistercian liturgy and calendar were introduced there. Certain matters, however, seem reasonably clear. Abelard established the Paraclete some time between 1129 and 1131, and among its earliest nuns were Heloise and some of his relatives. Abelard preached to raise money to support the foundation and exhorted the male deacons there. Abelard wrote books for Heloise and the nuns and provided much of the liturgy. There is no reason to think that he did not have a hand in the abbey's acquisition of a charter of privilege from Pope Inncccent II which established the abbey's independence from any ecclesiastical control but that of the pope; there is no evidence that the Paraclete was ever subjected to the authority of any neighboring abbey, and if any man had responsibility for the early direction of the Paraclete, that man was surely Abelard. During the early years of the abbey it is inconceivable that it should follow a rule not acceptable to Abelard.

Why then should Heloise, in Ep. VI, ask Abelard for a new rule, fearing that a later director 'may be less likely to feel concern for us,' and why should she not then immediately institute the rule which Abelard provided at such length in answer to her supposed request? I cannot answer these questions with certainty, but I believe they deserve an answer. One possible answer now seems likely. It is that when Abelard established the Paraclete, he was the man in control. After time had passed and he was further removed from the affairs of the abbey, he began to fear that Heloise and the nuns needed male control from outside the convent, and he offered a new rule as the concluding letter of an exemplary correspondence which stressed his own role in the foundation of the convent and demonstrated the carnal weakness of a woman without proper male direction. The internal evidence of quotations and repetitions suggests that Heloise did not herself write the letter requesting a new rule. To this internal evidence should be added an additional reason for thinking that Heloise did not request or desire

---

[10] Muckle, 'Personal Letters,' pp. 55–56, calls attention to the striking similarity between a passage in Abelard's *Ethica* and a statement in Ep. IV: 'Nulla quicquid meriti apud Deum obtinent quae reprobis aeque ut electis communia sunt' (p. 82 of his edition). Fr. Muckle deals with this 'difficulty' by pointing out that the *Ethica* is one of the latest of Abelard's works and suggesting that 'the *Ethica* borrowed from thé letter.' With this argument in mind it is worth noting the appearance in the Monte Cassino manuscript of the *Sic et Non* of a passage attributed to 'Abaielardus' which contains the sentence, 'Exteriora autem opera aeque reprobis sicut sanctis communia sunt' (ed. Boyer and McKeon, p. 609).

a new rule, and that is the apparent fact that she and her successors did not follow it.

We began this inquiry with three possibilities, that the letters are the record of an actual interchange between Abelard and Heloise (though possibly modified by Heloise), that they are a 'literary fiction' written by Abelard (possibly slightly altered in transmission), or that they were written by a third party. The 'third party' hypothesis now seems to me much weaker than it did at Cluny. The theory of a literary fiction written by Abelard has never been shown to be in opposition to established facts, though individual arguments in its support have been rejected. It is consistent with the apparent Abelardian authorship of Ep. VI, and it explains various discrepancies which have long troubled different commentators. The theory of authenticity of exchange which requires that Heloise wrote all the letters attributed to her has, on the other hand, never been established on the basis of positive evidence, arguments in support resting largely on the risky basis of psychological realism. The theory of authenticity is weakened if Heloise did not desire and request a new rule for the Paraclete, and external evidence exists which suggests that Abelard's rule was not followed at the Paraclete. Though as I wrote this paper doubts and problems still remained in my mind, it is possible that those present at this conference may develop together a solution to the long-standing question of authenticity.

25

The Correspondence of Abelard and Heloise

Questions of authenticity and forgery are particularly susceptible to the influence of personal patterns of perception. Just as in an ambiguous drawing one observer may see a duck and another a rabbit, so in a given piece of writing one historian may see an authentic text (though possibly with minor interpolations or scribal or editorial revisions), while another declares the same work to be a fiction or a fraud (though possibly based on and preserving some authentic material)[1]. Historians and other critics frequently try to settle such issues by imagining conditions of composition which seem plausible or even compelling, or by analyzing the presumed psychology of a supposed author. I have myself engaged in such arguments, and while they are often fun and sometimes useful heuristically, I can attest from experience that it rarely convinces others who bring different perceptions and presuppositions to the texts and who are also adept at making up plausible hypotheses and psychological explanations.

When the scholarly community reaches agreement that a given document is a forgery, that consensus is almost always based on technical arguments, frequently involving anachronism. Lorenzo Valla may have convinced himself that it would not have been in character for Constantine to give away his empire to the pope, but the arguments which were most convincing to posterity were those demonstrating the anachronism of a document which could not possibly have been written in the fourth century. Again, though its authenticity was seriously questioned, Yale's Vinland Map was accepted as a genuine product of the fifteenth century by a large group of knowledgeable experts until 1974, when particle analysis showed that the ink contained a chemical not in use before 1920. And even then one committed specialist proclaimed, "I feel

---

1) On the philosophical problem of world-views and non-terminating disagreements, illustrated by an example comparable to the problem we face in evaluating the correspondence of Abelard and Heloise, see W. T. JONES, Philosophical Disagreements and World Views, Proceedings and Addresses of the American Philosophical Association 43 (1971) p. 24–42. For his (and my) reference to rabbits and ducks, see Ludwig WITTGENSTEIN, Philosophical Investigations, trans. G. E. M. Anscombe (1953) II.xi, 194e; or cf. E. H. GOMBRICH, Art and Illusion: A Study in the Psychology of Pictorial Representation (^{2}1961) p. 5.

surprised ... but not shaken in the least; I accept the microchemical findings, but not the inference drawn from them"[2].

Judgments about the authenticity of the correspondence of Abelard and Heloise are affected not only by our personal orientation towards disputed documents and the canons of proof needed to establish either falsity or authenticity, but also by our personal feelings about Abelard and Heloise themselves. I have been told that Fr. Muckle, who raised many questions about Heloise's authorship, had a sister who was a nun, and that he could never quite believe that a respectable nun would write letters like those he had edited. Charlotte Charrier, on the other hand, cordially disapproved of Abelard and concluded that he composed the correspondence "par fatuité d'homme"[3]. Such personal reactions must be expected; we would be bloodless creatures indeed if we did not respond emotionally, one way or another, to such powerful personalities as those of Heloise and Abelard. And yet, how little has been securely established about these two people as compared to the amount that has been written about them. As much as we may try, we cannot come to this subject fresh, without preconceptions, without such images as those of Alexander Pope's Eloisa to Abelard affecting our understanding. Sentimental fantasies about the two lovers dominated the literature of the seventeenth and eighteenth centuries, and Pope himself based his poem, not on the letters which we read and debate today, but on a translation which included completely fictitious letters and a fanciful reworking of the Historia calamitatum known as the Lettre à Philinthe. The later literary history of Abelard and Heloise is so full of sentimentality, misrepresentation and fraud that we must begin any research in the field by questioning the presuppositions inherited by our culture[4].

---

2) For the initial favorable consensus see Proceedings of the Vinland Map Conference, ed. Wilcomb E. WASHBURN (1971). For the quotation see G.D. PAINTER in: Helen WALLIS et al., The Strange Case of the Vinland Map, Geographical Journal 140 (1974) p. 194, with further comments cited in an editorial in Antiquity 48 (1974) p. 81. Painter's tenacity (though not his logic) has apparently been justified, for a new and more extensive scientific analysis has effectively challenged the 1974 finding; see Thomas A. CAHILL et al., The Vinland Map Revisited: New Compositional Evidence on Its Inks and Parchment, Analytical Chemistry 59 (1987) p. 829–833.

3) Charlotte CHARRIER, Héloïse dans l'histoire et dans la légende (1933) p. 24.

4) For the "modern" history of Heloise and Abelard, see CHARRIER, Héloïse, and D. W. ROBERTSON, Jr., Abelard and Heloise (1972). The dupe who purchased the letter (in French) from Heloise to Abelard forged by Vrain Lucas is an extreme but not unique example of romantic credulity; Peter GANZ kindly pointed out the letter in Henri

The existence of differing world-views and personal reactions does not, in my opinion, mean that disputes about the authenticity of this correspondence will necessarily be a non-terminating dialogue of the deaf. But if we are to avoid unnecessary misunderstanding, we must take particular care to comprehend the arguments of others and to treat them with respect. In addressing a topic like this one, emotional rhetoric, debaters' points and ad hominem arguments can easily obscure significant issues of logic and evidence. After reading most of the vast amount written about the issue of the authorship of this correspondence, I have become convinced that the capacity of imaginative scholars (including myself, of course) to find psychologically satisfying reasons for practically any hypothesized activity is limitless. If we are ever to settle the major issue of the authorship of these letters, it will not be through discussions of what might be plausible behavior for people of either the twelfth century or today, but on the basis of the most technical and indeed unemotional issues, questions of style, dating, sources and so on.

The organizers of the congress on "Fälschungen im Mittelalter" pleasantly told me that they had picked me to address this topic because they expected that I "could see both sides of the matter". In 1972 at Cluny I presented arguments in support of the hypothesis that the correspondence as we have it now was produced by a thirteenth-century forger who made use of a significant amount of twelfth-century material, including work genuinely written by Abelard[5]. My hypothesis at this time was largely based on questions of possible anachronism and the historicity of certain details contained in the text, for example, the inclusion of meat in the diet authorized for the nuns in Letter Eight. In the following seven years I found nothing further to support my original hypothesis, which I came to consider defective in a number of ways and which had found favor with only a few members of the scholarly community, most notably Professor Hubert Silvestre, who has maintained and extended the hypothesis of a thirteenth-century forger[6]. In 1979 at Trier I criticized

---

BORDIER and Émile MABILLE, Une fabrique de faux autographes ou récit de l'affaire Vrain Lucas (1870) p. 80–81.

5) John F. BENTON, Fraud, Fiction and Borrowing in the Correspondence of Abelard and Heloise, in: Actes du Colloque International Pierre Abélard – Pierre le Vénérable (1975) p. 469–511. See above, chapter 22, pp. 417-53.

6) For his most recent discussion of this problem, see Hubert SILVESTRE, L'idylle d'Abélard et Héloïse: la part du roman, Bulletin de la Classe des lettres et des sciences morales et politiques de l'Académie royale de Belgique, 5e sér. 71 (1985) p. 157–200,

my earlier hypothesis, and while I admitted to considerable uncertainty, I accepted as likely the proposition that Abelard was indeed the author of the Historia calamitatum and the other letters in the correspondence attributed to him. I also suggested, though I did not develop a detailed argument, that there are good reasons to think that Abelard also wrote the letters attributed to Heloise, that is, I reluctantly came back to the old position of Bernhard Schmeidler that the correspondence is a literary "fiction" written by Abelard[7].

The international congress on "Fälschungen im Mittelalter" has provided an occasion to consider this topic after another seven years. In my discussion this time, more emphasis has been given to stylistic matters, such as word frequency and choice. Let me reassure the reader from the beginning that I am not here arguing for some new, third position. Instead, the major goal of this paper is to present the evidence of a fresh, computer-assisted analysis of the text of the letters, evidence which accords with the conclusion that Abelard was the author of the Historia calamitatum and all of the letters in the correspondence, including those supposedly written by Heloise[8]. Since none of our manuscripts

---

now translated into German and published in this collection[*] (see p. 121–165). To respond appropriately to this learned and challenging article, of which Prof. Silvestre very kindly sent me an advance copy of the proofs, would require a very different paper than the one I have written here, and I have decided not to attempt a partial commentary. The heart of our difference, as I see it, turns on the fact that I can no longer believe, as I did in 1972, that any medieval forger could write an extended work using so many of Abelard's favorite phrases and quotations, and most certainly that a thirteenth-century forger could avoid any clearly demonstrable anachronisms. Not that I believe the Hist. cal. accurately recounts "what actually happened", but that I consider all the errors and distortions can be attributed to Abelard himself.

7) Petrus Abaelardus (1079–1142): Person, Werk und Wirkung, ed. Rudolf THOMAS (Trierer Theologische Studien 38, 1980) p. 41–52. SCHMEIDLER also revised his opinion somewhat over the decades; for his final paper see: Der Briefwechsel zwischen Abälard und Heloise dennoch eine literarische Fiction Abälards, Revue bénédictine 52 (1940) p. 85–95. Peter VON MOOS has provided an excellent survey of the literature of this controversy through 1972: Mittelalterforschung und Ideologiekritik. Der Gelehrtenstreit um Héloise (1974).

8) I am embarrassed that this conclusion differs markedly from that of J. F. BENTON and Fiorella PROSPERETTI ERCOLI, The Style of the Historia Calamitatum: A Preliminary Test of the Authenticity of the Correspondence Attributed to Abelard and Heloise, Viator 6 (1975) p. 59–86. For that study we estimated the number of words (minus quotations) in the Historia calamitatum, using a procedure explained on p. 78. That procedure gave us a total of approximately 6 400 words, less than two-thirds the number now established by computer-assisted counting. All of the percentage-based conclusions

[*] *Fälschungen im Mittelalter*, MGH Schriften, 33, v (1988).

is earlier than the late thirteenth century, the possibility of thirteenth-century interpolation exists, but with the exception of a few disputed phrases or passages which have been considered possible evidence of anachronism, the text appears to be consistent with twelfth-century authorship and bears the mark of Abelard's style and thought[9]. I should state clearly at the beginning that this analy-

---

about the Historia in that article are therefore erroneous. There are also, I regret to say, some small errors in the absolute word-counts. The figures in the present article have been verified from a concordance generated by the Oxford Concordance Program. It should be noted that the frequency counts cover only 1 000-word units; the word *saltem*, for example, appears eight times in the whole of the Hist. cal., but two of those appearances are in the last few hundred words (out of a total of 10,391) and therefore are not counted in the statistics in this paper. In the earlier article, the word-count for *facile* includes *facilius*, but here the count is only of words read individually by the computer.

9) In 1972 (Fraud, Fiction and Borrowing [as n. 5] p. 442-3). I considered that the numbering of a chapter of the Bible, which was close (though without an exact fit) to the thirteenth-century system of Stephen Langton, provided strong support for my hypothesis of thirteenth-century composition or interpolation; Prof. SILVESTRE (L'idylle [as n. 6] p. 178) now considers this issue "un des arguments les plus nets contre l'authenticité de l'Historia calamitatum". Since I introduced this argument, I feel a special obligation to show why I no longer consider it valid. In Abelard's day the citation of Biblical passages by book and chapter was uncommon; Abelard did it infrequently and only twice in the Hist. cal. In the first case (ed. Jacques MONFRIN [1978] line 618) he labeled as *Lib. Numeri, cap. LXXIIII* a verse which we now cite as Lev. 22:24. A confusion between *Leviticus* and *ad Levitas* (that is, Numbers – see Commentaria in epistolam Pauli ad Romanos, in Petri Abaelardi Opera Theologica, ed. Eligius M. BUYTAERT [CC Cont. Med. 11, 1969] p. 88 and 137), was an easy one to make, and in the standard chapter numbering of Abelard's time, Leviticus, cap. LXXIIII would be our modern Lev. 22. The numbering of the verse is therefore that appropriate to a Bible of Abelard's day, as demonstrated by Abelard's usage in Comm. Rom., p. 234. This instance, in other words, supports the case for Abelard's authorship of the Hist. cal. The second citation is much less clear-cut. In Hist. cal. (ed. MONFRIN, lines 620–1) a verse we now call Deut. 23:1 is labelled *Deuteronomii, cap. XXI*. In the most common numbering system of Abelard's day, the same verse would be numbered *cap. CVII. Cap. XXI* is so close to Stephen Langton's *cap. XXIII* and so far from *Cap. CVIII* that I felt confident that the reference had been written (with a slight error, of course) in the thirteenth century. What I did not realize in 1972 is that there was great inconsistency in the chapter numbers of pre-Langton Bibles, and no one system which he replaced. In Theologia Christiana 2, 18, ed. BUYTAERT (CC Cont. Med. 12, 1969) p. 140, Abelard called the modern Deut. 4 *capitulo Deuteronomii XV* and modern Deut. 7 *capitulo XXIII*. In Comm. Rom. (p. 251) modern Deut. 30:11–13 was *capitulo LVII* and Deut. 30:14 was *capitulo LVIII*. But in Sic et non, q. 138, c. 56, eds. Blanche BOYER and Richard McKEON (1976–77) p. 479, a verse which is now Deut. 16:19 was labeled *cap. LXXXI*. If modern Deut. 30 could be *Cap. LVII* and modern Deut. 16 *Cap. LXXXI,* then Abelard or his

sis does not prove, in a positive way, that Abelard wrote the entire correspondence, but my results do show that on the basis of the words studied there is no statistically significant difference between the letters attributed to Abelard and those attributed to Heloise. I will present the evidence under five headings: the cursus, word-frequencies, quotations, concepts, and patterns of phrasing.

In 1979 Peter Dronke presented the first statistical analysis of the cursus in the correspondence and distinguished the practice of Heloise from that of Abelard, though he concluded, "I do not know if Heloise's keen adherence to *tardus* cadences, exceptional as it is, is sufficiently distinct from Abelard's practice to differentiate her prose style decisively from his"[10]. Tore Janson has recently re-examined the question, analyzing a larger sample than Dronke did. He has concluded, in an as-yet unpublished paper[11], that the evidence of the cursus patterns suggests that all the letters were written by one person, or at least edited by one person, though his approach does not permit him to say whether that person was Abelard or Heloise. The pattern of the cursus in the Historia cala-

---

copyists were quite capable of being imprecise or of using a variety of numbering systems. The reference to *cap. XXI* in Hist. cal. does not fit the usage of any identified manuscript or numbering system; it could be a distortion of Stephen Langton's system, but it could also have been derived from a Bible or citation used by Abelard. In short, the citation of Deuteronomy proves nothing about dating, and the citation of Leviticus supports twelfth-century authorship, not thirteenth-century.

10) Peter DRONKE, Heloise's Problemata and Letters. Some Questions of Form and Content, in: Petrus Abaelardus (1079–1142) (as n. 7) p. 55. Though he presents his conclusions vigorously, stating that "from these tests results emerged that were more decisive and more startling than I could have surmised simply from an attentive reading of the letters", the figures which Dronke supplies do not support a differentiation between two authors.

11) I am extremely grateful to Professor JANSON for sending me an advance copy of his paper: Schools of Cursus in the Twelfth Century and the Letters of Heloise and Abelard, to appear in the Acta of the Congress on rhetoric and literature in the 12th and 13th centuries held in Trento in October, 1985, ed. Claudio LEONARDI. In his statistical analysis, which Janson incorporated in his own study, Dronke used two different editions, that of Monfrin for Letters Two and Four and that of Muckle for a portion of Letter Six and the letters attributed to Abelard. The two editors differ significantly in their systems of punctuation (Muckle uses more periods, Monfrin more semi-colons). At my request Professor Janson very kindly recalculated the results using Muckle's edition throughout, and in a letter of 5 November 1986 wrote me that "in practice it does not matter which edition is chosen. The preferences are exactly the same in both samples. This is encouraging for me because it means that the method as such is not very sensitive to variations in editorial style".

mitatum parallels that in Abelard's other letters, while the style of Letters Two to Eight is closer to that of Abelard's sermons. In Janson's opinion, the cursus patterns used in the correspondence are distinctively those of the first half of the twelfth century, providing a very strong argument against the hypothesis of a thirteenth-century forger.

Let us turn now to a second body of evidence. My own stylistic analysis, based on a computer-assisted frequency count of vocabulary and a concordance of the entire correspondence, supports Janson's conclusion that there was a single author. To summarize a complex procedure and an even more complex set of data generated by this procedure, I can say briefly that for the words I have studied so far[12], there is no case where the frequency in the letters attributed to Heloise differs from that in the letters of Abelard by as much as two standard deviations (that is, by an amount which would have statistical significance). The 24 words listed in the appendix in rates per thousand include the most frequent words and those which for one reason or another have been discussed in the literature. When one compares the letters of "Heloise" (Two, Four and Six) with Letters Three, Five and Seven, only one word (*etiam*) differs by as much as one standard deviation[13]. That is to say, on the basis of the frequencies

---

12) In The Style of the Historia Calamitatum (as n. 8) p. 74, I stated that to match the thoroughness of Frederick Mosteller and David Wallace's analysis of the Federalist papers, one might have to study over 100 words, but that with the assistance of a computer "such a survey is well within the range of possibility". The present study is limited to only 24 words, partly because many words in the sample were either context-sensitive or so uncommon as to be statistically uninteresting, but largely because even with the assistance of a computer, compiling accurate statistics by 1 000-word units is still laborious. Robert L. OAKMAN, Computer Methods for Literary Research (^{2}1984) p. 139–171 is a very sensible and useful introduction to this relatively new field.

13) In this paper, as in the previous ones I have written on this subject, I have followed the numbering of the editio princeps, in which the Hist. cal. is treated as Letter One and the first letter of Heloise is Letter Two, rather than that used by J. T. MUCKLE in his edition in Mediaeval Studies 15 (1953). The procedure used here was to divide each letter into units of 1,000 words, ignoring any words left over at the end of a letter. Frequencies per thousand words were calculated for the Hist. cal., for Letters Two, Four and Six as a unit, and for Letters Three, Five and Seven as a third unit. I have omitted from these calculations the very long Letter Eight, which to all appearances follows the same style as Letter Seven. Standard deviations within each unit were also calculated. Two frequencies are considered to be within one standard deviation of each other if the the difference between their means is less than the amount created by squaring the two standard deviations and then taking the square root of the sum. For example, in Letters

I have analyzed so far, the style of the two sets of letters is virtually identical. There is, however, a small but perceptible difference between the frequencies in both sets of letters on the one hand and those found in the Historia calamitatum on the other. When one compares Letters Three, Five and Seven with the Historia calamitatum, five of the 24 words differ by as much as one standard deviation; no word differs by two standard deviations. Those words which are not within one standard deviation of each other are marked between the columns in the final table. The differences between the Historia calamitatum and Letters Three, Five and Seven are not large enough to indicate two different authors[14], but they do suggest that the Historia may have been written for a different audience, or at a different time, or as if it were in a different genre, or when the author was in a different mood. On this point too my evidence accords with that of Janson; there is something different about the Historia.

A study based on a comparison of means and standard deviations has the advantage of measuring variation within a text as well as the difference of frequency of usage between two or more texts. It is also a simple form of comparison, so that those who are relatively unsophisticated statistically can compare the numbers and make up their own minds as to whether two samples seem different or similar. It should be noted that there is an arbitrary element to my calculations, because the degree of differentiation would vary with the size of the base, for example, if I had made calculations on the basis of 500 or 2 000 words. To objections raised on that point I can reply that my choice of 1 000 words is arbitrary but not unreasonable; a sample of 500 words is so small that the results would be of reduced significance, and a sample of 2 000 words would be

---

Three, Five, and Seven the mean for *obsecro* is 0.7 and the standard deviation 1.1, while in Letters Two, Four, and Six the mean is 1.9 and the standard deviation 0.9. Since the difference between 1.9 and 0.7 (1.2) is less than 1.42 (the square root of the sum of 1.1 and 0.9 squared), *obsecro* is not a statistically significant word in these letters for distinguishing one author from another. Étienne GILSON, Héloïse et Abélard (³1964) p. 187, noted that CHARRIER (Héloïse [as n. 3] p. 577–8) had counted thirteen cases of *obsecro* for Heloise and nine for Abelard and wittily asked, "... qu'est-ce que cela prouve? Que la tendance à l'obsécration est un peu plus forte chez une femme amoureuse que chez l'homme qui cherche à la calmer?". With that psychological argument in mind, it is worth stressing that statistically the two sets of letters cannot be distinguished by the frequency of use of *obsecro*.

14) A rule of thumb of statistical significance is that in measurements of two samples of the same population one can expect to find differences of two standard deviations five percent of the time.

too large for Letter Three and would obscure any measure of variation in Letters Two and Four.

I have been asked what results a chi-square test on these figures would give. For comparisons of this sort, the appropriate chi-square test is essentially equivalent to a t-statistic test for differences of proportions[15]. Since such tests obscure differences of frequency within a given sample, I do not consider them as useful as the mean and standard deviation figures given here, but I have calculated t-statistics for these numbers. The results show a greater difference between the Historia calamitatum and Letters Three, Five and Seven (the letters of "Abelard") than between those letters and Letters Two, Four and Six[16]. Whatever the value of this test, it does not support the hypothesis that the letters of "Heloise" were written by a different person than the author of the letters of "Abelard."

A third approach to questions of authorship, the issue of the quotations used in the letters attributed to Heloise, has long been a subject of scholarly discussion, since there is both a general similarity and in some cases also a striking textual relationship between those quotations and passages cited by Abelard in other works. Except for Persius, all the authors cited in the letters of "Heloise" are favorites of Abelard, as shown by his use of their writings in other works. For example, Lucan is an author for whom he had a particular fondness[17], Cicero's De inventione he cited in Letter Eight, Sic et non, Theologia Christiana, and other works[18], and Seneca he called *ille maximus morum edificator et conti-*

---

15) See Thomas H. and Ronald J. WONNACOTT, Introductory Statistics for Business and Economics (^{2}1977) p. 223–227 and 501–508. I am grateful to my colleagues Philip Hoffman, J. Morgan Kousser, and Leonard Searle for their advice on statistical questions.

16) In a comparison between Letters Two, Four and Six with Letters Three, Five and Seven, *ad, etiam, non, quasi, saltem* and *ut* have t-statistics of over 1.95. When comparing the letters of "Abelard" with the Hist. cal., *a+ab, autem, cum, de, diligenter, est, etiam, facile, obsecro, penitus, quae,* and *vehementer* are all above that level of significance. I should repeat here that in my opinion these differences are amply explained by variations of frequency of usage within the two samples (as the statistics for standard deviation show), and do not therefore provide evidence that Abelard was not the author of the Hist. cal.

17) See Peter VON MOOS, Lucan und Abelard, in: Hommage à André Boutemy, ed. Guy CAMBIER (1976) p. 413–443.

18) See among other places Abelard's Rule for Religious Women, ed. Terence P. MCLAUGHLIN, Mediaeval Studies 16 (1956) p. 242; Sic et non, prologue, eds. BOYER and

nentissime[19]. Now that almost all of Abelard's works have appeared in modern critical editions, a full study of his use of quotations would be enlightening. Though the evidence of the quotations in the letters of "Heloise" has been subjected to various interpretations, they are entirely consistent with the hypothesis that Abelard was the author of the entire correspondence. But since these matters are familiar, I will not develop them further here[20].

Those who argue that the correspondence is an authentic exchange rather than a literary fiction which had not been given a final editorial polish, have difficulty – or should have difficulty – explaining how Abelard, in Letter Seven, could address his wife as *O fratres et commonachi*[21] or repeat in Letter Eight practically verbatim two passages supposedly written by Heloise in Letter Six[22]. But such passages do accord with Abelard's known style of composi-

---

McKeon (as n. 9) p. 89; Theol. Christ. 3, 133, ed. Buytaert (as n. 9) p. 245; and the references cited in these editions.

19) Dialogus inter Philosophum, Iudaeum et Christianum, ed. Rudolf Thomas (1970) p. 99.

20) In A reconsideration (see n. 7) 484, I argued that an error in a long quotation from St. Augustine's De Bono Coniugali indicated that the Sic et non or another Abelardian fichier was the source of the quotation in Letter Six. In his excursus, Did Abelard Write Heloise's Third Letter? in: Women Writers of the Middle Ages (1984) p. 140–143, Peter Dronke counters that it indicates nothing of the source and that I have ignored "the two contexts of the Augustinian quotation". Prof. Silvestre has replied effectively and forcefully to this objection in L'idylle (as n. 6) p. 185–186. Prof. Dronke considers my reference to an Abelardian fichier as "a questionable and perhaps anachronistic assumption". I consider it obvious that Abelard, a peripatetic who spent much of his working life at places with very limited library resources (like Saint-Gildas and Le Paraclet), possessed a volume (or a number of volumes) of quotations which he had copied out for himself and then used in his writings; the various versions of Sic et non are examples or descendants of such volumes. I regret that Dronke has introduced into his discussion assumptions about the psychology and unstated beliefs not only of Heloise and Abelard but of myself (he characterizes what he conjectures to be my underlying argument as "purest prejudice"); the danger of this approach, besides its irrelevance and unfortunate ad hominem quality, is that a critic may erroneously interpret a conclusion as a presupposition.

21) Ep. VII, ed. Muckle (as n. 13) p. 269. It still seems to me likely that the existence of this phrase indicates the incorporation of some material from the lost Exhortatio ad fratres et commonachos; see Fraud, Fiction and Borrowing (as n. 5) p. 491–492.

22) Ep. VI, p. 245 = Ep. VIII, p. 269; Ep. VI, p. 247 = Ep. VIII, p. 270. Dronke, Women Writers (as n. 20) p. 143, deals with this problem by writing "one can only say that in the portions shared by Epp. VI and VIII there is a strong likelihood of contamination,

tion, to repeat himself and to include in one work quotations and passages which he had earlier developed elsewhere[23].

Other passages in the letters attributed to Heloise go beyond repetition to suggest a true unity of thought, providing a fourth type of evidence. One example, included in the appendix, is the expression of Abelard's doctrine of intention in the first letter attributed to Heloise: "Justice does not weigh what is done but the spirit in which it is done" (*Nec quae fiunt sed quo animo fiunt aequitas pensat*), an idea and indeed practically the very phrasing which also appears in Abelard's Theologia Christiana, his Commentary on Romans, his Ethics, in the treatise *Adtendite a falsis prophetis* recently discovered by Louk Engels, and as in Letter Eight[24]. A similar concept, also included in the appendix, is that of the moral indifference of those things common to both the elect and the damned, *quae reprobis aeque ut electis communia sunt*, as Letter Four puts it; this idea is also stated in much the same words in Letter Six and two times each in Abelard's Commentary on Romans and his Ethics[25]. A parallel of a different sort is the image in Letter Two comparing Le Paraclet to a newly planted vineyard in need of watering; this metaphor is very similar to one in Abelard's sermon De eleemosyna for the nuns of his new foundation[26].

Striking, aphoristic phrases might be evidence of either single authorship or the influence of one author on another. More commonplace "Abelardian"

---

and that some passages, which do not seem to fit into either argument, may well have been interpolated".

23) See Louk J. ENGELS, Abélard écrivain, in Peter Abelard. Proceedings of the International Conference Louvain, May 10–12, 1971, ed. E. M. BUYTAERT (1974) p. 16–23, and ENGELS, Adtendite a falsis prophetis (Ms. Colmar 128, ff. 152v/153v). Un texte de Pierre Abélard contre les Cisterciens retrouvé? in: Corona Gratiarum: Miscellanea patristica, historica et liturgica Eligio Dekkers O.S.B. XII lustra completenti oblata (1975) 2, p. 213.

24) Ep. 2, p. 72; Theol. Christ. 5, 41, ed. BUYTAERT (as n. 9) p. 366; Comm. Rom. (as n. 9) p. 65, lines 644–5, and p. 306, lines 324–5; Ethics, ed. David O. LUSCOMBE (Oxford Medieval Texts, 1971) p. 28, lines 9–10; Adtendite, ed. ENGELS (as n. 23) p. 226, 11.19–20. MUCKLE discusses the passage in Mediaeval Studies 15 (1953) p. 55 and ENGELS in Adtendite p. 207–208.

25) Ep. 4, p. 82, lines 9–10 and ep. 6, p. 248, lines 28–29; Comm. Rom., p. 65, lines 629–30 and p. 304, lines 262–3; Ethics, ed. LUSCOMBE p. 2, lines 13–14 and p. 44, lines 30–31.

26) Ep. 2, p. 70: *novella plantatio cuius adhuc teneris maxime plantis frequens ut proficiant necessaria est irrigatio*; sermon 30 in Abelard's Opera, ed. Victor COUSIN (1849–59, rpt. 1970) 1. 552: *Sed novella ejus adhuc et tenera plantatio vestris, ut crescat. colenda est eleemosynis.*

phrases are stronger evidence of Abelardian authorship, since they are not in themselves especially memorable. A concordance allows one to identify in the letters attributed to Heloise a number of turns of phrase which also appear in the letters of Abelard and others of his works. Many of these phrases are the magisterial locutions of an experienced Biblical expositor and teacher, and while some can doubtless be found in other authors as well, others seem to me to be personal peculiarities of style. Abelard frequently rephrases a quotation after writing *Ac si aperte dicat* or some variant[27]. He regularly introduces a quotation with some form of *Quod diligenter attendens* or *Ut praedictus doctor meminit*. The only times in his letters when he uses the adverb *magnopere*, it appears in negative phrases with the verb *curare*[28]. This same usage appears three times (once with *pensare*) in Letter Six. There is, of course, nothing unusual about *ut supra memini* or its equivalent, but I thought it worth recording that both „Heloise" and „Abelard" make use of both *memini* and *meminimus*. My choice of most of the examples given in the appendix is based on my impression that they are relatively unusual, but whether a given locution is a useful marker of Abelardian authorship depends, of course, on whether it appears in many works unquestionably written by Abelard and whether it is not a commonplace among medieval authors. The first question can best be determined with the help of a computerized text of Abelard's opera omnia, and may therefore be answered relatively soon[29]. The second question can be answered statistically with the help of other computerized texts[30], or impressionistically

---

27) In his sermons Abelard most commonly uses the phrase *ac si diceret*, but in sermons V, XI, XXI, and XXII he introduces variety with the phrase *tanquam si diceret*. Sermon XI contains three examples of *ac si* and one of *tanquam*, the later following a quotation from St. Augustine (Sermon CLXXX) beginning *Tanquam diceretur*. While awaiting the edition being prepared by Louk ENGELS, see Opera, ed. COUSIN, 1, p. 394, 432, 443, 451–452, 501–2. Possibly variations in style like this one will permit a relative dating of works like the sermons.

28) In this usage Abelard followed Augustine; see Theologia 'Summi Boni' 3.1.10, ed. Heinrich OSTLENDER (1939) p. 80, citing De Genesi ad litteram 4.4.9, ed. J. ZYCHA (CSEL 28, 1, 1894) p. 101 or MIGNE PL 34, col. 300.

29) As I learned when I presented this paper orally, Prof. Udo Kindermann and his colleagues at the Institut für Alte Sprachen of the Universität Erlangen-Nürnberg have prepared such a computerized text, based on Cousin's edition.

30) The new volumes of the Corpus Christianorum, like the Chronicon of William of Tyre, ed. R.B.C. HUYGENS (CC Cont. Med. 73, 1986), with its microfiche instrumenta lexicologica, are an invaluable resource for comparisons of this sort.

by those with lexicographic memories. The examples in the appendix are offered in the hope of stimulating answers to both questions.

If the letters were written by different authors, how can one account for such similarity or identity in so many different forms? Similarities of phrasing and patterns of quotation have long been noted by such scholars as Schmeidler, Charrier and Muckle, and they have regularly been dismissed on the grounds that as a teacher and husband Abelard naturally influenced his wife's literary style. To affect not only Heloise's reading and choice of phrasing but even her use of the cursus, that influence must have been strong and continuing. The hypothesis of mutual influence has recently been stated succinctly by Peter Dronke: "The most natural basic assumption is that they read certain texts together at one stage of their lives, and that, when they were separated, they still read texts in the same manuscripts, exchanging these (or sometimes perhaps making copies for each other) when necessary"[31].

If, however, we accept the chronology given in the Historia calamitatum and the following correspondence, a chronology which is supported by other evidence, the opportunities for intellectual and literary contact between Abelard and Heloise in the period before the composition of the correspondence were slight. The two met about 1116, when Heloise was probably sixteen or so and already had a basic formation in Latin; as Abelard wrote in the Historia, *per habundanciam litterarum erat suprema*[32]. According to both Abelard and his critics, the tutor was initially more involved in seduction than education. When Heloise soon became pregnant, she took refuge separately in Brittany, and when she returned to Paris they lived apart, with Heloise eventually entering Argenteuil. Abelard's castration and their mutual conversion to monastic life probably occurred in or about 1118. There really was little time or occasion in those early years for Abelard to teach Heloise his personal style of cursus and his favorite constructions. Moreover, Abelard's style and reading matter changed significantly after his conversion, and the style of the letters attributed to Heloise is that which Abelard used in the mid-1130s, not that of the works he has left us from the period when he was in close contact with Heloise[33].

---

31) DRONKE, Women Writers (as n. 20) p. 141.
32) Hist. cal., ed. MONFRIN (as n. 9) p. 71.
33) This statement is admittedly impressionistic and not based on a computer-assisted or statistical study. The style of the Hist. cal. and the letters in the correspondence (at least through Letter Seven) seems to me to be strikingly different from that of the Dialectica, ed. L. M. DE RIJK (²1970), of which major portions appear to have been

We really do not know how much contact the two had after their entry into monastic life and before the period in the second half of the 1130s when Abelard was deeply involved in writing for Le Paraclet, producing a set of writings which apparently began with the "correspondence." According to Roscelinus, in the period shortly after his conversion Abelard frequently visited Heloise while he was teaching away from Saint-Denis. It is p o s s i b l e that he talked with her often, wrote her long and learned letters which have not survived, and sent her manuscripts of his own and other works. After 1129, when Heloise was installed at Le Paraclet, but before the time of the composition of the correspondence, Abelard m a y have had even more contact with her, both personally and through manuscripts, though both propriety and their monastic rule did not authorize a close relationship. Abelard himself says that he undertook to look after the sisters at Le Paraclet in person (*corporali quoque presentia eis invigilare*), apparently acting as the *magister* of the house[34]. But while the possibility of significant personal and intellectual contact existed, it must be said that it is a major function of the correspondence we are discussing to deny that any such contact took place. The first letter of "Heloise" states the matter categorically in asking "why ... have you so neglected and scorned me that you neither hearten me with conversation when you are here nor console me with a letter when you are away?"[35]. Paradoxically, if Heloise had enough intellectual contact with Abelard to be able to write in his style, using his pattern of cursus and his favorite quotations, she would not have needed to write a letter complaining of neglect, a letter which appears on this major point to be a fic-

---

written before c. 1118 and in the period of Abelard's courtship of Heloise. The style of the letters is closer to that of Theologia 'Summi Boni', written about 1120 after Abelard became a monk of Saint-Denis, but there are still noticeable differences between that work and those of the 1130s. One I find intriguing is that the phrase *verbi gratia* does not appear in Hist. cal. or Letters Two through Seven, though Abelard used it often in Theologia 'Summi Boni'. One might object, of course, that the differences among these works are the product of the genre or subject matter rather than of a development of Abelard's style, but I consider this argument insufficient to explain all the differences, and in any case, if the adolescent Heloise learned to imitate the style of her mature teacher, she presumably was influenced by the style he was writing at the time.

34) Hist. cal., ed. MONFRIN (as n. 9) lines 1479–80.

35) Ep. 2, ed. MUCKLE in Mediaeval Studies 15 (1953) p. 72: *cur ... in tantam tibi negligentiam atque oblivionem venerim ut nec colloquio praesentis recreer nec absentis epistola consoler*; I have used active constructions in my translation, but in the Latin Heloise is the passive recipient of Abelard's neglect. Cf. ibid. p. 70: *nec ... vel sermone praesentem vel epistola absentem consolari tentaveris.*

tion. Here is a serious problem for those who accept the authenticity of the letters, for the more contact one hypothesizes in order to explain the style of the letters attributed to Heloise, the more difficult it is to explain their content. Theoretically, of course, Heloise could have misrepresented her situation when writing authentic letters to Abelard, but it is hard to imagine a motive for doing so, whereas Abelard, as he makes clear in the Historia calamitatum, was sensitive about the charge that his relationship with Heloise at Le Paraclet was improper[36].

If in writing these letters Abelard created a literary fiction to present ideas which he attributed to his wife, it would not have been the only time he appeared to do so. It has long been known that five of the quotations supposedly used by Heloise to dissuade Abelard from marriage, as reported in the Historia calamitatum, also appear in the Theologia Christiana, and it seems overwhelmingly likely that when Abelard wrote the Historia he felt quite free to create an imagined conversation. He also "reported" the words of Heloise, in both direct and indirect discourse, in his preface to the Hymnarius Paraclitensis, where he uses Heloise's criticism of existing hymns to justify his own composition[37]. We cannot know for certain, of course, whether or not Heloise wrote Abelard just those words which he attributes to her, but if she did, she wrote precisely what he needed her to say to counter a charge of presumption for writing his own liturgical compositions[38].

In this paper I have deliberately avoided a discussion of questions of motivation and psychology, of why Abelard might have undertaken to write a literary fiction, to what degree he might have been representing the actual words or thoughts of Heloise, and what reactions Heloise might have had to such a composition. That limitation keeps the emphasis of discussion where it should be in the present state of scholarly disagreement, not on speculation about the psychology of Heloise and Abelard, but on the more technical issue of whether the correspondence was written by one author or two.

---

36) Hist. cal., p. 101.

37) Peter Abelard's Hymnarius Paraclitensis, ed. Joseph Szövérffy (1965) 2. 9–13. Szövérffy wrongly closes the quotation at the bottom of p. 9, but Abelard continues to "quote" or paraphrase up to p. 13, beginning to speak in his own voice again with *His vel consimilibus vestrarum persuasionibus rationum* ...

38) It is also within the realm of possibility that Abelard composed the letter "from" Heloise which introduces the Problemata, but I can think of no way to establish with certainty who wrote it. Since the answers to the questions are his, it might be said that Abelard had the final say over what was written.

Statistical evidence of the sort presented here cannot disprove the hypothesis of two separate authors, though the cumulation of such evidence makes the hypothesis less und less likely. It is my conclusion that the letters of "Heloise" and the letters of "Abelard" were written by a single person, and it seems to me reasonable to ask the champions of dual authorship to offer some relatively unsubjective means of distinguishing between the writing of one author and the other[39]. The large number of locutions and quotations common to both sets of letters and to other works surely written by Abelard makes me think that a single author was Abelard rather than Heloise or a third person.

It is difficult to marshal one's forces on two fronts at once, and in this paper I have been more concerned to address the question of single rather than dual authorship than to deal with the issue of forgery rather than Abelardian authorship. Any hope for a convincing answer to that second question, it seems to me, will depend on whether a full analysis of the style of the Historia calamitatum and the following letters accords distinctively with that of other works written by Abelard. If further analysis does confirm the case for Abelardian authorship, we would then be faced with the challenging task of understanding, not the moral but the literary and psychological basis[40] for writing such a curiously contradictory work and how Abelard could have felt free to build a monument to his own reputation on a foundation of his beloved wife's intimate revelations[41].

---

39) DRONKE frankly states in Heloise's Problemata (as n. 10) p. 55 that the characteristics which he considers indicate the "individuality" of Heloise's style "can occur at times, too, in Abelard's letters". Passages expressing deep emotion (and even, to use Gilson's phrase, obsecration) could as well be produced by Abelard writing a literary fiction as by Heloise writing authentic letters.

40) Whatever the history of its composition, this correspondence calls out for explanation. For scholars, however, issues of morality, of whether we end up considering Heloise and Abelard admirable people or not, seem to me to be questions of only minimal interest. What is important and challenging is not to judge these two people but to understand them.

41) After this paper was completed, Chrysogonus WADDELL published The Paraclete Statutes 'Institutiones Nostrae': Introduction, Edition, Commentary (Cistercian Liturgy Series 20, 1987). In his extensive commentary, Fr. Waddell argues learnly that Institutiones nostrae was almost certainly written in the twelfth century, probably in the mid-twelfth-century, and most likely by Heloise herself. He also shows that the redactor of this brief customary for the Paraclete and its daughter houses was familiar with the Rule which is such an important component of Abelard's correspondence, but that while s/he used some of Abelard's unusual phrasing and incorporated some of his

Appendix

1. Comparative Passages

Ep. 6, p. 243.15	Ac si aperte dicat: ...	
246.23	Ac si aperte diceret: ...	
Ep. 5, p. 83.29	Ac si aperte dicatur, ...	
84.29–30	Ac si apertius dicat: ...	
85.25	Ac si diceret: ...	
93.44	Ac si aperte diceret: ...	
Ep. 7, p. 255.37	Ac si diceret: ...	
259.11	Ac si aperte diceret: ...	
266.37	Ac si aperte dicat: ...	

---

ideas, on the whole his prescriptions were not followed at the Paraclete. If Waddell is correct in his conclusions (as I believe he is) that Institutiones nostrae is a twelfth-century text which clearly shows familiarity with the disputed correspondence, and that Heloise herself very likely used Abelard's Rule as one of her sources, the authenticity of Abelard's authorship seems to be established by the best witness possible. On the other hand, the conclusion that the Rule was known by Heloise but that so many of its unusual and often impractical provisions did not become part of the customary life at the Paraclete suggests that Heloise was not as eager to follow Abelard's advice as Letter Six proclaims; indeed, it is consistent with this evidence to imagine that Heloise loved Abelard and cherished his memory after his death, but largely ignored the "correspondence" and Rule he created, though this is a possible conclusion that Waddell does not press. We have no reason to believe that either the letters or the Rule were treated as edifying reading for the nuns or were circulated to the Paraclete's dependencies. Fr. Waddell, who cites an earlier version of this present paper, concludes that Abelard was the sole author of the entire correspondence. We have exchanged ideas and information on this topic since 1972, I have learned a great deal from him, and I find it very gratifying that, starting from different positions and following different lines of investigation, our conclusions have become so closely interwoven. I should add that in The 'Letters' of Abelard and Heloise: A Source for Chrétien de Troyes? in Studi Medievali, 3rd. ser. 27 (1986) p. 123–146, Helen C.R. LAURIE asserts on the basis of similar concepts that Chrétien was familiar with the correspondence in question, but since she also shows that many of these common ideas could also be found in such authors as Ovid, Quintillian and Cicero, I have not been convinced that she has made her case. In my opinion there is still no evidence that a copy of the correspondence was ever known outside the Paraclete before the late thirteenth century, when Jean de Meun and his Parisian circle became aware of the text.

Ep. 8, p. 244.15	ac si diceret ...
247.26–27	Ac si aperte dicat: ...
268.36	Ac si diceret: ...
Ep. 5, p. 245.7	Ex quibus quidem verbis aperte colligitur ...
250.30	Ex his liquide verbis colligitur ...
Ep. 8, p. 269.4	Ex quibus videlicet Apostoli verbis manifeste colligitur ...
Ep. 11, p. 251.72	Ex quo liquide colligitur ...
Ep. 6, p. 248.26–27	Non enim magnopere sunt curanda quae ...
251.10	Non itaque magnopere ... pensandum est,
251.33–34	non magnopere curanda esse docemur
Ep. 8, p. 276.19–21	nec etiam ... magnopere curarent.
Ep. 11, p. 253.100	Nec magnopere curandum est, ...
Ep. 6, p. 242.28–29	Quod et beatus praecavens Hieronymus ... meminit dicens:
Ep. 8, p. 254.23	Quod studiose praecavens Apostolus:
Ep. 6, p. 242.28–29	Quod et beatus praecavens Hieronymus ... meminit dicens:
246.1–2	Unde et Macrobius Theodosius ... meminit his verbis:
247.18–19	De quo et maximus ille sapientum in Proverbiis meminit dicens:
Ep. 6, p. 244.44	... beatus non immemor Benedictus ...
Ep. 6, p. 246.41	ipse quoque beatus non immemor Benedictus ...
Ep. 8, p. 271.39	Hinc et beatus non immemor Benedictus ...
Ep. 4, p. 80.33–34	Quod beatus exponens Gregorius: inquit
Ep. 7, p. 264.1	Quod quidem beatus exponens Hieronymus:
Ep. 8, p. 290.27–28	Quod beatus exponens Gregorius ... ait:
Sermo 11, p. 443	Quem quidem locum beatus exponens Augustinus ait:
Ep. 4, p. 80.39–40	beatus diligenter attendens Ambrosius:
Ep. 6, p. 243.35–37	Quod diligenter beatus papa Gregorius attendens ... ita distinxit:
246.28	... si diligentius attenderent, ...

Ep. 6, p. 249.45–46	Quod diligenter attendens beatus Augustinus ...
HC p. 202.5	si diligentius apostolicam attendamus auctoritatem ...
211.7–8	Quae diligenter beatus attendens Hieronymus ... ait:
Ep. 3, p. 74.5	Quod diligenter attendens Apostolus
Ep. 8, p. 245.9–10	Apostolus Jacobus diligenter attendens ait:
250.30–31	insignis ecclesiae doctor Hieronymus diligenter attendens ... dicens:
261.41	Ecclesiastes diligenter attendens ait:
264.27–28	Quod diligenter beatus attendens Augustinus ... meminit:
270.5–7	Quod maximus ille sapientum diligenter attendens ... dicens:
274.7–9	Quod et diligenter beatus attendens Augustinus ... breviter expressit:
280.40–41	Quod beatus diligenter attendens Gregorius ...
284.9–10	quod beatus Antonius admonet dicens:
Rom. p. 191.159	Quod quidem et Dominus ipse diligenter attendens
Ethics p. 6.18–19	si diligentius adtendamus
58.30–31	Quod diligenter beatus Stephanus adtendens
Sermo 5, p. 394	Quae duo diligenter idem apostolus attendens,
Sermo 13, p. 462	Quod et beatus Apostolus diligenter attendens
Ep. 4, p. 81.43	Per Isaiam Dominus clamat:
82.1–2	Et per Ezechielem:
82.3–4	E contra autem per Salomonem dicitur:
Ep. 5, p. 91.33	ipse etiam per Ieremiam fideles adhortatur, dicens:
Ep. 5, p. 91.39–40	Et quod per Zachariam prophetam ... praedictum est comple:
Ep. 8, p. 245.1	Hinc autem per Salomonem dicitur:
270.32	Dominus per Joel dicit:
290.40	... per Eliphaz dicitur:
Rom. p. 55.284	Per Ieremiam Dominus dicit:
Ep. 6, p. 248.5–6	Legerat ni fallor quod in Vitis Patrum scriptum est his verbis:
Ep. 8, p. 274.12	Legerat, ni[si] fallor, illud beati Athanasii ...:
290.43	Legerat iste, ni[si] fallor, magni Christianorum philosophi Origenis homelias ...
HC, p. 181.1658	Legerat, ni fallor, praedictus sanctus illud Suetonii

Ep. 6, p. 250.34–35	Unde et ipsos legimus apostolos ita rusticane ...
HC p. 187.21–22	... beato attestante Hieronymo, monachos legimus in veteri Testamento.
206.28–29	Legimus et potentem illum reginae Candacis eunuchum ... praeesse
208.24–25	... quos frequenter legimus, vel etiam vidimus, monasteria quoque feminarum constituere ...
Ep. 3, p. 74.6	Legimus Dominum Moysi dixisse:
Ep. 7, p. 254.5	Legimus in Evangelio murmurantem Pharisaeum ...
280.24	Legimus et Dominum ipsum ... exhibuisse ...
281.7–8	Sicut de beata legimus Eugenia ...
	+ 12 other instances of legimus in Ep. 7
Ep. 8, p. 274.1–2	... ut ait Hieronymus, monachos legimus in Veteri Testamento ...
271.26	Unde in Vitis Patrum scriptum legimus:
281.27–28	Legimus Dominum in Joanne, ut iam supra meminimus, vilitatem ... laudasse.
	+ 6 other instances of legimus in Ep. 8
Sermo 23, p. 505	beatus Hieronymus quodam loco meminit, dicens Filii prophetarum, quos monachos legimus in Veteri Testamento, etc.

HC p. 194.27	... ut praedictus doctor meminit, ...
207.9	et ut beatus meminit Augustinus in sermone quodam
Ep. 5, p. 85.42	ut beatus etiam meminit Augustinus
Ep. 7, p. 255.9	sicut et Hieronymus in psalmo XXVI meminit
256.2	ut Marcus meminit
274.11	ut enim Lucas meminit,
Ep. 8, p. 242.13	ut in Rhetorica sua Tullius meminit
242.18	ut praedictus meminit doctor,
253.36	Ut enim beatus quoque meminit Benedictus:
254.20	et ipse alibi meminit dicens:
263.13–14	sicut in Vitis quoque Patrum quidam ipsorum meminit dicens:
263.17	Hinc Apostolus de diaconissa meminit dicens:
264.1–2	ut beatus quoque meminit Benedictus
264.11–13	beatus Gregorius ... meminit dicens:

Ep. 8, p. 264.27–28	Quod diligenter beatus attendens Augustinus ... quodam loco meminit:
279.10–12	Hic quippe magnus ecclesiae tam rector tam doctor ... ita meminit:
280.1–3	quam et beatus Hieronymus ... ita quodam loco meminit:
289.32–34	Qui ... quodam loco sic meminit:

Ep. 2, p. 71.7	in ea quam supra memini ad amicum epistola
Ep. 6, p. 251.22	ut supra meminimus, Timotheo scribit ...
HC p. 181.10	ut supra memini,
184.18	ut supra memini,
197.10	ut supra memini,
Ep. 3, p. 76.13	sicut supra memini
Ep. 5, p. 91.28	ut iam supra memini
93.17	ut supra memini,
Ep. 7, p. 265.25	ut iam supra meminimus.
Ep. 8, p. 273.15	quod supra meminimus:
281.27	ut iam supra meminimus,
284.42–3	quod supra meminimus
287.21–2	ut supra meminimus:

Ep. 2, p. 72.15–16	Nec quae fiunt sed quo animo fiunt aequitas pensat.
Ep. 8, p. 265.34–5	Nec tam quod fiat, quam quod quomodo vel quo animo fiat, pensandum est.
Rom. p. 65.644–6	... non tam attendant quae fiunt quam quo animo fiant.
306.324–5	Deus namque, qui cordis inspector est, non tam quae fiunt quam quo animo fiunt attendit.
Ethica, p. 28.9–10	Non enim quae fiunt, sed quo animo fiant pensat Deus,

Ep. 4, p. 82.9–10	quae reprobis aeque ut electis communia sunt.
Ep. 6, p. 248.28–29	Haec vero sunt omnia quae exterius geruntur, et aeque reprobis ut electis, aeque hypocritis ut religiosis communia sunt.
Comm. Rom. p. 65	remuneratio tam electis, ut dictum est, quam reprobis
304	Quaecumque enim exterius bene fieri videntur ... aeque reprobis ut electis communia sunt et hypocritis sicut veris fidelibus.

Ethics p. 2 44.30	Quae quidem omnia cum eque reprobis ut bonis eveniant Opera quippe quae, ut prediximus, eque reprobis ut electis communia sunt, omnia in se indifferentia sunt,
Ep. 6, p. 248.21–22	in his quae media boni et mali atque indifferentia dicuntur,
Ep. 6, p. 251.33	ea, quae fiunt exterius, et indifferentia vocantur,
Ep. 8, p. 278.28–29	intermedia boni et mali, hoc est indifferentia computantur,
Ep. 4, p. 81.22–22	qui cordis et renum probator est, et in abscondito videt.
Ep. 6, p. 251.11	qui cordis et renum probator est, et in abscondito videt, ...
Rom. p. 78.61–62	Unde et ipse probator cordis et renum in abscondito videre dicitur.
Sermo 14, p. 468	In abscondito magis quam in manifesto Deus videre dicitur, quia probator cordis et renum, non tam quae fiunt, quam quo animo fiant attendit, nec tam opera quam intentionem remunerat.
	[This phrase may be a quotation and has Biblical overtones; cf. Jerem. 11: 20 and 20: 12.]
Ep. 6, p. 243.26–27	Sed et cum omnium virtutum discretio sit mater, et omnium bonorum moderatrix sit ratio, ...
Ep. 8, p. 274.28	omnium virtutum mater discretio
Sermo. 30, p. 551	Est enim discretio mater omnium virtutum.
	[Cf. Cassian, Collationes 2, 4 (PL 49, 528): omnium namque virtutum generatrix, custos moderatrixque discretio est.]
Ep. 4, p. 82	Non coronabitur nisi qui legitime certaverit. Non quaero coronam victoriae.
Sermo 26, p. 521–2	Non coronabitur nisi qui legitime certaverit, ab omnibus se abstinet, ne coronam scilicet victoriae perdat.
	[See Vulgate 2. Tim. 2: 5: Nam et qui certat in agone, non coronatur nisi legitime certaverit.]

2. Word count of correspondence

Ep. 1 (=HC)	text:		10,391	(89%)	
	quotations:		1,265	(11%)	11,656 (19%)
Ep. 2	text:		2,125	(96%)	
	quotations:		96	(4%)	2,221 (4%)
Ep. 3	text:		1,526	(93%7	
	quotations:		182	(7%)	1,708 (3%)
Ep. 4	text:		2,099	(89%)	
	quotations:		260	(11%)	2,359 (4%)
Ep. 5	text:		4,541	(90%)	
	quotations:		520	(10%)	5,061 (8%)
Ep. 6	text:		3,425	(67%)	
	quotations:		1,672	)33%)	5,097 (8%)
Ep. 7	text:		8,197	(71%)	
	quotations:		3,303	(29%)	11,500 (18%)
Ep. 8	text:		15,716	(70%)	
	quotations:		6,887	(30%)	22,603 (36%)
total text:			48,020	(77%)	
total quotations:			14,185	(23%)	
grand total:					62,205 (100%)

Historia calamitatum (Ep. 1)

	A	B	C	D	E	F	G	H	I	J	m	s.d.
a + ab	15	3	6	5	11	3	3	3	5	10	6.4	4.2
ad	17	13	6	14	15	21	23	12	17	13	15.1	4.8
amplius	5	7	5	0	2	0	1	1	0	5	2.6	2.6
autem	8	4	7	8	10	8	13	5	6	6	7.5	2.6
cum	10	9	7	5	8	14	18	12	15	11	10.9	4.0
de	12	7	9	7	4	6	3	7	7	10	7.2	2.7
diligenter	0	0	0	2	0	0	0	0	0	0	0.2	0.6
est	10	8	6	7	3	8	8	6	4	6	6.6	2.1
et	30	27	46	26	36	39	33	38	36	33	34.4	6.0
etiam	2	0	6	4	3	0	0	3	2	9	2.9	2.9
facile	1	1	4	1	0	0	2	0	3	0	1.2	1.4
in	21	30	24	16	21	18	16	25	30	24	22.5	5.1
non	7	12	12	10	3	12	3	12	6	4	8.1	3.9
obsecro	0	0	0	0	0	0	0	0	0	0	0.0	0.0
penitus	2	2	2	1	3	2	3	1	1	2	1.9	0.7

										m	s.d.
quae	1	6	5	7	4	1	3	4	6	2	3.9	2.1
quam	1	5	14	16	15	5	3	13	13	13	9.8	5.6
quasi	4	2	1	0	2	5	5	3	5	2	2.9	1.8
quod	5	5	9	9	13	15	12	10	6	5	8.9	3.6
saltem	0	0	0	3	0	1	0	0	1	1	0.6	1.0
si	0	4	7	5	1	8	2	5	4	5	4.1	2.5
tanto	6	2	1	1	2	1	0	1	3	4	2.1	1.8
ut	19	9	9	8	9	12	10	5	17	12	11.0	4.2
vehementer	1	2	6	4	3	1	3	1	1	1	2.3	1.7

A, B, c etc. = 1000-word-units
m = mean
s.d. = standard deviation

Ep. 2, 4 and 6 ("Heloise")

	2 A	2 B	4 A	4 B	6 A	6 B	6 C	m	s.d.
a + ab	3	5	3	10	15	7	11	7.7	4.5
ad	12	8	8	7	12	6	10	9.0	2.4
amplius	1	2	2	3	1	0	0	1.3	1.1
autem	4	5	4	6	3	2	0	3.4	2.0
cum	4	7	9	5	6	6	11	6.9	2.4
de	9	4	5	5	14	9	15	8.7	4.4
diligenter	1	0	0	1	3	0	1	0.9	1.1
est	7	11	8	16	10	9	18	11.3	4.2
et	36	22	31	34	31	42	52	35.4	9.5
etiam	2	2	1	6	5	5	8	4.1	2.5
facile	0	0	0	1	2	1	0	0.6	0.8
in	20	22	31	29	18	21	17	22.6	5.4
non	11	28	8	18	16	13	11	15.0	6.6
obsecro	2	3	3	2	1	1	1	1.9	0.9
penitus	0	1	1	2	1	1	0	0.9	0.7
quae	6	10	8	8	7	7	13	8.4	2.4
quam	9	25	11	11	11	9	8	12.0	5.9
quasi	2	2	0	0	0	4	2	1.4	1.5
quod	8	9	14	11	13	13	3	10.1	3.8
saltem	4	1	1	3	1	0	0	1.4	1.5
si	4	11	3	7	8	8	2	6.1	3.2
tanto	4	1	7	2	1	0	2	2.4	2.4
ut	12	11	22	10	17	15	13	14.3	4.2
vehementer	0	1	1	0	0	0	1	0.4	0.5

The Correspondence of Abelard and Heloise

Ep. 3 and 5

	3	5 a	5 B	5 C	5 D	m	s.d.
a + ab	6	5	12	12	7	8.4	3.4
ad	14	10	10	13	15	12.4	2.3
amplius	0	3	7	2	0	2.4	2.9
autem	7	4	3	0	1	3.0	2.7
cum	4	10	10	10	9	8.6	2.6
de	10	8	10	3	8	7.8	2.9
diligenter	3	3	0	0	0	1.2	1.6
est	12	16	23	6	21	15.6	6.9
et	48	24	33	49	38	38.4	10.5
etiam	4	5	9	10	8	7.2	2.6
facile	1	1	0	0	1	0.6	0.5
in	15	37	23	26	20	24.2	8.2
non	9	6	12	12	21	12.0	5.6
obsecro	1	0	3	0	3	1.4	1.5
penitus	0	0	2	2	1	1.0	1.0
quase	5	10	9	6	8	7.6	2.1
quam	5	11	17	16	8	11.4	5.1
quasi	3	3	0	2	3	2.2	1.3
quod	20	4	15	11	7	11.4	6.3
saltem	0	0	2	1	0	0.6	0.9
si	9	4	8	6	6	6.6	1.9
tanto	2	2	10	3	0	3.4	3.8
ut	8	11	11	13	8	10.2	2.2
vehementer	0	2	0	1	0	0.6	0.9

Ep. 7

	A	B	C	D	E	F	G	H	m	s.d.
a + ab	18	13	9	2	8	11	8	9	9.8	4.6
ad	5	7	15	15	14	14	17	8	11.9	4.5
amplius	0	0	0	0	3	3	2	8	2.0	2.8
autem	3	4	2	0	3	2	3	4	2.6	1.3
cum	8	14	9	9	5	6	3	4	7.3	3.5
de	10	18	16	17	7	18	7	8	12.6	5.1
diligenter	1	3	2	4	0	0	0	0	1.3	1.6
est	10	11	14	7	17	10	8	9	10.8	3.3
et	29	46	36	47	34	35	40	29	37.0	6.9
etiam	6	11	16	12	10	7	16	8	10.8	3.8
facile	0	0	0	1	0	0	1	0	0.3	0.5
in	32	23	30	18	26	26	29	20	25.5	4.9

non	7	7	11	8	10	7	6	19	9.4	4.2
obsecro	1	0	0	0	1	0	0	0	0.3	0.5
penitus	0	0	0	1	0	0	0	1	0.3	0.5
quae	10	7	7	11	3	10	6	10	8.0	2.7
quam	12	8	13	16	9	10	7	10	10.6	2.9
quasi	1	4	5	2	2	6	3	2	3.1	1.7
quod	6	10	8	8	6	2	6	11	7.1	2.8
saltem	0	0	0	0	0	0	0	1	0.1	0.4
si	2	2	3	5	6	2	3	6	3.6	1.8
tanto	2	0	0	0	2	3	2	6	1.9	2.0
ut	8	8	10	9	7	8	17	13	10.0	3.4
vehementer	0	0	0	1	0	1	0	0	0.3	0.5

	Historia calamitatum (Ep. 1)			Ep. 3, 5 and 7			Ep. 2, 4 and 6	
	m	s.d.	dif.	m	s.d.	dif.	m	s.d.
a + ab	6.4	4.2		9.2	4.1		7.7	4.5
ad	15.1	4.8		12.1	3.7		9.0	2.4
amplius	2.6	2.6		2.2	2.7		1.3	1.1
autem	7.5	2.6	1	2.8	1.9		3.4	2.0
cum	10.9	4.0		7.8	3.2		6.9	2.4
de	7.2	2.7		10.7	4.9		8.7	4.4
diligenter	0.2	0.6		1.2	1.5		0.9	1.1
est	6.6	2.1	1	12.6	5.3		11.3	4.2
et	34.4	6.0		37.5	8.1		35.4	9.5
etiam	2.9	2.9	1	9.4	3.7	1	4.1	2.5
facile	1.2	1.4		0.4	0.5		0.6	0.8
in	22.5	5.1		25.0	6.0		22.6	5.4
non	8.1	3.9		10.4	4.8		15.0	6.6
obsecro	0.0	0.0		0.7	1.1		1.9	0.9
penitus	1.9	0.7	1	0.5	0.8		0.9	0.7
quae	3.9	2.1	1	7.8	2.4		8.4	2.4
quam	9.8	5.6		10.9	3.7		12.0	5.9
quasi	2.9	1.8		2.8	1.6		1.4	1.5
quod	9.9	3.6		8.8	4.8		10.1	3.8
saltem	0.6	1.0		0.3	0.6		1.4	1.5
si	4.1	2.5		4.8	2.3		6.1	3.2
tanto	2.1	1.8		2.5	2.8		2.4	2.4
ut	11.0	4.2		10.1	2.9		14.3	4.2
vehementer	2.3	1.7		0.4	0.7		0.4	0.5

Index

This is primarily an index of subjects, weighted more to persons than to places in accordance with the author's stress. *Note well* that chapters 12 and 13 have their own indexes of persons and places; no attempt is made here to duplicate them. Manuscripts (under MANUSCRIPTS CITED) and classical allusions (by author) are indexed, but not Scriptural citations. Modern authors are indexed for opinions. The abbreviations are: abp. = archbishop; abt. = abbot; ar. = *arrondissement*; bp. = bishop; c. = *canton*; ch.-l. = *chef-lieu*; ct. = count; ctess. = countess; dép. = *département*; k. = king.

Abelard, Peter (1079-?1142) 320, 332-3, 343, 347; and Heloise 455-73; commentaries on: Ezechiel 432, 482; Romans 425, 438; correspondence, authenticity of 411-12, 415, 438-53, 475-86, 488-512; date of death 472-3; *Dialectica* 432; *Ethics* 338, 348; *Exhortatio: ad fratres* 317, 419, 439, 440; *ad sorores* 445, 446, 447; *Hist. calam.* 329-30, 418, 420, 430-8, 441-8, 469, 477-83, 494; *Soliloquium* 439; *Theol. christiana* 438, 439, 441, 444, 469; on women 317; style of 478-9, 484, 492-511
Adam, abt. of Saint-Denis (d. 1122) 390, 391, 436
Adam of Eynsham, *Life of St Hugh of Lincoln* 333-4
Adam de Perseigne 34-6, 38, 40
Adam of Saint-Victor 45, 46, 51-2, 54, 55-8
adultery 39-40, 102, 104-10, 119
Aldobrandino of Siena 325
Algrin 394
Alix de Mareuil 38
allegory 175
André de Luyères 81, 84-7
Andreas Capellanus 7, 30-4, 39, 81-8, 113, 119, 120, 172
anonymous authors 30
Anthony, Saint (d. 356) 505
Aquinas, Saint Thomas (1225-74) 102, 112, 318, 424
Arbois de Jubainville, Henri d' 3-4, 280, 281n
Argenteuil (Val-d'Oise, ch.-l. ar.), priory 393, 433-5
Ariès, Philippe 359
Arnoul, bp. of Lisieux (1141-79; d. 1182) 9
Aubouin de Sézanne 37
Augustine, Saint (354-430) 15, 484, 504-7; *City of God* 111; *Confessions* 294, 328-9, 354
Augustinian Rule 345
Auxerre (Yonne, ch.-l. dép.), church of 123-8

Bamberg Apocalypse 341
Barres, Catherine des 426-7
Battle of Maldon 159
Bautier, R-H 392n
Beaumanoir, Philippe de 103, 107
Becker, Philipp A. 13n
Bede (673-735) 15, 27, 481
Bédier, Joseph 148
Benedict (Saint) of Nursia (d. *c.* 547-55) 504, 506; *Rule* of 344, 424
Benoît de Sainte-Maure, *Roman de Troie* 168, 178
Beowulf 320
Bernard (Saint) of Clairvaux (1090-1153) 7, 28, 125-7, 318, 323, 327, 329, 332, 350, 392; compared with Suger 402

Bernard of Provence 378
Bezzola, R.R. 14n, 174
Bible 15, 17, 18, 26, 27, 50, 353, 442-3, 477
Biche Guidi 260
biography 333-4
Blanche de Navarre, ctess. of Champagne (d. 1229) 288; cartulary of 167, 282
Bloch, Marc 100, 119, 276, 277, 287n, 294, 311
Boccaccio, Giovanni (1313-75), 255-6
Boethius (*c.* 480-*c.* 525) 304
Boncompagnus de Signa 111, 120-1
Boniface, Saint (d. 754) 105
Bonnard, Jean 15
Bouvet, Jean (Canon) 35
Brocéliande (forest) 171, 173. *See also* fantasy
Brussel, Nicolas 206, 286
Bur, Michel 357
Burckhardt, Jacob 314

Cadurc 394-5
Caesar (d. 44 B.C.) 399
'Calendre', *Les empereors de Rome* 169-70, 178
Carmen ad Astralabium 473
'Cartulary of Countess Blanche' (*c.* 1220) 282-3
Cassian, John (*c.* 360-*c.* 435) 343
cathars 116, 117, 118
Celestine III, pope (1191-8) 107
Cepperello da Prato 255-7; accounts of tax on *nouveaux acquêts* 257-74
Champagne, *cour des barons* of, disproved 206-10; court of 3-43, 77. *See also Jours de Troyes*
Chanson de Roland, see *Song of Roland*
Charité-sur-Loire, La (dép. Nièvre, ar. Cosne, ch.-l. c.), priory 126-7
Charlemagne, k. of Franks (768-814) 156-8
Charrier, Charlotte 458, 471, 475, 488
Chaurand, Jacques 295
Chennevières-lès-Louvres (Val-d'Oise, ar. Montmorency, c. Gonesse) 387-8, 404-8
Chicago, Judy, *The dinner party* 365
child-rearing 298-301, 324-5, 350-1, 355
Chrétien de Troyes (*fl.* 1165-90) 13-15, 39, 110-11; *Perceval* 169, 175, 178; *Yvain* 174, 179
church 335, 352, 354-5
Church, Joseph 357-8
Cicero (106-43 B.C.) 399, 503, 506

Cîteaux, Order of 424
Clanchy, M.T. 279, 284-5
Clermont-en-Beauvaisis (Oise: ch.-l. ar.) 297, 298, 305
Collingwood, R.G. 135
computer revolution (analogous to systematising of feudalism) 285-7
Conan, provost of Lausanne 183, 188-90
conformity 321-3
Conon de Béthune (d. 1219-20) 29
Constantine the African (d. *c.* 1087) 365, 386
contraception 117
councils 348; of: Aix (816) 412, 425n, 429, 430; Chalcedon (451) 425; Lateran (1112) 390; Mâcon (585) 317; Merton (1236) 103; Paris (1248) 415; Provins (1251) 415; Rouen (1231) 411-6, 429, 449n; Sens (1140) 332-3, 415, 467, 470, 473; Soissons (1121) 431, 433-4, 435
Cour des Barons, *see* Champagne
courtesy, 118, 179
courtly love 3, 32-4, 39-43, 99, 114, 120
courts of love 82, 119, 172
Cowper, Frederick 20-1
Cum auctor (medical treatise) 365-7, 374, 376, 378, 379, 380, 381-2, 385
cursus 492-3

Dante Alighieri (1265-1321) 346
De aegritudinum curatione 373-4, 376
De amore, *see* Andreas Capellanus
De ornatu (medical treatise) 366-8, 378, 379, 380, 381-2, 385, 386
De secretis mulierum 383
dietary rules 423-5, 489
dreams 176, 331
Dronke, Peter 457, 492, 496n
Dyggve, H.P. 19nn

Eadmer, *Life of St Anselm* 333
Edmund of Lancaster (d. 1296) 194
education 37-8
Einhard, *Life of Charlemagne* 333
Eleanor of Aquitaine (d. 1204) 33, 119
Eleazar ben Nathan, rabbi 353
Elias Cairels 112
enculturation 149-65
Engels, Louk 497
'epic stroke' 150-1, 173
Eracle 39, 42
Erdmann, Carl 154
Erec, *see* Chrétien de Troyes

Erikson, Erik 321, 358, 362
Eructavit (Ps. 44) 18, 34-6, 39, 40, 108, 175
Étienne 'de Alinerra' 10-12
Eudes Rigaud, abp. of Rouen (1248-75) 415
Eudoxia (d. 1187), 108
Étienne de Provins 11, 12, 38
Eusebius (*c*. 263-*c*.340) 15, 302
Evergates, Theodore 261
Evrat 15-18, 39, 42, 175
exempla 89, 90, 94

fantasy 169-80
Fawtier, Robert 19n, 184
Feoda Campanie 283-4
feudalism 275-9; feudal system 284
fidelity 155-6, 161-2
Flahiff, G.B. 477
Flanders 184
Fontevrault (Maine-et-Loire, ar. Saumur, c. Saumur-Sud), abbey 421, 422, 434, 448n
forgery 476, 487
fortune-telling 348
Francia 160
Francis of Assisi, Saint (1182-1226) 323; rules of 344
Frappier, Jean 15
fraud 476
Frederick I, k. of Germany, emperor (1152-90) 37
Fulbert, bp. of Chartres (d. 1029) 277-8, 345
Fulk of Deuil 456, 469
Fulk Nerra, ct. of Anjou (987-1040) 107

Gace Brulé (*fl*. 1185-1210) 18-19, 37, 39
Galen (d. *c*. 200) 365, 366
Ganshof, F.L. 276
Gautier d'Arras (d. 1185) 20-2, 39
Gelasius II, pope (1118-19) 398
genealogy 25, 150
Genesis, see Evrat
Geoffroi de Villehardouin (*c*. 1150-*c*. 1213) 12
Gerald of Wales (1146-1223) 330
Gesta pontificum Autissiodorensium 126
Gilbert de la Porée, bp. of Poitiers (1142-54) 10, 462-4, 466, 472
Gilson, Etienne 419, 475, 484
Goitein, S.D. 315, 352n
Grancey, Guillaume de 200
Gratian (*fl*. 1130-50), *Concordance of discordant canons* 337
Gregory the Great, Saint and pope (d. 604) 504, 505
Gregory of Tours (d. 594) 353
Guibert of Nogent (*c*. 1064-*c*. 1125) 329, 351; *De pignoribus sanctorum* 294, 304, 332; *Gesta Dei per Francos* 295, 296, 299, 309, 310; personality, *Monodiae*, of 293-312, 329, 331
Guigo, prior of La Grande Chartreuse (d. 1136) 327, 336
Guillaume de Mantes 259
Guillaume de Nointeau, canon of Tours 259, 260
Guillem de Montanhagol (*fl*. 1239-57) 114
guilt 335-6
Guiot de Provins 29; his *Bible* 29
Guy of Bazoches 24-5, 38, 329
Györy, Jean 177

Häring, Fr. Nikolaus 460n, 464n
Haskins, C.H. 120, 294
Hatto, bp. of Troyes (d. 1145) 49
Heloise (d. *c*.1164) 420, 426, 428, 433, 434, 443, 448, 455, 499-501; epitaph of 457n; love of Abelard 457-9; *Problemata* of 440, 448
Henry I, k. of England (1100-35) 396, 397
Henry II, k. of England (1154-89) 37, 184
Henry V, k. of Germany (1106-25) 396
Henry the Liberal, ct. of Champagne (1152-81) 3, 5-43, 77, 282
Herbert of Bosham 27
heresy, heretics 116-7, 118, 311
Herrad of Landsberg, abbess of Hohenbourg 339-40
Hiersemann, Conrad 369
Higounet, Charles 403, 405
Hildegard of Bingen (1098-1179) 331-2, 347, 384-5
Hippocrates (d. *c*. 377 B.C.) 365, 378
Hirsch, Rudolf 132
Historia calamitatum, see Abelard
history, Pierre de la Palu's conception of 133-5
Holmes, U.T. 13
Homer (s. x B.C.?) 462
honor 148, 161-5, 307, 335
Hugh of Mâcon, bp. of Auxerre (1137-1151) 124-7
Hugh of St. Victor (d. 1141) 8, 111, 346n
Huon III d'Oisy 29
Hurd-Mead, Kate Campbell 365

'identity-crisis' 358, 362
ideology (political) 178-9
individualism 313-26, 328, 333-55; criteria for 316
Institutiones nostre (rule for nuns) 421-5, 448
intention 336-9
irony 110-11
Isidore of Seville (d. 636) 361
Islam 318-9, 320, 342
Ivo, bp. of Chartres (1090-1115), *Panormia* 429

Jackson, W.T.H. 103
Jacques de Vitry (d. 1240) 89-97, 347
James (Saint) the Apostle 505
Jaynes, Julian 328n
Jean de Trie, *bailli* of Auvergne 257
Jeanne of Navarre (d. 1305) 193-4, 204
Jehan le Nevelon 22-3
Jehan le Venelais 22-3
Jenkins, T.A. 34, 35
Jerome, Saint (c. 331-420) 15, 27, 424, 484, 504, 505, 506, 507
Jews 296, 311, 318, 352-3
Jocelin of Brakelond (d. after 1215) 333-4
John Chrysostom (348-407) 27
John of Le Thoult 285, 287-9
John of Salisbury (c. 1115-80) 25-7, 37-8, 395n, 464, 465, 467
John the Scot (d. c. 879) 26n, 461
Joinville, Jean de (c. 1225-1317) 192, 193, 199, 200, 202, 208, 330
Josephus (37-c. 93) 15
Jours de Troyes 191-254; attendance in 239-46; registers of 213-38

Kantorowicz, E.H. 172
Karnein, Alfred 172
Keller, Hans-Erich 157
Kelly, Amy 32n
Kempe, Margery (c. 1373-after 1438) 330
Kennan, Elizabeth 176
Kohlberg, Lawrence 358-9
Kohut, Heinz 402n
Kraut, Georg, *De passionibus mulierum* 367-8, 369
Kristeller, P.O. 26n

Laetabundus exsultet 53-5, 56
Lancelot, *see* Chrétien de Troyes
Landnámabók 352
Landry, Bernard 294, 295
Laudes crucis attollamus 54, 55

Leclercq, Jean 47, 176-7
Lefranc, Abel 294, 295, 296, 309
Lejeune, Rita 36
Lewis, C.S. 99
Liber bellorum domini, *see* Pierre de la Palu
Liber feudorum maior 284
Linus 462
Louis VI, k. of France (1108-37) 162, 183, 390-1, 394, 395
Louis VII, k. of France (1137-80) 29, 37, 127, 395-6; revenues of 183-90
Louis IX, k. of France (1226-70) 196, 210
love 19, 99-120, 350; 'of friendship' 114, 116
Lubac, Henri de 304-5

Mabillon, Jean 297
Macrobius (c. 360-c. 435) 171, 468, 504
Mahoney, John F. 81, 83, 84
Maitland, F.W. 275
MANUSCRIPTS CITED:
ASSISI Com. 695: 54n
AUBE, A.D. 24H 6: 425n
AVRANCHES, B.M. 149: 413n
BALTIMORE, John Hopkins Institute of H. & M. 3: 368n
BERLIN, Deutsche Staatsbibl. Phillipps 1719: 47n, 79, 80, 123; Phillipps 1852: 457n
BERN, Burgerbibl. 211: 457n; B 219: 189n
BRUGES, Stadsbibl. 593: 368n
CAMBRAI, B.M. 916: 366n
CAMBRIDGE, Trinity 0.1.20: 368n, 382n
CHÂLONS-SUR-MARNE, B.M. 583: 416n, 433n
CHAUMONT, B.M. 31: 478-9
CLERMONT-FERRAND, B.M. 623: 257n
COLOGNE, *see* KÖLN
CÔTE-D'OR, A.D. B 10423: 281n
ERFURT, Wissensch. Bibl. Amplon. Q204: 366n
HEIDELBERG, Univ. Pal. germ. 112: 150n
KÖLN, Schnütgen-Mus. Ludwig XIII 5: 348n
LA CHARITÉ, MS cited: 22n
LEIPZIG, 1215: 373n
LONDON, British Library: Burney 216: 459n; Cotton Vitellus C VIII: 459n; Harley: 978: 459n, 460-1; 3073: 8, 47, 53, 59; 3542: 367n, 378n, 386; Royal 6E III: 27n; Sloane: 1124: 366n, 373n; 2463: 382n
LUXEMBOURG, Bibl. nat., MS of Gui de

Bazoches: 24n
MADRID, Bibl. nac. 3356: 368n; Univ. Complut 119: 374n, 375
MARNE, A.D. H 1381 (cart. de Huiron); H Supplém. (cart. Hôtel-Dieu, Provins): 247
MUNICH, Staatsbibl. Clm 444: 367n; Clm 5426: 113n; Clm 23499: 120
NEW YORK, Acad. Medicine SAFE: 367n 373n
ORLEANS, B.M. 284 (*olim* 238): 338n, 456n
OXFORD, Bodl. 483: 368n; (Bodl.) Digby 23: 151-2) (Bodl.) Douce 37: 368n, 382n; Exeter 35: 367n, 386
PARIS, AN: KK 1064: 282n; LL 1158 (Cart. blanc de St-Denis): 393n; BN: fr. 794 (Guiot): 167-8, 178; fr. 920: 445n; fr. 12021: 6n; fr. 12456: 15n; fr. 12576: 169n; fr. 14410: 418, 422n, 429n, 435n, 436n, 438n, 448n, 482n; lat. 2445: 436n; lat. 2447: 436n; lat. 4893: 457n; lat. 4998: 24n; lat. 5992: 282n; lat. 5993A: 342n; lat. 7056: 365n, 380n; lat. 8654: 111n, 120; lat. 9187: 107n; lat. 9688: 37n; lat. 11003: 403; lat. 15002: 189n; lat. 16089: 366n, 378n, 381n, 386; lat. 17098: 35n, 85n; n.a. fr. 7412: 214; n.a. lat. 603: 366n; Coll. de Champagne 45: 93; 67: 214; Coll. Dupuy 761: 242; Coll. Moreau 50: 433n; Coll. Bastard, Ad 144a folio: 340n; Bibl. Ste-Geneviève 356: 466n; 865: 131, 135n; 1057: 368n; fr. 1327: 368n.
PHILADELPHIA, Univ. Pa. Lea 45: 132-45
REIMS, B.M. 1602: 10n
SAINT-OMER, B.M. 710: 459n, 461n
SALZBURG, Mus. Carolino-Augusteum 2271: 367n, 386
SEINE-ET-MARNE, A.D. H 492: 35n
SOISSONS, B.M. 7: 286n
STRASBOURG, Bibl. publ., MS of Herrad of Landsberg: fig. O.
TOURNAI, B.M. 101: 483n
TROYES, B.M. 403: 330n; 802: 411-6, 418, 419n, 475
VATICAN CITY, Arch. S. Pietro H. 13: 120; Vat. Reg. lat. 547: 130
WROCLAW, lost MS of *c.* 1200: 373-5
ZÜRICH, Zentralbibl. C58/275: 457n
Map, Walter (*c.* 1140-*c.* 1208) 28, 170
Marcabru (*fl.* 1128-50) 114

Marie, ctess. of Champagne (d. 1198) 3, 5-43
marriage 16, 34, 100-9, 323-4
Martianus Capella (*fl.* early s. v) 461-2, 464, 468
Mason-Hohl, Elisabeth 365
Matthew of Vendôme (*c.* 1130-*c.* 1200), 346-7
Mause, Lloyd de 358
McLaughlin, Mary M. 435
Mécringes, Agnès de 426
medicine 363-86
Metamorphosis Goliae 459-73
Michelet, Jules 314
Mignon, Robert (*fl.* early s. xiv) 257, 259
Misch, Georg 294, 310
Misset, Eugène 57-8
Molesme (Burgundy) 323n, 422-3
monastic rules 344-5, 420; for women 420-1, 423, 429-30
Monfrin, Jacques 419n, 429, 444n, 445n, 478
Monod, Bernard 295
Morris, Colin 314, 315, 325
Muckle, Fr. J.T. 459, 471, 484, 488
Musciatto Guidi 255
Muslims 296, 311, 318, 320

names 341-3
nations 295
Nicholas I, pope (858-67) 107
Nicolas of Clairvaux (d. 1175-8) 7-9, 38, 45-75, 77-80, 123-8
nobility 305-307
Nogent (sous Coucy, Aisne), abbey of 303
Nogent (-sur-Seine: Aube, ch.-l ar.) 437
Norbert, Saint (d. 1134), 28, 431n-2
Normandy 184, 211-2
nouveaux acquêts, see Cepperello da Prato

Oignies (dép. Pas-de-Calais, ar. Lens, c. Carvin) 90
Orderic Vitalis (1075-*c.* 1142), 278, 331, 371
Origen (*c.* 185-*c.* 254) 27, 311, 505
Othloh of St Emmeram 331
Otto, bp. of Freising (d. 1158) 456
Ovid (43 B.C.-17 A.D.) 50, 62n, 111, 113, 302, 368, 461, 503

Pacaut, Marcel 185-90, 395n
Painter, Sidney 99, 315
Paraclet(e), oratory near Troyes (Aube), 411-6, 418-30, 432-7

Paris, schools of 347, 445
Paris, Gaston 3, 14n, 36, 99, 147
Parlement (of Paris) 191, 195-7, 201-6, 211-2
patriotism 147-9, 155-6, 158-60, 295, 312, 320
patronage 178
Paul, Saint 101
Pepo, Master 336
perception 487-8
Persius (34-62) 386
Peter the Chanter (d. 1197) 107n, 113
Peter Lombard (d. 1160) 104, 464-5
Peter the Venerable, abt. of Cluny (d. 1156) 127, 329, 448
Petit Moustier 428, 436, 480
Philip II 'Augustus', k. of France (1180-1223), 183, 188-90
Philip III, k. of France (1270-85) 194-7, 199, 210, 258
Philip IV ('the Fair', k. of France, 1285-1314) 193-5, 198-206, 210-12, 259, 261
Philip, ct. of Flanders (1163-91) 40, 108, 178
Philippe de Harveng 27, 37
Piaget, Jean 358
Pierre de Celle 9-10, 26, 38, 40
Pierre de la Palu, O.P. (*c.* 1275-1342), 129-45, 155
Pierre Riga 28-9
plagiarism 47, 50
Plato (428-348 B.C.) 8n, 50n, 468
Portejoie, Paulette 207
portraiture 338-41
Practica, see Trotula
'Premier budget' (1202-3) 186-8
Prémontré, statutes of 413, 424
Priscian (*fl.* early s. vi) 12
Prisée des sergents 186-7
Pseudo-Ambrose, *Acta Sancti Sebastiani*, 50
Pseudo-Turpin, *Historia Karoli magni* 158n
psychohistory 325-6, 331-2, 358

Quintilian (*c.* 35-*c.* 100) 503
Quinze Joyes de Mariage 115

racism 443
Radding, Charles 337n, 359
Raftis, J. Ambrose 322
Rajna, Pio 31, 82, 83
Ralph of Vermandois (d. 1152) 394, 396
Ramon Vidal 108
rationalism 294, 296, 304, 309-11

realism 174-5
reforming values 307
relics 294, 303-4, 310-1, 353
Rémusat, Charles de 359, 471
revenue, of: Anglo-Norman realms 184, 188; Louis VII, 183-90
Richard the Lion-Hearted (k. of England, 1189-99) 19-20
Rigaut de Barbezieux 36-7, 41
Roach, William 14n
Robert of Arbrissel (d. 1117) 434, 440, 448
Robert of Flamborough 337
Robertson, D.W., Jr. 14n, 110, 176, 475
Rohmer, Eric, *Perceval le Gallois* (film) 173
Roman de la Rose 418 427n, 482-3
Roscelin of Compiègne (*c.* 1050-*c.* 1125) 431, 432, 434, 456, 469, 480-1, 500
Rougemont, Denis de 99
Rowland, Beryl 369
Runciman, Steven 321
Rupert of Deutz (d. 1129) 343

Saint-Denis (Seine-St-Denis), abbey of 157, 389, 391-5; Abelard and 433, 434, 435-6
Saint-Etienne (Troyes: Aube) 85, 86, 87
Saint-Germer of Fly (Oise, ar. Beauvais, c. Le Coudray), abbey of 301, 303, 305, 307
Saint-Médard (Soissons: Aisne) 311
Saint-Victor (Paris) 51
Salerno, medicine at 366, 371, 378-9
Schlösser, Felix 33n
Schmeidler, Bernhard 438, 475, 478
self consciousness 327-56
sequence 45, 51-9
sexology 115n, 383
sexuality 115, 298-9, 302, 306, 308-9, 311, 424, 470
shame 307, 321, 335-6
Silvestre, Hubert 489-90, 491n, 496n
Simon Chèvre d'Or, Master (*fl.* 1150-60), 22, 38, 397
Song of Roland 114, 147-65, 320; audience of 163-5, 335-6; dating of 151-2, 163-4
Southern, R.W. 463n
Spanke, Hans 55
Stendhal 99
Stenton, D.M. 118
Stephen, canon of Auxerre 124-6
Stephen of Garland 392
Stephen (Saint) of Obazine 334
Stephanus (magister) de Aliorra 11

Stephen (master) of Reims 12
Strayer, J.R. 257
Stronski, Stanislaw 109n
Suger (1081-1151) 127, 157, 387-407;
    compared with: Bernard 402; Guibert,
    401-2; *De administratione* 400; family of
    387-9, 403-7; *Life of Louis VI* 390, 395,
    399; *Life of Louis VII* 399; royal service
    394-7
Symonds, J.A. 332

Taylor, H.O. 120
Terence (*c.* 185-159 B.C.) 302
Thibaut IV, ct. of Blois-Champagne (1125-
    52) 37, 40, 282, 397
Thibaut le Chansonnier, ct. of Champagne
    (1222-53) 167, 282, 288
Thierry of Chartres (d. 1150-5) 463-4, 465,
    466; *Heptateuchon*, 469
Thomas de Marle 309, 397
tolerance 321
Trachtenberg, Joshua 296
Trotula (Trota) 363-86; her work *Practica*
    374-7, 379, 385
Troyes (Aube: ch.-l dép.), *bailliage* of 259,
    260, 261, 262; castellany of 262-3

Ullmann, Walter 314, 315
Ulrich von Zatzikhoven, *Lanzelet* 110
Ut de curis (medical treatise) 365-7, 372,
    374, 376, 378, 379, 380, 381-2, 385

Valerius Maximus (early s. i) 37
Valéry, Paul 174

Van den Eynde, Fr. Damien 412-3, 416,
    421-2
Vegetius (*fl.* late s. iv) 38n
Venjance Alixandre 23, 38, 41n
Vergil (70-19 B.C.) 462; *Aeneid* 22; *Bucolics*
    302
Vitry-en-Perthois (Marne, ar. and c. Vitry-
    le-François) 91-2

Wace (d. *c.* 1175), *Roman de Brut* 168, 171,
    178-80
Waddell, Fr. M. Chrysogonus, O.C.S.O.
    49n, 476, 478-9, 481, 502n
warfare 152-6
Weakland, Rembert, O.S.B. 69
Wetherbee, Winthrop 460, 468-9, 470-1
William II, k. of Sicily (1172-89) 37
William VIII, lord of Montpellier
    (d. 1202) 108
William IX, duke of Aquitaine (d. 1126)
    106
William fitz Stephen 325
Williams, J.R. 12, 23
wine, of Auxerre 77-80
Winton Domesday 342
witness lists 5, 7, 22, 31, 465n, 466
Wolf, H.K. 369
women 16, 18, 316-17; medicine and
    363-86; sexuality of 115, 383-5; status of
    117-19
written records 275-90

Zacour, Norman 133

Things to Make and Do for H